# Applying Educational Psychology in the Classroom

# Applying Educational Psychology in the Classroom

## Fourth Edition

## by Myron H. Dembo

*University of Southern California*

**Longman**
New York & London

**Applying Educational Psychology
in the Classroom, fourth edition**

Copyright © 1991, 1988 by Longman Publishing Group.
All rights reserved.
No part of this publication may be reproduced,
stored in a retrieval system, or transmitted
in any form or by any means, electronic, mechanical,
photocopying, recording, or otherwise,
without the prior permission of the publisher.

Longman, 95 Church Street, White Plains, N.Y. 10601

Associated companies:
Longman Group Ltd., London
Longman Cheshire Pty., Melbourne
Longman Paul Pty., Auckland
Copp Clark Pitman, Toronto

Senior editor: Naomi Silverman
Editorial assistant: Karen Philippidis
Production editor: Halley Gatenby
Text design: Betty Sokol
Cover design: Joseph DePinho
Text art: J & R Services, Inc.; Maryland Composition
Text photographs: Jeff Sedlik

**Library of Congress Cataloging-in-Publication Data**

Dembo, Myron H.
    Applying educational psychology in the classroom / Myron H. Dembo.
    —4th ed.
       p.   cm.
    Includes bibliographical references and index.
    ISBN 0-8013-0484-9
    1. Educational psychology.   2. Learning, Psychology of.
3. Classroom management.   I. Title.
LB1051.D369   1991
370.15—dc20                                             90-41523
                                                           CIP

ABCDEFGHIJ-VH-99  98  97  96  95  94  93  92  91  90

# Copyright Acknowledgments

To Nancy

*Who has been a friend and loving wife during our 25 years of marriage. Her support and encouragement have been important to me in all my endeavors.*

# Contents Overview

# Contents

_Introductory_

# PART FOUR

## Measurement and Evaluation   501

# Classroom Applications

# Preface

Many good educational psychology textbooks are available to students. However, in speaking with instructors and students in teacher education throughout the country, I continue to be influenced by two major concerns. First, recent textbooks appear to represent one of two extremes. Some authors attempt to provide an encyclopedic knowledge of content with little attention paid to how that knowledge can be *used* by teachers. Other authors take the opposite approach, emphasizing tips and suggestions for teachers but neglecting to provide sufficient theory and research to support the suggestions.

Second, students often read about specific variables in the instructional process but don't understand how these variables are related. For example, readers may learn about individual differences in one chapter and about planning for instruction in another chapter, yet read nothing about how to plan for individual differences in instruction. In general, instructors and students both see the need for a better-organized educational psychology textbook.

I wrote this book with the above concerns in mind. First, I provide concise coverage of imporant theory and research in educational psychology while focusing on how teachers can *apply* this knowledge in the classroom. The emphasis is on improving teachers' decision-making ability. Second, I use a model of the teaching-learning process that serves two important functions: It illustrates how knowledge of educational psychology can be used in teaching, and it helps to integrate the material from different chapters.

## CONTENT ORGANIZATION OF THE FOURTH EDITION

As in the previous editions of the book, an instructional model identifying six major variables in the teaching-learning process is used to organize psychological content: instructional objectives, individual differences, teacher behavior, principles of learning, method of instruction, and evaluation of learners' behavior. The schematic diagram of the model in Chapter 1 has been revised for greater clarity. The book is divided into four parts: Development and Individual Differences, Learning Theories and Instructional Applications, Preparing for Effective Teaching, and Measurement and Evaluation. For instructors familiar with the previous editions of the book, note that the part on Learning Theories and Instructional Applications now precedes Preparing for Effective Teaching. This reorganization allows me to show how learning theory is used to plan for instruction, motivate students, and manage classrooms.

I discuss development and individual differences in Chapters 2 to 5. Chapter 2, Intelligence and Cognitive Development, has been revised to include the psychometric, Piagetian, and information-processing approach to intelligence. Chapter 3, Cognition, Culture, and Language, emphasizes approaches to teaching the increased number of immigrant and culturally different students entering schools in the United States. Chapter 4, Personal and Social Development, now includes Marcia's contribution to Erikson's theory of personal and social development and covers new material on divorce, child-rearing, child abuse, latchkey children, and television viewing. Chapter 5, Exceptional Children, updates legislation and deals with current issues in special education.

In Part Two I emphasize learning theory and instructional applications. I include chapters on Behavioral Psychology (Chapter 6) and Cognitive Approaches to Learning (Chapter 7). A new appendix, Teaching Learning Strategies in the Content Areas, follows Chapter 7. The behavioral chapter traces the development of behavioral psychology from classical and operant conditioning and social learning theory to cognitive behavior modification. The chapter on cognitive psychology updates the work on learning strategies. Chapter 8, the Humanistic Perspective, deals with current issues in character or citizenship education and includes an expanded discussion of how to prepare students to work cooperatively. Sample lesson plans are provided for direct instruction, discovery, and cooperative learning.

Part Three includes Planning for Instruction (Chapter 9) and new chapters on Motivation (Chapter 10) and Classroom Management and Discipline (Chapter 11). The chapter on motivation focuses on the teacher's role in changing student motivation, while the chapter on classroom management focuses on techniques for preventing problems from occurring and for dealing with problems once they occur.

The final part of the book includes Standardized and Teacher-Made Measurement Instruments (Chapter 12) and Analyzing Test Scores and Reporting Student Progress (Chapter 13). These chapters help to prepare the future teacher for the many measurement and evaluation tasks in classroom instruction.

## PEDAGOGICAL FEATURES OF THE BOOK

Each chapter begins with a brief Chapter Overview outline, and an Orientation describing the relevance of the material to the teaching-learning process. At the end of the Orientation you will find a list of chapter objectives and Focus Questions. For the most part, the objectives emphasize actual teaching skills or behavior that should be acquired after reading the chapter. The Focus Questions help to ensure that you learn important content in the book related to the objectives. In addition, these questions appear in the margins by the pertinent material. In some cases, material from earlier sections of the book is relevant to a particular focus question. If you can't answer a focus question after reading a particular section in the book, you should go back and review the material. Although the Focus Questions emphasize important material in the book, they do not include all the information you will learn.

Important terms are **boldfaced** and listed at the end of each chapter in the Key Terms section with the page number where each term *first* appears. In some cases a term that was boldfaced earlier may be italicized later in the text if it appears with a list of terms that are boldfaced. A Glossary is included at the end of the book in case you have any question concerning the definition of any boldfaced term. You will also find Key Points at the end of each chapter, summarizing the most important information in the chapter.

I have included 26 Classroom Applications in this edition. These sections, based on current research, help you develop actual competencies for the classroom. That is, they describe how to apply concepts or skills in the classroom. These sections are identified by color shading in the text and are listed following the Contents.

A section, Thinking about the Teaching-Learning Model, is included at the end of each chapter. These sections focus specifically on the integration of material in various chapters by emphasizing the relationship among the major variables in the teaching-learning process: instructional objectives, individual differences, teacher behavior, principles of learning, method of instruction, and evaluation of learners' behavior.

The Suggestions for Further Reading provide a list of important books and journals for additional reading on major topics in each chapter.

Follow-Up Activities at the close of each chapter provide opportunities to debate or discuss important issues, to complete research projects, and to involve you in a variety of experiential activities. The variety of activities allows your instructor to select exercises to complement his or her class presentations.

As you read the book you will want to learn the (1) theories of learning and development, (2) major research findings, (3) important terms, and (4) procedures for applying theory and research in the classroom. The pedagogical features in this book are designed to help you meet the objectives of your course. Have a successful semester!

## TO THE INSTRUCTOR

Two *new* supplements are now available: an *Instructor's Manual with Test Items* and a *Student Guide*. In addition, a *Computerized Test Bank* with all the test items for the text can be obtained from the publisher by instructors adopting the textbook.

## ACKNOWLEDGMENTS

I would like to thank my daughter, Lisa, for her help in checking references, and graduate students at the University of Southern California who reviewed specific chapters and provided research and/or draft material for various chapters in the book: Lucinda Boswell, Phyllis Maguire Dunmire, Val Kirkus, Mi Chin Liu, Marilyn Mantz, John McGowan, Priscilla Porter, Julie Scott, and Jennifer Sevilla. Thank you, Sidney Blake and Brenda Sugrue for preparing the test questions for the instructor's manual. I also appreciate the reviews by my colleagues at USC: Richard Clark, Dennis Hocevar, Reynaldo Macias, and Robert Rueda. My writing was also influenced by helpful reviews from the following individuals: Livingston Alexander, Georgia Southern College; Carolyn Anderson, Humboldt State University; Christopher Clark, Michigan State University; Bonnie Cramond, University of Georgia; J. Kent Davis, Purdue University; Thomas Fetsco, Northern Arizona University; William Gnagey, Illinois State University; Gay Goodman, University of Houston; Juanita Hire, Western Kentucky University; James Kaatz, San Diego State University; James Kahn, University of Illinois; Charles Lester, Alaska Pacific University; Sharon McNelley, Northeastern Illinois University; Richard Mueller, Northern Illinois University; Protima Roy, Drury College; and Toni Santmire, University of Nebraska.

A number of individuals played an important role in obtaining the photographs in the book. I am grateful to the following individuals for their assistance: Eva Hain, director of the Public Information Unit in the Los Angeles Unified School District, who provided approval to use teachers and students in the LAUSD; Polly McDowell and Linda Zimmerman at Wilbur Elementary School and Cindy Hiller at the Sherman Oaks Center for Enriched Studies, for allowing us to use classroom time for the photos; the many students and teachers at these schools who allowed their photos to be used in the textbook; and Jeff Sedlik, a talented photographer who took all the photos in the book.

Several individuals at Longman deserve special mention: Naomi Silverman, senior editor, and her editorial assistant, Karen Philippidis, who have provided excellent support throughout the project; and Halley Gatenby, associate managing editor, who helped turn a red-penciled manuscript into a quality book.

Finally, I would greatly appreciate knowing *your* reactions to this book. I welcome your praise and criticism. Write to me at 600 Phillips Hall, University of Southern California, Los Angeles, CA 90089-0031.

# CHAPTER 1

# The Teacher
# as Decision Maker

## ORIENTATION

Teaching and learning are related but independent processes. Sometimes teaching leads to learning but not always. Although the teacher may facilitate learning, each student must take charge of his or her own learning.

Smith (1960) defines **teaching** as a "system of actions intended to induce learning" (p. 230). **Learning** is often defined as a process by which behavior is either modified or changed through experience or training.

To facilitate learning in others, teachers must learn the major variables that influence the success of the teaching-learning process. This is no easy task, for the classroom is a complex meshing of simultaneous activities and events. I have organized this book around an instructional model that identifies some important decisions a teacher must make during the instructional process so that you, the teacher, will better understand the relation between teaching and learning. This introductory chapter explains the model and discusses the ways you can use psychological content to improve your teaching effectiveness. The major goals of this book are to help you:

- examine the effects of your decisions on your students' learning.
- examine your personal beliefs about the teaching-learning process.
- evaluate your beliefs and practices so that you can modify your teaching behavior.

Teachers espouse hypotheses, or beliefs, about the nature of the teaching-learning process that influence their classroom behavior. These beliefs lead them to make important decisions that set the conditions for behaviors under which students live and learn at school (Greenwood & Parkay, 1989; Mayer, 1985a). Shavelson (1973) has emphasized the importance of teachers' decisions during instruction by stating: "Any teaching act is the result of a decision, either conscious or unconscious. . . . *the* basic teaching skill is decision making" (p. 144).

Careful observation of teacher practices in the classroom can provide insights into a teacher's belief system and will reveal that not all teaching decisions are supported by empirical research or are consistent with sound educational theory or practice.

Let's look at a comment from a student observer who questioned a teacher about a particular teaching behavior:

> She reads to the class because she feels that lecturing "over their heads" is not good and that they will learn nothing from it. She feels that if students understand what she says, they will learn much better. After reading to the class, she asks questions to test their comprehension.

This teacher's beliefs about learning prompted her to read to the class. What classroom experiences led her to this decision? If she had lectured "over their heads" in the past, what was the cause of her behavior? Did the students not understand important knowledge? Was her vocabulary too difficult for the students' level of development? The answers to these questions should help to explain why her lecturing was ineffective. Although she feels that her students will learn better by being read to than by being lectured at, the solution to the problem may prove to be as ineffective as her original strategy.

McDonald (1965) provides a good example of how a teacher's decisions can shape what students will learn:

> A fourth-grade teacher was introducing a unit on "Pioneer Life." He asked the students what they wanted to study about "Pioneer Life" and what kinds of questions they should raise concerning the subject. As the discussion proceeded, the children suggested the usual categories for studying a history unit—namely, the pioneer's food, shelter, and clothing. One child mentioned that he had seen a Western movie in which a man accused of horse stealing was immediately hanged. This comment on the movie evoked considerable interest in the group, and one of the children asked why the man was hanged right away. The teacher dismissed this question as irrelevant to a discussion on pioneer life. The decision not to utilize this question in effect set the stage for the kinds of things that the pupils would talk about. Had the teacher chosen to capitalize upon this question, topics concerning pioneer conceptions of justice and due process of law, the function of law-enforcing bodies, and the validity of citizens' arrests could have been developed. These topics did not emerge in the ensuing discussion, nor were they included as relevant points in the outline of topics to be studied under the headline of "Pioneer Life." The teacher's decisions at this point, then, determined the character of what the children could learn. (pp. 63–64)

McDonald asks whether this teacher would have profited by examining his decisions in the light of his teaching hypotheses.

These examples illustrate the importance of examining and testing teaching hypotheses, or beliefs, so that you can make necessary modifications in educational procedures and practices. Teachers must learn to ask questions about their own teaching practices in order to self-monitor and self-regulate their behavior (Corno, 1989).

Educational psychology includes research findings, theories, and principles that you can use to formulate and test your personal beliefs about teaching and learning (see the appendix following this chapter for information on using library resources to locate relevant journal articles on your area of interest). Notice the emphasis on the word *use*. Many people believe that the more knowledge teachers possess, the more effective they will be in the classroom. Cohen (1973) discusses this belief as "to know good is to do good" (or the "mythstake"). Unfortunately, research studies have failed to demonstrate a relationship between measures of classroom teaching behaviors and the teacher's knowledge of psychological information (Aspy, 1972; Silverman & Kimmel, 1972). Perhaps one reason for this finding is that many teachers simply memorize psychological material without attempting to internalize and to apply it in any meaningful way. Surely, we would be dissatisfied with an attorney who knew the law but had difficulty defending clients because of the ambiguities in the law.

Teaching is not an exact science. The teacher must apply personal knowledge to the complex world of the classroom and make decisions that lead to improved student performance. Teaching will then lead to learning.

To help you internalize the psychological information presented in this book, I have interspersed questions throughout the text and provided follow-up learning activities at the end of each unit with suggestions for further reading. Take time to consider the questions and activities, and discuss them with your classmates. Avoid the tendency to be a passive learner by simply underlining sentences with a Magic Marker. Remember, in a short time you will have to apply educational psychology in the classroom. Why not begin now? Finally, please read the preface to this book if you skipped it earlier, especially the section on the pedagogical features of the book. This information is important in helping you to use the book successfully.

By the time you master the material presented in this chapter, you will be able to:

- Use a model of the teaching-learning process to analyze a teacher's instructional behavior.
- Observe student behavior in classrooms.

## FOCUS QUESTIONS

1. How do the major variables in the teaching-learning process impact the effectiveness of instruction?
2. What type of problems do beginning teachers confront?

## INSTRUCTIONAL DECISIONS MADE BY TEACHERS

Before studying the teaching-learning process, you should understand the major variables in the process. The use of an instructional model best accomplishes this purpose. Lembo (1969) identified an adequate instructional model as *diagnostic, prescriptive,* and *normative.*

It is diagnostic in that it provides for (1) identification of the learners' present level of functioning or cognitive ability; (2) the appropriate kinds of instructional objectives and activities for the learners' level of cognitive abilities and style of learning; and (3) solutions to the problems resulting from instructional activities. The model thus points out the direction for remediation when learning does not occur. A good instructional model is also prescriptive in that it provides some procedural guidelines for establishing learning conditions. Last, a good instructional model is normative in that it provides general criteria for determining whether learning conditions have been met. Figure 1.1 is an instructional model meeting these criteria. It has been adapted from Hunter (1971), who has applied it to the education of both preservice and inservice teachers.

An important aspect of this model for teachers is that it integrates the major variables in the teaching-learning process: the students whom they teach, the objectives they hope to attain with them, and the methods and behaviors they use to this end. Because each variable is separated, you can study each one and relate research findings to your teaching decisions during instruction. The model also emphasizes that teachers' behavior causes learning and directs teachers to different areas in which they must become proficient.

Let's look at the variables in the model and the decisions that a teacher must make. Each component is numbered for easy identification.

## The Learning Task

One of the important decisions to make in teaching is deciding on an **instructional objective.** What is to be learned? (See box No. 3 in Figure 1.1.) A number of earlier decisions must intervene during this process. Teachers' familiarity with the content area and particularly their ability to determine what the learners already know about the content are examples (box No. 1).

Some psychologists refer to the knowledge the learners already know as their **entry behavior.** Assessing entry behavior requires at least two kinds of measurement, according to Hunter (1971). The first is the continuum—easy to more difficult—that exists in most content areas. For example, a child who can multiply by a single-digit number may not be able to multiply by two- or three-digit numbers. Starting at the proper level of difficulty is an important condition of any instructional program.

The second dimension of a learning task is its level of complexity. For example, the *Taxonomy of Educational Objectives—Cognitive Domain* (Bloom et al., 1956; discussed in Chapter 9) categorizes knowledge into a number of levels that allow the teacher to determine if the learner will merely possess knowledge, understand and summarize it, apply it, analyze it, synthesize it with other knowledge, evaluate it, or some combination of these.

## The Behavior of the Learner

Before determining the instructional objective, you must also consider the behavior of the learners (box No. 2). What must they do to learn—read, write, list? The behavior must be relevant to the objective (students can't learn to debate merely by reading books on debating, nor can they solve chemistry problems simply by memorizing formulas). And the behavior must be relevant to the learner. If a child is a poor reader, your reliance solely on a social studies textbook for factual material is not an appropriate teaching behavior.

The synthesis of the first two teaching decisions—what the students will learn and how they will learn it—constitutes the instructional objective of a lesson (box No. 3). The determination of this objective will help you

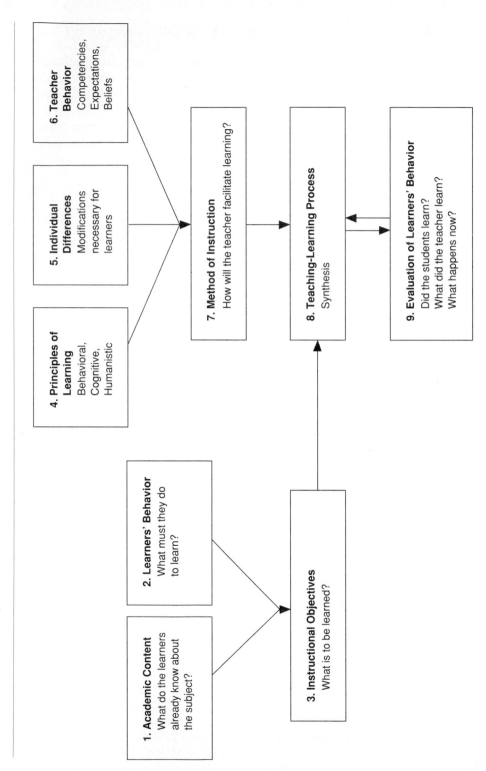

Figure 1.1   The Decisions That Make Up the Teaching-Learning Process.

*Source: Adapted from Hunter, 1971, in Allen and Seifman.*

to decide later whether you have been successful in changing the learners' behaviors.

The model identifies some important responsibilities for you to consider before you even begin teaching a lesson. Too often, teachers start out with instructional techniques or strategies before they know what they are trying to teach, or they identify objectives before they analyze the individual abilities of the students. Planning objectives without first assessing the needs and abilities of the learners is a risky procedure that often leads to inappropriate, irrelevant, or unnecessary teaching.

## The Behavior of the Teacher

Another major decision is answering the "how" question in the instructional process (box No. 7). How will the teacher facilitate learning? Teachers differ greatly in their styles of teaching. These differences involve the degree of planning, the amount of control of student behaviors, the method of presentation of material, types of grouping, and so forth.

The model shown in Figure 1.1 identifies a number of variables that should influence a teacher's instructional methodology (box No. 7), *principles of learning* (box No. 4), *individual differences of students* (box No. 5), and *teacher behavior* (box No. 6).

Principles of learning (box No. 4) can help the teacher to determine which variables and what conditions will help students to improve their performances. R. Gagné (1985) points out that not all learning is the same and that the instructor needs to teach differently to effect different kinds of learning. Repetition is an important principle in learning multiplication tables, but it is less useful in learning to solve mathematical equations. Knowledge of the principles of learning can improve a teacher's decisions in selecting appropriate teaching methodologies. It will also help a teacher better to understand the assumptions that lie behind various educational procedures and practices.

Another variable to consider in deciding how to teach is the individual differences of students (box No. 5). I pointed out earlier that this information is also important when deciding what is to be learned (box No. 3). For example, teachers have to make some modifications because of their students' level of attention, memory and language development, and motivational differences (Short & Weissberg-Benchell, 1989). With experience, teachers sometimes discover that procedures effective at one grade level are less effective at another. Many differences abound even among students of the same age or stage of development. There are differences in styles of learning, personality, aptitude, and motivation in 1st-grade as well as in 12th-grade students. Teachers find that they must continually modify their lessons for particular students in order to attain instructional objectives.

The third variable influencing how to teach is teacher behavior (box No. 6). Like students, teachers also differ greatly in their teaching styles,

One of the major challenges in teaching is instructing students with varied abilities, interests, and cultural and ethnic backgrounds.

personalities, personal concerns and adequacy, expectations, and so on. The literature on teaching effectiveness has confirmed the relationship between specific teacher variables and student achievement within several domains of teacher behavior—classroom management, instructional organization, and lesson presentations. However, teacher behaviors must be appropriately matched to student differences if they are to have their intended effects. Some teaching methods work successfully for some objectives or for some types of students but are less effective for other objectives and students (Englert, 1984).

Teachers hold differing expectations for students (Good & Brophy, 1990). They do not treat all students alike in the classroom. Some students are called on more frequently, asked more thought-provoking questions, or reinforced more often. If a teacher expects a student to achieve at a lower level than another student, this expectation affects the teacher's behavior toward both students.

Classroom management is another important component of teacher behavior. Lemlech (1988) views classroom management as the orchestration of classroom life: planning curriculum, organizing procedures and resources, arranging the environment for working efficiency, maintaining student progress, and anticipating potential problems. Research indicates that teachers who are good classroom managers also tend to produce more student learning (Good & Grouws, 1975; McDonald & Elias, 1976; Rosenshine & Berliner, 1978).

Although evaluation (box No. 9) is a separate variable, it is manifested during the planning of objectives and continues throughout the instructional process. As a teacher, you must know how to measure student behavior at various points before the start of instruction (to organize an appropriate instructional program for students), during each segment of instruction (to facilitate student progress), and at the end of instruction (to determine how well instructional objectives were met and to decide where to go from there).

**How do the major variables in the teaching-learning process impact the effectiveness of instruction?**

You should pay particular attention to the evaluation of learning outcomes at the end of instruction: Did the students learn anything from the instructional lesson or unit? If you failed to develop any specific objectives at the beginning of the lesson, you may be hard-pressed to answer the question. When the expected does not occur, you must ask yourself: What went wrong? Were the objectives appropriate for the students? Was my teaching method appropriate for the objectives? Should I reteach all or part of the lesson? Should the class move on to another topic? With this self-questioning technique, a teacher can properly evaluate the students' learning and revise different components of the teaching-learning process.

## DECISIONS, DECISIONS . . .

Using the teaching-learning model, we can now summarize the major decisions that make the teaching-learning process work. Keep in mind that each decision does not operate independently but interacts with the others in an ongoing manner (Hunter, 1971).

- What learning task can the student handle at the entry stage of learning?
- What learner behavior and characteristics are relevant to the task and to the learner's characteristics?
- What is the primary instructional objective of the lesson?
- What principle(s) of learning can a teacher apply to the learning task?
- What modifications does a particular learner require?
- How can the teacher's own competencies and personality be used to translate teaching decisions into effective action?
- What is the best method of accomplishing the instructional objective?
- How will the teacher synthesize the preceding decisions into the teaching-learning process?
- How successful was the teaching-learning process? What happens now?

## USING THE TEACHING-LEARNING MODEL TO ANALYZE INSTRUCTION

Let's look at two different teaching incidents to give you an opportunity to use the teaching-learning model in analyzing classroom instruction. As you read each incident, identify the variables (i.e., *instructional objectives, individual differences, teacher behavior, principles of learning, methods of instruction,* and *evaluation*) that influence the amount of learning in the classroom. Identify the type of decisions made by both teachers. I will comment on each incident at the end.

### An Elementary School Classroom

Mr. Walker is a fourth-grade teacher whose class was observed during the first month of school. The lesson is part of a unit on the history of Los Angeles.

Teacher: Math time is over. Quietly go back to your regular seats, and put away your math books. (*There is much noise in the classroom. Some children stop right away; others keep working in their books.*)

Aaron: (*Walking over to Carl's desk*) I saw a great movie last night.

Teacher: (*In a loud, threatening voice*) Aaron, what do you think this is, time to play with friends? Did I say go visit a neighbor and talk?

Aaron: (*No response*)

Teacher: You're holding up the entire class. (*By now most of the class has settled down; some students are still quietly talking.*)

Teacher: Now, will everyone please take out the social studies book.

Julie: What social studies book?

Teacher: The books I passed out yesterday—the history of Los Angeles.

Julie: Oh, I didn't know that was social studies.

Teacher: Well, if you spent a little more time listening instead of talking to Susan, maybe you would learn something.

Adam: I can't find my book.

Teacher: Well, you'd better find it because I don't have any more, and these books need to be used next year. We waste so much time changing subjects. When we change, there should be no talking. You don't need to visit with a neighbor or sharpen your pencil. Now, open your books to page 50 and read the chapter to yourself.

Phil: (*To Steve after 10 minutes*) I've already finished. Where are you?

Steve: (*Whispering*) I'm almost finished.

Teacher: Phil, Steve, stop talking. (*At this point they had already stopped.*) Phil, you're a good student, but you need to learn to control your mouth. (*To the class*) Has everyone finished reading? (*Students respond yes and no.*)

Teacher: Okay, let's get started. Who can tell me a main point from the chapter? (*Many hands go up, and students begin whispering for attention.*) There is no need for sound effects.

*2* Lisa: (*Calling out*) They were telling about prehistoric animals.

Teacher: Good. What kind of animals?

*1* Tom: (*Calling out*) Dinosaurs.

Teacher: No, there weren't any dinosaurs in Los Angeles. At least we haven't found any dinosaur bones yet. What other animals did they have?

*2* Pam: Elephants.

*3* Ralph: Camels.

Teacher: Right. Did the camels look like the camels today?

Class: No-o-o!

Teacher: How many humps did they have?

*5* George: Two.

Teacher: Wrong. Don't you pay attention to what you read? They had one. What other animals were there? (*Wesley drops his pencil box.*)

*4* Jimmy: Hawks.

Teacher: Wesley! What do you think you're doing? What did I just say? What kind of prehistoric animals did we have in Los Angeles?

*1* Wesley: Dinosaurs.

Teacher: You haven't listened to a thing I've said all morning.

*4* Bill: (*Raises hand*) Mr. Walker? Mr. Walker?

Teacher: What is it?

*4* Bill: I just wanted to tell you about hawks.

Teacher: Let me finish with Wesley, then we'll talk about it. (*Many students are fidgeting and appear to be daydreaming. No hands are raised. Mr. Walker glances at the clock and realizes it's time for lunch.*) It's lunch time. We'll have to finish tomorrow.

Mr. Walker's general goal was to teach his students what life was like in Los Angeles many years ago. More specifically, he wanted the students to identify the kinds of prehistoric animals that lived in Los Angeles (*instructional objective*). However, he failed to tell his students the objective before they began reading the textbook. In addition, he didn't prepare them for the lesson by evoking their curiosity or interest in the topic, nor did he consider the *individual differences* in reading speed and comprehension. After the class observed how he responded to incorrect answers, the students did not appear eager to respond. When one of the class thought that dinosaurs had lived in Los Angeles, he could have used this response as an opportunity to explain about the discovery of bones and the kind of bones that were found. He also could have led a discussion concerning why there were not dinosaurs in Los Angeles (*methods of instruction*). Instead, he told the student he was wrong.

A major problem was Mr. Walker's classroom management (*teacher behavior*). As you will learn later in the book, effective classroom managers develop concise procedures in the classroom that reduce the possibility of problems during transition from one subject to another. It is clear that Mr. Walker had not established any rules or procedures, and, in fact, he mentioned to the class that they were unruly during transition periods. Yet he did nothing to help them improve their behavior. Instead of using positive reinforcement to change his students' behavior, he used ridicule and criticism, which are not good *learning principles* to change behavior.

## A High School Classroom

Mr. Barratt's ninth-grade class has been studying the functions and decisions of the Supreme Court to help students identify and analyze factual and value problems using our legal-ethical framework.[1] To accomplish this purpose, he selects a contemporary issue for class discussion. This morning he has rewritten a newspaper article for his students to read.

> Teacher: Okay, folks, let me give you an overview of what we're going to do this morning and, in fact, most of this week. First, we're going to read about the Fort Lauderdale senior citizen who was sentenced to prison for murder. Then we will review our chart on American legal-ethical values, and later, we will begin our discussion and research.

Mr. Barratt passes out the article, and the students begin to read silently. He moves around the room and helps several students with unfamiliar words. The news story is about a 76-year-old man, Roswell Gilbert, who has been sentenced to life imprisonment in Florida with no possibility of parole for 25 years. Mr. Gilbert had shot his wife, to whom he had been married for 51 years. His wife had Alzheimer's disease and osteoporosis (a bone disease) and was in a great deal of pain all the time. Gilbert knew that he was breaking the law, but he could no longer stand to see his wife in pain. His neighbors testified at the trial that his wife had begged him to kill her and end her suffering. Florida governor Bob Graham asked his cabinet for "an act of mercy" to free Gilbert while he appealed the decision. A member of the governor's cabinet responded to the governor: "I don't want to send a message that it's all right to take a person's life because that person is ill." At the time this incident was presented in class, Gilbert was in prison, and his daughter feared that he would die there.

---

[1] This incident was written by Johanna Lemlech of the University of Southern California.

Teacher: What are the issues here? What are the facts of this case?

Susan: The man killed his wife.

Bill: He knew he was breaking the law.

Bennett: The jury found him guilty of murder.

Ann: His wife was sick and wouldn't get better.

Sam: Hey, we don't know that a cure wouldn't be found.

Ann: Well, she was in a lot of pain. Maybe he couldn't stand that.

Bob: There aren't any cures for Alzheimer's disease. Everybody knows that.

Teacher: We're straying from the facts now. Remember, our task right now is just to identify the facts of the case. We'll discuss the conflicts later. Are there some additional facts?

Gilbert: We know that his neighbors testified for him that his wife begged him to end her suffering.

Ann: The governor asked for an "act of mercy."

Teacher: Why don't we move ahead? Using our chart to help us remember our legal-ethical framework, begin to identify values and value conflicts.

Jared: Well, the law says murder is wrong, so the big issue is the rule of law.

Teacher: Good thinking, but what are some other basic values at stake?

Maria: Well, I think due process is an issue.

Bill: Why? I don't understand that.

Todd: Well, lots of times even supposed murderers are allowed out on bail. He wasn't some kind of kook or mass murderer. He should be allowed out on bail. He is being treated differently from others.

Teacher: Todd, do you know for a fact that other murderers are allowed out on bail to appeal their cases?

Todd: Well, no. But I do know that it is awfully unusual for someone who is not a menace to society to be imprisoned for 25 years without bail.

Jan: Mr. Barratt, isn't the issue whether or not there is evil intent? His motive wasn't evil.

Teacher: Interesting point. Are you saying that there is a difference between his motive and that of other murderers?

Jan: Yes, I guess so. He believed that he was acting in a moral way.

Teacher: It's all right to kill someone, then, if you claim to be moral?

Jan: Well, I don't know.

Teacher: Does anyone else want to respond to that point?

Jared: I do. I heard my parents talking about this case. Isn't he saying that there is a higher authority than society for certain acts, that some laws have to be broken if you are a moral person?

Teacher: Do you think that our legal system should be responsive to moral values?

*3* Sharon: Well, it isn't fair that he should go to jail for mercy killing.

*5* Sam: Do you mean anyone can decide when someone else should die?

Teacher: It sounds like we are ready to take a position and discuss the consequences. Who can identify the value conflict in this issue? (*Mr. Barratt continues by helping the students to focus on the value conflicts pertaining to the issue and asks them to prepare for a debate on the issue in two days.*)

It is clear from the incident that Mr. Barratt was involved in some long-term planning in his class. He stated that the students would read, review prior material, discuss, and research the topic. The primary *objective* was to identify value conflicts. He rewrote the newspaper article for his students to read and moved around the class to monitor the reading activity (*individual differences*). As the instruction began, he guided the discussion through planned questions (*teacher behavior and instructional methodology*). He told the students that the initial discussion should focus on "facts." By remaining silent, he encouraged multiple responses. When the students began to stray from the immediate objective of identifying facts, he reminded them and asked if there were some additional facts. He then used Sam's statement as a cue that the next phase of the lesson should begin. He brought out the chart of American legal-ethical values and value conflicts. At no time did Mr. Barratt respond with a personal opinion. He continued to probe and guide the inquiry—for example, "Is it all right to kill someone, then, if you claim to be moral?"

Mr. Barratt planned distinct phases of his lesson The students first read the prepared material and were encouraged to identify the facts and, then, the value conflicts. Later, he asked students to *evaluate* and synthesize their discussion into two conflicting positions and to do group research to prepare for a class debate (these phases were not reported in the brief transcript you read).

You have read brief descriptions of two teachers with different instructional skills. Although the high school teacher appeared to be more successful in attaining his goal, I easily could have presented a situation in which an elementary school teacher used a similar teaching strategy with great success. I mention this because I don't want you to think that teaching effectiveness is related to any particular level of instruction. I will present examples of effective and ineffective teaching at all levels in school.

## A Final Comment

Before I leave this introduction to the use of the teaching-learning model, it is important that I clarify my position on an important issue in teacher education. The education literature is filled with debates regarding the best way to educate teachers. Some experts believe that any attempts to quantify and sequence teaching as a predictable step-by-step process is doomed to failure (see Costa, 1984; Eisner, 1983). The critics of this approach believe that focusing on the holistic, or total, aspect of teaching is a more effective method of educating teachers. For example, Eisner (1983) states: "Teachers are more like orchestra conductors than technicians. They need rules of thumb and educational imagination, not scientific prescriptions" (p. 5). My position is that beginning teachers need help in identifying the major variables relating to the teaching-learning process. In this way, they will have a better understanding and awareness of that process. As teachers develop greater awareness of the variables influencing learning, there can be more emphasis on the "big picture." Although variables initially are discussed here in a linear fashion to help you better understand the teaching-learning process, you need to recognize that in the real world of teaching, everything happens at once!

Another related issue in teacher education is whether teaching is more an art than a science. At one extreme of this continuum, there are those who believe that "good teachers are born, not made." This position relies on intuition as a basis of action. At the opposite side of the continuum, there are those who believe that good teaching is based on a science of instruction whereby teachers learn effective teaching behaviors. I find it difficult to subscribe totally to either perspective. There may be certain natural traits or abilities in people that make them good teachers. Yet I am convinced that there are important teaching skills that can be learned to enhance teaching effectiveness. I also believe that a sound empirical data base will improve the artful teacher's performance. Thus I believe that good teaching involves both an art and a science.

Finally, some teacher educators have used this particular teaching-learning model (Figure 1.1) in a rigid manner, believing that only one type or method of teaching should be used in all situations. I believe that the use of the model doesn't prevent the teacher from employing a variety of methods and approaches in the classroom.

## THE COMPLEXITY OF CLASSROOM LIFE

Good and Brophy (1987) have pointed out the complexity of classroom life and have explained why teachers are unaware of or misinterpret classroom behavior. They attribute lack of awareness to three factors: First, so much happens so rapidly that it is difficult to be aware of all events. Second, there is no formal system to provide teachers with information on how to behave in the classroom. Finally, teachers do not acquire the observational skills for analyzing and labeling classroom behavior in their teacher education programs. The Classroom Application in the next section provides you with helpful information about observing students in the classroom—an important skill for decision making.

## CLASSROOM APPLICATION: OBSERVING IN THE CLASSROOM

It is important for a teacher to learn as much as possible about individual students in the classroom. Observation of student behavior is an important method of collecting information. Keen observation of all important classroom events is not an easy task, since in one day a teacher may engage in more than a thousand interpersonal exchanges with students (Jackson, 1968). To make matters even more difficult, teachers also have to *interpret* complex behavior as it happens. A teacher cannot become a good observer in one day or one week. A teacher must learn the skills of observation and practice them over a long time.

Almy (1969) identifies three aspects of observation: *description, feelings,* and *inferences.* First, description refers to how the student looks, and to what the student says or does. Second, our own feelings and emotions about what we observe influence what we see and hear. Finally, we infer what the behavior means from what we see and hear and from what we feel and know from past experiences.

Almy points out that when teachers study students to get to know them better, they need to discriminate between actual behavior of the students and the feelings and emotions of the teacher that influence the interpretations of the behavior. This distinction will help the teacher to see behavior more clearly and to reach conclusions about a student that are more likely to be based on factual evidence. For example, if a student has a past history of problems in the classroom and becomes involved in an altercation with another student, the teacher may infer from observation that the "problem" student was responsible for the disagreement. Yet another observer who knew nothing about the students involved may interpret the situation differently.

Another concern in classroom observation is that teachers often react not to what they hear but to their interpretation of what the student said (Good & Brophy, 1987). For example, two students of different abilities can complain about a homework assignment. Even though their comments may be similar, a teacher's reaction to the lower achiever may be more negative than the reaction to the same comments made by the higher-achieving student. Think about how your past experience with a friend, family member, or classmate has influenced how you interpreted something that person has recently said.

In summary, it is very easy for an observer to misinterpret classroom behavior. The observer's past experiences, biases, and prejudices can lead to interpretations that are incorrect. Consequently, a classroom observer has to examine and become aware of any personal perceptual blinders. It is important that you learn to observe behavior as accurately as possible before interpreting what you think you see. If you don't observe or listen objectively, you may end up finding exactly what you expected to find and not realize that you made an invalid inference.

There are many different types of observation that can be made in the classroom. One of the most useful types of observation is the anecdote—a narrative account of a situation as seen by an observer. The first step is to decide what you want to observe. I have already mentioned that classrooms are busy places. It is best, therefore, to focus on one area at a time (e.g., social interaction, behavior during seatwork, or progress in oral reading). If you are aware of the purpose of the observation, you can observe students in appropriate situations to obtain adequate samples of their behavior. Consider such variables as the periods and times of the day, subjects that the students like and dislike, and the size of the instructional group. Make observations inside and outside of class. John Holt (1982), in *How Children Fail*, reminds teachers: "If we look at children only to see whether they are doing what we want or don't want them to do, we are likely to miss all the things about them that are the most interesting and important" (p. 36).

Keep a running log of the students' behavior during the observation periods. The observations should be dated and distinct from one another in the log. The log should contain narrative descriptions of behavior along with interpretations about its possible meanings. Keep in mind that interpretations may change as more information is collected. This is another reason why it is important to separate subjective interpretations from descriptions of behaviors. A good procedure is to use only the left half of the page for keeping the log of behavior. Put interpretations on the right side of the page. When recording data, note specific behaviors, including body language such as facial expressions and posture. Avoid interpretations that are not supported by facts. In reviewing behavioral comments, look for relationships and contradictions. Try to identify behavioral patterns, and look for places where a particular pattern might have been expected but did not occur (Good & Brophy, 1987).

## PROBLEMS ENCOUNTERED BY BEGINNING TEACHERS

**What type of problems do beginning teachers confront?**

All teachers are faced with problems. Bluming and Dembo (1973) state that teachers rarely leave their profession as a result of inadequate training in their discipline. However, many do leave because they are discouraged by aggravations that interfere with normal teaching situations and find themselves unable to make effective decisions about the problems that arise in their classrooms.

What are the concerns of a beginning teacher? Veenman's (1984) review of literature on the topic indicates eight problems—classroom discipline, motivating students, dealing with individual differences, assessing students' work, relationship with parents, organization of classwork, in-sufficient and/or inadequate teaching materials and supplies, and dealing with problems of individual students. He finds that the problems of ele-mentary and secondary teachers are similar. This textbook will deal with all the problems Veenman found except those regarding teaching materials and supplies.

Ryan (1970) describes the first year of teaching in a book with an in-teresting title, *Don't Smile until Christmas*. He points out that the novice teacher faces many situations and events without adequate preparation:

> They find high school students are hard to reach; they underestimate the difficulty of motivating them and overestimate their own skills as disci-plinarians. They do not anticipate the amount of time and work necessary to keep up with students. The volume of administrative tasks surprises them. They are unprepared to handle classes *and* take roll, write tardy slips, read notices from the office, and execute the dozens of ever-present administrative details. The emotional and physical drain of teaching five periods a day leaves them little energy for anything else. . . . Of course, the first year of teaching is not always unpleasant. Some beginners are tremendously relieved to discover that their fantasies of failure do not come true. They are surprised to find out that they can teach, that they like what they are doing, and that students do respect them. For some, anticipated sources of trouble turn out to be their strengths; they *do* have a good command of their subject matter; they *can* be fair to all the students and avoid playing favorites. . . . But whether the first year of teaching is a sad one or a joyous one, it is a year of intense learning for all. (pp. 172–173)

Fuller and Brown (1975) divide teacher concerns into three phases: the *entry stage*, the *stage of teacher situation concerns*, and the *stage of pupil concerns*.

They call the first, or entry, stage of teaching the "survival stage." This stage is marked by anxiety and trepidation because the teacher is concerned with personal adequacy: Do my students like me? What do other teachers think of me? Does my principal think I am doing a good job? Preservice teachers have more concerns of this type than inservice teachers. There is research evidence that some teachers become more impersonal, negative, and authoritarian during their initial orientation to the real world of teaching (Dutton, 1962; Kahn & Weiss, 1973). Hoy (1967) has shown that beginning teachers change from a humanistic orientation to a custodial one, stressing bureaucratic order and control. He believes that this change is due to the socialization processes in schools where teachers are expected to manage well-behaved and controlled students. As a result, beginning teachers want to become good classroom managers and tend to become less humanistic in accomplishing this goal.

I was reminded of the strong effects of teacher socialization when I visited the classroom of a teacher who had been in my educational psy-chology course a few years earlier. The student was one of the more "nontraditional" students I had in the class. He often spoke of the radical changes that needed to occur in the classroom and mentioned that he would take steps to ensure that his classroom would be different. He would teach students effective learning strategies, would de-emphasize rote learning, and would involve parents in the learning process—all excellent teaching practices! However, when I observed his classroom, it appeared that he either had modified his beliefs or had found it difficult to practice what he believed, because his classroom was one of the more traditional ones in the school! Could the desire to succeed during the "survival stage" of teaching alter teaching beliefs and practices?

When teachers feel that they are surviving the demands of teaching, they become more concerned with student achievement and enter stage two, the stage of teacher situation concerns. These concerns pertain to the frustration and limitations regarding teaching various subject areas. Concerns about class size, time pressures, and lack of instructional materials are examples of frustrations evoked by various teaching situations. Inservice teachers have more concerns of this type than preservice teachers.

Until the first two stages have been dealt with adequately, teachers don't appear to aspire to the third, which Fuller and Brown identify as the stage of concern about pupils (e.g., recognizing the social and emotional needs of children at different developmental levels, identifying individual differences in the classroom, and realizing the inappropriateness of some material for certain students). Based on Fuller and Brown's findings, it is not surprising that some teachers are not able to deal with individual student needs. In fact, Cruickshank and Callahan (1983) believe that some teachers never get to stage three because they leave the profession psychologically defeated, or they struggle for years in stage two "preoccupied with themselves and with what they teach" (p. 154). The important implication of Fuller and Brown's work is that beginning teachers need to be concerned about their own personal development and how their own needs may influence both awareness and interaction in the classroom.

The following excerpt from "Diary of a Beginning Teacher" (Morris, 1968) records the personal concerns of a teacher in the early teaching phase. As you read the diary, make a list of the various topics mentioned, and discuss them with students in your class. What problems might give you the most trouble?

> *September 7.* I'm exhausted today. I gave them all back their papers which, thank goodness, took up part of the class time. I also assigned them four questions to do for homework. I didn't write the questions on the board, which was a mistake; I ended up repeating everything five or six times.
>
> I feel so pushed, preparing and correcting papers; hope things calm down soon.
>
> *September 9.* I tried playing a game with them in class today. It didn't go very well. One of the biggest problems was that I didn't have a firm enough control over the class to do it. I had them asking each other

questions. They were divided into two teams and all that. I even set up a panel of judges who decided whether the answer to a question was right.

I also gave them a pop quiz at the beginning of the period. I tried it in one class at the end, but that didn't work as well; they were too excited from the game to settle down.

One real catastrophe today. The map fell on my head during fourth period. The class went wild; luckily the assistant principal was right outside the room and came in and rescued me.

*September 13.* I gave the quiz today and they did pretty well and then I finished up discussing geography—I hope. I only gave them twenty of the spelling words and left off the longest and most difficult. They were very upset because they said they had all learned that one. The day has finally come. Despite all of the work and how tired I am, I think I am really going to like teaching.

*September 26.* I'm having a problem getting the classes to keep quiet now. For a while they were pretty good, but now they're beginning to get to me. Even the good students are starting to talk during class. I don't think it's because they're not interested because the talk is almost always about what I'm discussing, but still they're talking without permission. If it was only a little I wouldn't mind, but it's beginning to get to the point where I can't go on because of the talking.

*September 27.* The assistant principal came and visited one of my classes today. Before class I was talking at my desk with one student and all of a sudden I heard this deathly silence hit the class. (I guess that's not the right way to say it, but anyway) I looked up and there he was. I started the class. I'd ask a question and there was absolute silence. Nothing. It was terrible! It's bad when they're all talking at once, but it's horrible when they're afraid to move.

*September 29.* I've been getting bored, teaching the same thing over and over and so today I did different things in different classes. I discussed with some, gave some a quiz and had others writing. I tried discussing with my sixth-period class, but they're just impossible after about ten minutes. I got really mad at them and told them to take out their books and study quietly for ten minutes and then I would give them a quiz. While they studied, I made up the quiz and it was a dilly—only four people passed. I suppose it isn't good educational psychology to do that, but it made me feel much better, and at that point it was either them or me.

*October 14.* I have now firmly and purposely gotten my classes separated. That is, I am no longer doing the same thing five times a day. At first it was a big help being able to prepare only one lesson each night. But I realized that it was terribly boring for me, and my boredom would be reflected in the kids. Once I felt that I had my bearings, I decided to change all that. Well, it's taken me this long to carry out my plan. Although I use much of the same material in all of my classes, I do not use it all at the same time or in the same manner. I can really see the difference in the classes.

*October 19.* Tonight was the PTA open house. I was pleased at how well it went. I guess that parents are not really ogres after all. But it was an awfully long day. I really do love teaching and I look forward to all of my classes, but I often feel that I am not doing my best for these kids. Teach and learn—and have I learned a lot in these seven weeks.

*November 4.* Teacher's Convention—WHAT A FARCE!

*November 9.* Every day I learn so much. I hope that the children are learning some too, but they couldn't possibly learn more than a fraction of what I have. I think there is hope for me yet. I already know so much more than I did in September. Sometimes I feel the huge mountain of things yet to learn pressing down on me, but I think I've made a significant dent in the mountain. I may live through the year. But then again, it seems overwhelming.

*December 8.* Ugliness! Nothing went well at all. Jabber, jabber, jabber—I don't know. Sometimes I get so upset and depressed it's horrible. They don't listen or follow instructions, or learn anything. I guess it's a normal feeling for new teachers.

*December 12.* Almost the end of the period before vacation. I guess not really but it seems like it must be. Happiness! They announced that all evaluation meetings are cancelled until after Christmas. Hurray! Except for the faculty meeting Thursday.

The diary provides some good examples of typical problems faced by a beginning teacher. Ryan (1970) describes the first year of teaching as an emotional roller coaster. Did you detect the swings in the teacher's emotions as she progressed throughout the semester? Your first impressions of this teacher might lead you to the conclusion that all is lost! However, if you return to the teaching-learning model, you will see that her problems can be identified. There are three obvious areas that are causing her problems: *teacher behavior* (particularly management problems—failing to write questions on the board, classroom control, questioning, and maintaining attention); *evaluation* (constructing a poor test and using evaluation as a discipline technique); and *methods of instruction* (lack of variability in lessons). After identifying these problems, she could take steps to acquire information and skills to alleviate them. Think about the type of advice you would give her as you read about the variables comprising the teaching-learning process.

## KEY POINTS

1. All teachers have personal hypotheses or beliefs about the teaching-learning process even if they are not consciously aware of them.
2. Teacher beliefs lead them to make important classroom decisions that affect how students learn in school.
3. Teachers need to (a) examine the effects of their decisions on learning, (b) examine their personal beliefs about the teaching-learning process,

(c) evaluate the effectiveness of beliefs and practices, and (d) modify teaching behavior when necessary.

4. Educational psychology includes content that the teacher can use to formulate and test personal beliefs about teaching and learning.
5. An instructional model that identifies the major variables in the teaching-learning process includes the variables of individual differences, teacher behavior, instructional objectives, principles of learning, teaching methods, and evaluation of student behavior.
6. Some teachers become discouraged because they are unable to make effective decisions about the problems that arise in their classrooms.
7. Teachers need to learn to analyze their problems so they can put their knowledge of educational psychology to use. Thus teachers must both understand and apply psychological knowledge.
8. In observing student behavior, teachers must learn to separate description of behavior from their feelings and inferences.
9. Beginning teachers appear to be most concerned with their personal adequacy in meeting the demands of teaching. Other concerns involve classroom discipline, motivating students, dealing with individual differences, assessing student work, handling relationships with parents, and organizing the classroom.

## KEY TERMS

teaching, p. 2
learning, p. 2
instructional objective, p. 5
entry behavior, p. 5

## SUGGESTIONS FOR FURTHER READING

Boyer, E. L. (1983). *High school: A report on secondary education in America.* New York: Harper & Row. Discusses the results of a major study of the American high school.

Bullough, R. V. (1989). *First-year teacher.* New York: Teachers College Press. An in-depth case study of the first year-and-a-half of a seventh-grade teacher's experience. Three appendixes include advice on selecting a school and surviving the year.

Emmers, A. P. (1981). *After the lesson plan: Realities of high school teaching.* New York: Teachers College Press. Provides helpful insights into secondary teaching.

Goodlad, J. (1984) *A place called school: Prospects for the future.* New York: McGraw-Hill. An excellent description of classroom instruction that provides proposals for improving the effectiveness of schools.

Greenwood, G. E., & Parkay, F. W. (1989). *Case studies for teacher decision making.* New York: Random House. Provides typical teaching situations for students to develop their decision-making skills.

Kowalski, T., Weaver, R. A., & Henson, K. T. (1989). *Case studies on teaching.* White Plains, NY: Longman. Presents cases on first-year teachers that provide insight into the major problems facing them.

The following references are good sources for developing observational skills in the classroom:

Almy, M., & Genishi, C. (1979). *Ways of studying children: An observation manual for early childhood teachers.* New York: Teachers College Press.

Boehm, A., & Weinberg, R. A. (1987). *The classroom observer: Developing skills in early childhood education.* New York: Teachers College Press.

Cartwright, C. C., & Cartwright, G. P. (1984). *Developing observation skills* (2nd ed.). New York: McGraw-Hill.

Cohen, D. H., Stern, V., & Balaban, N. (1983). *Observing and recording the behavior of young children* (3rd ed.). New York: Teachers College Press.

Good, T. L., & Brophy, J. E. (1987). *Looking in classrooms* (4th ed.). New York: Harper & Row.

## FOLLOW-UP ACTIVITIES

### 1. Analyze Common Myths about Teaching

Combs (1979) believes that myths are the greatest source of failure in the schools. Since people behave in terms of their beliefs, behavior based on false or inaccurate information often results in false or inaccurate outcomes.

Read each of the following statements and determine whether you agree with, disagree with, or are not sure about the accuracy of each statement. After identifying your beliefs, discuss how they might lead to certain teaching or classroom practices.

|  | Tend to Agree | Tend to Disagree | Not Sure |
|---|---|---|---|
| 1. A person needs to feel some pressure to be motivated to learn. | | | |
| 2. Children have a natural desire to learn. | | | |
| 3. Younger children need more structure than older children. | | | |
| 4. Competition is a great motivator. | | | |
| 5. Human intelligence is fixed by the time a child begins school. | | | |
| 6. Failure is helpful in motivating students. | | | |

### 2. Think about Teaching Problems

Discuss some teaching problems that your previous teachers have had. Did they realize that a problem existed? What strategies did they use to attempt to solve the problem? What types of teaching problems do you think will give you the most trouble? Why do you feel this way?

### 3. Use Library Reference Sources to Identify Information about Teaching and Learning

Use *Psychological Abstracts, Resources in Education,* or *Current Index to Journals in Education* to locate articles on a topic or issue of interest (see Appendix: Using Library Reference Sources and Reading Journal Articles). If an article includes ideas about methods and techniques in teaching, summarize it and mention how you might use the ideas discussed in the article. Don't hesitate to criticize the author if you disagree with the ideas presented in the article. If the paper reports a research investigation, write an abstract of the article following the outline below:

- Author(s)
- Title of article
- Journal in which article appears (include date, volume number, and pages)
- Purpose of the study (found in the first few paragraphs)
- Subjects
- Procedures (or methods)
- Results
- Conclusions

### 4. Analyze the Teaching-Learning Process   *write*

Make arrangements to observe a teacher presenting a lesson. Keep detailed notes on both the teacher's and the students' behavior during the lesson, and analyze the lesson by answering the following questions:

a. Was there a perceivable objective? Did the teaching focus on a particular learning target, or did it include a little bit of everything or anything?

b. Was the objective appropriate for this group of learners? Had the objective already been achieved by the learners, or was it so difficult that there was little possibility of achieving it?

c. Was the objective achieved? Was there evidence of progression toward advancement or attainment of the objective?

d. What did the teacher do that facilitated learning?

e. What did the teacher do that interfered with learning?

f. What problems arose during the lesson? How did the teacher handle these problems?

g. What suggestions do you have for improving the lesson? (Hunter, 1973)

## APPENDIX: USING LIBRARY REFERENCE SOURCES
## AND READING JOURNAL ARTICLES

It is important for you to get acquainted with the library facilities at your college or university. Reading books and journal articles will help you keep up with developments in your field long after you attain your degree. The following reference sources can be useful in locating research and applied articles in your field of specialization: *Psychological Abstracts, Resources in Education, Current Index to Journals in Education.*

### Psychological Abstracts

*Psychological Abstracts* is published monthly by the American Psychological Association and contains abstracts of articles appearing in more than 500 journals in psychology and related areas. Each issue has sections covering various topics of psychology. The section on child development and adolescence and the section on educational psychology, which include abstracts in areas such as attitude and adjustment, testing, special education, counseling and guidance, school learning and achievement, and curriculum programs, are most relevant for the teacher.

The December issue contains both an author and a subject index of all articles in the previous 11 issues of the year. A semiannual index is also available. When using cumulative indexes, check the subject index for articles pertaining to the topic. The subject of the article appears in a concise form. After the description of the subject, you will find one or more numbers referring to the abstract included during the preceding year. The information will help you find the abstract in the appropriate monthly issue.

### Resources in Education

Another important reference source has been established by the Office of Education: the Educational Resources Information Center (ERIC), which collects, stores, and disseminates information on education. ERIC abstracts include papers presented at educational conferences, progress reports of research in progress, final reports of federally funded studies, and abstracts of some documents listed in *Psychological Abstracts*. The advantage of the ERIC system is that it includes many documents not usually published in journals and provides the best compilation of current educational research.

All the abstracts in ERIC appear in a monthly publication called *Resources in Education*. Each abstract is classified by subject area, author, and institutional and accession (identification) number. To locate an abstract, first select key research terms in your area of interest. If you are interested in teaching procedures, you might look under teaching methods, educational strategies, or teaching techniques.

To help identify appropriate search terms, ERIC has published the

*Thesaurus of ERIC Descriptors*. This publication includes all terms used to classify ERIC documents. Once the key search terms have been identified, you should then examine the semiannual or annual cumulative indexes for the titles or pertinent references and locate the abstract in a monthly issue of *Resources in Education*.

Most educational libraries have the ERIC collection in microfiche—small sheets of microfilm—that require special readers to enlarge the image to normal page size. Therefore, once you identify the accession number of the document from *Resources in Education* (for example, ED 013 371), you can locate the corresponding numbered microfiche of the complete article. If you wish to obtain a copy of the document, you can order it through the ERIC Document Reproduction Services.

### Current Index to Journals in Education

Another important resource is the monthly journal *Current Index to Journals in Education* (CIJE), compiled by specialists of the ERIC system. Articles from more than 500 journals are classified and listed according to the same system developed in the ERIC *Thesaurus*.

The CIJE is divided into four sections: subject index, author index, journal contents index, and main entry section. The procedures for selecting an entry are similar to those for *Resources in Education*. Locate articles in the main entry section by checking the subject index to find the titles and numbers of the articles. If the title of an article is not sufficient to convey the main meaning of the article, the CIJE staff provides a brief annotation under the title.

### Journals in Psychology and Education

As you locate various educational journals, you will see that they fall into various categories. Some journals include only research articles; other journals include papers on general issues in education and some research articles. Specialized journals are available in specific teaching areas and focus on teaching techniques and research reports. *Psychological Abstracts* focuses on journals reporting research investigations, and the *Current Index to Journals in Education* includes research and applied journals. Some journals have articles listed in both reference sources. *Resources in Education* includes papers presented at conferences and special reports that are not listed in the other two reference sources.

The following are examples of types of journal. Refer to the listing of journals included in the CIJE for a *complete* list of available journals in education and psychology.

### RESEARCH JOURNALS
- *American Educational Research Journal*
- *Child Development*
- *Developmental Psychology*
- *Journal of Educational Psychology*
- *Journal of Applied Behavioral Analysis*
- *Journal of Educational Research*

- *Journal of Experimental Education*
- *Psychology in the Schools*

## GENERAL JOURNALS

- *Educational Leadership*
- *Elementary School Journal*
- *Phi Delta Kappan*
- *Teachers College Record*
- *Theory into Practice*
- *Journal of General Education*

## SPECIALIZED JOURNALS

- *American Biology Teacher*
- *American Business Educator*
- *American Music Teacher*
- *Arithmetic Teacher*
- *Art Education*
- *Coach and Athlete*
- *Educational Theatre Journal*
- *Elementary English*
- *German Review*
- *Journal of Reading*
- *Journal of Secondary Education*
- *Mathematics Teacher*
- *Physical Education*
- *School Science and Mathematics*
- *Social Education*

### Reading Research Articles

Although the format of research articles varies depending on the particular journal, some common components can be identified:

- *Abstract.* This section is found on the first page of the article and briefly reviews the purpose, procedures, results, and conclusions in less than 150 words. By reading the abstract, you can quickly determine whether you are interested in the article. Some research journals do not include an abstract.
- *Introduction* (often not labeled). The first few paragraphs of a research article review previous literature on the topic to provide a rationale for why the investigation was undertaken. The last paragraph in this section usually includes the questions or hypotheses to be investigated.
- *Method.* This section describes how the study was conducted and includes a number of subsections—for example, the subjects, procedures, and instrumentation used in the investigation.
- *Results.* This section summarizes the data collected, describes the statistical tests used to test the hypotheses, and reports whether or not the hypotheses were confirmed or rejected.

- *Discussion*. This section examines and interprets the results of the investigation. The author usually discusses the conclusions reached and the implications for future research. Some research articles combine the results and discussion sections.

Students who have not had a course in statistics or introduction to research may have some difficulty reading the results section of a research article. Researchers use various procedures to conduct investigations on various issues in education. In **experimental research** (studies that explore cause-and-effect relationships), the researcher uses **control groups** and **experimental groups** to test hypotheses. A **hypothesis** is a statement about the relationship among variables in a study. An example of such a statement is: "If students participate in cooperative learning, they will develop more positive attitudes about mathematics." In some investigations, researchers will identify questions that they want to answer rather than use a hypothesis. For example: Does cooperative learning improve attitudes toward mathematics? The experimental group(s) use(s) the particular method or technique that the researcher wants to investigate (cooperative learning) and the control group(s) use(s) the normal, or typical, learning method for learning mathematics (e.g., the lecture-discussion method).

Two other terms usually found in research articles are **independent variables** and **dependent variables.** The independent variable is the variable that the experimenter is manipulating. In the foregoing example, it is a method of instruction—cooperative learning. The dependent variable is the variable that the researcher uses to measure the effect of the independent variable. The dependent variable in the study on cooperative learning could be an instrument measuring attitude toward mathematics that is given to the subjects in the study before and after the investigation.

To test whether or not a hypothesis has been confirmed, researchers use various statistics based on the laws of probability. For example, suppose that at the beginning of the study, the control and experimental groups have the same average score on their attitude toward mathematics—let's say, 85.4. However, at the end of the study, the control subjects score 90.4 and the experimental subjects 95.7. Is this difference large enough to confirm the hypothesis? The only way to determine this is by a statistical test. Thus, when you read about a researcher identifying a **significant difference,** the term refers to a statistical probability determined before the study. Common levels of significance established in research studies are $p < .01$ or $p < .05$. These probability levels can be interpreted as follows: A probability of less than .05 means that for a finding to be significant, it can happen by chance only 5 times out of 100. Stating this finding in another way, if the investigation was conducted 100 times, the size of the difference in attitude scores between the control and experimental groups would likely occur 95 times out of

100. If the statistical test indicates that the probability is greater than .05, the researcher would then state that there was no significant difference between the groups. As a result, the hypothesis could not be confirmed.

Even if you do not understand the statistical tests used in a research article, you will be able to determine whether significant results were attained by reading the text or tables in which significant differences are identified by the probability levels for each statistical test.

Some studies use correlational methods to investigate educational issues. A **correlation** between two variables is a statistical indication of their relationship. It is determined by a mathematical formula (see Figure 12.1, page 512). Because correlations are used extensively in educational research, it is important that you be able to interpret the meaning of a correlation.

If two variables increase proportionately (for example, children's age and weight), their correlation is positive. A negative correlation signifies that as one variable increases, the other decreases (for example, a car's increase in age and decrease in price).

The symbol used to denote a correlation is $r$, which ranges from $-1$ to $+1$. The closer $r$ is to $-1$ or $+1$, the higher the correlation. The closer $r$ is to zero, the smaller the correlation. We almost never obtain a perfect negative or positive correlation (-1 or +1), but we do find that variables correlate to some degree. For example, we might refer to $r = .50$ as a moderately positive correlation, to $r = .95$ as a high positive correlation, and to $r = -.91$ as a high negative correlation. Correlations near zero denote no or minimal relationships between the variables. If no sign ($+$ or $-$) is present in front of the correlation, it is assumed to be positive.

Finally, correlations do not imply causality. That is, two variables may correlate (e.g., smoking and lung cancer), but one variable is not necessarily the cause of the other. There is a high positive correlation between the number of liquor stores and churches in urban areas. I would hope that one is not the cause of the other!

When you take courses in research design and statistics, you will learn more about the different ways to conduct research in education. In the meantime, this brief introduction will get you started reading research articles. For more information, locate books on introduction to research, such as *Educational Research: An Introduction* (Borg & Gall, 1989) and *Research Methods in Education* (Sowell & Casey, 1982).

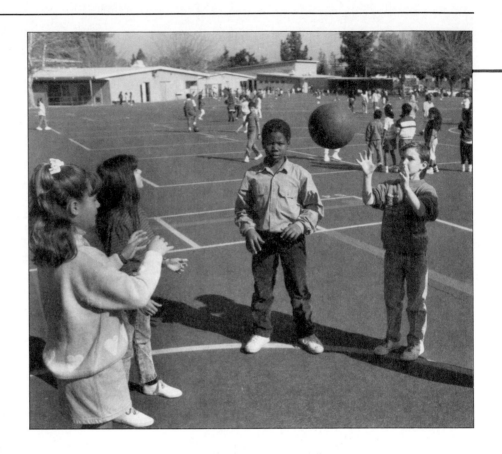

# P A R T   O N E

# Development and Individual Differences

## PART OVERVIEW

One of the most important variables influencing the effectiveness of instruction is individual differences. The variety of student abilities, developmental, language, and cultural differences, learning styles, interests, and attitudes found within any classroom leads to a wide variety of results. Some students will enjoy more success in school and experience more favorable teacher and peer interaction than other students.

Teaching would be much easier (but less interesting) if all students were alike. Instructional decisions would be greatly reduced. Lesson plans would not have to be modified, teachers would not have to consider alternative instructional procedures, and teacher-student interaction would probably be more uniform. However, the reality of teaching is that student differences present one of the greatest challenges to teachers.

Think back to your own elementary and secondary school days. These types of students were probably acquaintances of yours: the student who was always the first to answer the instructor's question; the student who infuriated the teacher by asking different or unusual questions; the student from a different cultural background who had difficulty learning; the student whose primary language was not English; the student who always panicked during exam time; the student who always sat in the back of the classroom, rarely said anything, and had an implicit "contract" with the teacher stating: "You don't bother me and I won't bother you." Try to recall additional types of students who had varying success in school. Try to pinpoint the characteristics that appeared to help or hinder them in the classroom.

From the teacher's perspective, it is important to understand what student characteristics should be considered in planning and implementing instruction. Chapters 2 deals with intelligence and cognitive development; Chapter 3 with cognition, culture, and language; Chapter 4 follows with a discussion of personal and social factors influencing learning. Finally, Chapter 5 discusses exceptional children who often differ in both cognitive and social attributes. As you read the next four chapters, identify the individual differences that would influence the types of decisions you might make in the classroom.

# CHAPTER 2

# Intelligence and Cognitive Development

### ORIENTATION

The study of intelligence—its general nature and measurement—is one of the most emotional issues in educational psychology. Probably no other area is more discussed and less understood by educators. In this chapter, I will discuss three major perspectives of intelligence: the psychometric, the Piagetian, and the information-processing.

Briefly, the **psychometric** perspective attempts to understand intelligence by identifying the factors or mental structures (e.g. reasoning ability, spatial ability, and verbal ability) that are responsible for individual differences on intelligence tests. The Piagetian perspective focuses on qualitative developmental changes in children's thinking by identifying how children think and reason differently from adults. The focus in this approach is on the development of intellectual processes that are common to all children rather than on individual differences. Finally, the **information-processing** perspective looks at the specific processes that underlie intelligent behavior. Information-processing psychologists ask the following questions: What are the underlying aspects in thinking in specific areas? How do individuals with superior ability differ from individuals who are less competent in the area? Do they change with age? Do people differ in their skill in using different abilities?

The three perspectives should be considered complementary rather than mutually exclusive since they deal with different but overlapping aspects of intelligence (Wagner & Sternberg, 1984). In general, the psychometric perspective assesses *what* we know (the product). Although the specific approaches are different, the Piagetian and information-processing perspective emphasize *how* we think (the process). Each perspective has different implications for designing intervention strategies for intellectual growth and academic success.

By the time you master the material presented in this chapter, you will be able to:

• Identify the psychometric, Piagetian, and information-processing approaches to intelligence.
• Explain how the theory of intelligence a person adopts can influence intervention strategies designed to enhance intellectual development and academic achievement.

1. Is intelligence a unitary trait or a composite of traits?
2. How is intelligence measured?
3. Are intelligence tests fair to all students?
4. Is intelligence fixed, or can it be changed?
5. Is intelligence determined by environment or heredity?
6. According to Piaget, what are the major characteristics of children thinking at the preoperational, concrete, and formal operation stages?
7. What are the criticisms of Piaget's theory?
8. What instructional practices would Piaget recommend?
9. How do neo-Piagetian theories modify Piaget's theory?
10. How do information-processing theorists criticize the psychometric approach to intelligence?
11. How do information-processing theorists approach the study of intelligence?

## THE PSYCHOMETRIC PERSPECTIVE

### The Composition of Intelligence

**Is intelligence a unitary trait or a composite of traits?**

Introductory textbooks usually provide a definition of the concept under discussion to clarify any misconceptions regarding its meaning. An intelligent definition of **intelligence** would probably comprise a booklet. The definition of intelligence varies with each psychologist's philosophy regarding its nature. In general, intelligence is viewed as the capacity or set of capacities that allows any individual to learn, to solve problems, and/or to interact successfully with the environment. For the most part, theories of intelligence have been viewed from one of two perspectives. The first takes the position that one general factor accounts for most of our mental ability. In 1927, Spearman was one of the first psychologists to propose that intelligence involves a high degree of general ability. He hypothesized an intellect composed of a general factor ($g$) underlying all mental functions and a multitude of specific factors ($s$) related to a given task or situation.

According to Spearman's theory, people differed in the degree of the general factor as well as in the quality of the specific factors involved in a given task, so that a person could be relatively "more intelligent" than another person because of a superior $g$ but less capable in a given area (for example, science) because of deficient or inferior $s$ factors in that area. However, since $g$ represented a form of mental ability included in all mental operations, a person who was grossly lacking in general intelligence would probably not be gifted in a specific field.

Teachers are often surprised that various intelligence tests ask different questions and wonder how students who take these tests can be compared. Psychologists who support Spearman's theory would explain to them that it does not matter what particular combination of mental tests or performances any given test calls for, because they all tap the same general factor.

Any reading and arithmetic test will result in an overlap of the general abilities common to both tests. The *g* factor in both reading and arithmetic tests is vocabulary and word meaning. The measure of intelligence in this case is general ability, although specific abilities that are not common to both tests (that is, computational skills and reading speed) also enter into play.

The second basic psychometric approach to intelligence, one that has received more attention in recent years, is the study of specific abilities, especially as they relate to success in various subject areas. Thorndike (1927), unlike Spearman, believed that intelligence was the sum of specific abilities. He identified intelligence as (1) *abstract ability*—the ability to deal with ideas and symbols, (2) *mechanical ability*—the ability to deal with mechanisms and tasks involving sensory-motor activities, and (3) *social ability*—the ability to deal effectively with people.

Thurstone (1938) also disagreed with Spearman after his battery of 56 tests produced no common intelligence factor. Thurstone concluded that there was no general factor; he conceived of intelligence as a number of *primary mental abilities*. His research indicated that mental ability could be grouped into seven factors and that intelligence could be measured by sampling individual performance in seven areas: number, word fluency, verb meaning, associative memory, reasoning, space, and perceptual speed.

One of the most extensive multifactor theories of intelligence was presented by Guilford (1959, 1988), who used the statistical technique of **factor analysis** to develop his **Structure of Intellect** (SOI) model. He hypothesized that the human intellect was composed of a three-dimensional system of numerous intellectual abilities classified on the basis of (1) the material or **contents** processed, (2) the processes or **operations** performed with the material, and (3) the forms or **products** of the processed information.

Figure 2.1 represents the three kinds of factors by means of a cubical model. Theoretically, 180 different factors, or abilities, can be generated from the model (5 contents × 6 operations × 6 products), because any operation can be performed on any content and can result in any product. This model implies that an individual's intelligence cannot be adequately assessed by means of a single score.

The first dimension of Guilford's model, content, has five subcategories: (1) *visual* content refers to concrete objects directly perceived (e.g., shapes, diagrams); (2) *auditory* content represents stimuli that can be heard; (3) *symbolic* content pertains to letters, numbers, or other conventional forms; (4) *semantic* content takes the form of verbal meanings or ideas; (5) *behavioral* content is social intelligence—the ability to perceive and interpret the thoughts and feelings of others from their overt behavior.

The second dimension, operations, contains six subcategories: (1) *evaluation* is the decision-making process relative to the accuracy and appro-

*Guilford model*

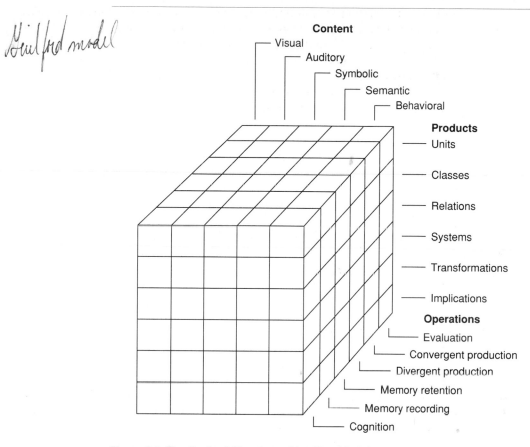

Figure 2.1  The Revised Structure of Intellect Model.

*Source: Guilford, 1989.*

priateness of the information that has been cognized; (2) *convergent production* is the process of producing a correct or conventional answer from known and remembered information; (3) *divergent production* is the process of thinking in different directions, sometimes seeking variety, from known and remembered information; (4) *memory retention* is the retention of information over a period of several days; (5) *memory recording* is the retention of information immediately after memorizing a set of items; (6) *cognition* is the discovery and recognition of information.

The application of mental operations to the content dimension results in certain kinds of product, the third dimension of Guilford's model. Products are divided into six subcategories: (1) *units* are segregated items of mental work, such as a specific word or image; (2) *classes* are groupings of units of information according to common characteristics; (3) *relations* refer to the relationship between units of information, such as "bigger than" or "next to"; (4) *systems* pertain to the structuring of complex information; (5) *transformations* refer to changes in preexisting information; (6) *implications* refer to inferences or predictions drawn from current knowledge and applied to future actions.

Meeker (1969) has used Guilford's original (1959) model to assess the curriculum and abilities of children. She believes that when educators discuss intelligence, they must ask: Intelligence? In what area? Meeker further states that when a child of average ability fails to learn, the intelligence test score neither explains nor accounts for the failure. According to Meeker, we need theoretically based tests that provide the teacher with diagnostic information on which instructional decisions for a given child can be made.

Guilford's model sets forth one way of organizing abilities in a school's curriculum. Examine any traditional school curriculum, and you will find that some abilities receive more attention than others. In the field of content, for instance, the stress is on semantic and symbolic abilities to the detriment of figural and behavioral skills. Three of the five operations—cognition, memory recording, and convergent production—are stressed over the other two—divergent production (associated with creative thinking) and evaluation. Among the six products, a disproportionate amount of emphasis falls on units and classes.

## Individual Intelligence Tests

**How is intelligence measured?**

The first intelligence test was developed in the early 1900s by Alfred Binet, a French psychologist, who was commissioned by the Ministry of Public Instruction in Paris to identify retarded children who could not benefit from a traditional French education. The target of this investigation was the establishment of special schools for children who needed help.

Binet had no particular theory of intelligence but had been working on a series of tests that appeared to be reasonable samples of children's behavior and that distinguished abilities at different age levels. He found that at each age level, some children performed better than others. The children who performed the best on these tests were also rated by their teachers as "bright." Conversely, those children who performed poorly on the tests were rated by their teachers as poorer students.

Binet based his tests on the comparison of a particular child with the child's age group. A child who was above average in intelligence could answer more questions than the average child in the age group. If the child answered about the same number of questions as the average child in the group, the child was considered average in intelligence. The child whose performance was below average for the age group was considered below average in intelligence.

Binet established the use of the term **mental age** as a basis for determining the level of a given child's mental functioning. A child of 8 years who could answer questions that the average 10-year-old child could answer would have a mental age of 10 years.

There were many translations of Binet's test in this country. Lewis Terman created one in 1916 at Stanford University that became widely used. His test, known as the Stanford-Binet, is still used today in revised form. Terman defined intelligence as the ability to think in abstract terms, and this definition served as the basis for establishing test items.

The popular term **intelligence quotient (IQ)** was first used by the psychologist William Stern, who proposed that a child's mental age should be divided by his or her chronological age, the most important factor being the relationship, or ratio, of the two numbers. Therefore, *IQ* = Mental Age *(MA)* ÷ Chronological Age *(CA)* × 100 (to remove the decimal).

Stern believed that the IQ would be relatively stable throughout an individual's life. For example, a child of 6 years (CA) with a mental age of 8 years has an IQ that equals 133 (8 ÷ 6 × 100). Stern theorized that at age 12 the child's mental age would be 16 and the IQ would still equal 133.

Later research on the growth of intelligence did not support this linear relationship, and psychometrists (measurement specialists) disregarded the IQ formula in determining mental ability.[1] Presently, a table of deviation scores is used in determining an IQ (this score is discussed in more detail in Chapter 13). A child's score reflects its deviation from the average score of the children of the same chronological age in the standardization (comparison) group.

Other reasons for disregarding the use of the IQ ratio have to do with mental age, which loses its meaning for adults. It cannot be used to compare results on different tests, as can the deviation score. I present more information on intelligence tests in Chapter 12 when I deal with the evaluation aspect of the instructional process.

Most intelligence tests are constructed to have an average score of 100. Approximately two-thirds of a random sample of people score between 85 and 115; about 2 percent score above 130 and below 70. The most widely used **individual intelligence tests** are the Revised Stanford-Binet and the Wechsler Intelligence Scale for Children (WISC-R). These tests are administered to a single student at a time by a trained examiner, usually a school psychologist.

The WISC-R includes 10 subtests divided into two groups—*verbal* and *performance*. Each type of question in each subtest goes from very easy to very difficult. Unlike the Binet, which has separate tests for children of different age groups, the WISC-R uses the same questions for all children. The following is a list of the subtests, with examples similar to actual items on the subtests (Bee, 1989):

**Verbal Tests**
*General information.* "How many eyes have you?"
*General comprehension.* "What is the thing to do when you scrape your knee?"

---

[1] We still use the term *IQ* to indicate intelligence, or a score on an intelligence test.

*Arithmetic.* "James had ten marbles and he bought four more. How many marbles did he have altogether?"

*Similarities.* "In what way are a pear and an orange alike?"

*Vocabulary.* "What is an emerald?"

**Performance Tests**

*Picture completion.* The child is shown pictures of familiar objects in which a part has been left out. He has to identify the missing part, such as a tooth missing from a comb.

*Picture arrangement.* Pictures like the frames of a comic strip are laid out in the wrong order in front of the child. The child has to figure out the right order to make a story.

*Block design.* Sets of special blocks (red, white, or half red, half white on the different sides) are given to the child. Using these blocks, she has to copy designs. The first problems involve only four blocks; harder problems include nine blocks.

*Object assembly.* Large pictures of familiar objects like a horse or a face have been cut up into pieces—rather like jigsaw puzzles, but in bigger pieces. The child has to put them together in the correct configuration as rapidly as possible.

*Coding.* A series of abstract symbols like balls and stars or curved lines are shown in pairs. The child must learn which symbols go together, because he is given several rows of boxes that show only one of each pair, and he must fill in the paired symbol in each box as quickly as possible. (p. 191)

The WISC-R provides three separate IQs: verbal, performance, and total. More can be said about the persons at the extremes of the distribution than those in the middle. Although there are other factors involved in the classification, students with IQ scores above 130 are frequently identified as gifted, and those with scores below 70 are classified as **mentally retarded**. I will discuss both students identified as **gifted and talented** and mentally retarded in Chapter 5.

## Uses of Intelligence Tests

Individually administered intelligence tests are most frequently used for making decisions about educational placement, since intelligence test scores generally are good predictors of academic achievement (Sattler, 1988). For example, if students are having difficulty in class, they may be given an IQ test to determine whether they may have some specific learning problems or may be retarded. There are also intelligence tests for young children to help predict whether they will be able to handle kindergarten work.

Gronlund (1985a) cautions those making educational decisions that intelligence test scores are less dependable for the following types of students:

- Those whose home environment does not provide the opportunity to learn the types of task included in the test.
- Those who are little motivated by school tasks.
- Those who are weak in reading skills or have a language handicap.
- Those who have a poor emotional adjustment. (p. 308)

## Some Misconceptions about Intelligence Tests

You, among many others, may be confused about what intelligence tests measure. They do *not* measure "innate" or "natural" ability to learn new behavior. An intelligence test measures present ability—specifically, the behavior required by the test at the time the test is given. Since the environment interacts with heredity at the time of conception, it is impossible to determine the exact contributions of each.

Many psychologists question whether a child's intelligence test score is even an accurate reflection of learning ability. The argument is that children's performances on an intelligence test are based on the faulty assumption that equivalent chronological age implies equivalent learning opportunities. An intelligence test compares what a child has learned over some period of time to what his or her peers have learned. However, not all children of the same chronological age have had an equal opportunity to learn the material tested by an intelligence test. Because of this inequity, psychologists argue that the teacher who concludes that a student with a low intelligence test score simply lacks the capacity to learn is making a serious error in interpreting the meaning of the test score.

Some people mistakenly believe that once an individual's IQ is determined, the score doesn't change. Research has determined that intelligence tests given to infants do not correlate well with their scores when they become children or adolescents (Kopp & McCall, 1982). In fact, there are even fluctuations in IQs throughout childhood and adolescence.

Another mistaken belief is that intelligence tests measure all educators need to know about human abilities. Earlier I mentioned some of the abilities identified by Guilford that are not emphasized in school. Later in this chapter I will discuss the work of Robert Sternberg (1988), who has serious concerns about the limitations of traditional intelligence tests. Intelligence test scores, in general, correlate fairly highly with academic achievement in school and can be used to predict scholastic success. However, the skills measured by intelligence tests are limited to a narrow range of human abilities.

## Intelligence Test Bias and Fairness

**Are intelligence tests fair to all students?**

The issues of bias and fairness regarding intelligence tests have been debated for years. Fairness is a philosophical issue and most often relates to how tests are used (or misused); test bias is concerned with the controversy over the items contained on the tests and whether they provide a true measure of ability within the socioeconomic or ethnic group tested. Test experts often disagree about both issues.

White students tend to score higher than black students, and middle-class students tend to score higher than lower-class students (Jensen, 1980). Critics argue that the poor performance on IQ tests by some black students stems from bias in the test items and administration. Let's review the arguments and responses by the proponents of IQ testing (Fogel & Melson, 1988).

It is argued that IQ tests require verbal responses and since some black students do not speak standard English, they may be reluctant to respond freely in front of white adults. Also, since many black students are criticized for their language skills, they may feel unmotivated or discouraged when they take a test. These conditions can lead to poor test performance. On the other hand, advocates of intelligence tests counter that black children's performance is not influenced by whether the examiner is white or black, and in some situations, black children score higher when the examiner is white (Sattler & Gwynne, 1982). Second, the proponents indicate that black children tend to score lower on performance rather than verbal items (where language bias would be most evident) (Reynolds & Jensen, 1983).

Another argument relates to the fact that there may be bias in the test items. That is to say, black and Hispanic children may perform more poorly on items that are more familiar to white children. Jensen (1980) has pointed out that when the most culturally specific items are removed from tests, racial differences in test results still exist. In addition, he reports that when white and black students are compared on the most culturally biased items, black children do not respond more poorly.

The responses to the critics of IQ tests do not "close the book" on further criticism, for there may be more subtle sources of bias that have yet to be uncovered (Fogel & Melson, 1988). More recently, other racial differences in IQ performance have been found. We are now seeing Japanese children scoring higher on IQ tests than whites (Lynn, 1982). In many areas of the country, certain Asian-American students are now the top students in school and gaining admission into major universities in record numbers. Could their performance be due to the emphasis by their parents on the importance of school, amount of time spent studying, and their own motivation to succeed?

Another major concern is that some teachers use intelligence test scores, consciously or unconsciously, to label children as poor students. A teacher who has noticed that a student has a low intelligence test score may hold a low expectation for the student's classroom performance and may be less likely to provide remedial instruction. The teacher may even act in ways that contribute to the fulfillment of the expectation, such as calling on the student less often. Chapter 10 will give you detailed information on teacher expectations.

A final concern is that intelligence tests are often a basis for discriminatory practices in school, especially in the placement of poor and minority students in special classes for mentally retarded or slow students. Mercer (1971) studied the distribution of ethnic group members in classes for the mentally retarded in the public schools of Riverside, California. Although the ethnic group distribution of children in the classes tested by psychologists closely approximated the ethnic group distribution of the entire school population, a disproportionate number of Mexican-American and black children had intelligence test scores below 80. In addition, more Mexican-Americans than Anglo-Americans were recommended for and finally placed in classes for the mentally retarded. Mercer stated that neither genetic factors nor environmental deficiencies could account for the large percentage of low test scores among minorities. However, children from low **socioeconomic status (SES)** groups or from ethnic minorities are more vulnerable to being labeled mentally retarded because clinical measures (primarily intelligence tests) are interpreted from a culture-based perspective. Federal legislation now provides guidelines for identifying students needing special education (see Chapter 5). The purpose of these regulations is to reduce the probability of unfair testing procedures and improper placement of students in special education classes.

The controversy over the benefits of IQ testing has reached the courts. In one of the most widely publicized cases, a lawsuit was initiated in the state of California because of the overrepresentation of blacks in classes for the mentally retarded. The plaintiff charged that the intelligence test was a biased assessment of the students' abilities. The judge ruled in *Larry P. v. Riles*, in 1979, that school officials in California could not use an intelligence test for identification of black educable mentally retarded children. After the U.S. Court of Appeals for the Ninth Circuit upheld, by a 2–1 margin, the judge's ruling, the California State Department of Education issued a directive to prohibit all individually administered intelligence tests for use in the assessment of black children referred for any special education placement.

In two other court cases, judges ruled that intelligence testing was not discriminatory against black children. In *PASE v. Hannon* (1980), a judge in Chicago stated that he could find little evidence that intelligence tests were biased. The judge found only eight test items on the WISC-R and one item on the Stanford-Binet to be biased against black children. He also noted that the judge in *Larry P. v. Riles* failed to analyze the items on the intelligence tests. Finally, in *Georgia Conferences of NAACP v. Georgia* (1985), both the trial court and the Court of Appeals rejected the claims that intelligence tests were discriminatory.

It is obvious that the issue of bias in mental testing is not resolved. Some jurists have noted that the courts may not be the most appropriate place to resolve complex issues concerning the fairness of tests in educational decision making (Sattler, 1988).

Can the issue of bias in testing be solved by developing "culture-free" tests? There have been a number of attempts to develop a "culture-free" test (e.g., *Davis-Eells Games*) or at least a "culture-fair" test (e.g., *Culture-*

*Fair Intelligence Tests*). These measures are nonverbal tests that use pictures and diagrams common to many cultures. Unfortunately, these tests have not been successful because, first, lower socioeconomic status and some minority students score lower than white, middle-class students; and, second, the tests fail to predict scholastic achievement as well as do other intelligence tests (Jensen, 1980).

## Educational Interventions to Increase Intelligence and Academic Performance _____

**Is intelligence fixed, or can it be changed?**

One of the important educational implications of the psychometric perspective is to develop intervention programs aimed at improving intellectual skills related to school success as indicated by scores on achievement tests. Since the mid-1960s considerable federal funding has been used to establish preschool programs (for example, Head Start, which services students from age 3 to school entry), summer programs, special educational equipment, tutoring, trips, and other extracurricular activities for children from poverty-stricken and low socioeconomic areas. Much of this funding has come from Title 1 of the Elementary and Secondary Education Act of 1965. Since 1981 the funds have come from federal legislation called Chapter 1. Much of the support for special funding was and continues to be based on the belief that children reared in poverty areas are not motivated to learn in school and are deprived of the stimuli that affect intellectual and cognitive development. General sensory deprivation results from lack of sufficient auditory and visual stimulation, and poor verbal skills stem from arrested language development in children's speech at home.

The goal of these special programs was to compensate for the inadequacies of deprived children through a planned enrichment program of various sensory experiences and language skills. Thus, *culturally deprived* and *compensatory education* became widely used terminology in educational circles. Numerous books and journal articles were written in the 1960s and 1970s on the problem of and possible solutions for educating "disadvantaged" children. Today, educators are more likely to use the term *culturally different* than *culturally deprived*.

The proponents of compensatory education believed that improved environmental conditions could influence children's intellectual and academic development, and they attempted to equalize individual differences that existed before the children started school. In fact, Hunt (1961), a crusader for early childhood programs, argued that "with a sound scientific educational psychology of early experience, it might become possible to raise the level of intelligence . . . by thirty points" (p. 267).

The research on Head Start has been mixed. One problem is that there is no one type of Head Start program; the term represents a label for many different types of programs using a variety of instructional methods—some of which have been more successful than others. In general, for the programs that had significant impact on children's intellectual and academic performance, the gains were lost by the time the students were in the primary grades (Haskins, 1989; McKey et al., 1985). However, there is evidence that children benefit in other ways by attending preschool programs. Lazar and his colleagues (1982) found that students who had participated in preschool programs were less likely to be assigned to special education classes, less likely to be retained in school, and had more positive attitudes toward achievement. Another investigation of students at age 19 showed that students who attended a particular preschool program were more likely to finish high school, had a lower rate of delinquency, and were earning more money (Barnett, 1985).

In 1967 a program called Project Follow Through was established to service children in kindergarten through the third grade and to build upon Head Start programs. Unfortunately, due to budget cuts, this program remained small and ended up funding demonstration projects throughout the country to determine what programs worked best. In one investigation, Becker and Gersten (1982) studied Project Follow Through students in grades 4 and 5. They found that the Follow Through students scored significantly higher in reading, spelling, and math than students who were not involved in the program. However, when they compared the achievement scores of the Follow Through students with a national sample of students, they found that the Follow Through students' achievement scores steadily declined from the third grade (when they left the program) to the sixth grade.

In both the Head Start and Follow Through programs, students' IQ and/or achievement gains diminished once they left the program. Bjorklund (1989) sees the implications of this finding as follows:

> Intelligence is not something that once you "get it," you necessarily keep it. Intelligence, as measured by IQ tests, is a reflection of a person's intellectual functioning at a given time. Once established, intelligence (or any other complex behavior, for that matter) must be maintained. If the environmental supports responsible for establishing competence are removed, one should not be surprised that intelligence suffers. (p. 246)

**Is intelligence determined by environment or heredity?**

*A Critic of Compensatory Education Programs.* In 1969 a highly controversial article was written by Arthur R. Jensen, entitled: "How Much Can We Boost IQ and Scholastic Achievement?" In this article, Jensen concluded that the main reason compensatory education programs have failed is that they concentrated on environmental experiences as the determining factor in intellectual development. He presented data to support the position that about 80 percent of variations in IQ occur because of genetic differences, with environmental factors contributing to only a small portion of the differences among individuals.

Jensen raised an old controversy in psychology, **heritability**—the extent to which differences in a trait (such as intelligence) are attributed to inheritance. Psychologists refer to heritability in terms of a percentage that can range from 0 (none of the differences in the trait are related to inheritance) to 1 (100% of the differences in a trait are attributed to inherit-ance). The present estimate of the heritability of intelligence is .50, meaning that, on the average, 50% of the differences in intelligence test scores in a population of people can be attributed to inheritance (Bjorklund, 1989). The relationships among people increase as genetic similarity increases. For example, the intelligence correlations of identical twins (i.e., they come from the same zygote or egg) reared together is .86; reared apart, .72, whereas the correlations of fraternal twins reared together is .60; siblings reared together, .47; reared apart, .27 (Bouchard & McCue, 1981).

Although there is evidence that inheritance plays an important role in determining intelligence, there also is evidence that environmental fac-tors similarly play an important role. For example, there are adoption stud-ies demonstrating that when children from impoverished environments are reared in more affluent environments, the children's IQ scores are 10 or 15 points higher than those of their birth mothers (Scarr & Kidd, 1983; Skodak & Skeels, 1945). Also, the Transracial Adoption Study of Scarr and Weinberg (1976; 1983) reported that when black children born of parents from low-income environments were adopted by white, upper-middle-class parents, the average IQ of the adopted children was 20 points higher than the average IQ of a comparable group of children reared in the local black community.

Current evaluation studies have failed to change Jensen's opinions regarding the success of preschool educational programs. In a more recent article, Jensen (1985) points out that preschool programs have had success in such areas as involving parents in school and improving children's self-esteem and their attitudes toward school, but he continues to question the impact of preschool programs on intelligence and academic achievement. He believes that more research needs to be done to learn how compen-satory education influences children's *thinking processes* (or information pro-cessing). In the past, the research focus has been on children's deficiency in *knowledge*, which involved the erroneous belief that intelligence is iden-tified with the content of the test items found in intelligence tests—that is, if a child learns the material tested, the child will become more intel-ligent. Jensen believes that intelligence is related to thinking processes, not the amount of acquired knowledge.

## THE PIAGETIAN PERSPECTIVE

Through analysis of the processes involved in the organization of knowl-edge, the Swiss psychologist, Jean Piaget developed a theory of how a child's thinking process gradually shifts from concrete to abstract intellec-tual functioning. Piaget is considered a developmental psychologist be-cause of his study of the developmental stages, or age-level changes, that determine what children can learn at various ages. The unique aspect of

Piaget's theory is that it separates and identifies stages of intellectual, or cognitive, development. The child's stage of development sets limits on learning and influences the type of learning that can take place.

Piaget is one of the few psychologists who present a comprehensive theory of the development of intelligence, or the thought process. His theory is different from the psychometric perspective discussed earlier in the chapter. The first part of the following discussion deals with the development of the stages in the thinking process; the second part derives the instructional and learning implications of the theory.

## The Process of Cognitive Development

From the Piagetian perspective, mental growth means the acquisition of new mental abilities not previously present. Intellectual growth is not a quantitative but a qualitative process in which there are significant differences between the thinking of children and adolescents, as well as between preschool and school-age children (Elkind, 1974).

Biologists are hard-pressed to explain how structures evolve so that organisms can adapt to their environment. Piaget has explored this same problem in regard to human adaptation and has researched a theory of intellectual or cognitive development based on the premise that intellectual structures—organizational properties of thought—are formed in the individual during interaction with the environment. The emerging structures enable the individual to cope better with the increasing demands of the environment.

Piaget uses the term *scheme* almost interchangeably with *structure*.[2] A scheme is a repeatable behavior pattern. Initially, scheme relates to inborn reflexes such as the "sucking scheme"; during adolescence schemes are mental, as in the "scheme of classification," "scheme of probability," and "operational schemes," or "operations" for short. The acquisition of a scheme implies that there has been a change in the child's intellectual development.

Although Piaget's overwhelming concern is with the structures of intelligence, he stresses two other aspects of intelligence: content and function. *Content* refers to the child's specific patterns of behavior that surface in the responses given by the child to various problems or situations. Early in his career (during the 1920s and 1930s), Piaget's research interest focused on the content of children's thoughts—such phenomena as changes in reasoning ability from early to late childhood, moral behavior and judgment, the child's conception of the world (the origin of trees, dreams, sun, and moon), and the conception of certain natural phenomena (the movement of clouds and rivers). However, later in his career Piaget's research

---

[2] I am using the terminology suggested by Ginsburg and Opper (1988), who state that Piaget's French term *scheme* is usually translated as *schema* (plural: schemata). They suggest that because Piaget has used the French word *schema* for another purpose, the retention of the French word *scheme* in English is preferable.

interest deepened and focused on the analysis of the basic processes underlying and determining the content (Ginsburg & Opper, 1988).

*Function* refers to the manner in which an organism makes intellectual progress. According to Piaget, all organisms inherit two basic tendencies, or "invariant functions": *organization* and *adaptation*. (Ginsburg and Opper, 1988, provide an excellent discussion of these tendencies.)

The term **organization** describes the ability of organisms to systematize, or to organize, their physical or psychological processes into coherent systems. In the physical realm, for example, fish possess a number of structures that allow them to function effectively in water: gills, a circulatory system, and temperature mechanisms. All these structures work together efficiently to maintain fish in their environment. This physical coordination is the result of the organization tendency. This same organizational tendency characterizes the psychological level. An infant has separate behavioral structures for visual focusing and grasping. At some point in development, the infant is able to organize both of these behavioral structures into a higher-order structure by grasping an object while looking at it. Organization, then, integrates physical and psychological structures into higher-order systems.

The second aspect of functioning is **adaptation.** All organisms are born with a tendency to adapt to their environment. The ways in which adaptation takes place differ from organism to organism. Adaptation may be considered in terms of two complementary processes—**assimilation** and **accommodation.** Assimilation refers to the process by which an individual uses an existing structure or ability to deal with some problem in the environment. Accommodation is a process by which the individual must change in response to environmental demands. This adaptation necessitates a modification, or rearrangement, of the individual's existing mental structures.

The following example illustrates the relationship between assimilation and accommodation. A child who has learned to open cabinets by pulling on them will have to develop a new sequence of hand movements in order to open a cabinet with a handle that must be turned. The child will have to accommodate to the environment. However, once this new response has been learned, the child will be able to recall the sequence of behaviors when opening this particular type of cabinet door. The child will have assimilated the new experience. In review, if an individual has an existing behavior pattern for interacting with the environment, this behavior is assimilated. If the individual does not have an appropriate set of behaviors to deal with a situation, the pattern of response must change to allow accommodation to the environment.

To Piaget, adaptation is a balance of assimilation and accommodation. If, in the process of assimilation, the individual cannot adapt to the environment, a state of **disequilibrium** exists. Accommodation is the result of this disequilibrium, and either the individual's present structures are altered or new ones emerge. Intellectual growth is a continual process of equilibrium-disequilibrium states. However, when equilibrium is restored, the individual is at a higher intellectual level than before (Sullivan, 1967).

Adaptation can also be applied to classroom learning. Cognitive progress depends partly on accommodation for development. The student must enter an area of the unknown in order to learn. One cannot study only what one already knows—one cannot rely on assimilation. In a situation in which the student's existing cognitive processes are not used, accommodation but no assimilation occurs. In courses that present you with nothing new, you have probably overassimilated; in courses that you don't grasp, you have overaccommodated. Neither situation will facilitate your cognitive growth.

In summary, there are three aspects of intellectual growth: structure, content, and function. As the child develops, structure and content change but functions remain the same. The organization and adaptation functions create a series of stages, each possessing particular psychological structures that determine the child's thinking ability. Intelligence for Piaget, then, is the sum of available structures an individual has available at a particular point in development.

## PIAGET'S DEVELOPMENTAL STAGES

A question often asked about Piaget's stages is, "What causes an individual to move from one stage to another?" Piaget (1964) identifies four factors that influence this transition.

1. *Maturation.* The development of the central nervous system, brain, motor coordination, and other physical manifestations of growth influence cognitive development. Until the child's motor coordination is developed to a certain extent, walking cannot occur, and if the child is limited in exploring the environment, not much will be learned about it. Although maturation is an important factor in intellectual development, it does not sufficiently explain it. If it did, teachers would play a very minor role in influencing intellectual development.
2. *Physical experience.* The child's interaction with the physical environment can increase the rate of development because observation and manipulation of objects aid the emergence of more complex thinking.
3. *Social transmission.* This marks the influence of language, formal instruction, and reading, as well as social interaction with peers and adults. These experiences also influence cognitive development.
4. **Equilibration,** or self-regulation. This factor incorporates the ability to re-establish equilibrium states during periods of disequilibrium.

It is a process by which the individual attains higher levels of cognitive functioning through a step-by-step assimilation and accommodation.

**According to Piaget, what are the major characteristics of children thinking at the preoperational, concrete, and formal operation stages?**

Let us now explore the various stages and corresponding structures identified by Piaget. The stages are presented in Table 2.1. It should be noted that these age ranges are only approximations. (You may encounter slightly different classifications in other readings, especially for middle childhood.) All children proceed through each stage but at different rates. Thus it is possible for a 6-year-old child to be at the concrete operations stage or an 8-year-old child still to be at the preoperational stage in thinking. However, the sequence of development is the same for all children. Each successive stage is built in a hierarchical fashion on the preceding stage. Structures belonging to earlier stages become integrated and incorporated as part of the stages that follow.

## Sensorimotor Stage (0–2 Years)

**Sensorimotor** thought occupies approximately the first two years of life, when infants experience the environment primarily through their senses and motor activity. The infant begins life with innate reflexes, schemes that are modified and combined with other schemes to form more complex behavior. By the end of this stage, babies begin to acquire a primitive symbol system (such as language) to think about and represent events in their lives.

During this time, the infant has no conception of **object permanence.** When an object is hidden from view, the infant fails to look for it. As

Table 2.1 **PIAGET'S STAGES OF COGNITIVE DEVELOPMENT**

| Stage | Approximate Age | Characteristics |
|---|---|---|
| Sensorimotor | 0–2 years | Begins to make use of imitation, memory, and thought. Begins to recognize that objects do not cease to exist when they are hidden. Moves from single reflex actions to purposeful activity. |
| Preoperational | 2–7 years | Gradual language development and ability to think in symbolic form. Able to think operations through logically in one direction. Thought and language both egocentric. |
| Concrete operational | 7–11 years | Able to solve concrete problems in logical fashion. Understands laws of conservation and is able to classify and seriate. Reversibility attained. |
| Formal operational | 11–15 years | Able to solve abstract problems in logical fashion. Thinking becomes more scientific. Solves complex verbal and hypothetical problems. |

*Source: Wadsworth, 1989.*

infants continue to experience the environment, toward the end of the sensorimotor period, they behave as though they realize that a hidden object still exists and begin looking for it after they have seen it hidden. Other primitive concepts not present at birth—space, time, causality—develop and become incorporated into the child's behavior patterns.

Our interest in the school-age child prompts us to move on to the remaining stages in Piaget's theory. We shall spend more time on these later stages.

## Preoperational Stage (2–7 Years)

Although the child makes rapid cognitive growth during the first two years of life, abilities are limited to objects that can be seen in the environment. The child's "thinking" acts on objects that can be perceived directly. However, toward the end of the second year, the child begins using symbols to represent various aspects of the environment. For example, the child can use the word *ball* to represent a real ball when it is not in immediate view. This symbolic ability adds a new dimension to the child's thinking ability (Ginsburg & Opper, 1988).

A great deal of Piaget's research on childhood concerns understanding the nature of a class—a set of objects that are united by some relationship, such as girls, dogs, balls, or red circles. The ability to add classes together, multiply classes, and break down classes into subclasses is necessary for conceptual thinking. The child at this period has a difficult time with such classification tasks and is capable of formulating only primitive concepts that are referred to by Piaget as "preconcepts."

Phillips (1969) has summarized some of the limitations of **preoperational** thought under six headings.

1. *Concreteness.* The preoperational child is capable of manipulating symbols and, when compared with the child in the sensorimotor period, is rather abstract in his or her thinking. Nevertheless, when compared with an adolescent or adult, the preoperational child is still oriented toward the concrete.

2. *Irreversibility.* **Reversibility** is the ability to return to the point of origin, to do and undo, to go in one direction and compensate for it in another direction. Every mathematical or logical operation is reversible: $4 + 8 = 12$, and $12 - 8 = 4$; all boys + all girls = all children, and all children − all girls = all boys. The preoperational child does not have the ability to deal with problems that necessitate reversible thinking.

   Phillips (1969) illustrates this limitation from one of his own observations. He asked a 4-year-old boy "Do you have a brother?"

   "Yes."
   "What's his name?"
   "Jim."

"Does Jim have a brother?"
"No." (p. 61)

Another example, commonly referred to as the **conservation** experiment, further illustrates the lack of reversible thought, or irreversibility. The idea that the amount or quantity of a matter stays the same regardless of any changes in shape or position is incomprehensible to the child. Though a child observes two small glasses, A and B, identical in size and shape and filled with an equal amount of water, and in turn observes as the water from glass A is emptied into another glass, C, which is taller and narrower, the child tends to conclude that the quantity of water has changed. Glass C contains more water than glass A because "it is higher," even though the child readily admits that no water has been added or removed.

In another conservation experiment, two clay balls of equal size are shown to the child. The child is asked if they are the same size, after which one of the balls is rolled into a sausage shape. The child

To understand that the amount of liquid does not change when it is poured into different-size beakers, the child must consider both the length and width of the beakers at the same time. According to Piaget, volume conservation is not usually present until the concrete operations stage.

Around the age of 6 or 7 the child learns to conserve number. Even though the child sees one row lengthened without any change in the number of pennies, she declares that both rows are equivalent.

is then asked the same question, the usual response being that the sausage-shaped ball is larger.

A child presented with two rows of pennies states that the rows contain the same number of pennies. However, if one row is elongated without any change in the number of pennies, the child usually declares that the rows are no longer equivalent.

Conservation does not take place at the same time in all subject areas. The child usually grasps conservation of numbers (age 5–6) before conservation of substance, or mass (age 7–8), and weight (age 9–10), followed last by conservation of volume (age 11–12).

3. *Centering*. The characteristic of centering is also related to the previous problems. The child's tendency is to focus on only one dimension or detail of an event to the neglect of other important aspects. In the water-level problem demonstrating the child's irreversible thinking, one reason for the difficulty is that the child focuses on length—the taller glass—and forgets about width. The preoperational child cannot **decenter,** or focus back and forth between details, and reasoning is necessarily distorted.

4. *Egocentrism*. Many of Piaget's readers have misunderstood the term **egocentrism** (sometimes called *perspective taking*). It is not used in a derogatory sense to describe the child's personality. It simply means that the child has difficulty taking another person's point of view. Egocentrism enters the arena of language and communication. Watch any group of preschool children playing together, and you will hear egocentric speech. You may hear children repeating words merely for the pleasure of pronouncing them or talking "toward" each other without really expecting the others to listen or reply.

5. *States versus Transformations*. The preoperational child focuses on the static aspect of an event rather than on the transformations from one state to another. In the water-level problem, the child is intent on the height of the water, not on the act of pouring. In the conservation-of-substance problem with the clay balls, the child retains the image of the shape of the clay and ignores the transformations— the change from the round to the sausage shape. In one experiment (Flavell, 1963), the child is asked to "depict the successive movements of a bar which falls from a vertical, upright position to a horizontal one" (p. 158). Although the solution of this problem is obvious to the adolescent, the preoperational child fails to draw the intermediate positions of the bar.

6. *Transductive Reasoning*. Deduction is reasoning from the general to the specific. Assuming that all children are good, if we see a child, we deduce that the child is good. Induction proceeds in the opposite direction, establishing generalizations from specific instances: If we meet a large number of good children, we can conclude that they are all good.

According to Piaget, the preoperational child's thinking is somewhere in between, moving from the particular to the particular without touching on the general. The child sees some relationship between particular instances when there is none. Piaget calls this **transductive reasoning.** The child who walks through the forest, not knowing whether a succession of turtles is appearing or whether the same turtle is reappearing time and time again, is thinking transductively. This is an example of the preconcept I discussed earlier.

Piaget (1952) reported an example of transductive thinking, when his daughter failed to take a nap one afternoon. She said to him, "I haven't had my nap, so it isn't afternoon" (p. 232). It is very common for children at this age to see relationships between particular instances, such that if $A$ causes $B$, then $B$ causes $A$.

## Concrete Operations Stage (7–11 Years)

The **concrete** operations stage marks the beginning of operational thought. That is, the child acquires logical thought processes (operations) that can be applied to concrete problems. When faced with a discrepancy between thought and perception, as in the conservation problems, the child in the concrete operations period opts for logical decisions instead of the perceptual decisions a child in the preoperational period makes.

The following mathematical symbols are examples of operations: $=$ (equal), $+$ (combining), $-$ (separating). Each of these operations has its counterpart in logic; for example, $+$ is equivalent to *and*, $-$ is equivalent to *except* (Phillips, 1969). Piaget uses the structure of logic as a model for explaining the qualitative differences in children's thinking ability during both the concrete and formal operations periods.

The operations of this period are tied to personal experience. They are concrete but not formal operations. The child is still unable to deal with abstract material such as hypotheses and verbal propositions. The following are an important set of concrete operations:

- **Combinativity,** or classification, is an operation by which two or more classes are combined into a larger group: all boys $+$ all girls $=$ all children. Relationships such as $A > B$ and $B > C$ can be combined into a new relationship, $A > C$. For the first time, the child can form a variety of class relationships and understands that some classes can be included in other classes.
- *Reversibility* is the major criterion for operational thought in Piaget's system. It implies that every logical or mathematical operation can be canceled by an opposite operation. All children $-$ all girls $=$ all boys; or $7 + 3 = 10$ and $10 - 7 = 3$.
- **Associativity** is an operation by which several classes can be combined in any order $(1 + 3) + 5 = 1 + (3 + 5)$. In reasoning, this

operation allows a child to arrive at answers in many different ways.
- **Identity** is an operation in which there exists a null element that, when combined with any element or class, produces no change: 10 + 0 = 10. Also, a quantity can be nullified by combining it with its opposite: 10 − 10 = 0; or, if I walk 3 miles east and 3 miles west, I end up where I started from.

It is not that children at the concrete operations stage are "brighter" than preschool children but that they have acquired certain abilities (operations) for solving problems that they could not solve correctly before. Concrete operational thinking is stable, compared to the highly impressionistic and static thinking of the preoperational period.

Concrete operational children can bring these operations to bear on such problems as class relationships. If you ask preschoolers if there are more girls or more children in the room, they may respond that there are more boys than girls, for young children have difficulty dealing with classes and subclasses at the same time. They cannot conceive that it is possible to belong to two classes at the same time (e.g., boy and children). However, 6- or 7-year-old children will have no difficulty with this problem. They are capable of deducing the following: boys + girls = children (combina-

The manipulation of concrete objects can provide an important foundation for higher-level thinking.

tivity), since children − boys = girls (reversibility); thus, children ≠ boys (Elkind, 1968).

Using these same operations, the child develops an awareness of the principles of conservation. The child can focus on both length and width (decentration) and can recognize that pouring water into different-size beakers does not change the amount of water because the amount of water is the same as in the beginning (identity and reversibility).

The child in this period can now rank in order a series of objects, such as wooden dolls or sticks, according to their size. Piaget refers to this operation as **serializing.** However, the child can do this only as long as the problem is presented concretely; it is not until adolescence that such a problem can be solved mentally using verbal propositions.

Language also changes at this time. The child becomes less egocentric and more sociocentric in communication. The child now makes an attempt to understand other people and communicate feelings and ideas to adults and peers. Thought processes also become less egocentric, and the child can now take another's point of view.

### Formal Operations Stage (11 Years and Above)

At approximately 11 years of age, a new operations period emerges in which the older child can use concrete operations to form more complex operations. Inhelder and Piaget (1958) and Flavell (1963) provide excellent detailed discussions of the operations available to the adolescent during this period.

Flavell (1963) discusses some characteristics of **formal** operational thought. First, the adolescent uses **hypothetico-deductive reasoning.** Many alternative hypotheses in dealing with a problem can be formulated, and data can be checked against each of the hypotheses to make an appropriate decision. Children in the concrete operations stage also can reason deductively, but their thinking is limited to events and objects with which they are familiar. The adolescent's major advance during this stage is that it is now no longer necessary to think in terms of objects or concrete events; he or she now has the ability to think *abstractly.*

Second, this period is marked by **propositional reasoning.** The adolescent is not limited to concrete objects or events in reasoning but can deal with statements or propositions that describe these concrete data. The adolescent can even deal with contrary-to-fact propositions. If you ask a child in one of the other developmental stages to pretend to be the president of the United States and then ask the child a question about a hypothetical situation he or she might encounter as president, the child is likely to say, "But I'm not the president of the United States." The adolescent has no trouble accepting contrary-to-fact propositions, and reasoning from them (Elkind, 1968).

Last, the adolescent engages in **combinatorial reasoning.** When considering solutions to a problem, the adolescent can isolate individual factors and possible combinations of factors that may figure in the solution.

## CLASSROOM APPLICATION: ASSESSING CHILDREN'S
## LEVEL OF COGNITIVE DEVELOPMENT

Piaget used an interview method to determine the nature of a child's reasoning. This interview consists of (1) demonstrating a fact in the physical world or some relationship that may or may not really exist; (2) asking the children or adolescents what they think will happen; and (3) exploring their answers with them. The method requires that the examiner or interviewer allow the children to use their own words to describe what is happening (Gordon, 1966).

Although some standardized paper and pencil tests have been developed to assess levels of cognitive development in a group testing situation (see Milakofsky and Patterson, 1979, for such a test used in science education), most Piagetians are critical of standardized paper and pencil tests because they do not believe that tests, which ask the same questions of all students, are able to determine *how* a child arrived at an answer.

It takes some practice to assess cognitive development using an interview procedure. The examiner follows certain guidelines, making sure that the child is relaxed and motivated to respond to the task before the interview begins, asking questions about the event or situation, making a hypothesis about the child's conceptual ability, following up with further questions based on the examiner's hypothesis that has been formed, and allowing the child enough time to think about responses. Most important, the examiner needs to avoid leading the child to the right answer and must realize that "wrong" answers are of as much interest as "correct" answers (Wadsworth, 1978).

There are four criteria for assessment using the clinical interview. In order to be considered at a specific reasoning level, the child must (1) make a "correct" judgment, (2) logically justify that judgment, (3) successfully resist a verbal countersuggestion, and (4) produce a successful performance on a related behavioral task (Strauss, 1972).

The following interview (Wadsworth, 1978, pp. 236–237) is an example of how the procedure is conducted. Notice how the examiner uses equivalence questions to include the notion of difference and similarity, and requires reasoning after each answer the child gives to an equivalence question, whether the question was correct or incorrect. The examiner evaluates the child's reasoning as well as the child's answer.

### A Piagetian Interview

A row of nine blue blocks, each about an inch apart, is arranged between the examiner and the child.

Examiner: "Will you make a row of blocks using the red ones just like my row, and right in front of you?" (*The child makes a row below the examiner's row by first placing two end blocks in position, then placing eight blocks between those two without any careful comparison.*)

Examiner: Does one row of blocks have more blocks than the other, or do they both have the same number?

Child: They're the same.

E: Are you sure?

C: Yes.

E: How do you know they're the same number of blocks? (*request for reasoning*)

C: I can count them. (*Child proceeds to count the blocks in each row. He counts nine for the blue row and ten for the red row.*) They're different. There are more reds.

E: Can you make them so they have the same number? (*Child removes one of the red blocks from the middle of the row and lines the other red ones up corresponding to the blue ones.*)

E: Now both rows have the same number of blocks?

C: Yes.

E: Okay, I'm going to move my blue blocks together like this. (*The row of blue blocks is collapsed so that they are about one-half inch apart.*) Now, are there more blocks in my row or in your row, or do we both have the same number of blocks?

C: I have more.

E: How can you tell? (*request for reasoning*)

C: My row sticks out more. (*preoperational reasoning*)

E: Okay, I'm going to make my row just like your row again. Who has more blocks now, or do we have the same number of blocks? (*Examiner makes his row of blocks as long as child's.*)

C: Same.

E: How do you know? (*request for reasoning*)

C: See, they both come out to here and here. (*The child points to the ends of each row.*)

E: Now if I move your blocks together (*child's row of blocks is collapsed the way examiner's row was previously*), do we both have the same number of blocks, or does one of us have more blocks than the other?

C: You have more.

E: How do you know I have more? (*request for reasoning*)

C: Same as before; your row is bigger.

E: Why don't you count the number of blocks in each row? (*Suggestion is made to determine whether counting influences reasoning. Child counts nine blocks for each row.*)

E: How many blocks in your row?

C: Nine.

E: How many blocks in my row?

C: Nine.

E: Which row has more blocks, or do they both have the same number of blocks?

C: You have more.

E: Tell me why I have more blocks than you have. (*request for reasoning*)

C: You have more blocks. They come out more. (*pointing to the ends of examiner's row*)

Countersuggestions would have been employed to test the resistance of the child's answers to suggestions if the child had given correct answers. For example, the interviewer might remove an object from one of the rows while the child is observing and say, "The rows still have the same number of blocks, don't they?" or "Now this row (the longer one) has more blocks than this one (the shorter one)."

## CRITICISMS OF PIAGET'S THEORY

**What are the criticisms of Piaget's theory?**

Although Piaget's theory has made important contributions to the understanding of cognitive development, there are a number of criticisms of his theory: Piaget's notion of structurally distinct stages has come under considerable criticism. More specifically, his critics argue that he has underestimated the intellectual abilities of the preschool child and has overestimated the formal operations thinking of adolescents and adults. The clinical method that Piaget used to interview children may have contributed to this situation. Some researchers have found, for example, that children's performance on conservation tasks is influenced by the types of question that are asked of them. Gelman and Gallistel (1978) have found that children as young as 2½ years already understand certain number principles even though they cannot correctly perform Piaget's conservation task. Also, researchers have shown that conservation can be accelerated by a variety of training procedures (e.g., Field, 1987). Under some conditions children much younger than 11 have displayed formal operations reasoning (Hawkins et al. 1984; Slater & Kingston, 1981).

A large portion of the adult population may never go beyond concrete thinking (Schwebel, 1975). Research as shown that Piaget may have overestimated the ability of adolescents and adults to use formal operations thinking. For example, Kuhn et al. (1977) administered a battery of formal operations tasks to 265 adolescents and adults. They found that only about 30% of adults could be classified in the formal operations stage.

Although Piaget describes in detail the quality of children's thinking at various developmental stages, he fails to explain in the same detail how these changes in structure come about. Why does the child move from the preoperational to the concrete operational stage? Piaget's explanation is that when children acquire the necessary schemes, or intellectual structures, they move to the next stage. This explanation involves circular reasoning: "Children don't conserve because they are in the preoperational stage, and we know they are in the preoperational stage because they don't conserve."

The sequencing from one stage to another may be only an artifact of the evaluation procedure Piaget used. Given the way in which children's knowledge is assessed, it would be difficult for them to demonstrate any other pattern of cognitive development than that which is found (Brainerd, 1978). The issue is whether the sequence of stages is dependent upon some innate maturational blueprint or whether the stage sequence can be explained by other means (Gross, 1985). Learning theorists argue that higher-order skills require prerequisite knowledge that can be *learned*. Therefore, the educator does not have to rely on the development of schemes but instead needs to *teach* the necessary prerequisite skills.

In general, many psychologists believe that the stages of cognitive development are not as clear-cut as Piaget has proposed and that new research is needed to explain some of the discrepancies found in his theory (Bjorklund, 1989). Psychologists who are making modifications in Piaget's theory are called neo-Piagetians and are discussed under information processing.

I don't believe that Piaget's theory has been discredited by recent research. He was not totally correct about the characteristics of the stages of development but appears to have been on target concerning the notion of a sequence in cognitive development and in the identification of qualitative changes in children's thinking between preschool children and adolescents. In general, he has made considerable contributions to understanding children's cognitive development.

## IMPLICATIONS OF PIAGET'S THEORY FOR EDUCATION

**What instructional practices would Piaget recommend?**

There are two major aspects of Piaget's theory that have influenced educators. One idea is that children are active thinkers who construct their own understanding of the events in the world around them. This notion implies that the school curricula should involve students as active participants in the learning process rather than absorbing knowledge by passively listening to teachers. The development of **open education** or open classrooms (see Chapter 8), in which students work on projects in different learning centers, is one attempt to apply Piagetian concepts. Another teaching strategy consistent with Piaget's theory of cognitive development is

**discovery learning,** in which students acquire concepts on their own rather than by explanation by the teacher.

The second major idea of his theory is that knowledge is constructed by systems of "logico-mathematical operations" (e.g., reversibility and associativity) that develop through a series of stages. Piaget's delineation of the relationship between a child's level of conceptual development and the complexity of the subject matter implies that teachers should heed what and how they teach. Piagetians maintain that the ideal learning situation arises from the match between the complexity of the subject matter and the child's level of conceptual development. A teacher who uses the best textbooks available and develops the most interesting and stimulating lesson plans can still fail to reach a majority of students who do not have the necessary structures (operations) to enable them to "understand" the presented material. This means that the classroom teacher must be able to (1) assess a child's level of cognitive development and (2) determine the type of abilities the child needs to understand the subject matter.

## Teaching Strategy

A teaching strategy developed from Piaget's theory is to "confront the child with the illogical nature of his point of view" (Siegel, 1969, p. 473). During the discussion of the assimilation-accommodation process, I mentioned that when assimilation fails, the child is in a state of disequilibrium and must begin to accommodate in order to adapt to the environment. You create disequilibrium in a child when you ask questions about some illogical statement the child has made. The child's attempts to reconcile this disequilibrium create new plateaus in cognitive development. The confrontation strategy implies that a student's incorrect answers should receive as much teacher attention as do correct answers.

In reacting to this same confrontation, the child advances from egocentric to sociocentric thought. Children have difficulty conceiving of a point of view different from their own. When they locate other individuals standing at different vantage points, the discovery plays an important role in modifying their point of view (Ginsburg & Opper, 1988).

Confrontation takes many forms, including questions, demonstrations, and/or environmental manipulations. Duckworth (1964) quotes Piaget:

> Good pedagogy must involve presenting the child with situations in which he himself experiments, in the broadest sense of that term—trying things out to see what happens, manipulating things, manipulating symbols, posing questions and seeking his own answers, reconciling what he finds one time with what he finds at another, comparing his findings with those of other children. (p. 2)

The preceding statement also emphasizes the active role of children in the learning process. The Piagetian type of classroom de-emphasizes the transmission of knowledge through the lecture-discussion method and encourages the teacher to act more as a catalyst in situations in which children do their own learning.

Piaget was constantly asked (particularly during his travels in the United States) whether educators can speed up the transition between stages by teaching the operations or structures, such as reversibility, necessary for logical thinking. His statement (quoted in Duckworth, 1964) makes his position on the matter clear:

> The question comes up whether to teach the structure, or to present the child with situations where he is active and creates the structures himself. The goal in education is not to increase the amount of knowledge, but to create the possibilities for a child to invent and discover. When we teach too fast, we keep the child from inventing and discovering himself. . . . Teaching means creating situations where structures can be discovered; it does not mean transmitting structures which may be assimilated at nothing other than a verbal level. (p. 3)

## Discovery Learning

Piaget's recommendation for giving children an active role in their classroom learning finds favor with many cognitive psychologists who advocate learning by discovery. Much of the credit for encouraging the use of discovery learning goes to Jerome Bruner (1960), a Harvard psychologist who came into prominence after the publication of *The Process of Education*. In this book he reported the outcomes of a conference of scientists, scholars, and educators on the teaching of science.

Bruner set down some controversial statements about curriculum development. The following statement is widely quoted and debated: "Any subject can be taught effectively in some intellectually honest form to any child at any stage of development" (p. 52). Bruner's adversaries were quick to point out that a child could *not* learn any subject at a particular age: Could the first grader learn calculus? Bruner's reply to this criticism was that he had phrased his statement in terms of the possibility of teaching meaningful aspects of a subject at a certain age level. Perhaps we can teach some aspect of calculus to a first grader.

The real issue is: How can educators develop more effective instructional programs for the young child? Bruner's answer is to coordinate the mode of presentation of the material with the way in which the child can learn it. The child progresses from sensory (**enactive**) representations to concrete (**iconic**) representations and, finally, to abstract (**symbolic**) representations; the teaching sequence should be the same. Curriculum organization should be ordered so that the child first experiences the material, then reacts to concrete aspects of it, and, finally, symbolizes it.

Another statement in *The Process of Education* emphasizes how subject matter should be taught: "The curriculum of a subject should be determined by the most fundamental understanding that can be achieved of the underlying principles that give structure to the subject'' (p. 31). The basic thesis of this statement is that the bare bones of any discipline can and should be exposed to reveal its structure—its most basic elements. Instead of memorizing factual material and isolated content, students should learn the principles that the discipline builds on. Once students know these principles, they can then independently inquire into and solve the problems in the discipline.

Bruner also mentions that teachers must allow students to become problem solvers, to function in the same way as a scientist, historian, or mathematician. Let students discover meaning for themselves, and you enable them to learn concepts in the language they understand.

The critics of discovery learning strongly question its use with slow learners (e.g., Wittrock, 1966). Also, special programs founded on Piagetian-based models designed for disadvantaged children in grades 1–6 generally have demonstrated little achievement gains compared to similar programs that teach students specific language and mathematical concepts in a prescribed curriculum. It appears that there are limitations in allowing students to choose activities related to their developmental levels and learn language and mathematical concepts through experience rather than direct instruction (Slavin, Karweit, & Madden, 1989). More will be said about direct and indirect methods of instruction in later chapters.

## Curriculum

Some educators suggest that Piaget's observations can aid in the structure and sequencing of subject matter in the curriculum. Elkind (1980) identified problems that can occur when students are asked to deal with subject matter requiring formal operations. Consider a student attempting to understand $(a + b)^2 = a^2 + 2ab + b^2$. The student understands the equation for two numbers, say, 4 and 5, but cannot understand that the equation holds for all numbers. In other words, the student believes that the letters stand for specific numbers rather than all numbers.

Another problem involves interpreting literature. Reading good literature is an important goal in English, but requiring students in the concrete stage to describe what a poet had in mind when a certain poem was written or why an author approached a story in a particular way is likely to lead to failure. These types of question ask a student to hypothesize about intentions—a difficult task for a student in the concrete operations stage. Elkind believes it is difficult enough for young people to deal with complex plots and metaphorical language without dealing with another person's intentions. He believes that a teacher must understand that there are different levels of understanding in literature.

Last, Elkind points out that the formal operations stage is necessary for understanding experimental science. He states that students are introduced to experimental science too early, since it presupposes an understanding of quantification along one or more dimensions, propositional logic, and the ability to analyze reality and to distinguish between reality and appearance (e.g., to recognize that two liquids of the same color can have different compositions). In sum, experimentation presupposes a level of thinking that many young students simply do not possess. Elkind believes that more appropriate scientific activities for students in the concrete operations stage are classifying and describing.

## THE INFORMATION-PROCESSING PERSPECTIVE

One attempt to provide an alternative perspective to explaining children's cognitive abilities is information-processing theory. In this approach, the human mind is viewed as a type of computer that processes various types of information. This theory, of which there are different kinds, attempts to explain "how information is taken into the organism, interpreted, represented, transformed, and acted upon (Gross, 1985, p. 19).

In studies of children's thinking, there are at least two branches to the information-processing approach. One group of researchers believes that children's thinking develops in stages, but suggest different structures and processes from those proposed by Piaget (see Sternberg, 1987a, for a review of these neo-Piagetian theories). These psychologists integrate the Piagetian perspective with the information-processing perspective. Another group of researchers investigate basic information-processing strategies to learn more about the processes that are the basis of human abilities or intelligent behavior. Many of these information-processing psychologists use the mental structures identified by the psychometric perspective to study the specific mental processes that constitute intelligent behavior.

### Neo-Piagetians

**How do neo-Piagetian theories modify Piaget's theory?**

Fischer (1980; Fisher & Pipp, 1984) has suggested a modification of Piaget's developmental stages into 10 levels. He places greater emphasis on the role of the environment than Piaget did in explaining cognitive development. Fischer believes that children develop *skills* that are specific to particular objects and tasks. Thus he would not find it unusual for a child to be at one level on one task, and at a higher level on another task.

Another neo-Piagetian researcher is Pascual-Leone (1970, 1989), who believes that the development of memory capacity is the major reason why children demonstrate different thinking at different ages. He finds that younger children are much more limited in the amount of information they can deal with at any one time than are older children or adults. For example, if one can think about only two or three things at once, rather than six or seven, this limitation will influence one's thinking and problem-solving ability. As capacity increases with increasing age, the child can deal with more information, and cognitive growth can occur. More specifically, Pascual-Leone found that the developmental transition from the preoperational to the concrete operational stage requires an increase of one information chunk in the child's memory. Until the child's mental capacity increases by that one unit, the change in developmental stage will not occur. Thus mental space (M-space) and its growth is an alternative approach to explaining cognitive development.

Case (Case & Griffin,1989) also uses the notion of mental space in formulating his own theory of cognitive development, but emphasizes that working memory is not the only constraint on the quality of children's thinking. Although he proposes four stages, and three substages within each stage, the difference between his and Piaget's theory is that he does not assume that each new stage involves totally new types or forms of thinking; he assumes only that each stage requires more complex levels or integrations of the same basic processes. Case hypothesizes that children actively process and transform information by the use of a central conceptual structure, an internal network of concepts and conceptual relations that permit children to problem-solve and develop new structures for dealing with more complex situations. Case's notion of structures is different from Piaget's use of the term in that Case's structures are potentially teachable and are domain-specific (i.e., related to specific tasks or subject matter).

Case points out that the rate at which children progress through his developmental sequence can vary from one domain (or area) to the next. This development is influenced by the child's experience exploring and solving problems in the domain. Thus, if a child conducts basic scientific experiments at home, reads books on science, and/or asks questions about scientific phemonenon, he or she is going to be a more advanced thinker in science than another child who has not had such experiences.

## Information Processing and Human Abilities

**How do information-processing theorists criticize the psychometric approach to intelligence?**

I have pointed out that psychometric theorists attempt to understand intelligence in terms of factors, or mental structures, and show how individuals differ on these factors. Sternberg (1987b), a proponent of the information-processing approach, criticizes the psychometricians by pointing out that:

> When one says that a person is better on a reasoning test because he or she has a higher score on a reasoning factor, it does not seem to go much beyond saying that the score is higher because it is higher. So what we ask is: What are the underlying mental processes that contribute to individual differences in intelligence? (p. 194)

**How do information-processing theorists approach the study of intelligence?**

Let's use an example from intelligence testing to better understand the information-processing approach. Inductive reasoning ability is a factor or structure that is measured in almost all intelligence tests and has been shown to be a good indicator of general intelligence. Induction is the establishment of general rules or ideas from sets of specific instances or examples. Inductive reasoning tasks have similar characteristics. The learner is presented with a set of stimuli and asked to infer the pattern or rule for the task. One of the most common tasks is the verbal analogy, such as: BOY is to GIRL as FATHER is to (a. WORKER, b. MOTHER, c. MAN, d. BROTHER).

The information-processing psychologists would begin with the following question: "What are the basic psychological processes involved in solving inductive reasoning problems?" In solving verbal analogies, the person must *encode,* or think about, the different terms in the analogy, identifying each and decide the attributes that may be relevant to a solution. Next, a person *infers* the relationship between the two terms (BOY and GIRL); *maps* or connects the higher-order relationship that links the first half of the analogy with the second half (the boy half with the father half); *applies* the relationship inferred between the first two terms (BOY and GIRL) to create the best completion to the analogy (MOTHER); *justifies* the answer option as preferable to the others, even if it is not the ideal response; and, finally, responds with the answer that seems best (Sternberg, 1988).

Next, researchers would attempt to propose a theory as to how these processes are performed and executed, the sequence of the processes, length of time needed to solve each item, and which items were more difficult. Finally, they would attempt to determine how individuals differ in the speed and accuracy of executing separate mental processes. When information-processing psychologists are finished, they plan to have a good understanding of inductive reasoning and hope to develop training programs to improve this human ability.

Let's look at another example. Mathematical ability is another human structure, or factor measured on intelligence tests. The psychometrician would identify mathematical ability as the ability to score well on tests of mathematics problems. In contrast, the information-processing approach would attempt to identify the mathematical components (e.g., skills, knowledge, mental operations) that are necessary to solve problems.

Consider the cognitive processes and knowledge required to solve simple word problems such as: "John has a nickel. Pete has 3 more cents than John. How many cents does Pete have?" Table 2.2 identifies two major parts—*problem representation* (changing a problem from words into an internal representation) and *problem solution* (applying mathematical knowledge to the internal representation to arrive at an answer). Five types of knowledge are used in solving such a problem (Mayer, 1985b):

1. *Linguistic knowledge* refers to knowledge about the English language, such as how to parse a sentence into parts of speech, or what various words mean.
2. *Factual knowledge* refers to knowledge about the world, such as units of measure.
3. *Schema knowledge* refers to knowledge of problem types, such as the difference between word problems and motion problems.
4. *Strategic knowledge* refers to knowledge of how to develop and monitor a solution plan.

TABLE 2.2 **TYPES OF KNOWLEDGE REQUIRED IN PROBLEM SOLVING**

*Sample problem:* John has a nickel. Pete has 3 more cents than John. How many cents does Pete have?

| Step | Knowledge | Examples from Sample Problem |
|---|---|---|
| Problem representation | | |
| Translation | Linguistic | "Pete has 3 more cents than John" means "$P = J + 3$" |
| | Factual | A nickel equals 5 cents. |
| Integration | Schema | This is a "comparison" problem, consisting of two subsets and a superset. |
| Problem solution | | |
| Planning | Strategic | The goal is to add 3 plus 5. |
| Execution | Algorithmic | Counting-on procedure. |

*Source: Mayer, 1985b.*

5. *Algorithmic knowledge* refers to a procedure for carrying out a planned operation, such as how to compute in long division. (p. 131)

The mathematical ability of students to solve algebra word problems can be analyzed according to their translation, integration, planning, and execution abilities and related knowledge. Since students often demonstrate different patterns of strengths and weaknesses with respect to these abilities, the instructor can provide different training for individual students to improve their mathematical ability to solve these types of problems (and their intelligence). Chapter 7 and its appendix discuss how you can teach students similar learning strategies to become more successful learners.

*Sternberg's Triarchic Theory of Intelligence.* Sternberg (1988) believes that human intelligence is a dynamic process that is used in all aspects of our lives—at work, at social gatherings, at home, and at school. His position is as follows: We are constantly attempting to make sense of and solve problems to function successfully in our environment. Unfortunately, present intelligence tests measure only a small part of "mental self-management skills." To fully understand intelligence, we need to go beyond the current tests and see how intelligence operates in our everyday lives. The type of intelligence needed to succeed in school only partly determines success in out-of-school situations.

Sternberg (1985, 1988) proposes that individuals are governed by three aspects of intelligence—*componential, experiential,* and *contextual*—that are exercised in different domains. Componential intelligence identifies the mental components involved in analytical thinking (e.g., planning, organizing, remembering facts, and applying them to new situations). This component includes what is normally measured on IQ or achievement tests.

Experiential intelligence refers to how individuals face new situations in which intuition, insight, and creativity are brought to bear on situations. Contextual intelligence is the environment in which intelligence functions (e.g., the classroom, home, work). Some individuals call this component "social intelligence" or "street smarts." Sternberg believes that there are various ways of being intelligent, or smart. In the best situation, an individual uses basic thinking or analytical skills, applies them to experience, and uses the resulting ability to adapt to and shape his or her environment.

Some individuals may have a good deal of ability in all three components, others may have strength in only one or two of the three components. Sternberg is concerned that present intelligence tests measure only the componential component. However, in the real world, experiential and contextual intelligence may be more in demand than the kind of intelligence emphasized in school (Bee, 1989).

On the basis of his theory, Sternberg is currently working on a new type of intelligence test—the Sternberg Multidimensional Abilities Test—that will measure intelligence in a much broader way than current tests. In his 1986 book, *Intelligence Applied*, he discusses how people can be trained to be more intelligent. Earlier approaches to intelligence have made few contributions in this area. Only time will tell if Sternberg's approach is more successful.

## THINKING ABOUT THE TEACHING-LEARNING MODEL

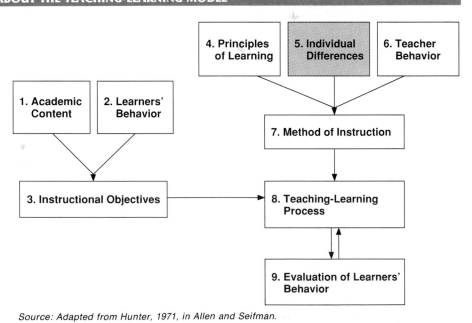

Source: Adapted from Hunter, 1971, in Allen and Seifman.

The psychometric approach to intelligence has dominated educational practice since the 1940s and illustrates how the assessment of individual differences (Box No. 5 in the teaching-learning model) influences instructional procedures (Box No. 7) and teacher behavior (Box No. 6) toward different students. The mental-ability conceptions of student functioning led to the thinking that when students were tested, they could be classified and placed in the proper instructional group in elementary school or achievement tracks in secondary schools. It is important to review the research on the effectiveness of tracking and grouping students for instruction.

*Tracking* involves the placement of students with similar educational needs and abilities into separate classes and programs. Curriculum tracking is common in high schools in which students are assigned to college preparatory, vocational, or business programs and expected to complete a specified sequence of courses. Another form of tracking, used in the upper-elementary and junior high schools as well as high schools, is *ability grouping*. In this school organization, the academic subjects—usually English, mathematics, science, and social studies—are organized into classes for students at different ability levels. In some schools, students are placed in the same ability groups for all subject areas; in other schools, a student may be in the high-ability level in mathematics but in the low ability level in English. In many schools, tracking and ability grouping overlap so that a student in the college preparatory track may be in an honors class in mathematics and in an average English class (Oakes, 1987)

Two conflicting points of view dominate educational thinking about tracking. One view is that tracking is an effective way to deal with the individual differences of students by providing programs for students at different ability levels. More specifically, it is argued that high-ability students need special programs if they are to develop their talents fully. In addition, low-ability students need to be educated together to avoid the stress from trying to keep up with their more talented peers. The opposing view is that tracking has little benefit for high-ability students and locks low-ability students into programs and classes in which they are stereotyped as weaker students and given an inferior education (Oakes, 1987).

The research evidence indicates few benefits of tracking students. The results in the succeeding paragraphs are based on reviews by Gamoran and Berends (1987) and Oakes (1985; 1987). First, while there is evidence that *some* tracking programs (e.g., gifted or accelerated classes) do benefit students in the higher tracks, these positive effects are not universally found (see Noland, 1985). Moreover, when there are positive effects, they tend to be more related to variations in students' academic experiences (e.g., quality of teaching) than the fact that they were homogeneously grouped. Most important, the research evidence indicates that students at all ability levels can achieve as well in heterogeneous as in homogeneous classes. In particular, students who are identified as average or low-ability usually exhibit higher achievement in mixed groups.

Second, tracking appears to be academically detrimental to students in the lower tracks. In fact, students who are placed in vocational tracks in which they are supposed to attain the skills for immediate employment do not benefit from this placement, since they often are less employable (because of the quality of their education) and earn lower wages than other high school graduates.

Third, there is no support for the argument that lower-ability students will suffer emotional strains from their enrollment in mixed-ability classes. In fact, the *opposite* has been found to result. Students experience more negative social and emotional effects from placement in lower tracks than placement in mixed-ability groups.

Finally, tracking widens the initial differences among groups rather than serving as a solution to narrow the gap among them. Some educators argue that lower-ability track students need slower pacing of material. The problem is that slow pacing usually leads to less material covered and less proficiency in mathematics, English, and foreign languages. As a result, the students in the lower tracks don't have the academic courses needed to apply for admission into college even if they decide in their junior or senior year that they want to go to college. An important point to consider is that students in lower tracks rarely move to higher tracks.

Let's now turn to ability grouping. Despite the widespread use of between-class ability grouping in schools, the research does not support its value because the disadvantages tend to outweigh its advantages (Good & Marshall, 1984; Rosenbaum, 1980). A number of explanations are given for this conclusion. First, the primary purpose of between-class grouping is to give teachers the opportunity to work with a smaller range of ability so they can more effectively adapt their instruction to the needs of their students. However, students are usually assigned to different classes or groups on the basis of test scores. As a result, the reduction in the range of differences in ability often is not great enough to make a difference in how the students are instructed or how much the students learn. Second, the quality of instruction generally is not as high in low-track groups as it is in high-track groups. Teachers of low-track classes often do not cover as much material, are less enthusiastic, and are less organized than teachers of high-track classes. Third, labeling or stigmatizing students assigned to lower tracks in school is a major problem. Students in these tracks tend to believe that they are less capable, and often they are treated differently by teachers and other students in school. In addition, they are more likely to drop out of school and become delinquent than students in higher tracks (Slavin, 1988).

The research on within-class ability grouping tends to be more positive (Slavin, 1988). One reason is that within-class grouping is usually more flexible, whereas between-class grouping tends to be more rigid. For example, if a high school student is assigned to a low-track class, the probability of being moved to another class during the year is rather low, whereas the student placed in a low group within a class is more likely to be assigned to a higher group if the teacher observes an increase in achievement. Another factor contributing to greater success of within-class as opposed to between-class grouping is the opportunity for students in within-class grouping to participate in different types of ability groups during the day. A student in a lower group in mathematics may be in a higher group in reading. This opportunity reduces the possibility of negative feelings about being in a low-ability group.

When you become involved in making decisions concerning individual differences in school or in your own classroom, consider the positive and negative outcomes of different instructional designs. The research reported in this section encourages all educators to reconsider some traditional methods of attempting to deal with student diversity in schools.

## KEY POINTS

1. The psychometric approach to intelligence attempts to identify the content and structure of mental abilities.
2. Intelligence is defined as a single or multifactor trait.
3. Guilford's multifactor theory of intelligence lists 180 characteristics or capacities that contribute to intelligence.
4. Binet developed the first intelligence test and based it on the concept of mental age.
5. Individual intelligence tests are primarily used for placement decisions.
6. The Stanford-Binet and Wechsler are two individually administered intelligence tests.
7. Teachers must not be hasty in interpreting intelligence scores of students who have not had an opportunity to learn tasks included in the test, are unmotivated, have poor reading skills, or are not well adjusted emotionally.
8. Some common *misconceptions* of intelligence tests are that they measure "innate" or "natural" abilities, are an exact indicator of all learning abilities, and provide unchangeable scores.
9. White students tend to score higher than black and other minority students, and students from high socioeconomic backgrounds score higher on intelligence tests than do students from low socioeconomic backgrounds.
10. Intelligence tests are criticized for emphasizing verbal ability over other types of mental ability.
11. Educators as well as the courts disagree whether intelligence tests provide biased scores for minority students.
12. Teachers and schools may use low intelligence test scores as a basis for discriminatory practices in school.
13. Intelligence tests may not adequately measure the academic potential of minority-group children.

14. Attempts at developing culture-free intelligence tests have not been successful.

15. Preschool programs were established to increase the intellectual development and academic performance of children from impoverished backgrounds. Although there are many personal and social benefits from these programs, research has shown that academic and cognitive gains diminish once students leave these programs.

16. Jensen questions the ability of preschool programs to accomplish their objectives because of their focus on academic knowledge or skills rather than thinking processes.

17. According to Piaget, children proceed through four distinct stages of cognitive development.

18. Critics of Piaget question the validity of distinct stages of development, believe that he overestimated the ability of adolescents and adults to move into formal operations thinking, and challenge his methodology.

19. Information-processing theorists studying cognitive development believe that children can be taught problem solving at an earlier age than Piaget's theory would predict. They also tend to disagree with Piaget's notion that each stage of development involves a totally new form of thinking.

20. Piaget's theory can be used as a guide in the structuring and sequencing of subject matter in the curriculum.

21. Teachers should be conscious of the cognitive-developmental level of their students.

22. Teachers should analyze tasks in the curriculum to determine the level of reasoning required for the successful solution of each task.

23. Teachers should use concrete learning experiences whenever possible and not move into abstract levels of thinking too quickly.

24. Because of its emphasis upon the processes and strategies individuals use in intelligent behavior, the information-processing approach has been particularly useful in suggesting directions for training intelligent performance.

25. Sternberg's triarchic theory of intelligence focuses on three different aspects of intelligence exercised in different domains. The implication of this theory is that current intelligence tests only tap a small part of intelligent behavior.

## KEY TERMS

psychometric, p. 34
information processing, p. 34
intelligence, p. 35
factor analysis, p. 36
Structure of Intellect, p. 36
contents, p. 36

operations, p. 36
products, p. 36
mental age, p. 38
intelligence quotient (IQ), p. 39
individual intelligence tests, p. 39
mentally retarded, p. 40
gifted and talented, p. 40
socioeconomic status (SES), p. 43
heritability, p. 45
organization, p. 48
adaptation, p. 48
assimilation, p. 48
accommodation, p. 48
disequilibrium, p. 48
equilibration, p. 49
sensorimotor stage, p. 50
object permanence, p. 50
preoperational stage, p. 51
reversibility, p. 51
conservation, p. 52
decenter, p. 53
egocentrism, p. 53
transductive reasoning, p. 54
concrete operations stage, p. 54
combinativity, p. 54
associativity, p. 54
identity, p. 55
serializing, p. 56
formal operations stage, p. 56
hypothetico-deductive reasoning, p. 56
propositional reasoning, p. 56
combinatorial reasoning, p. 56
open education, p. 60
discovery learning, p. 61
enactive, p. 62
iconic, p. 62
symbolic, p. 62

## SUGGESTIONS FOR FURTHER READING

Bjorklund, D. F. (1989). *Children's thinking: Developmental function and individual differences.* Pacific Grove, CA: Brooks/Cole. A review of the theories and research of intellectual and cognitive development.

Sattler, J. M. (1988). *Assessment of children.* (3rd ed.) San Diego: Sattler. A comprehensive assessment of intelligence tests currently in use.

Wagner, R., & Sternberg, R. J. (1984). Alternative conceptions of intelligence and their implications for education. *Review of Educational Research, 54,* 179–223. Compares three major views of intelligence: the psychometric, the Piagetian, and the information processing.

Select any of the following for more detailed study of Piaget:

Flavell, J. H. (1985). *Cognitive development.* (2nd ed.) Englewood Cliffs, NJ: Prentice-Hall.

Ginsburg, H. P., & Opper, S. (1988). *Piaget's theory of intellectual development* (3rd. ed.). Englewood Cliffs, NJ: Prentice-Hall.

Labinowicz, E. (1980). *The Piaget primer.* Menlo Park, CA: Addison-Wesley. Uses illustrations to explain children's responses to different tasks.

Phillips, J. L., Jr. (1975). *The origins of intellect: Piaget's theory* (2nd ed.). San Francisco: Freeman.

Wadsworth, B. (1978). *Piaget for the classroom teacher.* White Plains, NY: Longman. Good discussion of how Piaget's theory relates to teaching reading, mathematics, science, and social studies. Part III deals with cognitive-developmental assessment.

Wadsworth, B. (1989). *Piaget's theory of cognitive and affective development* (4th ed.). White Plains, NY: Longman.

Wolman, B. B. (Ed.) (1985). *Handbook of intelligence: Theories, measurements, and applications.* New York: Wiley. Includes chapters on various approaches to intelligence.

To learn more about Sternberg's work:

Sternberg, R. J. (1985). *Beyond IQ: A triarchic theory of human intelligence.* Cambridge: Cambridge University Press.

Sternberg, R. J. (1986). *Intelligence applied: Understanding and increasing your intellectual skills.* San Diego: Harcourt Brace Jovanovich.

Sternberg, R. J. (1988). *The triarchic mind: A new theory of human intelligence.* New York: Viking.

## FOLLOW-UP ACTIVITIES

**1. Compare and Evaluate the Psychometric, Piagetian, and Information-Processing Perspectives of Intelligence**

Suppose a psychologist representing each of these perspectives is asked to train a student to solve analogy problems in the form A: B :: C: (D1,D2). Compare and contrast how a psychometric, Piagetian, and information processing-psychologist would approach the task (see Wagner & Sternberg, 1984 for an explanation).

**2. Analyze a Piagetian Quotation**

The goal in education is not to increase the amount of knowledge, but to create the possibilities for a child to invent and discover. When we teach too fast, we keep the child from inventing and discovering himself. . . . Teaching means creating situations where structures can be discovered; it does not mean transmitting structures which may be assimilated at nothing other than a verbal level. (Piaget, 1964, p. 3)

What does Piaget mean by teaching too fast? Can you relate this statement to your own learning?

### 3. Assess a Child's Level of Cognitive Development

In Piaget and Szeminska (1952, p. 165), Piaget places 20 beads (18 brown and 2 white) in a box, the child acknowledging that they are all made of wood. Piaget asks the following question: "In this box, which are there more of, wooden beads or brown beads?" (All the beads are visible.) The child replies that there are more brown beads, "since there were only two white ones." Piaget then asks the child, "Are all the brown ones made of wood?" The child responds, "Yes." Piaget questions further, "If I take away all the wooden beads and put them in a second box, will there be any beads left in the first box?" The child replies, "No, because they are all made of wood." The child is then asked, "If the brown ones are taken away, will there be any beads left?" The child responds, "Yes, the white ones."

In which period is the child? What operation(s) is Piaget testing? Why does the child respond as described?

### 4. Try a Piagetian Experiment

**Conservation of Quantity**
*Material:* A ball of clay.
*Presentation:* Give the child a ball of clay and ask the child to make another exactly like it—just as big and just as heavy.
*Activity:* After the child has done the activity, retain one of the balls as a standard of comparison. Change the other one by stretching it into a sausage, flattening it into a cake, or cutting it into smaller pieces. Ask if the amount of clay, its weight, and its volume have changed or remained invariant (conserved) as a result of the transformation. "Do the two pieces of clay have the same amount of clay?"
*Justification:* "How do you know?"

# CHAPTER 3

# Cognition, Culture, and Language

ORIENTATION

In this chapter we shall explore three interrelated variables—**cognition, culture,** and language—that can have considerable impact on learning. Cognition refers to mental processes such as thinking, perceiving, and problem solving. There are many aspects of cognition: Intelligence is one, **cognitive style,** or how individuals process information, is another.

Culture can influence how we think and the linguistic processes we use to communicate with each other. There are many different definitions of culture. Casanova (1987) states that culture is the "sum total of ways in which a group of people think, feel, and react in order to solve problems of living in their environment" (pp. 372–373). Throughout history, Anglo-Americans have responded in diverse ways to explain the school failure of culturally different children: They were genetically inferior, their culture was viewed as deficient, and/or their cultural traits were incompatible with the dominant culture (Sue & Padilla, 1986). Today, there is more concern about **multicultural education,** emphasizing the advantages of a pluralistic society. The thinking by many educators is that society, and its institutions (e.g., the school) should change to assist immigrants' adaptation to a new culture. The purpose of changing the structure of educational institutions is to allow all students—regardless of their gender, social class, or racial, ethnic, and cultural background—the opportunity to achieve success in school (Banks, 1989). An objective of this chapter and the next two chapters is to provide you with the knowledge and competencies to help you achieve this goal.

Educational anthropologists have focused on psychocultural factors in teaching and learning. Students from some minority groups have had considerable success in U.S. schools, while other immigrant groups have had a difficult time achieving in school. Students who enter school are also entering a new cultural setting. Much of a student's success in school depends on his or her success in making the transition from the home or community culture to the school culture (Casanova, 1987). In this chapter, I explore some of the issues involved in understanding differences in educational achievement and the steps that some educators are taking to ease the transition to the school culture.

English is not the primary language of most of the immigrant children entering school. For example, in California, one out of six children entering public school in the fall of 1989 did not speak English. Thus educators are challenged to provide effective methods of language instruction. Furthermore, since culture is transmitted primarily through language, teachers must be concerned with **sociolinguistics**—the study of language in its social context. Linguistic rules of the classroom may differ from students' linguistic behavior at home. As a result, teachers need to be sensitive to these differences and not underestimate the academic abilities of students who display different linguistic behavior.

By the time you master the material presented in this chapter, you will be able to:

- Modify instructional procedures based on different cognitive/learning styles of students.
- Develop culturally compatible classrooms.
- Enhance the language development of students.

1. How can cognitive/learning style impact student learning?
2. Why do some divergent thinkers have difficulty in the classroom?
3. What problems do students from different cultural backgrounds face when entering schools in the United States?
4. How can modifications in classroom organization, sociolinguistics, cognition, and motivation help culturally diverse students?
5. What is the difference between Piaget's and Vygotsky's approach to cognitive development?
6. According to Vygotsky, what role does social interaction have on language and cognitive development?
7. How does Krashen's approach to language acquisition differ from traditional approaches?
8. What are the issues involved in developing bilingual rather than English-only language programs?

## COGNITIVE/LEARNING STYLES

**How can cognitive/learning style impact student learning?**

An area of individual differences that has received considerable attention in education is *cognitive style,* or **learning style.** Sometimes these terms are used interchangeably. Cognitive styles refer to the consistent ways in which an individual responds to a wide range of perceptual and intellectual tasks. Messick (1976) identified more than 20 dimensions of cognitive style that have derived, for the most part, from the research in laboratory investigations studying cognitive differences in humans.

Whereas ability (i.e., intelligence) is viewed as unipolar (i.e., having more ability is better than less ability), cognitive styles tend to identify one element or dimension with two polarities. As you will soon learn, one polarity of a cognitive style is not necessarily better than another. There is some debate as to the extent that cognitive style and ability are related. For the most part, it appears that cognitive style is relatively independent from ability. However, certain cognitive styles may be more related to ability than other cognitive styles.

Educators and psychologists became interested in the implications of cognitive-style research for adapting instruction for different types of students. In some cases they have used cognitive-style instruments in educational settings to assess learning style. They also have developed special assessments for use by educational practitioners. As a result, the term *learning style* was used to identify this new orientation. Although the definitions of learning styles differ, most definitions focus on individual differences that influence *learning in classroom situations.* For example, DeCecco (1968) identifies learning styles as "personal ways in which individuals process information in the course of learning new concepts and principles" (p. 75). Keefe (1982) states: "Learning styles are cognitive, affective, and physiological traits that serve as relatively stable indicators of how learners perceive, interact with, and respond to the learning environment" (p. 44). In this section I use the terms interchangeably and focus on cognitive and learning styles that have implications for classroom learning.

The major focus of the research on learning styles is to attempt to provide students with a specific instructional environment that is based on their learning style. Think about your own learning style for a moment. Suppose you had to prepare for an examination next week on this chapter. How would you prepare for such a task? Does your learning style

- Involve studying with other students, or do you work independently?
- Include studying for short periods during the week, or would you wait for the night before the exam to begin studying?
- Involve taking notes on the chapter during your initial reading, or do you rely on your Magic Marker underscores?
- Depend on the type of exam—essay or multiple choice—that is scheduled?
- Call for studying under quiet conditions, or do you require a minimum level of noise—a radio tuned to your favorite station?
- Require working under pressure? Without tests as a prod, would you study as much?

What additional aspects of your learning style are important to your learning? Compare them with those of other students in your class.

Table 3.1 includes a number of learning-style factors that may influence a student's adjustment to classroom instruction and, possibly, to academic success. Dunn and Dunn (1972) believe that teachers should assess students on these dimensions.

As you talk to other students about their learning styles and observe the behavior of your roommates and friends, the range of differences becomes apparent. I have always been intrigued by the metamorphosis of student behavior during final exam time. Some students sleep during the day and study at night, don't bathe, and don't shave. They change their regular study behavior in many ways, as if the new behavior change will make a difference. Why do students make these changes? Do the changes have certain psychological effects on them?

Let's analyze why knowledge of some of the characteristics listed in Table 3.1 would be useful to a teacher's decision making (Shumsky, 1968).

TABLE 3.1 LEARNING-STYLE DIAGNOSIS

*Self analysis*

| 1. Time | When is the student most alert? In the early morning, at lunchtime, in the afternoon, in the evening, at night? |
|---|---|
| 2. Schedule | What is the student's attention span? Continuous, irregular, short bursts of concentrated effort, forgetting periods, etc.? |
| 3. Amount of Sound | What level of noise can the student tolerate? Absolute quiet, a murmur, distant sound, high level of conversation? |
| 4. Type of Sound | What type of sound produces a positive reaction? Music, conversation, laughter, working groups? |
| 5. Type of Work Group | How does the student work best? Alone, with one person, with a small task group, in a large team, a combination? |
| 6. Amount of Pressure | What kind of pressure (if any) does the student need? Relaxed, slight, moderate, extreme? |
| 7. Type of Pressure and Motivation | What helps to motivate this student? Self, teacher expectation, deadline, rewards, recognition of achievement, internalized interest, etc.? |
| 8. Place | Where does the student work best? Home, school, learning centers, library media corner? |
| 9. Physical Environment and Conditions | Floor, carpet, reclining, sitting, desk, temperature, table lighting, type of clothing, food? |
| 10. Type of Assignments | On which types of assignment does the student thrive? Contracts, totally self-directed projects, teacher-selected tasks, etc.? |
| 11. Perceptual Strengths and Styles | How does the student learn most easily? Visual materials, sound recording, printed media, tactile experiences, kinesthetic activities, multimedia packages, combinations of these? |
| 12. Type of Structure and Evaluation | What type of structure suits this student most of the time? Strict, flexible, self-determined, jointly arranged, periodic, self-starting, continuous, occasional, time-line expectations, terminal assessment? |

*Source: Dunn and Dunn, 1972.*

Students vary in their attention span (item No. 2 of Table 3.1). Some students can work on activities for long periods without distraction, whereas other students find it difficult to maintain attention for more than 15 or 20 minutes. Such information can be useful to the teacher in determining when it may be necessary to stop and check whether certain students are still "with it." Understanding the attention span of various students also can help the teacher plan the length of assignments for them.

It is important for the teacher to know who can work independently with little direction and who needs considerable help in beginning an assignment (No. 10). The teacher needs to know the students who need intermittent help (even if they don't ask for it) and those who consistently need assistance. Such information is useful in making decisions regarding grouping of students. For example, if certain students need help in beginning tasks, it would make little sense to place them in a self-directed activity without providing the information that would allow them to begin the activity. Some students can plan their work schedules and complete assignments on time, whereas other students need help planning for effective use of time.

Reaction to new situations can influence a student's success in that activity (No. 6 and No. 10). A teacher should observe students to determine differences in how they accept new situations and challenges. Some students panic with the introduction of new material and need time to become acquainted with the activity before they learn to handle a task with confidence; other students dive right into new situations without any hesitation.

## Conceptual Tempo

Kagan et al. (1964) noticed that some students take a long time to think about a question or problem before they respond, whereas other students respond almost immediately to the questions posed. They have developed a test called the Matching Familiar Figures Test (MFFT) to obtain measures of student response rates and errors.

As a result of their findings, Kagan and his colleagues proposed a stylistic dimension called **conceptual tempo,** referring to the speed with which subjects make a response to their tasks and the number of errors they make in the response. Rapid responders, who make a fair amount of errors, are called **impulsive.** Slower responders, who tend to make fewer errors, are called **reflective.** Kagan believes that impulsiveness or reflectiveness is a consistent and relatively stable personality trait that may be evident by the time the child is 2 years old. Research on conceptual tempo has established that reflective students perform better on a number of academic-type tasks than impulsive students, including reading and memory tasks (Bjorklund, 1989).

Holt (1982) describes the behavior of some of his students that is typical of the impulsive individual:

> It used to puzzle me that the students who made the most mistakes and got the worst marks were so often the first ones to hand in their papers. I used to say, "If you finish early, take time to check your work, do some problems again." Typical teacher's advice; I might as well have told them to flap their arms and fly. When the paper was in, the tension was ended. Their fate was in the lap of the gods. They might still worry about flunking the paper, but it was a fatalistic kind of worry; it didn't contain the agonizing element of choice—there was nothing more they could do about it. Worrying about whether you did the right thing, while painful enough, is less painful than worrying about the right thing to do. (pp. 74–75)

Both overly reflective students and impulsive students are likely to have trouble in the classroom—the impulsive student because of a too-

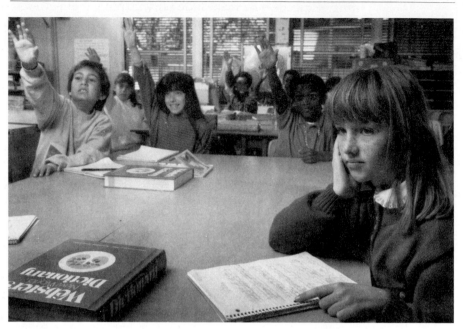

Although a student may not respond as rapidly as other students, a teacher should not judge him or her less capable.

quick response to questions and tasks without thinking, and the reflective student because of endlessly pondering questions. The important implication here is that impulsiveness, not intellectual deficiency, is partly responsible for poor reading and low scores on intelligence and achievement tests.

Depending on how the teacher puts them through their paces, both reflective and impulsive students can have trouble with certain types of task. The impulsive teacher will overwhelm the reflective child with a barrage of information or questions that the child cannot handle—for example, in speed games. However, the impulsive child, who delivers a volley of responses to straightforward questions, is in just the right situation. The more reflective classmate wastes time mulling over answers that do not require much attention.

The reflective child shines in dealing with questions when there is a great chance of error. This kind of person will suppress the incorrect answers that occur and will unearth other possibilities that escape the more impulsive child, who has already quickly given answers.

Kagan (1966) provides an excellent example to illustrate the advantage that the reflective child holds. Suppose a reflective and an impulsive child must remember whether the formula for the circumference of a circle is $2\pi r$ or $\pi r^2$. The impulsive child selects one formula quickly, with even odds for selecting the correct formula. The reflective child pauses to evaluate the validity of each formula and might remember that the area of a rectangle involves the square of a number. The child then decides that $\pi r^2$ applies to the area of a circle; thus, $2\pi r$ is probably the correct formula for the circumference.

How many times have we heard a teacher say, "Why don't you take time to think?" or "Why can't you move a little faster?" What the teacher doesn't realize is that a student's learning style is part of the personality and can be modified only with specific training (see Chapter 6, for a discussion of how self-instruction training is used to modify impulsive behavior).

## Field-Independent/Field-Dependent

One of the most widely investigated forms of cognitive style is the **field-independent/field-dependent** dimension. This dimension is a measure of the extent to which individuals are able to overcome effects of distracting background elements (the field) when they attempt to differentiate the relevant aspects of a particular situation (item No. 11 of Table 3.1). The more independent the person is of distracting elements, the more analytical, or field-independent, that person is. The more dependent on or incapable the individual is of ignoring the distracting elements, the more global, or field-dependent, the person is. For example, an individual who has difficulty reading a diagram to assemble a bicycle or barbecue set may be field-dependent. Figure 3.1 presents an example from the Hidden Figures Test used to determine a person's cognitive style in the field-independent/field-dependent dimension.

In a paper reviewing the research in this area, Witkin et al. (1977) pointed out the characteristic orientation of individuals classified as field-dependent and field-independent. Field-dependent persons are particularly attentive to the social field and will look to others in defining their own attitudes and beliefs. They reflect a considerable degree of social sensitivity. In contrast, field-independent persons show greater interest in the more impersonal, abstract aspects of various stimuli.

These two types of individual interact differently with the environment. Field-dependent persons are drawn to people, favor occupations, such as teaching, that require involvement with others, and prefer academic areas, such as the social sciences, that are more people-oriented. Field-independent persons prefer occupations such as astronomy and engineering, in which there is less emphasis on interpersonal interaction. They also favor school subjects, such as mathematics and the physical sciences, that stress the impersonal and abstract. Field-dependent persons are better at learning and remembering social material, and field-independent persons are better at learning and remembering impersonal material.

Another difference—not surprising, after we learn about their differences in social orientation—is that social reinforcement has a greater impact on field-dependent than on field-independent people. This finding may

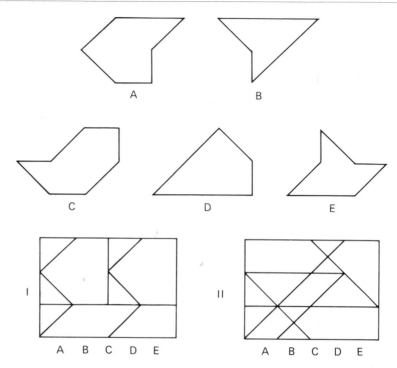

Figure 3.1 A Hidden Figures Test of the Type Used to Assess Field Dependence/Field Independence. The student is asked to identify which of the five simple figures (A–E) is hidden within the embedding context of the more complex patterns.

*Source: Educational Testing Service, 1962, 1975.*

be one factor in explaining students' differential responses to different types of reinforcement in the classroom.

Finally, field-independent and field-dependent persons respond differently to material in terms of its degree of structure. When the learning material is unstructured, the learner must organize it. Field-independent persons are better able to internalize the structure needed to organize and learn the material. When the material is structured, field-independent and field-dependent people are equally matched in their learning ability.

Table 3.2 identifies field-dependent and field-independent learning and teaching styles as well as methods to use to motivate each type of student. Generally, field-independent teachers encourage independent student achievement and competition between individual students. In contrast, field-dependent teachers are more interpersonally oriented and prefer situations that allow them to use personal, conversational techniques while interacting with students.

TABLE 3.2 **FIELD-DEPENDENT AND FIELD-INDEPENDENT LEARNING STYLES**

### Learning Styles

| Field-Dependent | Field-Independent |
|---|---|
| Perceives globally | Perceives analytically |
| Experiences in a global fashion; adheres to structures as given | Experiences in an articulated fashion; imposes structure or restrictions |
| Makes broad general distinctions among concepts; sees relationships | Makes specific concept distinctions with little overlap |
| Social orientation | Impersonal orientation |
| Learns material with social content best | Learns social material only as an intentional task |
| Attends best to material relevant to own experience | Interested in new concepts for their own sake |
| Requires externally defined goals and reinforcements | Has self-defined goals and reinforcements |
| Needs organization provided | Can self-structure situations |
| More affected by criticism | Less affected by criticism |
| Uses spectator approach for concept attainment | Uses hypothesis-testing approach to attain concepts |

### Teaching Styles

| Field-Dependent | Field-Independent |
|---|---|
| Prefers teaching situations that allow interaction and discussion with students | Prefers impersonal teaching situations such as lectures; emphasizes cognitive aspect of instruction |
| Uses questions to check on student learning following instruction | Uses questions to introduce topics and following student answers |
| Uses student-centered activities | Uses a teacher-organized learning situation |
| Viewed by students as one who teaches facts | Viewed by students as encouraging them to apply principles |
| Provides less feedback; avoids negative evaluation | Gives corrective feedback; uses negative evaluation |
| Strong in establishing a warm and personal learning environment | Strong in organizing and guiding student learning |

### How to Motivate Students

| Field-Dependent | Field-Independent |
|---|---|
| Through verbal praise | Through grades |
| Through helping the teacher | Through competition |
| Through external rewards (stars, stickers, prizes) | Through choice of activities, personal goal chart |
| Through showing the task's value to other people | Through showing how the task is useful to them |
| Through providing outlines and structure | Through freedom to design their own structure |

*Source: Garger & Guild, in* Curriculum Review, *1984.*

## Hemisphericity: Left-Brain versus Right-Brain Processing

Another area of of individual differences is **hemisphericity** (sometimes called *brain lateralization*). This controversial dimension of cognitive style pertains to an individual's supposed preference for processing information and solving problems using different parts of the brain (Bjorklund, 1989). The human brain is divided into two hemispheres. Although the two halves look alike, they do not function in the same manner. The two halves appear to house different functions, although they are connected and work together. The right side of the brain has been identified as the more intuitive side, whereas the left side is the more logical side. The left side focuses on such domains as speech, abstraction, logic, reading, and mathematics. The right side focuses on emotion, innovation, creativity, intuition, and spatial relationships.

The major issue presented by some educators is that the secondary schools tend to ignore the activities involved in the right side of the brain. The argument goes as follows: The curriculum of the high school emphasizes sequenced, verbal, numerical, and analytical skills—all left-brain functions. The right brain is more difficult to work with, and in fact less valued, because it includes activities that do not lend themselves to grades, tests, and well-organized activities. Furthermore, the adolescent who functions better in a nonverbal, intuitive, or nonsequential manner is likely to have difficulty attaining success in school. As a result, more attention should be given to nurturing both halves of the brain (Fuhrmann, 1986).

Claims about the benefits of stimulating the right brain are made in conferences, workshops, and self-help books such as *The Right Brain* (Blakeslee, 1980) and *Drawing on the Right Side of the Brain* (Edwards, 1979). Levy (1982) believes it is wrong to make a sharp distinction between the functioning of the two parts of the brain because they work together. He states that although there are individual differences among people to the extent that one hemisphere is more differentially aroused than the other, it is wrong to state that students learn with only one side of the brain. For example, the appreciation of literature depends on learning the meaning of words and sentences as well as responding to the rhythm of language, imagining and feeling the scenes and moods, and empathizing with the characters. This total experience cannot be accomplished by either side of the brain alone but represents an integrative activity. It is difficult to say which side of the brain contributes to what activity.

Harris (1985) criticizes educators for misunderstanding and, in many cases, not reading basic neuropsychological literature. He states: "If educators are unsatisfied with the educational *curriculum,* they ought to present the case for change on its *own* merits, and not seek to win scientific respectability for their arguments by cloaking them in neuropsychological jargon" (p. 267).

One new development based on controversial brain research (Das,

Kirby, & Jarman, 1975) is an instrument by Kaufman and Kaufman (1983), the Kaufman Assessment Battery for Children (K-ABC), which measures children's intelligence (defined as learning potential and preferred learning style) and achievement. It is based on two different types of information processing—sequential (or successive) and simultaneous (or holistic). Sequential processing places stimuli into sequences to solve a problem, whereas simultaneous processing synthesizes separate elements into spatial groupings. Although the instrument has been criticized on theoretical and methodological grounds (see Sattler, 1988), it is an attempt to improve upon standard intelligence tests.

Does knowledge of the functions of both sides of the brain have any implications for understanding the learning styles of students? Levy (1983) believes that in time there may be some important implications for education. For example, the evidence of differential arousal suggests that whole-brain learning may be attained by different individuals using different methods. In learning algebraic equations, some students may better understand the concept if they are first taught the structure of the equations and the methods of symbol manipulation and then learn to visualize the equations on an X and Y axis, whereas other students might better understand the concept if they are first taught the visual, geometric relationships and then the symbolic equations. Levy (1983) states: "I am suggesting only that the *gateway* into whole-brain learning may differ for different children, *not* that one hemisphere or the other should be the object of education" (p. 70).

The exciting aspect of research on the functioning of the brain is that it has brought more attention to the various abilities that can be developed as well as pointing out individual differences in functioning. We may learn how to increase the potential of human capacity in all aspects of functioning.

## Convergent and Divergent Thinking

Guilford (1959) was among the first psychologists to suggest that intelligence and **creativity** were not synonymous. In the Structure of Intellect model presented in Chapter 2, Guilford distinguished between **convergent thinking** and **divergent thinking.** Convergent thinking produces a well-determined answer to a routine problem, whereas divergent thinking generates new ideas and solutions to problems that have more than one correct answer.

Convergent thinking would produce the answer "16" to the question "What is the square of 4?" Divergent thought production might entail finding unusual uses for a knife. In theory, the latter form of thinking is associated with creativity. Some students are better at divergent tasks than convergent tasks and vice versa, while some students are strong in both types of thinking.

Guilford identified four characteristics of divergent thinking:

- Fluency—coming up with a large quantity of ideas, words, and ways of expressing things.
- Flexibility—thinking up a variety of ideas and new ways of dealing with situations.
- Originality—thinking of uncommon, clever, and novel ideas and images.
- Elaboration—packing detail into the response.

**Why do some divergent thinkers have difficulty in the classroom?**

Many creative-thinking tests use these criteria in evaluating the responses of students. In a recent review of creativity measures, Hocevar and Bachelor (1989) reported that different creativity instruments do not measure the same traits. Thus it is not always easy to identify creative individuals through paper and pencil tests.

The following are some behavioral characteristics of creative children, as summarized from Torrance (1962, 1972):

- Work characterized by humor, lack of rigidity, and playfulness.
- Willingness to attempt difficult tasks.
- Long attention span, concentration, and interest.
- Likely to express unconventional ideas and engage in imaginative activities.
- More sensitive and independent than the average child.
- Lack of preoccupation with what the classroom group thinks.
- Sometimes labeled by their peers as having "silly" or "crazy" ideas.

An important issue for the teacher is whether the classroom activities provide opportunities to develop both convergent and divergent thinking skills. Students with excellent divergent thinking abilities often have difficulties in a classroom where the instructor emphasizes primarily convergent-thinking activities. In addition, divergent thinkers may be viewed by the teacher as troublemakers or difficult students because they approach learning tasks differently than other students.

## Learning Styles: A Concluding Statement

Much of the focus on learning styles has been to match instruction to the individual differences of students. Although such attempts may contribute to student enjoyment of the classroom situation, and in some cases may improve academic performance, teachers need to be aware of the current status of the research in this area. Doyle and Rutherford (1984) point out some of the difficulties in attempting to match instruction to learning styles. First, the teacher must decide which of the many learning styles is most important. Then the styles must be measured. And finally, because some of the instruments generate hundreds of possible combinations for matching learning style and instruction, the teacher must make decisions regarding how to apply the information.

There is not much support of the idea that matching instructional methods to different learning styles increases achievement (see Cohen et al., 1989; Cronbach & Snow, 1977; Kampwirth & Bates, 1980). Cronbach and Snow have reported the most extensive literature on what is called **aptitude by treatment interaction (ATI)** research. This type of investigation studies how aptitudes interact with instructional treatments or methods to affect student learning. The strongest evidence for ATI involves measures of general ability (i.e., intelligence). The major conclusion of the review by Cronbach and Snow was that students with high ability learn best in an educational setting in which they are free to impose their own structure on the educational tasks. Individuals with low ability, on the other hand, appear to learn best when the instructor imposes the structure on the learning task.

Learning-style instruments focus on student preferences for learning in different environments. Clark (1982) has studied the relationship between students' achievement and their preference for or enjoyment of various instructional methods. He found that students often report enjoying the method from which they learn the *least* because they underestimate the amount of effort needed to attain success. Students with low ability like more permissive methods of instruction (e.g., independent study or small-group activities) because they can maintain a low profile that makes their failure less visible. However, these students need more direction and attention to achieve success in academic tasks. Students with high ability like more structured methods (e.g., lecture-recitation sessions) that they believe help them to learn more efficiently. However, the research indicates that students with high ability actually learn more from permissive methods, which allow them more independence in using their abilities. Although this research is limited to structured and permissive environments and to students with high and low ability, it does suggest that a teacher should consider whether it is always advantageous to match student preferences and instructional environment—not only because the preferences may not lead to improved academic achievement but because students simply may benefit from certain instructional approaches whether they like them or not.

## PSYCHOCULTURAL FACTORS IN LEARNING

The diversity of the cultural backgrounds of students in American schools and the low academic achievement of many of these students require greater understanding of how cultural factors may influence educational achievement. There have been two major explanations for the academic difficulties that some minority students have had in school: cultural difference and secondary cultural discontinuity (Jacob & Jordan, 1987). Proponents of the cultural differences approach point to the disparity between the students' home and school culture and the difficulties that minority students have in adjusting to a classroom with different social interaction, linguistic, and cognitive styles. The argument is that these differences can lead to cultural conflicts that interfere with minority children's abilities to perform well in school.

The secondary cultural discontinuity approach differs from the cultural differences position. Ogbu (1987), the leading advocate of this approach, points out that the learning problems of minority students involve much more than cultural discontinuity between the school and the home. He states that some minority groups have been very successful in school whereas others have not been. He differentiates between minority groups (termed *castelike* or *involuntary*) (e.g., certain Hispanics and blacks) who were incorporated into U.S. society against their will and who tend to do poorly and minority groups (termed *immigrant*) (e.g., certain Asian-Americans) who come to the United States by their own choice and do well in school. While the immigrant groups view education as a means to improve their position in society, the castelike groups who have experienced limited occupational opportunities are less enthusiastic about education as a means to social mobility. As a result, the tendency of the parents of castelike groups not to communicate the importance of education to their children leads to less interest and involvement in formal education. Thus Ogbu would argue that to improve the educational process for certain minority groups, one must focus on the general society as well as the classroom. This means that the same economic opportunities open to Anglos must be available to minority groups if these groups are to view formal education more favorably.

Gibson (1987) provides some additional insights into the education of minority students that can be helpful to educators. She points out that involuntary minorities often equate school learning with the loss of their own cultural and ethnic identities, while immigrant groups view school learning and acquisition of the majority culture as an additional set of skills to use when appropriate. Therefore, some minority groups see school learning and acculturation as leading to assimilation, whereas other minority groups view school learning and acculturation in a broader perspective, in which new knowledge is incorporated into their own culture, transforming but not replacing it.

## The Changing Face of America

Neil Diamond sings: "Everywhere around the world, they're coming to America." This lyric appropriately describes the influx of immigrant students into American public schools. This migration presents a major challenge for teachers as they attempt to educate large numbers of language minority students. The number of legal immigrants, refugees, and undocumented immigrants entering the United States between 1981–1990 is estimated to be the largest migration in history. The result is that we now have one of the most ethnically and culturally diverse societies in the history of the United States.

Kellogg (1988) presents demographic information about the new immigrants. They come primarily from Asia (34%), Latin America (34%), and Europe (16%) (Muller & Espenshade, 1985) and have concentrated in California (28%), New York (16%), Texas (9%), Florida (8%), Illinois (6%), New Jersey (4%), Massachusetts (3%), Pennsylvania (2%), Michigan (2%), Ohio (1%), and in the remaining 40 states (21%). Fifty percent of the undocumented immigrants are estimated to be in California.

One of the characteristics of today's migration is its youth. Approximately 60% are between the ages of 16 and 44, with the median age of many Southeast Asian immigrants between 13 and 21 (Muller & Espenshade, 1985). The implication of the young age of the immigrants is that they are coming to America at their prime working and childbearing years. As a result, their fertility rates will have an important impact on the population of the public school system. Whereas white Americans average 1.7 children and black Americans average 2.4 children per lifetime, the Hmong (immigrants from Southeast Asia) average 11.9 children, Cambodians average 7.4 children, the Vietnamese average 3.4 children, and Mexican-Americans average 2.9 children (Rumbaut & Weeks, 1986).

This new immigration is predicted to change the population demographics as follows: By the year 2020, whites will comprise 70% of the U.S. population. By the year 2050, this percentage will have dropped to 60%. The black population will increase slightly, to about 16% of the total population. The Hispanic population will more than double (from 6.4% to 15%), and Asians will climb from 1.6% of the total population to as much as 10% (Bouvier & Agresta, 1987). Figure 3.2 presents the projected pro-

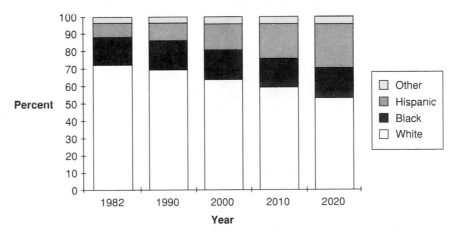

Figure 3.2 Projections of the 0–17 Population by Race/Ethnicity U.S. Total, 1982–2020.

*Source: Pallas, Natriello, and McDill, 1989.*

portions of the population 0–17 years old by race/ethnicity between 1982–2020.

## Challenge for the Schools

**What problems do students from different cultural backgrounds face when entering schools in the United States?**

The current migration brings a variety of backgrounds, languages, and cultures—many of which are new to the United States. The immigrant students bring to the public schools unique life experiences, different skills, and a new set of problems that pose many challenges for teachers. The language roots of many of the new immigrants are not similar to English, their religions may not stem from the Judeo-Christian heritage, and their parents may have a value system different from that of the mainstream American society (Kellogg, 1988).

You may be concerned about the necessity of educating undocumented immigrants. The U.S. Supreme Court ruled in 1982, in *Plyler v. Doe,* that the state has an obligation to educate the children of undocumented immigrants. Thus there are no legal grounds to deny an education to any group of immigrant children.

The diversity of students in public schools presents challenges to teachers, who must learn about their culture, help them acquire English, and deal with their emotional problems. Olsen (1988) illustrates this challenge by the following incident:

> In a San Francisco elementary school, a teacher plays hangman with her students to enliven a spelling lesson. As the class eagerly shouts out letters, one child bursts into tears. A Cambodian immigrant recently arrived from a Thai refugee camp, the child speaks little English. Another child is found who can interpret, and the hysterical child finally manages to communicate that she had witnessed the hanging of her father in Cambodia. (p. 211)

Teachers need to remember that many of these students may not understand even basic classroom or school rules and procedures. Opening a locker, standing in line for lunch or eating strange food, moving to another room when a bell rings, or participating in unfamiliar games may be new experiences. Many students come to school alone, frightened, and frustrated. An eighth-grade girl from Vietnam described her experience as follows:

> I felt so out of place that I felt sick. I didn't know where to sit or eat or where the bathroom was or how to eat the food. I felt that all around me activities were going on, but I was not a part of anything. (Olsen, 1988, p. 214)

Can you imagine how difficult it is for an immigrant high school student who has no or limited English to prepare for a test or participate in other academic activities he or she doesn't understand?

Even the most talented teachers often are challenged by the degree of student diversity in the classroom. Olsen (1988) describes a situation in which a teacher working with many new arrivals from Mexico began planning the annual holiday play in November. But by the first week in December, her students stopped coming to school and by the time the play was scheduled for a school assembly, almost two-thirds of her class had disappeared. Her students and their parents had begun the annual pilgrimage back to Mexico to visit family and friends and might not return until February. When they did return, many would enroll in a different school.

## Cultural Differences, Not Deficits

The typical North American classroom has certain distinct characteristics: The teacher usually is at the center of attention instructing students in a large group. The rules of communication that dominate include a pattern of question and answer sessions, in which the teacher asks a question, obtains a response from a student, and then reacts to that response. Spontaneous speech on the part of students is generally disencouraged. For the most part, the classroom organization is representative of the field-independent cognitive style (see Table 3.2), with individualism and competition providing an important framework for instruction.

For many students, the educational process described in the preceding paragraph is consistent with their experiences in their home and community. For other students, the classroom is incongruent with their home experiences. Hilliard (1989) identified a number of problems that can arise when teachers do not understand cultural differences. Although these problems are discussed separately, they often interact to cause considerable difficulties for students. What follows is a discussion of these differences, along with examples to illustrate their effect in the classroom.

## Low Expectation for Success

A teacher's error in estimating a student's or a cultural group's academic potential can lead to a low expectation for success. In one investigation, Deyhle (1987) studied tests and test-taking behaviors among Navajo students in a Bureau of Indian Affairs day school and Anglo students in a large Western city. Unlike the teachers of the Anglo students, the teachers of Navajo children were angry that their students didn't seem to care about low grades. Of particular concern was the fact that the students threw away their test papers after receiving them. The teachers concluded that the academic failure of the Navajo students was caused by a culture that didn't value academic achievement.

After visiting classrooms and interviewing both the Anglo and Navajo students, Deyhle found that the Navajo students did not relate the test to learning. They did not understand that results on tests were indicative of their personal progress in school. The Anglo students, however, understood the importance of testing, which was probably conveyed to them by parents and siblings who had been socialized by a formal educational system. As the Navajo students moved into the upper elementary grades, they began to view tests in the same manner as the Anglo students. Unfortunately, they also developed test anxiety and became more frustrated as they developed more negative self-perceptions of ability because of their lack of achievement.

## Sociolinguistics

Misunderstanding of cultural differences can lead teachers to misjudge their students' language abilities. When students and teachers differ in language abilities, teachers are more likely to use their own language as the proper form of expression. The most obvious differences in the use of language are those indicated by dialects, which are noticeable in the communication of individuals in different regions of the country (Casanova, 1987).

*Nonstandard English.* One of the most widely discussed language patterns is called Black English, or **Nonstandard English,** a dialect that deviates from Standard English in pronunciation, vocabulary, and grammar. Some educators believe that Nonstandard English is a defective form of Standard English and that it is detrimental to learning. As a result, these educators urge teachers to instruct students in Standard English and to avoid any recognition of Nonstandard English. On the other side of the issue are linguists such as Labov (1970), who has studied the language patterns of black youths and reports that they use an English vernacular that is grammatically complex and capable of expressing abstract concepts. Unfortunately, teachers perceive this form of language to be an inferior product of environmental conditions. Labov further points out that early childhood education programs such as Head Start, which were designed to overcome lower- and middle-class language differences, aggravated the black students' learning difficulties in school.

Labov does not say that children using Nonstandard English do not need additional verbal skills, some of which are characteristic of middle-class verbal behavior: precision in spelling, practice in handling abstract symbols, the ability to define words explicitly, and a broader vocabulary. The differences in pronunciation and grammar often create problems in the classroom. For example, Nonstandard English distinguishes between a continuing state and a temporary condition: "He working" corresponds to "He is working right now," whereas "He be working" means "He usually works" or "He has a steady job" (Labov, 1969). Another characteristic of the nonstandard language is the tendency to omit what linguists call the *medial r,* which the listener interprets as a "lost" syllable. The pronunciation of *sto'y* (story) and *ma'y* (marry) can lead to misunderstandings as to meaning (Adler, 1979). Labov (1974) questions whether all middle-class verbal habits are functional and desirable in school:

> Before we impose middle-class verbal style upon children from other cultural groups, we should find out how much of it is useful for the main work of analyzing and generalizing, and how much is merely stylistic or even dysfunctional. In high school and college, middle-class children spontaneously complicate their syntax to the point that instructors despair of getting them to make their language simpler and clearer. (p. 160)

The basic point of view expressed by Labov is that the school faced with individual differences should change its orientation. Rather than seek ways to modify students' behavior, educators should consider how the school can accommodate its instructional program to students' strengths. In terms of language instruction, teachers could use Nonstandard English as a springboard for teaching Standard English instead of criticizing students for speaking and writing "incorrectly." This means that instead of insisting that speakers of Nonstandard English follow phonetic rules in reading Standard English materials, teachers would permit children to read standard materials in their own dialect. Many teachers are reluctant to follow this advice because they fear that children will not learn Standard English. Linguists arguing for this approach point out that speaking and understanding have been shown to be separate aspects of language development. Children can understand written or spoken Standard English without producing standard pronunciations and grammatical forms in their own speech (Jackson, Robinson, & Dale, 1977).

*Classroom Interaction.* The linguistic processes in a classroom may differ from the oral discourse experienced by students from different cultural backgrounds (Ainsworth, 1984). An example of this linguistic conflict is described by Philips (1983), who studied how native American children's lack of responsiveness in the classroom influenced their academic achievement.

Teachers at the Warm Springs Indian Reservation in central Oregon complained that the native American children would not talk in front of the class and participated less and less in verbal interaction as they proceeded through school. Philips pointed out that teachers use classroom recitation to allow students to learn from their own public mistakes. The problem is that the native American children do not learn this way at home and come to the classroom unprepared to learn under this condition. The children's home learning involves watching an adult perform a task or skill and practicing it alone, unsupervised. When the children are successful, they perform the skill in front of the adult who taught it. When the task or skill is fully developed, only then is it demonstrated publicly. The use of speech in the learning process from instruction to evaluation plays a minor role, because verbal instruction is confined to corrections or answering questions.

This process provides some insight into the native American children's reluctance to speak in front of their peers. The assumption by the teacher that students learn more effectively by making mistakes in front of others is inconsistent with the children's background. The native American children have no opportunity to observe others performing successfully before they attempt a task or skill, and they don't have the freedom to determine whether they know enough to demonstrate their knowledge because the teacher determines when they must respond. Finally, competence is demonstrated verbally in the classroom rather than nonverbally.

Philips found that the children's classroom participation increased when the teacher interacted privately with individual students and when students worked together in small groups. Many teachers eventually changed their methods to include the participation structures that increased the children's oral discourse. However, Philips questions the desirability of complete accommodation to the children's learning preferences, because such change may not prepare the children to succeed in later grades, when they would be with Anglo children. She suggests that the children gradually be taught the traditional classroom discussion procedures so that they would be able to cope effectively in other classroom environments.

*Nonverbal Interaction.* Misunderstanding of cultural differences can influence the quality of teacher-student interaction. If you have taken courses in anthropology or read books such as *The Silent Language* (Hall, 1959) or *The Hidden Dimension* (Hall, 1966), you are already aware of important cultural differences in social interaction, time, space, and materials. Hall (1969) has also written about cultural differences in listening behavior, a topic of particular interest to teachers. He states that there exists in black cultures a series of responses governing the use of the eyes, the hands, the orientation and position of the body, and the tone of voice. Many of these characteristics are frequently misread by whites. Hall notes an informal rule in black culture: "If you are in the room with another person or in a context where he has ready access to you, there are times when there is no need to go through the motions of showing him you are listening because that is automatically implied" (p. 380). This behavior causes some difficulty when blacks and whites interact. Whites expect some visible or audible sign that one is listening, but blacks, according to Hall, have no such expectation. So when a polite black child casts his eyes downward as a sign of respect, instead of looking straight at his teacher, he might hear his teacher angrily state, "Johnny, look at me when I talk to you!"

There are many other nonverbal cultural distinctions that may affect classroom behavior and interaction. For example, for most Asian students, crossed fingers are not a sign of good luck; they are considered an obscene gesture. Folded arms or tightly crossed legs indicate that the individual is not interested in communication. Calling a person by gesturing with an index finger is an insult, since such a motion would be applied only to animals (Divoky, 1988).

## Cognition

Many psychologists believe that when the cognitive functioning of a minority group's members is congruent with that expected by the school, they will perform more successfully (Anderson, 1983; Tharp, 1989). A number of researchers have investigated the relation between culture and cognitive functioning.

A series of investigations was undertaken by Lesser and his colleagues (Lesser, Fifer, & Clark, 1965; Stodolsky & Lesser, 1967) to study the patterns of various mental abilities in children from different cultural backgrounds and social classes. Lesser believed that one's cultural background would influence an individual's intellectual abilities, thinking styles, and interests. In their first investigation, they studied four mental abilities—verbal, reasoning, number facility, and space conceptualization—in first-grade children in four cultural groups in New York City: Chinese, Jews, blacks, and Puerto Ricans.

The tests were carefully constructed to include only objectives and experiences common to all social and cultural groups in an urban area. In addition, the tests were individually administered by an examiner belonging to the same cultural group as the child and required no reading or writing. The tests consisted primarily of pictures and games that each child was asked to manipulate or to label. Each child was familiarized with the testing procedures and was given time to become acquainted with the testing situation. The researchers attempted to improve upon the testing situation of previous cultural-group studies so that their results would engender greater confidence.

The findings were quite interesting. On all mental abilities, middle-class children performed better than lower-class children, a result consistent with similar research on different SES levels. However, these differences in social class did not influence the patterns among the abilities. Each cultural group exhibited a particular pattern of strengths and weaknesses that was the same regardless of social class.

Figure 3.3 shows the patterns of the mental abilities by cultural groups. The ranking on the four measures of mental abilities, from high to low, was as follows: verbal ability—Jews, blacks, Chinese, and Puerto Ricans; reasoning—Chinese, Jews, blacks, and Puerto Ricans; numerical ability—Jews, Chinese, Puerto Ricans, and blacks; spatial ability—Chinese, Jews, Puerto Ricans, and blacks. Within each cultural group, the scores were almost exactly parallel for the middle and lower classes. Only the Puerto Rican children departed slightly from this trend.

Typically, studies of culture and mental abilities do not separate social class and cultural or ethnic groups but, instead, treat them equally. The investigators do not know whether the differences found among children of various groups arise from social class or from cultural background. In the Lesser study, the investigators demonstrated that these two variables do not have the same effect on the pattern of mental abilities. Conditions

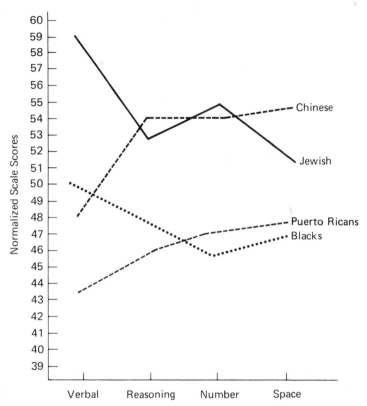

Figure 3.3 **Patterns of Normalized Mental Abilities by Cultural Group.**

*Source: Lesser, Fifer, and Clark, 1965.*

arising from social class failed to alter patterns of mental ability associated with cultural-group membership.

    The investigators believe that the differences are manifested because each cultural group attaches importance and emphasis of varying degrees to different mental abilities. These differences are influenced by "the reinforcement parents provide for different types of intellectual performances, opportunities inside the home to learn various skills, the value placed on different forms of intellectual performances, work habits developed in the home, and the parents' intellectual aspirations for the child" (Stodolsky & Lesser, 1967, p. 580). If you have had contact with members of any of the cultural groups in the study, can you identify specific behaviors that could account for the pattern of mental abilities found by the investigators?

    Stodolsky and Lesser (1967) suggest that an implication inherent in these findings is the need for a change in educational methods to suit the learning strengths of different ethnic or cultural groups. The matching of methods with strengths could be accomplished in two ways. The first way is to assess the particular patterns of mental abilities and to build an instructional strategy to capitalize on the child's intellectual strengths. For example, when teaching mathematical functions to children strong in spatial conceptualization but weak in numerical facility, the teacher would use more graphical than numerical presentations. A second way is to identify the child's intellectual skills to modify or develop the specific skills necessary to learn the task.

*Cognitive Style.* Students' dominant cognitive styles may conflict with the cognitive style orientation of the teacher and/or classroom organization. Since most classrooms function according to a field-independent cognitive style (Buenning & Tollefson, 1987), culturally diverse groups that do not emphasize verbal/analytic problem solving may have difficulty in school. For example, some researchers have found that Mexican-American students tend to be more cooperative and affiliative than Anglo-American students in their interpersonal relations because of their field-dependent cognitive style. Although many investigators have found Mexican-American students to have a more cooperative orientation than Anglo-American students in the classroom, the explanations vary as to the causes of the development of this social motive. Family size, birth order, parental practices, and classroom structure have all been suggested as possible factors (Kagan, 1984). Also, the cooperativeness of Mexican-Americans appears to lessen with successive generations (Knight & Kagan, 1977). Another way to state the same findings is that Mexican-American students appear to become more competitive as they become acculturated into American society.

An orientation for cooperative behavior has been noted for other ethnic and cultural groups—blacks (Shade, 1982), Filipinos (Kubany, Gallimore, & Buell, 1970), Hawaiian (Gallimore, Boggs, & Jordan, 1974), and native American students (Wax, 1969). Because most school environments reflect the field-independent style (i.e., competitive and individualistic), Mexican-American children and other children socialized in field-dependent cultures often are handicapped in school. Ramirez and Castaneda (1974) believe that teachers should help students to fulfill their bicognitive development. (i.e., to learn to feel at home with both field-independent and field-dependent styles)(see Table 3.2).

Shade (1982) reviewed research on black students and reported that they have a cognitive style preference that emphasizes a *person* rather than an *object* orientation. Although a person orientation is useful in social and interpersonal situations, it may not be conducive to success in certain school tasks or types of classroom environment. An example of Shade's finding was reported by St. John (1971), who found that black children demonstrated improved conduct, higher attendance records, and improved attitude toward their teacher if taught by a child-oriented teacher.

The behaviors of a child-oriented teacher included optimism, kindliness, and understanding. A similar finding was reported by Cazden et al. (1980) in their research with Hispanic children.

One characteristic of a "good student" is to be "on time" in such behaviors as arrival at school and completing assignments and tests. Sando (1973) points out how a difference in time orientation among native American children affects school performance in terms of low attendance, unwillingness to plan ahead, low scores on timed tests and assignments, and lack of attention to teacher-designed schedules.

The foregoing examples of cultural differences and cognitive style indicate that some students may have difficulty in the classroom not because of their academic ability, but because the organization of the classroom environment is not consistent with their cultural experiences and styles of learning. The implication is that with certain modifications in instructional procedures, these students may be more successful in the classroom. A word of caution needs to be stated at this point. Although there is evidence that certain learning styles tend to be more dominant in specific cultural groups, one should not conclude that all Mexican-Americans, blacks, or members of any ethnic or cultural group will always possess that particular style. There is the danger of using learning styles as a procedure for categorizing and labeling students.

I have provided a few examples of how cultural differences can cause a teacher to misinterpret behavior of students from another ethnic group. It is imperative that a teacher interacting with children from other cultures learn about cultural influences by reading about the ethnic groups, visiting families, and attending community events. As you learn more about your students' cultural backgrounds, you may be hesitant to jump to conclusions regarding the reasons for their classroom behavior. Can you identify any incidents from your own experiences in school when problems arose that were partially attributable to misunderstandings about cultural differences?

## Developing Culturally Compatible Classrooms

**How can modifications in classroom organization, sociolinguistics, cognition, and motivation help culturally diverse students?**

There is evidence that when schools and classrooms are changed to adapt to the students' cultural background and experiences, students' academic achievement increases. An example of the impact of classroom modifications for instruction is the Kamehameha Early Education Program (KEEP), designed to develop a culturally compatible language arts program for Hawaiian children in the primary grades. Tharp (1989) explains how the KEEP program made modification in four areas to make the classroom more compatible with the Hawaiian culture: *social organization, sociolinguistics, cognition,* and *motivation.*

First, teachers had difficulty maintaining the attention of Hawaiian students in the traditional classroom structure, in which students are asked to work independently. Since the Hawaiian students begin learning social responsibility by taking care of their siblings, they are used to collaboration, cooperation, and assisting others rather than working individually and competitively. As a result, the directors of the KEEP program designed an instructional situation in which almost all the instruction is in small groups (four to five students of mixed sex) emphasizing peer interaction. Students move to different learning centers (see discussion of open classrooms in Chapter 8) located throughout the classroom every 20 to 25 minutes. They work together at these centers on different language activities.

Second, Tharp distinguishes between a holistic/visual and verbal/analytic cognitive style. In holistic thought, the parts derive their meaning from the whole. In analytic thought, one understands the whole through the unfolding of the parts. This distinction is similar to the field-independent/field-dependent cognitive style discussed earlier in the chapter. Tharp believes that the holistic/visual pattern is associated with certain cultural learning that tends to emphasize learning by doing rather than through verbal instructions as well as involvement in adult activities.

Instead of focusing on phonics, a process of teaching reading by identifying letters and the sounds represented by them (an analytic approach), the KEEP program focuses on whole-story discussions and general themes (a holistic approach). The students begin by reading small segments of each story silently, after which they discuss the meaning of the events in the story and relate them to their own lives. At the end, they put the smaller parts together and discuss the overall meaning of the story. Word identification skills are not taught separately but are always presented in the context of sentences, emphasizing meaning over the sounds of letters (Vogt, Jordan, & Tharp, 1987).

Third, an important linguistic process in the classroom is **wait-time,** or pauses in interaction. One type of wait-time is the amount of time given the student to answer questions; another is the amount of time following a student response that the teacher waits before making another response (Rowe, 1974). It appears that students from different cultures have different preferences for the way they respond.

White and Tharp (1988) report that Hawaiian children have a negative wait-time; they tend to talk as the teacher is responding. Although this behavior would be considered a rude interruption by some observers, in the Hawaiian culture it demonstrates involvement and concern. If a teacher attempts to curtail the behavior, the classroom participation of the students would be inhibited. In the KEEP program, researchers developed an instructional format whereby each day the students meet in a small group with the teacher for a 20-minute discussion of some text. The "one person at a time" rule of interaction was dropped to allow students to participate in interaction characterized by "rapid-fire response, liveliness, mutual participation, interruptions, overlapping volunteered speech, and joint narration" (Tharp, 1989, p. 352). Researchers have found that this type of communication pattern leads to higher academic achievement than lessons taught in a more traditional manner (Au & Mason, 1981).

Finally, researchers found that many of the competitive techniques used to motivate students were not effective with the Hawaiian students. The students are more involved in academic tasks when teachers used school-based praise and incentives rather than individual praise and incentives. The KEEP project trains teachers to be both warm and firm. To be accepted in one's peer group, Hawaiian children must show warmth and also prove toughness. Teachers are evaluated by their students using the same criteria (D'Amato, 1986).

What do you think about the attempt to develop culturally compatible classrooms? Zeuli and Floden (1987) raise a number of issues for teachers as they consider how best to educate culturally different students: Is cultural congruence the solution to the inequities of schooling? How does a teacher determine which classroom practices obstruct the learning of culturally different students? Are all cultural differences significant enough to warrant changes in instruction? Do students sometimes benefit from instruction that forces them to deal with content from perspectives that are unfamiliar to them? Think about these issues and discuss your views with other students in your class.

## LANGUAGE ACQUISITION

One of the most remarkable aspects of human behavior is language acquisition. The average child learns most of the sounds of his or her first language before the age of 3 and uses most of its grammatical patterns before the age of 5 or 6 (Gleason, 1985 ). Theories of language acquisition include both social and biological explanations. In short, some linguists argue that language is learned in the same way we learn other forms of behavior (Skinner, 1957), primarily through **imitation** and **reinforcement** (see Chapter 6 for a detailed discussion of these learning principles). Other linguists believe that humans are born with a language acquisition device, which allows them to derive different grammatical structures from the speech of adults (Chomsky, 1965). This innate structure provides the ability to comprehend and produce sentences that were never heard before. Thus a child can take a sentence such as "I like to walk" and can generate sentences: "I like walking," "I like to take walks," and so forth.

For a long time, linguists believed that different theories were needed to explain first and second language acquisition. Today, many linguists support the view that there are sufficient similarities between first and second language acquisition to support a common theory on how language is acquired (e.g., Ellis, 1986; Krashen, 1982).

In this section I would like to focus on two related perspectives that stress the importance of social interaction and cognitive processes in language acquisition. Both of these perspectives have important implications for the classroom teacher. The first perspective is Vygotsky's (1978) **zone of proximal development;** the second perspective is Krashen's (1982) i + 1 concept and its application to his natural approach to language acquisition (Krashen & Terrell, 1983).

## Vygotsky's Zone of Proximal Development

**What is the difference between Piaget's and Vygotsky's approach to cognitive development?**

Lev Vygotsky (1978) views language as an important mediator between learning and development. Language develops initially because of a child's need to communicate with people in the environment. During the child's development, language is converted to internal speech as it becomes an internal process and organizes the child's thoughts.

Piaget and Vygotsky differ on the relation between development and learning. Piaget believes that development proceeds learning, whereas Vygotsky believes that learning proceeds development. According to Piaget, an individual's developmental stage determines the quality of thinking and that instruction above this level would not produce learning. On the other hand, Vygotsky believes that developmental processes lag behind the learning processes. He points out that children can often complete tasks with the help of peers or teachers that they could not accomplish working independently. The abilities that children can demonstrate when given assistance are not yet developed; they are in the process of becoming internalized. The zone of proximal development is the difference between an individual's current level of development and his or her potential level of development.

Vygotsky (1978) points out that mental tests measure children's current level of development, or what they can do on their own. However, with some questioning or prodding, children often can demonstrate considerably more ability. In fact, what children can do with the assistance of others may be more indicative of their true abilities than what they can do alone. Vygotsky argues that we cannot really understand children's development unless we consider *both* their actual development and their potential developmental level. The following is the basis of his argument:

Suppose I investigated two children upon entrance into school, both of whom are ten years old chronologically and eight years old in terms of mental development. Can I say that they are the same age mentally? Of course. What does this mean? It means that they can independently deal with tasks up to the degree of difficulty that has been standardized for the eight-year-old level. If I stop at this point, people would imagine that the subsequent course of mental development and of school learning for these children will be the same, because it depends on their intellect. Of course, there may be other factors, for example, if one child was sick for half a year while the other was never absent from school: but generally speaking, the fate of these children should be the same. *Now imagine that I do not terminate my study at this point, but only begin it.* These children seem to be capable of handling problems up to an eight-year-old's level, but not beyond that. Suppose that I show them different ways of dealing with the problem. Different experimenters might employ different modes

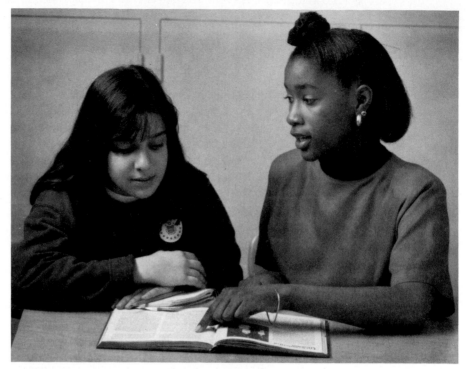

Peer tutoring can be beneficial for both tutor and tutee.

of demonstration in different cases: some might run through an entire demonstration and ask the children to repeat it, others might initiate the solution and ask the child to finish it, or offer leading questions. In short, in some way or another I propose that the children solve the problem with my assistance. Under these circumstances, it turns out that the first child can deal with problems up to a twelve-year-old's level, the second up to a nine-year-old's. Now, are these children mentally the same? (pp. 85–86, italics added)

**According to Vygotsky, what role does social interaction have on language and cognitive development?**

Since Vygotsky believed that higher-level thinking develops best in social contexts, he encouraged learning situations in which teachers, parents, and more capable peers interact directly with students who are at lower levels of thinking. The significant people in one's environment can help guide their thinking by providing hints as to how they should proceed when they cannot manage on their own. More specifically, the expert can describe what needs to be done, taking the student through the problem, while demonstrating appropriate strategies. Also, the expert can reduce some of the demands of the task by taking responsibility for some parts while allowing the student to concentrate on other parts. In this way, students can learn even though they can't solve the whole problem on their own. They employ those skills that they have acquired and with help begin to internalize other relevant skills and knowledge. Over time, the students assume more responsibility for completing the task (Day, Cordon, & Kerwin, 1989).

Wood, Bruner, and Ross (1976) described the tutoring process in terms of providing a scaffold that

> enables a child or novice to solve a problem, carry out a task or achieve a goal which would be beyond his unassisted effort. This scaffolding consists essentially of the adult "controlling" those elements of the task that are initially beyond the learner's capacity, thus permitting him to concentrate upon and complete only those elements that are within his range of competence. (p. 90)

Think about the teaching implications of Vygotsky's theory and the role of scaffolding. What instructional recommendations would you make?

## Krashen's i + 1 Concept

**How does Krashen's approach to language acquisition differ from traditional approaches?**

One of the major approaches to second language acquisition is the interactional approach—an approach that emphasizes interesting and relevant subject matter in low-anxiety classroom environments. One such program, called the *natural approach*, is proposed by Stephen Krashen (Krashen, 1982; Krashen & Terrell, 1983). The following discussion of Krashen's approach follows the explanation by Richard-Amato (1988) in *Making It Happen: Interaction in the Second Language Classroom.*

Krashen distinguishes between two different linguistic systems: *acquisition* and *learning*. He believes that acquisition is subconscious and is developed through natural communication, in which the emphasis is on meaning. Learning occurs through conscious study of the formal aspect of the language. Language information that is learned (i.e., the formal rules of the language) is used in speech production only if it is relatively simple and if the speaker in concerned with form and has time to apply the information. According to Krashen, one acquires the rules of language not by studying it but by exposure to the language.

Krashen believes that the teacher does not have to focus on formal instruction in the target language. Instead, she should provide optimal input that is comprehensible, interesting and/or relevant, not grammatically sequenced, and in sufficient quality. The teacher's input must approximate the student's i + 1. It must be comprehensible in that it is near the student's actual level of development (i), but then it must stretch beyond that to include concepts and structures that the student has not yet acquired (i + 1).

Think for a moment how a child learns a primary language. Parents use a simplified form of communication called **motherese.** They don't worry about grammar or correct form; their primary concern is to communicate with their child. Why shouldn't the classroom use a similar model? If the language teacher treated "errors" as evidence that the language was being acquired, the learner might be more willing to take risks of being wrong and might be more uninhibited in developing competency in the language (Ellis, 1985). Observe the instruction in the following dialogue:

> Student: I Throw it—box. (He points to a box on the floor.)
> Teacher: You threw the box.
> Student: No, I threw *in* the box.
> Teacher: What did you throw in the box?
> Student: My . . . I paint . . .
> Teacher: Your painting?
> Student: Painting?
> Teacher: You know . . .painting. (The teacher makes painting movements on an imaginary paper.)
> Student: Yes, painting.
> Teacher: You threw your painting in the box.
> Students: Yes, I threw my painting in box. (Richard-Amato, 1988, p. 40)

Krashen would say that the teacher is speaking near the student's i +1. The vocabulary is simple, repetition is frequent, and the focus is on meaning, not form. Notice how the teacher produced changes in the child's speech (e.g., *throw* became *threw*) without teaching grammar.

What about all the errors students make in learning a language? Doesn't the teacher need to correct students? Although Krashen believes there is a role for error correction in language acquisition, he doesn't believe error correction is an important factor in learning a language. Sutherland (1979) provides support for Krashen's position in stating that both accuracy and fluency can't be achieved in the early stages of learning a language. Sutherland contends that students develop very little proficiency in a language when teachers emphasize accuracy over fluency. He believes that many language teachers mistakenly feel that if they don't correct their students' mistakes, they will never accurately learn the language.

Krashen also minimizes the role of output (what the learner says) in the acquisition process. He believes that comprehension precedes production. "We acquire spoken fluency *not* by practicing talking but by understanding input by listening and reading" (Krashen, 1982, p. 59). The implication for the teacher is that there is a "silent period" during which children acquire a great deal of understanding in a language but can't achieve an equal amount of production. Thus, the teacher can't always judge a student's progress in a language by what he or she says in class.

Although Krashen's approach to language acquisition has been well received by teachers, there have been some criticisms of his theory and instructional approach (see Ellis, 1986; Higgs & Clifford, 1982; McLaughlin, 1978). One concern is based on the role of grammar in learning a language.

If little or no attention is paid to grammatical inaccuracies through corrective feedback early in the language acquisition process, students may not be able to advance to higher levels of proficiency. What do you think about Krashen's approach? What type of experiences did you have learning a language? What changes in language instruction would you recommend?

## Bilingual Education

**What are the issues involved in developing bilingual rather than English-only language programs?**

Another important issue in language development is how to instruct the increasing number of students entering school in the United States whose primary language is not English. Many of these students come from backgrounds where Spanish, Vietnamese, or any one of many other tongues is the primary language spoken at home. For example, administrators in the Los Angeles Unified School District report that they have students from over 80 different language backgrounds.

There are already over 30 million individuals living in the United States whose primary language is other than English (Hakuta & Garcia, 1989). Figure 3.4 shows estimated or projected figures for the years 1982 to 2020 for the number of children speaking a primary language other than English. This increase will present a great challenge to educators to increase the effectiveness of all language programs.

A major debate among educators is how best to teach non-English-speaking students: Should they be taught in their primary language? Should they be encouraged to speak English? Should they receive **bilingual education** (i.e., instruction in both English and their primary language)?

One of the early approaches to language diversity was the "sink-or-swim" method. Children were put into English classes and expected to succeed in school. In some cases, children were punished if they were

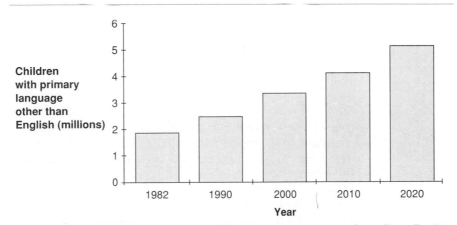

Figure 3.4 Projected Number of Children With a Primary Language Other Than English U.S. Total, 1982–2020.

*Source: Pallas, Natriello, and McDill, 1989.*

found speaking Spanish in the classroom or on the playground. Can you imagine being placed in a classroom in Mexico, Germany, or France and being expected to compete with the other students in the class without being able to speak the dominant language? How do you think you would describe your predicament—unpleasant, frustrating, traumatic? How do you think your teachers would judge your ability? How would you feel about yourself and your culture? The chances are that such an experience would not be positive if you were left on your own to learn the language without any support system. Would you stay in school? Spanish-speaking students have faced this problem for decades. As late as 1966, over 80 percent of them were school dropouts (Cardenas, 1986). Cummins (1981) believes that schools have contributed directly to the problems that minority students have in school by undermining their cultural identity, diminishing the value of their primary language, and providing them with English material that makes little sense to them.

Many educators are opposed to bilingual education because they believe students would learn English more rapidly if they spent more time exposed to the language (Rossel & Ross, 1986). Other educators have concerns regarding the role of minority groups in society: fear that cultural groups would retain their primary language and not assimilate into American culture; belief in the unwillingness of immigrants to speak the English language; and belief that allowing individuals to speak their native language in school would interfere with their learning English (a phenomenon called the *interference theory*) or cause confusion in their thinking (Cardenas, 1986). The first two reasons are emotional issues that cannot be logically refuted. Some countries function very well when citizens and other residents speak more than one language. The United States is among the few countries in the world in which students are not proficient in more than one language upon graduation from high school (National Commission on Excellence in Education, 1983). As for the third issue, there is no evidence that bilingualism interferes with performance or thinking in either language. In fact, bilingual education increases achievement in areas other than the language studied (Hakuta, 1986).

One of the problems of conducting research in this area is that both the programs and the language proficiency of teachers vary widely. For example, many bilingual programs are implemented with only the classroom aide speaking Spanish. Therefore, it is easy to find bilingual programs that have little impact on students. Troike (1978) and Willig (1985) found that when programs were well organized and had proficient teachers, bilingual instruction was more effective than English-only instruction in developing English academic skills. More recent research (e.g., Carter & Chatfied, 1986; Krashen & Biber, 1988) has identified specific instructional procedures that produce bilingual students who succeed in school.

How does bilingual education benefit students? Cummins (1981) posits a common proficiency dimension that underlies the development of academic skills in both languages. This means that either language can promote the development of a basic proficiency in both languages. As students learn English, they continue to develop their cognitive skills by receiving instruction in content areas in their primary language. As a result, limited English skills do not impede the intellectual or academic progress of the students, as would occur in an all-English program. Furthermore, the students are less likely to feel alienated in school and are more likely to develop a positive self-concept.

Many states have mandated bilingual education. In 1971 Massachusetts was the first state to legislate bilingual education. That state required that a program be instituted whenever 20 or more students of the same language background were present in the same school. In addition, the law stipulated a three-year period for preparing students for a monolingual English classroom. California requires a bilingual program whenever there are 10 or more students of the same language in the same grade and school. At present, the states vary as to the requirements of establishing bilingual programs and the types of program developed. If you are interested in bilingual education, you will find the work by Ambert and Melendez (1985) and Alatis and Staczek (1985) to be good background reading.

## CLASSROOM APPLICATION: IMPROVING CHILDREN'S LANGUAGE

You can play an important role in helping students to develop their language skills. Following are some recommendations for classroom practices (adopted and quoted from Jackson, Robinson, & Dale, 1977, pp. 5–6):

1. *"Give young children ample opportunities to play and talk with one another and with adults."* Although children talk a great deal among themselves, they sometimes are less verbal near adults. Teachers should ask questions about situations that interest children rather than always appearing to ask questions to "test" their knowledge. Also, when teachers show more interest in *what* children say than *how* they say it, children are more likely to talk in the future.

2. *"Create situations in which children want and need to formulate and elaborate their messages. When they have difficulty with this task, help them by asking probing questions ('What else did it look like?' 'What did you do then?') and by providing examples of good messages."* Much of what a young child says can be understood only if the listener knows the present or past events leading up to the current situation, because the speaker omits much of the information needed by the listener. For example, a preschooler may go to the teacher and state: "I want the big one!" Young children fail to communicate clearly because they often don't understand

what the listener needs to know or how to relay the information. Therefore, learning to use language effectively requires an understanding of the needs of the listener. An important classroom strategy is to give children opportunities to play the role of both speaker and listener. Several communication games can be designed to meet this objective. For example, two children might sit at a table with a screen blocking their view of each other. One child is given objects with which to make a design that must be described to the other child, who then attempts to draw the design. The children can take turns being speaker and listener (Bartlett, 1972).

3. *"Provide children with extended exposure to the meaning of words such as* more, on, before, *and so on in a variety of contexts. In your own use of these words, check to make sure that the children understand the meanings you intend."* Certain vocabulary words such as *more, less than*, and *under* deal with relationships that are useful in many learning situations. These words, or the concepts they express, are difficult to learn because they convey ideas that require children to attend to the unchanging feature or relationship that must be separated from the specific situation in which the word is used. Teachers need to be careful in assuming that children understand a word merely because they use it correctly in one situation.

4. *"Provide examples of good English in your own speech, but resist the impulse to nag children about their grammar."* Teachers often become frustrated in attempting to change children's grammar or pronunciation. Research investigations have indicated that correcting students' errors in language usage does not lead to immediate changes in behavior (Dulay, Burt, & Krashen, 1982). Sometimes children will modify their grammar simply by listening to an adult model the correct usage. However, the child must be ready to imitate or to accommodate the change. In many situations, it may take weeks or months before a child will make the change. Providing opportunities for children to hear correct adult speech is a good way to improve the use of grammar. However, expecting children to use grammar or pronunciation too far from their own level will lead to disappointment.

5. *"In teaching reading to all children, but particularly to children who speak Nonstandard English, begin by emphasizing comprehension rather than Standard English phonetics [pronunciation]. Adapt phonics lessons in spelling and reading to the pronunciation used by children in class."* Emphasis on Standard English phonetic reading may lead to anxiety and frustration for both teacher and student. If the purpose of reading instruction is to enable students to comprehend messages, then overemphasis on pronunciation is not the best ap-

proach. This approach assumes, of course, that the student's pronunciation can be understood.

6. *"Don't assume that children from disadvantaged backgrounds are 'non-verbal' or that they lack the verbal skills necessary for thinking."* Adler (1979) points out the problems with the following reasoning: "Language is inferior; therefore, thought is inferior" (p. 76). There is little evidence that any one dialect or language enables an individual to reason more successfully. Therefore, beliefs that lead to negative attitudes and behavior toward students' language can have a detrimental effect on classroom interaction.

## THINKING ABOUT THE TEACHING-LEARNING MODEL

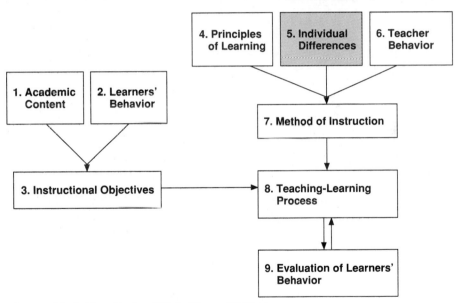

Source: Adapted from Hunter, 1971, in Allen and Seifman.

Teacher behavior (box No. 6) plays an important role in dealing with the diversity of student differences presented in this chapter. Teachers often have different attitudes toward the academic potential and future success of students from different races and cultural groups. They generally hold more negative attitudes about most minority-group students than about white, middle-class students (Datta, Schaeffer, & Davis, 1968; Lea-cock, 1969). In addition, teachers give more praise and attention to white students than to students from other cultural groups (Baron, Tom, & Cooper, 1985). These research results can change with better teacher education and positive experiences working with students from different cultural and ethnic backgrounds. The material in Chapter 10 is relevant to the topics discussed in this chapter. Later in the book you will learn how teacher beliefs about students' achievement can influence their motivation and academic success.

Different instructional procedures (box No. 7) may be needed with culturally different students. The research in this chapter indicated that cooperative rather than competitive learning environments may be beneficial for some students. Chapter 8 includes a discussion of cooperative learning methods.

Linguists have found that student motivation, anxiety, and self-esteem are important personal variables that can influence second language acquisition (see Brown, 1987). Chapter 4 discusses self-esteem, and Chapter 10 deals with factors influencing student motivation. Also, the material in Chapter 8 on humanistic education will be helpful. According to Brown (1987): "Understanding how human beings feel and respond and believe and value is an exceedingly important aspect of a theory of second language acquisition" (p. 101). All this information will help you realize that methods of instruction (box No. 7) are not the only factors that influence learning.

In Chapter 2 I first raised issues about the mental testing of children from diverse cultures. Since teachers use a variety of formal and informal procedures to evaluate student progress (box No. 9), attention must be given to cultural factors that might influence student response to assessment devices. (Remember the study by Deyhle, 1987, on the meaning of tests for Navajo children.) Be especially careful judging the responses of children whose primary language is not English.

## KEY POINTS

1. Cognitive styles can influence student learning.
2. Some researchers do not believe that educators should make sharp distinctions between the functioning of the two parts of the brain because the two parts work together.
3. Some teachers may emphasize convergent over divergent thinking.
4. Divergent thinking is associated with creativity.
5. Creative students are characterized by such traits as lack of rigidity, humor, willingness to attempt difficult tasks, and expression of unconventional ideas.
6. Using student preferences for determining methods of instruction is not always an appropriate procedure.
7. The learning environment in U.S. schools may be incongruent with the learning experiences at home for many cultural groups.
8. The reasons for certain minority groups coming to the United States, and the economic and political conditions existing at the time they

arrive, may be factors influencing the level of their motivation and achievement.

9. Recent increases in immigration to the United States has led to one of the most ethnically and culturally diverse societies in history.

10. All states are mandated by law to educate undocumented immigrants.

11. Many immigrant children need special help because of their experiences with violence and war in their native country.

12. Many problems can arise when teachers do not understand cultural differences. They may underestimate students' academic potential, believe that their language is inferior, or misinterpret their classroom behavior.

13. Children from different cultural backgrounds exhibit cultural patterns of strengths and weaknesses on various tests of mental ability.

14. There is some evidence that cognitive style develops from various socialization practices.

15. Cognition, classroom organization, sociolinguistics, and motivation are factors that need to be considered in developing culturally compatible classrooms.

16. Culture, cognition, and language are interrelated variables.

17. Piaget believes that development precedes learning, whereas Vygotsky believes that learning precedes development.

18. Vygotsky believes that educators should consider *two* levels of development—an individual's current level and potential level.

19. Vygotsky believes that current intelligence testing may not predict future academic attainment because it doesn't consider what a person can attain with help.

20. Helping a student solve a problem by taking responsibility for some parts of the task while allowing the student to concentrate on other parts can be an effective instructional procedure.

21. Krashen believes that the key to language acquisition is comprehensible input rather than formal instruction in the rules of the language.

22. Optimal input must be near the learner's actual level of development, but it must stretch beyond that to include concepts and structures that the learner has not yet acquired.

23. According to Krashen, the grammar of a language is learned best by speaking the language and hearing the appropriate form rather than by studying rules.

24. Some linguists believe that students develop very little proficiency in the early stages of language acquisition when the teacher emphasizes accuracy over fluency.

25. Krashen minimizes the importance of output (what the learner says) in the acquisition process because of his emphasis on comprehension.

26. Some linguists criticize Krashen's de-emphasis on the importance of formal instruction of the rules of a language.

27. There is no evidence that bilingual education interferes with language proficiency or thinking in either language.

28. There is no evidence that any dialect or language is inferior to another.

## SUGGESTIONS FOR FURTHER READING

The following references provide a good discussion of cognitive and learning styles:

Goldstein, K. M., & Blackman, S. (1978). *Cognitive style: Five approaches and relevant research*. New York: Wiley.

Matching teaching and learning styles. (1984, Winter). [Special issue]. *Theory into Practice, 23.*

*Student learning styles: Diagnosing and prescribing programs.* (1979). Reston, VA: National Association of Secondary School Principals. This book includes articles by researchers who are involved in developing learning-style instruments.

The following references focus on language differences and bilingual education:

Adler, S. (Ed.). (1985). *Cultural language differences: Their educational and clinical-professional implications*. Springfield, IL: Thomas.

Alatis, J. E., & Staczek, J. J. (Eds.). (1985). *Perspectives on bilingualism and bilingual education*. Washington, DC: Georgetown University Press.

Ambert, A. N., & Melendez, S. E. (1985). *Bilingual education: A sourcebook.* New York: Garland.

Feagans, L., & Farran, D. C. (Eds.). (1982). *The language of children reared in poverty.* New York: Academic Press.

Richard-Amato, P. A. (1988). *Making it happen: Interaction in the second language classroom. From theory to practice.* White Plains, NY: Longman.

The following journal articles or books are helpful in understanding the culturally different student:

November 1988 issue of *Phi Delta Kappan.* A special section on educating immigrant children.

Spindler, G. (Ed.). (1982). *Doing the ethnography of schooling.* New York: Holt, Rinehart and Winston. Provides examples of field studies done by anthropologists on educational issues.

Trueba, H. T. (1987). *Success or failure?: Learning and the language minority student.* Cambridge, MA: Newbury House.

For information on multicultural education:

Banks, J. A. (1988). *Multiethnic education: Theory and practice* (2nd ed.). Boston: Allyn & Bacon. Identifies actions that educators can take to develop programs related to ethnic and cultural diversity.

Banks, J. A., & Banks, C. A. (Eds.). (1989). *Multicultural education: Issues and perspectives.* Boston: Allyn & Bacon. The book describes how race, social class, gender, exceptionality, language, and religion must be considered in teaching.

## FOLLOW-UP ACTIVITIES

### 1. Recognize Learning Styles

Would you have been more successful in certain classes if teachers had been more cognizant of your learning style? Give specific examples of how teacher awareness of student differences could have helped you.

### 2. Identify Differences in Learning Styles

*Use for obs.*

This observational activity will awaken you to the range of individual differences in the classroom. The following list gives pairs of terms that summarize opposite types of thinking, perceiving, and reacting. Observe students in a public school or college class and pick out—for as many of the listed opposites as you can—a student who exemplifies each extreme. Then briefly describe that style of behavior. Add any additional information from the Learning-Style Diagnosis (Table 3.1). Finally, analyze the appropriateness of the teacher's behavior toward the student (Biehler, 1974).

- *Impulsive*—gives the first answer, is eager to respond quickly. *Reflective*—thinks things over, is deliberate and cautious in responding.
- *Short attention span*—is unable to stick with an assignment or pay attention for more than a few minutes; is easily distracted. *Long*

*attention span*—is capable of concentrating on an assignment for an extended time; has a high degree of resistance to distractions.

• *Resistance to change*—is unwilling to accept unexpected or unconventional views or evidence. *Flexibility*—adapts well to new, different, or unexpected points of view.

• *Convergent production*—seeks or provides the one right answer or a conventional answer. *Divergent production*—responds in a nonconventional, unexpected way.

## 3. Debate the Value of Bilingualism

In recent years, some political figures have lobbied for a constitutional amendment that would make English the country's single official language. Governor Richard Lamm of Colorado was quoted by *Time* magazine in the August 25, 1986, issue as stating: "We should be color blind but not linguistically deaf. . . . We should be a rainbow but not a cacophony. . . . We should welcome different people but not different languages."

What is your position on bilingualism and bilingual education? Is bilingualism a barrier to a unified nation? Does it allow immigrants to avoid learning English and form self-perpetuating ghettos? Is bilingualism a positive factor in American society? Does our country benefit from the diversity of languages spoken in various cultures?

## 4. Debate the Best Approach to Cultural Literacy

With the increasing diversity of the student population in U.S. schools, some educators are concerned that students are not becoming literate in the American culture. Hirsch, in *Cultural Literacy* (1987), lists 500 things every American adult should know; more recently, in *A First Dictionary of Cultural Literacy* (1989), he lists 2,000 things he thinks grade school students should know.

What do you think it means to be culturally literate? Do we need a common body of information to ease the assimilation of culturally diverse individuals? Is Hirsch's approach to cultural literacy useful or is it dangerous? Will it reinforce the beliefs among minority students that certain people don't belong or that aspects of their culture are not worthy of consideration? (See the December/January 1988 issue of *Educational Leadership* for articles by Hirsch and his critics.)

## 5. Evaluate the Benefit of Culturally Congruent Classrooms

Zeuli and Floden (1987) state: "making classrooms more culturally congruent is only one, and not necessarily the best alternative" (p. 13). What are the other alternatives? Read their article and research the different approaches to educating culturally diverse students.

# CHAPTER 4

# Personal and Social Development

Physical Growth and Development
School Experiences

Socialization and the Family _____

Child-Rearing Practices
Child Abuse and Neglect
Student Stress
Maternal Employment
Divorce
Latchkey Children

Television as a Socialization Agent _____

CLASSROOM APPLICATION: HELPING PARENTS MONITOR
THEIR CHILDREN'S TELEVISION VIEWING

**ORIENTATION**

In Chapters 2 and 3 I focused primarily on cognitive factors influencing
learning. In the second section of Chapter 3 attention shifted to the relation
between culture and learning. You learned how social factors can shape a
student's academic adjustment and performance in school.

This chapter begins with a discussion of Erikson's theory of psychosocial development which provides a framework for how personal identity
or self-concept develops through experiences in the home, school, and
community. Special attention is given to gender differences.

Although teachers don't have control over many of the developmental
factors influencing their students' classroom behavior, they must deal with
the outcomes of family socialization. One factor influencing the teacher's
role is the major changes in family functioning during the last few decades.
Many of these changes have weakened and modified the traditional position and function of parents.

Economic developments have caused both mothers and fathers to join
the labor force keeping them away from their homes and children for much
of the day. This condition, in many cases, has lead to children being unsupervised before and after school. Occupational opportunities have
caused married children to move away from their parents to face child-
rearing without the support of an extended family. In addition, divorce
and various patterns of custodial arrangements are no longer considered
atypical family transitions.

As you read this chapter I would like you to consider how the family,
school, and peers influence the personal and social development of children and adolescents. Think about how family transitions may require
greater attention to the adjustment of certain students, how you may need
to reorganize your time to schedule parent conferences, how you may need
to communicate with both custodial and noncustodial parents, and how

you can make recommendations to parents who indicate that they need to improve their child-rearing skills.

By the time you master the material presented in this chapter, you will be able to:

- Use Erikson's theory of personal and social development to explain students' identity formation.
- Reduce sex-role stereotyping in the classroom.
- Explain how different child-rearing practices influence students' behavior.
- Identify child abuse and neglect.
- Identify warning signs for possible suicide.
- Interact with students facing family transitions.
- Provide guidelines to parents who want to monitor their children's television viewing.

## FOCUS QUESTIONS

1. How do parents, teachers, and friends contribute to the identity development of an individual?
2. How does the psychosocial development of a parent influence a child or adolescent's development?
3. How do socialization experiences influence different behavior for males and females?
4. How can teacher expectation and interaction with males and females influence their motivation and achievement?
5. Why do most attempts to change students' self-concepts fail?
6. What factors in a school or classroom contribute to students' self-concepts?
7. How do parents' child-rearing styles influence their children's social behavior?
8. What type of parent is likely to abuse his or her child?
9. How can a teacher deal with students exhibiting stress?
10. How can divorce impact students of different developmental ages?
11. How can a teacher help families of latchkey children?

## ERIKSON'S THEORY OF PERSONAL AND SOCIAL DEVELOPMENT

**How do parents, teachers, and friends contribute to the identity development of an individual?**

Erik Erikson (1963, 1968) has delineated eight major **psychosocial crises,** or dilemmas, that have their roots in the demands of society and that individuals experience over the course of life. Each crisis represents an important turning point in which major psychological issues are faced and resolved on a continuum from a positive (desirable) pole to a negative (undesirable) pole. The resolution of each crisis adds a new dimension to one's identity. Table 4.1 summarizes each of these crises.

TABLE 4.1 **ERIKSON'S EIGHT STAGES OF THE HUMAN LIFE CYCLE**

| Stage | Ages | Central Conflict | Primary Implications for Optimal Development |
|---|---|---|---|
| 1 | Infancy | Trust versus mistrust | Developing general security, optimism, and trust in others (based on consistent experiences involving satisfaction of basic needs) |
| 2 | Toddlerhood | Autonomy versus shame and doubt | Developing a sense of autonomy and confident self-reliance, taking setbacks in stride (based on consistent experiences involving encouragement and limit setting without rejection or blame) |
| 3 | Early childhood | Initiative versus guilt | Developing initiative in exploring and manipulating the environment (based on consistent experiences of tolerance, encouragement, and reinforcement) |
| 4 | Middle childhood | Industry versus inferiority | Enjoyment and mastery of the developmental tasks of childhood, in and out of school (based on consistent experiences of success and recognition of progress) |
| 5 | Adolescence | Identity versus identity confusion | Achievement of a stable and satisfying sense of identity and direction (based on consistent personal experiences involving success and satisfaction combined with social acceptance and recognition) |
| 6 | Young adulthood | Intimacy versus isolation | Development of the ability to maintain intimate personal relationships (based on personal openness and confidence complemented by consistently rewarding experiences with intimate others) |
| 7 | Adulthood | Generativity versus stagnation | Satisfaction of personal and familial needs supplemented by development of interest in the welfare of others and of the world in general (based on achievement of a secure and rewarding personal life and a freedom from pressures which limit one to self-preoccupation) |
| 8 | Aging | Ego integrity versus despair | Recognizing and adjusting to aging and the prospect of death with a sense of satisfaction about the past and readiness about the future (based on consistent success in prior stages which provides a real basis for satisfaction in having led a full and good life and for accepting death without morbid fears or feelings of failure) |

*Source: Good and Brophy, 1990.*

A central theme in Erikson's theory is that the way individuals resolve developmental dilemmas in one stage will influence the resolution of developmental dilemmas in other stages. As a result, our past experiences influence the way we resolve our present developmental crises.

The fact that developmental crises are resolved on a *continuum* means that the resolutions are not necessarily all positive or all negative. A variety of possible developmental outcomes emerges as individuals interact with significant others in their environment. Each of the crises identified by Erikson is discussed in the following section.

## Basic Trust versus Mistrust

A sense of trust develops in an infant through the social care and comfort provided by the primary care giver. The infant, who has experienced the warmth and protection of the uterus, faces the reality of discomfort and hunger immediately on contact with the outer world. To develop a sense of trust, the infant requires a feeling of physical comfort and a minimum of fear and uncertainty. Erikson emphasizes the underlying emotional and attitudinal themes that motivate the parent handling and caring for the infant, rather than any particular method of care. Once this feeling of trust is established, it generalizes to new experiences. However, if the infant does not receive the necessary physical warmth and care, a sense of mistrust develops that leads to apprehension or fear in novel situations.

## Autonomy versus Shame and Doubt

During this stage, society makes demands on the child to do things alone. For example, parents make their first major demands on the child when they require that toilet-training be accomplished. The manner in which this crisis is handled influences whether children feel that they are effective and able to control their environment (autonomy) or are ineffective and controlled by others (shame or doubt). The parent-child relationship again is important in the resolution of this crisis. Warm and accepting parents are likely to structure the environment so that children can experience success and a sense of autonomy, whereas hostile and overly controlling parents can promote a sense of doubt. Toilet-training is important because the process often involves emotional overtones. The child who has difficulty in this task and is criticized by his or her parents does not separate the difficulties and incompetence of the toilet-training situation from other life experiences. The lack of success in toilet-training can cause the child to develop a sense of shame and doubt regarding his or her competency.

## Initiative versus Guilt

During this period, children gain greater freedom in exploring their environment and often attempt tasks of which parents do not approve. When children master these new tasks, they feel a sense of self-responsibility, establishing a sense of purpose. As a result, they are likely to attempt to meet new challenges in the future. Guilt occurs when the initiation of these acts or tasks either exceeds the limits of their capabilities or is constantly held in check by parents who want their children to curtail their initiative.

A difficult aspect of child rearing is to determine how much freedom and protection children should be given as they develop their competence.

## Industry versus Inferiority

The major theme of this period reflects the determination of children to master whatever they are doing. Erikson believes that many individuals' later attitudes toward work and work habits can be traced back to the degree of a successful sense of industry fostered during this phase. In acquiring a sense of industry, children must feel competent in what they are doing while accepting their limitations. A sense of inferiority is caused when the child is not ready for the challenges of school and/or is unable to measure up to the expectations of parents, teachers, or friends.

## Identity versus Identity Confusion

The critical issue that adolescents must resolve is the question "Who am I?" Children enter adolescence in a diffuse state. They are not sure of their attitudes, beliefs, and values. During this period, they experience various situations, meet many people, experiment with various identities, and begin to integrate their previous and present identities into a meaningful sense of self. On the negative side, they have a sense of confusion about their identity or role in society. Some adolescents become delinquents—choosing an identity that is the opposite of what society expects—because they would rather have a negative identity than remain a nonentity.

Erikson points out that adolescents are provided with a **psychosocial moratorium,** a period of delay that is granted to someone who is not ready to meet obligations. A psychosocial moratorium is a permissiveness on the part of society that allows young people to try different identities and to fail or have difficulties but that protects them from many of the consequences of their actions. It may be a time of adventure, academic study, troublesome pranks, wandering, or social action. For example, youths who tell their parents that they plan to quit their job because it's boring or because they simply don't want to work anymore expect that their parents will provide shelter and other support until they find another job. Middle-class youths generally have more protection from the demands of society than lower-class youths. The differences in the way some courts treat juvenile offenders from various socioeconomic backgrounds provide further evidence of the differential impact of society's psychosocial moratorium.

*Marcia's Identity Statuses.* Marcia (1980) has provided more information about the development of identity by distinguishing four different patterns and common issues that adolescents experience during the psychosocial crises of identity versus identity confusion. According to Marcia, the criteria for the attainment of a mature identity are based on two factors: *crisis* and *commitment*. "Crisis refers to times during adolescence when the individual

Social relations play an important role in the development of identity.

seems to be actively involved in choosing among alternative occupations and beliefs. Commitment refers to the degree of personal investment the individual expresses in an occupation or belief" (Marcia, 1967, p. 119). The following is a brief discussion of the four identity statuses.

Adolescents begin in a state of **identity diffusion** (or confusion)—a situation in which the individual has not made any firm commitments to any ideology, occupation, or interpersonal relationship and is not currently thinking about such commitments (no crisis, no commitment).

As adolescents develop and have greater interpersonal, work, and educational experiences, they may begin to reflect on the kinds of long-term commitments that could be made. This status is called **identity moratorium**—a situation in which alternative choices are considered and different roles are experienced, but final decisions are deferred during a period of uncertainty (crisis, no commitment).

Sometimes the uncertainty of thinking about one's future can produce a great deal of anxiety, especially when one doesn't have the answers to the questions from parents and friends about future careers and educational options. For this reason, some adolescents choose to remain in a state of identity diffusion, during which they stop thinking about choices and commitments, or opt for **identity foreclosure.** In this status condition, the individual selects some convenient set of beliefs or goals without carefully considering the alternatives. The best example of this status is the high school student whose mother is a doctor or lawyer and answers the typical question: "What do you want to study in college?" by stating "pre-law" or "pre-med" when he really hasn't considered the implications of the career in detail. Such a response gets people to stop asking further questions about life goals and is satisfying to the individual (for the time being) because he can stop worrying about what course of study to pursue (no crisis, commitment).

As a result of additional experiences that help clarify attitudes, values, and self-evaluations, the adolescent eventually resolves the identity crises and settles on the relatively stable commitments that constitute **identity achievement.**

These four identity statuses may be perceived as a developmental transition, but one stage is not a prerequisite for another, as in Erickson's eight stages. Only the moratorium status appears to be necessary for identity achievement, since one can't develop a mature identity without considering alternative options. Waterman (1982) has identified possible patterns in identity formation. For example, one model may be diffusion to moratorium or identity achievement; another model may begin with foreclosure, moving to moratorium and then toward identity achievement. The latter model often occurs when individuals find out in college that they really don't have the interest or aptitude for a particular goal. Still another model may be identity diffusion to moratorium to identity achievement to identity diffusion. In this situation, the individual may lose a sense of purpose as a result of some life experiences and fail to seek new commitments.

## Intimacy versus Isolation

The development of a sense of intimacy results in an integration in the form of sexual union and close friendship. According to Erikson, an individual cannot develop a fully intimate relationship until he or she has established a clear identity. (Erikson has focused on the identity development of males, saying little about females—a shortcoming of his theory.) In other words, individuals must know who they are before they can develop a shared identity with another person. The negative polarity is a sense of isolation that is characterized as self-absorption. Because of a fear of losing oneself in the identity of another, some individuals are incapable of developing a strong intimate relationship.

Individuals who trust others, feel a sense of autonomy, are willing to take initiatives, and have a good sense of their abilities and beliefs are more likely to maintain intimate relationships. Individuals who show a mistrust of others and who fear making decisions or taking the initiative in new situations are often less willing to establish intimate relationships.

## Generativity versus Stagnation

**How does the psychosocial development of a parent influence a child or adolescent's development?**

A sense of generativity involves a sense of responsibility to parents and the community for the improvement of oneself and society. Parenting and teaching the young in order to improve the quality of life for the next generation is an important responsibility for an adult. These activities reflect a sense of productivity and creativity. On the negative polarity is the adult who cannot find any meaning or purpose in life and who has little interest in self-improvement or making contributions to society.

## Ego Integrity versus Despair

Successful resolution of this crisis leads to feelings of accomplishment and fulfillment of one's life cycle. Adults with ego integrity can look back on their lives and feel that they were worthwhile. Unsuccessful resolution leads to feelings of despair, of incompleteness, and an unfulfilled life.

## Gender Differences in Identity

A criticism of Erikson's theory is that his description of identity development may not accurately describe the development of women. For example, there is evidence that females tend to focus on interpersonal aspects of identity formation, whereas males focus on intrapersonal aspects. As a result, late adolescent females are more likely to learn about themselves through the individuals with whom they have good relationships, whereas late adolescent males are more likely to develop an identity on the basis of skills and competencies they develop rather than on interpersonal relations (Marcia, 1980). The result of different paths toward identity development may cause researchers using criteria for assessing the identity of males to conclude erroneously that some women may lag in their development.

Erikson also has suggested that women have a different developmental trend in the achievement of identity than men. While he indicates that men move from identity to intimacy, he thinks that for women, identity and intimacy are interrelated. For a woman following a *traditional* role, identity comes from marriage because her identity is closely tied to the man she marries. Many feminists are critical of Erikson's perspective of the process of women's identity, arguing that the demands of modern society make such an alternative route of identity achievement (i.e., waiting for marriage to develop an identity) unsatisfactory. With the necessity for women to work, increased divorce, and single living, women can no longer delay their identity development until they become wives and mothers. Instead, like men, they must develop the knowledge, competencies, and values necessary to attain unique identities (Fuhrmann, 1986).

## IMPLICATIONS OF ERIKSON'S THEORY FOR EDUCATION

A good way to understand any developmental theory is to attempt to apply it to your own development. How do you think you resolved the major psychosocial crises in your life? What effect did your parents, teachers, and peers have on your early development? Did your parents encourage autonomy and initiative? Were you successful in your early schooling? Did you develop a sense of industry? A positive identity? Can you evaluate your own identity development according to Marcia's stages?

Erikson provides some good advice if you are currently involved in a relationship. He believes that a truly intimate relationship depends on a shared identity. This type of identity occurs when each partner develops a strong self-identity rather than one partner losing his or her identity in the relationship. The implication for enhancing a relationship or marriage is for both partners to develop their own abilities and interests to the maximum.

Erikson's stage theory can help teachers to understand the types of conflict students face in the developmental periods. Students in the early grades are resolving the crises of initiative versus guilt and industry versus inferiority. They need support as they attempt new tasks and meet new challenges.

Elkind (1986) believes that the development of a sense of initiative is more likely to occur when adults allow children to become more self-directed in choosing their own learning activities. For example, the danger of directing young children to read before they are ready may cause them to "become dependent on adult direction and not to trust [their] own initiative" (p. 635).

Erikson's theory helps the teacher to understand why young adolescents may have personality or social adjustment problems in school if their psychosocial crises have been resolved toward the negative polarities—mistrust, shame, guilt, and/or inferiority. Teachers and parents must be concerned with healthy adjustment throughout the developmental stages.

A teacher can help to establish a classroom climate in which failure is seen as a natural part of the learning process and where it is appropriate to be understanding and helpful to others. In junior and senior high school, where students are attempting to develop a sense of identity, teachers should understand that students need numerous opportunities to experience various situations and to evaluate their behavior, attitudes, and beliefs. It is important to provide opportunities for students to talk with teachers about educational and career concerns. In addition, teachers can often use certain course assignments such as diaries, position papers on controversial issues, and field experiences in the community to help students to learn more about themselves.

Finally, teachers need to help female students achieve the knowledge and skills necessary to help them develop realistic occupational goals while they make decisions concerning the nature of their spousal and maternal roles (Fuhrmann, 1986). I shall now discuss gender differences to help you understand how the school contributes to the socialization of males and females.

## GENDER DIFFERENCES

### The Development of Sex-Role Stereotyping

**How do sociali-
zation experi-
ences influence
different be-
havior for
males and
females?**

Most psychologists and sociologists view gender differences in terms of role training and social expectations. For example, despite the fact that developmental psychologists report few differences in the behavior of infant girls and boys, parents soon begin to interact with them differently. As children grow, mothers talk more to female toddlers and encourage them to stay near them when they play. Boys are allowed to explore and wander farther away from their mothers' grasp, and they demonstrate more aggression than girls. When a little boy falls, he is told to get up and "try it again," whereas a little girl is picked up and cuddled. It is clear that passivity and dependency training for most girls begins very early in their lives (Brooks-Gunn & Matthews, 1979).

As children grow, they learn what is "appropriate" male and female behavior from their family, teachers, friends, television, and books. This learning often emphasizes that the female-male relationship is not equal and that each sex has certain gender-related roles.

Many of the reported differences (e.g., dependency, passivity, or conformity) between males and females in the personality and social domain appear only in late adolescent and college-age women. A number of investigations identify differences in socialization experiences that may account for differences in achievement and behavior.

One of the classic studies on the socialization of females to lower their achievement goals is Komarovsky's *Women in the Modern World* (1953), which contains reports by college women describing advice not to set their sights too high and not to reveal their intellectual abilities or goals to potential boyfriends until they anticipate a favorable reaction. We must wonder about the number of outstanding women who have been talked out of (by themselves or by others) high educational and occupational achievement.

In a more recent book, *The Cinderella Complex*, concerning the socialization of women, Dowling (1981) writes that women have not entirely freed themselves from some of the traditional aspects of sex-role stereotyping in society. She believes that women are still being socialized to feel that they are not successful unless they have someone to take care of them. This form of psychological dependence is a major factor preventing women from achieving according to their potential. Dowling states that the need to be taken care of formerly began at age 16 or 17, when girls relinquished their desire to go to college and opted for early marriage. Today the desire to be "saved" begins after college, when the initial sense of freedom subsides and anxiety begins to arise.

Dowling traces the socialization pattern of boys and girls and points out that "girls . . . are trained *into* dependency, while boys are trained out of it" (p. 105). This trend begins in infancy and continues throughout the girl's family life and school career. If you have a brother or sister or know a family of male and female siblings, think about incidents in which parents treated them differently. For example, is the boy told after he falls to stop crying, brush himself off, and get on with the activity, whereas the girl is picked up and consoled after the same incident? Are the two siblings receiving equal encouragement for independence? Are they protected by the parents in the same or different ways? Are they both encouraged to experience various activities and value systems to help establish an identity? Would they receive similar reactions if they told their parents they were leaving home?

Research findings indicate that bright women have problems of self-confidence and that they consistently underestimate their own ability. There are important differences in how males and females explain the causes for their successes and failures. In general, females are more likely than males to attribute their success to factors such as luck or the ease of the task rather than to their own ability. Females are more likely than males to use lack of ability as an explanation for their failures. These research findings are used to explain how differences in children's achievement-related beliefs might influence boys and girls to seek and persist in various types of academic task. Boys are more likely than girls to select difficult rather than easy tasks and persist until the tasks are completed. In contrast, girls are more likely than boys to avoid the possibility of failure (Licht & Dweck, 1983).

## Androgyny

For a long time psychologists viewed certain traits as either masculine or feminine. For example, aggression, independence, competitiveness, and adventurousness were traits attributed to males, whereas sensitivity, gentleness, dependence, and submission were traits attributed to females. More recently, the concept that masculinity and femininity possess dual sets of traits has been stressed (Bem, 1974; Spence & Helmreich, 1978).

Bem (1974) has developed an instrument, the Bem Sex-Role Inventory, that classifies individuals into four categories. One category consists primarily of males who are high in traits that are considered masculine and low in traits that are regarded as feminine. A second category consists primarily of females who are high in feminine traits and low in masculine traits. A third category consists of individuals who are low in both masculine and feminine traits. The fourth category consists of individuals who are high in both masculine and feminine characteristics. Bem identifies individuals in this last category as *androgynous*.

**Androgyny** means, literally, "man-woman" and comes from the Greek *andro* (male) and *gyn* (female). The term describes individuals who are able to choose the most appropriate response to a given situation. For example, androgynous individuals can be either assertive or tender or perhaps a combination of the two qualities, depending on which is the appropriate response to the situation facing them. Androgynous women and men are high in *both* independence and nurturance (Bem, 1974, 1975).

More recently, Bem (1981, 1984) has developed the Gender-Schema Theory to describe how individuals differ in the ways they use culturally based definitions for appropriate female and male behaviors as guides for evaluating behavior. She believes that some children view the world through "gender-colored glasses" because they learn to process information in terms of a schema—a network of associations that organizes and guides individuals' perception. This schema imposes meaning on incoming stimuli and influences decisions and judgments, as well as the acquisition of knowledge and content. The gender schema also influences certain aspects of one's self-concept (Liben & Signorella, 1987).

## Aptitude and Achievement Differences

The pattern of aptitude and achievement between males and females indicates the following: There are no gender differences in general intelligence; girls excel at verbal tasks and boys at mathematical and visual-spatial tasks. On standardized achievement tests, girls score higher than boys in subjects requiring verbal abilities, and boys surpass girls in subjects requiring various reasoning and spatial skills. Girls receive higher grades throughout elementary school, with boys closing the gap during high school. More boys are nonreaders and are more likely than girls to receive special education services (Harvey, 1986; Linn & Petersen, 1985; Maccoby & Jacklin, 1974).

In 1972, data from the National Center for Educational Statistics supported the fact that girls outperformed boys in subjects that require verbal ability and boys outperformed girls in mathematics and related subjects (Harvey, 1976). However, between 1972 and 1980 a different picture began to emerge. The advantage of girls over boys in reading and vocabulary was eliminated. The data also indicated that in high school achievement test scores, males scored higher than females in vocabulary, reading, math, and science. The scores on the Scholastic Aptitude Test (SAT) in 1989 indicated that males averaged 13 points higher than females on the verbal section and 46 points higher on the quantitative (math) section. In contrast, the results of the National Assessment of Educational Progress (NAEP), a program that attempts to determine national achievement in various academic areas, have shown that females score higher than males in reading ability.

Recently, the New York State Board of Regents decided to stop using the SAT scores as a basis for determining college scholarships given by the state of New York when it became known that girls received only 28% of the awards while males received 72%. What is interesting is that whereas there is a large gap in the SAT math scores of males and females, the state of New York found no gender differences in statewide math tests given at the ninth-, tenth-, and eleventh-grade levels.

The current data on the achievement of males and females fail to confirm some of the traditional differences that have been identified in the past. The data also provide more questions than answers. For example, why has the achievement of females declined since 1980? If females score lower than males on most achievement tests, why do females attain higher grades than males in the same subject areas? How does the educational experience differ for males and for females?

## Mathematics Achievement

A great deal of literature focused on the issue of why males perform better than females on math aptitude and achievement tests. Benbow and Stanley's (1980) investigation received considerable media attention because the researchers suggested (in interviews but not in the article) that biological factors accounted for differences in math aptitude between gifted males and females. The researchers gave the verbal and quantitative sections of the SAT to gifted boys and girls in the middle of the seventh grade who had not studied algebra. The boys were matched with girls by intellectual ability, age, grade, and willingness to participate in the study. There were almost no differences in the verbal ability between boys and girls, but the boys scored on the average 30 points higher than the girls on the math section. The *implication* was that because the students' previous background in math education was similar and because they had not reached high school, where social values influence interests in various subject areas, superior math reasoning by the boys at this age indicated superior ability.

A number of researchers have challenged the genetic basis for male-female differences in math performance (see Eccles & Jacobs, 1986, and Lips, 1988, for critical reviews of the genetic explanation). The major argument is that social, not biological, factors are responsible for sex inequality related to the learning, valuing, and career implementation of mathematics. Boys take more higher mathematics courses, have more confidence in their ability to learn math, and perceive math as a more useful subject than do girls. In addition, there is evidence that counselors, parents, and teachers do not provide the same amount of support for females

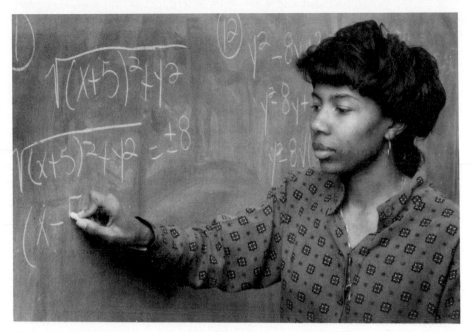

Both girls and boys who receive encouragement and good instruction in mathematics can be highly successful.

that they do for males in studying and valuing math. Last, there is evidence that math is perceived by females as a male domain since the main users of math in careers are males. Thus, if females believe that the study of mathematics is inappropriate for them, they will feel anxious about succeeding in the area.

Fennema (1983) reported on a special school program, Multiplying Options and Subtracting Bias, which attempts to encourage more female involvement in mathematics. The investigators developed four workshops that focus on stereotyping of mathematics as a male domain and other social factors limiting female involvement in mathematics. Students, teachers, and counselors participated in the program. The evaluation indicated that the program influenced female students' attitudes toward mathematics, decreased mathematics stereotypes, and influenced their willingness to take more courses in the subject.

## Reading Achievement

For years teachers have noticed that boys do not learn to read as well as girls in elementary school. Some educators have argued that because girls mature more rapidly than boys, they develop longer attention spans, which help them learn to read more effectively. However, cross-cultural studies in England and Germany have reported that males surpass girls in reading achievement and have fewer problems of reading disability (Johnson, 1972; Preston, 1962). Thus the maturational hypothesis is not supported by research.

A number of alternative hypotheses have been identified as possible explanations for differences in reading achievement at the elementary school level. The reading materials do not appeal to boys, female teachers give preferential treatment to girls, and reading is considered a passive activity that is more appropriate to the female sex role (Bank, Biddle, & Good, 1980). The current evidence relating to these hypotheses does not provide a definitive explanation for differences in achievement. For example, many readers and other curriculum materials used in the elementary grades provide male-oriented themes, and teachers of both sexes appear to act in similar ways toward boys and girls.

The resolution of this issue may be found in research focusing on teacher instructional behavior and on cultural factors. For example, when more attention is given to reading instruction for boys and they are reinforced for their progress, their reading performance increases (Leinhardt, Seewald, & Engel, 1979). Thus it appears that cultural factors can be influenced when boys observe more models of males as readers.

## Personality and Social Differences

In regard to personality differences, girls are generally more dependent and have a higher degree of anxiety, whereas boys are more aggressive and have a higher expectation of success. The differences between the sexes in aggressiveness and expectancy of success are the most conclusive finding among these traits. There is considerable disagreement on the other two traits, dependency and anxiety (Linn & Petersen, 1985; Maccoby & Jacklin, 1974). It is only on self-report studies on dependency and anxiety that girls score consistently higher than boys. As a result, we do not have conclusive evidence that boys *are* less anxious or less dependent than girls, only that boys consistently report less anxiety and dependency. Another factor that needs to be considered in interpreting these findings is that personality and social differences are influenced by contextual or situational factors. Thus females are likely to exhibit more anxiety and less self-confidence in situations they perceive as more threatening or of less interest (e.g., math) than in situations in which they perceive themselves as being more competent and having greater interest (e.g., English).

In summary, although researchers do not have all the answers as to the causes of gender differences, present evidence indicates that nothing in the intellectual or social-emotional makeup of either sex imposes limits on what members of that sex may hope to become or achieve. However, societal expectations can impose limits on achievement and vocational success. Parents and teachers need to make decisions based on the characteristics of a particular child rather than on sex-role stereotypes.

## The School's Response to Gender Differences

**How can teacher expectation and interaction with males and females influence their motivation and achievement?**

Many educators believe that the combination of courses, materials, and student-teacher interaction makes the majority of female students passive, shy, and dependent but provides male students with learning experiences that help them become self-assured, competitive, and independent. Marland (1983) views the school as a "sexist amplifier" because many conscious and unconscious decisions are made by teachers that magnify, or amplify, sex differences (e.g., the selection of learning material, subject content, division of tasks in the class, and different interaction with males and with females). Marland states: "Not only do schools treat boys and girls differently, but they actually make girls and boys more different than would normally happen" (p. 2).

Content analyses of textbooks used in various subject areas reveal that females are portrayed in stereotyped ways (see Gollnick, Sadker, & Sadker, 1982; Klein, 1985). Sadker (1974) stated: "A female student desiring to read about another female who is intelligent, creative, powerful, interesting, or charismatic will have to wade through many books before meeting one" (p. 277).

Here is how researchers have found males and females portrayed in reading texts (Gollnick, Sadker, & Sadker, 1982, p. 65):

| Males | Females |
|---|---|
| ingenious | dependent |
| creative | passive |
| brave | incompetent |
| persevering | fearful |
| achieving | victims |
| adventurous | docile |
| curious | concerned with domesticities |
| autonomous | objects of scorn and ridicule |
| athletic | aimless |
| self-respecting | concerned about physical appearance |
| problem solver | spiritless |

Although conditions improved during the 1980s as a result of the development of guidelines by local and state textbook adoption committees who review new textbooks, many books still used in the schools reflect stereotyping.

One of the major developments leading to more sex equity in the schools has been the passage of Title IX of the 1972 Education Amendments:

> No person shall, on the basis of sex, be excluded from participation in, be denied the benefits of, or be subjected to discrimination under any education program or activity receiving federal financial assistance.

This law makes it illegal to treat students differently or separately on the basis of sex. The regulations cover such areas as course offerings, counseling services, extracurricular activities, athletic programs, facilities, and financial assistance.

Do teachers view the classroom behavior of males and females differently? Brophy and Evertson (1981) studied teachers' attitudes toward male and female students and found that females were seen as "calmer, more careful, more mature, higher achieving, more persistent, happier, more attractive, more likely to maintain eye contact, and more cooperative" (p. 113). Males were more likely to be described as aggressive, active, or inattentive.

What have researchers found about teacher-student interaction with male and female students? The research in the 1960s and 1970s emphasized the difficulties boys had in elementary school. The main reason for this focus was that little research was available on secondary education and the problems of girls (Brophy, 1985b). Research evidence indicated that teachers criticized boys more frequently (Jackson & Lahaderne, 1967) and gave them lower grades than their actual achievement deserved (Carter, 1952; Hess et al., 1969). Several studies also indicated that female teachers were more favorably disposed toward girls and female qualities than toward boys and male qualities (Arnold, 1968; Jackson, Silberman, & Wolfson, 1969). There is also evidence that teachers overestimated the achievement potential and intelligence of girls, underestimated the abilities of boys, and held lower expectations for boys than for girls of equal ability (Doyle, Hancock, & Kifer, 1972).

It is important to analyze the apparent bias against males that was discussed during the 1960s and 1970s. Lee (1973) pointed out that the reasons for differential treatment of boys and girls were related to the fact that schools socialize their personnel to suit their own goals, placing constraints on the behavior of teachers and thereby accounting for certain institutional demands often erroneously identified with the "feminization of the schools." One such institutional demand are compulsory attendance laws, which require schools to educate students who may not be enthusiastic about school. Pupil control becomes an important aspect of school life, and teachers bear the onus of imparting the disciplines and regulations that smooth the path of school routines. Teachers' ability to maintain control of their classes is one measure of their success, so they strive for docile, obedient, and quiet behaviors and attitudes on the part of students. Another demand is the grade-level organization of the school, binding the teacher to a prescribed amount of material to impart to students over a nine-month period. Strict adherence to schedules and the socialization of children to respect and obey the schedules are the teacher's pre-eminent task.

But what about the questions of female bias against male students? The literature indicates that female teachers cannot be blamed for their differential interaction with males and females because male teachers treat boys in the same way that females teachers treat them (Brophy & Good,

1974; Brophy, 1985a). As a result, the presence of more male teachers in the elementary school without any other changes in teaching methods or procedures would not make a difference in the behavior or achievement of boys, other than perhaps having some benefit for fatherless boys.

Brophy and Good (1974) have argued that gender differences are more a result of student effects on teachers than teacher effects on students. Because males are more salient and active in the classroom, they are more likely to receive teacher attention to all types of behavior. Males are both praised more and punished more by teachers, are asked more questions, initiate more contact, and are called on more often by teachers. The fact that teachers interact more with males does not necessarily suggest bias on the part of the teacher. The fact is that boys are more forceful in gaining their teachers' attention. Sadker and Sadker (1986) report that in their research in both the elementary and secondary schools, boys are eight times as likely as girls to call out answers in class. They also found that teachers responded differently to call-outs from males and females. Teachers tended to accept call-outs from males but remediated the behavior of girls and advised them to raise their hands when they called out answers.

Sadker and Sadker suggest that one reason boys may score higher than girls on tests like the SAT is that boys receive more attention in the classroom. In content areas like science and math, where inquiry and questioning are important conditions of learning, lower rates of initiation and general interaction during instruction would place females at a disadvantage.

The research of the 1980s has focused more on the classroom experiences of females at all educational levels. For the most part, the findings at the elementary level are similar to the findings of the 1970s with two possible exceptions: First, there is some evidence that girls may receive better instruction in reading and boys receive better instruction in mathematics. Second, teachers may be socializing boys to be more independent and self-reliant and socializing girls to be more conforming (Brophy, 1985b).

## CLASSROOM APPLICATION: REDUCING SEX-ROLE STEREOTYPING

Sex-role stereotyping in the classroom is often referred to as the "hidden curriculum." Teachers are often unaware of how their own expectations and behaviors contribute to sex-role stereotypes and the development of different academic abilities and behaviors between male and female students (Serbin, 1983). Eccles and Blumenfeld (1985) point out that although teachers may not be the major source of sex-role stereotypes, they do not play an active role in changing them or providing boys and girls with the types of information that might lead them to change their sex-stereotyped beliefs. As a result, teachers passively reinforce the sex-typed academic and career decisions made by their students that contribute to the differences in the levels of educational attainment achieved by males and females.

The following are some guidelines for taking a more active role in developing a sex-equitable classroom environment (adapted and heads quoted from Shapiro, Kramer, & Hunerberg, 1981, pp. 8–15):

### Help children become more aware of sex-role stereotyping and of the variety of forces that influence attitudes, thinking, and behavior

Teachers often hear comments like "You can't expect girls to do that," "I don't want to sit with the boys," "Only girls do that." The teacher might respond immediately to these types of statement by replying, "Who said girls or boys can't do that?" or "In this class, people sit together." Sometimes using comments from students as a basis of discussion can be effective. This provides an opportunity for boys and girls in the class to point out examples of males or females accomplishing tasks that are considered stereotypical by some individuals.

Teachers can also discuss how individuals develop ideas about appropriate male and female behaviors. Assignments can be given in which children analyze television programs and commercials, books, and magazines for sex-role stereotypes.

Another area that can be explored in the classroom are children's attitudes and feelings about members of the opposite sex. "I hate those boys; they always mess up our game" and "Girls are so emotional" are examples of comments often heard in school or at home. Activities or discussions are not likely to change attitudes overnight, but in time students learn that many of their criticisms apply to people in general, rather than specifically to males or females.

### Change school practices that contribute to the separation and stereotyping of children by gender

Teachers often do not realize that certain school rules, procedures, or casual remarks contribute to expectations regarding sex-role behavior. The following are some practices that need to be eliminated:

- Establishing classroom seating arrangements and lines by sex.
- Using techniques that needlessly emphasize sex in managing groups of children (e.g., "Boys, be quiet," or "The girls can go first because . . .").
- Assigning classroom or school jobs on the basis of sex (e.g., boys are assigned to moving equipment, and girls are given clerical chores to complete).
- Perpetuating stereotyping while talking or disciplining students (e.g., "How pretty you look today," "Boys should be more polite with girls," or "Girls don't behave like that!").
- Allowing students to self-select facilities, materials, and people

with whom they work and play (e.g., "The girls will cook today while the boys will work on their woodworking projects").

- Using sexist terms when referring to girls or women (e.g., *darling, doll, cutie, sweetie*).
- Creating needless competition between the sexes (e.g., "Who will finish their work first—the boys or girls?" or "The girls do their homework so neatly").
- Requesting parental cooperation focused on the mother and assuming, sometimes erroneously, that fathers and mothers perform stereotypical jobs inside and outside the home (e.g., "Please invite your mothers to attend our show," "Please ask your mother to bake a cake for our party," "We need a class mother to go on a trip with us").

For each of these practices, suggest some nonsexist alternatives that could be used.

### Help children see that sex-role definitions change with time and vary in different cultures

Another important way to demonstrate that sex roles are not inherited or unchanging is for children to learn how sex roles vary in different cultures as well as how roles have changed in our own culture. Children can ask their mothers or fathers about sex-role behavior when they were growing up and discuss present conditions in their families and communities.

Lessons can be developed to study the responsibilities that men and women have in different cultures. For example, in many agricultural communities in the United States, both men and women work in the fields, but in China field work is largely women's work. In the United States, doctors are primarily men (although the percentage of women in medical schools is increasing), whereas in the Soviet Union there are more women than men physicians.

### Help children understand that there is a difference between sex roles, gender identity, and sexual preference

When children begin learning about roles for women and men, they may fear that the modification of the roles assigned to a gender will affect their gender identity or sexual behavior. The important point that must be taught is that human feelings or characteristics do not belong uniquely to one gender, nor do they influence one's sexual preference. For example, women can be assertive or men can be sensitive without its having any impact on their "femaleness" or "maleness." While you are dealing with this issue, be sensitive to the fact that students from some cultural groups experience clearly defined sex-role behaviors in their home and community.

It is helpful for children to see pictures of men taking care of children and pictures of women engaging in nonstereotypical occupations. I was in a classroom some years ago when a teacher brought in a picture of a football player who took up knitting for relaxation. The students were quite surprised by this.

### Encourage children to learn to work and play together and experience a variety of roles within a group

The teacher can provide opportunities for males and females to work together in completing assignments, to learn to help each other, and to enjoy activities together. Unless the teacher plans for such activities, however, they are unlikely to occur. Current research indicates that sex segregation among children may have social consequences that persist into adulthood (Lockheed & Klein, 1985). The sex segregation that typically occurs at the elementary school level may not simply represent a "harmless" developmental stage (Serbin, 1983) but may provide the foundation for further interaction patterns. Boys dominate the interaction patterns when working in mixed-sex, problem-solving groups in elementary school, and men dominate the interaction and decision making in mixed-sex groups (Lockheed & Hall, 1976). It appears that stereotyped expectations regarding the relative abilities of males and females begin in childhood and persist into adulthood. Furthermore, Webb and Kenderski (1985) reported differential behavior in high-achieving, mixed-sex groups in which males have higher attainment than females. They found that males were more likely to help males when they requested help, but males did not reciprocate when females asked for help.

By allowing the sexes to segregate and not cooperate with each other, the teacher may be communicating to children a normal acceptance of sex segregation and its consequences. It is important for the teacher to increase the opportunity for cross-sex interaction. Using cooperative cross-sex learning and discussion groups, reinforcing cross-sex play, and making use of seating and team assignments that place males and females in close proximity to each other can contribute to more positive interaction between the sexes. When students work in groups, teachers can assign different roles (e.g., leader, recorder) to students in each group, so that all students experience roles of different responsibility and status (Lockheed & Klein, 1985).

## SELF-CONCEPT

**Self-concept,** one's ideas or perceptions about oneself, is a very important factor affecting behavior (Combs & Avila, 1985). Educators have become increasingly aware of the impact that an individual's self-concept and **self-**

**esteem** have on classroom behavior and achievement.[1] Students' problems in school may have their sole source in the lack of a positive self-concept.

A number of investigations have provided important data to help explain the characteristics of the self-concept (Marsh, Byrne, & Shavelson, 1988; Marsh & Shavelson, 1985; Shavelson, Hubner, & Stanton, 1976). First, self-concept is *organized*. Individuals collect a great deal of information on which to base their perceptions of themselves. To arrive at a general picture of the self, the individual organizes the information into fewer and fewer broad categories.

Second, self-concept is *multifaceted;* we should not regard it as a single entity. Individuals categorize self-perceptions into such areas as social acceptance, physical attractiveness, athletic ability, and academic ability. For a long time it was commonly accepted and supported by some research that the self-concept of children from impoverished backgrounds was lower than that of more advantaged children. Miller and Woock (1970) suggest that poor children may score higher than, or at least as well as, more advantaged children, on tests of general self-concept but score lower on tests of self-concept related to achievement (i.e., the self measured against the standards and expectations of the school). One should identify the specific type of self-concept when referring to a student.

Third, the multifaceted structure of self-concept may be *hierarchical* on a dimension of generality. One possible representation of the organized, multifaceted, and hierarchical nature of self-concept is shown in Figure 4.1.

Fourth, self-concept is *stable*. Notice, however, that as one ascends the self-concept hierarchy, self-concept depends increasingly on specific situations and thus becomes less stable. This fact is supported by Ludwig and Maehr (1967), who found that success and failure in an athletic task changed subjects' self-concept of specific physical ability but did not change their general self-concept.

**Why do most attempts to change students' self-concepts fail?**

Many special programs have been developed by schools to improve students' self-concepts but have failed to demonstrate any change. Two of the major problems are the weak intervention programs and the poor relationship between the intended goals of the intervention and the specific dimensions of self-concept being evaluated. To improve the possibility of producing effective interventions, one must first establish the specific type of self-concept to be changed, develop activities and experiences related to the dimension of self-concept selected, and, finally, measure the specific dimension (Marsh, 1990).

---

[1] Many psychologists believe that the self has two aspects—self-description and self-evaluation—and therefore distinguish between *self-concept* and *self-esteem*. Self-concept is the total organization of the perceptions an individual has of the self. Self-esteem is the value or judgments the individual places on self and behavior. However, other psychologists fail to make the distinction and refer to *self-concept* as a global term that includes personal judgment. For this reason, *self-concept* and *self-esteem* have been used interchangeably in psychological literature.

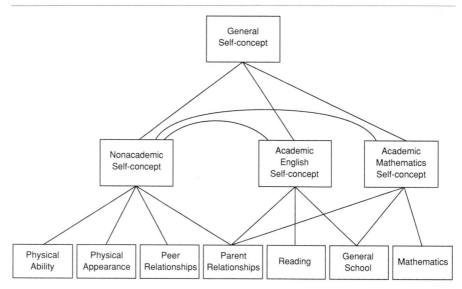

Figure 4.1 A Hierarchical Organization of Self-concept.

*Source: Adapted from Marsh and Shavelson, 1985.*

Another factor to consider in developing intervention programs is that interventions that improve performance or skill in a particular area may not improve self-concept in the same area. For example, Marsh and Peart (1988) compared the impact of a cooperative and competitive physical fitness program on self-concept of physical ability. They found that in the competitive program, physical fitness improved but self-concept of physical ability decreased. In the cooperative program, both physical fitness and self-concept of physical ability were enhanced. The researchers attributed the results to the differences in the participants' frames of reference in both programs (i.e., competition affected perceptions of self differently from cooperation).

Fifth, the self-concept hierarchy is *developmental.* As children mature, they develop concepts and categories for organizing events and situations. During the preadolescent years, self-concept becomes increasingly differentiated with increasing age. Also, during preadolescence and early adolescence, self-concept declines with age (Marsh, 1990). Students "learn" to regard themselves positively or negatively as they assimilate their experiences with significant people in their life—parents, peers, and teachers. By the time they reach school, they have acquired a good deal of information about themselves from others and begin to act like the type of person they conceive themselves to be. Their initial school experiences often reinforce these beliefs.

Last, self-concept is *evaluative.* Not only do individuals form a description of themselves in a particular situation, but they also form evaluations of themselves in the situation. Some students see themselves as successful achievers, but others believe they are inadequate and inferior to their classmates. Frame of reference can be an important factor in how an individual evaluates his or her self (Marsh, 1990).

In an extensive investigation of the antecedents of self-esteem among 1,700 fifth- and sixth-grade children, Coopersmith (1967) found that persons with positive self-esteem viewed themselves along the following general lines:

> I consider myself a valuable and important person, and am at least as good as others of my age and training. I am regarded as someone worthy of respect and consideration. . . . I'm able to exert an influence upon people and events, partly because my views are sought and respected and partly because I'm able and willing to present and defend those views. I have a pretty definite idea of what I think is right . . . and have a fairly good understanding of the kind of person I am. I enjoy new and challenging tasks and don't get upset when things don't go well right off the bat. (p. 47)

At the same time, a similar monologue by an individual with negative self-esteem might proceed as follows:

> I don't think I'm a very important or likeable person, and I don't see much reason for anyone else to like me. I can't do many of the things I'd like to do or do them the way I think they should be done. I'm not sure of my ideas and abilities, and there's a good likelihood that other people's ideas and work are better than my own. Other people don't pay much attention to me and given what I know about myself, I can't say I blame them. I don't like new or unusual occurrences and prefer sticking to known and safe ground. . . . I don't have much control over what happens to me and I expect that things will get worse rather than better. (p. 47)

The characterization of a person with moderate self-esteem falls between these two descriptions and is less precise in its evaluation of competence and expectations.

## Self-Concept and Achievement

The relationship between self-concept and achievement has been discussed extensively in the psychological literature. The guiding question is: "Which comes first—positive self-concept or high achievement?" One could argue that doing well in school is likely to enhance the student's positive self-concept. On the other hand, it also can be argued that students who develop positive self-concepts feel better about themselves and their ability, and as a result they do better academically. It is difficult to resolve this issue because there is evidence to support both positions. Although it is difficult to determine which comes first, high achievement or high self-concept, it is likely that a positive change in one facilitates a positive change in the other (Hamachek, 1985).

Students' self-concept can be an important aspect in understanding how young people deal with academic tasks. Many students are caught in a vicious cycle. They believe they can't perform well in a certain activity and they avoid it. Because they avoid it, they fail to get practice in the activity and don't perform well when they are asked to respond in class. The negative experiences caused by the inability to respond correctly only reinforce their initial belief about their inability. This dynamic process is called the **self-fulfilling prophecy.** Adults as well as children are victims of the beliefs they hold about themselves. My main point is that a negative self-image can be self-perpetuating, and over time it can have a negative effect on academic achievement.

Have you ever considered the consequences of attending a high school with high academic standards and ranking toward the middle of the class or attending a less demanding school and ranking near the top? Marsh (1989; Marsh & Parker, 1984) has investigated the impact of what he calls "the big-fish-little-pond effect" on academic self-concept. He finds that equally able students have lower academic self-concepts in high-ability schools than in low-ability schools. This result is attributed to social comparison processes with a reference group that is perceived to be more able or less able than oneself. This research presents a dilemma for parents who are dissatisfied with public schools and want to send their children to high-achieving private schools: The private school environment is likely to challenge students to excel. However, the early formation of a self-image as a poor student may be more detrimental than attendance at a mediocre school. Can you relate this research to your experiences in high school?

Two factors especially mold various dimensions of students' self-concepts: physical growth and development and school experiences. The next two sections focus on these topics.

## Physical Growth and Development

There is a strong correlation between self-image and body image for both boys and girls. In our society, having an acceptable body build is an important factor in evaluating ourselves. Most of us are well aware of adolescents' concern over their changing bodies. There is evidence that quite young boys and girls are also well aware of different body builds and often have negative reactions to their own physique (Lerner & Gillert, 1969; Staffieri, 1967).

*The Impact of Others.* The self-concept is influenced by the reaction of others concerning physical appearance and body size, as well as by activities in which success is contingent on body size and/or physical skills. For example, the awkward child or adolescent who does not possess the athletic agility that is highly valued by the child's peers will not be accepted with open arms when the time comes to select team members. Do you know what it feels like always to be selected *last* for team competition? In addition to awkwardness or lack of ability, physical features—height, weight, complexion, or general body proportions—are very much related to feelings about one's self.

Children and adolescents of both sexes are influenced by mass media stereotypes of the beautiful body. Television, movies, and magazines such as *Playboy* and *Playgirl* reinforce ideas about body build with which individuals compare themselves. Jourard and Secord (1955) found that the ideal height and weight for college women were 5 feet 5 inches, 120 pounds, with a bust, waist, and hip measurement of 35, 24, and 35 inches, respectively. The more a woman's dimensions deviated from this ideal, the more she disliked her physique. During different historical periods in our society, certain aspects of the ideal body build have changed. Since the 1980s considerable attention has been given to the illness **anorexia nervosa,** in which adolescent girls often starve themselves to maintain a slim figure. In studies of men's perceptions of satisfactory body builds, men consistently rate the wide-shouldered, narrow-hipped, athletic type of body build over the obese or thin body build (Brodsky, 1954).

*Rate of Development.* Another area of growth that can affect the self-concept is one's rate of development (i.e., early versus late maturation). The

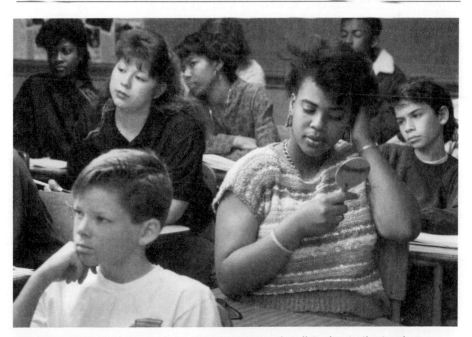

Sometimes students have more important concerns than listening to the teacher.

emergence of **puberty,** the biological changes that lead to reproductive maturity, has important psychological and social implications for the adolescent. Early-maturing males have been found to be more relaxed, less dependent, more self-confident, and attractive to both adults and peers than late-maturing males (Jones & Bayley, 1950; Mussen & Jones, 1957).

What types of experiences do early-maturing males have that influence a more positive self-esteem? First, because females mature approximately two years earlier than the average male, the early-maturing males are more likely to begin dating and developing social relationships with girls in junior high school and high school, whereas their late-maturing peers do not develop these social skills until late in their high school career. As a result, the early-maturing males develop important social skills that give them a sense of confidence when interacting with people, particularly members of the opposite sex. Second, because early-maturing males tend to be bigger and stronger than late-maturing males, they are more likely to gain prestige from participating in athletics, a major source of pride for males. Third, again because of their size, early-maturing males are more likely to be given more responsibility by parents and teachers, at an earlier age, which adds to their confidence and positive self-image.

For females, the research is more ambiguous and confusing (Jones & Mussen, 1958). The advantages to females of early or late maturation are not always clear-cut. Many of the same advantages of early maturation accrue to girls in the same way as they do to boys. However, it can have some disadvantages such as lack of popularity and greater internal turbulence, because early-maturing girls feel and often look different from their peers. For girls, lacking the support of a peer group also going through puberty can be difficult. In a recent investigation, Tobin-Richards, Boxer, and Petersen (1983) reported that boys who matured earlier perceived themselves more positively than boys who were either on time (in relation to their peers) or late in their development. However, girls who were in mid-development or who perceived themselves to be on time in their physical maturation felt more attractive and more positive about their bodies than the girls who were early or late developers. The researchers also found that the late maturers felt more positive about themselves than the early maturers. The differential effects of early or late maturation for girls in various investigations may depend on different value systems and attitudes among peer groups in different communities.

## School Experiences

**What factors in a school or classroom contribute to students' self-concepts?**

The teacher can exert considerable influence on the direction of a child's self-concept by establishing a positive learning environment and by communicating effectively with students in the classroom. An important point to remember is that a student's concept of ability develops mainly from performance on classroom tasks, and the teacher can enhance the self-concept of ability by helping students to select learning objectives according to their abilities.

Another important factor in school experience that can have a strong effect on self-esteem is the school setting. Blyth, Simmons, and Bush (1978) found that for girls the discontinuity of moving from the sixth grade to the seventh grade in a new school can have a negative effect on self-esteem. In contrast, girls who stayed in the same school from kindergarten through the eighth grade showed no negative effects. In another investigation, Simmons, Rosenberg, and Rosenberg (1973) reported that 12-year-old girls in the seventh grade were more likely to demonstrate negative self-images than 12-year-olds in the sixth grade who were in elementary school. The researchers found no differences in the self-images between 11- and 12-year-olds in the sixth grade or between 12- and 13-year-olds in the seventh grade. The key factor leading to a negative self-image for girls was being in a traditional junior high school at the time of puberty. Boys do not appear to be as affected by the transition from one type of school environment to another.

Why do you think that girls experience more stress by moving to a new school during the time of puberty? (Think about this question before reading the rest of this paragraph.) Simmons et al. (1979) believe the differences between pubertal boys and girls may be understood by exploring their value systems at this developmental period. Girls value sociability and appearance because these traits determine popularity. Therefore, girls rely more on the opinions of others to determine their self-esteem and position in their peer group. When girls move to a new school, they are faced with an entirely new reference group, in which the peers who are evaluating them are less well known. If a girl is engaged in dating during the change in schools, she is even more vulnerable to developing a negative self-image.

The impact of school transition is different for boys, who rely less on "looks" as a factor in their total evaluation of themselves. In addition, the nature of the change in body image is different for the sexes. Girls develop a figure, which makes them different from the way they were in elementary school. Boys become taller and more muscular and athletic-looking, a less dramatic change, which is more in line with their existing values concerning athletics and body strength. Thus boys are more likely to view the changes as an improvement in their own appearance, whereas girls are less sure whether their particular figure will be viewed by others in a positive manner (Simmons et al., 1979).

While Simmons and her colleagues have argued that the *timing* of the transition to junior high school results in more disruption to the individual than would occur if the school change were made later in adolescence, Eccles and Midgley (1989) point out that the *nature* of the transition should be considered. They believe that it is the developmental mismatch between young adolescents and the traditional junior high school environment that causes the decrease in students' motivation and achievement-oriented beliefs about themselves. If the junior high school environment was supportive and less competitive, the change could have a positive impact on how adolescents view themselves.

Eccles and Midgley's analysis of the research is as follows: The junior high school student experiences more teacher control, competition and social comparison, and whole-class instruction, less personal contact with the teacher, and fewer opportunities for student decision making and self-management than the elementary school student. At the same time, adolescents are more self-conscious and concerned about comparing themselves to others and desire more freedom in decision making. The consequence in this mismatch is an increased focus on ability assessments and anxiety over one's relative ability and performance levels, and a decreased sense of personal control. This situation causes many adolescents to have lower self-esteem and negative attitudes toward school and learning.

The research just recounted has important implications for dealing with junior high students. Are you convinced that more attention needs to be given to how the school environment meets the developmental needs of students? Perhaps encouraging dating behavior and developing activities that model the high school is not the best course for students in early adolescence. Does society push young adolescents to exhibit "grown-up" behavior too early? Think back to your own junior high school days. We can now laugh at certain awkward social experiences, but they were not funny when they occurred. Can you think of ways in which parents and teachers can be more supportive during this difficult developmental period?

## SOCIALIZATION AND THE FAMILY

### Child-Rearing Practices

**How do parents' child-rearing styles influence their children's social behavior?**

A number of researchers have shown that parents' child-rearing practices influence children's behavior. Erikson's theory of identity formation provides some insight into child-rearing practices as they pertain to important psychosocial crises at different developmental periods. In particular, providing a sense of trust, allowing children to explore their environment, and encouraging them to try new situations while providing support if they fail are important parenting behaviors in developing children's identity. Coopersmith (1967) found three child-rearing conditions to be related to a high self-esteem: parental acceptance of children, parental enforcement of clearly defined behavioral limits and rules, and parental respect for the freedom of their children's actions within the established limits.

Baumrind (1966, 1967, 1971) demonstrated how different parenting styles influence the social/personality development of children. She studied the impact of child-rearing practices by observing the behavior of preschool children age 3 and 4. After studying the children's social behavior, she observed and interviewed the parents of the children and identified three categories of parenting styles—the **authoritarian,** the **permissive,** and the **authoritative**—and described typical behavior patterns of the children raised according to each style.

Authoritarian parents attempt to control their children's behavior and attitudes to conform to strict rules of conduct. These parents value obedience and favor punitive measures when their children attempt to behave contrary to their parents' expectations. They don't like to discuss standards with their children, are more detached, more controlling, and less warm than other parents; their children are more discontented, withdrawn, and distrustful.

Permissive parents make few demands on their children, allowing them to regulate their own behavior. They hardly ever punish their children for misbehavior, make few demands for responsibility at home, and avoid the exercise of control; their children are the least self-reliant, explorative, and self-controlled.

Authoritative parents try to direct their children's activities by establishing firm rules and standards but are willing to discuss the reasons behind their regulations. They don't threaten their children, are loving, consistent, and respectful of their children's independent decisions; their children are the most self-reliant, self-controlled, explorative, and contented.

Although there are many different explanations for antisocial behavior, Patterson, DeBaryshe, and Ramsey (1989) have constructed a developmental model (see Figure 4.2) that emphasizes the role of faulty child-rearing methods as the basis for later antisocial behavior. Research indicates that the families of antisocial children use harsh and inconsistent discipline, have little positive interaction with their children, and don't adequately monitor and supervise their activities (Loeber & Dishion, 1983; McCord, McCord, & Howard, 1963). These parents are not consistent in the use of rewards for appropriate behavior and punishment for deviant behavior. Of particular concern is that they allow their children to be aggressive with other members of the family. The result of this early family experience is that the children learn to control their environment through coercive means and fail to learn appropriate social behaviors. When they go to school, their difficulty in conforming to classroom regulations leads to difficulties with teachers and peers, and ultimately to poor academic

Figure 4.2 Developmental Progression for Antisocial Behavior.

*Source: Patterson, DeBaryshe, and Ramsey, 1989.*

achievement. Finally, at early adolescence, the children's antisocial behavior and peer rejection motivate them to seek out a deviant peer group with which to identify. Many of these individuals become adolescent delinquents and adult offenders.

Many schools provide either parent education courses or information where parents in the community can obtain help. One problem is that parents who need the most help often don't contact schools or social agencies for assistance. Since there is evidence that successful interventions occur at the preadolescent stage (Kazdin, 1987), it is important for teachers and mental health professionals to identify children who exhibit antisocial behavior at an early age. In addition to parent training, there are interventions that include teaching children academic and social skills.

A number of books and programs are available for parents who want guidance in child rearing. Some of the more popular books include *P.E.T.: Parent Effectiveness Training* (Gordon, 1975); *Children: The Challenge* (Dreikurs & Soltz, 1964); *Systematic Training for Effective Parenting* (Dinkmeyer & McKay, 1976); and *Living with Children* (Patterson & Guillion, 1971). These books can be useful to the teacher who may be asked questions by parents regarding specific approaches to dealing with child-rearing problems. Readers interested in an evaluation of some of the major parent education programs will find Dembo, Sweitzer, and Lauritzen's (1985) review helpful. Lastly, many of the methods discussed in Chapter 11 regarding classroom management also are applied to child-rearing techniques.

## Child Abuse and Neglect

**What type of parent is likely to abuse his or her child?**

In Section 3 of the Child Abuse Prevention and Treatment Act (P.L. 93-247), *child abuse* and *neglect* are defined as "the physical or mental injury, sexual abuse, negligent treatment, or maltreatment of a child under the age of eighteen by a person who is responsible for the child's welfare under circumstances which indicate that the child's health or welfare is harmed or threatened thereby."

According to the National Center for Child Abuse and Neglect, approximately 1 million children are abused or neglected each year. More than 2,000 children die each year because of abuse or neglect by their adult caretakers. Many individuals incorrectly believe that child abusers come from some particular type of background. The fact is that child abusers come from all religious, ethnic, occupational, and socioeconomic groups. Furthermore, many child abusers were themselves abused as children.

McNeese and Hebeler (1977) have stressed that prerequisites to an incident of abuse are "a *child* who is difficult to manage (or is merely considered difficult by parents), a *parent* or *family* that has the potential to abuse, and a *stressful event* that precipitates the abuse" (pp. 5–6). Infants who are born with low birthweight, congenital malformations, and other developmental deviations and handicapped children often are vulnerable to abuse because they may not live up to their parents' expectations or may be difficult to rear (Morgan, 1987). Researchers have found that certain family and/or personal problems of mothers and fathers can be an important determinant in child abuse. For example, stress, isolation, poor information about child-care procedures or unrealistic expectations concerning child development (e.g., expecting a child to be toilet-trained by the first birthday), serious marital problems, unemployment, and crises involving separation or divorce can all be possible factors that cause an adult to abuse or neglect a child (Gelardo & Sanford, 1987).

Because teachers spend considerable time with children, they are in an excellent position to identify signs of abuse and neglect, provided they know what to look for (Cartwright, Cartwright, & Ward, 1984). Teachers should be alert to the following symptoms (Kline, 1977):

| Symptoms of Abuse | Symptoms of Neglect |
|---|---|
| Evidence of repeated injury | Clothing inappropriate for weather |
| New injuries before previous ones have healed | Torn, tattered, unwashed clothing |
| Frequent complaints of abdominal pain | Poor skin hygiene |
| Evidence of bruises | Rejection by other children because of body odor |
| Bruises of different ages | Need for glasses, dental work, hearing aid, or other health services |
| Welts | Lack of proper nourishment |
| Wounds, cuts, or punctures | Consistent tiredness or sleepiness in class |
| Scalding liquid burns with well-defined parameters | Consistent very early school arrival |
| Caustic burns | Frequent absenteeism or chronic tardiness |
| Frostbite | Tendency to hang around school after dismissal |
| Cigarette burns | |

It is not always easy to determine clear-cut cases of abuse or neglect. For example, a child who is consistently tired or sleepy in class may have some illness. However, every state requires that suspected child abuse be reported. For example, in California, teachers and other professionals who have contact with children are required by law to report child abuse immediately by telephone to a child protection agency and send a written report within 36 hours of learning about an incident. Failure to comply with this law is a misdemeanor punishable by six months in jail and/or a $500 fine. The reporting teacher is not required to provide proof of the abuse. The agency that receives the report has that responsibility.

Many school districts have formal procedures to report cases of child abuse and neglect. It is important that you ask about the procedures and regulations regarding the reporting of child abuse in your school district. All states now provide immunity for those who report suspected cases of child abuse in good faith.

*Child Sexual Abuse.* Recently, there has been a great deal of attention in the mass media on the sexual abuse of children. Many schools have developed special educational programs for young children emphasizing primary prevention (keeping the abuse from occurring in the first place) and detection (encouraging disclosure of past and present abuse so that children can receive intervention and protection). Unfortunately, there is insufficient research in this area to determine whether these prevention programs are effective (Reppucci & Haugaard, 1989).

An important concern is the possibility of teachers and other school personnel being falsely accused of improper behavior. As a result, teachers need to avoid situations in which their interaction with children could be questioned. The following are some do's and don'ts (adapted from Morgan, 1987, pp. 97–98):

- Never give a child a ride in your car, even in an emergency.
- Never take children on field trips away from the school unless at least two parents are present.
- Never go into a bathroom alone with children.
- Never touch children, except on the shoulder to lead them to their seats or wherever it is you want them to be.
- Never hug, kiss, or pat a child on the bottom, and do not allow students to give you extended hugs or allow them to kiss you.
- Never let students into your home.
- Always document for your file any false accusations a child makes, such as: "You are mean to me. You hate me."
- Always take a child immediately to the school nurse if he or she acquires an injury, whether self-inflicted or accidental.

In reading this list, you might conclude that educators may be overreacting to isolated incidents. Unfortunately, present circumstances require greater awareness on the teacher's part to prevent false accusations regarding professional conduct.

## Student Stress

**How can a teacher deal with students exhibiting stress?**

Important variables influencing learning are student **stress** and **anxiety**—terms that identify factors associated with apprehension or fear. Some psychologists debate whether stress and anxiety are the same, or whether stress causes anxiety, or vice versa. I will avoid this issue and define stress as a stimulus situation and anxiety as an emotional state. I will discuss stress in this section and anxiety in Chapter 10 when I focus on factors influencing student motivation.

Some of us can tolerate more stress than others and react differently to stressful situations. In fact, there is some indication that an individual's personality may influence the ways in which he or she responds to stress factors. Friedman and Rosenmann (1974) identified Type A and Type B behavior in the way individuals respond to their environment. Individuals with Type A behavior tend to be aggressive and ambitious and to have a sense of time urgency in their quest to excel. Individuals with Type B behavior also may be aggressive or ambitious, but they are more easygoing and relaxed in their quest for excellence. Friedman and Rosenmann believe that Type A individuals are more likely to have heart attacks and other physical ailments.

Some psychologists believe that many children are currently being reared in an environment that fosters Type A behavior. David Elkind (1981) has described the socialization factors that cause stress in children in his book *The Hurried Child: Growing Up Too Fast Too Soon.* According to Elkind, the "hurried child" is often forced to assume adultlike behaviors before being prepared to do so. We dress our children like adults, allow them to view sex and violence in the media, make unreasonable demands on them to attain goals beyond their ability, and expect them to deal with changes in the family such as divorce and single parenthood without any difficulty. Elkind states that pediatricians report a greater incidence of chronic psychosomatic complaints such as headaches, allergic reactions, stomachaches, and even ulcers in today's children than in the past.

The following scale (Table 4.2) reported by Elkind (1981) provides an estimate of the impact of various stressful changes in a child's life. He estimates that for a given year, if a child scores below 150, the child is about average with respect to stress load. If the child's score is between 150 and 300, the child has better than an average chance of demonstrating some symptoms of stress. If the child's score is above 300, there is a strong possibility that some changes in health and/or behavior will be observed. These numbers should be used only as guidelines, because a child may show symptoms of stress with a much lower score. As you talk to children, be cognizant of the stressors in their lives. Such information may provide you with insights as to why certain students may not be performing up to standards.

An important factor for teachers to consider is that children do not deal with stress as well as adults. In many ways, society permits more acceptable outlets for adults than it does for children. For example, a teacher can be angry with a student, but it is inappropriate for a student to display anger toward a teacher; adults can walk away from a stressful situation, but children often do not have this option at home or in the classroom; adults can daydream or become involved with some other activity to reduce the effects of stress, but children are expected to maintain their attention on school-related tasks; adults can get a prescription drug for "nerves" from a physician, but it is inappropriate for children to deal with stress in the same manner (Youngs, 1985).

*Controlling Stress through Relaxation.* Psychologists have developed programs to help children understand and become aware of stressors in their lives as well as to help them manage their stress (see Humphrey & Humphrey, 1985, and Youngs, 1985, for a detailed discussion of various programs). One of the most common strategies for reducing stress is to alleviate its symptoms. In this regard, relaxation techniques have been successful in dealing with many psychosomatic illnesses such as migraine

TABLE 4.2 ASSESSMENT OF STUDENT STRESS

|  | Points | Child's Score |
|---|---|---|
| Parent dies | 100 | |
| Parents divorce | 73 | |
| Parents separate | 65 | |
| Parent travels as part of job | 63 | |
| Close family member dies | 63 | |
| Personal illness or injury | 53 | |
| Parent remarries | 50 | |
| Parent fired from job | 47 | |
| Parents reconcile | 45 | |
| Mother goes to work | 45 | |
| Change in health of a family member | 44 | |
| Mother becomes pregnant | 40 | |
| School difficulties | 39 | |
| Birth of a sibling | 39 | |
| School readjustment (new teacher or class) | 39 | |
| Change in family's financial condition | 38 | |
| Injury or illness of a close friend | 37 | |
| Starts a new (or changes an) extracurricular activity (music lessons, Brownies, and so forth) | 36 | |
| Change in number of fights with siblings | 35 | |
| Threatened by violence at school | 31 | |
| Theft of personal possessions | 30 | |
| Changes responsibilities at home | 29 | |
| Older brother or sister leaves home | 29 | |
| Trouble with grandparents | 29 | |
| Outstanding personal achievement | 28 | |
| Move to another city | 26 | |
| Move to another part of town | 26 | |
| Receives or loses a pet | 25 | |
| Changes personal habits | 24 | |
| Trouble with teacher | 24 | |
| Change in hours with baby sitter or at day-care center | 20 | |
| Move to a new house | 20 | |
| Changes to a new school | 20 | |
| Changes play habits | 19 | |
| Vacations with family | 19 | |
| Changes friends | 18 | |
| Attends summer camp | 17 | |
| Changes sleeping habits | 16 | |
| Change in number of family get-togethers | 15 | |
| Changes eating habits | 15 | |
| Changes amount of TV viewing | 13 | |
| Birthday party | 12 | |
| Punished for not "telling the truth" | 11 | |

*Source: Elkind, 1981.*

headaches. For example, controlling one's breathing is an effective way to relax. Many experts in stress reduction teach individuals breathing exercises that involve a long, slow exhalation. Your diaphragm expands and tenses when you take in air and relaxes when you let the air out. Thus one way to relax is to increase the time you spend exhaling. This process is called *diaphragmatic breathing*. Certain measures of anxiety can be lowered as a result of using relaxation procedures (Johnson & Spielberger, 1968; Keat, 1972). The following is a simple exercise to teach individuals to relax (Youngs, 1985). Experience the following technique by asking a friend to read each step as you attempt it:

1. Get comfortable. Move your arms and legs around to make your muscles loose.
2. Close your eyes.
3. Take a deep breath in and count slowly one . . . two . . . three . . . four . . . five . . . six.
4. Let the air out very slowly, counting one . . . two . . . three . . . four . . . five . . . six.
5. Repeat the above, but this time place your hands on your stomach and feel it filling up with air (pushing out) when you breathe.
6. Breathe in deeply one . . . two . . . three . . . four.
7. Let the air out slowly one . . . two . . . three . . . four . . . five . . . six . . . (feel your stomach pull back in).
8. Repeat this a few more times.
9. Open your eyes.
10. Now how do you feel? (p. 117)

Don't get too relaxed. You have more material to cover in this chapter!

*Suicide.* Sometimes student stress reaches a point that it can't simply be alleviated by rest or relaxation. A concern of parents, educators, and mental health practitioners is the increasing rate of suicide among adolescents, caused, in part, by the stressors in their lives. The number of adolescents who commit suicide has increased 300% since the 1960s (National Center for Health Statistics, 1985). Many adolescents have maladaptive coping strategies to handle their problems. Instead of dealing directly with problems, they seek methods that temporarily give them relief (e.g., experiment with alcohol and other drugs or engage in other risk-taking behaviors). The result, however, is that these behaviors do not resolve the problems that they face (Frymier, 1988).

The problems that suicide victims face usually are common to most adolescents (e.g., failing grades, difficulties with peers, tension at home, and so forth). What makes the situation different is that the accumulation of stress is so great that they come to believe that suicide is the only solution open to them. There are, however, some stressors that can be particularly dangerous. For example, a history of physical and sexual abuse is associated with a higher rate of self-destructive behaviors (Frymier, 1988).

Schools are preparing materials and programs for students and their parents dealing with this issue. In addition, many teachers participate in staff development workshops on suicide and are trained to present workshops for students. The student-centered programs usually focus on teaching the warning signs of an impending suicide, promoting listening skills on the part of the students, and stressing how to get professional help for suicidal peers. The five warning signs identified by the American Association of Suicidology are

(a) a suicide threat or other statement indicating a desire or intention to die, (b) a previous suicide attempt, (c) depression, (d), marked changes in behavior, including eating and sleeping patterns, acting out, hyperactivity, substance abuse, or high risk taking behavior, and (e) making final arrangements or saying good-bye to possessions and/or individuals. (Davis, Wilson, & Sandoval, 1988, p. 560)

Other types of programs available for adolescents include peer counseling in schools, mental health consultation by school psychologists and other professionals, screening to identify students at risk, and special programs to provide information on life skills, with a focus on helping young people cope with the stressors in their lives.

There are some steps that teachers can take if they suspect that a student may engage in self-destructive behavior. Your first step is to find out if there are specific procedures established by your school district. If there are no specific guidelines, consider the following (Frymier, 1988):

- Tell the principal, guidance counselor, and/or school psychologist about your concern.
- With one of these individuals confront the student to discuss what is causing him or her to consider suicide.
- Alert the student's family and with the principal or mental health professional meet with them to discuss your concerns.
- Monitor the student's behavior.

The process for dealing with students who need special attention differs from school to school. Sometimes a principal will prefer that the school psychologist handle the situation without direct involvement with the classroom teacher. In other situations, the teacher may work together with the school psychologist. Don't ever try to handle the problem alone. Get the help of professionals in your school for advice on how to proceed.

## Maternal Employment

With the increasing number of single-parent families and dual-career parents, more mothers are working today than ever before. It is estimated that 71% of mothers with school-age children from two-parent families are presently working outside the home.

Hoffman (1989) has reviewed the research on the effects of maternal employment in two-parent families and has found the following: First, children of employed mothers have less gender stereotypes. Second, employed mothers teach their children to be more independent than nonemployed mothers. Third, employment has the potential to increase a mother's sense of contentment if she likes her job, has adequate support from her husband for working, and is satisfied with the quality of child care. Finally, there are few differences in parent-child interaction between employed and nonemployed mothers. Although employed mothers spend less time with their children during the week, they often compensate by spending more time with them on weekends. Thus, in general, if a mother receives the necessary support while working, there doesn't appear to be any detrimental effects for either the mother or child.

## Divorce

At one time relatives and friends were shocked to hear about a divorce. Today divorce is no longer considered atypical, but instead viewed as a normal process of family change (Ahrons & Rodgers, 1987). It is estimated that 40% to 50% of schoolchildren will experience their parents' divorce and will spend an average of five years raised by single parents before a parent remarries (Glick & Lin, 1986).

Although there is more acceptance of divorce in society, the negative impact on children has not changed. In general, parent conflict is associated with adjustment problems among children—especially boys, who react less well to divorce than girls. This is not to say that all children from divorced families are maladjusted. In some cases, a supportive one-parent household is more beneficial for children than a two-parent household with conflict (Hetherington & Anderson, 1988).

**How can divorce impact students of different developmental ages?**

It is difficult to predict how a specific child or adolescent will respond to parental separation and divorce. Such factors as the age of the child at the time of separation, the child's personality, the degree of parental conflict, the economic position of the child's residential family, and the quality of the child's relationship with his or her residential parent are factors to be considered. It is not the simple event of divorce itself that produces the negative impact, but the subsequent events—the inconsistent parenting, conflict between parents, economic hardships on the family—that have the greatest effect on the child's development and adjustment (Emery, 1988).

It does not appear that there is a "good time" for a divorce, since it affects children at all ages. In some cases, delayed responses are observed many years after the event. At one time it was believed that adolescents handled marital transition better than younger children. However, Wallerstein, Corbin, and Lewis (1988) reported data from the 10-year follow-up of the California Children Divorce Study indicating that contrary to earlier findings, older children appear to suffer the greatest from divorce.

They found that large numbers of young men and women had personal problems, and one-third of the women were very concerned about commitment and were fearful of being betrayed.

Wallerstein and Kelly (1980) provided information on some common responses to divorce related to the developmental level of the child. Preschool children were likely to regress in the area of recent achievement such as toilet-training, dressing, and going to school. They feared routine separation, had trouble sleeping, became concerned with abandonment, and were irritable and demanding. Some preschool children blamed themselves for the divorce.

Children between 5 and 8 years of age cried a great deal and were preoccupied with feelings of rejection. Boys, in particular, missed their father and expressed anger at their mother for causing him to leave. The school performance of these children declined.

Children between 9 and 12 were angry, particularly at the parent they saw as causing the divorce, and tended to align with one parent against the other—most frequently with the mother against the father. They grieved, were anxious and lonely, and some also had academic problems.

Adolescents, who were already experiencing their own developmental difficulties, acquired additional problems with the separation. They became anxious as they realized their parents were not perfect, were concerned with their own futures and with the possibility of their own sexual and marital failure. Finally, they tended to disengage from their families and sought support from peers and other significant adults.

*Implications for Teaching.* The teacher should be prepared for the possibility of adjustment problems following parental separation, especially if custodial changes are involved. The tendency for diminished parenting following a divorce (Hetherington, Cox, and Cox, 1982; Wallerstein & Kelly, 1980) can lead to less parental discipline and more independence given to the child. The result can influence the student's classroom behavior and academic achievement.

Hamner and Turner (1985) developed the following guidelines for teachers (based on Black, 1979, and Hammond, 1981):

- Talk with the child, encouraging expression of feelings, and be a willing and receptive listener.
- Recognize emotions and accept them.
- Deal openly in class with a variety of family situations. Avoid referring only to nuclear families. Be sensitive to language used. Avoid stereotyping terms such as "broken homes."
- Do not expect children from one-parent homes to fail; children live up to expectations.
- Make information on divorce available to children and their parents.
- Establish communication with both parents, if possible.

- Learn about custodial and other arrangements for the children.
- When possible, place young children without fathers in classrooms with male teachers. (p. 179)

## Latchkey Children

One serious problem resulting from the increase in dual-career and single-parent families is the growing number of children and adolescents caring for themselves after school. Estimates of **latchkey children** range from 2 million to 6 million. The term *latchkey* originated in the 18th century and denoted the implement used to lift the door latch to gain entry into one's house.

Many families cannot afford the pay for child care before or after school; even if they can, they often can't arrange for suitable care. A 1987 Harris poll reported that teachers considered the lack of adequate child care as the number 1 problem in schools, surpassing drug use, truancy, and discipline.

Although not all latchkey children are maladjusted or do poorly in school, there is evidence that as parental supervision declines, the possibility of psychological and behavioral problems increases. For example, latchkey children report more fear and anxiety, have more academic and social problems, and are more susceptible to peer pressure to commit antisocial acts than children who are supervised after school (Long & Long, 1989). Richardson et al. (1989) found that eighth graders who took care of themselves for 11 or more hours a week were at twice the risk of substance use—alcohol, tobacco, and marijuana—as those who did not take care of themselves at all. This relationship held for all levels of socioeconomic status, gender, ethnicity, extracurricular activities, or sources of social influence (e.g., whether the parents smoked or drank). The significance of this investigation is that it demonstrated that the likelihood of becoming a substance abuser is not limited to children of any one type of family.

**How can a teacher help families of latchkey children?**

Schools and communities are making attempts to help children and their families deal with the problem. Some communities have organized hot lines where children can speak to adults about their fears or concerns. *The Handbook for Latchkey Children and Their Working Parents* (Long & Long, 1983) should be recommended to parents who need advice about reducing the dangers of unsupervised care. One of the most important steps parents can take is to establish a contact person, a parent or some other adult, for the child to call once he or she comes home. Other advice in this book is to provide the child with structured activities to complete while alone in the house.

Teachers can also play an important role by listening to students' concerns and providing information about personal safety. In addition, advising parents how to monitor students' homework and television viewing can be helpful in assuring normal academic progress.

## TELEVISION AS A SOCIALIZATION AGENT

Television has both positive and negative influences on children. It teaches academic and cognitive skills and social behaviors, and targets children as a market for advertising toys, cereals, and other foods (Huston, Watkins, & Kunkel, 1989). Steinberg (1985) reported that the average television set is on more than 7 hours a day. In fact, the average high school graduate will have watched up to 20,000 hours of TV (much more time than in the classroom) (Kaye, 1979). Have you thought about what life would be like without TV? Can you imagine family members having to talk to each rather than watching TV? In some homes, family members each have their own TV and often watch the same program by themselves. There have been many investigations of television's effects on young people (see Liebert & Sprafkin, 1988, for a comprehensive review of these studies). The research to date indicates that TV violence is *a* cause of aggressiveness and that parents need to monitor their children's viewing behavior; young children do not understand the purpose of advertising and are, therefore, especially vulnerable to its appeals; there is a great deal of stereotyping of minorities, women, and the elderly. On the positive side, programs can teach important academic skills (e.g., *Sesame Street*) and important **prosocial behaviors** (e.g., *Mr. Rogers' Neighborhood*), such as generosity, helping, cooperation, and self-control (Hearold, 1986).

Can you identify some of the social behaviors or attitudes you developed from watching television? Did your parents place any restrictions on your viewing? The following Classroom Application (quoted from Berns, 1989, p. 296) can serve as a guide for your discussions with parents as they consider how they should deal with their children's television viewing.

## CLASSROOM APPLICATION: HELPING PARENTS MONITOR THEIR CHILDREN'S TELEVISION VIEWING

**Know what your children watch and when**

A log of how much time in front of the tube will often speak for itself about whether TV is playing too large a role in their lives.

Be alert to the content of the program as well as the commercials. Notice ways in which viewing affects your children's behavior. Do they become transfixed after watching for a while? Or does viewing make them tense and lead to fighting? What effects does it have on family communication when you all watch together?

How are ethnic groups, sex roles, age groups presented? How are conflicts resolved?

**Choose what to watch**

Don't leave watching to chance—you wouldn't put a refrigerator in your children's rooms and allow them to eat what they wanted on the chance they would eventually meet their nutritional requirements. Learn to turn off the set when your choice is over.

**Set limits**

Talking over a set of guidelines with family members, agreeing upon them, and sticking to them is effective in establishing a new routine for viewing TV. For example, your family may choose to ban TV during dinner, to allow viewing only after other responsibilities (homework, chores) have been done, or to allow each family member to have a choice of selecting a program each week.

Help children choose activities to do when the TV is off (read a book, draw a picture, play a game).

**Whenever possible, view with children**

When watching with young children, point out what is real and what is fantasy.

When values presented on TV conflict with your family values, say so! When values agree, say so too!

- Discuss the differences between fantasy and reality.
- Discuss conflict situations and how problems could be solved without violence.
- Discuss situations involving cooperation and note behaviors your child might imitate.
- Point out characters who represent a variety of ethnic groups.
- Point out men/women who represent a variety of occupations.
- Discuss food advertisements in terms of what is healthy and nutritious.
- Discuss toy advertisements in terms of play potential, safety, and age appropriateness.

**Use the time in front of TV to benefit the child**

Television can be a rich source of vocabulary development. Explain new words to children.

Television can expand a child's horizons. Talk about other places in the world, other cultures, new experiences.

Television programs can stimulate reading of related material, if the child is encouraged.

Television can stimulate discussions on sensitive topics by older children—such as drugs, rape, teenage pregnancy—and thus may provide the opportunity for parents to discuss such topics.

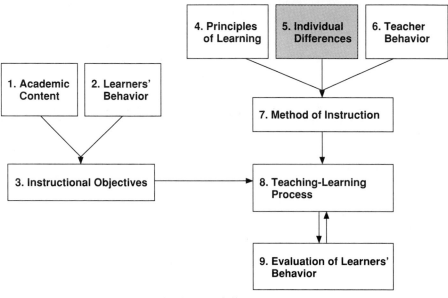

*Source: Adapted from Hunter, 1971, in Allen and Seifman.*

In this chapter I have discussed a number of personal and social factors that are likely to influence students' interaction with teachers (box No. 5 and box No. 6) and their involvement in academic tasks. These characteristics will influence your decision making in determining how you can best facilitate learning (box No. 7).

You will learn in Chapter 10 (Motivation) the importance of a student's self-concept of ability. This self-perception greatly influences the student's selection of academic tasks, persistence, and willingness to try different learning strategies to succeed. Teachers must strive to develop a positive self-concept of academic ability among their students. Despite beliefs to the contrary, failure has little or no effect on motivating low-achieving students.

Consider how students from different cultural groups may think about the roles of males and females. Remember that some cultural groups have traditional patterns of expectations for males and females that may be contrary to what you might teach in class. Also, parents of different cultural groups have different goals of parenting and child rearing. In some families, children are not to question their parents' authority. Parents from immigrant groups often have difficulty raising their children when they exhibit behavior accepted by the dominant cultural group but considered inappropriate by the standards of the immigrant group. How does the teacher mediate problems between parent and child under such circumstances?

Before you leave this chapter, I would like you to think about possible organizational and instructional decisions that you might make using your knowledge of students' cognitive, personality, and social differences. A good exercise would be to make your own list of educational implications under each of the topics discussed in Chapters 2, 3, and 5.

## KEY POINTS

1. Erikson has identified eight major psychosocial crises that individuals experience over a life span.
2. Teachers can play an important role in helping students to develop a sense of initiative and industry.
3. There is little evidence to support any argument for innate differences between gender in the cognitive and social areas.
4. Socialization experiences appear to account for most differences in performance among males and females.
5. Classroom practices can contribute to sex-role stereotyping.
6. Individuals' self-concepts embody the ideas they have about themselves and the value they place on their behavior.
7. The self concept is organized, multifaceted, hierarchical, stable, developmental, and evaluative.
8. It is incorrect to assume that students from poverty backgrounds have poor self-concepts.
9. It is more useful to refer to specific types of self-concept than to general self-concept.
10. Special programs designed to change self-concept generally have not been successful.
11. Students with negative beliefs and feelings about themselves are likely to be underachievers or failures in school.
12. The transition from elementary to junior high school can be particularly stressful for some females.
13. The rate of physical development can influence students' self-concepts of physical appearance.
14. A description of parenting styles includes the authoritarian, permissive, and authoritative parent.
15. Parenting styles influence different social/personality development of children.
16. Teachers have a legal responsibility to report suspected cases of child abuse.
17. Teachers should avoid situations in which they can be falsely accused of unprofessional conduct.
18. Stress can have a detrimental effect on an individual's health.
19. Teachers should be alert to the warning signs of an impending suicide.

20. In general, there is no evidence that maternal employment has any detrimental effect on children, assuming the mother wants to work and receives the necessary support while working.
21. Divorce takes its toll on all children and may have delayed effects on adolescents.
22. Children's adjustment to divorce depends on such factors as age at the time of divorce, personality, degree of parental conflict, the family's economic situation, and relationship with custodial parent.
23. Boys generally have a more difficult time adjusting to divorce than girls.
24. Latchkey children tend to be at a higher risk for substance abuse, report more fear and anxiety, and have more academic and social problems than children who are supervised after school.

## KEY TERMS

psychosocial crises, p. 119
psychosocial moratorium, p. 122
identity diffusion, p. 123
identity moratorium, p. 123
identity foreclosure, p. 124
identity achievement, p. 124
androgyny, p. 129
self-concept, p. 138
self-esteem, p. 138
self-fulfilling prophecy, p. 142
anorexia nervosa, p. 143
puberty, p. 144
authoritarian parenting style, p. 146
permissive parenting style, p. 146
authoritative parenting style, p. 146
stress, p. 150
anxiety, p. 150
latchkey children, p. 157
prosocial behavior, p. 158

## SUGGESTIONS FOR FURTHER READING

Emery, R. E. (1988). *Marriage, divorce, and children's adjustment* (Vol. 14). Newbury Park, CA: Sage. A helpful review of literature on family transition.

Grusec, J. E., & Lytton, H. (1988). *Social development: History, theory, and research.* New York: Springer-Verlag. Provides excellent discussions of family socialization, prosocial behavior, and divorce.

Hamner, T. J., & Turner, P. H. (1985). *Parenting in contemporary society.* Englewood

Cliffs, NJ: Prentice-Hall. A comprehensive review of parenting techniques, family variations, and support systems for parents.

The following books focus on the role of self-concept in school achievement:

Beane, J. A., & Lipka, R. P. (1986). *Self-concept, self-esteem, and the curriculum.* New York: Teachers College Press. Shows how curriculum planning can lead to improved self-perceptions.

Canfield, J., & Wells, H. C. (1976). *100 ways to enhance self-concept in the classroom.* Englewood Cliffs, NJ: Prentice-Hall.

Hamachek, D. (1978). *Encounters with the self* (2nd ed.). New York: Holt, Rinehart and Winston. Discusses the many factors influencing an individual's self-concept.

For more information on the treatment of male and female students in school:

Sadker, M., & Sadker, D. (1986). Sexism in the classroom: From grade school to graduate school. *Phi Delta Kappan, 67,* 512–515. Reviews classroom research on teacher interaction with males and females.

Shapiro, J., Kramer, S., & Hunerberg, C. (1981). *Equal their chances: Children's activities for non-sexist learning.* Englewood Cliffs, NJ: Prentice-Hall. A good reference for making changes in the treatment of male and female students.

The following references deal with student stress:

Blom, G. E., Cheney, B., & Snoddy, J. E. (1986). *Stress in childhood: An intervention model for teachers and other professionals.* New York: Teachers College Press. Provides an intervention model that can be applied in school.

Humphrey, J. H., & Humphrey, J. N. (1981). *Reducing stress in children through creative relaxation.* Springfield, IL: Thomas.

Humphrey, J. H., & Humphrey, J. N. (1985). *Controlling stress in children.* Springfield, IL: Thomas.

Kuczen, B. (1982). *Childhood stress: Don't let your child be a victim.* New York: Delacorte Press.

The following work is on child abuse:

Brassard, M. R., Germain, R., & Hart, S. N. (Eds.). (1987). *Psychological maltreatment of children and youth.* New York: Pergamon Press. Focuses on various forms of physical and psychological mistreatment of children.

## FOLLOW-UP ACTIVITIES

### 1. Debate Gender Differences in Behavior

Read some books and articles on sex-role behavior. Decide which of the following positions (Gall & Ward, 1974) is closest to your point of view on sex-linked differences in behavior and defend your position:

    a. Everyone, whether male or female, should have an opportunity to develop full intellectual potential. Teachers and others should strive to eliminate traditional sex-role stereotypes, because these biases influence what is learned by boys and girls, and thus prevent them from reaching their full potential.

b. Many differences in the behavior of boys and girls are desirable. They should not be eliminated even if it means some individuals will not achieve their full potential. For example, achievement of a woman's full intellectual potential may not be desirable if it, in turn, necessitates the loss of her sensitivity to others. (p. 263)

## 2. Analyze Texts for Sex Stereotyping

A number of studies have uncovered sex stereotyping between the covers of books used in public schools. For example, the authors often depict boys as ingenious, creative, brave, and adventurous and depict girls as lonely, frightened, and poorly motivated.

Examine at random three books used at the elementary level in a local school or in the curriculum materials section of your college library. Ask a class member of the opposite sex to examine the same books and record the titles and grade levels of the books. Indicate the number of times males and females are the central characters and put a tally mark next to the words listed below that you feel reflect the behavior of characters portrayed in the texts. Include some direct quotes or situations that illustrate sex stereotyping (Biehler, 1974).

**Males**                                                          **Females**

Number of main characters
Adventurous
Ambitious
Creative
Dependent
Engaged in home chores
Engaged in important,
   exciting work
Helpless
Self-confident

What conclusions do you draw from your analysis?

## 3. Learn about Child-Rearing Methods

Read one of the following books on child rearing: *P.E.T.: Parent Effectiveness Training* (Gordon, 1975); *Children: The Challenge* (Dreikurs & Soltz, 1964); *Systematic Training for Effective Parenting* (Dinkmeyer & McKay, 1976); or *Living with Children* (Patterson & Guillion, 1971). Summarize the major ideas in the book and report how they can be helpful to parents.

# CHAPTER 5

# Exceptional Children

A sizable group of students possesses individual differences that require special types of education. At one time, classroom teachers had little to do with handicapped children because they were rarely included in the regular classroom. Instead, they were educated, if at all, by special education teachers in self-contained classrooms or residential schools separated from their nonhandicapped or nonexceptional peers.

A federal law passed in 1975, the **Education for All Handicapped Children Act (P.L. 94-142)** mandated many changes in the education of exceptional students. These changes require that such students have the right to due process, protection against discriminatory testing in diagnosis, individualized program plans, and placement in an educational setting that is the least restrictive environment.

The concept of **least restrictive educational environment** has especially important implications for the classroom teacher because it implies that handicapped children should be educated with their nonhandicapped peers in regular settings whenever possible. As a result, it is not uncommon to observe a student who is mentally retarded, learning disabled, or visually impaired in a regular classroom for all or part of the day. It is now essential for all teachers to acquire knowledge about exceptional children.

Three terms—**exceptional, disabled,** and **handicapped**—are widely used by educators to identify children who need special educational services. *Exceptional* refers to any student whose performance significantly departs from the average or typical student, either below or above, to such an extent that special education is needed. As a result, the exceptional student includes both the intellectually gifted and the severely retarded. *Disability* (or impairment) is a particular condition that limits a student's functioning in certain tasks (e.g., visual, motor, or auditory). *Handicap* refers to the difficulties that an individual who is disabled faces because of possible limitations encountered in the interaction with the environment. *Handicapped* is a more restrictive term than *exceptional* and does not include the intellectually gifted (Heward & Orlansky, 1988).

It is important to remember that a disabled person can be handicapped in one situation but not another. For example, a person in a wheelchair is not handicapped when participating in a debate tournament but is handicapped when encountering a flight of stairs that must be ascended.

Most special educators classify exceptional students as falling into one or more of the following categories:

1. Mental retardation
2. Learning disabilities
3. Behavior disorders (emotional disturbances)
4. Communication (speech and language) disorders
5. Hearing impairments
6. Visual impairments

7. Physical and other health impairments
8. Severe and multiple handicaps
9. Gifted and talented

The purpose of special education is to develop educational programs to help exceptional children to achieve the greatest possible self-sufficiency and academic success—goals that are appropriate for all students (Heward & Orlansky, 1988).

Before you start reading this chapter, you should be aware of a number of points: First, books and journal articles are available for all categories of special education. This chapter does not attempt to provide all the information you will need to know about a particular student. It will provide you with a good foundation on which to build your knowledge concerning exceptional children. Second, although areas in special education are discussed separately for clarity, many children have multiple handicaps and must be dealt with accordingly. Third, exceptional children represent a heterogeneous group. For example, even though two children may be identified as mentally retarded, they will differ as much as two of their non-handicapped peers. Students with a similar handicap have individual personalities, interests, and educational needs. Fourth, the limitations resulting from a handicap can be lessened by positive interaction and assistance from teachers and peers. As a teacher, you can greatly influence the quality of your students' educational and social experiences. Don't underestimate your impact! Fifth, think about your past and present experiences with handicapped individuals. Were these experiences positive? Have you been in situations that you found uncomfortable? Why? How do you feel about teaching exceptional children?

After you master the material in this chapter, you will be able to:

- Identify students who may need special education assistance.
- Identify the legal requirements and issues in special education.
- Identify the teacher's role in referral, assessment, and placement procedures.
- Implement intervention strategies that can help exceptional students succeed in the regular classroom.

## FOCUS QUESTIONS

1. What are the advantages and disadvantages of special education labels?
2. What are the issues involving the identification of learning disabled and mentally retarded children?
3. What factors differentiate a student who is a low achiever from a student who is mentally retarded or learning disabled?
4. What are the behavioral characteristics indicating that a student should be assessed for possible special education in the following areas: be-

havior disorders, hearing impairment, visual impairment, and communication disorder?

5. What are the advantages and disadvantages of educating exceptional students in and outside the regular classroom?

6. What are the important issues and concerns of parents of special education students?

7. In what ways can a teacher assist special education students to maximize both their academic and social behavior in the classroom?

## EXCEPTIONAL CHILDREN—AN OVERVIEW

It is difficult to determine exactly how many handicapped children there are among the estimated 40 million students enrolled in United States public schools (preschool through grade 12). The *Eleventh Annual Report to Congress on the Implementation of the Education of the Handicapped Act* (U.S. Department of Education, 1989) presents data on the percentage and number of students *enrolled* in special education in 1986 to 1987 (see Table 5.1). Of the 4,127,568 served in various school programs, the largest number were classified as learning disabled (47%), followed by speech or language impaired (23.2%).

The report, however, contains no estimates of the total number of handicapped children in the United States. Educators and government officials often debate whether all or nearly all handicapped students are being served by special education programs. Recent data indicate that the number of students identified as learning disabled has increased every academic year since 1976–1977, when the federal government first required states to count their special education students in order to receive federal

### TABLE 5.1  NUMBER OF HANDICAPPED CHILDREN BY EXCEPTIONALITY

| Exceptionality | Percentage Enrolled in Special Education | Number Enrolled in Special Education |
|---|---|---|
| Learning disabled | 47.0 | 1,941,731 |
| Speech or language impaired | 23.2 | 956,140 |
| Mentally retarded | 14.6 | 601,288 |
| Behavior disordered | 9.1 | 374,730 |
| Multihandicapped | 1.9 | 79,132 |
| Hard of hearing and deaf | 1.4 | 56,937 |
| Orthopedically impaired | 1.1 | 47,409 |
| Other health impaired | 1.1 | 45,865 |
| Visually handicapped | 0.6 | 22,864 |
| Deaf-blind | 0.0 | 1,472 |
| Total | 100.0 | 4,127,568 |

*Source: U.S. Department of Education, 1989.*

financial assistance. Some educators believe this steady increase is caused by inaccurate assessment that leads to overplacement, whereas others believe that students with handicaps other than learning disabilities are being placed in the wrong category. For example, a decreasing number of children are being identified as mentally retarded, a fact that may be related to the increase in the identification of learning disabled children (*Education of the Handicapped*, 1986). On the other hand, many special educators believe that social influences since the 1970s, such as the breakup of the family unit and the use of drugs by parents, may contribute to the *actual* increase in learning disabilities found in children.

One of the major debates in special education involves the pros and cons of using categories, or labels, to distinguish one type, or group, of students from another. Some educators argue that a system of classification is needed in order to provide the special education services to meet the students' unique needs in the classroom, to educate teachers and give them the necessary skills to maximize the achievement of students with various handicapping conditions, and to document the prevalence of specific disabilities to guarantee continued funding for special educational programs. For example, the federal government has spent as much as $1 billion a year for special education. Unless categories are established to determine who should get these funds, there could be a decrease in the support for special education. Other educators believe that the labels are not helpful in providing educational services for students and, in fact, may be detrimental for some.

## Labeling: Pro and Con

**What are the advantages and disadvantages of special education labels?**

Heward and Orlansky (1988) provide a comprehensive list of the arguments raised for and against the classification of exceptional children. As you read about different types of exceptional children, think about whether the benefits of labeling outweigh the disadvantages.

### Possible Benefits of Labeling

1. Categories can relate diagnosis to specific treatment.
2. Labeling may lead to a "protective" response, in which nonlabeled children accept certain behaviors of their handicapped peers more fully than they would accept those same behaviors in "normal" children.
3. Labeling helps professionals to communicate with one another and to classify and assess research findings.
4. Funding of special education programs is often based on specific categories of exceptionality.
5. Labels allow special interest groups to promote specific programs and spur legislative action.
6. Labeling helps make the special needs of exceptional children more visible in the public eye.

### Possible Disadvantages of Labeling

1. Labels usually focus on negative aspects of the child, causing others to think about the child only in terms of inadequacies or defects.
2. Labels may cause others to react to and hold expectations for a child based on the label, resulting in a self-fulfilling prophecy (see Chapter 10 for information on the way this process operates).
3. Labels that describe a child's performance deficit often mistakenly acquire the role of explanatory constructs (e.g., "Sherry acts that way *because* she is emotionally disturbed").
4. Labels used to classify children in special education emphasize that learning problems are primarily the result of something wrong within the child, thereby reducing the likelihood of examining instructional variables as the cause of performance deficits.
5. A labeled child may develop a poor self-concept.
6. Labels may lead peers to reject or ridicule the labeled child.
7. Special education labels have a certain permanency about them. Once labeled as "retarded," "learning disabled," it is difficult for a child ever again to achieve the status of being "just like all the other kids."
8. Labels often provide a basis for keeping children out of the regular classroom.
9. A disproportionate number of children from minority culture groups have been inaccurately labeled as handicapped, especially as educably mentally retarded.
10. The classification of exceptional children requires the expenditure of a great amount of professional and student time that could better be spent in planning and delivering instruction. (p. 11)

## CATEGORIES IN SPECIAL EDUCATION

In this section I briefly discuss the various categories of exceptional children. Each category includes a definition, methods of classification, characteristics and etiology (causes) of the handicap, and some suggestions for the regular classroom teacher for helping the student. As you read this section, keep in mind that in some categories identification and diagnosis is not always clear-cut (especially in the areas of mental retardation, learning disability, and behavior disorders) and that each category of exceptionality is not necessarily independent. For example, the child with a hearing impairment may also exhibit a learning disability and/or a behavior disorder, making it difficult to sort out a specific causality and making it necessary to employ a wide variety of intervention strategies. Thus, educating exceptional students requires much more that identifying the correct label and providing a prescribed intervention.

## Mental Retardation

The American Association of Mental Deficiency (AAMD) defines *mental retardation* as follows (Grossman, 1983):

> Mental retardation refers to significantly subaverage general intellectual functioning resulting in or associated with concurrent impairment in adaptive behavior, and manifested during the developmental period. (p. 11)

This definition includes two important characteristics—*below average intellectual functioning* and *deficits in adaptive behavior* (i.e., how one deals with the demands of one's environment). Both criteria must be met for a child to be labeled mentally retarded. This definition attempts to protect individuals from improper diagnosis and labeling.

In the past, many children (especially from minority groups) were identified as retarded inside the school but were functioning very effectively outside the school (i.e., the students were not deficient in adaptive behavior skills) (Landesman & Ramey, 1989). This condition led the President's Committee on Mental Retardation to entitle its 1970 report *The Six Hour Retarded Child.* Many individuals, such as sociologist Jane Mercer (1973), believe that it is the individual's social system that determines whether the person is considered retarded. Remember the discussion in Chapter 2 regarding the large number of black and Hispanic students that Mercer found in special education classes in Riverside, California. Many educators don't realize that "mental retardation is an arbitrarily defined diagnostic category." . . . [and the] actual practices used to identify children with mental retardation vary dramatically across states and school districts" (Landesman & Ramsey, 1989, p. 409).

The research by Mercer and others has focused more attention on cultural diversity in special education. According to Kamp and Chinn (1982), about one-third of the entire population of special education students in the United States consists of students from diverse cultural groups. Educators have a responsibility to ensure that culturally diverse students receive a fair assessment of their ability and that instruction be sensitive to their cultural background.

The words "significantly subaverage general intellectual functioning" in the AAMD's definition usually refer to performance on an individually administered standardized test of intelligence. This level of functioning is generally defined as an IQ of 70 or below. However, this upper limit is intended only as a guideline and can be raised according to the type of test used or if a psychologist determines that an individual's deficits in living in the environment are caused by impaired intellectual functioning. The AAMD distinguishes the severity of retardation as mild, moderate, severe, or profound. Mildly retarded children and adolescents are sometimes referred to by educators as **educable mentally retarded (EMR).** The majority of students who are mentally retarded are identified in the mild category and can become independent and learn to read, write, and use basic mathematics.

An important aspect of the mental retardation definition is that it recognizes the influence of adaptive behavior. A person may score low on an intelligence test but have adequate adaptive ability. These behaviors are age- and situation-specific (e.g., eating, toilet use, money handling, shopping skills, and language development). Many adaptive behavior scales have been developed; two commonly used scales are the AAMD Adaptive Behavior Scale and the Vineland Social Maturity Scale. Mercer (Mercer & Lewis, 1978) has developed a comprehensive system designed to evaluate the current level of functioning and the potential of children from various cultures. The System of Multi-Cultural Pluralistic Assessment (SOMPA) is especially useful in identifying the potential for learning of students who may not have had the opportunities to learn the skills measured by individual tests of intelligence. The SOMPA includes a measure of intelligence, but its interpretation is based on the students' cultural background.

In most cases of mild retardation, the causes are unknown. However, psychologists believe that the combination of poor social and cultural environment early in a person's life may lead to retarded development. Psychologists are particularly interested in studying the impact of diet and certain prenatal influences such as drugs, alcohol, and smoking on fetal abnormalities and intellectual development.

There are many known causes of moderate, severe, and profound retardation. The AAMD has identified the following categories: infections, trauma, and physical agents (such as accidents before, during, and after birth), metabolism and nutrition, and gross brain disease (such as tumors). An example of an infection that can cause retardation is rubella, or German measles. When contracted by a woman during the first three months of pregnancy, it may cause visual impairments, hearing impairments, mental retardation, and/or other birth defects in her child. Additional categories include prenatal influence (such as hydrocephalus, a condition involving an enlarged head caused by accumulated cerebrospinal fluid), chromosomal abnormality (such as Down syndrome[1]), and gestational disorders (such as premature birth) (Heward & Orlansky, 1988).

The most common characteristics that you may notice with students classified as having varying degrees of mental retardation are social and academic learning problems. They need more practice and experience than others of the same age to retain information previously learned, to generalize or transfer recently learned skills to new situations, to learn language, and to develop self-care skills and peer interactions. They often display immature and inappropriate classroom behavior and often are subjected to teasing and isolation by their nonhandicapped peers. The teacher

---

[1] *Down syndrome* (sometimes called *mongolism*) is a condition resulting from a chromosomal abnormality characterized by such physical signs as slanted-appearing eyes, flattened features, shortness, and a tendency toward obesity.

must be aware that because of the history of failure that many of these children experience, they tend to become overly dependent upon others to tell them what to do, or may develop a general reluctance to engage in new learning situations. As with other handicaps, mental retardation may co-occur with any number of additional handicaps, such as hearing, visual, or motor deficits.

Hallahan and Kauffman (1988) provide a number of suggestions for the regular teacher who may have students with mental retardation in the classroom:

1. Separate learning tasks into small steps, sequence them in the proper order, and teach one skill at a time (see the discussion of task analysis in Chapter 9).
2. Use drill and repetition.
3. Ask the students to rehearse orally what they learn. This procedure will help their memory.
4. Use different motivational strategies. Novelty in presenting lessons is a good strategy, but too much change can be confusing to students who are mentally retarded because they need a sense of structure and familiarity.
5. Use consistent reinforcement, especially in the development of learning skills (e.g., working independently and completing assignments).
6. Assess the students' progress on a regular basis so that changes in objectives and/or instruction can be made.
7. Provide continuous and immediate feedback for all learning activities.

## Learning Disabilities

There is much controversy in the area of **learning disabilities** about the identification of its population, primarily because the term *learning disability* is not a unitary concept and does not represent a homogeneous population. The Education for All Handicapped Children Act (P.L. 94-142) includes the following definition:

> "Specific learning disability" means a disorder in one or more of the basic psychological processes involved in understanding or in using language, spoken or written, which may manifest itself in an imperfect ability to listen, think, speak, read, write, spell, or to do mathematical calculations. The term includes such conditions as perceptual handicaps, brain injury, minimal brain dysfunction, dyslexia, and developmental aphasia.[2] The term does not include children who have learning problems which are primarily the result of visual, hearing, or motor handicaps, of mental

---

[2] *Dyslexia* is an impairment of the ability to read. *Aphasia* is the loss or impairment of the ability to understand or formulate language and is caused by neurological damage.

retardation, or of environmental, cultural, or economic disadvantages. (*Federal Register*, December 29, 1977, p. 65083)

**What are the issues involving the identification of learning disabled and mentally retarded children?**

Chalfant (1989) identifies five terms in use nationally to define this population of children experiencing school learning problems: *learning disabled, learning disabilities, specific learning disabilities, perceptually impaired,* and *perceptual communication disorders.* He also notes that the criteria for classification to receive special education services under this category vary from state to state. Most states require that two to five of the following criteria be met: a task failure component, an exclusion factor component, an etiological component, a discrepancy component, and a psychological process component. Like the area of mental retardation, a student can be labeled learning disabled in one state but not in another.

The *task failure criterion* identifies children as having a learning disability if, in spite of all normal efforts by the teacher in the regular education program to provide a variety of instructional opportunities and strategies, they still demonstrate learning problems. The *etiological criterion* limits the label *learning disability* to those children whose learning problems are not explained by other diagnostic categories (e.g., mental retardation or visual impairment) or by a social and/or environmental deprivation causing a lack of opportunity to learn. The *psychological process criterion* focuses on dysfunctions in one or more of the psychological processes, such as attention, memory, or perceptual-motor abilities. The *discrepancy criterion* attempts to protect against misidentifying children as having a specific learning disability. For example, if a child has a minor or temporary problem in learning a mathematical concept, the child should not be labeled as having a learning disability. However, if the child consistently functions significantly below the expected level of achievement and his or her academic potential is at least average, he or she may have a learning disability.

Even with these definitions there is confusion. For example, what constitutes a discrepancy between intellectual potential and academic achievement—one year or two years or more below grade level? Is a one-year discrepancy at the third grade the same as at the eighth grade? What about preschoolers or first graders who have learning problems but the comparison of intelligence and achievement tests indicates that the students are only slightly below expected achievement levels? Based on this criterion, they would not receive special services until they "qualify" by falling further behind their classmates. Also, in states where the psychological processing dysfunction is used as a criterion, there is little consensus as to which psychological processes should be considered and few accurate instruments for measuring process dysfunctions (Chalfant, 1989).

The literature identifies many characteristics of learning disabled children. Tarver and Hallahan (1976) list the 10 most often cited traits:

1. Hyperactivity
2. Perceptual-motor impairments

3. Emotional lability (ups and down, moodiness)
4. General coordination deficits
5. Attentional disorders (distractibility)
6. Impulsivity
7. Memory and thinking disorders
8. Specific academic problems
9. Speech and hearing disorders
10. Equivocal neurological signs (e.g., abnormal brain wave patterns that are difficult to explain or interpret) (p. 13)

**What factors differentiate a student who is a low achiever from a student who is mentally retarded or learning disabled?**

A child *may be* identified as having a learning disability if the child exhibits one or more of the foregoing characteristics. The key determiner is whether or not he or she meets the specific criteria designated by the state or local school district. Table 5.2 identifies specific classroom behaviors that the teacher should be concerned about. Again, it is important to note that if a child possesses any of the identified characteristics but is achieving normally in school, the child would not be considered learning disabled.

TABLE 5.2 WAYS TO RECOGNIZE A LEARNING DISABLED STUDENT

| Classroom Behavior | Spelling |
|---|---|
| Moves constantly | Uses incorrect order of letters in words |
| Has difficulty beginning or completing tasks | Has difficulty associating correct sound with appropriate letter |
| Is often tardy or absent | Reverses letters and words (mirror image) |
| Is generally quiet or withdrawn | |
| Has difficult with peer relationships | *Writing* |
| Is disorganized | Cannot stay on line |
| Is easily distracted | Has difficulty copying from board or other source |
| Displays inconsistencies in behavior | Uses poor written expression for age |
| Seems to misunderstand oral directions | Is slow in completing written work |
| | Uses cursive writing and printing in same assignment |
| **Academic Symptoms** | |
| *Reading* | *Verbal* |
| Loses place, repeats words | Hesitates often when speaking |
| Does not read fluently | Has poor verbal expression for age |
| Confuses similar words and letters | |
| Uses fingers to follow along | *Motor* |
| Does not read willingly | Displays poor coordination |
| *Arithmetic* | Has problems of balance |
| Has difficulty associating number with symbol | Confuses right and left |
| Cannot remember math facts | Lacks rhythm in movement |
| Confuses columns and spacing | Has poor muscle strength |
| Has difficulty with story problems | |
| Fails to comprehend math concepts | |

*Source: Summers, 1977.*

The suspected causes of learning disabilities fall into three major categories: minimal brain damage, biochemical imbalance, and environmental factors (Heward & Orlansky, 1988). Some specialists (particularly in the medical profession) believe that learning disabled children suffer from some form of brain injury. Because the injury is not extensive enough to cause serious intellectual impairment (i.e., mental retardation), the term **minimal brain damage** is used in discussing learning disabled children. Special educators do not like this label because it is misleading. First, the problems faced by many students with learning disabilities are far from small. Second, the label conveys little hope for improved learning through effective intervention strategies. Finally, there is a lack of clear evidence to support brain damage as a cause for all learning disabilities. Research studies have identified children with brain damage who are not learning disabled and learning disabled children who do not display clinical (medical) evidence of brain damage ( Coles, 1978; Nichols & Chen, 1981).

Some specialists claim that biochemical disturbances within children lead to learning disabilities. Feingold (1975a, 1975b) has received a good deal of publicity regarding his claims that hyperactivity and learning problems are caused by artificial colorings and flavoring in many of the foods children eat. He claims that placing hyperactive children on special diets will bring about a change in behavior. In a similar vein, Cott (1972) hypothesized that learning disability can be caused by a vitamin deficiency. Many physicians supporting this contention began megavitamin therapy with learning disabled children. This therapy involves massive daily doses of certain vitamins to overcome the suspected deficiencies. Research investigations on food additives (Kavale & Forness, 1983) and vitamin deficiency (Kershner, Hawks, & Grekin, 1977) have failed to show that such specific corrective actions improve the performance of learning disabled children.

Another group of specialists believe that the quality of instruction and the student's emotional and motivational state greatly influence academic performance (e.g., Engelmann, 1977; Lovitt, 1978). These researchers think that the best way to help students with learning disabilities is to focus on the specific deficiencies in reading, math, or language that are causing the academic problems.

There are several approaches to planning educational programs for learning disabled students. A complete discussion of these techniques is beyond the scope of this book. For the most part, these approaches are related to the specialist's belief in the causes of the disability and the student's specific problem. For example, educators who believe that the learning problem is caused by dysfunctional psychological processes would provide training in these areas. Thus a student believed to have reading problems because of difficulties in visual perception would receive training in visual perception rather than in reading techniques (see Lerner, 1984, for a discussion of these methods). Don't confuse perceptual problems with visual acuity problems, which will be discussed later in this chapter. A child may have 20/20 vision but have difficulty in organizing and interpreting visual stimuli. Likewise, a child may have normal hearing (acuity) but still have a problem with interpreting or discriminating sounds (auditory perception).

Today, many educators are taking a more direct approach in working with students with learning disabilities. That is to say, rather than training psychological processes that are linked to learning, they emphasize techniques that are directly related to learning subject matter. Behavioral psychologists (see Chapter 6) focus on breaking subject matter into small steps and carefully teaching the prerequisite knowledge necessary for learning. Cognitive psychologists (see Chapter 7) emphasize techniques based on information processing. This approach stresses learning strategies to teach students "how to learn." One example of such a program for secondary learning disabled students is the Learning Strategies Curriculum (Schumaker et al., 1983; Schumaker, Deshler, & Ellis, 1986). It emphasizes strategies for acquiring information from written material, teaching students techniques for remembering information, and methods for improving written expression.

Current research indicates that techniques that stress careful instruction in the academic areas and the information processing approaches tend to be more successful than the earlier indirect approaches that attempted to train students in the dysfunctional process interfering with learning

Special equipment is available to help students improve their listening skills.

(Lloyd, 1988). These new programs offer considerable assistance for helping students with learning disabilities become successful learners.

The classroom teacher needs to keep in mind a number of special considerations when working with learning disabled students (Hallahan & Kauffman, 1988):

1. Set reasonable goals. Because some students may have a relatively high IQ, you may assume they can do more than they are actually capable of doing. Since students with learning disabilities often find it difficult to tolerate failure, find opportunities for them to experience success.

2. Provide clear instructions for the students and assume that your directions may not be understood. Be aware that students with learning disabilities often look as if they understand what is being said, when in fact they are confused.

3. Make special physical arrangements for the highly distractible and hyperactive student (e.g., place the student's desk in a corner or use walls to form a "cubicle"). (The teacher must be sure to communicate to the student and parents that these procedures are not punitive.) Also, to reduce overstimulation, remove extraneous materials from the student's desk so that the student can concentrate on the immediate task.

4. Be prepared for emotional outbursts by learning disabled students; set guidelines for appropriate classroom behavior and help the students work toward them.

## Behavior Disorders

**What are the behavioral characteristics indicating that a student should be assessed for possible special education in the following areas: behavior disorders, hearing impairment, visual impairment, and communication disorder?**

Many labels are used as general terms for emotional and behavior problems (e.g., *emotionally disturbed, behavior disorders, socially maladjusted, emotionally handicapped, psychologically disordered*).

"Seriously emotionally disturbed" was the term used when P.L. 94-142 was passed. However, many special educators prefer the term **behavior disordered** because it focuses attention on the most obvious problem of these children—disordered behavior (Hallahan & Kauffman, 1988). Although there are many definitions and classification procedures to identify these individuals, P.L. 94-142 uses the following:

(i) The term means a condition exhibiting one or more of the following characteristics over a long period of time and to a marked extent, which adversely affects educational performance:
  (A) An inability to learn which cannot be explained by intellectual, sensory, and health factors;
  (B) An inability to build or maintain satisfactory relationships with peers and teachers;
  (C) Inappropriate types of behavior or feelings under normal circumstances;

(D) A general pervasive mood of unhappiness or depression;

(E) A tendency to develop physical symptoms or fears associated with personal or school problems. (*Federal Register*, August 23, 1977, p. 42478)

Behavior displayed by behavior-disordered students is characterized by *excesses* and *deficits* (Whelan & Gallagher, 1972). Behavior excesses are outcomes that are exhibited to a great extent (e.g., too many fights or tantrums). Deficits are behaviors that are exhibited very infrequently or not at all (e.g., few social contacts or homework assignments not completed). The problem in diagnosis is that it is not always easy to determine when a behavior is excessive or when there is a deficit in behavior.

Many teachers are most concerned with behavioral excesses. However, lack of interest, laziness, daydreaming, and general passivity can be more serious problems. It is important for the teacher not to neglect the polite, shy student who never says anything in class or appears withdrawn. That student may need help.

Students with behavior disorders are usually identified first by the classroom teacher, followed by direct classroom observation of the behavior by a school psychologist. Personality tests are used frequently in the diagnosis and classification process. Teachers are not always correct in their initial identification. Kelly, Bullock, and Dykes (1977), in a study of teachers' perceptions of behavioral disorders in their classrooms, found that regular classroom teachers nominated about 20% of their students as exhibiting mild to severe behavior disorders.

You may be interested in some other data regarding the prevalence of behavior disorders in school. First, more boys than girls are labeled as behavior-disordered. Second, more low-socioeconomic and minority-group students are classified as behavior-disordered. Third, most behavior-disordered students have academic problems (note that part [A] of the behavior disorders definition could also apply to a student with learning disabilities) (Smith, Wood, & Grimes, 1988).

The suggested causes of behavior disorders are many. However, parent-child, teacher-child, and school-child interactions have been identified as important determinants of behavioral problems. Also, some psychologists believe that inborn temperament may predispose some students to problems (Heward & Orlansky, 1988).

Many educational strategies for behavior-disordered children have been developed. Nelson and Rutherford (1988) and Carpenter and Apter (1988) provide a detailed explanation of these procedures. Most schools use a variety of approaches such as behavior modification (see Chapter 6), individual and group counseling, and humanistic school climates (see Chapter 8) for students who have difficulty functioning in traditional educational settings.

Hallahan and Kauffman (1988) provide helpful information for regular classroom teachers who have behavior-disordered students:

1. Ask the special education teacher for advice concerning behavior management and teaching techniques.
2. Let the students know from the beginning that you expect a reasonable standard of conduct to be maintained in the classroom.
3. Communicate your expectations to the students clearly and firmly.
4. Provide consistent and appropriate consequences for behavior. Reward desirable behavior immediately and ignore or, if necessary, use mild punishment for inappropriate behavior.
5. Develop realistic expectations concerning the students' academic goals. Tasks should be challenging but within the students' capacity. Modify objectives if the work is too difficult.
6. Empathize with the students and understand how negative aspects of their social environment (e.g., abuse or criticisms at home or in school) may contribute to the inappropriate behavior. Attempt to improve the quality of their interaction with parents, teachers, and peers.

## Hearing Impairment

**Hearing-impaired** children are in two major categories—the deaf and the partially hearing (or hard-of-hearing). The categories are defined as follows (Report of the Ad Hoc Committee to Define Deafness and Hard-of-Hearing, 1975):

> A *deaf* person is one whose hearing disability precludes successful processing of linguistic information through audition, with or without a hearing aid. A *hard-of-hearing* person is one who, generally with the use of a hearing aid, has residual hearing sufficient to enable successful processing of linguistic information through audition. (p. 509)

Sound is measured in units that identify its intensity and frequency. The decibel (db), a unit for measuring the loudness of perceived intensity of sound, is used as a means of classifying the degree of functional hearing. The classification is based on the degree of hearing loss in five categories, from mild to total, and is done by an audiologist, a specialist in the identification and measurement of hearing disorders. The frequency, or pitch, of sounds is assessed in cycles per second, or hertz units. Many hearing loses are only in the pitch range for certain speech sounds. For example, a student whose hearing loss is more serious in the higher frequencies will have difficulty in discriminating the /s/ sound (Heward & Orlansky, 1988).

The major causes of hearing impairment in childhood stem from rubella, meningitis (a viral infection that can destroy the sensitive acoustic apparatus of the inner ear), prematurity and complications of pregnancy, and heredity. Moores (1987) estimates that 30% of the school-age population have deaf relatives.

Hearing impairments hinder the development of language and communication ability because individuals learn language through hearing, interpreting, and imitating it. If an individual receives inadequate auditory feedback when making sounds and is unable to hear an adult model adequately, communication problems are likely to develop. The age of onset of the hearing impairment is one of the most important factors in determining the child's language development.

Because language plays such an important role in school learning, one can understand why hearing-impaired children frequently have academic problems. In particular, their reading achievement may be below grade level.

For a long time, many individuals believed incorrectly that hearing-impaired children, especially those identified as deaf, were also intellectually deficient. The thinking processes of deaf children are similar to those of hearing children, although their verbal intelligence test scores are generally lower than their performance (nonverbal) test scores (Moores, 1987). Unless a hearing-impaired child has other disabilities, as with brain damage, there is no causal relationship between deafness and intelligence. However, a child may not reach full potential unless effective communication training is given.

Language deficiencies can also influence the hearing-impaired child's personality and social development because these factors are greatly dependent upon the communication process. Social interaction, by definition, comprises the communication of ideas between individuals. The hearing-impaired child may respond inappropriately in play situations because of lack of understanding of the rules of games or others' intentions. Furth (1973) believes that the greatest disability facing the hearing-impaired individual is not the hearing disability but the failure of parents, professionals, and people in general to understand and accept the person with the disability. Through the use of a total communication method involving a combination of speech therapy, speechreading (also called *lipreading*), and sign languages, hearing-impaired children can function more effectively today than ever before (Hallahan & Kauffman, 1988).

The teacher needs to be alert to possible hearing problems in the classroom. It is not unusual for a child with a mild hearing loss to remain undiagnosed throughout elementary school. The child learns to compensate for the hearing loss so that parents and teachers are unaware of the problems. What is even more distressing is that the children themselves are often unaware of their hearing loss and, as a result, become frustrated and anxious learners as they attempt to adjust to the social and educational demands of the classroom. These children are often inappropriately labeled as slow learners, unmotivated, shy, or lazy.

The following are some of the situations in which the regular classroom teacher should recognize possible symptoms of auditory impairment:

- A child misses school frequently because of earaches or sinus congestion; these illnesses can be a source of temporary or permanent hearing loss.

- A child suffers from allergies and develops head congestion severe enough to bring about reduced hearing acuity for a short time.
- A child appears inattentive or seems to be daydreaming and may not hear the teacher's directions.
- A child who is reluctant to participate in class activities may be fearful of failing because of inability to understand.
- A child who has problems speaking or understanding language should be suspected of having a hearing problem.
- A child who demonstrates unusual behavior in response to oral directions may be hearing-impaired.

A teacher should notice specific behaviors indicative of hearing problems, such as cupping the hands behind the ears when attempting to listen or turning one side of the head toward the speaker to favor the better ear (Dunn, 1973; Hallahan & Kauffman, 1988).

With enactment of P.L. 94-142, it is not uncommon for the regular classroom teacher to have hard-of-hearing children in class. The following are some suggestions for helping these students succeed (Hallahan & Kauffman, 1988):

1. Allow the students the freedom to move their chairs around the room so that they can position themselves to take advantage of visual and auditory cues.
2. Keep to a minimum all auditory and visual distractors such as noises from the hall, other rooms, and outside. These distractions are also a problem for students with hearing aids because all noises are amplified for them.
3. Optimize the students' opportunities to speechread by maintaining a distance of about 6 feet between yourself and the students. Face the students when talking to them.
4. Facilitate speechreading by speaking naturally. Some individuals have a tendency to exaggerate movements of the mouth when speaking to hearing-impaired children. These children are trained to read lips that form words naturally, so any deviation from normal speech patterns may confuse them rather than help them.
5. Be aware that some hearing-impaired students withdraw from class discussions because they do not hear everything that is said or may be self-conscious about their imperfect speech. Involve them in groups in which they can get support from other students. Ask questions that require only short answers to build their confidence.
6. Be aware that some hearing-impaired students have learned coping skills that help them look as if they understand what is going on when in fact they do not. Many of these skills involve imitating their peers (e.g., raising their hands when other students in the class do or laughing when their classmates laugh). Call by name each student before they speak to alert the hearing-impaired student as to who is about to talk.

Extracurricular activities can provide opportunities to develop special talents.

7. Encourage the students to ask questions.
8. Make every effort to use visual aids (e.g., overhead projector or chalkboard). Providing hearing-impaired students with a written outline of what will be covered in a lecture or asking a classmate to take notes using carbon paper (the copy to be given to the hearing-impaired) can be helpful to the students.

## Visual Impairment

There are both legal and educational definitions of **visual impairment.** The legal concept is defined by visual acuity—that is, the ability to discriminate details at a specific distance. The term *20/20* means that at a distance of 20 feet the normal seeing eye should be able to discriminate objects or letters of a certain size. A person with 20/30 or 20/40 vision has a minor visual problem. As the bottom number of the fraction increases, visual acuity decreases. A person whose visual acuity is 20/200 or less in the better eye after correction is legally blind. Persons may also be considered legally blind if their field of vision is extremely restricted.

When looking ahead, a normal eye is able to see objects within a range of approximately 180 degrees. An individual who has extremely restricted vision, 20 degrees or less is considered legally blind even though the visual acuity in the small area may be good (Heward & Orlansky, 1988).

According to the legal classification system, partially sighted individuals are "those whose visual acuity falls between 20/70 and 20/200 in the better eye with correction" (Hallahan & Kauffman, 1988, p. 310). The educational definition of visual impairment considers the extent to which a student's visual impairment influences learning and the need for special equipment and materials. Educators distinguish between blind and partially sighted, or low vision, students. Blind students are almost totally without sight and can learn to read Braille, using the tactile sense in their fingertips to feel the raised dots of the Braille alphabet. Partially sighted students are able to see the visual print even though they need to use magnifying devices or books with large print.

The federal regulations for P.L. 94-142 define *visually handicapped* for school purposes in such a way that functional vision is primary: "Visually handicapped means a visual impairment which even, with correction, adversely affects a child's educational performance. The term includes both partially seeing and blind children" (U.S. Office of Education, 1977, p. 42479). Educators have determined that functional visual efficiency—the way in which children use their vision—is more important than visual acuity alone in determining the educational needs of the children.

The most common visual problems are the result of errors of refraction. That is, the structure and/or malfunctions in the eye prevent the light rays from focusing correctly, causing myopia (nearsightedness), hyperopia (farsightedness), and astigmatism (blurred vision). These conditions can generally be corrected with glasses or contact lenses. More serious problems are a result of glaucoma (caused by excessive pressure in the eyeball) and cataracts (caused by a clouding of the lens of the eye), which result in blurred vision, and diabetic retinopathy (caused by interference in the blood supply to the retina). There are many other causes for visual problems. It has been estimated that about 64 percent of the visual impairments of school-age children are caused by prenatal factors (U.S. Department of Health, Education and Welfare, 1970).

Early identification of visual problems is important because students can benefit from specialized intervention as soon as they begin school. Most schools provide services for testing visual acuity. More thorough visual examinations can be conducted by an ophthalmologist (a licensed medical doctor who specializes in the diagnosis and treatment of eyes) or an optometrist (a licensed specialist in vision who is trained to examine eyes and enhance vision by nonsurgical means such as glasses and contact lenses).

As a teacher, you must be alert to possible visual disabilities in children. The following are symptoms to watch for (National Society to Prevent Blindness, 1977):

**Behavior**
- Rubs eyes excessively
- Shuts or covers one eye, tilts head, or thrusts head forward
- Has difficulty in reading or in other work requiring close use of the eyes

- Blinks more than usual or is irritable when doing close work
- Holds books close to eyes
- Is unable to see distant things clearly
- Squints eyelids together or frowns

**Appearance**
- Crossed eyes
- Red-rimmed, encrusted, or swollen eyelids
- Inflamed or watery eyes
- Recurring sties

**Complaints**
- Eyes itch, burn, or feel scratchy
- Cannot see well
- Dizziness, headaches, or nausea following close eye work
- Blurred or double vision

There are a number of ways a teacher can help visually impaired students in the classroom. Harley (1973) points out that seeing is affected by factors such as brightness, size of image, contrast, time, and distance. Brightness, or proper illumination, is necessary for students to be able to function successfully in visual tasks. Some students function better with a decrease in normal lighting. Proper seating in the classroom can prevent glare that may be present near the windows. The size of printed symbols is very important to students with visual impairment. Books with large print can be obtained from many publishers. In addition, optical aids for magnification are useful to many visually impaired children. The amount of contrast between an object and its background also affects visual acuity. Nolan (1961) stated that black on white or white on black provides the best contrast for partially seeing students. Time is another important factor in visual acuity. Some students need frequent periods of eye rest, and with their limited field of vision, partially seeing students often proceed at a slower rate. As a result, the teacher should provide the necessary time for these students to complete academic tasks. Last, distance is a factor in determining what should be considered when organizing student seating patterns and presentations of lessons. Visually impaired students should be moved closer to the front of the room and chalkboard, or seated so that they can see more effectively.

Hallahan and Kauffman (1988) make some additional suggestions for helping visually impaired students in the classroom:

1. Require the students to care for their own materials in order to foster a sense of independence.
2. Assign sighted students in the class to act as a guide as long as the visually impaired students do not become too dependent upon them.
3. Treat the students the same as their sighted peers; the same expectations should be maintained for all students.

4. Encourage interpersonal interaction between blind students and their sighted peers.

5. Encourage the students to participate in as many activities as possible. Alternative activities should be arranged if it is impossible for them to join in with the rest of the class.

6. Give the students the same kinds of special tasks or responsibilities that are given to other students in the class.

## Communication Disorders

According to Van Riper (1978), a person has a communication problem when that person's speech differs from the speech of others to the extent that it calls attention to itself, interferes with the intended message, or causes the speaker or listener to be distressed. The term *speech-impaired*, as defined under P.L. 94-142, describes someone with "a communication disorder, such as stuttering, impaired articulation, a language impairment, or a voice impairment which adversely affects a child's educational performance" (*Federal Register*, August, 23, 1977, p. 42479). The speech and language problems referred to in the federal definition can be summarized as problems of articulation, voice, fluency, and language disorders.

**Speech disorder** and **language disorder** are related, but they are not the same thing. Cartwright, Cartwright, and Ward (1984) state: "Speech problems are those associated with the production of the oral symbols of language, whereas language problems are difficulties with the linguistic code or rules and conventions for linking the symbols and symbol sequences" (p. 115). The Speech and Language Checklist in Table 5.3 serves as a useful guide for helping the classroom teacher to identify students who may need speech or language services. The diagnosis of speech and language disorders is a complex process that requires extensive training. It is conducted by a speech pathologist, a clinician who applies medical and behavioral science to the correction of speech and language disabilities.

The inability to articulate speech sounds correctly can be caused by biological factors (e.g., brain damage, damage to the nerves controlling the muscles used in speech, or gross abnormalities of the oral structures, such as a cleft palate). Other possible conditions contributing to communication disorders are environmental factors—primarily the quality of parent-child communication, emotional disturbances, and hearing loss.

As a teacher, you should be aware of the potential negative consequences in interpersonal relations and the possible development of a poor self-concept by speech-impaired students. For example, the student who stutters is usually subjected to extensive criticism and demands for better speech production.

The following teaching practices can help students with communication disorders in the classroom (Hocevar & Arnold, 1979):

1. Provide a model of acceptance for the students to follow. Show by actions that a communication disorder makes no difference

TABLE 5.3 **SPEECH AND LANGUAGE CHECKLIST**

### Communication
Talks very little to adults and/or peers
Uses poor eye contact
Avoids situations in which communication is imperative

### Articulation
Omits sounds in words (e.g., says ouside/outside; tar/star)
Distorts sounds in words (e.g., sounds are not precisely on target)
Substitutes one sound for another in words (e.g., wed/red; motha/mother; thit/sit; dod/dog)
Sounds are unintelligible because of multiple articulation errors

### Language
Uses poor sentence structure or has multiple grammatical errors
Appears to have limited vocabulary
Has difficulty explaining what is intended
Frequently gives inappropriate responses
Unable to understand the meaning of words, gestures, and/or expressions
Unable to understand or follow directions, and asks for frequent repetitions
Unable to comprehend or sequence word problems or information presented orally
Easily distracted by ambient noises

### Fluency
Repeats or prolongs the first sound or syllable of words
Repeats whole words or phrases
Has difficulty getting some words started (i.e., sound appears blocked)
Gets upset when speaking is difficult
Frequently looks away while talking
Pauses a long time before responding even when the answer is known

### Voice
Has constant hoarse or husky voice
Sounds unusually high or low in pitch for age and sex
Has excessively loud or soft voice
Has a nasal sounding voice most of the time

### Hearing
Uses little or no speech
Appears shy or withdrawn in a group setting
Relies heavily on visual clues (watches speakers' lips, watches and follows movements
  of others)
Asks to have information repeated
Lacks clear or distinct speech

*Source: Developed by Bernice Sedlik, speech pathologist.*

    with respect to friendship, academic status, or any other relationship in school.
2. Encourage the students with speech impairments to talk about activities they are involved in outside the school.
3. Children with communication disorders may need to hear a word, expression, sound, or concept used appropriately many times before they will be able or willing to use it.

4. Give the students opportunities to speak without interruption or pressure. Don't finish sentences for the students or add words.
5. Ask the students open-ended rather than yes-no questions. If you get no response, repeat the question or statement, using natural gestures.
6. Listen to what students have to say, and listen attentively with active interest. Do not look away from the students. (p. 175)

## Physical and Health Impairment

This category of exceptionality involves a broad range of disabilities, including functional (e.g., hand use or mobility), medical, or additional handicaps associated with emotional, social, or educational needs. The guidelines for PL 94-142 define *orthopedic impairments* as those having:

a severe orthopedic impairment which adversely affects a child's educational performance. The term includes impairment caused by congenital anomaly (e.g., clubfoot, absense of some member, etc.), impairments caused by disease (e.g., poliomyelitis, bone tuberculosis, etc.), and impairments from other causes (e.g., cerebral palsy, amputations, and fractures or burns which cause contractures. (*Federal Register*, August 23, 1977, p. 42478)

Also identified are those students with *health impairments*, who may exhibit

limited strength, vitality, or alertness, due to chronic or acute health problems such as a heart condition, tuberculosis, rheumatic fever, nephritis, asthma, sickle cell anemia, hemophilia, epilepsy, lead poisoning, leukemia, or diabetes, which adversely affect a child's educational performance. (*Federal Register*, August 23, 1977, p. 42478)

Table 5.4 presents identifying information regarding the major categories of physical disabilities and health impairments.

Many students with physical health disorders are not placed in special education classes; they remain in regular classrooms. The teacher working with these students must remember that they are frequently absent from school for long periods, sometimes need special medication, and raise many concerns for their peers. As a result, the children's social and emotional development, especially their self-esteem, can be influenced by the health problem. The teacher needs to plan carefully both the academic and social aspects of classroom activities to ensure maximum participation.

A number of recommendations for the regular teacher who may have students in the classroom with physical and health handicaps follow (Glass, Christiansen, & Christiansen, 1982):

1. Review student records at the beginning of the year, noting which students have unusual health problems. If you will have a student

TABLE 5.4 COMMON PHYSICAL HEALTH DISORDERS OF CHILDHOOD

| Name | Diagnostic Description | Important Characteristics |
|------|------------------------|---------------------------|
| Cerebral palsy | A crippling condition of the neuromuscular system; disorder of movement and posture; central characteristic is neurological motor dysfunction caused by brain damage (birth injury, congenital defect, infection); not a clear-cut syndrome but includes children with a variety of symptoms, such as muscle weakness or involuntary muscle movements. | Brain damage involved in CP may also affect IQ but not inevitably; however, a greater proportion of CP children are mentally retarded than is case with general population; since condition involves brain damage, it cannot be cured, but physical therapy and surgery can improve function. |
| Epilepsy | A condition of the neuromuscular system involving recurring attacks of loss of consciousness, convulsive movements, or disturbances of feeling and behavior; also known as *seizure* or *convulsive disorder*; caused by as yet undetermined brain damage. | Focus of treatment is the control of seizures; many effective anticonvulsant medications are now available; although many mentally retarded individuals suffer from seizures, the seizures themselves do not seem to cause mental retardation. |
| Spina bifida | A congenital defect of the spinal column; in its more severe forms, paralysis of lower limbs is virtually inevitable without surgical intervention; condition is evident at birth; most severe form is termed *myelomeningocele.* | Children are susceptible to hydrocephalus; if not surgically corrected, it can cause mental retardation and related behavior problems. |
| Muscular dystrophy | A degeneration of the muscles; disease is progressive and grows worse with age. | These children typically require a wheelchair in the normal course of the disease; cognitive abilities are not affected. |
| Limb deficiencies | Caused by genetic birth defects, amputations due to disease, or accidents. | Mechanical limbs (prosthetic devices) can frequently be fitted, but considerable training in use of limb as well as supportive attitudes are necessary. |
| Cystic fibrosis | Symptoms include generalized dysfunction of the exocrine glands, very high salt concentrations in sweat, and chronic pulmonary dysfunction with repeated episodes of pneumonia (with severe bouts of coughing); most lethal hereditary disorder of children in U.S.; specific cause unknown; no known cure, and illness is inevitably fatal; many patients, however, survive into adolescence and young adulthood. | These youngsters are encouraged to lead active lives and no physical restrictions are placed on behavior; cognitive development is normal and they typically remain in regular school placement; extensive therapeutic regimen is required in the home; patients frequently feel emotionally inhibited due to mucous excretions, chronic coughing, and breathing difficulty. |
| Leukemia | A group of diseases characterized by sudden increases of white blood cells in the bone marrow and peripheral blood; most common form of | Many children can be treated with medication on an outpatient basis; others require surgery, radiation therapy, or bone marrow |

*(continued)*

TABLE 5.4 (*continued*)

| Name | Diagnostic Description | Important Characteristics |
|------|------------------------|---------------------------|
| | childhood cancer; in the late 1970s, the disease was considered fatal; recent advances in chemotherapy have made it possible to expect cure or at least long-term leukemia-free survival. | transplantation; fear of death is frequent concern of child and family, even in remission, and an atmosphere of normalcy should be stressed, with emphasis on positive aspects of living. |
| Asthma | Causes unclear; involves both psychological and somatic factors; often described as *psychophysiologic* illness; characterized by difficulty in breathing due to narrowing of airways; involves severe and life-threatening attacks of wheezing; may cause death because of inability to breathe. | Sometimes described as the "vulnerable child syndrome"; breathing attacks are frightening and parents may tend to overprotect the child; drug therapy can be very effective in preventing attacks and aerosol (fine mist spray) can be helpful in controlling attack. |
| Diabetes | Characterized by an inability to store sugar in the blood because of dysfunction of the pancreas; symptoms include loss of weight, frequent urination, and excessive thirstiness; treatment involves diet management and insulin therapy as needed. | With proper management, diabetes can be brought under control; risks involve diabetic coma (excess of sugar in blood causing nausea, abdominal pain, labored breathing) and insulin reaction (lack of sugar causing hunger, sweating, tremors, drowsiness). |
| Spinal cord injury | Accidents are the most common cause of injury. The extent of disability is determined by where the damage occurred. Paralysis and loss of sensation occur below the location of the injury. | Students with major injuries require wheelchairs for mobility; those with quadriplegia may also have difficulty breathing and lack bowel and bladder control. |
| Sickle cell anemia | A hereditary blood disorder found more commonly in the black population; red blood cells distorted and don't circulate properly; results in severe pain to abdomen, arms, and legs. | Many orthopedic problems may result that affect full participation in certain physical activities; frequent absences from school can impact academic achievement. |

*Source: Adapted from Suran and Rizzo, 1979.*

with a health problem, develop an understanding of the problem by reading and by consulting the school nurse. Since some conditions require modifications in the classroom environment and/or instructional procedures, you should make preparations for the students before the start of school. Consulting previous teachers of the students to find out about successful procedures also is helpful.

2. Many students with physical and health impairments suffer from excessive pity or overprotection. Other such students are excluded from class activities or rejected by their peers. It is important that you treat these students as worthwhile, competent students who have interests and needs like any other students. As a result, never

expect them to do less than they are capable of. Develop reasonable objectives and expect them to be attained.

3. Spend time helping the class develop realistic attitudes about physical and health impairments and ways of interacting with their handicapped peers.

4. Because of fatigue, students who are handicapped or health-impaired may not be able to participate in all class activities or finish certain assignments on time. Provide suggestions for parents for home tutoring, and provide opportunities if possible for rest during the school day for students who tire easily.

5. If a student is hospitalized during the school year, it is helpful to communicate with the hospital's teachers or to send work home for the student to complete if possible. The goal should be to continue to support the student's contact with the school and to prevent the child from falling too far behind, while at the same time not making demands that cannot be attained because of the student's health condition.

6. Make the student feel welcome on return to school from an illness, and allow sufficient time for makeup work.

## Gifted and Talented

Although P.L. 94-142 does not specifically apply to the *gifted and talented*, these exceptional children also need special educational services to reach their potential. The classification covers a wide range of abilities and traits and is defined by the Gifted and Talented Children's Act of 1978, Section 902:

> Gifted and talented children means children, and whenever applicable, youth, who are identified at the preschool, elementary, or secondary level as possessing demonstrated or potential abilities that give evidence of high performance capability in areas such as intellectual, creative, specific academics, or leadership abilities, or in the performing and visual arts, and who by reason thereof require services or activities not ordinarily provided by the school.

The definition of the term and the identification of gifted and talented children, like other areas of exceptionality, have been characterized by controversy stemming from the following questions:

1. What are the different ways in which these children excel in such areas as intelligence, creativity, and special talents?

2. How should one measure the areas of students' expertise—with standardized tests, teacher judgments, past performances, and so on?

3. To what degree must a child excel to be considered gifted or talented?

4. Who should comprise the comparison group?

As you might expect from the possible answers to these questions, giftedness can be identified in many ways. The 1987 *State of the States Gifted and Talented Education Report* (Council of State Directors, 1987) showed that each state has its own procedures for identifying and establishing special services for these children. At the time this report was published, 22 states did not mandate programs for the gifted and talented. However, those states that do have programs are providing greater financial support for them than they provided in the past.

There is still considerable confusion over who should be labeled as gifted and talented. In one publication, 17 different conceptions of giftedness were identified (Sternberg & Davidson, 1986)! Many school districts use multiple criteria for identifying students, such as achievement test scores, intelligence test scores, teacher nominations, parent nominations, student interviews, grades, classroom performance, and creativity. The problem regarding diverse definitions is that often the definition used in identifying students is not consistent with the instruments used to select students or with the type of program provided for students. For example, many definitions incorporate statements about the levels of motivation, creativity, and/or leadership, yet use an individual intelligence test as the sole indicator to select students. The inconsistency between the definition and type of program occurs when students are selected because of their high intelligence but then placed in gifted programs that emphasize independent work or special talent that is not necessarily related to high intelligence. It is important to realize that just because students are labeled as gifted or talented does not mean that they will be placed in a program suited to their unique abilities and needs (Hoge, 1988; Sosniak, 1987).

*Intelligence as an Indicator of Giftedness.* The traditional definition of *giftedness* is based on general intelligence in that a student with an intelligence test score of 130 or above would be selected for special education in most schools. Terman and Oden's (1925, 1954) study of highly gifted children (those with a score over 140) is still considered to be one of the classic works in the field. An important aspect of their study was that in addition to high academic achievement, gifted children's physical and social development was found to be above average when compared to that of their normal peers. Furthermore, contrary to popular notion, gifted children become gifted adults. They do not burn themselves out. Also, children identified as gifted according to intelligence test scores tend to score above average on tests of special ability (Gallagher, 1975).

*Creativity as an Indicator of Giftedness.* In Chapter 3, I discussed the difference between convergent and divergent thinking, pointing out that the latter is associated with creativity. It is important that you understand the distinction between intellectual giftedness and creativity. The results from a number of studies (Getzels & Jackson, 1962; Wallach & Kogan, 1965) indicate that although persons above average in intelligence are more likely to be creative, this does not mean that above average or highly intelligent persons are necessarily creative. In fact, Torrance (1962) states that "if we were to identify children as gifted simply on the basis of intelligence tests, we would eliminate from consideration approximately 70 percent of the most creative" (p. 5).

Students with high grades in school may or may not be creative. Many noncreative, highly intelligent individuals perform very well in school or on the job but never generate any original ideas. There are also students who do poorly in school and demonstrate little motivation but have a high degree of creative talent.

During the 1960s, a number of issues regarding the traditional means of identifying the gifted were raised. Some educators became concerned that many gifted children were going unidentified, especially those from various cultural groups, because of the biased nature of intelligence tests. As a result, many states placed more emphasis in their selection process on teacher and parent nomination and on work samples (particularly in talent areas such as the visual and performing arts), in addition to intelligence and achievement tests. Furthermore, many psychologists and educators believed that high intelligence was not the only trait needed for outstanding accomplishments in society.

*Special Talents as an Indicator of Giftedness.* Although *giftedness* and *talented* are often used interchangeably, *talent* usually refers to specialized ability in such areas as art, music, drama, science, mathematics, and leadership. Although psychomotor ability is not mentioned in the federal definition of giftedness, it was identified as an area of giftedness as defined in a U.S. Office of Education report to the Congress (Marland, 1972). Table 5.5 identifies characteristics of children with special talents.

*An Integrative Perspective.* Renzulli (1982) has suggested a multiple-criterion definition of giftedness that includes high ability (including high intelligence), high creativity, and high task commitment (a high level of motivation and the ability to see a project through to its conclusion). He believes that all three characteristics are necessary for truly gifted performance in any field. Using this definition, a student who has an average intelligence test score but is talented in areas not measured by an intelligence test would be included in gifted programs. On the other hand, the definition excludes children who have high intelligence test scores but are not exceptionally creative or committed to a field of interest (Berdine & Blackhurst, 1985).

*Programs for Gifted and Talented Students.* Two of the most common programs for gifted and talented students include *enrichment* and *acceleration* (Heward & Orlansky, 1988). Enrichment experiences are those that allow each student to investigate topics of interest in depth. Some of these activities are completed in the regular classroom, whereas others are expe-

TABLE 5.5 CHARACTERISTICS OF CHILDREN WITH SPECIAL TALENTS

| Talent Area | Abilities | Personality Attributes |
|---|---|---|
| Mathematics | Ability to manipulate symbolic material more effectively and more rapidly than classmates | Highly independent<br>Enjoy theoretical and investigative pursuits<br>Talented girls less conforming than general population |
| Science | Ability to see relationships among ideas, events, and objects<br>Elegance in explanation: the ability to formulate the simplest hypothesis that can account for the observed facts | Highly independent<br>"Loners"<br>Prefer intellectually rather than socially challenging situations<br>Reject group pressures<br>Methodical, precise, exact<br>Avid readers |
| Language arts | Capability of manipulating abstract concepts, but sometimes inferior to the high general achiever in working with mathematical material<br>Imagination and originality | Highly independent<br>Social and esthetic values (girls)<br>Theoretical and political values (boys)<br>Avid readers |
| Leadership | Ability to effect positive and productive change<br>Good decision-making ability<br>Proficiency in some area, such as athletics or academics<br>Ability to communicate | Empathic<br>Sensitive<br>Charismatic—can transform the group through their enthusiasm and energy<br>Superior communication skills |
| Psychomotor ability | Gross motor strength, agility, flexibility, coordination, and speed<br>Excellence in athletics, gymnastics, or dance<br>Fine motor control, deftness, precision, flexibility, and speed<br>Excellence in crafts—jewelry making, model building, mechanics, working with electronic equipment, etc.<br>Ability to use complicated equipment with little or no training | Enjoy and seem to need considerable exercise<br>Competitive<br>Interested in mechanics, electronics, or crafts<br>Have hobbies such as model building, origami, pottery |
| Visual or performing arts | Ability to disregard traditional methods in favor of their own original ones<br>Resourcefulness in use of materials<br>Ability to express their feelings through an art form<br>Attention to detail in their own and others' artwork | Self-confident<br>Competitive<br>Prefer working alone<br>Sensitive to their environment<br>Gain satisfaction through their feelings artistically<br>Responsive to music, sculpture |

*Source: Pendarvis, in Berdine and Blackhurst, 1985.*

rienced in special classes, field trips, camps, and hobby clubs. Acceleration programs provide a child with learning experiences that are usually given to older children. It means speeding up the usual presentation of content— early admission to school, grade skipping, concurrent enrollment in both high school and college, advanced placement tests, and early admission to college.

Were you or any of your friends identified as gifted? What did you think of the educational program? Did it help you develop your potential or was it a waste of time? Do you think gifted and talented students should be educated separately? What are some of the possible consequences of such action?

The following are teaching practices that can help gifted and talented students in the classroom (Glass, Christiansen, & Christiansen, 1982; Hallahan & Kauffman, 1988):

1. Periodically review the characteristics of students in your class to determine whether certain students show particular ability, creativity, and task commitment. Give special concern to culturally diverse students who may be gifted or talented but who are not achieving at a high level. Refer students who show indications of giftedness to the school psychologist for testing and observation.

2. Analyze your instructional program for gifted students. It is common for gifted children to become bored with the school routine because the work is not challenging. Teach the students independent research skills. Because many gifted and talented children are self-motivated, they are able to work independently for long periods. Develop specific goals and objectives for the students that provide an organized program of instruction.

3. Use instructional methods and procedures that encourage students to be creative and to explore their environment. These activities will benefit all the students in the class.

4. Be a good model. If you accept intellectual and personal differences, the students in your class are likely to imitate your behavior. If you show excitement about exploring new areas of knowledge, so will your students.

## LEGAL RIGHTS OF EXCEPTIONAL CHILDREN AND THEIR PARENTS

During the 1960s and 1970s, questions of the rights of students were raised in such areas as hair length, corporal punishment, discipline, and confidentiality of records. The student rights movement also influenced the schools' treatment of exceptional children. This movement began in many states by litigation that prevented the exclusion of exceptional children from certain educational programs and that instituted due process in deciding how and where a child was to be educated.

To understand the significance of the right to due process, you must understand the way many handicapped children were treated in the past. At one time, a school administrator or school psychologist could decide without any consultation with others whether a handicapped child could attend school and where in school the child was placed. These decisions were often made with little or no supporting data, on no legal basis, and with no parental involvement. This same person could exclude a child from school if the person believed that the child could not benefit from a public education or did not meet arbitrarily designated ability and behavior standards. Stated simply, one person could decide the educational destiny of a child or adolescent.

Handicapped children faced many problems in obtaining an appropriate education. First, they often remained in special programs throughout their educational careers. This was especially true of students classified as mildly mentally retarded. The tendency was to consider special education placements as permanent assignments rather than short-term options designed to help the individual prepare for return to the regular class.

Second, a disproportionate number of minority children were assigned to special education classes without consideration of the cultural and educational backgrounds contributing to their academic and intellectual deficiencies. As a result, many children were inappropriately placed in special classes.

In general, there were few protective safeguards to ensure the application of due process for the handicapped. Schools often labeled children, subjected them to psychological assessments by an individual, and placed them in educational programs without appropriate supporting data and often without parental consent.

## Public Law 94-142

In 1975 a major federal law pertaining to handicapped children, the Education for All Handicapped Children Act (P.L. 94-142), was passed. This law has had a major impact on special education. The key aspects of the law are as follows:

1. A free, appropriate public education is mandated for all handicapped children.
2. School systems must protect the rights of handicapped children and their parents.
3. The placement of handicapped children must be in the least restrictive educational environment (i.e., handicapped children must be educated with nonhandicapped children to the maximum extent possible).
4. An **individualized education program (IEP)** must be developed and implemented for every handicapped child.
5. Parents of handicapped children must be involved in the decision-making process affecting the education of their child.

## Free and Appropriate Education

This provision mandates that all special education needs and related services must be provided to students and parents by schools without cost. The term *appropriate* addresses the issue of *quality* of education and is in part guaranteed by other provisions of the law, such as the annually reviewed IEP, parental participation in decision-making processes, and due process. *Appropriate* has thus far been interpreted by the courts to imply an adequate, not necessarily optimum, program.

## Due Process

P.L. 94-142 attempts to protect against abuses such as permanent placement in special education programs, improper diagnosis, disproportionate placement of minority children in special education classrooms, and low-level educational services. The law does this by requiring the following (adapted from Meyen, 1988):

1. All school records must be open to parents.
2. Assessment of children considered for special education programs must be "nondiscriminatory." This means that children must be tested in their native language, using multiple criteria for decision making. The child cannot be placed in a special education program on the basis of the results of a single test.
3. Parents may obtain evaluations of their children from specialists outside the school.
4. A child advocate must be appointed if the parents or guardian of the child are not known or available. The child advocate cannot be an employee of the school district.
5. Parents must receive written notice in the parents' native language whenever the school proposes a change in the identification, evaluation, or educational placement of their child.
6. Parents must be given the opportunity to present complaints on any matter pertaining to the identification, evaluation, or educational placement of their child. The school must provide parents with information on the specific procedures they should follow to voice their complaints.
7. If parents are not satisfied with the educational program provided by the school, they can request a due process hearing. Guidelines for these hearings are specified in the law.

## Individualized Education Program (IEP)

The IEP is a written educational program agreed upon by parents and specialists at a meeting at which each handicapped child's educational needs are discussed. It is important to note that an IEP must be written for each child rather than for a class or group of children. A number of steps must be taken before an IEP is written. First, a teacher must initiate a *referral* for a student who is having difficulties in the classroom. This referral may go to the principal or to the special education teacher (sometimes called the *resource specialist teacher*). Second, a team of professionals identified by various names (e.g., *local review committee* or *student study team*) is established to *review the request for referral and conduct a preliminary screening* to determine whether there is enough evidence to accept or reject the referral (i.e., whether the problem appears serious enough for special education services). The team reviews the student's school records and meets with the referring teacher and other school personnel who may know the student. If the team accepts the referral, it requests parental permission for a comprehensive assessment to analyze the problem in depth. Third, the *comprehensive assessment* is usually completed by a school psychologist, special education teacher, and other specialists when particular expertise is needed (e.g., an audiologist or speech therapist). The assessment includes both achievement tests and special diagnostic tests to attempt to pinpoint the student's particular learning problems. Finally, when the comprehensive assessment is completed, the evaluation team (1) determines whether the student is eligible for special education and then (2) makes a decision as to the best type of placement for the student (keeping in mind the least restrictive environment provision in the law). The team may decide that the regular classroom teacher can work with the student without additional special education services. If it does determine that special education services are needed, the team will *prepare an IEP* for the student. The parents or guardian must sign the IEP to indicate agreement with the placement and type of educational program. If the parents disagree with the conclusions of the assessment team, they can appeal the decisions through the guidelines established by the school district. Each student's IEP must be re-evaluated yearly. Although school districts use various formats, most IEPs include a statement of the following:

> The child's present educational level or performance.
> The annual goals, including short-term objectives.
> The anticipated duration of the specific educational services, appropriate objective criteria, evaluation procedures, and schedules for determining, on at least an annual basis, whether instructional objectives are being met.

The law requires that at least four individuals be involved: the parents or guardian, the child's teacher, a representative of the local educational agency who is qualified to provide or supervise special education (usually a principal or director of special education or a representative), and, whenever appropriate, the child. In many situations, additional teachers who interact with the child and certain specialists (e.g., speech therapists, nurses, physicians, and psychologists) are also present at the meeting. The parents may invite an additional person familiar with their child to the meeting.

## Least Restrictive Educational Environment

The requirement for placement in the *least restrictive educational environment* attempts to reverse traditional procedures for dealing with handicapped children. Historically, handicapped children were referred out of the regular classroom for special services. The law now states that to the maximum extent appropriate, handicapped children are to be educated with children who are not handicapped. Removal of the student from the regular class for part or all of the day should occur only when the nature or severity of the handicap is such that education in the regular class with supplementary aids and services cannot be achieved satisfactorily. This aspect of the law is often called **mainstreaming.** The emphasis has shifted to the regular classroom as the preferred instructional base for all children. The law does not state that all handicapped children be placed in regular classrooms, but it puts the burden of proof on the schools when placement is other than the regular classroom. A child's IEP must show cause if and when the child is moved from a least restrictive educational environment.

Hallahan and Kauffman (1988) point out that in studies of the effectiveness of mainstreaming, *temporal integration* (i.e., the amount of time spent in a regular classroom) and *physical placement* have been the focus of research, often to the exclusion of what goes on in that physical setting. This makes the literature evaluating the efficacy of different programs somewhat suspect and difficult to compare, offering no clear-cut answers.

Mainstreaming considers the continuum of educational options available to the handicapped child. The purpose of mainstreaming is to match more effectively the characteristics and needs of the child and the type of educational environment in which the child is placed, while at the same time attempting to maximize interaction with children who are not handicapped. Merely including a handicapped child in a regular classroom will not eliminate the child's problems. For example, the research on mildly retarded students indicates that their social acceptance does not necessarily improve by placing them in regular classrooms. In fact, placing handicapped and nonhandicapped children together can actually result in lower acceptance for the handicapped (Strain & Kerr, 1981). However, when teachers structure their classrooms to help these students exhibit more appropriate classroom behavior and individualize instruction, acceptance can be improved and achievement can increase (Madden & Slavin, 1983).

Figure 5.1 illustrates the continuum of educational alternatives for handicapped children, from least restrictive environment (regular classroom) to the most restrictive environment (specialized facility.) Notice that educators have five options (Levels 1 through 5) for placing children in regular classrooms before considering full-time placement in a special class or school. The regular classroom teacher for these children may have the assistance of a consultant teacher, itinerant teacher (a specialist—for example, a speech therapist, who may work with the child individually and offer curriculum materials and/or other instructional support for the classroom teacher), resource teacher, or special day teacher. Children at Level 6, who attend special classes on a full-time basis, still have some interaction with their nonhandicapped peers—at lunch and recess—if their class is in the same facility as a regular education program. Although more restrictive than the regular class, the special class is less restrictive than placement in a special school or residential institution (Heward & Orlansky, 1988).

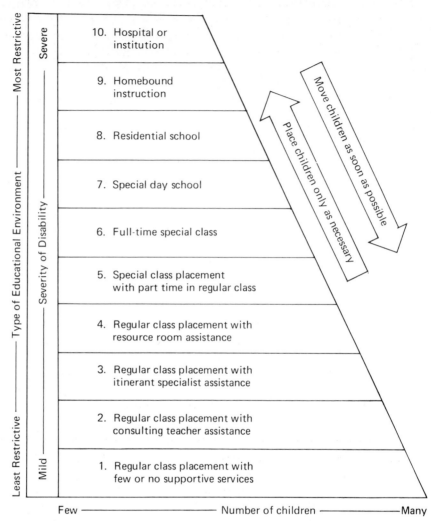

**Figure 5.1** Continuum of Special Education Services.

*Source: Berdine and Blackhurst, 1985, based on Reynolds, 1962, and Deno, 1973.*

A common educational service for mildly handicapped students is Level 4, the **resource room**, a special classroom within a school in which a special education teacher provides services for exceptional children. Depending upon the needs of the student, instruction can be from 30 to 60 minutes two to five times a week, or as much as half of the school day. The teacher assesses the needs of the students and works with them individually or in small groups to remediate the identified deficiencies. The resource teacher works closely with the regular classroom teacher.

**What are the advantages and disadvantages of educating exceptional students in and outside the regular classroom?**

*The Regular Education Initiative.* Even with the least restrictive environment stipulation in the law, many educators and researchers still argue that special education is too separate from general education. Today some advocate what has been called the **regular education initiative,** an alternative to special education. The goal is to restructure the regular classroom to be more responsive to students with special needs, benefiting not only handicapped students but economically disadvantaged, non-English-speaking, gifted, and other special needs students.

The major arguments for this approach include the following: the regular classroom is the best place to remediate academic deficiencies; educating students in separate "pull-out" programs (e.g., resource room instruction) results in substantial reduction in classroom instruction (often because of the lack of coordination between the resource and regular classroom teacher); and the procedures for classifying students for special education are flawed. Research demonstrates that the same instructional methods that produce achievement gains are appropriate for all groups of students. Thus, why not focus on effective instruction in a heterogeneous environment rather than segregate students into separate groups (Wang, Reynolds, & Walberg, 1988)?

The regular education initiative has engendered opposition as well as support (Chalfant, 1989). A major concern of individuals opposed to the initiative is that today's general education teachers are not well prepared to meet the special needs of handicapped students, and, as a result, the plan would lead to a less than adequate education for special needs students. Also, it is argued that changes in the present program can be made to improve it without overhauling the total system of instruction.

## CLASSROOM APPLICATION: PREPARING AN INDIVIDUALIZED EDUCATION PROGRAM (IEP)

The following example is a case study of the development of an actual IEP. The names and some minor data have been changed to maintain the confidentiality of the family involved. Notice the following steps: referral, review of the request for referral, comprehensive assessment, preparation of the IEP, and placement. Remember that the procedures may differ somewhat from one school district to another. In addition, because prevailing learning problems and student characteristics differ greatly, there is no such thing as a typical IEP.

Frank Davis, a fourth-grade teacher at Wilson Elementary School, was concerned about one of his students, Billy Fields, who was having difficulty with math and language arts. Billy read below grade level and had difficulty completing follow-up work. Mr. Davis moved Billy's seat to the front of the room to alleviate any hearing difficulty he might have when instructions were given to the entire class, to facilitate any copying from the blackboard, and to observe his behavior more closely. In addition, he worked individually with Billy as time permitted. Unfortunately, none of these remediations seemed to help.

Mr. Davis decided to review Billy's school records to see if any other teacher had noted similar problems. He learned that retention had been recommended in the first grade but was refused by the parent, and that the second- and third-grade teachers had noted that Billy was deficient in many basic academic skills and needed a great deal of attention.

Mr. Davis decided to discuss the problem with Mrs. Gordon, the resource specialist teacher at the school. He expressed his concern that Billy was beginning to fall behind in all subjects. Mrs. Gordon suggested that he complete the school's formal referral form with all the information he could address and attach work samples and anecdotal observations he had made to identify the problem. In addition, Mrs. Gordon agreed to observe Billy's classroom behavior.

Billy was observed during three basic periods—physical education, math, and spelling. In physical education, Mrs. Gordon noted that Billy was the third person chosen for a position on a team. His physical coordination and gross motor skills were excellent. Therefore, there was no reason to refer him to the adaptive physical education teacher (an individual trained to assess and work with children with physical and motor handicaps). In a conversation with Mrs. Gordon during his wait for a turn at bat, Billy exhibited clear articulation, normal vocabulary, and good sentence formation for a fourth-grade student. As a result, Mrs. Gordon did not believe that there was any reason to refer him to the speech and language consultant for evaluation. Observations during math indicated that Billy was having left-right sequencing problems. He was adding three-column figures of three digits and reversing numerals when regrouping (e.g., the first column of numbers totaled 24; Billy wrote 2 and carried the 4, instead of writing 4 and carrying the 2). During spelling he had good recall for basic reading words but did not get one word correct that involved simple phonic rules for long vowel sounds (e.g., *grat* instead of *great* and *trid* instead of *tried*).

After these observations Mrs. Gordon met with Mr. Davis to discuss her findings. She took his referral form, the formal request for assessment, and presented it at the team assessment meeting, which is held every other week at her school. Attending this meeting are the principal, school psychologist, Mrs. Gordon, and teachers who had referred children for various problems since the last meeting. The committee members discussed Billy's problem and decided that a formal assessment was necessary to determine whether Billy had a specific disability and was in need of special education services. They reached this decision on the basis of Mr. Davis's attempts to remediate the problem on his own, the observational reports by Mrs. Gordon, the indication by previous teachers that Billy needed special attention, and the fact that Billy was dropping further behind his classmates in all academic areas.

Billy's mother was contacted by Mrs. Gordon to request a conference to discuss Billy's academic problems and the recommendation by the evaluation team. Mrs. Fields stated at the conference that she was extremely worried about his learning problems. She believed that his problems were originally caused by emotional stress at age 6, when she and Billy's father were divorced. She regretted that she had not allowed Billy to be retained in the first grade, as recommended by the school. After her rights were explained, Billy's mother signed the permission form allowing for the assessment of her son. A copy of these rights accompanied her copy of the signed assessment. She was told that she would be notified as soon as the testing was completed and a school assessment team meeting for the IEP would be held.

The individual battery of tests given to Billy were divided into two sections: an intelligence test given by the school psychologist (the Wechsler Intelligence Scale for Children, Revised (WISC-R),* and achievement tests in the content areas given by Mrs. Gordon (see Chapter 12 for a discussion of intelligence and achievement tests). The school psychologist reported the following:

> He is presently functioning within the average range of intellectual abilities, but there is a significant discrepancy between his high average verbal skills and his average performance skills. He has difficulty with tasks requiring part-whole relationship and flexibility for new material and information. Billy is performing significantly below his ability level in language and mathematics. As a result, it appears that he would benefit from a more individualized instructional program to remediate those areas. It is recommended that he participate in a special education program for part of the school day.

Mrs. Gordon used both the Peabody Individual Achievement Test (PIAT) and the Basic Achievement Skills Individual Screener (BASIS). Although both tests are achievement tests, they differ in the procedures of testing. The PIAT uses a visual selection process in which the student need only point to one of four responses to each of the examiner's questions in math, reading recognition and comprehension, and spelling. No written work is necessary for scoring. The BASIS requires written work in math, spelling, and written composition (from the third grade up). This test was selected because Mrs. Gordon believed that Billy's written work in math and spelling would best document her observations regarding reversals in math sequencing and poor spelling and writing patterns.

---

* The WISC-R is an intelligence test that measures ability in verbal and nonverbal, or performance, areas such as visual-spatial competency.

When the assessment report was completed, the school assessment team meeting was scheduled for the formal IEP meeting. Present at this meeting were the school psychologist, Mrs. Gordon representing special education, a teacher (Mr. Davis), the principal, and the parent (Mrs. Fields). All the findings were explained to Mrs. Fields. The school psychologist explained that Billy had high average skills but was not achieving close to his potential academic ability. Mrs. Gordon explained that her observations and assessments were in agreement with those of the school psychologist and further explained some of the particular problems she had observed in the classroom and documented on the BASIS. The committee discussed Billy's social and emotional behavior and answered numerous questions that Mrs. Fields had about the special education services at the school. Mrs. Fields and the committee agreed that Billy should be placed in the resource program for two periods a day (at least two hours), when he would receive special instruction related to his particular needs. The rest of the day he would receive instruction in his regular classroom, with Mr. Davis working closely with Mrs. Gordon to provide academic activities that would further Billy's academic progress. Mrs. Fields was satisfied with the established program and signed the IEP. A copy of the educational objectives for the IEP is shown in Figure 5.2. Notice that it was signed for the duration of one academic year, with goals of 6 and 12 months. Mrs. Fields received a copy of this sheet along with a summary and interpretation of Billy's test scores, and a copy of the signature sheet signed by all the participants.

Mrs. Fields was told that she would be called for regular conferences and could at any time call the resource teacher if she had any questions. At the end of the 12-month period there would be another assessment to review Billy's progress. Another IEP meeting would be held, and a decision would be made to determine whether full remediation had been achieved or whether a new IEP with new goals should be written (again with parental consent) if additional special education was required.

## Public Law 99-457

In 1986 an amendment to P.L. 94-142 was passed. The law, P.L. 99-457 (Part H), Services for Infants and Toddlers with Handicapping Conditions, provides funding for eligible children from birth to age 2 who need early intervention services because of a developmental delay or who have a diagnosed condition that could result in developmental delay. This condition can be in cognitive, physical, psychosocial, language, or speech development. The purposes of the law are:

1. To enhance the development of handicapped infants and toddlers and to minimize their potential for developmental delay.

PUPIL NAME: _Billy Fields_    B/D: ___/___/___    Date of Meeting: ___/___/___

(Use of a number/code system for writing of goals/objectives must first be approved by the Division of Special Education and, if approved explanatory material shall be attached to the IEP for parent and service provider.)

## G. ANNUAL GOALS AND SHORT TERM OBJECTIVES

| Goals/Responsible Personnel | Short Term Objectives | Evaluation Criteria For Objectives |
|---|---|---|

**1.** ☐ Instruc. Area: _Math_  ☐ DIS Area: ___

Goal: _To add and subtract to the thousands with re-grouping in correct right - left sequence to the 80% level_

Responsible Personnel: _Resource Specialist Teacher_

Beginning date: ___/___/___   Ending date: ___/___/___

If RSP ☑ or DIS ☐

indicate frequency and total minutes per week: _4X / 50 min_ _200 min per week_

Short Term Objectives:
a. _Billy will use correct right - left sequence in addition and subtraction. He will begin with two columns of numbers and progress to five columns re-grouping accurately at the 80% level_

b. _He will recite the multiplication tables 1-10._

Objectives: 6   a ___ b ___
Expected date of achievement: _end / year_
Observation ☑ ☑
Informal Assess. ☑ ☑
Formal Test ☐ ☐
Other _selected work samples._ ☑ ☑
Date achieved ___
Not achieved ☐ ☐
Comment: ___

---

**2.** ☐ Instruc. Area: _Reading_  ☐ DIS Area: ___

Goal: _To read and write from dictation all short CVC and long CVCV vowel silent 'e' words at 80% level._

Responsible Personnel: _Resource Specialist Teacher_

Beginning date: ___/___/___   Ending date: ___/___/___

If RSP ☑ or DIS ☐

indicate frequency and total minutes per week: _4X / 80 min_ _200 min per week_

Short Term Objectives:
a. _Billy will use basic phonic reading rules beginning with short vowel words combined with consonant digraphs and consonant blends by verbally. From dictation at the 80% level._

b. _He will learn all silent 'e' long vowel words combined with consonant digraphs and consonant blends by writing them from dictation at the 80% level._

Objectives: 6   a ___ b ___
Expected date of achievement: _mon. / year_
Observation ☑ ☑
Informal Assess. ☑ ☑
Formal Test ☐ ☐
Other _selected work samples_ ☑ ☑
Date achieved ___
Not achieved ☐ ☐
Comment: ___

---

**3.** ☐ Instruc. Area: _Reading Comprehension_  ☐ DIS Area: ___

Goal: _To read paragraphs and correctly respond to questions at 80% level._

Responsible Personnel: _Classroom Teacher_

Beginning date: ___/___/___   Ending date: ___/___/___

If RSP ☐ or DIS ☐

indicate frequency and total minutes per week: ___/___

Short Term Objectives:
a. _Billy will read short paragraphs and identify who, what, when, where, and why (questions)._

b. _He will read more than one paragraph and properly respond to the comprehension questions by following the passage at the 80% level._

Objectives: 6   a ___ b ___
Expected date of achievement: _mon. / year_
Observation ☑ ☑
Informal Assess. ☑ ☑
Formal Assess. ☐ ☐
Other ☐ ☐
Date achieved ___
Not achieved ☐ ☐
Comment ___

---

**4.** ☐ Instruc. Area: ___  ☐ DIS Area: ___

Goal: ___

Responsible Personnel: ___

Beginning date: ___/___   Ending date: ___/___

If RSP ☐ or DIS ☐

indicate frequency and total minutes per week: ___/___

Short Term Objectives:
a. ___

b. ___

Objectives:    a ___ b ___
Expected date of achievement: ___/___
Observation ☐ ☐
Informal Assess. ☐ ☐
Formal Test ☐ ☐
Other ☐ ☐
Date achieved ___
Not achieved ☐ ☐
Comment: ___

FORM 27.808-2 (Rev. 6/81) P.O. 12D-62108-1

Figure 5.2 Individualized Education Program. *Source: Los Angeles Unified School District, Division of Special Education, 1981.*

[1] CVC refers to consonant-vowel-consonant words (e.g., *hat, hit, hot*); CVCV, to consonant-vowel-consonant-vowel words (e.g., *hate, cape, tape*).

[2] Consonant digraphs are "*sh, wh, th*" sounds. Consonant blends are "*bl, dr, cr*" sounds.

2. To reduce the educational costs to our society . . . by minimizing the need for special education and related services after handicapped infants and toddlers reach school age.
3. To minimize the likelihood of institutionalization of handicapped individuals and maximize the potential for independent living in society.
4. To enhance the capacity of families to meet the special needs of their infants and toddlers with handicaps. (paragraph 671a)

The legislation allows each state to define "developmental delay" as it sees fit. In addition, the law recognizes that it is often difficult to diagnose accurately the precise handicapping condition at such a young age. As a result, the law allows the states to serve "at risk" children—that is, medically at risk or environmentally at risk or both (Gallagher, 1989).

Among those infants and toddlers considered to be at risk are those that have been exposed to street drugs (e.g., cocaine, PCP, crack) in utero or who were born drug-addicted. It is too early to determine what, and if any, educational disabilities will become manifest in these children in a predictable way. The important aspect for you to understand is that, regardless of the etiology (cause) of their condition, these children, whether or not they are labeled as exceptional children, as well as regular education children who may be experiencing temporary disruptions in their lives, will be a part of your classroom. It is up to you to be sensitive to and recognize their special needs.

One of the major purposes of the legislation is to help families deal with infants and toddlers who have special problems. For this reason, the individualized family service plan (IFSP) requires the participation of a parent or guardian in the development and review of the program. The IFSP identifies the child's development, the family's ability to deal with the situation and its needs, and the intervention services that will be provided to help the family deal with its needs.

## PARENTS OF EXCEPTIONAL CHILDREN

**What are the important issues and concerns of parents of special education students?**

The importance of involving parents in their children's educational program cannot be overemphasized. In particular, parents of exceptional children can play an important role in helping to teach their handicapped children and in being active in the assessment and decision-making process regarding their children. Remember that P.L. 94-142 requires parents' involvement in developing an instructional plan for their child. Unfortunately, parents tend to be rather passive in the IEP meetings (Gilliam & Coleman, 1981) and often don't know (or don't feel qualified to comment upon) how their children are functioning in school (Abramson et al., 1983). To fulfill their roles adequately, it is important that parents acquire the knowledge and skills to do so. The schools must provide the necessary parent education.

Research has indicated that when parents are involved in their children's education, the children do better in school (Bailey & Worley, 1984; Bronfenbrenner, 1974; Zigler & Valentine, 1979). In addition, although P.L. 94-142 applies to all families, parents who are more involved in the school or are more articulate in expressing their point of view often are more successful in obtaining the services they want for their children. Many school districts and private educational consultants offer special seminars on the rights of parents and the IEP procedure to equalize the impact of politics in the process.

As a teacher, you need to be sensitive to the pressures of a parent of an exceptional student. Remember that parents face extra responsibilities when raising handicapped children. They may feel overwhelmed, anxious, or stressed (Peterson & Cooper, 1989) and often have more marital and family conflict (Moroney, 1981). Some parents adjust well to learning about their child's handicap, but other parents have a difficult time accepting the realization of their child's problem. As a result, you will meet various types of parent. At one extreme you will find parents who are very supportive of your instructional program; at the opposite extreme you will find parents who question almost everything you do and are less supportive. In general, parents will be cooperative with you in helping their child or adolescent receive a good education.

Teacher-parent conferences are an important source of information for both you and the parent. After all, the parent has a great deal of information that can be useful in the classroom. In addition, you can provide assessment of the child's progress and make recommendations for parental involvement at home. In Chapter 13, I provide detailed information for conducting parent-teacher conferences that will help you in dealing with all parents.

## THE CHALLENGE TO THE REGULAR CLASSROOM TEACHER

**In what ways can a teacher assist special education students to maximize both their academic and social behavior in the classroom?**

Classroom teachers play important roles in the identification, diagnosis, referral, and instruction of exceptional students and are important members of the assessment team. First, they must be able to identify students who can be considered at risk for academic failure. Teachers have a role in screening students to identify possible handicapping conditions. Second, they must learn to use informal and formal assessment methods to obtain precise information about students' academic skill (i.e., they must develop the ability to diagnose). Third, they must decide when a student should be referred to a school psychologist, speech therapist, or other professionals for more intensive evaluation. Fourth, they must contribute to the assessment team's deliberation concerning the type of educational services the diagnosed student needs (Moran, 1978). Finally, the teacher must implement the specialized program in the classroom.

When you are concerned about a child's progress, the first avenue that must be investigated is always physical. It may seem too obvious to mention, but a child who, for example, is experiencing reading difficulties needs to have his or her vision checked. Visual acuity deficits are common, and even children who already wear corrective lenses should have a vision screening. All too often the obvious or simple causes are overlooked.

It is important to realize that not every student who demonstrates some handicap will fall under the guidelines of P.L. 94-142 and receive an evaluation by an assessment team. A student may have low achievement in an academic area but because the gap between the student's scholastic aptitude and actual achievement is not large enough (e.g., an eighth-grade student with normal intelligence functioning at the seventh-grade level in mathematics), he or she generally will not qualify for special education services. This means that the responsibility for developing an appropriate educational program for low achievers often rests entirely with the classroom teacher. Assistance from other professionals is usually limited to consultation on methods and materials.

When students do qualify for special services and remain in the regular classroom for part or all of the day, it is the responsibility of the teacher to implement the classroom program as specified in the student's individualized education plan. Research on regular teacher attitudes toward mainstreaming shows that many teachers are not positively disposed toward having handicapped children in their classrooms and feel unprepared to teach them effectively (Madden & Slavin, 1983; Semmel, Gottlieb, & Robinson, 1979). Some teachers view mainstreamed students with academic handicaps as an additional burden placed on them. Teachers appear to be most concerned about (1) their own ability to provide an instructional program according to the needs of handicapped students and (2) the social acceptance of handicapped students by their peers. Fortunately, teachers are now receiving more training in exceptional education in both preservice and inservice education. In addition, more books and materials are available as resource information for teaching exceptional children. As a result of these efforts, many educators expect that regular teachers will develop greater confidence and expertise in teaching exceptional children.

Madden and Slavin (1983) identified a number of teaching methods that have been successful in improving handicapped children's social acceptance and/or academic achievement in the regular classroom. Problems of social rejection of mainstreamed students can be remedied by providing *social skills training* (i.e., training students in the social skills necessary for forming friendships). Examples of social skills that can be taught are learning to recognize that one interrupts at the pause or at the lowering of the voice, learning how to deal with conflict and anger, learning how to interpret the nuances of facial expressions and body postures, and learning to use polite words (Gresham, 1984, 1988a, 1988b). (See Chapter 11 for specific ideas about how to implement social skills training.) Another type of intervention used for improving both social acceptance and academic achievement is *cooperative learning*, in which handicapped and nonhandicapped students work in teams on academic and class projects. (Detailed discussion of various cooperative learning procedures is found in Chapter 8.) Finally, *individualized instruction* is a widely used method for accommodating the needs of low-achieving and handicapped students. For example, Wang (1980) has developed the Adaptive Learning Environments Model (ALEM), which takes into consideration the fact that students learn in different ways and at different rates. The program provides several types of instruction for a variety of student differences. You will learn to use successful teaching practices. What is most interesting is that these same practices have proven to be successful with regular students as well as with exceptional children (Larrivee, 1985).

In summary, laws can be passed to protect the rights of students. However, the quality of the implementation of educational programs ultimately determines the benefits of these programs. The teacher's attitudes and skills play a major role in determining the success of mainstreaming.

The major theme of this chapter is that teachers will have to make adjustments in their methods when dealing with exceptional children. Such children cannot be placed in a regular class and be expected to learn by the same methods every other child is using. The reason these children have been identified as being exceptional is that they cannot profit from *only* the normal methods of instruction. Another important implication is that teachers need to be concerned with the children's personal and social development as well as their academic progress.

## THINKING ABOUT THE TEACHING-LEARNING MODEL

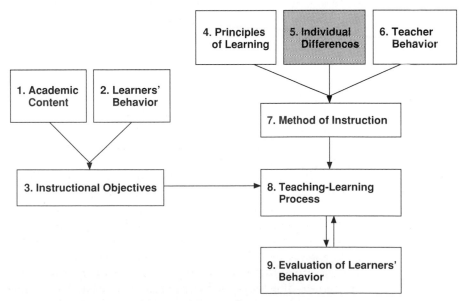

*Source: Adapted from Hunter, 1971, in Allen and Seifman.*

One of the requirements of P.L. 94-142 is that an individualized education program be written by a committee for each student who is receiving special education services. The IEP is a system of accountability that requires specific learning objectives (box No. 3). Because as the student's teacher you will be one person on this committee, it is important that you learn how to write specific objectives (Chapter 9), translate them into effective teaching strategies (box No. 7), and evaluate their outcomes (box No. 9). The succeeding chapters in this book will provide the background to help to accomplish these tasks.

The discussion of self-concept in Chapter 4 has important implications for the student with learning disabilities. Recent research indicates that students with learning disabilities do not have a low general self-concept. They appear to have a lower academic self-concept than their nonhandicapped peers. There also is evidence to indicate that these students believe that they don't have the ability to achieve and have low expectations for future achievement (Chapman, 1989). Since students with learning disabilities have the potential to succeed, teachers need to be especially sensitive to negative perceptions by these students as they attempt to help them succeed. The discussion of maladaptive self-perceptions in Chapter 10, (Motivation) is especially relevant to some exceptional students.

Knowledge of teacher behavior and classroom management (box No. 6), discussed in Chapters 10 and 11, will provide insights for organizing the classroom and for managing and interacting with students. As mentioned in this chapter, the teacher's attitudes regarding exceptional children in regular classrooms can play an important role in successful mainstreaming. Therefore, it is important that you explore your attitudes and beliefs about special education and handicapped children. Read carefully the section on teacher expectations in Chapter 10, because there you will learn how your beliefs or expectations often determine the ways students are treated and how much they will learn.

Last, exceptional students probably are subjected to more testing than average students. Information derived from various assessments can help the classroom teacher to develop the most appropriate instructional program for the student. Therefore, because the classroom teacher has to make important decisions regarding instructional strategies, it is important that you understand what the diagnostic instruments indicate so that you can teach more effectively.

## KEY POINTS

1. Labeling children's disabilities has advantages and disadvantages.
2. Children must score below 70 on an intelligence test *and* have deficits in adaptive behavior before they can be labeled as mentally retarded.
3. Educable mentally retarded (EMR) students are often "retarded" only

in school. In addition to functioning well outside school, they can generally master very basic academic skills.

4. There is no one universal definition of *learning disabilities*.

5. Using direct instructional approaches rather than training psychological processes appears to be more successful for helping students with learning disabilities.

6. Behavior displayed by children with behavior disorders is characterized by excesses and deficits.

7. Teachers tend to overestimate the number of behavior-disordered students in their classrooms.

8. More males, low-SES, and minority-group students are classified as behavior-disordered than are females and middle-SES students.

9. Hearing-impaired children usually have language and communication problems.

10. There is no causal relationship between deafness and intelligence.

11. Teachers need to recognize signs of possible auditory and visual impairment.

12. There are both legal and educational definitions of visual impairment.

13. The visually impaired child is affected by such factors as brightness, size of image, contrast, time, and distance.

14. The teacher should be aware of potential negative interpersonal relations and poor self-concept of speech-impaired children.

15. Speech and language disorders are related but are not the same disability.

16. Children with physical and health impairments may need special equipment and other modifications for learning in a regular classroom.

17. Gifted and talented students possess a wide range of abilities and traits.

18. Although persons above average in intelligence are more likely to be creative, persons of average or high intelligence are not necessarily creative.

19. The Education for All Handicapped Children Act (P.L. 94-142) provides for a free, appropriate public education for all handicapped children, the right to due process, protection against discriminatory testing in diagnosis, individualized education programs (IEPs), and placement in an educational setting that is the least restrictive environment.

20. Teachers play an important role in the development of an IEP in terms of referral, assessment, placement, and instruction.

21. Mainstreaming is a term used to describe programs that educate handicapped children, whenever possible, with their nonhandicapped peers.

22. Some educators believe that special education should be implemented within the regular school program, whereas others believe that general education teachers are not trained sufficiently to meet the needs of exceptional students.

23. The pull-out or resource approach to special education has not had positive effects on student achievement.

24. Public Law 99-457, an amendment to P.L. 94-142, provides funding for eligible children from birth to age 2. The purpose of this funding is to furnish early intervention services because of a developmental delay or for a diagnosed condition that could result in a developmental delay.
25. Parents need to be more involved in the education of their exceptional children.
26. Teachers need to be sensitive to the child-rearing pressures of parents with handicapped children.
27. Teacher attitude toward mainstreaming is an important factor in determining the success of a student's placement.
28. Training in social skills, cooperative learning, and individualized instruction are important methods of educating exceptional children.
29. The regular class teacher should meet with the special education teacher to determine specific strengths, weaknesses, and needs of exceptional children.

## KEY TERMS

Education for All Handicapped Children Act (P.L. 94-142), p. 166
least restrictive educational environment, p. 166
exceptional, p. 166
disabled, p. 166
handicapped, p. 166
educable mentally retarded (EMR), p. 171
learning disabilities, p. 173
minimal brain damage, p. 176
behavior disordered, p. 178
hearing-impaired, p. 180
visual impairment, p. 183
speech disorder, p. 186
language disorder, p. 186
individualized education program (IEP), p. 196
mainstreaming, p. 199
resource room, p. 200
regular education initiative, p. 201

## SUGGESTIONS FOR FURTHER READING

The following books are good basic references for special education:

Bauer, A. M., & Shea, T. M. (1989). *Teaching exceptional students in your classroom.* Needham Heights, MA: Allyn & Bacon.
Cartwright, G. P., Cartwright, C. A., & Ward, M. E. (1989). *Educating special learners* (3rd ed.). Belmont, CA: Wadsworth.

Gearheart, B. R., & Gearheart, C. (1989). *Learning disabilities: Educational strategies* (5th ed.). Columbus, OH: Merrill. Contains a good chapter on programs for adolescents and adults.

Gearheart, B. R., Weishahn, M., & Gearheart, C. J. (1988). *The exceptional student in the regular classroom.* (4th ed.). Columbus, OH: Merrill.

Hallahan, D. P., & Kauffman, J. M. (1989). *Exceptional children: Introduction to special education* (4th ed.). Englewood Cliffs, NJ: Prentice-Hall.

Heward, W. L., & Orlansky, M. D. (1988). *Exceptional children: An introductory survey of special education* (3rd ed.). Columbus, OH: Merrill.

Kerr, M. M., Nelson, C. M., & Lambert, D. L. (1987). *Helping adolescents with learning and behavior problems.* Columbus, OH: Merrill.

Kirk, S. A., & Gallagher, J. J. (1989). *Introduction to special education* (6th ed.). Boston: Houghton Mifflin.

Long, D. (1978). *Johnny's such a bright boy. What a shame he's retarded: In support of mainstreaming in public schools.* Boston: Houghton Mifflin. An experienced teacher writes about the effects of labeling.

Wang, M. C., Reynolds, M. C., & Walberg, H. J. (Eds.). (1987). *Handbook of special education. Vol. 1: Learner characteristics and adaptive education.* New York: Pergamon Press. Has chapters on research on learning characteristics of handicapped students, differential programming in serving handicapped students, and noncategorical programming for mildly handicapped students.

Wang, M. C., Reynolds, M. C., & Walberg, H. J. (Eds.). (1988). *Handbook of special education. Vol. 2: Mildly handicapped conditions.* New York: Pergamon Press. Includes chapters on research on mild mental retardation, behavioral disorders, and learning disability.

The following books are helpful references for the regular class teacher working with exceptional children:

D'Zamko, M. E., & Hedges, W. (1985). *Helping exceptional students succeed in the regular classroom.* West Nyack, NY: Parker.

Kroth, R. L., & Otteni, H. (1985). *Communicating with parents of exceptional children: Improving parent-teacher relationships* (2nd ed.). Denver: Love.

Moran, M. R. (1978). *Assessment of the exceptional learner in the regular classroom.* Denver: Love.

Schulz, J. B., & Turnbull, A. P. (1984). *Mainstreaming handicapped students: A guide for classroom teachers* (2nd ed.). Boston: Allyn & Bacon.

Shea, T. M., & Bauer, A. M. (1985). *Parents and teachers of exceptional students: A handbook for involvement.* Boston: Allyn & Bacon.

Turnbull, A. P., Strickland, B. B., & Brantley, J. B. (1982). *Developing and implementing individualized education programs.* Columbus, OH: Merrill.

Wood, J. W. (Ed.). (1989). *Mainstreaming: A practical approach for teachers.* Columbus, OH: Merrill.

## FOLLOW-UP ACTIVITIES

### 1. Educate Exceptional Children

Give a brief report to the class on how a teacher can help an exceptional child learn more effectively in a regular classroom. Select material for this report from books on exceptionality listed in the Suggestions for Further Reading section of this chapter or in the following journals:

*Exceptional Children*
*Journal of Special Education*
*American Journal of Mental Deficiency*
*Mental Retardation*
*Journal of Learning Disabilities*
*Behavioral Disorders*
*Behavior Therapy*
*Journal of Speech and Hearing Disorders*
*The Volta Review* (about hearing problems)
*Journal of Visual Impairment and Blindness*
*Education of the Visually Handicapped*
*Journal of Rehabilitation*
*The Gifted Child Quarterly*
*Journal of Creative Behavior*

### 2. Observe an Exceptional Child in the Classroom

Identify an exceptional student to observe in a special education class or in a regular classroom. After observing the student's behavior, ask the teacher to discuss attitudes and perceptions about the student's academic progress. Briefly report on your observation and discussion with the teacher. Include in your report the specific behavior you observed, any problems the student had in the classroom, how the teacher attempted to help the student, and recommendations for educating the student more effectively in the classroom.

### 3. Interview a Handicapped Adult

Interview a handicapped adult and ask about personal educational experiences. What were the most pleasant and unpleasant experiences? How did teachers react toward the individual? What recommendations does the person have for helping students with the same handicap?

### 4. Report on a Current Issue in Special Education

Identify a current issue in special education from your reading in journals and textbooks (e.g., instructional approaches, labeling, legal rights of the handicapped, and mainstreaming). Write a report about your research on the issue and include the following (Test, Howard, & Orlansky, 1980):

1. Define the issue.
2. Describe the various viewpoints covering the issue; compare and contrast these viewpoints.
3. Discuss your personal reactions to the issues.

## 5. Teach Students about Exceptional Children

Develop a lesson plan that could be taught when a handicapped student joins a class. Assume that the students have never had a handicapped student in class. Select the grade or subject area related to your teaching specialization. Use the reference material in the Suggestions for Further Reading section of this chapter.

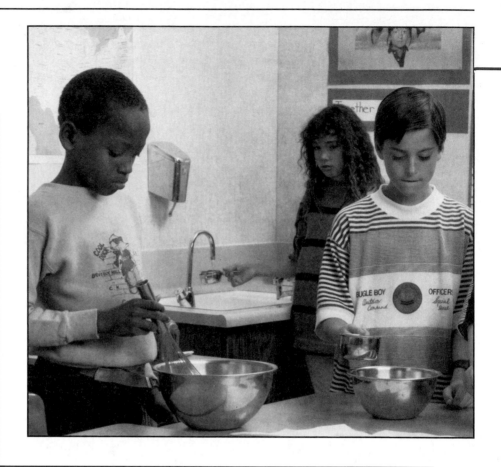

# P A R T   T W O

# Learning Theories and Instructional Applications

## PART OVERVIEW

The primary responsibility of teachers is to help students learn. Teachers' selection of educational goals, instructional procedures, and classroom organization and behavior are based in part on their conceptualization of the teaching-learning process. Chapter 1 discussed how a teacher's beliefs can influence the nature of teacher-student interaction. In this section you will learn that teachers' beliefs about their role can have an important impact on instructional decisions.

All teachers have a belief or theory about learning that is the very fabric of their teaching strategy. By watching teachers behave in the classroom, we can usually infer their basic assumptions about the teaching-learning process, even though those teachers may not be able to articulate their beliefs. For example, the teacher who directs and controls all student activities is operating under a set of beliefs different from those of the teacher who establishes conditions under which students make many of their own decisions about how they will learn.

I believe that one of the objectives of teacher education is to help teachers to see the relationship between beliefs and practices. Throughout the history of education, practices have changed as we have learned more about the learning process. Years ago teachers had it drummed into their heads that the best way to ensure learning was through repetition, a principle from behavioral learning theory that dominated educational thinking for some time. Students spent their time copying spelling words, historical information, and mathematical formulas over and over again until they learned the information. Teachers began to change some of their methods when they were confronted with views based on research findings that repetition was not the best strategy for attaining higher-level learning objectives.

Before proceeding, let's identify some of your beliefs about learning. Check whether you agree or disagree with the following statements (adapted in part from Seaberg, 1974, pp. 7–8):

| Agree | Disagree | I believe that: |
|---|---|---|
| \_\_\_\_ | \_\_\_\_ | 1. Learners need grades, gold stars, and other incentives as motivation to learn and to accomplish school requirements. |
| \_\_\_\_ | \_\_\_\_ | 2. Learners can be trusted to find their own goals and should have some options or choices in what they learn in school. |
| \_\_\_\_ | \_\_\_\_ | 3. Teachers need to determine what students are thinking about while solving math problems. |
| \_\_\_\_ | \_\_\_\_ | 4. Students should be graded according to uniform standards of achievement, which the teacher sets for the class. |
| \_\_\_\_ | \_\_\_\_ | 5. Students should set their own individual standards and should evaluate their own work. |
| \_\_\_\_ | \_\_\_\_ | 6. Curriculum should be organized along subject matter lines that are carefully sequenced. |
| \_\_\_\_ | \_\_\_\_ | 7. The teacher should help students to monitor and control their own learning behavior. |
| \_\_\_\_ | \_\_\_\_ | 8. The school experience should help students to develop positive relations with peers. |

For the most part, statements 1, 4, and 6 would be supported most strongly by behavioral psychologists, statements 3 and 7 by cognitive psychologists, and statements 2, 5, and 8 by humanistic psychologists. Did your responses fall into any particular pattern? Let's briefly review each of these theoretical positions.

Contemporary *behaviorists* (often called S-R psychologists) view environmental factors in terms of *stimuli* and resultant behavior in terms of *responses*. They attempt to demonstrate that behavior is controlled by environmental contingencies of external reward or reinforcement, which are links between behavioral responses and their effects (or stimuli). Teachers who accept the behavioral perspective assume that the behavior of students is a response to their past and present environment and that all behavior is learned. For example, classroom troublemakers "learn" to be disruptive because of the attention (reinforcement) they get from peers; withdrawn students "learn" that their environment does not reinforce gregariousness, and they become reserved and silent. As a result, any behavior can be analyzed in terms of its reinforcement history. The logical extension of the behavioral principle of learning is a method to change or modify behavior. The teacher's responsibility, therefore, is to construct an environment in which the probability of reinforcing students for correct or proper behavior is maximized. This goal is best attained by carefully organizing and presenting information in a designed sequence.

In contrast to the behavioral perspective, *cognitive psychologists* focus more on the learner as an active participant in the teaching-learning process. Those who adhere to this perspective believe that teachers can be more effective if they know what knowledge the learner already has acquired and what the learner is thinking about during instruction. More specifically, the cognitive approach tries to understand how information is processed and structured in an individual's memory. Many cognitive psychologists believe that teachers should instruct students in ways to use techniques or strategies to learn more effectively. Weinstein and Mayer (1985) state that effective instruction "includes teaching students how to learn, how to remember, how to think, and how to motivate themselves" (p. 315).

*Cognitive-developmental psychologists* such as Piaget (Chapter 2) study the steps in children's thinking and believe that it is quite different from adult thinking. They stress that teachers must understand the nature of thought processes in planning for instruction.

*Humanistic psychologists* believe that how a person "feels" is as important as how the person behaves or thinks. They describe behavior from the standpoint of the believer rather than of the observer, and they are especially concerned with "self-actualization"—the growth of persons in whatever area they choose. The humanistic teacher is interested in creating an educational environment that fosters self-development, cooperation, and positive communication, because of the belief that these conditions will foster greater learning.

In the next three chapters we investigate theories of learning and their instructional applications in educational settings. I would like you to keep the following three points in mind while you are reading the next three chapters:

1. There is no *one* behavioral, cognitive, or humanistic theory. Individuals within each of these systems differ on various points.
2. Not all educational practices are backed by one specific theory. In fact, more recently, there have been attempts to integrate various orientations that incorporate cognitive-humanistic or cognitive-behavioral methods.
3. You need to learn *when* to use ideas from various perspectives because each has strengths and weaknesses, depending on the particular purpose you may have in mind. There is no intent to have you adopt any one position.

# CHAPTER 6

## Behavioral Approaches to Learning

Computer Competence
Research on CAI
Mastery Learning and Personalized System of Instruction
**CLASSROOM APPLICATION: DEVELOPING AND IMPLEMENTING
A MASTERY LEARNING PROGRAM**

## ORIENTATION

The principles of behavioral psychology are used both in designing instruction and in behavior therapy to treat numerous personal and social problems such as anxiety, fear, aggression, and depression. In this chapter, I will present these principles and focus on their use in an instructional setting. In chapter 11, on classroom management and discipline, I will illustrate how these principles can be used more directly in managing classroom behavior.

The chapter is organized around four major perspectives: **classical conditioning, applied behavior analysis,** which relies on techniques derived from **operant conditioning, social learning theory** (which introduces internal or cognitive processes in behavior), and **cognitive behavior modification** (procedures based on cognitive processes and behavioral principles). Thus you will see how behavioral psychology moved from working with only observable behavior to the incorporation of cognitive processes (e.g., thoughts, beliefs) within its framework.

After mastering the material in this chapter, you will be able to:

- Describe the procedures used in applied behavior analysis for modifying behavior.
- Use shaping to develop complex behaviors.
- Use behavioral principles in designing a lesson.
- Develop and implement a mastery learning program.

## FOCUS QUESTIONS

1. How does Skinner's view of learning differ from that of other behaviorists?
2. What is the difference between classical and operant conditioning?
3. What is the role of discrimination training in instruction?
4. What is the difference between negative reinforcement and punishment?
5. Why is shaping needed in behavior change programs?
6. How are cognitive processes used in observational learning?
7. What is the difference in the role of reinforcement in operant conditioning and Bandura's social learning theory?
8. When is social learning theory a more effective approach to instruction than operant conditioning?

9. How does cognitive behavior modification depart from the traditional behavioral approach to behavior change?
10. How do programmed instruction and computer-assisted instruction employ behavioral principles of learning?
11. What are the similarities and differences between Bloom's mastery learning and Keller's Personalized System of Instruction?

# CLASSICAL CONDITIONING

## Pavlov

A Russian physiologist, Ivan Pavlov (1849–1936), accidentally came upon an interesting learning phenomenon while working with dogs in his laboratory. If a bell was sounded a few seconds before a hungry dog was presented with food, after several trials the dog would salivate simply at the sound of the bell. Pavlov identified the food as an **unconditioned stimulus** and salivation as an **unconditioned response** (an example of a stimulus that produces some observable response without prior learning). The bell, which originally had no particular meaning for the dog, took on meaning, or became a **conditioned stimulus**, because of its association, or pairing, with the food, which elicited a **conditioned response**—salivation.

This kind of learning is called *classical conditioning*, or stimulus substitution, because the conditioned stimulus, after being paired with the unconditioned stimulus often enough, can then be substituted for it. Figure 6.1 is a schematic representation of classical conditioning.

Pavlov found that when a dog was conditioned to salivate at the sound of a bell, it would also salivate at other similar sounds, such as that of a siren, even though the new stimuli were never used in training. Once a particular conditioned stimulus was associated with a response, other sim-

**Before conditioning**

CS (bell) ————————————————➤ no response or irrelevant response

US (food) ————————————————➤ UR (salivation)

**During conditioning**

CS (bell)
US (food) ————————————————➤ UR (salivation)

**After conditioning**

CS (bell) ————————————————➤ CR (salivation)

Figure 6.1 A Schematic Representation of Classical Conditioning.

ilar stimuli also were able to elicit the response. He called this phenomenon **stimulus generalization.**

## Watson

John B. Watson (1878–1958) was the first psychologist in the United States to use Pavlov's research findings as a basis for a learning theory. Watson believed that learning was a process of conditioning reflexes (responses) through the substitution of one stimulus for another. According to Watson, humans are born with a few reflexes and the emotional reactions of fear, love, and rage. All other behavior is established by building new S-R connections through conditioning.

In one of his most famous experiments, Watson conditioned an 11-month-old child to fear a white rat that he had made friends with. Watson made a loud noise (unconditioned stimulus, or US) whenever the rat was presented to the boy, which resulted in a fear response (unconditioned response, or UR). Within a short time, the boy became fearful (conditioned response, or CR) at the sight of the rat (conditioned stimulus, or CS).

Watson also demonstrated that the boy's fear could be unlearned by the process called **extinction.** This is accomplished by repeating the CS without following it up with the US: presenting the rat without making the loud noise.

Many students' attitudes are learned through classical conditioning. For instance, they may learn to acquire negative attitudes toward foreign languages because they associate these languages with the unpleasant experience of being asked to translate sentences aloud in class. Being asked difficult questions in class (US) elicits anxiety (UR). Students who are conditioned to fear foreign languages may generalize their fear to blanket other subjects of the school's curriculum or the institution of school. The same learning process operates in other school experiences.

## APPLIED BEHAVIOR ANALYSIS

### Early Developments—Thorndike

For the first several decades of this century, the learning theory of E. L. Thorndike (1874–1949) dominated educational practice in the United States. His theory became known as **connectionism** because he posited that learning was a process of "stamping in," or forming, connections between a stimulus and a response.

Thorndike developed his theory from extensive research on the effect of reward on the behavior of various animals. One of his major studies used cats that he placed in a "puzzle box"—a small cage with a door that would open if the cat pulled a string hanging inside the cage. The cat's task was to get out of the cage to obtain food (reward) placed outside the cage. Usually the cat went through the process of walking around, clawing at the floor, jumping at the sides of the cage, and other similar movements until, by chance, he pulled the string opening the door of the cage. Thorndike repeated the experiment several times. The cat still stalked around his cage but pulled the string much sooner. After several trials the cat centered his behavior around the string, eventually pulled the string immediately, and collected his reward (food).

Thorndike explained the process of learning as follows: After the cat hit upon the correct response and was rewarded for it, a connection was gradually strengthened between the situation (stimulus) and the response.

From animal learning, it was only a step upward (maybe more!) to human learning, which Thorndike saw as comprising the same elements. His research with various animals gave him his most important principle of learning, the **law of effect** (Thorndike, 1913):

> When a modifiable connection is made between a situation and a response and is accompanied or followed by a satisfying state of affairs, the strength of that connection is increased. When an annoying state of affairs goes with or follows a connection, the strength of that connection is decreased. (p. 71)

The main factor influencing all learning was **reward,** or a "satisfying state of affairs." In his later writings, Thorndike eliminated the negative or "annoying" part of the law of effect because he found that punishment did not necessarily weaken bonds and did not have the opposite effect of reward.

The **law of exercise** was his second important learning principle. In general, it stated that the more a stimulus-response connection was practiced or used, the stronger it would become; the less it was used, the weaker it would become. He also modified this law in his later writings because he found that practice without reward was ineffective. Connections were strengthened only by rewarded practice.

Thorndike's learning theory led to a number of educational practices. His general advice for teachers was "Put together and exercise what should go together, and reward desirable connections" (p. 70).

Thorndike showed one bond between stimulus and response that occurred in mathematics. Constant repetition of multiplication tables with the teacher providing the reward formed bonds between the stimulus (What is 7 x 7?) and the response (49). In reading, repetition was also emphasized by having students learn the most frequently used words at various grade levels.

The more S-R bonds subjects had, the more intelligent they were considered to be, because they had more bonds at their disposal in problem situations. The law of effect led to the use of concrete rewards such as gold stars placed on students' papers and emphasis on verbal praise. The law of exercise led to much repetition, practice, and drill for all subjects.

So far in our discussion of S-R psychologists, we have viewed learning from the perspective of forming connections, or associations, between a stimulus and a response. I have identified two vantage points in this approach: learning through the simultaneous occurrence of stimulus and response (Pavlov and Watson) and learning through the act of being rewarded (Thorndike).

Since the early explanations of learning by these psychologists, many individuals have contributed to these perspectives. Few have made as much impact on educational practice as B. F. Skinner (1904–1990), who is considered the contemporary advocate for the behavioral position.

## Skinner

**How does Skinner's view of learning differ from that of other behaviorists?**

Like Thorndike, Skinner views reward, or reinforcement, as the most important element in the learning process. We tend to learn a response if it is immediately followed by reinforcement. Skinner prefers the term *reinforcement* to *reward* because *reward* is a subjective interpretation of behavior associated with a pleasurable event, whereas *reinforcement* is a neutral term, defined simply as an effect that increases the probability of a response. The use of *reinforcement* removes any subjective interpretation from the concept and, like Skinner's other concepts, is discussed in terms of observable and measurable events. Skinner (1986) states: "a reward is compensation or remuneration for services performed and is seldom immediately contingent on behavior. We reward people; we reinforce behavior" (p. 106). His purpose is to establish relationships between behavior and environmental stimuli that would lead to a science of human behavior. Skinner calls his approach the *experimental analysis of behavior.*

Skinner believes that the purpose of psychology is to predict and control behavior. Because all behavior is learned, it follows that a teacher or psychologist can apply the same principles of learning to change behavior (Skinner, 1953).

Skinner identifies two types of response in the learning process: **respondents** and **operants.** Respondents are elicited by specific stimuli such as Pavlov's bell. Earlier we read about Pavlov's classical conditioning theory and found that an individual can learn by the pairing of association of stimuli. In a respondent situation, an individual learns merely by being in the situation, by responding to the environment.

Although humans learn some behavior by classical conditioning, Skinner thinks that most human behavior takes the form of operant responses that the individual emits. Such behaviors as writing a letter, picking up a book, and driving a car are operants—responses that an individual makes to no known stimulus.

**What is the difference between classical and operant conditioning?**

Initially, an individual's responses in a given situation are random, but after a time certain responses (operants) become more dominant than others because of selective reinforcement. Skinner calls this process *operant conditioning*—a learning situation in which a response is made more probable or frequent as the result of immediate reinforcement. A kindergarten student during the first week of school emits a number of responses: talking with other students, paying attention to the teacher, walking around the room, and bothering other students. As the teacher begins reinforcing certain responses—by smiling when the student pays attention, for example—some of the responses begin to occur more frequently. Of all possible responses that could be emitted in a given situation, some responses become more dominant than others.

An important difference between Pavlov's classical and Skinner's operant conditioning is that in classical conditioning the consequences of a behavior carry no weight in the learning of that behavior. Reinforcement is unnecessary because the stimuli bring about the desired response.

Operant conditioning, although closer to Thorndike's theory than to Pavlov's, is different from Thorndike's explanation of learning. Thorndike felt that reward strengthened a bond that existed between a stimulus and a response, whereas Skinner feels that what is strengthened is not an S-R bond but the probability that the same response will occur again.

*From Operant Conditioning to Applied Behavior Analysis.* Skinner initially developed the principles of operant conditioning with animals—rats and pigeons. Later in his career he wrote about the generalizability of operant principles and their applicability to complex behavior. *Walden Two* (Skinner, 1948) is a novel about a utopian society based upon operant principles. In *Science and Human Behavior* (Skinner, 1953) he pointed out how these same principles functioned in social institutions like government, law, religion, economics, and education.

By the early 1960s psychologists began using operant principles for clinical purposes in shaping or modifying human behavior in applied settings. They worked in hospitals, schools, prisons, and other institutions. This major change in emphasis from basic laboratory research with animals to applied applications led to the formal acknowledgment of what is now called *applied behavior analysis.* A major development in the formal recognition of applied behavior analysis as a separate research entity was the appearance in 1968 of a new journal, the *Journal of Applied Behavior Analysis,* which served as an outlet for research and defined the field. In the journal's first article, Baer, Wolf, and Risley (1968) defined *applied behavior analysis* by stating that the research is *applied* if it was directed toward clinically or socially significant behavior and the psychologist attempted to bring about behavior change of applied significance. Teaching a mentally retarded individual to cook and live independently or teaching a delinquent youth to interview for a job is an example of socially significant behaviors.

Whether the research constitutes *behavior analysis* is determined by the methodological approach in implementing and evaluating treatment interventions. This methodology is marked by a distinct approach toward assessment, experimental design, and data evaluation (Kazdin, 1978). Assessment in applied behavior analysis is conducted by the objective evaluation of overt responses. This means that the psychologist must identify the specific behavior to be changed and determine the frequency or duration of the response before the intervention begins. This level of responding is called the **baseline.** Behavior change is measured by comparing the baseline behavior with behavior after the intervention. The psychologist then attempts to demonstrate that the change is the result of the specific intervention (e.g., reinforcement ) rather than some other factor. This plan for demonstrating the cause of the change is called the *experimental design.*

One of the many types of designs used is to alternate the environmental contingencies over time. The absence of the intervention is called the *baseline* (or *A*) *phase,* while the intervention is called the *experimental* (or *B*) *phase.* One of many different designs used is ABAB, because A and B phases alternate (see Figure 6.2). After the behavior in one phase is stabilized (i.e., it is relatively uniform), the psychologist moves to the next phase. The final step in applied behavior analysis is data evaluation, the determination of whether a change in behavior was made. The purpose of moving back to the baseline phase is to ensure that a cause and effect relationship exists between the behavior and reinforcement. If the researcher stopped after the initial intervention, he or she could not be sure that the change in behavior was the result of reinforcement. The behavior could be attributed to some other environmental condition.

I recommend that teachers using applied behavior analysis employ the two phase AB design: the baseline (A) and intervention phase (B). Although the design has weaknesses in proving a definite cause and effect relationship, it provides the teacher with a relatively easy way of comparing behavior before and after some intervention. Furthermore, I don't feel it

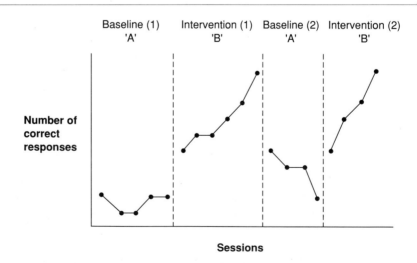

Figure 6.2 Reversal design demonstrating a functional relation between variables. *Note:* At Baseline (2) the reinforcement is stopped and begun again at Intervention (2).

is appropriate for the classroom teacher to halt a successful intervention that works!

Two important criteria are used to evaluate the success of applied behavior analysis: experimental and therapeutic. The change agent must show that the client's behavior during the treatment phase is significantly different from that at the baseline phase. Finally, the change agent must report on the importance of the change in behavior. For example, did the reduction in aggressive behavior by a student allow him or her to function successfully in the classroom? If the aggressive behavior was reduced, but not enough to allow the individual to function in the classroom, the intervention would not be considered successful.

In the literature describing behavioral interventions, you will see both the terms **behavior modification** and *applied behavior analysis* used. Most behavioral psychologists prefer the term *applied behavior analysis*, because it describes the change of behavior by application of behavioral principles. They argue that *behavior modification* is a general term to identify many procedures used to change behavior, including hypnosis, drug therapy, and electroconvulsive shock treatments (Alberto & Troutman, 1990). Most behaviorists would like to dissociate themselves from these other procedures. Yet you will still find books with titles like *Behavior Modification: What It Is and How to Do It* (Martin & Pear, 1988), whose authors prefer that term.

## Discrimination, Stimulus Control, and Generalization

**What is the role of discrimination training in instruction?**

Operant conditioning can be adequately explained without the presence of a stimulus initiating a response. However, we can talk about a response being brought under the control of a **discriminative stimulus** ($S^D$), a cue or signal that increases the probability of a response. This situation is best illustrated in Skinner's early research with rats placed in a small apparatus called a *Skinner box*, which is equipped with a lever, light, food tray, and food-releasing mechanism. By providing a **reinforcing stimulus** ($S^R$), food, the researcher can train a rat to push the lever only when the light ($S^D$) is turned on. If the rat pushes the lever when the light is off, it receives no reinforcement. The light is a cue that makes the response of lever pushing more likely to occur. Later the rat can be taught to push the lever only when the light is off. People, also, respond differently to different stimuli. For example, college students often use different language around their friends from what they use at home with their parents. Behavior is said to be under stimulus control when the response varies depending on what stimulus is present.

Earlier I discussed stimulus generalization in classical conditioning. We also can identify stimulus generalization in operant conditioning. Sometimes behavior learned in one situation will be performed in other, similar situations even though the behavior is not reinforced in the new situations. For example, stimulus generalization occurs when a child responds politely to a teacher in the same way he responds to his parents. The behavioral psychologist who teaches a child to use appropriate social behaviors in a clinic is interested in the transfer or generalization of these same behaviors with peers, at home, and in school.

Events occurring before and after a student makes a response can determine when and where that response will occur. The teacher wants students to learn certain responses under specific conditions. When a student receives the stimulus (4 + 3 = ) and responds (7), reinforcement follows. We say that **discrimination learning** has taken place. An important part of teaching is to present stimuli so specific that only one response is correct. If reinforcement is contingent upon only the correct response, more learning transpires. Another type of generalization involves responses rather than stimulus situations. Changing one response can inadvertently influence other responses. The term **response generalization** describes this condition. For example, adolescents who are taught to reduce their physical aggression when they get mad might also learn to speak in a lower voice and be more patient with others.

The following examples illustrate the stimulus-response processes in learning:

| Teacher Presents Preceding Stimulus ($S^D$) | Child Responds | Teacher Presents Consequent Stimulus ($S^R$) |
|---|---|---|
| "Who was the first president of the United States?" | "Washington." | "Good." |
| "How many times will 4 go into 16?" | "Three." | "No, that's wrong." |
| Teacher shows the letter *B* and asks: "What sound is this?" | No response | No consequence |
| Teacher then says, "This is *Bbbb* say '*Bbbb*.'" | "Bbbb." | "Good, that's much better." |

*Applied Behavior Analysis in Teaching.* The basis of applied behavior analysis in teaching is to ensure responses to stimuli. Unless the learner emits responses to stimuli, it is impossible to guide the student's behavior toward a behavioral goal. Teachers play an important role in the classroom by controlling and directing the learning activities. Behaviorists urge the use of instructional objectives (i.e., objectives stated in terms of actual behaviors such as *list, recite,* and *compare*) because teachers must know what they are trying to accomplish before they plan a sequence of behaviors directed toward a goal. After identifying the objective, the teacher would determine the most logical order of presenting the material in small steps (Chapter 9 includes a discussion on how to write behavioral objectives and plan a sequence of instruction) and then provide reinforcement immediately after the learner responds. The following teaching practices would be encouraged by behaviorists: returning and discussing all exams promptly, questioning students regularly and reinforcing correct answers, checking student work continually, and generally making an attempt to reinforce all behavior conducive to the development of good attitudes toward learning.

## Consequent Stimuli

**What is the difference between negative reinforcement and punishment?**

A number of consequences occurring after a response are discussed in this chapter. Table 6.1 presents a four-cell classification identifying types of reinforcement and punishment. We have already discussed *positive reinforcement*—the presentation of a stimulus that, when added to a situation, increases the probability of a response occurring (cell A). Second, an individual can receive **negative reinforcement**—the termination of an unpleasant stimulus (such as isolation) that, when taken away from a situation, also increases the probability of a response occurring (cell B). In the case of isolation, it may be maintained until the student promises to cease misbehaving. In another example of negative reinforcement, a child becomes sick just as the teacher hands out an examination. The sickness results in removal from class. Thus the response of getting sick has been followed by a negative reinforcer because it discontinued the test, an aversive (unpleasant) stimulus. We might expect "sickness" behavior to increase in frequency in similar test situations. Third, a child can receive **punishment**—the presentation of an unpleasant stimulus (such as contradiction or reprimand) that decreases the probability that a response will occur at all (cell C). Another form of punishment attempts to decrease behavior by taking away a pleasant or reinforcing stimulus (cell D). This type of punishment is used by teachers when they remove students from class activities or even the class itself, until the students are ready to demonstrate proper behavior. The procedure is called **time-out** and will be discussed in Chapter 11 (Classroom Management and Discipline). Note that positive and negative reinforcement seek to increase the probability of a response, whereas punishment aims to suppress the response.

In the studies of operant conditioning with animals, **primary reinforcement** (food or water) is a factor. These reinforcing stimuli work toward

---

TABLE 6.1 **TYPES OF REINFORCEMENT AND PUNISHMENT**

|  | Present Stimulus | Remove Stimulus |
|---|---|---|
| Response Increase | A<br>Positive<br>Reinforcement | B<br>Negative<br>Reinforcement |
| Response Decrease | C<br>Punishment 1 | D<br>Punishment 2<br>(Time-out) |

the satisfaction of the animals' physiological needs. Most reinforcement in educational environments is **secondary reinforcement**—learned. It is reinforcing because it has been paired with (or is exchangeable for) a primary reinforcer. Money, for instance, is not reinforcing to an infant, but later it becomes influential in affecting behavior when the child learns that it can be exchanged for candy.

Behaviorists identify three classes of secondary reinforcers: *social reinforcers* (social acceptance, smiles), *tokens* (physical objects like money, grades, prizes, points), and *activities* (free play, listening to music, trips). The premise behind using activities is **Premack's principle** (1959): Given two activities, the more preferred may be used to increase the rate of the less preferred. In other words, an interesting activity on which a person spends a good deal of time can reinforce behavior in an activity in which the person is less interested and on which the person spends less time. If a child likes to build model airplanes but does not like to read, telling the child he can work on his project after he successfully completes his reading assignment accomplishes reinforcement of the reading behavior.

Havighurst (1970) points out that people react differently to various types of reinforcer. Some students are motivated by being praised verbally in front of their peers; others shun such attention. A reinforcing event is not inherently effective, so it is wise for a teacher to make a list of possible reinforcers for various students in the class. The expression "different strokes for different folks" best summarizes this point.

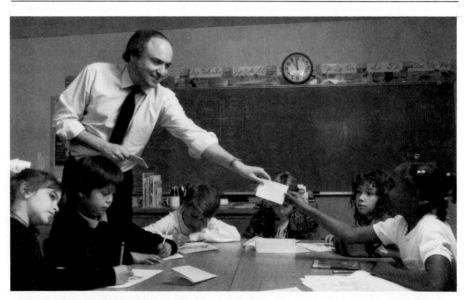

Teachers can use tokens as secondary reinforcers. In the situation above, the teacher gives slips of paper to students for appropriate behavior. These slips are worth points that can be traded for classroom privileges.

Teachers who learn about applied behavior analysis invariably ask, "How do I know what will be reinforcing to a student?" The only sure way is to observe the student and to recognize which stimuli increase the frequency of the response that follows. In a class of 30 or more students, the burden entailed is staggering. Instead, ask the students to fill out a questionnaire that includes such questions as: What special things do you like to work with or play with in the classroom? What are three jobs in this classroom that you like to do most? If you went to a store to buy three games that you like, what would they be? You can modify these questions for the age level of the students in the classroom.

Age difference should be a factor in the teacher's selection of reinforcer. You can use a five-cent eraser as a reinforcer for a young child, but an adolescent demands a reinforcer of greater value. Activities like helping the teacher, using a tape recorder, or doing puzzles are potentially reinforcing for elementary students; for junior high and high school students, more appropriate reinforcing activities are talking to a friend, playing video games, reading a magazine, or listening to music. Make a list of some potential reinforcing stimuli and events for the age level of students you will be working with.

## Schedules of Reinforcement

A *schedule of reinforcement* refers to when or how often a response is reinforced. Through experiments with rats, pigeons, and then humans, Skinner has been able to identify some important relationships between the way in which reinforcement is administered and the rates of learning, response, and extinction.

Reinforcement can be continuous or intermittent; the teacher reinforces correct responses each time or periodically. An experimenter or teacher using an intermittent schedule of reinforcement has two choices: reinforcing a proportion of responses (a ratio schedule) or reinforcing responses following a lapse of time from the previous reinforcement (an interval schedule). There are two types of ratio and interval schedules: fixed and variable.

A **fixed-ratio schedule** is based on presenting the subject with a reinforcer after the subject emits a specified number of responses. In a 4:1 ratio, for example, the subject is reinforced after each set of four responses. The teacher who tells the students that they can go to recess after completing four more problems is using a fixed-ratio schedule of reinforcement.

A **variable-ratio schedule** is based on presenting the subject with a reinforcer after an average number of responses. The exact number of responses may vary, from one reinforcer after every 3 responses to one reinforcer after every 20 responses. In this schedule the subject never knows the exact number of responses required for reinforcement. Outside the realm of education we find another example: Slot machines work on a variable-ratio schedule of reinforcement.

As noted, interval schedules are also fixed or variable. A **fixed-interval schedule** is based on a constant unit of time between reinforcements. Grading students on a 10-week period is an example of a fixed-interval schedule of reinforcement.

A **variable-interval schedule** provides reinforcement following the first correct response after a lapse of time. As in the variable-ratio schedule, the subject never knows when the next reinforcer is due. The student might be reinforced for remaining in her seat according to the following sequence: after 5 minutes of appropriate behavior, 3 minutes, 10 minutes, and 2 minutes. This reinforcement schedule is based on a variable interval, with an average of 5 minutes.

Each of the different schedules produces its own patterns of response. The continuous schedule of reinforcement is most effective in teaching new responses. Lower response rates accompany fixed-interval schedules because of the time lapse involved. The response rate picks up at the end of the time interval, as confirmed by college students' cramming for their final examinations. Fixed-ratio schedules are more conducive to constant response rates, and variable-ratio schedules are most effective for maintaining constant and high response rates.

Undesirable behavior is often unwittingly reinforced. When a teacher occasionally gives in to students' pleading for certain activities, the teacher is reinforcing them intermittently, a practice that contributes to the perpetuation of the behavior. The students learn that if they keep pleading, the teacher will eventually give them their way.

Here are some reinforcement rules to keep in mind:

- In teaching a new task, reinforce immediately rather than permit a delay between response and reinforcement.
- In the early stages of a task, reinforce every correct response. As learning occurs, require more correct responses prior to reinforcement; gradually shift to intermittent reinforcement.
- Reinforce improvements or steps in the right direction. Do not insist on perfect performance on the first try.
- Do not reinforce undesirable behavior.

## Extinction

It is possible to weaken behavior by removing the reinforcing events that maintain the behavior. Behaviorists recommend that extinction be used in conjunction with other techniques. Clarizio (1980) details the use of extinction with modeling and social reinforcement. A second-grade teacher faced a problem with overanxious children who continually blurted out answers without raising their hands. The teacher ignored all called-out answers and acknowledged only those children who raised their hands, with such comments as "Billy has his hand up and is waiting to answer the question" or "Mary has her hand up and is being considerate to the class." The teacher soon noticed a marked increase in hand-raising behavior. In addition, many students who had not participated in class discussions began raising their hands and had more opportunities to contribute to the class discussion.

Many teachers find extinction difficult to use because they must learn to ignore certain misbehaviors. Sometimes they admonish students about the improper behavior (often this attention is reinforcing to many students) and then ignore the behavior for the remaining time. On an intermittent schedule of reinforcement, the teacher's behavior is likely to cause the misbehavior to occur at a higher level than if extinction had not been attempted. Of course, there are many types of behavior teachers cannot ignore, especially behavior that is injurious to students. If the misbehavior consistently occurs, extinction procedures may not be advisable. Extinction works primarily when the reinforcement is attention. If a student is getting attention elsewhere, say, from peers, other changes in teacher-student interaction will have to discourage the behavior.

Another factor to consider is that even after the problem behavior has lessened, it may suddenly reappear. Such **spontaneous recovery** (or re-emergence) can cause difficulty for teachers if they are caught off guard and inadvertenly reinforce the student for the inappropriate behavior. Students often will test to see if the extinction rule is still in effect. Don't conclude that the procedure failed and revert to your previous behavior. The re-emergence of inappropriate behavior can be quickly terminated once again by ignoring it. However, it you don't ignore the behavior, the result may lead to rapid relearning on the part of the student (Alberto & Troutman, 1990).

Last, keep in mind that during the early stages of extinction, misbehavior may worsen before it improves. Kindergarten students who get their way with their teacher by throwing tantrums will become extremely frustrated when the teacher pays no attention to their behavior. However, they will quickly get the message.

The message for teachers regarding the use of extinction is: Be consistent, ignore certain misbehavior, and combine extinction with other methods such as reinforcement of appropriate behavior. Finally, choose behaviors for extinction in situations where you can tolerate the initial rise in intensity and frequency of the misbehavior.

## Shaping—A Method for Developing New Behaviors

**Why is shaping needed in behavior change programs?**

We have learned thus far that the key to learning is the immediate reinforcement of desired behavior. But what happens if the desired behavior is not part of students' behavioral repertoire? For example, how can you reinforce students for doing their homework if they don't take their books home? How can you reinforce students for performing complex behaviors if they never perform them? To solve this problem, behaviorists use a procedure called **shaping,** or **successive approximations,** in which reinforcement is applied to responses that successively approximate (or become increasingly closer to) the desired behavior.

Frazier (1969) reported the use of shaping to improve studying behavior in a residence home for children. The steps needed to attain this goal were broken down into the following components:

- Coming to class on time
- Participating in studying behavior and responding to the teacher
- Performing well on tests
- Completing homework
- Improving performance as time progressed

The students earned points for exhibiting each of these behaviors. Students exchanged their accumulated points for various toys and prizes in a store set up for this purpose. Students who earned enough points could participate in the many preferred activities available.

This behavior modification program increased the level of school attendance from about 50% to 86% after a few months. More important, the students became more cooperative in class and used their study time more effectively.

Students often need help responding appropriately at the lower or prerequisite levels in shaping behavior. This special help, physical, visual, or verbal, is called **prompting.** Basically, it is an additional stimulus that increases the probability that an appropriate response will be made in the presence of the discriminative stimulus ($S^D$). A teacher who holds up a picture of a president after providing biographical information on his life is providing a visual prompt. Another teacher might use a rule as a verbal prompt and define a verb, then present students with sentences and ask: "Is the underlined word a verb?" ($S^D$). "Does the word describe an action? Then it is a verb" (prompt). "Right, Susan, it's a verb" (Alberto & Troutman, 1990). Although prompts are effective ways to increase the probability of success, they should be withdrawn gradually, or faded, as instruction progress. Behaviorists use the term **fading** to describe the gradual removal of a prompt.

You need to consider the following in developing shaping procedures. First, if you are not sure about the desired behavior, you will have difficulty determining the prerequisite behavior, or steps necessary to get there. Second, you need to determine where to start. The students must be able to perform the prerequisite behavior you select so that shaping can begin. Third, you need to consider the size of the steps. If they are too small, you will be wasting a great deal of time; if the steps are too large, the students' behavior will not be reinforced and the desired behavior will not be learned. Finally, you need to be sure that the behavior at one level is acquired before you move to the next level.

## SOCIAL LEARNING THEORY

Since the early 1940s, behavioral psychologists have been interested in how children acquired social behaviors. These behaviors include cooperative, competitive, affiliative, assertive, aggressive, moral-ethical, and other social responses. Social responses are learned primarily from observing the behavior of others and are referred to as **modeling,** or observational learning.

Numerous behavioral explanations have been advanced based primarily on modifications of reinforcement theory (e.g., Baer, Peterson, & Sherman, 1967; Miller & Dollard, 1941; Mowrer, 1960). All of these theories have been criticized because they don't satisfactorily explain all forms of modeling. First, they don't account for the fact that children are usually selective in what they model; children don't imitate all behavior that has been reinforced. Second, children sometimes imitate models with whom they have had no previous interaction. A third problem is that the theories don't adequately explain why children first model new behavior days or weeks after their initial observation without being reinforced for the behavior and without seeing the model reinforced for the behavior.

In 1963, Bandura and Walters, in *Social Learning and Personality Development*, first stated that an individual could model behavior simply by observing the behavior of another person. They departed from the traditional operant conditioning explanation that the individual must perform and be reinforced for his or her responses for learning to occur. Later, Bandura (1969, 1977) proposed the most comprehensive and widely accepted theory of modeling, which he calls *social learning theory* (which also is known as **observational learning**). According to Bandura, children learn social behaviors by observing the actions of important people in their lives—their parents, siblings, teachers, peers, and television heroes. These observations are stored in the form of mental images and other symbolic representations that help them imitate behavior.

Bandura (1977) rejected the unidirectional view of the effects of the environment on the individual, the major premise of the S-R perspective. Instead, his central theme is **reciprocal determinism,** a process by which personal factors, environmental factors, and behavior all operate as "interlocking determinants of each other" (p. 10). In social learning theory, both behavior and the environment are changeable, and neither is the primary determinant of behavioral change. For example, aggressive children expect other children to react hostilely toward them. This expectation causes the aggressive child to act aggressively. The consequence is that other children respond to the child's aggressive behavior more aggressively, thereby strengthening the child's initial expectation (Bell-Gredler, 1986). "Aggressive children thus create through their actions a hostile environment, while children who favor friendly modes of response generate an amicable social milieu" (Bandura, 1977, p. 198).

Bandura's (1977) work helped bridge the behavioral and cognitive perspectives and contributed greatly to the practice of cognitive-behavior therapy. He studied the ways individuals can learn to control their own behavior (see the section on cognitive behavior modification later in this chapter) (Bandura & Perloff, 1967; Bandura & Kupers, 1964) and how modeling can be used to treat phobias (Bandura, Grusec, & Menlove, 1967). Today, self-control procedures and modeling are used in many programs to treat a variety of children's and adolescents' social and emotional problems.

## Types of Modeling

Bandura (1969) has organized modeling behavior into three categories: the **inhibitory-disinhibitory effect,** the **eliciting effect,** and the *modeling effect*. The inhibitory-disinhibitory effect makes a response less frequent or allows it to occur by influencing the response consequences of a model. Generally, we become inhibited when we observe others experience unpleasant consequences for engaging in behavior similar to ours. Bandura (1967) demonstrated how children could disinhibit their fear of dogs. He had children watch a film in which a child who did not fear dogs was playing with a dog in a party setting. He found that the children lost their fear after viewing the film.

A model can also have an eliciting effect on an observer by facilitating a response repertoire already present in the observer. Facilitation occurs when an unlikely response becomes more probable: Observing a friend donate time to collect for the annual cancer drive in your community may motivate you to volunteer your services for various charitable activities.

The final category, modeling effects, develops new responses through the observation of a model. This category has important implications for education. Children learn much new behavior from observing the behavior of parents, siblings, or peers. The small boy who watches his older brother move a kitchen chair to the cupboard to reach a cookie will probably attempt the same behavior later on.

## Processes in Observational Learning

**How are cognitive processes used in observational learning?**

Bandura (1977) identified four components of observational learning: The student must *attend* to the various aspects of the modeling situation, *retain* what has been learned from observing the modeling situation, *motorically reproduce*, or match, what has been observed in the modeling situation, and be *motivated* to perform the behavior observed.

*Attentional Processes.* Modeling will not take place unless the learner attends to and accurately perceives the behavior of the model. Several characteristics of the model and observer determine the extent of observational learning. Observers are more likely to attend to models who are similar to them and are perceived to be competent, warm, and powerful. Observers who are dependent, have lower self-concepts, and/or are anxious are more likely to model behavior. In general, individuals are influenced by the probability of reinforcement (or outcome expectancies) as they determine who and what they observe.

*Retention Processes.* Individuals will not be influenced by observation if they don't remember what they see. Observed behavior is represented in memory in symbolic form. Individuals use two representational systems— *imaginal* and *verbal*. Individuals store sensory images of what they see and use verbal coding to remember the information. For instance, an individual learns, retains, and later reproduces the correct route to a store more accurately by converting the visual information into a verbal code describing the correct series of left and right turns (e.g., RRLR) than by using only the visual imagery of the route. In addition to symbolic coding, rehearsal (e.g., repeating RRLR to oneself) serves as an important memory aid. An observer can increase proficiency and retention by visualizing and/or practicing the observed behavior.

*Motor Reproduction Processes.* The third component of modeling involves converting symbolic representations into appropriate actions. The individual must (1) select and organize the response elements and (2) refine the response on the basis of informative feedback. Thus Little Leaguers who try to model the swing of their favorite major league baseball players will not become good batters unless they practice and receive corrective feedback on their swing. An important factor influencing accomplished performance is the learner's **self-efficacy**—the belief that one can successfully execute the behavior required to produce a particular outcome. If learners don't believe they can master a task, they will not continue working on the task.

**What is the difference in the role of reinforcement in operant conditioning and Bandura's social learning theory?**

*Motivational Processes.* Social learning theory distinguishes between acquisition and performance because individuals do not model everything they learn. This situation led Bandura to employ a mediational interpretation of the effect of reinforcing consequences on behavior. He states: "Reinforcement does play a role in observational learning but mainly as an antecedent rather than a consequent influence" (1977, p. 37). Thus reinforcement is important not as a strengthener of behavior but as a source of information and an incentive. The anticipation of reinforcement influences attentiveness to the model's action and enhances retention of what was observed by motivating the observer to code and rehearse modeled valued behavior.

While direct reinforcement to the observer or model is one way to increase modeling behavior, direct reinforcement is not a necessary component for observational learning. Bandura identifies two other systems: **vicarious reinforcement** and **self-reinforcement.** In vicarious reinforcement, the model is reinforced for some appropriate behavior and the observer's performance of the same behavior increases in frequency even though the observer was not directly reinforced. An example is a teacher who reinforces a student for helping behavior and, as a result, the rest of the students in the class spend more time helping each other. A second function of vicarious reinforcement is the arousal of emotional responses. When an actor or actress does a TV commercial asking you to use a certain cologne or perfume and walks away with a handsome or attractive individual, the reinforcement to you is vicarious, if you intuit or experience the pleasure the actor or actress receives from the attention. The company manufacturing the item hopes that the reinforcement is sufficient for you to purchase the product. Vicarious reinforcement can have the same effect as direct reinforcement or an even stronger effect (Bandura, 1986).

Both direct and vicarious reinforcement involve consequences delivered by the environment. Self-reinforcement, on the other hand, is independent of the consequences delivered by society. It is consciously cultivated by individuals who develop performance standards for themselves and tend to respond to their behavior in self-rewarding ways if their performance matches or exceeds a standard. Thus students who take an extra year of a language establish performance standards for themselves and respond to their own behavior in self-rewarding or self-criticizing ways, depending upon the evaluation of their performance.

Do you have a hobby or interest that you pursue that is self-reinforcing? Do people have to tell you when your work in this special activity is at a high level of proficiency, or do you set your own standards?

## Social Learning in the Classroom

**When is social learning theory a more effective approach to instruction than operant conditioning?**

Children learn a great deal from observation in the classroom. The most obvious use of observation is instruction in new skills (e.g., math problems, art projects, science experiments). Other ways teachers can use modeling is to demonstrate logical thinking and problem-solving behavior by thinking out loud as they solve problems on the blackboard and by displaying intellectual curiosity, emotional control, respect for and interest in others, and good listening and communication habits. Teachers who model such characteristics tend to induce those same qualities in students. However, teachers who exhibit negative social behaviors also induce the same qualities in students (Good & Brophy, 1987).

Clarizio (1980) provides an excellent example of how a teacher used modeling to develop students' interest in English literature. The teacher made it a practice to be reading an interesting book as the students entered the room. Sometimes he laughed out loud, frowned, smiled, or exhibited other behaviors that conveyed interest in the book. Some student always commented about the teacher's interest in the book. The teacher reinforced the student's interest by telling the class a little bit about the book or by reading some of the more humorous or exciting passages. He also asked students to talk about interesting books they had recently read. As an English teacher, he not only talked about the pleasure gained from reading but demonstrated his own enjoyment and interest in reading. Can you think of other ways for a teacher to model important learning behaviors?

A good deal of classroom behavior is learned by vicariously experienced rewards and punishments. Kounin (1970) has found that interaction between a teacher and a student has an impact on other students who view the incident. When the teacher reprimands a student for inappropriate behavior, the whole class experiences the effect. You can encourage social control by discussing how one should behave in the classroom and pointing out how individual students and groups help to maintain this behavior. The identification and reinforcement of positive models provide clues for other class members. However, this same learning process works against the teacher if students see others getting away with misbehavior.

Modeling can be used to teach academic and motor skills and can have a strong effect on learning. It is especially useful when reliance on operant learning procedures would be less efficient or even dangerous. Would you want to be in a car in which the instructor was using a trial-and-error method of learning, waiting to reinforce the driver's correct response? In teaching by modeling, the instructor demonstrates how to perform the task or skill: the student observes this behavior and attempts to imitate the teacher or model. The student often is able to learn complete sequences of behavior in a much shorter time by modeling than by shaping.

Bandura (1977) states that the "failure of an observer to match the behavior of a model may result from any of the following: not observing the relevant activities, inadequately coding modeled events for memory representation, failing to retain what was learned, physical inability to perform, or experiencing insufficient incentives" (p. 29). Can you relate any of these factors to a specific instance in which an instructor's demonstration failed to result in learning? How does social learning theory help you suggest modifications in the instructor's approach?

## COGNITIVE BEHAVIOR MODIFICATION

**How does cognitive behavior modification depart from the traditional behavioral approach to behavior change?**

The latest development in behavioral psychology is the incorporation of various cognitive processes (i.e., thoughts, perceptions, expectancies, self-statements) within the behavioral framework. The theory behind these approaches is that children and adolescents have deficient cognitive processes that guide or control their behavior. If the cognitions that direct or control behavior can be altered, behavioral change will follow. These approaches are called *cognitive behavior modification, cognitive-behavioral therapy,* or *self-control.* As mentioned earlier, Bandura's (1977) social learning theory provided much of the theoretical support for the use of these approaches to the treatment of behavioral, emotional, and academic problems.

## Self-Management

Several self-management or self-control therapies were developed in the 1960s and 1970s. Although early self-control procedures were based on operant principles of learning, developments during the 1970s lead to more cognitive-oriented self-control procedures (Kendall & Braswell, 1985). In the traditional approach to applied behavioral analysis, the classroom teacher uses positive reinforcement and other procedures (e.g., modeling) to improve student behavior. Once the desired behavior changes are attained, a transfer of control is made from the teacher (external) to the student (self-regulation). The procedure involves *self-assessment,* whereby students determine whether they have performed specific behaviors, *self-monitoring,* whereby students monitor and record their performance of certain behaviors, keeping a record of how often and to what extent they engage in some activity, (e.g., how many times they talk out without permission); and *self-reinforcement,* whereby students give themselves reinforcement when they behave appropriately. After a period of time, the procedures permitting students to reinforce themselves for appropriate behavior are slowly removed, and control is shifted to reinforcers in the students' natural environment, like grades, social status, achievement feedback (Workman, 1982).

Some of you may be thinking: "Can a teacher actually trust students to record information honestly and reinforce themselves?" Several studies indicate that students can be effectively trained to monitor their own behavior. In the early stages of this training, students are told that their individual assessments will be observed by the teacher. Self-monitoring accuracy does improve when individuals are informed that their accuracy is being assessed by someone else ( Mace & Kratochwill, 1988). In fact, there is evidence that self-reinforcement procedures are generally as effective as teacher-administered consequences (Workman & Hector, 1978).

Today, more cognitively oriented self-control techniques are used. One way individuals have been taught to control their own behavior is through self-instruction, a type of self-control that is based on the work of Luria (1961) and Vygotsky (1962). Luria (1961) found that as children get older, they are able to inhibit behavior not only by following adult instructions but also by responding to their own self-directed instructions. Vygotsky (1962) described a progression from overt language to "internalized talking" and finally to silence. He pointed out that self-talk is important because it provides self-guidance.

## Self-Verbalization

The theory behind self-verbalization training is that an individual's inner speech influences cognition (thinking) and guides behavior. Some children have inappropriate self-verbalizations and, therefore, act in an inappropriate manner. Thus if more appropriate self-verbalizations are introduced, behavior can be changed.

Meichenbaum and Goodman (1971) developed a cognitive modification program called *self-instructional training* to teach impulsive children to work more slowly and carefully. Each child observed a model performing a task who simultaneously verbalized the procedures used. The model then verbally instructed the child while the child performed the task. Next, the child performed the task while instructing himself or herself and then tried the task while whispering the instruction to himself or herself. Finally, the child performed the task silently (using covert self-instruction).

The following (Meichenbaum & Goodman, 1971) is the verbalization produced by the model; the purpose of the statements is in parentheses:

> Okay, what is it I have to do (*problem definition*)? You want me to copy the picture with the different lines. I have to go slowly and carefully. Okay, draw the line down, down, good; then to the right, that's it; now down some more and to the left (*focusing attention and response guidance*). Good, I'm doing fine so far (*self-reinforcement*). Remember, go slowly. Now back up again. No, I was supposed to go down. That's okay. Just erase the line carefully. . . . Good. Even if I make an error, I can go on slowly and carefully (*self-evaluative coping skills and error-correcting options*). I have to go down now. Finished. I did it! (p. 117)

Initially, psychologists used cognitive behavior modification to help children in clinical settings with various behavior problems (e.g., impulsiveness, hyperactivity, aggression, and anxiety) to develop better self-control. More recent applications of self-verbalization training have been in the area of metacognition, to help students develop cognitive strategies in academically relevant tasks (see Meichenbaum & Asarnow, 1979; Schunk, 1986, for a review of this literature).

Meichenbaum and Asarnow (1979) describe a self-verbalization training program in an academic area. The study was designed to increase junior high school children's reading comprehension. The researchers began by using task analysis to determine the specific strategies that poor readers needed to complete in order to read effectively. They were guided by the following questions: What should poor readers say to themselves before, during, and after reading a selection that would help to enhance understanding? What should they say when trying to answer questions about the reading?

By the last training session (Meichenbaum & Asarnow, 1979) the poor reader's internal dialogue was similar to the following modeled passage:

> Well, I've learned three big things to keep in mind before I read a story and while I read it. One is to ask myself what the main idea of the story is. What is the story about? A second is to learn important details of the story as I go along. The order of the main events or their sequence is an especially important detail. A third is to know how the characters feel and why. So get the main idea. Watch sequences. And learn how the characters feel and why.

> While I'm reading I should pause now and then. I should think of what I'm doing. And I should listen to what I'm saying to myself. Am I saying the right things?
>
> Remember, don't worry about mistakes. Just try again. Keep calm, and relaxed. Be proud of yourself when you succeed. Have a blast! (pp. 18–19)

The researchers reported an improvement in the reading skills of students who received this training as compared to a control group who did not receive self-verbalization training.

# INSTRUCTIONAL APPLICATIONS OF BEHAVIORAL LEARNING PRINCIPLES

We shall now explore a number of instructional programs that have been developed from behavioral learning principles. As you read the material, see how each of the following behavioral principles is incorporated into the program:

- Identification of behavioral objectives
- Opportunities for frequent responding or practice
- Careful planning of the organization and sequencing of content
- Active student participation
- Immediate feedback and reinforcement

## Programmed Instruction

In 1954, Skinner published a paper, "The Science of Learning and the Art of Teaching," about his laboratory techniques that modified the behavior of both animals and humans. He stated in detail the principles of operant conditioning and described methods for automating instruction to improve human learning in school settings. This paper provided the theoretical basis and provoked the enthusiasm for **programmed instruction.**

Programmed instruction works as a self-instructional package that presents a topic in a carefully planned sequence and requires the learner to respond to questions or statements by filling in blanks, selecting from a series of answers, or solving a problem. Immediate feedback occurs after each response, and students can work at their own rate. The program can be incorporated into books, **teaching machines,** or computers. (The next section of this chapter discusses computer-assisted instruction.) Those who advocate programmed instruction stress that it can improve classroom learning, presenting even the most difficult subjects in small steps so that all students can succeed at their own rates. Figures 6.3 and 6.4 illustrate two types of programs. Figure 6.3 presents a **linear program,** in which the programmer lays out the route or sequence of frames for all students to

| Sentence to Be Completed | Word to Be Supplied |
|---|---|
| 1. The important parts of a flashlight are the battery and the bulb. When we "turn on" a flashlight, we close a switch which connects the battery with the _____. | bulb |
| 2. When we turn on a flashlight, an electric current flows through the fine wire in the _____ and causes it to grow hot. | bulb |
| 3. When the hot wire glows brightly, we say that it gives off or sends out heat and _____. | light |
| 4. The fine wire in the bulb is called a filament. The bulb "lights up" when the filament is heated by the passage of a(n) _____ current. | electric |
| 5. When a weak battery produces little current, the fine wire, or _____, does not get very hot. | filament |
| 6. A filament which is *less* hot sends out or gives off _____ light. | less |
| 7. "Emit" means "send out." The amount of light sent out, or "emitted," by a filament depends on how _____ the filament is. | hot |

**Figure 6.3** Part of a Program in High School Physics.

*Source: Skinner, 1958.*

follow in completing the program. To avoid any error, each frame or segment of the program includes a small piece of knowledge. The frames in linear programs rarely include more than one or two sentences.

Figure 6.4 represents a **branching program,** in which a student's responses determine the route followed. Alternative routes, called "branches," are predictors of the problems the student may have in completing the program. These branches allow the student who has answered a question incorrectly to go back and review pertinent information about a concept and find out why the response was not correct. Students who do not make mistakes never see these frames and can skip over material by moving to later frames in the program. The branching program typically presents more information per frame than the linear program: two or three paragraphs per frame, rather than one or two sentences per frame. Last, branching programs tend to use multiple-choice questions as the method of eliciting student responses. Students recognize the correct answer instead of constructing the response, as Skinner requires in his linear program. Each response to a question is keyed to a different page or frame in the program.

Programmed materials are not limited to pure linear or branching formats. For example, some branching programs can be modified for intelligence or achievement test scores. There are even "discovery programs,"

Page 6: A course *description* tells you something about the content and procedures of a course; a course *objective* describes a desired outcome of a course.

Whereas an objective tells what the learner is to be like as a result of some learning experiences, the course description tells only what the course is about.

The distinction is quite important, because a course description does not explain what will be accepted as adequate achievement; it does not confide to the learner the rules of the game. Though a course description might tell the learner which field he will be playing on, it doesn't tell him where the foul lines are, where the goalposts are located, or how he will know when he has scored.

It is useful to be able to recognize the difference between an objective and a description, so try an example.

Which of the statements below looks most like an *objective?*

*To be able to explain the principles for developing reading readiness in the primary grades* . . . turn to page 7.

*Discusses principles, techniques, and procedures in developing reading readiness in the primary grades* . . . turn to page 8.

Page 7: You said "To be able to explain the principles of reading readiness in the primary grades" was a statement of an objective.

You are correct! The statement describes an *aim* rather than a course. It doesn't do a very good job of it, but at least it does attempt to describe a goal rather than a process.

Now let us move on.                                                       TURN TO PAGE 10

Page 8: Oh, come on now! The collection of words that led you to this page is a piece of a course description, and not a very good description at that. I hope you are not being misled by the fact that college catalogs are composed of such phrases. They are *not* statements of intended learning outcomes and they are *not* what we are concerned with here.

Let me try to explain the difference this way. A course description describes various aspects of a PROCESS known as a "course." A course objective, on the other hand, is a description of a PRODUCT, of what the learner is supposed to be like as a *result* of the process.

Return to page 6 and read the material again.

Figure 6.4 Part of a Branching Program on Instructional Objectives.

*Source: Mager, 1984.*

which present an experiment or problem followed by a multiple-choice question that calls for the student to derive a conclusion, hypothesis, or generalization.

Skinner (1954, 1986) points out why teaching machines are needed in the classroom: First, a long time between a response and its reinforcement is common. If you accept the premise that the immediacy of reinforcement is an important variable in learning, then handing back test papers two or three weeks after the examination or being unable to answer students' questions is a serious instructional problem that needs modification. Second, he criticizes the relative infrequency of the use of reinforcement in many classrooms. Finally, there is a lack of organized instructional sequence in the teaching of complex skills. Teachers do not carefully arrange material (stimuli to shape the learner's behavior) toward instructional objectives. Skinner believes that teaching machines deal with these concerns.

The research on programmed instruction has not been positive (see Rothrock, 1982). Although the results of different studies vary somewhat, the general conclusion is that programmed instruction has not lived up to the expectations of its proponents. Attention is now directed to computer-assisted instruction, which uses the same basic learning principles.

## Computer-Assisted Instruction (CAI)

**How do programmed instruction and computer-assisted instruction employ behavioral principles of learning?**

The rapid development and dissemination of the microcomputer in the schools has created the opportunity for the use of these machines for individualizing instruction. **Computer-assisted instruction (CAI)** is an attempt to use the computer as a tutor to present information, give students opportunities to practice what they learn, evaluate student achievement, and provide additional instruction when needed. In many ways, CAI seeks to apply behavioral principles in a more efficient way than traditional programmed instruction.

In addition to instructional activities, the computer can be used for managerial purposes, such as determining error rates, student progress, and class averages, and making assignments based on the diagnosis of student weaknesses. These functions all fall under the heading of **computer-managed instruction (CMI)**.

Vargas (1986) identified three major uses of CAI in schools: (1) *drill and practice*, (2) *simulation*, and (3) *tutoring*. The key to the effectiveness of CAI is the quality of the software (the programs that run the computer). Poorly developed software, like a disorganized lecture, will lead to little learning.

*Drill and Practice Activities.* The predominant use of CAI has been with drill and practice activities in the basic skills areas. Such programs are used with skills already learned in order to improve speed or accuracy. Many programs attempt to motivate students with gamelike formats and graphics presented as reinforcers. One commercially available drill and practice series of programs is Milliken's *Math Sequences.* These programs cover the range of mathematical computation skills for grades 1 through 8. The CAI part of the program provides the student with practice in basic skills. This practice gives the student one or more chances to answer the question correctly. If the student fails to answer the problem correctly, the computer provides prompts that guide the student to the correct response. When the student responds correctly, a graphic representation of a cartoon animal praises the student, and the program moves to the next problem. When the student successfully completes the assignment, the student is again praised by the computer and is moved to the next level of the program. The CMI features of the Milliken programs allow the teacher to make individual and class assignments, review individual and class performance, set individual performance levels for each student, and provide a printed record of student performance. These functions performed by the computer free the teacher to work on higher-level skills. Vargas (1986) points out that some drill and practice programs subvert their own goals by preventing students from working at top speed. The reason is that students are forced to wait until the visual and auditory entertainment (i.e., the "reinforcement") is completed before the next problem is presented.

*Simulations.* Simulations are programs that attempt to simulate or imitate an actual experience to provide students with opportunities to learn specific skills or improve decision-making or problem-solving processes. For example, there are simulations available to learn how to fly an airplane, run a business, respond to a crisis situation. There is a simulation program available for elementary students called "Lemonade," in which students manage a lemonade stand and earn or lose money on the basis of various decisions they are asked to make. A simulation for high school students, "Revolutions Past, Present, and Future," is designed to teach students the development of revolutionary movements. Students use information from the American, French, and Russian revolutions to build a model of events leading up to a revolution. As more use is made of software that focuses on problem-solving skills in school, computers may contribute to the development of higher-level thinking as well as to practice in basic skills (Patterson & Smith, 1986). Vargas (1986) points out that simulations used properly can be an excellent teaching technique. However, it is often difficult to find a simulation to meet the particular instructional needs of the teacher. In addition, some programs may imitate very little of the actual events or decisions involved in a real-world situation.

*Tutorials.* The third category of CAI is tutorials, which are designed to teach new subject matter. These programs often consist of several screens of textual material, followed by exercises or questions. They are available in almost any subject area. Most tutorial systems can adapt instruction by using students' prior performance in the program to determine what material to present, its difficulty, and the rate of presentation. Vargas (1986) points out that many tutorials present several screens of text before calling for a student response and that often they do not break down a skill into small steps that would be easier for the student to master.

## Computer Competence

Martinez and Mead (1988) reported on the status of computer competence or computer literacy among school-age children in the United States. This evaluation involved black, white, and Hispanic male and female students in grades 3, 7, and 11 from different geographical regions around the country. The items on the questionnaire included information on computer background (e.g., exposure to computers, courses taken, and other general computer-related information) and attitudes regarding computer use, computer knowledge, computer applications, and computer science/programming. The data indicated that most children had some familiarity with and practical knowledge of computers. However, only a small fraction of the students were able to answer questions about important computer applications or about programming (no grade averaged at least 50 percent of the items correct). Table 6.2 identified student responses to the frequency of computer use in subject areas. The data indicate that computers are seldom used in the students' academic courses. When the machines are used, they are mainly confined to computing classes.

The following are important additional findings of the evaluation (Martinez & Mead, 1988):

- Most students like using computers and want greater access to them.
- Much learning about computers takes place outside of school and independent of formal instruction.
- Males, in general, demonstrate a slightly higher level of computer competence than females.
- There are clear racial/ethnic differences in computer competence, favoring white students over black and Hispanic students.
- Students whose parents are college graduates and from high socioeconomic backgrounds are more likely to have used a computer, to be studying computers in school, and to have a computer at home.
- Many computer coordinators have minimal training in computer studies and rate themselves mediocre in their ability to use computers. (p. 6)

TABLE 6.2  **FREQUENCY OF COMPUTER USE IN SUBJECT AREAS**

| How Often Do You Use a Computer to: | Almost Every Day | Several Times a Week | About Once a Week | Less Than Once a Week | Never |
|---|---|---|---|---|---|
| Frequency—Grade 7 | | | | | |
| Practice math | 5.7% | 4.7% | 9.8% | 17.5% | 62.3% |
| Practice reading | 3.1 | 3.8 | 5.9 | 8.8 | 78.4 |
| Practice spelling | 2.8 | 3.3 | 7.8 | 10.0 | 76.1 |
| Do science problems | 1.9 | 2.9 | 3.1 | 6.8 | 85.3 |
| Learn and make music | 2.4 | 3.0 | 6.2 | 10.3 | 78.1 |
| Play games | 19.4 | 15.4 | 16.3 | 24.6 | 24.3 |
| Frequency—Grade 11 | | | | | |
| Practice math | 3.4% | 3.0% | 3.6% | 12.1% | 77.9% |
| Practice reading | 1.8 | 2.1 | 2.0 | 6.9 | 87.2 |
| Practice spelling | 1.4 | 1.6 | 2.8 | 6.7 | 87.5 |
| Do science problems | 0.8 | 1.5 | 1.9 | 8.6 | 87.2 |
| Learn and make music | 1.4 | 1.7 | 2.2 | 9.0 | 85.6 |
| Play games | 8.5 | 9.8 | 14.0 | 33.9 | 33.8 |

Source: Martinez and Mead, 1988.

The evaluators were concerned with the equity issue relating to computer competence. That is, as knowledge and use of computers becomes increasingly important in the workplace, minority students will be at a serious disadvantage when they seek employment. As a result, it is important that educators develop policies to ensure that all students have equal access to computers and develop competency in their use.

## Research on CAI

In general, traditional computer-assisted instruction (i.e., the computer used as a personal tutor) has a moderately positive effect on student achievement (Bangert-Drowns, Kulik, & Kulik, 1985; Kulik, Kulik, & Bangert-Drowns, 1985). However, there is limited research on other uses of computers. CAI is more successful when it supplements the regular classroom instruction than when it is used to replace classroom instruction entirely. The positive effects of CAI appear to be greatest for elementary and secondary students and less effective for college students (Tobias, 1985). As of yet, we cannot determine the impact of computers on students (Lepper & Gurtner, 1989).

It appears that the computer revolution is years away. Two major problems limit the use of computers in the classroom: the availability of appropriate software and cost considerations. Most teachers are fortunate if they have one or two computers in their classrooms. Even in classes with

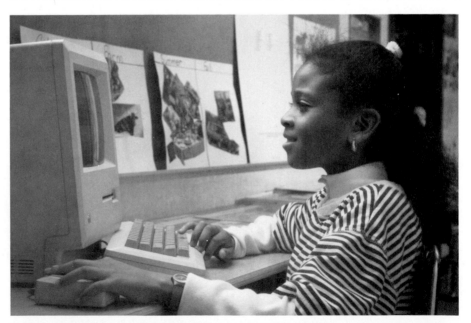

It is important that all students develop computer competence.

as many as eight computers, students spend a great deal of time waiting for a turn at the computer (Center for Social Organization, 1984).

In the 1950s and 1960s some educators believed that programmed instruction would replace teachers. Similar claims were made for motion pictures and instructional television. Today we hear that computers will revolutionize education because they have the ability to *interact* with students by allowing them to learn at their own rate and giving them practice on needed skills. Vargas (1986) states that computers have the ability to teach effectively if the programmers writing the software use features that are necessary for learning: "a high rate of relevant responding, appropriate stimulus control, immediate feedback, and techniques of successive approximations" (p. 744). All of these components are basic behavioral principles identified by Skinner decades ago.

With the vast amount of CAI software on the market, it is important that you carefully evaluate the effectiveness of software before making any purchase (see Lillie, Hannum, & Stuck, 1989, and Sloane et al. 1989, for some helpful hints). The evaluation checklist in Table 6.3 identifies important questions for you to consider. In addition, there are several magazines that evaluate software, such as *Electronic Learning*. Also, many large school districts have computer centers, where teachers can try out various computers and educational programs before ordering them for the classroom.

Finally, in using any technology for instruction, the teacher must keep in mind that there is nothing magical about devices like the computer. It is the instructional design of the learning activities that promotes learning. Clark (1983) has summed up this issue in an important review on the effectiveness of media in education by stating: "The best current evidence

---

**TABLE 6.3 EVALUATION CHECKLIST FOR EDUCATIONAL SOFTWARE**

\_\_\_\_\_ 1. Will the program run on the computer(s) you have available?

\_\_\_\_\_ 2. Do the objectives of the program match your classroom objectives?

\_\_\_\_\_ 3. Is the content accurate and at the appropriate level for your students?

\_\_\_\_\_ 4. Are instructions clear and easy to understand?

\_\_\_\_\_ 5. Do screen graphics enhance rather than interfere with learning?

\_\_\_\_\_ 6. Does the program encourage and allow students to work at their own rate of speed?

\_\_\_\_\_ 7. Are students required to decide between at least two responses when presented with a question?

\_\_\_\_\_ 8. Does the program provide accurate and corrective feedback?

\_\_\_\_\_ 9. Are students able to see their progress on a daily basis?

\_\_\_\_\_ 10. Does the program adjust to the performance level of the students?

\_\_\_\_\_ 11. Does the program handle student errors adequately?

\_\_\_\_\_ 12. Can the program keep records of student and class progress?

\_\_\_\_\_ 13. Is it possible for the teacher to add to the content of the program?

\_\_\_\_\_ 14. Is support or help available to the teacher through either the distributor or manufacturer?

---

*Source: Electronic Learning's Inservice Workshop, 1983, and Vargas, 1986.*

is that media are mere vehicles that deliver instruction but do not influence student achievement any more than the truck that delivers our groceries causes changes in our nutrition" (p. 445).

## Mastery Learning and Personalized System of Instruction

**What are the similarities and differences between Bloom's mastery learning and Keller's Personalized System of Instruction?**

In 1968 Bloom and Keller published important articles describing methods for increasing student mastery over content in a regular class or course. Bloom emphasized the importance of improving the achievement of students in elementary and secondary schools. Although the roots for his system of **mastery learning** initially came from the writings of Carroll (1963), the implementation of his system uses operant conditioning principles. Keller developed his **Personalized System of Instruction (PSI)** based on operant conditioning principles for use in college classrooms.

*Mastery Learning.* Mastery learning is a type of instruction that emphasizes student mastery of specific learning objectives and uses corrective instruction to achieve that goal. Mastery learning assumes that virtually all students can learn what is taught in school if their "instruction is approached systematically, if students are helped when and where they have learning difficulties, if they are given sufficient time to achieve mastery, and if there is some clear criterion of what constitutes mastery" (Bloom, 1974, p. 6).

Although the roots of mastery learning can be found in the writings of many educators as far back as the 1920s, John Carroll is credited with providing the theoretical background and Benjamin Bloom with designing the basic instructional process for mastery learning (Guskey, 1985). In 1963 Carroll published an article entitled "A Model of School Learning," in which he challenged the traditionally held view that student aptitude determined how much knowledge would be learned in a given course. Carroll pointed out that student aptitude reflected an index of learning rate. That is, most students have the ability to learn what is presented in school, but they differ in the time it takes them to learn the material. When aptitude is viewed as an indicator of learning rate, youngsters are not viewed as good or poor students, but rather as fast or slow learners.

Carroll proposed a model of school learning based on the belief that if each student was allowed the time needed to learn the material, and the time was spent appropriately, then the student would be able to achieve the specified learning objectives. However, if all students were given the same time to learn the material, many students would not attain the level of knowledge expected by the instructor. Carroll expressed the degree of learning attained by a student in the following equation:

$$\text{Degree of learning} = f \text{ (time spent/time needed)}$$

That is, the degree of learning is a function of the amount of time spent learning, relative to the amount of time the student needs to spend to learn the material.

Benjamin Bloom (1968, 1974) was impressed by Carroll's perspective on teaching and learning. If aptitude was related to the time a student needed to learn, then it would be possible to modify the nature of instruction to ensure that almost all students mastered the material presented in a given course.

Bloom noted that in traditional methods, teachers organized instruction into units that usually corresponded to chapters in a textbook. After the instruction, teachers tested students to determine how much knowledge they had acquired. Because of the cumulative nature of the knowledge, students who failed to master the material in the first unit were likely to have problems mastering the material in the second, third, and succeeding units. Thus, as the course proceeded, some students mastered less material and got further behind the rest of the class.

Bloom believed that dividing the instruction into small units and checking on learning progress at the end of each unit were useful instructional techniques. However, although the quizzes or tests at the end of the unit helped the teacher and students to determine what had been learned, the tests were of little value to the students in helping them to master more knowledge.

Bloom set out to develop an instructional approach that would produce better results. What was needed, he believed, was some type of feedback and corrective process that would diagnose individual learning difficulties (feedback) and prescribe specific remediation procedures (correctives) to help students learn the material.

In the section on Personalized System of Instruction, I identify an *individually based, student-paced* program in which students typically learn independently of their classmates. Bloom wanted to develop a system that was a *group-based, teacher-paced* approach to instruction, in which students learn, for the most part, cooperatively with their classmates (Guskey, 1985).

Bloom outlined his innovative teaching-learning strategy as follows: The content is divided into small learning units comprising one to two weeks of instructional time. After the material from the unit is presented, a **formative test** is administered to determine each student's progress and to identify areas in which more instruction is needed. A high level of performance is required (usually 80–90% correct) on each formative test for the student to move to enrichment activities or another unit of instruction. Students who have not mastered the material are engaged in corrective work for a class period or two following the formative test. Students are provided with alternative learning resources such as additional lectures, small-group instruction, different textbooks, filmstrips, study guides, or worksheets. Then they are administered another formative test to ensure that they have mastered the unit before moving on to the next unit. The students who demonstrate that they have mastered the material are given special enrichment activities to expand their knowledge. At the end of a series of units, the teacher evaluates the final competence of students by giving a **summative test** covering the objectives in the units. If the program is successful, almost all the students should attain a high score on the examination and would be more similar in their achievement levels as compared to traditional instructional programs. In addition to improved achievement, Bloom (1971) believed that mastery learning would lead to many important affective outcomes such as improved attitude toward the subject matter and a more positive academic self-concept.

## CLASSROOM APPLICATION: DEVELOPING AND IMPLEMENTING A MASTERY LEARNING PROGRAM

Block and Anderson (1975) recommend the following procedures for developing and implementing mastery learning in the classroom:

- *Develop instructional objectives* from the textbook using the *Taxonomy of Educational Objectives, Cognitive Domain,* to ensure that the objectives cover various levels of complexity (the Taxonomy of Educational Objectives is discussed in Chapter 9). The chapter headings and subheadings can be used as a guide in determining course objectives.
- *Construct the final examination* on the basis of the objectives of the course. The test results should be based on each student's mastery of the objectives (called *criterion-referenced testing;* see Chapter 13) rather than on how much each has learned relative to other students in the class. It is useful to write test items on separate 3-×-5 index cards for each objective in the course.
- *Select a mastery performance standard* that reflects the level of performance on the test that you would be willing to accept as indicating mastery over the course objectives. There are no specific guidelines for making this decision. Many teachers set the criterion for mastery at the percentage of correct answers needed to obtain a grade of A, which is usually 90 percent. In some cases, a teacher may establish mastery performance standards for different parts of the test that cover objectives of varied importance. If some students' performance is not indicative of mastery, you need to decide whether to give no grade or a grade of incomplete. If this cannot be done in your school district, then establish levels for B through F work. Discuss these standards with the students before implementing the mastery program.
- *Break the course into a series of units* of instruction and decide how you will teach the material in each unit. In most cases, whole-class instruction will be used.
- *Develop formative and summative quizzes* to determine student progress in meeting the objectives of the units. The quizzes should be parallel in that they should measure the same content,

be of the same level of difficulty, and not take more than 15 to 20 minutes to complete.

- *Give students either corrective instruction or enrichment activities*, depending on the results of the formative quiz. Providing corrective instruction for those students who did not attain mastery is the most important aspect of mastery learning. The corrective instruction can be given outside of the regular instructional time, either during the school day or after school. This is one way to deal with the time problem raised by the critics of mastery learning.
- *Give enrichment activities* to students who have mastered the material as demonstrated by their scores on the formative test. These activities should broaden the students' understanding of the material and may involve special reading assignments, writing essays in an area of interest, and other types of independent research.

Block and Anderson characterize different follow-up activities according to whether they can be used for (1) *individual* students or (2) a *group* of students, and whether they focus on different ways of (3) *presenting* the content or (4) *involving* students in learning the material. The following are the types of instructional materials and activities that can be used in the classroom:

- Alternative textbooks (1, 3) to give students a different presentation of the material, with the pages identified that provide a discussion of the relevant content.
- Workbooks (1, 3) to give students more familiarity with the textbook material.
- Flashcards (1, 3) to give students repeated exposure to the material covered in the unit.
- Reteaching (2, 3) to review material with any students who had difficulty with the material. It is important that reteaching involve examples or illustrations different from those first used.
- Audiovisual aids and materials (1, 2, 3) to provide instruction focusing on the visual and auditory sensory modalities.
- Token economies (1, 4) to stimulate interest by giving the students tokens or points in exchange for a particular level of academic performance.
- Academic games (2, 4) to create interest among students who have similar learning problems.
- Group affective exercises (2, 4) to deal with students' feelings and attitudes about learning (e.g., see the discussion of values clarification in Chapter 8).
- Programmed instruction (1, 3, 4) to provide a simplified presentation of the material.

- Tutoring (1, 3, 4) to involve students who have mastered the material as classroom aides. In some situations, cross-age tutoring may be used with older students working with younger students.
- Small-group study sessions (2, 3, 4) to enable students to discuss the material that is giving them problems (see the discussion on cooperative learning in Chapter 8).

*Present the summative quiz and report the scores to students* when you feel that the corrective instruction has been sufficient to remediate learning difficulties. If certain students still have not attained the specified mastery level, you can repeat the corrective instruction-summative test cycle.

*Grade student for mastery* at the end of the course, and evaluate the effectiveness of the program. Determine what changes need to be made before the next semester. Check the Suggestions for Further Reading at the end of this chapter for additional references on establishing a mastery learning program.

*Criticisms of Mastery Learning.* Arlin (1984) has raised an important issue regarding the use of instructional time in mastery learning. He argues that there is a time-achievement dilemma involved in mastery learning programs. By this he means that low achievers in group-based mastery learning do better because of corrective instruction, but faster students may be slowed down waiting for the other students to catch up. Arlin argues that the time needed to bring slow learners up to mastery must come from somewhere. If the corrective procedures are done during regular class time, then content coverage may be reduced. Cox and Dunn (1979) raise additional concerns about the implementation of mastery learning: First, not all teachers have the ability to identify prerequisite skills and begin instruction at the proper level. Second, some students may actually develop poor study habits from recycling by using the "principle of least effort," whereby they may risk failure on the first examination to discover the minimal knowledge that must be learned to pass the second examination. Also, constant recycling among slower students may cause them to develop negative self-concepts—exactly the opposite of what the proponents state mastery learning will eliminate! Third, if the teacher believes that mastery learning can solve most or all the problems of individual differences with a group of students who lack the intellectual skills and/or cognitive strategies to learn the material, the teacher may be taking on an unreasonable responsibility. Cox and Dunn state:

. . . certain instructional objectives have a higher probability of achievement for some learners than for others. Obviously, time and resources for recycling and building of the missing prerequisites are not unlimited.

So it naturally follows that some objectives or sequences of objectives differ in their appropriateness for various learners. (p. 28)

Fourth, there is a difference between earning an A in the course and attaining mastery of the material. Students may be led to believe that they know more than they really do because the criteria selected for mastery are low. In summary, the proponents of mastery learning believe that individual differences in achievement can be reduced or minimized by carefully designing instruction. Critics of the system believe that the proponents underestimate the difficulties of implementing the system in a class with diverse individual abilities and feel that time limitations prevent all or most students from mastering the same objectives without a decrease in content coverage.

*Research on Mastery Learning.* Since 1968, many school districts have implemented different types of mastery learning programs and researchers have conducted numerous investigations concerning the effectiveness of these programs (see Block, Efthim, & Burns, 1989). When reviewing research on mastery learning, it is important that you determine how the program is organized and implemented before you reach any conclusions regarding the effectiveness of the programs. For example, one major variable in the effectiveness of programs is the amount of time that is allotted to corrective instruction. Few differences have been found in evaluations of mastery and nonmastery programs when the instructional time was the same (Kersh, 1972; Slavin & Karweit, 1984).

One of the first major reviews of mastery learning was conducted by Block and Burns (1976), who found positive effects of the programs but not as large as mastery learning advocates often indicate. Almost all programs produced more learning and less variability in achievement than nonmastery approaches. In addition, the researchers found positive effects in the affective domain (i.e., students' attitudes toward the subject and how they felt about themselves as learners). Guskey and Gates (1986) completed an analysis of the research on group-based mastery learning in both elementary and secondary classrooms. Although they substantiated earlier findings of positive achievement gains compared to nonmastery approaches, they reported wide differences in gains from study to study.

More recently, Slavin (1987) completed a review of group-based mastery learning that was more critical than any of the past reviews. He found that long-term experiments lasting four weeks to months were not as effective as shorter studies of four weeks or less. The implication is that researchers need to show significant gains over longer periods of time to support interventions in schools. He also reported that standardized achievement tests showed fewer gains than did experimenter-made tests. This result may be caused by the fact that the experimenter-made tests emphasized the material in the mastery learning curriculum more than that in the conventionally taught curriculum. Finally, his data supported Arlin's (1984) criticism that slower-learning students are helped at the expense of faster-learning students.

*Personalized System of Instruction (PSI).* Keller (1968) established an individually based, student-paced form of mastery learning. Although there are many variations of Keller's program in use, most courses include the following five features: *self-pacing, unit mastery,* a *minimum of lectures,* an emphasis on *written assignments,* and the use of *undergraduate or graduate proctors* (Johnson & Ruskin, 1977).

*Self-pacing.* The students are given course assignments divided into small units of homework. The number and size of the units vary depending on the discipline and instructor. Students work at their own rate and decide when to complete their course assignments. Thus they take exams on material when they are ready—not when the instructor decides to give an exam!

*Unit mastery.* Students proceed to new course material only after demonstrating mastery of the previous unit or assignment. They are able to take tests as many times as necessary until mastery (as identified by each instructor before the course begins) is reached. In the original PSI courses, Keller graded students by the number of units they completed (75% of final grade) and their score on a final examination (25% of final grade).

*Lectures.* Lectures in PSI are not used as the main vehicle for information dissemination. In fact, students are not even required to attend lectures (. . . now you're getting more interested in this section!). Lectures are used as a motivational device to present new and interesting material not covered in the individual units. Students who complete specified units are permitted to attend and no examinations are given on the material.

*Written assignments.* Rather than passively listening to lectures, the students are actively reading, studying, and writing on their own. Study guides, prepared by the instructor and keyed to a specific text or supplemental readings, provide the goals or objectives for each unit, include an introduction section explaining how the new material relates to material already learned, suggest strategies for mastering the material, and often include sample quizzes for self-assessment to ensure mastery of the material.

*Proctors.* An important feature of PSI is the use of proctors who have passed the course with an A grade. In the early formulation of the course, Keller assigned 10 students to each undergraduate proctor. Today graduate student proctors also are used in most PSI courses. They maintain regular office hours and meet weekly with the instructor to discuss the course organization. In most PSI courses the proctor (1) scores and evaluates each student's quizzes over the units, (2) points out areas on the quizzes where material has not been mastered, (3) suggests ways to improve study skills, and (4) encourages consistent progress throughout the course.

*Criticisms of PSI.* In general, PSI has received positive reactions among college students. However, some students (see Gasper, 1980) would like more group discussions and interaction among students. Other students complain that the program demands more self-discipline than they are willing or able to exert. There is also concern that the program best fits courses with highly structured content, such as mathematics, chemistry, and engineering, but is less useful in courses like literature, history, and philosophy, in which analysis and evaluation activities are stressed. Jaynes (1975) expressed his dismay with PSI when he stated:

> I object to the too arrogant standardization that it imposes upon the mind. . . . What the Keller Method in complex subjects does is to grind down the individual student's particular style of going over things. It rebukes his wish to insert his own importances. (p. 631)

*Research on PSI.* Kulik, Kulik, and Cohen (1979) compared 75 courses taught both conventionally and by PSI and found that "PSI produces superior student achievement, less variation in achievement, and high student ratings on college courses, but does not affect course withdrawal or student study time in these courses" (p. 307). Most students enrolled in PSI courses appear to like the self-paced arrangements, the availability for personal tutoring, and the ability to obtain a high grade if specific requirements are met. However, the PSI format works best for students who have the self-discipline and motivation to learn independently (Johnson & Ruskin, 1977).

Would you like to take a mastery learning or PSI course? What factors seem most appealing to you? What factors would you be most concerned about? Think about these questions from the role both of a teacher and of a student.

## THINKING ABOUT THE TEACHING-LEARNING MODEL

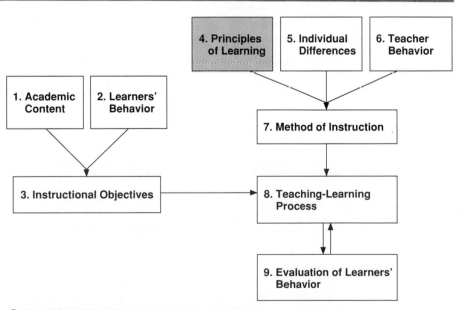

*Source: Adapted from Hunter, 1971, in Allen and Seifman.*

It is important for you to realize that behavioral psychologists view the role of the teacher (box No. 6) as a manager of instruction. They are strong proponents of using specific objectives and of sequencing instruction by presenting basic facts first, then moving to more complex information. Behaviorists believe that if teachers properly present and sequence information, students will learn more.

I have emphasized that individual differences (box No. 5) should influence a teacher's instructional decisions (box No. 7). The principles of applied behavior analysis have been employed successfully with many kinds of learners in a variety of learning situations. Various forms of individualized instruction have been used extensively to deal with student diversity in the classroom. Even if you do not establish a formal mastery learning program, the list of follow-up activities in this chapter can be useful when you ask yourself, "What do I do next?" Instead of simply repeating the same material in the same manner, you can move to alternative ways for students to learn the material.

Applied behavior analysis has been extensively used with exceptional children and low-achieving students both in managing classroom behavior and in designing effective instructional programs. You will find many articles in special education journals that deal with applied behavior analysis principles. Read a few articles to learn more about how to change behavior.

Most forms of technology in education (e.g., programmed instruction and computer-assisted instruction) cause changes in your instructional role. You need to be prepared for these changes because in many cases you will not present information to students. Instead, you may be spending more time diagnosing students' learning problems and deciding on alternative learning methods. These choices are as important as the decisions on how material should be presented in the first place. Do not reject technological developments simply because they are unfamiliar. School districts are now providing opportunities for teachers to learn more about technological developments in the classroom.

## KEY POINTS

1. Early behavioral psychologists viewed learning as forming connections or associations between a stimulus and a response.
2. Skinner believes that all behavior is learned. Most learning occurs because of operant conditioning—a situation in which a response is made more probable or frequent as the result of immediate reinforcement.
3. Applied behavior analysis is the extension of operant conditioning principles to change behavior of humans in natural settings. It is based on specific methodology and evaluation procedures.
4. The basis of applied behavior analysis in teaching involves (a) speci-

fying the desired instructional objective, structuring lessons in small steps, and presenting the steps in a sequence; (b) providing for involvement in a lesson by encouraging students to respond to various questions and problems; (c) providing immediate feedback to student responses to all questions, quizzes, and homework assignments; and (d) reinforcing students for correct answers, proper study habits, and other desirable classroom behavior.

5. Students may respond differently to various types of reinforcements.
6. Behavior is influenced by different schedules of reinforcement—fixed and variable ratio and fixed and variable interval.
7. In attempting to reinforce behavior, you should reinforce behavior immediately. Start by reinforcing appropriate behavior continuously, and then move to a variable schedule to maintain the behavior. Be sure not to reinforce undesired behavior.
8. Shaping and modeling are important procedures for developing new behaviors.
9. Observational learning can occur without any immediate reinforcement.
10. There are four important processes in observational learning: attention, retention, motor reproduction, and motivation.
11. Reinforcement in social learning theory is viewed as a source of information and an incentive rather than as a consequent condition of behavior.
12. Vicarious reinforcement and self-reinforcement can be effective alternatives to direct reinforcement.
13. Cognitive processes can be incorporated in behavioral approaches to help individuals guide or control their own behavior.
14. Programmed instruction and computer-assisted instruction use the principles of operant conditioning in presenting information to students.
15. Students seldom use computers in their academic courses.
16. Much learning about computers takes place outside of school and independent of formal instruction. Minority students have less access to computers.
17. Teachers need to evaluate the effectiveness of all computer software.
18. Mastery learning programs can be established to ensure higher levels of learning for most students.
19. Personalized System of Instruction is an individually based, student-paced form of mastery learning.

## KEY TERMS

classical conditioning, p. 222
applied behavior analysis, p. 222

operant conditioning, p. 222
social learning theory, p. 222
cognitive behavior modification, p. 222
unconditioned stimulus, p. 223
unconditioned response, p. 223
conditioned stimulus, p. 223
conditioned response, p. 223
stimulus generalization, p. 224
extinction, p. 224
connectionism, p. 224
law of effect, p. 225
reward, p. 225
law of exercise, p. 225
respondents, p. 226
operants, p. 226
baseline, p. 228
behavior modification, p. 229
discriminative stimulus, p. 229
reinforcing stimulus, p. 229
discrimination learning, p. 230
response generalization, p. 230
negative reinforcement, p. 231
punishment, p. 231
time-out, p. 231
primary reinforcement, p. 231
secondary reinforcement, p. 232
Premack's principle, p. 232
fixed-ratio schedule, p. 233
variable-ratio schedule, p. 233
fixed-interval schedule, p. 234
variable-interval schedule, p. 234
spontaneous recovery, p. 235
shaping, p. 236
successive approximations, p. 236
prompting, p. 236
fading, p. 236
modeling, p. 237
observational learning, p. 237
reciprocal determinism, p. 237
inhibitory-disinhibitory effect, p. 238
eliciting effect, p. 238
self-efficacy, p. 239
vicarious reinforcement, p. 239
self-reinforcement, p. 239
programmed instruction, p. 244

teaching machine, p. 244
linear program, p. 244
branching program, p. 245
computer-assisted instruction (CAI), p. 247
computer-managed instruction (CMI), p. 247
mastery learning, p. 252
Personalized System of Instruction (PSI), p. 252
formative test, p. 253
summative test, p. 253

## SUGGESTIONS FOR FURTHER READING

Hughes, J. N. (1988). *Cognitive behavior therapy with children in schools.* New York: Pergamon. An excellent discussion of cognitive-behavioral approaches for helping children who display emotional and behavioral problems.

Jenson, W. R., Sloane, H. N., & Young, K. R. (1988). *Applied analysis in education: A structured teaching approach.* Englewood Cliffs, NJ: Prentice-Hall. A good reference for how behavioral principles are used in instruction.

Kazdin, A. E. (1978). *History of behavior modification: Experimental foundations of contemporary research.* Baltimore: University Park Press. Provides a comprehensive review of the history of behavioral psychology.

Witt, J. C., Elliott, S. N., & Gresham, F. M. (1988). *Handbook of behavior therapy in education.* New York: Plenum. A detailed discussion of behavioral analysis and intervention in educational settings.

To learn more about Skinner's theory of learning:

Skinner, B. F. (1948). *Walden two.* New York: Macmillan. The novel in which Skinner conceives of a utopia based on the application of science to human behavior.

Skinner, B. F. (1968). *The technology of teaching.* New York: Appleton-Century-Crofts. Includes some of Skinner's most important writings.

The following books describe how to organize and implement a mastery learning program:

Block, J. H., Efthim, H. E., & Burns, R. B. (1989). *Building effective mastery learning schools.* White Plains, NY: Longman.

Block, J. H., & Anderson, L. W. (1975). *Mastery learning in classroom instruction.* New York: Macmillan.

Guskey, T. R. (1985). *Implementing mastery learning.* Belmont, CA: Wadsworth.

Issues in the use of computers in education are discussed in the following:

Lillie, D. L., Hannum, W. H., & Stuck, G. B. (1989). *Computers and effective instruction.* White Plains, NY: Longman. Includes a guide for assessing software.

Savas, S. D., & Savas, E. S. (1985). *Teaching children to use computers: A friendly guide.* New York: Teachers College Press. A clearly written introduction to programming.

Sloane, H. N., Gordon, H. M., Gunn, C., & Mickelsen, V. G. (1989). *Evaluating educational software: A guide for teachers.* Englewood Cliffs, NJ: Prentice-Hall. Offers guidelines for assessing student needs, evaluating instructional software, and evaluating the adequacy of a program.

White, C. S., & Hubbard, G. (1988). *Computers and education.* New York: Macmillan. A small book on the basics of computer uses in education.

## FOLLOW-UP ACTIVITIES

_____ 1. **Evaluate the Impact of Operant Conditioning**

According to Skinner, we are all products of operant conditioning. We learn appropriate and inappropriate behavior according to the same principles. To what extent do you agree with this statement? Can you use operant conditioning principles to explain some of your own behavior (both positive and negative)?

_____ 2. **Identify Appropriate Reinforcers**

The importance of choosing appropriate reinforcers was emphasized in the chapter. Assume that someone is going to reinforce one of your behaviors. Select two or three reinforcers that you believe would be effective in modifying your behavior.

_____ 3. **Use Shaping to Change Behavior**

Identify an individual with whom you have had contact (for example, a sibling or friend). Specify a behavior you would like to develop by using a shaping procedure. Outline the starting point you would select and the successive approximations you would go through (Martin & Pear, 1988).

_____ 4. **Discuss the Usefulness of Teaching Machines, Computers, and/or Programmed Textbooks**

How do you regard the use of teaching machines, computers, and programmed textbooks? Do they adequately solve the problem of providing efficient individualized instruction? In what situations would you prefer to be taught by a machine or a program rather than a teacher? What factors would influence your decisions?

_Due 11/26_

## 5. Plan a Lesson Using Applied Behavior Analysis

Plan a lesson, and point out how you can use principles of operant conditioning to improve learning. Be specific in identifying the principles used in your lesson.

# CHAPTER 7

# Cognitive Approaches to Learning

## ORIENTATION

Can stimulus, response, and reinforcement adequately explain the learning process? No! say cognitive psychologists, who believe that a person's behavior is always based on cognition, an act of knowing or thinking about the situation in which the behavior occurs. As a result, they are concerned with the organization of knowledge, information processing, and decision-making behavior—aspects of the cognitive realm.

An important goal of cognitive instruction is to help students process information in meaningful ways so that they can become independent learners (Jones, 1986). Cognitive psychologists have found that unlike less able students, more able students use effective learning strategies to attain various educational objectives (E. Gagné, 1985). They believe that less able learners can be taught to use appropriate learning strategies to become more successful in the classroom. The types of question that cognitive psychologists ask include: What are the students thinking about during problem solving? What cognitive processes do the students engage in? How might effective learning strategies be taught?

Another goal of cognitive psychologists is to develop independent, or self-regulated, learners. When given a learning objective to attain, self-regulated learners monitor and control their own behavior by setting manageable goals, using their prior knowledge, considering alternative strategies, developing a plan of attack, and considering contingency plans when they run into trouble.

Many students cannot function as self-regulated learners because they have never been taught how to learn. Corno (1986) describes how cognitive psychologists can help teachers develop more successful learners:

> Students can be taught to take "extension" notes from lecturers (rather than copying verbatim what is said). They can be taught to highlight the important points in texts; how to monitor comprehension as they read; how to use memory support devices . . . to retain strings of information; and to diagram, tabularize, or otherwise organize academic material. These strategies need also to be seen by students for what they are—the tools for learning from school tasks, tools and tricks that good learners use to make school work easier and increase the likelihood of success. (p. 17)

As you read this chapter, consider what you would do in the classroom to make your students more successful learners.

By the time you master the material in this chapter and the following appendix, you will be able to:

- Identify how the information processing system influences learning.
- Plan and implement lessons based on declarative and procedural learning tasks.
- Teach students learning strategies to make them more effective learners.

1. Why is it important to develop students' metacognitive abilities?
2. What are some methods that students can learn in order to increase their retention of factual material?
3. How can the use of learning strategies improve student achievement?
4. What advice would you give students about underlining?
5. How can you improve students' note taking?
6. How can a teacher help students improve their reading comprehension?
7. How can you help students improve their attentiveness to academic tasks?
8. What are the differences in teaching pattern-recognition knowledge and action sequences?
9. Can students be taught critical thinking skills?

## THE INFORMATION-PROCESSING SYSTEM (IPS)

Have you thought about any of the following questions: How does the human mind acquire information? What determines how much information is learned? Why is some information remembered and other information soon forgotten? What can be done to improve the retention of information? Cognitive psychologists have developed information processing models to identify how humans obtain, transform, store, and apply information in order to investigate these questions.

I first discussed information processing in Chapter 2, as an approach to understanding intellectual development. In this chapter, I take a broader perspective and focus on how the information processing approach can be useful in improving classroom instruction and student learning. Figure 7.1 shows a flowchart used to identify various components in the **information-processing system (IPS)**.

### Short-Term Sensory Store

As shown in Figure 7.1, the flow of information begins with input from the environment, such as the visual perception of words in a text. This information enters the **short-term sensory store (STSS),** referred to in some models as the *sensory register*. Information in the STSS is stored briefly until it can be attended to by the short-term memory. Information that does not enter short-term memory is quickly lost, usually in a fraction of a second. If the student does not attend to information, there is little concern about retention or retrieval because no information will have been acquired. Thus the importance of attention cannot be overestimated in any model of information processing.

Figure 7.1 An Information Processing Model of Learning.

*Source: Adapted from Mayer, 1981.*

## Short-Term Memory

In moving from the short-term sensory store to **short-term memory (STM),** information is changed to a verbal form involving a name coding. Shortly after seeing *A,* the student will no longer retain the visual pattern but instead will keep in short-term memory the verbal name of the pattern, the letter *A.* Similarly, TREEHOUSE will be held in short-term memory as *tree* and *house.* The STM is the active part of our memory system.

Some psychologists believe that another stage of memory exists between short-term and long-term memory components. This component is called the **working memory** and has been described as the center of consciousness in the IPS. Whenever we are consciously thinking about something, actively trying to remember a forgotten fact, or engaging in a fantasy, we are using our working memory.

The information processing capacity of STM is limited in two ways. First, at any one time, the STM of an adult can hold only five to nine chunks of information. This condition is referred to as the "7 ± 2 Magic Number" (Miller, 1956). New information coming into STM will, if it catches the attention of the student, tend to crowd out old information already there. For elementary children, this capacity is even less (Case, 1985). Second, without an active effort from the learner, STM holds information for only a brief time, often less than 30 seconds.

A number of control processes operate at the STM level that provide it with some flexibility in dealing with information. These processes focus attention, manipulate information, and organize and assist in retrieval of information. Some of these control processes operate automatically; others are subject to conscious voluntary control (Mayer, 1988).

Let's look at some of the control processes that are of particular interest to the classroom teacher. As I mentioned, the STM is limited in the amount of information it can deal with at any given time. **Chunking,** or grouping, information is one way of keeping more than nine pieces (7 $\pm$ 2) of information in working memory. For example, it is usually easier to remember a number such as "194781235" if the numbers are grouped in threes (194 781 235), because the original nine units are reduced to three chunks. When we read a word, we think of it as a single unit rather than as a collection of separate letters. A sentence can be thought of as a single unit, or chunk, instead of a series of letters and words. The STM can handle more information when it is organized into larger units of information because the organization reduces our memory load. Although the STM uses various chunking strategies automatically and unconsciously, these strategies also can be taught. The important implication for teaching is to minimize the load placed on a young child's working memory when you are trying to teach new information.

As the name implies, short-term memory holds information for only a brief time. The information entering the STM is quickly bumped out by new information, or it fades away. The longer information remains in STM, the more likely it will be properly organized and retrieved when it is needed. **Rehearsal strategies** are used to retain information for longer periods. They involve repeating or rehearsing the information we have in our STM. For example, after receiving directions on how to get to a location, a motorist may repeat "left-left-right-left" while driving down the road. In another situation, a person might try to visualize objects seen after they have faded away (disappeared from the STSS). Researchers are interested in studying the effectiveness of the kinds of rehearsal strategies that can be helpful to learners.

## Long-Term Memory

**Long-term memory** (LTM) stores all the information we possess but are not immediately using. It is generally assumed that storage of information in the LTM is permanent. That is, the information does not fade from long-term memory, nor is it ever lost except perhaps as a result of senility or some other physical malfunction. Thus cognitive psychologists view the problem of forgetting as the inability to retrieve or locate information from memory rather than the loss of information.

Information enters the LTM through the working, or short-term, memory. While information must be repeated or rehearsed to stay in short-term memory, it must be "elaborated" to be put into LTM. That is, it must be classified, organized, connected, and stored with information already in LTM. Once in LTM, the flow of information does not stop. It proceeds in two directions. Working memory nearly always calls up data stored in the LTM. For example, when we learn something new about representational government, working memory will call up our previously acquired knowledge, such as our understanding of the concepts "democracy" and "republic." Stored data also are called up as part of a problem-solving process—for instance, a student remembers a relevant theorem when performing a geometric proof. Also, information in LTM, as well as in STM, controls the ultimate output of the student's behavior. Certain behaviors are mastered to the point of **automaticity.** That is, they may be conducted without conscious thought. An example of such behavior in school is the **decoding** of words in text by expert readers. The advanced reader grasps the meaning of words or whole phrases without having to decode the sound of each letter.

**Encoding** is the process of transforming new information for integration into memory. The way in which new information is encoded and integrated into memory, as well as the depth and breadth of integration, affects the ease with which the information is retrieved. Information in the long-term memory is encoded for storage in one of two forms, episodic or semantic. **Episodic memory** is the recall of events in our lives. It allows us to recall images of what happened and what was said during these events, much like a videotape that we can replay for ourselves. **Semantic memory,** as the name implies, stores "meaning." Andre and Phye (1986) state that semantic memory "contains the generalizations we have drawn and acquired from experience" (p. 7). It contains our knowledge of concepts, rules, principles, and skills. Thus, when we read a sentence in a book, it is the meaning of the sentence that we save, not the particular words or grammatical characteristics of the sentence.

Anderson (1985) believes that semantic memory contains two types of knowledge: knowledge about things (called **declarative knowledge**), such as a date, a friend's address, and the information in a textbook, and knowledge about how to do things (called **procedural knowledge**), such as solving a math problem, driving a car, tying a shoe lace. The importance of distinguishing between these two kinds of semantic knowledge is that the conditions for learning declarative knowledge are different from those for learning procedural knowledge. I discuss these two types of learning in depth later in the chapter.

You now have some idea as to how information flows in the information processing system. Beginning with the environment, information flows to the short-term sensory store. The information that is attended to proceeds to the short-term, or working, memory, where it may be encoded and stored permanently in the long-term memory. Information then flows from the short-term, or working, memory to direct behavior.

## Executive Control

**Why is it important to develop students' metacognitive abilities?**

The last aspect of the information processing system to be discussed is the **executive processes,** which monitor and direct the cognitive activities in progress. These skills are responsible for assessing a learning problem, determining learning strategies to resolve the problem, evaluating the effectiveness of the chosen strategy, and changing strategies to improve learning effectiveness.

The functioning of the executive processes is based on **metacognition,** which has two separate but related aspects: (1) knowledge and beliefs about cognitive phenomena and (2) the regulation and control of cognitive behavior. Flavell (1976) states:

> "Metacognition" refers to one's knowledge concerning one's own cognitive processes and products or anything related to them, e.g., the learning-relevant properties of information or data. . . . Metacognition refers, among other things, to the active monitoring and consequent regulation and orchestration of these processes in relation to the cognitive objectives on which they bear, usually in the service of some concrete goal or objective. (p. 232)

Knowledge and beliefs about cognitive phenomena are involved whenever we assess our ability to perform a task or solve a problem. For example, when we are faced with a new learning situation, awareness of our learning strengths and weaknesses helps us to decide whether we are likely to succeed or fail in that situation. Thus one aspect of metacognition is the ability to realize our cognitive limitations or the complexities involved in any given task (Fry & Lupart, 1987). The second aspect of metacognition, the regulation and control of our cognitive behavior, directs our thinking processes during the learning situation. It helps us to plan an approach to the learning task, to monitor our progress, to check our understanding, and to evaluate our solution. Holt's (1982) observations of student learning in classrooms provide an excellent example of the importance of such skills:

> Part of being a good student is learning to be aware of the state of one's own mind and the degree of one's own understanding. The good student may be one who often says that he does not understand, simply because he keeps a constant check on his understanding. The poor student, who does not, so to speak, watch himself trying to understand, does not know most of the time whether he understands or not. Thus, the problem is not to get students to ask us what they don't know; the problem is to make them aware of the difference between what they know and what they don't. (p. 17)

Let's look at metacognition within the context of a particular task. Suppose the task is to read a chapter in American history. A student, Robert, realizes that knowledge of this material will be assessed by means of an essay test. Using metacognitive abilities, Robert assesses his own knowledge of the subject and decides it is necessary to plan out a study approach in order to gain a general understanding of the main ideas and to be able to recall the most important facts. Therefore, he paraphrases each section of the chapter, underlines the important facts, and monitors his own progress during study. Finally, Robert evaluates his knowledge of the material by writing answers to short essay questions.

*Learning strategies.* As you can see, metacognitive processes are important in helping us gauge the extent of our learning as well as in deciding how to learn. Planning a learning approach involves the use of what some psychologists (e.g., Pressley et al., 1989; Levin, 1986) call **learning strategies** (e.g., underlining and paraphrasing). Weinstein and Mayer (1985) define learning strategies as "behaviors and thoughts that a learner engages in during learning and that are intended to influence the learner's encoding process [so as to facilitate the way in which the learner] . . . selects, acquires, organizes, or integrates new knowledge" (p. 315). Flavell (1979) states that learning strategies are necessary to make cognitive progress but that metacognitive skills must monitor and direct the cognitive strategies.

Learning strategies can be specific to a particular learning task (e.g., knowing when to borrow in subtraction) or generalized to a wide variety of tasks (e.g., learning to answer the "Who? What? When? Where?" questions in any reading passage). In this chapter, I focus on Weinstein and Mayer's (1985) general learning strategies—*rehearsal strategies,* **elaboration strategies, organizational strategies, comprehension-monitoring strategies,** and **affective strategies.**

Good and Brophy (1990) summarize Weinstein and Mayer's five general types of learning strategies as follows:

- *Rehearsal strategies* involve actively repeating (saying, writing) material or focusing on key parts of it. For brief rote learning tasks

Students must be taught learning strategies so that they can become self-directed learners.

[i.e., arbitrary or unrelated factual information] rehearsal may involve nothing more than repeating the material aloud. For more complex learning from lectures or from studying, rehearsal may involve repeating key terms aloud (shadowing), copying the material, taking selective verbatim notes, or underlining important parts.

- *Elaboration strategies* involve making connections between the new and familiar. For rote learning, elaboration strategies include forming mental images to associate with the material, generating sentences that relate the items to be learned to more familiar items, or using mnemonic devices [to be discussed later]. . . . For more complex meaningful learning tasks, elaboration strategies include paraphrasing, summarizing, creating analogies, taking notes that go beyond verbatim repetition to extend or comment on the material, answering questions . . . and describing how the new information relates to existing knowledge.

- *Organizational strategies* involve imposing structure on the material by dividing it into parts and identifying superordinate-subordinate relationships. In simple rote learning tasks, organizational strategies involve breaking lists into chunks. Organizational strategies for complex meaningful learning tasks would include outlining the text, creating a hierarchy or network of concepts, or creating diagrams showing their relationships.

- *Comprehension-monitoring strategies* involve remaining aware of what one is trying to accomplish, keeping track of the strategies one uses and the success achieved with them, and adjusting behavior accordingly. Comprehension-monitoring strategies include self-questioning to check understanding, taking action when one does not understand something, using prequestions or statements of objectives to guide study, establishing subgoals and assessing progress in meeting them, and modifying strategies if necessary.

- *Affective strategies* include establishing and maintaining motivation, focusing attention, maintaining concentration, managing performance anxiety, and managing time effectively. (pp. 248–249)

I add the category *problem-solving strategies* to the list of learning strategies because many researchers have developed programs to teach students thinking and problem-solving strategies. I shall discuss general problem-solving programs in this chapter and specific problem-solving strategies related to subject areas in the appendix following this chapter.

From the cognitive perspective, one of the major goals of teaching is to help students to manage and control their own learning. If students do not have the strategies needed to learn, the teaching goal must be to help them to acquire the strategies. Good learners have been shown to have better metacognitive skills, more effective strategies for selecting and attending to important information in text and lectures, and the ability to organize material in a more efficient manner than poor learners (E. Gagné, 1985). There also is evidence that students can be taught to use learning strategies to improve their classroom learning (Pressley, Snyder, & Cariglia-Bull, 1987; Weinstein & Mayer, 1985). A major area of research in cognitive psychology is to determine the best way to provide instruction in learning strategy to students.

Keep in mind that very young children do not have the ability to think about their own thought processes. By first grade, however, students know that some learning tasks will be more difficult than others. Students in the third grade usually know when they have failed to comprehend something. However, these young students are limited in their ability to do anything about this knowledge. It is not until late childhood or early adolescence that students become capable of assessing a learning problem, devising a strategy to solve the problem, and evaluating their success (Flavell, 1985). This does not mean that the individual learning strategies discussed in this chapter are not important for the young learner, only that you will have to determine which strategies are most useful considering the developmental level of the learner.

I organize the remaining content in this chapter by showing how different learning strategies can be used with different types of learning tasks. An example is knowledge about things (declarative knowledge) and knowledge about how to do things (procedural knowledge) (Anderson, 1985). I first introduced these terms in the discussion of semantic memory's role in long-term memory, and I pointed out that the conditions for learning declarative knowledge are different from the conditions for learning procedural knowledge. Figure 7.2 identifies the decisions that need to be made in instruction.

In discussing the different types of knowledge and the kinds of instructional procedures that are appropriate to each type, we will follow the instructional decisions of two teachers, Mrs. Jones and Mr. Smith. Mrs. Jones teaches science at the junior high level and is applying cognitive principles in developing instructional lessons in a life science course. Mr. Smith teaches fifth grade and is applying cognitive principles in teaching mathematics. In the discussion to follow, I often refer to Tables 7.1 and 7.2, which illustrate the instructional objective, the type of knowledge each objective represents, the learning conditions appropriate to promoting each type of knowledge, and examples of relevant instructional techniques that include various learning strategies.

Figure 7.2 Process for Determining Learning Strategy Appropriate to Learning Objective.

TABLE 7.1 CONDITIONS PROMOTING LEARNING THE INSTRUCTIONAL OBJECTIVES IN MR. SMITH'S MATHEMATICS CLASS

| Learning Objective | Type of Knowledge | Conditions Promoting Learning |
| --- | --- | --- |
| Students will associate Roman numbers V, X, and C with 5, 10, and 100. | Declarative-Rote | Rehearsal: Spaced and frequent practice associating Roman and decimal numbers to overlearning.<br>Elaboration: Explanation of some Roman numbers as originating from counting on fingers. |
| Students will identify finite sets. | Procedural-Pattern Recognition | Provide a definition: "A finite set is one in which the members of the set are countable."<br>Provide varied true examples: {5, 10, 15}, the set of all people in the world, the set of all grains of sand in the world, all even numbers below 100.<br>Provide matched nonexamples: {5, 10, 15 . . .}, the set of all odd numbers below 100. |
| Students will divide fractional numbers using reciprocals. | Procedural-Action Sequence | Provide a written description of steps: "Invert the divisor, and multiply."<br>Check prerequisite knowledge: Does student understand "invert"? Can student identify the divisor? Can student correctly multiply fractions?<br>Provide practice: Frequent, spaced practice can make this procedure almost automatic.<br>Provide corrective feedback: Use students' verbal self-reports or error analyses to analyze source of errors. See Table 7.3. |

## DECLARATIVE KNOWLEDGE

The learning of declarative knowledge can be either meaningful or rote. **Meaningful learning** refers to learning concepts, procedures, or ideas from sources such as textbooks or lectures. The "meaning" in *meaningful learning* comes from the learner's ability to relate the new knowledge to old knowledge already in memory. **Rote learning** refers to mastering disconnected or arbitrary verbal material. Such tasks as learning lists of states and their capitals, the order of colors in the rainbow, or the vocabulary of a foreign language are examples of rote learning.

Let's focus first on rote learning and determine the factors that facilitate and interfere with learning. Then I'll show you how you can help students to develop strategies to improve their rote learning.

TABLE 7.2 CONDITIONS PROMOTING LEARNING THE INSTRUCTIONAL OBJECTIVES IN MRS. JONES'S LIFE SCIENCES CLASS

| Learning Objective | Type of Knowledge | Conditions Promoting Learning |
|---|---|---|
| Students will define the metric terms *kilo, deca, deci, centi, milli.* | Declarative-Rote | Rehearsal: Spaced and frequent practice in associating each term with its meaning to overlearning.<br>Elaboration: Using mnemonic and associating terms with familiar words. |
| Students will recall the eight life processes: food getting, respiration, excretion, response, secretion, growth, reproduction, movement. | Declarative-Meaningful | Elaboration: Encourage students to take notes, paraphrasing definitions of each life process. Prompt students to think about how they carry out each life process.<br>Organization: Activate schema. Prompt students to relate each function to their own respective bodily parts. |
| Students will classify living and nonliving objects. | Procedural-Pattern Recognition | Definition: Living things carry out all the life processes.<br>Provide varied true examples: demonstrate how diverse organisms (e.g., protozoa, mammals, plants) carry out the life processes.<br>Provide matched nonexamples: Compare living organisms with things that show only some of the life processes—for example, crystals that grow but do not get food, respire, respond, secrete, reproduce, or move. |
| Student will follow the scientific method in investigating a self-chosen question. | Procedural-Action Sequence | Provide a written list of steps—see Figure 7.6.<br>Provide practice: Have students describe each step they will take, and why, in investigating some life science phenomenon.<br>Provide corrective feedback. |

# ROTE LEARNING

## Types of Rote Learning

Rote learning can be categorized into three types:

- **Free recall** refers to recall of information without any specific order or without association with other stimuli. Remembering names of your classmates or the names of your favorite sport stars are free-recall tasks.
- **Serial recall** refers to remembering information in a particular order, such as the names of the planets in order from the sun, or the combination to a padlock.
- **Paired-associate learning** involves recalling information that is associated with some stimulus. The act of remembering the capital of

each state or the foreign language equivalent of an English word, is an example of paired-associate learning. Table 7.1 shows that Mr. Smith has one objective involving paired-associate material—teaching three symbols of the Roman numeration system. Thus the teaching task becomes a matter of associating one stimulus, such as *V*, with another, *5*. Mrs. Jones also has an objective involving paired-associate learning—defining metric terms such as *kilo, deca,* or *centi.*

When we think of rote learning, our image is of having information drilled into us through endless repetition. Whether memorizing a song or learning the capitals of each state in the United States, we have been told by our teachers that we must practice, practice, practice. But does it matter how we practice? Cognitive psychologists offer some advice as to how practice can be made more effective. Research has shown that **distributed practice** among frequent and short periods is more effective than a smaller number of sessions of **massed practice** (Underwood, 1961). If you want students to remember the presidents of the United States without error, they should practice for many short sessions, reading the list and saying the names over and over. The classic "all-nighter," of which I must admit I experienced a few during my undergraduate days, is the best example of massed practice. Although this practice method may be effective in learning a large amount of information in a short time, it is a poor method of learning *if* retention of information is the goal. Think about the examinations on which you used massed practice. How much of the content did you remember a few days after the examination?

In memorizing a list, you should be aware of the **serial position effect,** which results from the particular placement of information within a list. In general, a person is more likely to remember information placed at the beginning (*primacy effect*) or the end (*recency effect*) of a list than information placed in the middle.

Most people have difficulty learning a long list at one time and find it easier to break the list into small groups. This is called **part learning.** This method is appropriate, for instance, in teaching the multiplication tables. Students can start with the 2s table and work upward. Part learning is also useful in teaching the symbols for chemical elements.

The relationship of new and old knowledge can influence the difficulty of learning and recalling data. Learning a task that has the same stimuli and responses as a previously learned task will be easier than learning material with which you have no previous experience. This situation is called **positive transfer.** For example, a youngster who has learned how to keep a room tidy at home will find that skill helpful in meeting the same requirements at camp. **Negative transfer** occurs when two tasks have the same stimuli but require a different response. Learning Italian after learning Spanish can be difficult because it is easy to confuse the Spanish and Italian words for the same concept.

Forgetting is an overwhelming impediment to learning. A widely accepted explanation of this phenomenon is that interference from previous or subsequent learning occurs. When previous (early) learning interferes with subsequent (later) learning, **proactive inhibition** occurs. **Retroactive inhibition** takes place when subsequent learning interferes with previous learning. The child who has learned to spell *relief* may later experience proactive interference when learning to spell *receive*. In another situation, our ability to recall and use metric measurements can be hampered by our familiarity with the English measurement system. An example of retroactive interference is the difficulty experienced by a student who finds that learning in a second-period French class interferes with learning in a first-period Spanish class. Learning a second programming language, such as FORTRAN, may inhibit our ability to recall the commands and format of previously learned BASIC.

The chance of interference in rote learning is high. One means of reducing the effects on rote learning is the proper sequencing, variation, and organization of material so that interference can be minimized. For example, similar concepts should not be taught too closely in time. In teaching kindergarten children the alphabet, the letter *b* should be totally familiar to them before the letter *d* is introduced. When the letter *d* is introduced, the differences between the two letters should be pointed out. Research has shown that **overlearning** reduces the effects of interference on the learning of rote material (Underwood & Ekstrand, 1966). Overlearning occurs when practice or drill continues after the student reaches the desired level of performance.

## Using Learning Strategies for Improving Rote Learning

*Rehearsal.* I first mentioned the importance of rehearsal in describing how information, when repeated or rehearsed, can be retained when it enters short-term memory. The rehearsal is performed by repeating the information to oneself subvocally or out loud. When looking up a phone number, we often repeat it out loud until we have completed dialing. We do the same when learning the combination to a padlock. In class, students will often repeat to themselves the spelling of new vocabulary words or the words to a poem that are to be memorized.

One of the reasons that rote learning is often considered uninteresting is that it has a low level of meaningfulness. Few connections are made between the new information and old knowledge. Thus another way to facilitate rote learning is to increase the meaningfulness of the material by creating connections between the new data and information the student already knows. This goal is accomplished by elaboration and organization.

*Elaboration.* **Mnemonics** are elaboration techniques that impose a useful linkage between new data and visual images or semantic knowledge (see Belleza, 1981; Schneider & Pressley, 1989). They can be very useful for improving recall of names, categories, sequences, or groups of items.

**What are some
methods that
students can
learn in order
to increase
their retention
of factual
material?**

Mnemonics that are useful for serial recall learning are the loci method, acronyms, and the peg-word method. With the **loci method,** used since classical Greek times, the student creates a mental image of a familiar place, such as the classroom. In this image, several easily identifiable locations are determined. The student then associates each individual item on the list with a particular location in the image. A student studying the presidents might visualize George Washington sitting in the first seat inside the door of the classroom. Farther into the classroom would be John Adams, then James Madison, and so on. Then, during recall, the student imagines walking through the room, visualizing each president in his place. In this way, the list of presidents, in its proper order, is made more meaningful through the association with a visual image.

**Acronyms** use the first letter in each word to form a mnemonic. "ROY G. BIV" is an acronym that gives the order of the colors of the rainbow: *R*ed, *O*range, *Y*ellow, *G*reen, *B*lue, *I*ndigo, and *V*iolet. Similar to an acronym is the sentence mnemonic that uses the first letter of each term as the first letter of each word of a sentence. "*M*y *v*ery *e*fficient *m*other *j*ust *s*at *u*p *n*ear *p*op" gives the planets in order from the sun: Mercury, Venus, Earth, Mars, Jupiter, Saturn, Uranus, Neptune, Pluto. Another kind of acronym involves taking the first letters of a series of words to describe steps in a procedure. For example, the initial letters of the words *d*ad, *m*om, *s*ister, *b*rother can be used to help students remember the four steps in long division: *d*ivide, *m*ultiply, *s*ubtract, and *b*ring down.

The **peg-word method** uses visual imagery and semantic associations in remembering serial data. For instance, items in a list are associated, as in a visual image, with each phrase in a chant: "One is a bun, two is a shoe, three is a tree," and so on. The student who is studying a series of items imagines the first item stuck between the halves of the bun, the second item stuck in a shoe, the third item hanging in a tree, and so on.

A useful mnemonic for learning foreign language vocabulary is the **key-word method** (Atkinson, 1975), which involves the creation of an image that relates the English to the foreign word. For example, the Spanish word for *postal letter* is *carta*. An appropriate image might involve a huge postal letter being transported to the post office in a shopping cart. Thus the word carta would be encoded both as an idea and as an image. The student's subsequent attempts to recall the Spanish word for *postal letter* will stimulate the image of the letter in the cart, providing a concrete cue to the correct word. This method has been shown to have significant success in teaching foreign vocabulary (Atkinson, 1975).

*Organization.* A method for increasing the meaningfulness of rote .material is to provide an organizational structure. This is often useful with free-recall tasks. Hierarchical schemes of organization are especially effective. This type of organization reflects what some researchers believe is the hierarchical organization of information stored in long-term memory (Collins & Quillian, 1969). For example, students find it easier to recall the different types of rock when studying geology if an organizational structure is imposed. Learning the names of rocks can be difficult, as demonstrated by this list: granite, gabbro, peridotite, syenite, felsite, basalt, pumice, obsidian, shale sandstone, conglomerate, limestone, dolomite, evaporite, organic limestone, coal, slate, schist, phyllite, gneiss, quartzite, marble, and anthracite. Figure 7.3, however, shows how this list can be reorganized in a hierarchical fashion. Such organization has been shown to improve subsequent recall (Frase, 1973).

Mr. Smith has taken several steps in designing instruction on Roman numeration that reflect the cognitive principles of rote instruction. First, he has provided daily periods of instruction so that students have frequent opportunity to rehearse the association of Roman and decimal numbers. To aid in elaboration, Mr. Smith shows how some of the Roman numbers are related to counting on one's fingers. The *V* stands for the open hand (5 fingers), and *X* represents two open hands (10 fingers). The other symbols are more difficult to associate in this way. However, *C* can be remembered as *cent* (100).

Mrs. Jones's rote objective involves associating the decimal terms *kilo, deca, deci, centi,* and *milli* with their appropriate meaning. In addition to frequent rehearsal of this material, Mrs. Jones aids elaboration by use of mnemonics. First, to aid in encoding the descending order of value of terms, she devised the following sentence using the first few letters of each term in a word: "*Kill*ing *deci*nitely *deci*ases *centi*pedes and *milli*pedes." Further, Mrs. Jones associates several of the similar terms with familiar words that help to distinguish them. Thus *deca* is associated with *deca*de—10 years—and *deci* is associated with *deci*mals.

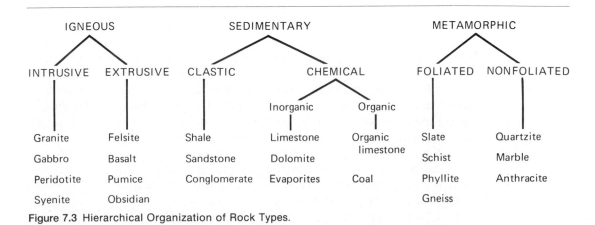

Figure 7.3 Hierarchical Organization of Rock Types.

## MEANINGFUL LEARNING

### Using Learning Strategies to Improve Meaningful Learning

**How can the use of learning strategies improve student achievement?**

For the most part, teachers deal with meaningful knowledge that is connected or interrelated, such as information from textbooks and lectures. Such knowledge gets its meaningfulness from our ability to relate the ideas of the text or lecture to knowledge we have stored in long-term memory. When we gain new information about something, such as "Columbus explored the Virgin Islands in 1493," what we store is the meaning, or main ideas, contained in the text. Unless we specifically attempt to encode it, information such as the grammatical structure of the preceding sentence is lost. In long-term memory we connect this knowledge with other things we know about America and Columbus. This makes it meaningful to us. Four strategies facilitate the storage of ideas in long-term memory: rehearsal, elaboration, organization, and comprehension monitoring.

**What advice would you give students about underlining?**

*Rehearsal.* A method of external storage and rehearsal of textual material is underlining. Underlining allows students to quickly locate and review important information in a text. Studies have shown that students learn more from a text if they underline important and relevant ideas in it (Fowler & Barker, 1974; Snowman, 1984). Rickards and August (1975) compared recall under different types of underlining conditions. They found that students told to underline any sentence in each paragraph recalled more than did students told to underline the most important sentence in each paragraph. Apparently, the free underlining condition allowed students to connect the passage to existing knowledge structures. It is important that students use underlining sparingly and underline only the information that they find important. How many times have you seen a student in a college course underline almost every sentence in the book with a Magic Marker? How is this underlining helpful?

Studies have found that underlining irrelevant information reduces recall of important data (Smart & Bruning, 1973). Because students below the sixth grade cannot reliably determine which information is important (Brown & Smiley, 1977), it is best to encourage underlining for older children only. An alternative is to teach underlining to younger students and older students who do not know how to underline. Such a program should begin with an explanation of what is important in a passage, such as the topic sentence. Younger or less able students may not have the knowledge structures necessary to allow them to underline freely. The next step would be to teach students to underline sparingly, perhaps only one or two sentences in a paragraph. Finally, students should be taught to review and paraphrase those passages underlined.

*Elaboration.* When someone asks us to elaborate on an idea we have expressed in discussion, they want us to add more information to what we have said to provide detail, give examples, make connections to other issues, or draw inferences from the data. The additional information makes our point more meaningful to the listener and also is likely to make the point easier to remember.

We can elaborate for ourselves when learning new information. As information enters working memory, the efficient learner thinks about the information: What does this new information mean? How does it relate to other ideas in the text and other information already learned? The learner may create examples that demonstrate the new knowledge. Thus, when encoding the information that Switzerland is politically neutral in international relations, the advanced learner might relate this to Switzerland's history of noninvolvement in the wars of the past several centuries. The learner may also draw conclusions as to the relationship of this neutrality to Switzerland's role as world banker.

A social studies lesson provides a second example of elaboration. A student learning that ancient Egyptian society depended on slavery may elaborate on this fact by adding details, making connections with other information, or drawing inferences. By way of providing detail, the student may notice that Egyptian slaves were largely prisoners of war. The student may connect the concept of Egyptian slavery with what is known of antebellum American slavery, noting similarities and differences. The student may infer that life for an Egyptian slave was hard and held cheaply by Egyptian society at large. In this way, the efficient learner integrates the new ideas into long-term memory by associating the new data with the old knowledge (Bransford, 1979). This procedure leads to improved understanding of the material and to an increased probability that the data will be remembered at a later time.

**How can you improve students' note taking?**

*Note Taking.* Students often find it difficult to learn a large amount of information in a short time. Consequently, when information is presented faster than students can encode it, they will not be able to keep up. Under such circumstances, competent students may choose a method of external storage, such as note taking.

Note taking is discussed here under elaboration because taking notes can do far more than create an external store of information for review. It can also encourage elaboration and integration of the new information. The kinds of notes taken affect the way in which the information is integrated and organized. Taking verbatim notes encourages encoding of verbatim data and amounts to little more than rehearsal. Taking summary notes encourages reorganization and integration (Anderson & Armbruster, 1984). Students should be taught to take brief notes, in their own words, that organize and summarize the important points of the lecture so that the notes make sense to the students themselves.

Although taking notes does help the encoding process, the most efficient and effective use of notes includes reviewing them. Students who take their own notes and review them learn more than do students who take notes but do not review them, and they also learn more than do students who review notes taken by another person (Kiewra, 1989). Part of the benefit of reviewing notes is that it allows further elaboration and integration of the material at that time. Therefore, students should be encouraged not simply to read over their notes but to think actively about the ideas in the notes and relate them to other information they already have. Also, the research supports the benefit of borrowing notes from a friend if you miss a lecture. You will benefit from reviewing a friend's notes.

In a review of note taking, Kiewra (1985) found that the types of notes taken affected the manner in which the information was encoded. Students should be encouraged to take conceptual notes that stress the main ideas of the lecture. Detailed notes are also related to performance and should be taken to supplement the lecture's main ideas.

Kiewra (1989) believes that teachers can improve students' note taking and review behaviors and, consequently, their achievement in the following ways:

- Lecture at a slower rate.
- Repeat complex subject material.
- Present cues for note taking.
- Write important information on the board.
- Provide students with a complete set of notes to review.
- Provide structural support for note taking such as skeletal outline

Students need to be taught how to take good notes.

(e.g., provide the students with topic headings under which they have to place major ideas) or matrix framework.

A good method of taking notes for comparing and contrasting information is to use **matrix notes,** a system in which notes are written in matrix form. Figure 7.4 provides an example of this system for a lecture passage on the topic moths and butterflies. As you can see in Figure 7.4, notes written in matrix form list major topics of information in the lecture (i.e., moths, butterflies) as vertical column headings, and the subtopics (e.g., growth, wings) as horizontal column headings. Cells within the matrix contain ideas representing the intersection of the headings. Kiewra (1989) states that matrix notes have several advantages over other form of notes (e.g., linear), including organizing lecture material for easier recall, integrating ideas within and across categories of information, and making it easier to identify missing information from lectures (e.g., the lecture failed to mention anything about the cocoons of butterflies). Kiewra suggests using matrix notes whenever two or more topics with several subordinate ideas are discussed. Did any instructor in high school or college teach you to take notes? Would you benefit from improved note-taking skills?

A final word about note taking: Not all students may benefit from taking notes. Note taking may be less productive for students of lower ability (Kiewra, 1989) or for students who have difficulty processing aural information (information they hear). Such students might do better if en-

LECTURE PASSAGE:

### Moths and Butterflies

A moth has two sets of wings. It folds the wings down over its body when it rests. The moth has feathery antennae and spins a fuzzy cocoon. The moth goes through four stages of development. A butterfly also goes through four stages of growth and has two sets of wings. Its antennae, however, are long and thin with knobs at the ends. When a butterfly rests, its wings are straight up like outstretched hands.

MATRIX NOTES BASED ON LECTURE PASSAGE:

|  | Moths | Butterflies |
|---|---|---|
| Similarities |  |  |
| Growth | 4 stages | 4 stages |
| Wings | 2 sets | 2 sets |
| Differences |  |  |
| Antennae | feathery | long and thin with knobs |
| Rest | wings over body | wings outstretched |
| Cocoon | fuzzy | ? |

Figure 7.4 Matrix Notes for a Lecture Passage on Moths and Butterflies.

*Source: Kiewra, 1989.*

couraged to listen carefully to a lecture and review notes provided by the teacher.

*Organization.* As was the case for rote learning, new meaningful information is easier to learn and remember if it is presented in an organized format, especially if the format is hierarchically arranged. Having a well-organized body of knowledge in long-term memory is characteristic of experts in any field; chess and science are examples. This organization allows the expert to manage data more efficiently in working memory and to quickly locate needed information stored in long-term memory.

One method of improving the organization of encoded data is to provide written outlines for students before lectures and readings. Glynn and Divesta (1977) provided college students with a hierarchically organized outline of material presented in a 15-paragraph passage on stones. The students who studied the outline before reading the passage recalled more specific information than did other students.

Textual material often provide cues regarding organization. Scanning text for chapter, section, and subsection titles has been recommended for many years as a preliminary reading technique for determining the organization of the material.

**How can a teacher help students improve their reading comprehension?**

*Comprehension Monitoring.* A major cognitive function in reading and study is comprehension monitoring. Skilled readers start this process at the beginning of a reading assignment and continue it until the assignment is completed (Brown, 1980). The skilled reader has a comprehension goal in mind, such as finding a particular fact or determining the main ideas of a text. Such a reader's strategy might then be to skim the text for the fact, or read the text for the main ideas. Following execution of this strategy, if the important fact has been located or the main ideas grasped, the skilled reader will experience satisfaction at reaching the goal. However, the reader's experience might instead be one of frustration at not finding the fact, or one of confusion because of not understanding the passage. If comprehension monitoring shows that the goal has not been reached, then a remedial step would be taken, such as reskimming the material, or perhaps reading the text more carefully.

As discussed earlier, good readers have skills that help them to decide whether they have understood textual material at the level necessary to reach their reading goal. Palincsar and Brown (1984) devised a remedial program called *reciprocal teaching* to teach these same skills to deficient readers. The teacher first modeled three skills of comprehension monitoring: (1) making predictions about what the text will say, (2) asking questions about the main ideas in the text, and (3) being aware of unclear passages. Students were then given practice in these same skills and were provided corrective feedback on their performance. Students were also given feedback as to their improvement in reading comprehension. Scores on comprehension tests for students in this four-week program rose from a be-

Effective readers have good metacognitive skills, allowing them to learn independently.

ginning average of 50% correct to 80% correct. See the appendix following this chapter for more detailed information about this procedure.

Researchers have found that many young children as well as college students are deficient in comprehension monitoring skills. Many students continue to rely on repetition (e.g., rereading, copying notes, using flashcards) as their major strategy in attempting to learn new knowledge from a textbook or lecture. To help such students, Devine (1987) suggests that they practice the following strategies for monitoring and improving comprehension of text:

- Change rate of reading to accommodate for differences in the comprehensibility of the text. Speed up for easier sections to quickly get an idea of the author's overall plan, but slow down for more difficult sections.
- Suspend judgment. If something is not clear, continue to read. The author will probably fill in the gaps, add more information, or clarify points in the text.
- Hypothesize. When something being read is not clear, make it a habit to hypothesize about the meaning of the unclear passage and read along to see if your guess makes sense.
- Reread difficult passages. This simple strategy can often be effective, particularly when information appears contradictory or ambiguous.

*Adjunct Questions.* One way of helping students check their comprehension is through the use of **adjunct questions**—questions added to text or lecture material to influence what is learned from the material (Hamaker, 1986). These questions can be asked before, during, or after the presentation of the material. (I have chosen to use adjunct questions—Focus Questions—at the beginning of each chapter and to repeat them in the margins at appropriate places throughout the chapter.) Adjunct questions also may be distinguished by type. Factual questions ask for verbatim information presented in the text. The student has only to find or recall the material to answer the question. Higher-order questions ask students to relate or manipulate information to create an answer. If Mrs. Jones's handout on the eight life processes used factual prequestions, a simple question at the beginning of the chapter could be, "What are the eight life processes?" A higher-order postquestion, such as "How do the eight life processes work together to sustain life?" could come at the end of the chapter.

The use of adjunct questions has been extensively investigated and found to be effective in a wide range of instructional settings (Hamilton, 1985). However, the types and the placement of questions are important. The placement of questions affects the material that is attended to. Prequestions alert the reader as to what material to look for. During reading, only material relevant to questions is processed. Consequently, prequestions facilitate the learning of targeted material but inhibit the learning of incidental information (material in the text that is not targeted by the questions or learning objectives) (Felker & Dapra, 1975). Postquestions do not alert the reader in this way. Postquestions facilitate learning because the reader is alerted as to what material to review *after* reading the passage; the reader will have already attended to incidental material in the first reading. Consequently, postquestions facilitate learning targeted material, but they do not have the detrimental effect on learning incidental material that prequestions have (Anderson & Biddle, 1975; Hamaker, 1986).

The type of question influences the form in which the information is encoded (Cook & Mayer, 1983). Using factual versus higher-order questions can be compared to rote versus meaningful learning. Factual questions lead the learner to review, or rehearse, important information (Rickards, 1979). After reading the factual question, Mrs. Jones's students might repeat over and over to themselves the eight life functions. This type of study would help the students to remember the labels for the life functions but little else. In general, asking questions about verbatim and specific facts encourages only verbatim recall (Felker & Dapra, 1975).

Higher-order questions not only encourage review but also cause learners to integrate and elaborate the material (Hamaker, 1986). Questions that encourage higher levels of processing (e.g., analysis, synthesis, and evaluation) also lead to higher levels of retention and to higher-quality inferences than do questions that do not promote higher-level thinking. (Felker & Dapra, 1975). Students in Mrs. Jones's class who received the higher-order question would be encouraged to establish relationships among the life processes. Activity such as this should not only increase students' recall but improve their understanding of the material.

While adjunct questions are effective in helping students comprehend new information, some research shows that they may not be as helpful when learning must be generalized to new situations (Andre & Thieman, 1988). This phenomenon apparently occurs when too few adjunct questions are used with a given body of text. Andre and Thieman point out that most textbooks, for example, employ only a small number of questions for the material presented. They feel that more than just one or two questions are needed if students are to understand those aspects of the material that are generalizable to new contexts.

Most texts are written without adjunct questions. However, these texts are not without clues as to what material the author considered important. School textbooks generally include a table of contents, chapter titles, and subsection headings. These sections give hints as to the important material contained in the text. From these clues, students can create their own adjunct questions.

Most of the research on adjunct questions has been done with questions relating to textual material. However, the teacher may use adjunct questions by giving students a list of questions regarding lecture material either before or after a lecture, or by asking students questions about the material during the lecture.

One method of study has incorporated adjunct questions for several decades: the **SQ3R system** (F. P. Robinson, 1970). This system encourages the student to *survey* the chapter headings and boldface type; to develop *questions* about the material; then to *read, recite,* and *review* the material. Dansereau and his colleagues (1979) found that training students to use reading strategies that called for paraphrasing, to construct idea networks, and to define main ideas and make connections between those main ideas significantly improved performance on short-answer and multiple-choice tests over control conditions. It is usually assumed that students possess these skills. However, most students could probably benefit from direct instruction in how to use each skill for both text and lecture material.

*Schemata.* Some researchers have investigated the use of **schemata** in comprehension monitoring and problem solving. *Schemata* (plural for *schema*) are cognitive structures that may be created through the abstraction of previous experiences or acquired through instruction. Schemata make learning easier by giving incoming information meaning and reducing the number of things we must attend to. They do this in two ways. First, schemata provide an organizational structure into which new information can be fitted. Hierarchical organizations of knowledge, as in the geology example discussed earlier, demonstrate this function. Second, schemata let us know what to expect from incoming information. For example, we know that a story will normally have at least one character, a conflict, a beginning, climax, and resolution. Gordon and Braun (1985) have developed a series of schema-related questions to help students to improve their reading comprehension:

- *Setting:* Where and when did the story take place? Who was in it?
- *Main goal:* What is the main goal?
- *Starter event:* What started the chain of events in the story (first episode)?
- *Inner response:* What does the character think, feel, or want?
- *Action:* What does the main character do?
- *Reaction:* What are the reactions of the characters?
- *Outcome:* What happened as a result of the main character's action? or reaction? (p. 70)

Related to the organizational and interpretive functions of schemata are what Armbruster (1986) calls *textual schemas* and *content schemas*. Textual schemas are structure or organizational patterns found in text to aid comprehension. Examples are patterns of comparison and contrast, cause and effect, and problem and solution. Armbruster has noted that skilled readers appear to know these conventional organizational patterns of text and adopt a strategy of seeking and using them as an organizational framework for understanding and recalling text information.

Content schemas involve knowledge of objects, events, and situations. They are generic characterizations of what we know about the world and, as such, help us to interpret new information. One way they do this is by providing an analogy or comparison by which new information can be understood. Armbruster (1986) provides an example by comparing the workings of a bread factory to the process of photosynthesis in a leaf:

> Have you ever been to a bread factory to see how bread is made? First, the materials needed to make the bread—flour, milk, and other ingredients—are transported to the factory. Then they are mixed together to form dough. Next, the dough is baked in ovens. In the ovens, heat energy is used to change the dough into the final product—bread.
>
> The leaf of a green plant is much like a bread factory. Just as flour and milk must be transported to a bread factory, so must water and carbon dioxide be transported to the leaf factory. Heat energy is used to make bread in the bread factory, while sunlight provides the energy to make the product in the leaf factory. Bread is the final product of a bread factory, and sugar, the food for green plants, is the final product of the leaf factory. The process by which green plants make their own food is called photosynthesis. (p. 262)

Using content schemas as a basis for interpreting new knowledge is an effective strategy for teachers to employ in designing lessons. For example, Mrs. Jones wants to design a lesson on the eight life processes, the functions all living things must fulfill: Food getting, respiration, excretion, growth, movement, response, secretion, reproduction. As can be seen in Table 7.2, this objective involves meaningful declarative knowledge. Consequently, the use of a relevant content schema may help in effectively teaching this material. To do this, Mrs. Jones will make use of a schema that all the students possess; she will prompt them to call up an image of their own bodies in thinking about each of the life processes. The familiar functions of their bodies can serve as a basis for understanding more general life processes. For example, when considering the life process "food getting," students will be prompted to think about how their bodies go about getting food, such as going to a restaurant, cooking their own dinner, or even growing food in a backyard garden. By calling up this schema of their own bodies, the students have something that the new information can be "attached" to. Students will then be asked to elaborate on food getting by thinking of what they eat, how it is important in staying alive, and what hunger is and why it is important. By integrating food getting with other concepts, such as hunger or nutritional value, they add additional meaning to the concept and make additional connections with previously learned information. These additional connections help in retention and subsequent recall of this information (Anderson, 1985; E. Gagné, 1985).

*Advance Organizers.* Another way in which schemata have proven useful in promoting comprehension is through the use of **advance organizers** (Ausubel, 1968). Advance organizers present information before a lesson to make the lesson content more meaningful and easier to understand. The information in an advance organizer is presented at a higher level of abstraction and generality than the lesson content to aid the learner in subsuming or integrating the new material. I have already stated that one of the conditions for meaningful learning is that the learners have relevant ideas in their cognitive structure to which they can relate the new material. An advance organizer serves this function. According to Joyce and Weil (1972):

> the organizer can be a statement, a descriptive paragraph, a question, a demonstration, or even a film. It might be one section or it might be an entire lesson which precedes the other lessons in a unit of work. The form of the organizer is less important than the fact that its solution must be clearly understood and continuously related to the material it is organizing.
>
> The instructor can use organizers at many stages throughout the lesson or unit. As the learner moves to new material, new organizers provide a framework for relating new ideas to information already studied. In this manner, the learner has a framework to organize his information, and relate and differentiate the many ideas he has learned. (p. 175)

Before students begin studying the caste system in India, for example, a brief presentation of *social stratification* as an organizer will help them to understand the nature and purpose of the caste system. This more abstract discussion is an organizing outline for relevant information in the lesson. In mathematics, teaching the number line before proceeding to the addition and subtraction of negative numbers is another example of the effective use of an organizer. In teaching literature, the model shown in Figure 7.5 can be presented as an organizer to explain the derivation of the similarities and differences in various literary forms or to explain the interrelationships of forms within any of the main subdivisions of literature.

It is important to realize that typical introductions or summaries of content presented before a lecture, a chapter in a book, or a film are not examples of advance organizers. The purpose of introductions and summaries is to orient students to the new material. In addition, they are typically presented at the same level of abstraction or generality as the new material. As a result, they do not provide the same framework as advance organizers do in helping students better organize and integrate new information.

There has been considerable discussion regarding the effectiveness of advance organizers for different types of learning as well as the conditions under which they should be used (see Barnes & Clawson, 1975; Lawton & Wanska, 1977; Mayer 1979a, 1979b). Advance organizers do not always increase the amount of learning. They appear to be most useful when the information is poorly organized or when the learners lack prerequisite knowledge or abilities.

Mayer (1987) has recently used advance organizers in the form of concrete models or analogies to effectively teach concrete representations for the main components in a computer system. For example, objects such as a scoreboard, a window, and a scratch pad are used to explain how the memory functions of a computer operate. Students who have been given these models prior to instruction about computers have done better in solving both familiar and novel computer problems than students who

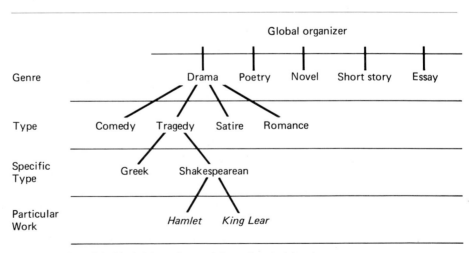

Figure 7.5 Possible Model for a General Organizer in Literature.

*Source: F. Robinson, 1970.*

have not had the benefit of the models. This effect has been particularly strong for low-ability learners, which suggests to Mayer that more skilled learners can invent their own models.

*Affective Strategies.* The importance of social and personal factors in learning was discussed in Chapter 4. In Chapter 10 you will learn more about motivational factors and learning. Learning strategies can be used to overcome certain personal factors that interfere with learning. For example, in Chapter 4 I discussed how relaxation training could reduce stress. In this section, I discuss how focusing attention and using self-verbalization can serve in a variety of situations to improve learning.

**How can you help students improve their attentiveness to academic tasks?**

*Focusing Attention.* The classroom environment frequently makes it difficult for some students to filter out appealing distractions and focus instead on educational tasks. Teachers often complain that students who have trouble maintaining attention in the classroom are immature, have an attention deficit, or are unmotivated to learn. Unfortunately, using different labels to describe students with attentional problems does little to improve their learning. Corno (1987) views attentional concerns as a self-management problem because the students have difficulty planning and controlling their learning. She believes that students need to be taught to self-manage or self-regulate their behavior by learning strategies to handle distractions, as follows:

- Keep objectives focal: "Pay attention to what you're doing."
- Set reward contingencies: "If I finish this, I'll get to . . ."
- Avoid visual contact with distractor.
- Isolate self: "I'd better go to the learning center."
- Protest: "Please, I'm trying to concentrate here!"
- Enlist help from teacher or other task-oriented peers. (p. 257)

Many psychologists believe that students lack knowledge about attention in the same way that they lack knowledge about mathematics or scientific concepts. If they can be taught techniques to self-regulate their attention, the teacher no longer needs to be totally responsible for the attention of all the students in the class. The students can use these skills both at home and at school to improve their learning. What do you do to self-regulate and control your attention?

Knowledge of the information processing system also can be helpful to the teacher concerned with student attention. Information available in the short-term sensory store will be lost if it is not attended to in short-term memory. Therefore, the first thing a successful teacher must do is to get students to attend to important material. The teacher can do this by helping students to pick out important material, motivating them to attend to it, reducing distractions, and teaching them the skills to cope with those distractions that do occur.

Efficiently picking out the important information in text or lecture material involves the use of a strategy on the part of the learner. It has been shown that faster learners have better methods for selecting the right information on which to focus (Thorndyke & Stasz, 1980).

Several strategies may be used by the teacher or student to determine which information is important. Teachers can use instructional objectives (see Chapter 9) to inform students of lesson goals. Students who are told at the beginning of a lesson what the goals and objectives of the lesson are attend to and retain verbatim information better than students without this advantage (Hamilton, 1985).

Many students determine what is important in a lesson by anticipating the kinds of question that will be asked on the next exam. This skill has been shown to lead to increased attention to relevant material (Rothkopf & Billington, 1979). Teachers generally hold students responsible for learning more information than they actually test for because tests only sample information in a particular area. Teachers do not want to "give away" exact test questions because if they did, students would learn only that material. Untested but important material would be ignored. However, teachers can reveal what kinds of question (e.g., multiple-choice or essay) will be on a test and what general areas of the subject will be covered. This allows the students to determine, for example, whether to study for recall of specific facts or to strive for an understanding of general concepts. Certainly, the teacher can tell students which material is less important so that they can more efficiently use their study time.

## PROCEDURAL KNOWLEDGE

Up to this time I have been focusing on declarative knowledge (knowledge about things), which is a major aspect of school learning. I now turn to ways to facilitate procedural learning, another important category of school learning.

Procedural knowledge tells us how to do something. To know how to do something, it is necessary to know not only the steps in the procedure but also the conditions under which the steps are to be taken. Procedural knowledge can therefore be thought of as being composed of conditional if-then statements, which take the form *if* certain conditions apply, *then* a specific action is to be taken. An example of an arithmetic procedure occurs in dividing by fractions: *If* dividing by a fraction, *then* invert the divisor and multiply. An *if-then* statement can be one step in a procedure, and many such steps can be chained together into quite complex procedures, because each step results in the necessary conditions for the next step in the chain. Long division of large numbers represents such a chain of conditional statements.

Procedural knowledge is used to transform information—in the foregoing example, transforming information about a divisor and a dividend into a quotient. As can be readily seen, procedural knowledge is essential for the basic skills of school and independent living. Basic to any success in school is the ability to execute successfully the procedures that transform numbers into other numbers (arithmetic) and symbols into meaning (reading). To succeed in independent living, the number of procedures the competent adult must master is innumerable: paying bills, cooking meals, shopping for food and clothing, solving problems, and so on. Procedural knowledge takes one of two forms: *pattern-recognition knowledge* or *action-sequence knowledge*.

## Pattern-Recognition Knowledge

**Pattern-recognition knowledge** pertains to the ability to recognize and classify patterns of stimuli. One important instance of pattern recognition is the ability to identify new incidents of a concept, or **concept learning.** A *concept* represents a group of ideas or things that share some common characteristics and have the same name (Merrill, 1983). Recognizing that a platypus is a mammal because it is a furred animal that suckles its young is an incident of a pattern-recognition skill. A second important incident of pattern recognition is identifying the conditions calling for a certain behavior or the application of a particular rule, such as when to "invert and multiply" (Anderson, 1985; R. M. Gagné, 1985).

Concepts and other pattern-recognition procedures are learned through a process of generalization and discrimination (E. Gagné, 1985). As an infant learns language, it often labels objects inappropriately because they share some nondefining characteristic. The child may learn to call the household pet "doggy" and then proceed to call all four-legged animals "doggy." The child has overgeneralized the concept "doggy" and will eventually learn to apply this label only to animals more like Fido. This process of reducing the range of situations to which the concept applies, based on some defining characteristic of the concept, is called *discrimination*.

*Generalization* is the process of broadening the situations to which a concept or pattern-recognition procedure is appropriate. For example, a child, after examining many animals classified as mammals, may come to hold a conception of a mammal as an animal with fur that suckles its young and bears live young. If the child is subsequently told that the platypus is a furry mammal that suckles its young but lays eggs, the concept of "mammal" will generalize to include the platypus by dropping that part of the concept concerning how the young are born.

In teaching children concepts and pattern-recognition procedures, the teacher defines the concept and gives examples that promote accurate application of the procedure. By *accurate* it is meant that the children will be able to apply the concept or procedure in all the appropriate situations and refrain from applying the concept in inappropriate situations. In other words, the teacher strives for accurate generalization and discrimination.

Two conditions promote accurate generalization. The first is the presentation of true examples of the concept that are similar on the defining attributes but greatly different on irrelevant attributes. The example of mammals meets these conditions because the attributes of furriness and suckling of the young were constant, and the irrelevant attribute of manner of birth was varied. The second condition is the successive presentation of examples so that they may be held in working memory simultaneously (Tennyson & Park, 1980). Thus, when teaching the concept of "mammal," it would be desirable to present successive examples not only of the platypus but also horses, dogs, humans, mice, and other mammals.

Accurate discrimination is stimulated when a known procedure does not work (E. Gagné, 1985), as in the example given previously of the child incorrectly labeling all animals "doggy." The conditions promoting accurate discrimination are the simultaneous presentation of examples and matched nonexamples. The matched nonexamples share relevant and irrelevant attributes but vary on at least one relevant attribute.

Mr. Smith wants to teach his class the concept of finite set. He defines a *finite set* as one in which the members can be counted. To promote generalization, Mr. Smith provides his class with the following examples of finite sets that vary on the irrelevant attribute of size of set:

- {5, 10, 15}
- Even numbers of less than 100
- All people in the world
- All grains of sand in the world

Some of these sets are very large, but they are, at least in theory, countable. To promote discrimination, Mr. Smith provides his class with the following matched nonexamples:

- {5, 10, 15, . . . }
- odd numbers greater than 100

Mrs. Jones also has an objective involving pattern-recognition learning. She wants students to be able to classify living and nonliving objects accurately. To do this, students will have to use the declarative knowledge regarding the eight life processes they learned earlier. The conditional statement representing the procedure the students will be learning is *"If an object carries out all eight life processes, then it is alive."* Generalization will be promoted through the use of varied examples of living organisms such as protozoa, fish, mammals, and plants. Mrs. Jones will show how each example carries out the eight life processes. To promote discrimination, Mrs. Jones will provide matched nonexamples, such as crystals, that grow but that do not carry out other processes, such as movement, respiration, and response.

## Action-Sequence Knowledge

The second type of procedural knowledge refers to knowledge of action sequences. An **action sequence** is simply a sequence of behaviors or cognitive actions to be taken to reach some goal (E. Gagné, 1985). The actual

What are the
differences in
teaching
pattern-
recognition
knowledge and
action
sequences?

procedure of regrouping, or borrowing, in subtraction is an example of an action sequence.

Action sequences are first learned as a list of steps comprising some procedure (Anderson, 1982). For example, the steps in a physical activity, such as starting a car, may first be learned as a series of instructions. The learner consciously proceeds through each step, one at a time, until the procedure is complete. For example, in starting a car, the learner might begin by thinking, "First, if the car door is closed, then open the door; second, if the car door is open, then sit in the driver's seat; third, if in the driver's seat, then put on seat belt; fourth, if the seat belt is on, then insert the key into the ignition."

As can be seen, if each step had to be consciously thought out before execution, very little work would be done. With practice, however, the procedures become almost automatic, and the driver carries them out with little thought. This frees working memory to perform other tasks, such as conversing with a passenger while starting the car. When procedures have been learned to the point of automaticity, however, another source of errors is introduced—the **set effect.** The set effect results when carrying out an automatic action sequence leads to a failure to process important information, which results in inefficient or incorrect performance. To continue the example, when driving home from work, how many times have you forgotten to make a special stop at a store to pick up something? Once the action sequence for driving home from work has been triggered, it can be difficult to interrupt. The benefit we get from making this procedure automatic is that it frees working memory for other tasks. We can ruminate on the happenings in the classroom or staff cafeteria while driving home. It often seems that we have to drive all the way home, however, and then make a special trip to the market.

There are two major roadblocks to learning a procedure. First is the limited capacity of working memory, especially troublesome in learning long and complex procedures. Any procedure that requires more than nine steps (remember the $7 \pm 2$ rule presented earlier in this chapter) usually is too long to keep in working memory. To overcome this limit, memory supports can be used. Instead of requiring the student to memorize the steps of a procedure, provide a written list of the steps. After all, it is the successful execution of the procedure that is important, not the memorizing of the steps.

A second potential problem in learning a procedure is the absence of prerequisite knowledge. It is essential to ensure that students already have the knowledge and skills necessary to learn the procedure. For example, it is difficult for a student to solve a geometric proof if the necessary axioms and theorems have not been mastered. The use of **task analysis** (discussed in Chapter 9) is helpful here. Through task analysis, necessary subordinate skills are identified. The teacher can then assess the students' abilities on the subordinate skills. If necessary, the teacher should provide remedial lessons on those skills in which students are deficient before teaching the skill itself.

When you teach action sequences, take care to avoid errors caused by the set effect. The simplest remedy for the set effect is to promote automaticity of only those procedures unlikely to be changed and used often enough so that increased speed is valued (E. Gagné, 1985). Basic academic skills, such as reading, arithmetic, and writing, are important candidates for automatic responses. When action sequences such as letter and word decoding become automatic, working memory is freed for other important tasks, such as comprehending what is decoded.

We all know how difficult some tasks can seem when we are first learning them and how easy these same tasks can become with practice, but good execution comes with good practice. Practice of incorrect procedures only leads to incorrect execution of those procedures. Therefore, feedback must indicate not only whether a response is right or wrong, but if it is wrong, how it can be corrected (Elwar & Corno, 1985).

A particular procedure that Mr. Smith is teaching in his fifth-grade math class is division by fractional numbers (see Table 7.1). His instructional program has four aspects. First, the procedure is written out for the students in the text: "Invert the divisor and multiply." Second, Mr. Smith gives a pretest to assess the students' prerequisite knowledge. Students must know several things to be able to follow this procedure. They must know the meaning of *invert* and *divisor,* and they must know how to multiply fractions. After modeling the procedure for the students, Mr. Smith ensures that division by fractional numbers is practiced for a short time each day. Finally, following this practice, Mr. Smith gives students corrective feedback.

To determine where students make errors, Mr. Smith has three alternatives. First, he can ask students to explain how they arrived at an incorrect answer by orally describing each step taken in attempting to solve the problem. Similarly, Mr. Smith can ask students to show all their work. Either of these two methods will allow Mr. Smith to pinpoint and correct the faulty step in the student's procedure.

These procedures are often not possible, as when Mr. Smith is correcting papers after class or when students fail to show their work. In such cases, Mr. Smith can resort to error analysis, which is the examination of student errors to determine where mistakes were made. Table 7.3 shows several types of error and their probable causes. It is important that Mr. Smith give this feedback to his students as soon as feasible so that they do not continue to practice the procedure incorrectly.

Although Mrs. Jones's teaching field is a content area (life sciences) rather than a basic skill and usually involves more declarative knowledge, she must also teach some action sequences. One such procedure is the scientific method. Like Mr. Smith, Mrs. Jones provides a written list of steps in the scientific method in the form of the flowchart in Figure 7.6. Mrs. Jones will also assess prerequisite knowledge by checking the students' understanding of basic vocabulary, such as *hypothesis, experiment,* and *theory*. Some practice will be given in using the scientific method by having students carry out investigations of issues of their own choosing.

TABLE 7.3 TYPICAL ERRORS IN DIVISION OF FRACTIONAL NUMBERS AND THEIR PROBABLE CAUSES

| Error | Cause |
|-------|-------|
| (a) $\frac{1}{2} \div \frac{1}{2} = \frac{1}{4}$ | Student failed to invert the divisor before multiplying. Check student's understanding of *invert* and *divisor*. Also check whether student recognizes that "÷" means *divide*. |
| (b) $\frac{1}{4} \div \frac{3}{8} = 1\frac{1}{2}$ | Student inverted the dividend. Check the student's understanding of *divisor*. |
| (c) $\frac{5}{8} \div \frac{2}{3} = \frac{15}{18}$ | Student multiplied incorrectly. |
| (d) $\frac{7}{8} \div \frac{1}{8} = \frac{3}{4}$ | Student did not recognize problem as one calling for division. Student subtracted instead. |

However, as automaticity is neither necessary nor desired, frequent practice is not required. More important for Mrs. Jones's purposes is that students appreciate the purpose and importance of each step of the scientific method.

Although pattern-recognition and action-sequence procedures have been discussed separately, they seldom function that way. The correct use

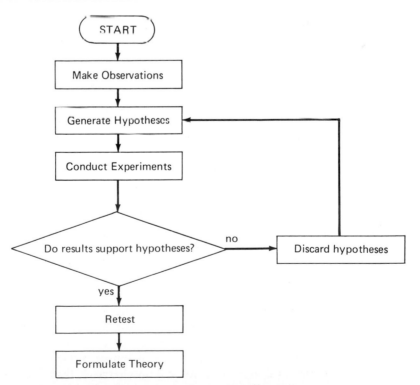

Figure 7.6 Flow Chart of Steps in Following the Scientific Method.

of an action sequence requires recognition of the proper conditions that call for it. Recognizing the conditions is a pattern-recognition process. For example, in subtraction, one must be able to recognize the pattern of numbers that call for regrouping if one is to execute this procedure correctly. In Table 7.3, error *d*, the student failed to recognize the stimulus pattern calling for division and mistakenly subtracted the numbers.

Procedural and declarative knowledge also interact. Declarative knowledge often provides data needed for a procedure. Comprehending the conditions calling for a procedure requires declarative knowledge. Mr. Smith's students must know the meaning of *divisor*, *invert*, and ÷ to carry out this procedure successfully. To use again the example of regrouping, the student must know that the upper number is less than the lower number in order to know that regrouping is required. Mrs. Jones's students must know the eight life processes before they can classify objects as living or inanimate.

*The Transfer Characteristics of Procedural and Declarative Knowledge.* In helping students generalize new learning, it is important to understand that procedural and declarative knowledge differ in their transfer characteristics (Gick & Holyoak, 1987). In general, procedural knowledge is more difficult to transfer than declarative knowledge because procedural knowledge is more closely related to the specific context, problems, or situations in which it is used. For example, the procedure for dividing fractions that Mr. Smith is teaching his fifth-grade math class is a procedure that works only for this task. It would not work for adding or subtracting fractions. While some forms of procedural knowledge are more generalizable than others, this knowledge is nevertheless highly task-related and not broadly applicable.

Because declarative knowledge is more conceptual and abstract, it can be more easily applied to a variety of contexts and situations. The Gordon and Braun (1985) schema-related questions presented earlier (e.g., "Setting: Where and when did the story take place?" "Action: What does the main character do?") illustrate this point. These questions, which are designed to aid comprehension, are declarative knowledge that can be applied to many kinds of reading situations. They can be used when reading fairy tales as well as other forms of fiction like folk tales, mysteries, and short stories.

The differences in the transfer characteristics of declarative and procedural knowledge can have important consequences for classroom learning (Schoenfeld, 1989). For example, researchers studying math instruction have noted that many teachers overemphasize the learning of procedural skill in math, while de-emphasizing the development of more conceptual math knowledge. The result is that students become skilled at manipulating numbers but not at solving real-world problems. Students need both procedural and declarative knowledge if they are to successfully apply what they have learned.

## Problem-Solving Strategies/Critical Thinking Skills

**Can students be taught critical thinking skills?**

In recent years many educators have become concerned with the fact that schools focus too heavily on basic facts and fail to emphasize higher-level thinking skills, such as analyzing, synthesizing, and evaluating. In addition, insufficient attention is given to how thinking skills can be used in problem solving. The following terms are often used to describe the focus of this type of instruction—*problem solving, critical thinking, thinking skills,* or *intellectual skills.* Many school districts are now incorporating the teaching of thinking in their curriculum.

Few educators disagree with the idea that thinking can be taught. The disagreement, however, is based on how best to teach these skills. Some educators believe that there should be separate programs or courses designed to teach thinking skills. One recent book (Costa, 1985) lists over 15 different programs to select from, including Feuerstein's (1980) Instrumental Enrichment, Lipman's (1985) Philosophy for Children, and de Bono's (1985) CoRT (Cognitive Research Trust).

Instrumental Enrichment is designed for junior high students and is presented as a separate curriculum in which students are trained with classroom and individual paper and pencil exercises. These exercises, called *instruments*, give students practice in abstract and logical thinking, analytical and abstract reasoning, and problem analysis skills. The goal of Instrumental Enrichment is to help students develop insight into their own intellectual processes and to make them more active thinkers. An important aspect of this program is the use of *bridging*, which relates skills taught in the program to real-world problems.

Philosophy for Children also teaches problem-solving skills, but does so within the context of short stories. The stories are based on different philosophical topics or issues that describe the activities of young children as they apply thinking to everyday problems and situations. A major assumption of this program is that children are naturally interested in philosophical problems in the area of values and ethics and can develop the thinking skills necessary to deal with these subjects.

The CoRT program shows 9-to-11-year-old-students how to develop original solutions to problems by teaching them to change their perceptions of problems that they will face outside of school. Students are taught to consider the aims, goals, and objectives in a situation and consider new ideas without immediately judging them as good or bad, right or wrong.

The research on general problem-solving programs indicates that they are only moderately successful in achieving their goals (Sternberg & Bhana, 1986). For example, students taught to solve problems show only modest gains in their problem-solving ability, and these gains appear limited in their generalizability. This limitation is seen in the Instrumental Enrichment program: Skills transfer to tasks on standard IQ tests but show little transfer to school work. Another problem is that the programs seem to work with only certain students. Philosophy for Children works best with bright students because of the extensive reading requirements of the program, whereas Instrumental Enrichment is better suited for average or below-average students. Few programs are useful for students of all ability levels (Adams, 1989).

Some researchers believe that many problem-solving skills are domain-specific (e.g., unique to a certain field or specialization) and should be taught only within the context of a specific field (Gagné, 1985). In this approach, mathematics, history, and science teachers would introduce thinking skills as part of the regular instruction in their content areas.

## CLASSROOM APPLICATION: APPLYING COGNITIVE LEARNING THEORY

You can improve the effectiveness of your teaching if you take advantage of what is known about the information processing system and learning strategies. This chapter refers to general learning strategies as those strategies that apply to all types of learning and whose design is based on the general functioning of the IPS (e.g., focusing attention, rehearsal, chunking). This chapter also discusses the types of knowledge stored in a particular part of the IPS (e.g., long-term memory). Strategies that are aimed at improving the learning of particular types of knowledge (e.g., declarative and action sequence) I call specific learning strategies.

Table 7.4 includes a checklist of important strategies that you should consider while developing lesson plans for various instructional objectives and helping students become independent learners.

If you are to change students' cognitive functioning, you must have a way of obtaining information about their internal cognitive events. Asking students to show their work is one way to begin this inquiry. Although this is traditionally done for mathematics assignments, it is often neglected in other academic areas. For example, research has found that it is beneficial to have students show their work at each of the four stages of the writing process: generating ideas, organizing ideas, writing the ideas as an essay, and revising the essay (Humes, 1983). Other methods of assessing cognitive functioning are error analysis, student oral reports, and student discussions regarding how they solve problems or think about various issues.

The first stage of the information processing system, the short-term sensory store, suggests that it is of primary importance to get students to attend to important material. Otherwise such material will not enter the IPS, and long-term storage will be impossible. Thus it is important that students' attention be focused on the appropriate material. Some helpful methods include ensuring that students understand the goals of the lesson, emphasizing or highlighting important data in the text or lecture material, modifying the environment to reduce distractions, and teaching monitoring and self-control procedures.

TABLE 7.4 CHECKLIST FOR APPLYING COGNITIVE PSYCHOLOGY IN THE CLASS-ROOM

### General Learning Strategies

**To focus attention:**
_____ 1. Make modifications in the physical environment to reduce distractions.
_____ 2. Inform students of the learning goals of the lesson.
_____ 3. Emphasize important information.
_____ 4. Teach students self-monitoring and self-control techniques so they can handle distractions.

**To reveal student cognitive processes:**
_____ 5. Ask students to show all their work.
_____ 6. Ask students about their thought processes (e.g., What were you thinking about when I presented this lesson? How are you going to solve the problem? Why do you think you are having difficulty?)

**To avoid limitations of short-term memory:**
_____ 7. Present material at a pace that does not overwhelm short-term memory.
_____ 8. Teach or prompt appropriate chunking and rehearsal strategies.
_____ 9. Prompt students to examine their cognitive processes; ask students what they are learning by completing the assignment. Similar to step 4, but do not only ask students to describe their thought processes, but teach them to monitor these processes as a regular part of problem solving.
_____ 10. Provide discussion periods wherein students can discuss their problem-solving methods.
_____ 11. Teach students self-instructional skills, such as prompting themselves to start a task, providing themselves encouragement to continue, and using self-reinforcement at the completion of each step.
_____ 12. Teach students how to paraphrase information, take notes, and underline important information.

### Specific Learning Strategies

**For rate-declarative knowledge:**
_____ 13. Keep practice sessions frequent and spaced.
_____ 14. Teach to overlearning.
_____ 15. Use mnemonics.

**For meaningful-declarative knowledge:**
_____ 16. Inform students of the organization of the material.
_____ 17. Provide outlines of lecture and text material.
_____ 18. Activate relevant schemata through analogies.
_____ 19. Teach and/or prompt elaboration.

**For pattern-recognition procedures:**
_____ 20. Define concept or conditions calling for an action sequence.
_____ 21. Provide varied true examples to promote accurate generalization.
_____ 22. Provide matched nonexamples to promote accurate discrimination.

**For action-sequence procedures:**
_____ 23. Provide a written list of the steps in the procedure.
_____ 24. Provide opportunity for practice.
_____ 25. Provide prescriptive feedback.

The limits of the second stage of the information processing system, short-term memory, can give students, especially young elementary age students, trouble. You can help to overcome the $7 \pm 2$ limitation by either reducing the amount of information presented at any given time or by teaching chunking and rehearsal strategies that will allow students to retain information in STM for a longer time. Students in the first or second grade may have to be prompted to use even the most basic rehearsal strategy.

Part of instructing students how to be good learners is to teach them learning strategies. These learning strategies can then be prompted by either you or the students' own cognitive processes. There are learning strategies for remembering information, for reading and studying, for problem solving, and for affective support. Many of these strategies have been discussed as part of various lesson plans. When directly teaching these strategies, it is important for you to recognize that they are procedures. Therefore, it is best when you teach both the procedure and its use.

The third stage of the information processing system, long-term memory, is composed of episodic and semantic knowledge. The goal of most educational activities is to increase the students' store of semantic knowledge in long-term memory. There are two types of strategy you can use that address the types of knowledge in long-term memory. First, you can pair episodic information with semantic knowledge to improve the learning of the semantic knowledge (Kulhavy & Swenson, 1975). You can use slides or pictures depicting important points in a lecture to help your students encode these points. It is important that the images, whether they are pictures in a book, slides projected on a wall, or images the students create in their minds, depict the important points in the material. Second, teaching the types of semantic knowledge in long-term memory, pattern-recognition knowledge, and action-sequence skills requires that you use strategies specific to that type of knowledge.

It is important to consider the type of semantic knowledge to be imparted to the students. Specific learning strategies are designed for specific types of semantic knowledge. Teaching rote-declarative knowledge involves frequent and spaced practice. Lessons should be of short duration and continue well beyond the point at which the learner demonstrates the desired level of competence. Rote lessons should be designed to reduce the negative effects of transfer and interference by ensuring proper sequencing and teaching to overlearning. Another way to promote learning of rote material is to add meaning to it. Use of mnemonics is one way to accomplish this goal.

Teaching meaningful-declarative knowledge is a matter of establishing connections between the new data and an organized body of old knowledge (elaboration). Making clear to students the principles around which new knowledge is organized is one way to promote the acquisition of an organized body of knowledge. Providing students with outlines of lecture and reading assignments is another way of promoting organization. Activating relevant schemata to which new information can be attached is a third way to promote organization. Elaboration is a way of making connections to old knowledge. Elaboration can be promoted by encouraging students to paraphrase new information, to make predictions and inferences about it, to relate the new information to other data, or to add missing details (E. Gagné, 1985).

When you teach procedures, it is important that you make clear to the students *when* to carry out a procedure as well as *how* to do so. Knowing when to carry out a procedure is a matter of pattern recognition. Students must know the pattern of conditions that require a certain procedure. Pattern recognition is also the basis for concept learning. Students must know the rules that call for the classification of an object or idea. Teaching pattern recognition involves three principles: defining the concept or the conditions calling for a procedure, providing varied true examples, and providing matched nonexamples.

Teaching an action-sequence procedure involves a written list of the steps in a procedure, practice, and feedback. For procedures that will be frequently used and probably not changed, practice should proceed to the point of automaticity. For less frequently used procedures and procedures subject to change, automaticity is not desired and less practice is needed. Feedback is important because incorrect practice will result in incorrect performance. Therefore, feedback should be prescriptive and point out how students can improve their performance.

## THINKING ABOUT THE TEACHING-LEARNING MODEL

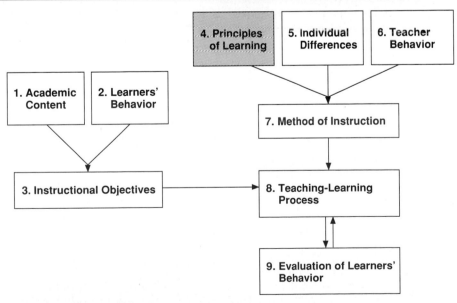

*Source: Adapted from Hunter, 1971, in Allen and Seifman.*

Individual differences (box No. 5) can have an effect on students' information processing. For example, anxiety can influence students' attention by preventing information from entering the short-term sensory store, limiting the rehearsal required to maintain stimuli in short-term memory, and interfering with cognitive processing as students attempt to use proper learning strategies (Tobias, 1979). Since students must carefully analyze a task and consider what learning strategies should be implemented, impulsivity can interfere with good strategy use because the impulsive student fails to delay his or her response long enough to consider the best approach to the task (Pressley et al., 1989).

The learning strategies discussed in this chapter have important implications for helping low-achieving and learning disabled students. Considerable evidence is available that these students are deficient in their use of learning strategies. That is, they are less adept at evaluating their ability to successfully undertake a task, plan effective strategies for completing the task, monitor their progress, identify and correct their errors, modify their approach as they proceed with the task, and evaluate their overall performance (Loper & Murphy, 1985). Thus classes that provide remedial instruction that simply reviews basic content or knowledge that has not been adequately learned while neglecting students' use of general or specific learning strategies will have limited impact on students' future achievement.

Cognitive psychology offers an approach to instruction different from that in behavioral psychology. Behavioral psychologists use reinforcement to encourage students to maintain task persistence. Although cognitive psychologists are also interested in having students engaged in instruction, they are more interested in what students are doing or thinking about *while* they are so engaged.

The role of the teacher (box No. 6) is different in behavioral and cognitive approaches to instruction. The research on effective teaching presented in Chapter 11 and the work on behavioral instruction discussed in Chapter 6 identify the teacher as an executive whose primary role is to manage student behavior and make instructional decisions that direct student activities. However, cognitive psychologists are more likely to view the role of the teacher as a mediator or facilitator, one who helps students to select appropriate learning strategies, monitor their understanding, and make decisions for future learning. This is not to say that behavioral approaches do not involve any of these functions, only that they do not emphasize them.

Teachers' beliefs regarding the role of learning strategies in student achievement are important factors is determining their outlook about students' success. Clifford (1986a, 1986b) found that when teachers are told that student performance is related to appropriate strategy use, they have more favorable perspectives about students' future performances than if they believed that achievement is caused by either ability or effort.

Another difference between behavioral and cognitive approaches to instruction is that behaviorists tend to emphasize external reinforcers, whereas cognitive psychologists emphasize internal reinforcers (e.g., self-satisfaction). Although either type of motivation may be appropriate in a specific situation, it is important that you realize how your instructional procedures foster one type of motivation over another.

## KEY POINTS

1. The information processing system (IPS) is a model that cognitive psychologists use to identify how individuals obtain, transform, store, and apply information. It comprises the short-term sensory store. the short-term (working) memory, and the long-term memory.
2. The flow of information through the IPS is monitored by control or executive processes (metacognitive knowledge).
3. Metacognitive knowledge is the process by which individuals think about their thinking. It involves both knowledge about one's cognitive processes and the active monitoring and regulation of these processes.
4. Successful learners have acquired the metacognitive skills necessary to become independent learners. Students can be taught metacognitive or learning strategies to manage and control their own learning.
5. Declarative knowledge is knowledge about things and can be either rote or meaningful.
6. Learning declarative knowledge is aided by rehearsal, elaboration, organization, and comprehension monitoring.
7. Mnemonics are elaborative techniques that help us remember rote material by connecting it to visual images or semantic knowledge. This connection makes the rote material more meaningful and thus easier to remember.
8. Although note taking helps the encoding process, notes can be even more effective when reviewed, as review promotes further elaboration and integration of the material to be learned.
9. A teacher can improve students' note taking by following certain procedures while lecturing.
10. Outlining text or lecture material helps learners manage information more efficiently in working memory, because it helps to organize knowledge. Having a well-organized body of knowedge in long-term memory is characteristic of experts in any field.
11. Comprehension monitoring helps readers decide whether they have understood what they have read at a level necessary to reach their reading goal.
12. Adjunct questions are most effective in promoting comprehension monitoring when they are placed after the text to be read, are of high level, and are of sufficient number to promote transfer.

13. Schemata are cognitive structures that help learners to organize and process information efficiently by providing an organizational structure into which new information can be fitted and by helping us to know what to expect from new incoming information.

14. Advance organizers can be used either to activate students' present cognitive structure or to equip students with the necessary cognitive structure they do not have.

15. Affective strategies motivate students, focus their attention, and help to reduce anxiety.

16. Listing instructional objectives and providing advance warning of possible test questions are ways to focus student attention.

17. Self-verbalization can be used to help students monitor and control their attention.

18. Procedural knowledge is knowledge about how to do things. Two types of procedural knowledge are pattern-recognition knowledge and action-sequence knowledge.

19. Pattern-recognition skills are involved in concept learning and in knowing when to execute an action sequence.

20. Pattern recognition is learned through the processes of generalization and discrimination.

21. Barriers to learning action sequences are limited short-term memory and the lack of prerequisite skills.

22. Problem-solving strategies demonstrate the interaction of declarative and procedural knowledge.

23. Procedural knowledge is more difficult to transfer than declarative knowledge.

24. A teacher should plan to teach students how to use different learning strategies in completing assignments and preparing for examinations.

25. The emphasis on the teaching of thinking has increased in recent years. Some thinking-skills programs are more effective than others. As a result, it is important that the teacher carefully evaluate available programs before deciding to implement a program.

## KEY TERMS

information-processing system (IPS), p. 268
short-term sensory store (STSS), p. 268
short-term memory (STM), p. 269
working memory, p. 269
chunking, p. 270
rehearsal strategies, p. 270
long-term memory, p. 270
automaticity, p. 271
decoding, p. 271
encoding, p. 271

episodic memory, p. 271
semantic memory, p. 271
declarative knowledge, p. 271
procedural knowledge, p. 271
executive processes, p. 271
metacognition, p. 272
learning strategies, p. 273
elaboration strategies, p. 273
organizational strategies, p. 273
comprehension-monitoring strategies, p. 273
affective strategies, p. 273
meaningful learning, p. 276
rote learning, p. 276
free recall, p. 277
serial recall, p. 277
paired-associate learning, p. 277
distributed practice, p. 278
massed practice, p. 278
serial position effect, p. 278
part learning, p. 278
positive transfer, p. 278
negative transfer, p. 278
proactive inhibition, p. 279
retroactive inhibition, p. 279
overlearning, p. 279
mnemonics, p. 279
loci method, p. 280
acronyms, p. 280
peg-word method, p. 280
key-word method, p. 280
matrix notes, p. 285
adjunct questions, p. 288
SQ3R system, p. 289
schemata, p. 289
advance organizers, p. 291
pattern-recognition knowledge, p. 295
concept learning, p. 295
action sequence, p. 296
set effect, p. 297
task analysis, p. 297

## SUGGESTIONS FOR FURTHER READING

Beyer, B. K. (1987). *Practical strategies for the teaching of thinking.* Needham Heights, MA: Allyn & Bacon. A guide for the teaching of thinking skills, K-12.

Beyer, B. K. (1988). *Developing a thinking skills program.* Needham Heights, MA: Allyn & Bacon. Provides ideas on how to develop and implement a thinking skills program.

Chance, P. (1985). *Thinking in the classroom: A survey of programs.* New York: Teachers College Press. Describes eight curriculum programs and instructional strategies intended to develop thinking abilities.

Gagné, E. D. (1985). *The cognitive psychology of school learning.* Boston: Little, Brown. Discusses how recent developments in cognitive instructional psychology are applied to the teaching of academic subjects.

Levin, J. R., & Pressley M. (Eds.). (1986). Learning strategies. [Special issue]. *Educational Psychologist, 21* (1, 2).

Pressley, M., Goodchild, F., Fleet, J., Zajchowski, R., & Evans, E. D. (1989). The challenges of classroom strategy instruction. *Elementary School Journal, 89,* 301–342. An excellent review article for learning strategies.

Tiedt, I. M., et al. (1989). *Teaching thinking in K-12 classrooms: Ideas, activities, and resources.* Needham Heights, MA: Allyn & Bacon. Provides strategies that can be incorporated in your regular lesson plans as well as providing over 70 lesson plans.

For review of research on teaching thinking:

Adams, M. J. (1989). Thinking skills curricula: Their promise and progress. *Educational Psychologist, 24,* 25–77.

Gick, M. L. (1986). Problem-solving strategies. *Educational Psychologist , 21,* 99–120.

McCormick, C. B., Miller, G. E., & Pressley, M. (Eds.). (1989). *Cognitive strategy research: From basic research to educational applications.* New York: Springer-Verlag.

Nickerson, R. S. et al. (1985). *The teaching of thinking.* Hillsdale, NJ: Erlbaum.

Schneider, W., & Pressley, M. (1989). *Memory development between 2 and 20.* New York: Springer-Verlag.

## FOLLOW-UP ACTIVITIES

### 1. Teach Students to Think

A common complaint among teachers is that some students refuse to think. They attempt to memorize information, easily forget concepts taught earlier in the course, and fail to relate previous learning to present situations. Holt (1982) illustrates his concern for this problem in the following description of one of his students:

> What she needs is a broom to sweep out her mind. She has so much junk in there, her filing systems are in such a mess that she can never find anything, and the file drawers and old trunks must be emptied out before they can be put into any kind of order. If she could only forget completely about nine-tenths of the facts and rules she has all mixed up in her head, she might begin to learn something. (p. 186)

How does this problem begin? Does the problem improve or get worse when students reach college? What advice would each of the learning theorists you have studied propose?

## 2. Think about Learning Strategies

Think about the learning strategies you used in school. How did you memorize rote material? How did you learn concepts in history, chemistry, and mathematics? If you had to do it over again, how would you improve your learning strategies in high school? Did you change your learning strategies in college?

Analyze the way you deal with problems of attention according to the following skills: monitoring your current attentional state, analyzing the attentional demands of the task, selecting an attentional strategy, and evaluating the attentional strategy. What would you teach your students to improve their attentional skills?

## 3. Plan a Lesson Using Learning Strategies

Develop a lesson in your teaching specialty. Describe how you would use the information in Table 7.4 to increase your student's learning. If you developed a lesson plan in an earlier chapter, describe how you could use cognitive psychology to improve the lesson.

## 4. Lead a Discussion to Explore Students' Thinking

Lead a discussion with your students about some important issue in your field. Structure the discussion according to the ideas discussed by Schoenfeld (1985) or Lester and Garofalo (1986) in the following appendix. Closely observe how your students respond to this type of exercise: Which students participated and which did not? How enthusiastic were the students in exploring their own thought processes? Did the students have difficulty? Why? What did you learn about the students' knowledge of the topic?

## 5. Help Students Improve Their Metacognitive Skills

Ask students to keep a daily learning log in which they write about material they don't understand, generate questions they would like to discuss in class, summarize insights learned from a lesson or reading assignments, and identify any other aspects of their learning (Bondy, 1984). Discuss the information in the logs with students at the end of the week and have other students or yourself model effective learning strategies raised from the information in the logs. Provide students with examples of what they might place in the logs before they begin.

## APPENDIX: TEACHING LEARNING STRATEGIES IN THE CONTENT AREAS

In Chapter 7, I emphasized the importance of teaching students learning strategies to help them become more effective learners. Learning-strategy instruction takes time and effort, but the research indicates that such instruction can make a difference in helping many unsuccessful learners achieve academic success. You already have learned about the importance of teaching students such strategies as note taking, underlining, summarizing, memorizing, outlining, as well as techniques for improving reading comprehension. My intent in this appendix is to discuss strategies for reading comprehension in more detail and provide examples of some developments in writing and mathematics. Information on learning strategies in other content areas (e.g., science, social studies, literature) also is available (see Hyde & Bizar, 1989; Jones et al., 1987; Resnick & Klopfer, 1989). Refer to the references included in this appendix as well as the list of Suggestions for Further Reading in Chapter 7 for more detailed study of specific learning strategies. Consider developing your own learning strategies curriculum.

Pressley et al. (1989) provide excellent resources for learning more about learning strategies and outline important steps in the implementation of strategic learning in the classroom. They recommend that the teacher start by finding out what strategies are available, selecting a few general strategies that can be used across subject areas and then moving to more specific strategies that are more domain-specific (i.e., unique to a certain field or specialization), and motivating students to use the strategies.

Winograd and Hare (1988) provide the following recommendations for teaching learning strategies:

- *What the strategy is.* Teachers should describe critical, known features of the strategy or provide a definition/description of the strategy.
- *Why the strategy should be learned.* Teachers should tell students why they are learning about the strategy. Explaining the purpose of the lesson and its potential benefits seems to be a necessary step for moving from teacher control to student self-control.
- *How to use the strategy.* Here, teachers break down the strategy, or reenact a task analysis for students, explaining each component of the strategy as clearly and as articulately as possible and showing the logical relationships among the various components.
- *When and where the strategy is to be used.* Teachers should delineate appropriate circumstances under which the strategy may

be employed. . . . Teachers may also describe inappropriate instances for using the strategy.

- *How to evaluate use of the strategy.* Teachers should show students how to evaluate their successful/unsuccessful use of the strategy, including suggestions for fix-up strategies to resolve remaining problems. (pp. 123–124)

## Reading Comprehension

Many students believe that the key to reading is learning how to decode words. The result is that they often don't learn how to comprehend what they read, make inferences, generate questions, answer questions, and paraphrase material as they read (Pressley et al., 1989). In other words, students don't realize that they must be active participants in the reading process. Pressley, Snyder, and Cariglia-Bull (1987) analyzed various learning strategies for students having reading comprehension difficulties and recommended two methods for instruction that have considerable research support—reciprocal teaching (e.g., Palincsar & Brown, 1984; in press) and direct explanation of strategies (e.g., Roehler & Duffy, 1984).

## RECIPROCAL TEACHING

In reciprocal teaching, students and teachers talk to each other about the meaning of text and take turns implementing various strategies during structured dialogues. The dialogue structure incorporates the use of four strategies: *summarizing, question generating, clarifying,* and *predicting.* Each strategy helps students monitor their reading comprehension (Palincsar, 1986):

- *Summarizing*—Identifying and paraphrasing the main ideas in the text.
- *Question Generating*—Self-questioning about the type of information that is generally tapped on tests of comprehension.
- *Clarifying*—Discerning when there has been a breakdown in comprehension and taking the necessary action to restore meaning (e.g., reading ahead, rereading, asking for assistance.)
- *Predicting*—Hypothesizing what the structure and content of the text suggest will be presented next. (p. 119)

The instructor introduces reciprocal teaching with a discussion of the many reasons text may be difficult to comprehend and explains the importance of strategic approaches to reading and studying. Students are then presented with a general description of the procedure and explained the benefits of reciprocal teaching. When the teacher leads the dialogue, he or she models the specific strategies. As the students assume responsibility for leading the dialogue, they practice the strategies within a familiar and meaningful context. Reciprocal teaching is best accomplished in groups of seven to eight students.

Palincsar, Brown, and Martin (1987) view the process of transfer of responsibility of group leadership from the teacher to students as a form of scaffolded instruction (Wood, Bruner, & Ross, 1976) (review Vygotsky's ideas in Chapter 3). The teacher can adjust each dialogue according to the support different students need in comprehending the text. As the students become increasingly knowledgeable in understanding the material, the teacher can provide less support to the students and, consequently, become less involved in the dialogue.

The following is a partial transcript from a lesson conducted with first graders who have listened to a paragraph about aquanauts. Student 1 begins facilitating (Palincsar, Brown, & David, in press):

Student 1:  My *question* is, what does the aquanaut need when he goes under water?
Student 2:  A watch.
Student 3:  Flippers.
Student 4:  A belt.
Student 1:  Those are all good answers.
Teacher:  Nice job! I have a *question* too. Why does the aquanaut wear a belt, what is so special about it?
Student 3:  It's a heavy belt and keeps him from floating up to the top again.
Student 1:  For my *summary* now. . . . This paragraph was about what the aquanauts need to take when they go under the water.
Student 5:  And also about why they need those things.
Student 3:  I think we need to *clarify* "gear."
Student 6:  That's the special things they need.
Teacher:  Another word for gear in this story might be equipment, the equipment that makes it easier for the aquanauts to do their job.
Student 1:  I don't think I have a prediction to make.
Teacher:  Well, in the story they tell us that there are "many strange and wonderful creatures" that the aquanauts see as they do their work. My *prediction* is that they will describe some of these creatures. What are some of the strange creatures that you already know about that live in the ocean?
Student 6:  Octopuses.
Student 3:  Whales?
Student 5:  Sharks!
Teacher:  Let's listen and find out! Who will be our teacher?

The following partial transcript comes from a lesson conducted with secondary students who have read a paragraph on salt mining. While it is useful to begin the procedure working with paragraphs, over time, the groups work with larger segments of text. Student C begins facilitating (Palincsar & Brown, 1984):

| | |
|---|---|
| Student C: | Name three different basic methods how salt is produced (*question*). |
| Student A: | Evaporation, mining, evaporation . . . artificial heat evaporation. |
| Student C: | Correct, very good. My *summary* on this paragraph is about ways that salt is being produced. |
| Teacher: | Very good. Could you select another teacher? (Student C selects another student and the next paragraph is read aloud.) |
| Student L: | Name two words that often describe mining salt in the old days. |
| Student K: | Back to the salt mines? |
| Student L: | No. Angela? |
| Student A: | Dangerous and difficult. |
| Student L: | Correct. This paragraph is all about comparing the old mining of salt to today's mining of salt. |
| Teacher: | Beautiful! |
| Student L: | I have a *prediction* to make. |
| Teacher: | Good. |
| Student L: | I think it might tell when salt was first discovered, well, what salt is made of and how it's made. |
| Teacher: | OK. Can we have another teacher? (Student L selects and the lesson continues. (p. 162) |

## DIRECT EXPLANATION

Roehler and Duffy (1984) believe that teachers who work with poor readers should explain explicitly the mental processing associated with strategies used by good readers. Direct explanation emphasizes the teacher's role in explaining the *process* of reading to students. The teacher using this approach explains to students how to implement the strategy, discusses the effects produced by the strategy, and describes when and where to use the strategy.

Duffy and Roehler (1987) provide the following examples of direct explanation of reading skills. The first example includes teaching word meaning; the second example includes teaching how to combine prior knowledge with current information in a text to make predictions.

*Skill:* Assessing word meanings
"My pillow is made from the *down* of geese."

T:   What word is confusing in there?

S:   Down.

T:   Down. Okay, what are you going to do to figure that out?

S:   It's like going down, or downstairs.

T:   All right. Going downstairs. You've already realized that that doesn't make sense. Now, what's next?

S:   Look for clues.

T:   Good. Are there any clues?

S:   Pillows and geese.

T:   All right. We looked for clues. Now we've got to think about what those clues tell us. The pillow is made from something of the geese. In your experience what would a pillow be made of?

S:   Feathers.

T:   How are you going to know if you're right or wrong, George?

S:   Read the sentence with the word in it.

T:   All right. Try it, George.

S:   My pillow is made from the feathers of geese.

T:   Does that make sense?

S:   Yes.

T:   Good. (p. 519)

*Skill:* Combining prior knowledge with current text to make predictions

T:   What do you think is going to happen next here? I mean, you're reading the story. What'll happen next, Candy?

S:   (responds)

T:   Oh, Okay. What do you think, Mark?

S:   (responds)

T:   Interesting. Why do you think what you think? How can you make these predictions like this? How can you predict what's going to happen next in the story?

S:   I thought about the story and Roberto and his problem.

T:   Yes, but how did you use that to predict? Did you use your own experience?

S:   Yea. I thought about what I thought would probably happen.

T:   That's right. Because you've been thinking about the story and you've been thinking about Roberto and his problem. And that's part of what reading is. It's making predictions about what's going to happen next. (p. 519)

Helping students become strategic readers requires explicit explanations about the mental processing involved. However, these explanations may be difficult to provide. It's necessary for teachers to decide how their students are reasoning and what the associated explanations should be. Duffy and Roehler (1989) don't believe that the techniques can be proceduralized (as in reciprocal teaching), since the dialogue unfolds in unpredictable ways depending upon how students restructure what their teachers say. As a result, direct explanation is a process that involves spontaneous and fluid interactional exchanges. See Duffy and Roehler (1990) for lesson plans for teaching various learning strategies in reading.

## Writing

Several national studies indicate that students in the United States have inadequate writing skills (Boyer, 1983; National Assessment of Educational Progress, 1986). Teachers find that students need assistance in each of the three stages in the writing process—generating content, organizing, and revising (Beal, 1989). Students complain that they can't think of enough material to include in a paper, have difficulty planning and organizing the paper, and don't know what to do when they are asked to revise their writing.

Cognitive psychologists have found that metacognitive processes play an important role in writing. As a result, cognitive strategies have been developed to help students better understand the writing process and the procedures for regulating writing performance.

The following are learning strategies for writing that can be applied in many different settings (adapted from Beal, 1989):

### Generating Content
- Select topics that are exciting or emotionally arousing.
- Help children set up a "future topics" file, to store information that is not appropriate for a present writing assignment but may be relevant for a future assignment.
- Train students to list single words on a topic to help them write more.
- Ask questions about stories.
- Give students cards with sentence openers such as "For example," or "Also," or "That's why" to use as they begin each sentence.
- Require students to use "dialogue" style of writing, in which the characters tell the story through conversation.

### Planning and Organizing Text
- Provide students with prepared "templates" for different text structures, with slots that can be filled in. For example, a "class news" article might have slots for the title, and for *who, where, when*, etc.

- Provide students with part of a narrative and ask them to complete it.

**Evaluating and Revising Text**
- Provide a guide to tell children precisely what to do while revising. For example, use advice printed on index cards that tells the child to first review a sentence and then to select an appropriate action.
- Help students question themselves about the comprehensibility and meaning of written material.
- Provide students with examples of different types of text problems and help them locate such problems in other written material.
- Provide the students with written text and model the revision process. Illustrate specific examples of additions, deletions, substitutions, and text rearrangement.

## Mathematics

For many students mathematics involves memorizing rote techniques for getting correct answers without learning how to think and problem-solve. Did you "understand" the mathematical concepts and principles of algebra, geometry, or calculus? Did you learn how to be an effective problem solver in mathematics? Many students are more concerned with "getting through" a course by memorizing mathematical procedures rather than understanding what they are doing.

Mathematics educators have identified many inappropriate processes and strategies commonly used by students and have recommended learning strategies that can be used to help students become more successful learners. The following material provides ways to develop effective learning strategies in mathematics.

## Process Monitoring

A problem that commonly occurs in math classes is that students appear not to attend to their own cognitive behavior (Romberg & Carpenter, 1986). Schoenfeld (1983) has found that expert problem solvers are "vigilant managers" who monitor their problem-solving performance but that novices are often unaware of their own thinking processes.

Lester and Garofalo (1986) suggest that mathematics teachers can help students to develop metacognitive knowledge by asking questions that require them to reflect upon their own mathematical thinking. In turn, the teacher can serve as a reactor and provide feedback to the students' responses. The following are examples of the types of question that can be asked:

- Think of everything you do when you practice solving math problems. Why do you do all these things?
- What things can you do to solve more problems correctly?

Why? Do you usually do these things?
- What kinds of errors do you usually make? Why do you think you make these errors? What can you do about this?
- What kinds of things do you forget to do when solving math problems?
- What kinds of problems are you best at? Why? What kinds of problems are you worst at? Why? What can you do to get better at these? (pp. 12–13)

Schoenfeld (1985) suggests two methods of group problem solving during which the teacher functions as manager or consultant in promoting students' awareness of their cognitive problem-solving processes. In the first method, the teacher poses a problem for the class and asks for suggestions as to possible methods of solution. Students' suggestions are not evaluated during this brainstorming session so that students feel free to speak up. Once all suggestions are in, the class is asked to evaluate the reasonableness of each suggestion. The teacher acts as manager in encouraging students to examine all aspects of a problem and all student suggestions for arriving at a solution. The purpose of this type of management is to demonstrate to students, through the classroom discussion, the executive control functions of assessing a problem, selecting a solution strategy, and evaluating the strategy's effectiveness.

Schoenfeld's (1985) second strategy involves small-group discussions of a problem posed by the teacher. The teacher acts as consultant with these groups by asking a series of questions, as follows:

- What (exactly) are you doing? (Can you describe it precisely?)
- Why are you doing it? (How does it fit into the solution?)
- How does it help you? (What will you do with the outcome when you obtain it?) (p. 374)

These questions are designed to promote the students' awareness of their cognitive processes and to stimulate the development of metacognitive skills.

Derry and Murphy (1986) recommend a third approach to teaching by providing instruction in general problem-solving models and supplementing the instruction with domain-specific strategies. They used such an approach in an arithmetic program, Training in Arithmetic Problem-Solving Skills (TAPS). The TAPS program incorporates a general problem-solving model, the Four C's problem: Clarification, Choosing a solution, Carrying out the solution, and Checking the results.

Once the students learn the general model, they are instructed in specific subroutines for executing each step. Under problem *clarification*, Derry and Murphy teach students to classify word problems into "problem schemata." Students also are taught to identify the goal of a problem and to eliminate irrelevant information. In *choosing* a solution, students are taught word problem heuristics, such as working backward, breaking up the problem into smaller segments and setting up subgoals, and means-end analysis. Under *carrying out* the strategy, students are taught the value of persistence, strategy, and careful work. For *checking* the results, students are taught how to estimate answers, and then to ask important questions about each step of the procedure to locate errors.

# CHAPTER 8

# The Humanistic Perspective

## ORIENTATION

The learning theories discussed thus far have emphasized the role of environmental and cognitive factors in the teaching-learning process. Although it is apparent that learning is affected by how students think and act, it is also apparent that students are influenced and guided by the personal meanings and feelings they attach to their learning experiences.

In this chapter we investigate humanistic psychology and its influence on educational thought and practice. Humanistic psychologists maintain that (1) the behavior of individuals is primarily determined by how they perceive themselves and the world around them, and (2) individuals are not solely the products of their environment, as the behaviorists would have us believe, but are internally directed, having free choice, motivated by the desire to "self-actualize," or fulfill their unique potential as human beings. Ryan (1986) states: "The role of the school is not simply to make children smart, but to make them smart *and* good. We must help them to live well and that will enable the common good to flourish. For schools and teachers to do only half the job puts the individual child and all the rest of us in danger" (p. 233).

From the humanistic perspective, educators should be concerned with making education more responsive to the affective needs of students. *Affective needs* are those needs that are related to the student's emotions, feelings, values, attitudes, predispositions, and morals (Beane, 1985/1986). These needs are evident in Combs's (1981) description of the major goals of humanistic education:

- Accepting the learner's needs and purposes and creating educational experiences and programs for the development of the learner's unique potential
- Facilitating the learner's self-actualization and feelings of personal adequacy
- Fostering the acquisition of basic skills and competencies (e.g., academic, personal, interpersonal, communicative, and economic) for living in a multicultural society
- Personalizing educational decisions and practices
- Recognizing the importance of human feelings, values, and perceptions in the educational process
- Developing a learning climate that is challenging, understanding, supportive, exciting, and free from threat
- Developing in learners a genuine concern and respect for the worth of others and skill in resolving conflicts

As you read this chapter, you will see how the goals of humanistic education have been incorporated into a number of alternative instructional approaches (e.g., **open education,** moral education, and cooperative learning). These approaches, although differing in certain respects, have in common the ideal of making education a more human, personal, and student-centered endeavor as opposed to the more traditional, teacher-centered kind of schooling. In Chapter 11, you will see how humanistic techniques are used to help students *and* teachers deal more effectively with problems of communication, interpersonal relations, social skills, and discipline.

It is important to keep in mind that although humanistic education emphasizes the value of learning that is personal and affective, it does not ignore or deny the necessity of acquiring basic knowledge and skills. As Combs (1982) has stated:

Humanistic education does not require the surrender of traditional goals and objectives. Quite the contrary. It is a way of making certain that students achieve them. I am not a humanist because I just want to go about being nice to people. I am a humanist because I know that when I apply humanist thinking to my teaching, students will learn anything better. (p. 135)

By the time you master the material in this chapter, you will be able to:

- Use humanistic principles to facilitate learning and human development.
- Lead a class discussion on a moral dilemma.
- Use values clarification exercises to help students better understand their own values.
- Develop an open classroom.
- Prepare students for cooperative learning.

## FOCUS QUESTIONS

1. How do humanistic psychologists view learning?
2. What classroom practices would humanistic psychologists encourage?
3. What factors do humanistic psychologists see as interfering with learning?
4. What is the difference between values clarification and Kohlberg's approach to moral education?
5. What is the controversy concerning direct and indirect approaches to moral character development?
6. How are humanistic principles and Piaget's theory of cognitive development used in the open classroom?
7. How do individual differences influence group functioning?

## HUMANISTIC PSYCHOLOGY

**How do humanistic psychologists view learning?**

During the late 1940s, a new psychological perspective emerged from the work of persons engaged in the application of psychology—clinical psychologists, social workers, and counselors—rather than from the work of those researching the learning process. The movement that grew out of this perspective became known as *humanistic, existential, perceptual,* or *phenomenological* psychology and attempted to understand behavior from the point of view of the behaver rather than of the observer.

**What classroom practices would humanistic psychologists encourage?**

To gain a better understanding of the principles of humanistic psychology and how they apply to the learning process, let's first examine the views of three of its major proponents: Arthur Combs, Abraham H. Maslow, and Carl R. Rogers.

**Combs** _____

Arthur Combs et al. (1974) explain how perceptual psychologists view behavior:

> To understand human behavior . . . it is necessary to understand the behaver's perceptual world, how things seem from his point of view. This calls for a different understanding of what the "facts" are that we need in order to deal with human behavior; it is not the external facts that are important in understanding behavior, but the meaning of the facts to the behaver. To change another person's behavior it is necessary somehow to modify his beliefs or perception. When he sees things differently, he will behave differently. (p. 15)

This statement is one of the credos of the humanists' concern for the individual's feelings, perceptions, beliefs, and purposes—the inner behaviors that make people different from one another. To understand another person, it is necessary to see the world as the behaver does, to determine how the behaver thinks and feels about him- or herself and his or her world.

To understand the behavior of a student, you must determine how that student perceives the way he or she acts in a situation. What appears to be strange or unusual behavior to you may not be so from the behaver's (student's) perspective. To the teacher, a student's wanton destruction of school material is inexplicable. To the student who cannot achieve recognition, status, or prestige in school, the behavior (although improper) is a purposeful act that may bring recognition from peers.

This is why perceptual psychologists state that to change behavior, one must change an individual's perception. Combs, Avila, and Purkey (1971) suggest that misbehavior is "the result of not wanting to do what one knows he should do because something else is more personally satisfying" (p. 96). When teachers complain that students are not motivated, the teachers really mean that the students are not motivated to do what the teachers want them to do. Yet if the teachers selected different activities, they might find totally different reactions on the part of the students.

Now let's see how a student's internal perspective relates directly to the learning process. Humanists see two parts to learning: the acquisition of new information and the individual's personalization of this information. Teachers make the mistake of assuming that students will learn if subject matter is properly organized and presented. But meaning is not inherent in the subject matter; it is the individual who instills subject matter with its meaning (Combs et al., 1971). The dilemma in teaching is not how to present subject matter but how to help students derive personal meaning from the subject matter. If they can relate it in some way to their lives, you will have succeeded.

Combs et al. explain the dominance of personal meaning over a person's information retention by drawing two concentric circles and labeling "perceptions of the self" in the center and "perceptions of the world" in the outer circle. The farther events are from the center of the circle (perceptions of the self), the less they will influence the individual. The closer events are perceived to be to the self, the more they will affect behavior. Now you may understand why so many of the things that we learn are soon forgotten: they have little relation to the self!

I often ask my students to write down main ideas from each of their courses of the previous semester. Every semester many students admit that their list is going to be a brief one because they cannot remember many worthwhile ideas from certain courses. Think about your own learning. Do you find a relationship between the amount of your learning and the degree of personal meaning you found in the subject?

## Maslow

Abraham Maslow has been long recognized as one of the leading proponents of humanistic psychology. His work in the area of gratification of needs has been influential in understanding human motivation. An important part of his theory is based on the assumption that within us are both forces that seek growth and forces that resist growth. Maslow (1968) states:

> One set [of forces] clings to safety and defensiveness out of fear, tending to regress backward, hanging on to the past, *afraid* to grow . . ., *afraid* to take chances, *afraid* to jeopardize what he already has, *afraid* of independence, freedom and separateness. The other set of forces impels him forward toward wholeness of self and uniqueness of self, toward full functioning of all his capacities, toward confidence in the face of the external world at the same time that he can accept his deepest, real, unconscious self. (pp. 45–46)

Think about these forces as they relate to an important decision that you made in the past or are presently contemplating. Identify these feelings that relate to safety and those feelings that relate to growth.

Maslow's **hierarchy of needs** (Figure 8.1) is helpful in understanding need gratification. Maslow believes that some human needs, especially physiological needs, are basic to others and that certain needs must be satisfied before the individual becomes concerned with higher needs.

According to Maslow, *physiological* needs (e.g., food, water, sleep) are the most demanding of satisfaction. Once these needs have been satisfied, needs at the next level emerge. These are *safety* needs—the desire for good health and for security from harm and danger. Satisfaction of safety needs is followed by motivation for *belonging and love*—to have friends and family, and to belong to a group. An inability to love and belong may motivate a person to behave in different ways to gain such acceptance. For example, some people attempt to use achievement as a substitute for love. The next

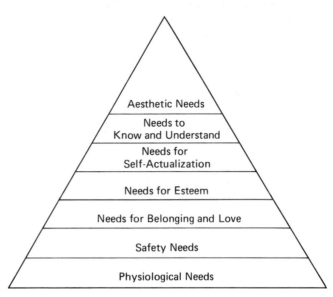

Figure 8.1 Maslow's Hierarchy of Needs.

need on the hierarchy is the need for *esteem*—the desire to have the respect, confidence, and admiration of others, and to gain self-respect. I discussed earlier in the book how a student's classroom behavior is related to a need for self-esteem.

Maslow assumes that if an individual has been able to satisfy all these lower needs on the hierarchy, then motivation is directed toward **self-actualization**—the need to develop one's potential, to become what one is capable of becoming. The manner in which self-actualization surfaces in people varies greatly. Developing a hobby, reading a book, driving a truck, raising children, becoming a professor are all paths to self-actualization. Self-actualization is "not so much a matter of what a person does, as how he feels about what he's doing" (Kolesnik, 1975, p. 42). In the choice of action, each person wants to improve in some way. The next need on the hierarchy is *to know and to understand*—to satisfy curiosity, seek knowledge, and gain understanding. Finally, Maslow proposed that some individuals have *aesthetic* needs—for order, symmetry, closure, and the completion of an act.

Maslow distinguished the first four needs in the hierarchy from the later ones. He identified the former as *deficiency* needs and the latter as *growth* needs. Generally, the gratification of deficiency needs depends on other people, whereas gratification of growth needs depends more on one's self.

*Instructional Implications of Maslow's Views.* Maslow's hierarchy of human needs has important implications that teachers should take into account while working with children. A teacher may have difficulty understanding why certain children do not do homework, are restless in class, or are completely uninterested in class activities. The teacher assumes that the desire to learn is an important need for all children, but Maslow suggests that interest or motivation to learn may not develop until other basic needs have been met. Children who come to school without breakfast or sufficient sleep, or with personal family problems, anxieties, or fears, are not interested in becoming self-actualized individuals.

## Rogers

**What factors do humanistic psychologists see as interfering with learning?**

Carl Rogers (1969, 1983) was a humanistic psychologist whose ideas have been influential in educational thought and practice. Through such popular books as *Freedom to Learn* and *Freedom to Learn for the 80's,* he has advocated an educational approach that tries to make learning and teaching more humanistic and thus more personal and meaningful.

Rogers's approach can best be understood from an examination of some of the important humanistic learning principles that he has identified as being central to his educational philosophy.

*The Desire to Learn.* Foremost among Rogers's beliefs is that human beings have a natural desire to learn. This desire is easily verified, says Rogers, by watching the curiosity and eagerness of young children as they explore their environment. The inherent eagerness of children to learn is a basic assumption in humanistic education. In the humanistic classroom, children are given the freedom to satisfy their curiosity, to pursue their interests unabated, and to discover for themselves what is important and meaningful about the world around them. This orientation is in sharp contrast to traditional classrooms, in which the teacher or the curriculum determines what it is children should learn.

*Significant Learning.* The second humanistic learning principle that Rogers has identified is that significant or meaningful learning occurs when it is perceived by students as being relevant to their own needs and purposes. As we saw earlier in our discussion of Combs, humanists consider learning to be a two-part process, involving both the acquisition of new information and the personalization of it. Students learn best and most rapidly, humanists feel, when learning is personally significant.

Examples of this kind of learning are not hard to find. Think of the student who quickly learns to operate a computer in order to enjoy a favorite game, or the student who rapidly learns to count change in order to buy a favorite toy. In both instances, learning is purposeful and certainly motivated by the need to know.

*Learning without Threat.* Another principle identified by Rogers is that learning is best acquired and retained in an environment free from threat. The process of learning is enhanced when students can test their abilities, try new experiences, or even make mistakes without experiencing the sting of criticism and ridicule.

*Self-Initiated Learning.* For the humanists, learning is most significant and pervasive when it is self-initiated and when it involves both the feelings and mind of the learner. Being able to choose the direction of one's own learning is highly motivating and gives the student the opportunity to *learn how to learn.* The mastering of subject matter is no doubt important but no more so than acquiring the ability to discover resources, formulate problems, test hypotheses, and evaluate the outcomes. Self-initiated learning focuses the student's attention on the process of learning as well as on the product.

Self-initiated learning also teaches students to be independent and self-reliant. When students learn on their own, they have an opportunity to make judgments, choices, and evaluations. They come to depend more on themselves and less on the evaluations of others.

In addition to being self-initiated, learning should involve all aspects of the person, cognitive as well as affective. Rogers and other humanists call this type of learning (i.e., learning from the "gut" rather than just from the neck up) *whole-person learning.* Humanists believe that if learning is personal and affective, it will induce feelings of belonging in the student. The student will feel more personally involved in learning, more excited over accomplishments, and, most important, more motivated to continue learning.

*Learning and Change.* The last principle that Rogers has identified is that the most socially useful learning is learning about the process of learning. Rogers notes that in the past, students could get by with learning a static set of facts and ideas. The world was slow to change, and what people learned in school was adequate to meet the demands of the time. Today, however, change is a central fact of life. Knowledge is in a constant state of flux. Yesterday's learning is no longer adequate to enable one to function successfully in the modern world. What is needed now, according to Rogers, are individuals who are capable of learning in a changing environment.

*Instructional Implications of Rogers's Views.* The learning principles and teacher characteristics that Rogers has identified as being central to his educational philosophy have been incorporated into an approach that he calls **person-centered education.** He feels that this approach results in learning that is deeper and that can be acquired more rapidly and pervasively than learning that occurs under traditional classroom approaches.

Rogers, like many humanistic educators, is not overly concerned with teaching methodology. The value of curricular planning, the scholarly expertise of the teacher, or the use of technology is not as important for the facilitation of learning as is responsiveness to the student's feelings or the quality of the interaction between students and teachers. Nevertheless,

Rogers (1983) feels that there are certain instructional strategies and methods that may be helpful in promoting humanistic learning.

One strategy suggested by Rogers is to provide students with a variety of resources that can support and guide their learning experiences. Resources can include such typical instructional materials as books, reference guides, and electronic aids (e.g., computers and calculators) as well as less typical ones, such as building materials, tools, cooking utensils, and the like. Resources can also include people, such as members of the community who may have an area of interest or expertise that they would be willing to share with students. Teachers can serve as resources by making their knowledge, skills, and experience available to students when requested.

Another strategy suggested by Rogers is peer tutoring—students teaching one another. There is much evidence that this experience benefits both the student doing the teaching and the student receiving the help (Devin-Sheehan, Feldman, & Allen, 1976).

Finally, Rogers is a strong proponent of discovery and inquiry learning, in which the student seeks answers to real questions, makes autonomous discoveries, and becomes engaged in self-directed learning.

*The Humanistic Teacher.* The humanistic principles that Rogers has identified focus primarily on the learning experiences of the student. However, Rogers's philosophy of education also gives attention to the role of the teacher. Humanistic education is only as successful as the teacher who implements it, and that success is largely dependent upon certain human qualities which that teacher brings to the classroom.

According to Rogers, the teacher in a humanistic classroom is primarily a *facilitator of learning.* In contrast to the traditional teacher who assumes full responsibility for the learning process, the humanistic teacher shares the responsibility for learning with students. Rather than telling students what to do or study, the facilitative teacher acts as a guide and model, helping students to decide what and how they will learn and providing them with the resources to do so. If, for example, students are interested in learning to program a computer, facilitative teachers may respond by providing instruction themselves or by helping students to find other sources of information or expertise.

Rogers has identified a number of personal qualities or attitudes that seem to enhance the teacher's role as a facilitator of learning. These include realness, trust, and empathic understanding.

*Realness,* or *genuineness,* refers to the degree to which teachers are honest in their relationships with students. Rogers believes that if teachers are to be effective, they must clearly and openly communicate their feelings and beliefs. In other words, they must be real people. As Rogers (1983) states:

> When the facilitator is a real person, being what she is, entering into a relationship with the learner without presenting a front or a façade, she is much more likely to be effective. This means that the feelings that she is experiencing are available to her, available to her awareness, that she

is able to live these feelings, be them, and able to communicate them if appropriate. (p. 121)

Humanists believe that being real with students encourages open communication in the classroom and helps students to become more connected with their own feelings.

Another quality that enhances the teacher's role as facilitator is *trust*. Rogers (1983) defines this quality as a basic confidence or faith in the student's potentiality for self-actualization. It is a conviction that students will naturally "wish to learn, want to grow, seek to discover, endeavor to master, desire to create, move toward self-discipline" (p. 127). This quality is also characterized by an honest acceptance of students as unique individuals, as individuals worthy of respect, and as persons who are fundamentally trustworthy.

By communicating trust and acceptance, the teacher conveys to students that they are free to take risks in their development as learners and human beings. They can explore, take chances, or even fail without the risk of losing the teacher's support and approval.

The last quality that Rogers identifies as important to the role of the facilitative teacher is **empathic understanding**—the ability to view the world through the students' eyes, to understand what the process of learning and education mean personally to the students.

Rogers (1983) observes that empathic understanding is seldom practiced in the traditional classroom. Instead, teachers tend to use an evaluative type of understanding that is often expressed as, "I understand what is wrong with you." This is understanding from the teacher's point of view, not the student's. On the other hand, when the teacher is empathic with how the student feels, the student's reaction is likely to be "At last someone understands how it feels and seems to be *me* without wanting to analyze me or judge me. Now I can blossom and grow and learn" (p. 125).

## INSTRUCTIONAL APPLICATIONS OF HUMANISTIC PSYCHOLOGY

Thus far in this chapter I have discussed how prominent humanistic psychologists view teaching and learning, and the teacher's role in teaching and learning. This section focuses on some specific applications of how humanistic psychologists have attempted to merge the traditional emphasis on skills and cognitive information with the affective area of feelings, values, and interpersonal behavior. The three programs discussed in this section are moral education, open education (also called *open classrooms*), and cooperative learning. I have decided to discuss some additional humanistic approaches—effective communication, interpersonal relations, and social skills training—in Chapter 11 because they relate to classroom management and discipline.

This discussion by no means covers the total field of humanistic education. It is intended to identify some of the most important and useful concepts for teaching and learning. The references at the end of the chapter are a good source for additional study in these areas.

## Moral/Character Education

At one time the responsibility for moral education (sometimes called *character education, values education, or citizenship education*) was taken by organized religion and the family. Today many people are questioning whether these two institutions can adequately do the job and believe the school can play an important role in moral education. If so, where should moral education be taught? As part of a special curriculum? Included within the regular school curriculum? How should it be taught, directly or indirectly? These are some of the issues that will be addressed in this section.

A person's values impact his or her behavior. Hanson and Ginsburg (1988) found that adolescents were likely to have high academic achievement when they placed a high value on education and had parents who were concerned about their activities and well-being. In fact, the researchers found that even when socioeconomic status was taken into consideration, values had a greater impact on school achievement than socioeconomic status.

Davis (1984) argues that it is impossible for the schools to avoid teaching values even if there is no formal curriculum. For example, values are apparent when schools address the following issues: Should evolution and creation be taught in science? What facts about human reproduction should we teach in biology? Should we ignore or include facts related to pregnancy, venereal disease, and other sexual problems among teenagers? Living in the classroom environment also involves civic or citizenship issues: Are the classroom rules fair? Is there a good balance between cooperation and competition? Are individual responsibilty and community responsibility both emphasized? Do students learn respect for self and others?

*Character Education and Clinical Intervention.* London (1987) believes that there must be a major change in the way society sees the role of schools in the development of citizens. At one time the responsibility of children's personal development, including mental health, fell on the home. Today, he argues, we are faced with a psychosocial epidemic affecting millions of schoolchildren—substance abuse, pregnancy, abortion, parenting among teenagers, low self-esteem, depression, and suicide. At the same time, we are seeing greater family disruption, causing an increase in the incidence of divorce and the number of single parents. Since young people are the main victims of this epidemic and the schools are where the young people spend much of their time, the schools are the place for major intervention to help promote healthy child development. Thus the schools must assume a broader approach to character development than they have in the past.

How do you think students can best learn to be good citizens and exhibit moral behavior?

London describes two components of character education: training in *citizenship,* including such topics as the duties of citizens in a democracy, personal integrity as the basis of citizenship, the notion of equality, and the concern for caring for others; and education in *personal adjustment,* the qualities that enable children and youth to become productive citizens. He believes that achievement, self-control, and self-esteem are essential ingredients for character development. He states:

> Children who, in the battle against boredom, fear, loneliness, drink or drug themselves or get pregnant cannot very well practice the virtues they have learned. It is a wonder that any of them can learn to read, master arithmetic, or pass exams in schools. (p. 672)

Since the family can't perform all the functions needed for character development, other agencies must assist in the task. London states that by viewing the adjustment problems of students as roadblocks to the development of character, educators and mental health professionals (i.e., social workers, counselors, physicians) should subsume the health care and social service delivery systems under the educational system. This approach would shift the focus of mental health from hospitals, clinics, and private offices to schools. One important implication of this approach would be to change the schools' focus on dealing only with the individual as the primary unit of concern to attending to families as well (Moynihan, 1986).

What do you think about this approach? Are you convinced such steps need to be taken? Should health clinics provide contraception information? Should the schools get involved in counseling services for students and their families? Would the schools be taking on more than they could handle? What social and political forces need to be considered for such a reorganization of human services? What are the alternatives?

**What is the difference between values clarification and Kohlberg's approach to moral education?**

*Indirect Approaches to Moral Education.* Indirect approaches to character education tend to encourage students to define their own values and the moral perspectives that support those values. The two most widely used indirect approaches are values clarification and Lawrence Kohlberg's cognitive-developmental theory.

*Values Clarification.* Sidney Simon has developed a program called **values clarification,** based on the premise that many young people do not know clearly what their values are. He believes that young people need help in examining their values to direct their insights into how they view choices and make decisions. Simon contends that values clarification does not focus on the content of a person's values but the process itself of valuing.

To accomplish the goal of helping students to clarify their values, the teacher uses special exercises that involve students in discussion. Simon, Howe, and Kirschenbaum (1972) have organized 79 values clarification exercises for use in the classroom. One of the first exercises in their book helps individuals to realize what activities they enjoy and whether they are finding time to participate in them. Why don't you try this exercise as I explain it? Make a list of 10 or 15 things that give you great pleasure or joy. Write after the name of each pleasure the date you last experienced it. Next, place a dollar sign after each activity that costs more than $5.00. Now go through the list again, and place a *P* after those activities that usually require considerable planning. Review your list, and place an *S* after activities that you share with others. Last, place an *A* after those activities that you do alone. What does this activity tell you about yourself? The teacher using this exercise can lead a discussion that may take the class into many areas: What are the activities people value? Why is it that some people find time to do the things they enjoy whereas others do not? What kinds of activities do people enjoy? Why? Do students feel that their values will change or remain the same? What steps can be taken to change the ways in which individuals use their time?

In another series of exercises, the teacher can use incomplete sentences to evoke discussion about aspirations, attitudes, feelings, and beliefs. Some examples follow:

- I'd like to . . .
- When I grow up . . .

- In about 10 years . . .
- I'm for . . .
- In my opinion . . .
- I really enjoy reading about . . .
- I get angry when . . .

Another approach is to take a controversial issue and place opinions at each end of a continuum. The teacher then asks the students to mark their position on the continuum and discuss the reasons for their selections. This activity is useful in dealing with such issues as sexual behavior, drugs, and other issues of interest to students.

*Criticisms of Values Clarification.* Although the technique of values clarification has been used widely in schools throughout the country, critics of the approach raise issues about the ethical relativism of the program (i.e., communicating to students that there is no one set of values that is better than another). Many educators believe that it is important to teach students a particular moral or value system. For example, both abortion rights advocates and anti-abortion groups state that they value life. Thus the same value can be used to support contradictory actions. In this case, developing a value would apparently not provide a clear guide to behavior—a goal of values clarification (Hersh, Miller, & Fielding, 1980).

What happens if the teacher has certain rules about cheating, and some students indicate that cheating is acceptable on tests? Does the teacher accept the values of these students, or tell them that they must conform to his or her value system? Should teachers limit discussion of values that conflict with their idea of how things should be run?

Another issue is whether students discuss what they really feel or instead make statements that are socially acceptable to their peers. Some critics question whether students actually explore their value systems in depth, as the proponents of values clarification feel that they do.

*Kohlberg's Theory of Moral Reasoning.* During the course of instruction, particularly in the humanities and social sciences, a teacher has opportunities to raise questions about ethical or moral situations or to respond to moral issues identified by students in the class. It is important to realize that students differ in their reasoning about these issues. Lawrence Kohlberg (1964) developed a theory of moral reasoning that can help a teacher to identify students' level of reasoning and to stimulate students' moral growth.

Traditionally, morality has been equated with one's character or behavior. However, Kohlberg's theory is based on the belief that morality is a set of rational principles for making judgments about how to behave. His basic principle is, justice: the regard for the dignity and worth of all persons. According to Kohlberg, children proceed through a series of stages during which they refine their concept of justice. The stages are organized systems of thought through which individuals proceed in a specified sequence. Table 8.1 presents **Kohlberg's stages of moral reasoning.**

TABLE 8.1 KOHLBERG'S STAGES OF MORAL REASONING

| Stage | Description | Example |
|---|---|---|
| Level I | *Preconventional level:* Children at this level reason in terms of their own needs. Answers to moral dilemmas are based on what they can get away with. Moral values reside in good and bad acts, not people or standards. Cultural rules and labels of good or bad, right and wrong, are interpreted in terms of punishment, reward, exchange of favors, or the physical power of those who advocate the rules and labels. Children are concerned about external, concrete consequences to themselves. | |
| Stage 1 | *Punishment-and-obedience orientation:* Children worry about avoiding punishment by adults or people with superior power and prestige. They are aware of rules and the consequences for breaking them. The physical consequences of an action determine its goodness or badness: "might makes right." | Heinz should not steal, because he would be punished by authorities. |
| Stage 2 | *Instrumental-relativist orientation:* Children want to satisfy their own needs (and occasionally the needs of others) if they can get away with it. They are motivated by self-interest and aware that relationships are dominated by concrete reciprocity (you scratch my back and I'll scratch yours), not loyalty, gratitude, or justice. They assume that everyone has to look out for himself and is obligated only to those who help him. | Heinz should steal, because he is worried about his wife and he will feel better if she isn't sick. |
| Level II | *Conventional level:* Moral value resides in performing good and right roles. Children are concerned with meeting external social expectations; they value meeting the expectations of family, group, or nation by conforming to the expectations of significant people and the social order. There is active support and justification of conventional rules and roles. | |
| Stage 3 | *Interpersonal concordance orientation:* Children earn approval by being "nice." They are concerned about living up to "good boy" and "good girl" stereotypes. Good behavior is what pleases or helps others and what is approved of by them. Children are aware of the need to consider the intentions and feelings of others; cooperation is seen in terms of the golden rule. | Heinz should steal, because good husbands care about their wives. Other people would disapprove if he let his wife die. |
| Stage 4 | *Authority-maintaining orientation:* Children are motivated by a sense of duty or obligation to live up to socially defined roles, and to maintain the existing social order for the good of all. They are aware that there is a larger social system which regulates the behavior of the people within it. They assume that the social order is the source of morality and that laws should be maintained, even at personal expense. | Heinz should not steal, because stealing is against the law and the laws must be maintained even at the expense of personal loss. |
| Level III | *Postconventional autonomous, or principled, level:* Children make a clear effort to define moral values and principles that have validity and application apart from the authority of groups or individuals and apart from their own identifications. There is a concern for fidelity to self-chosen moral principles. Moral value resides in conformity to shared standards, rights and duties. | |
| Stage 5 | *Social-contract, legalistic orientation:* Right actions tend to be defined in terms of general individual rights and standards that have been critically examined and agreed on by the whole soci- | Heinz should steal, because society places more value on the right to have medicine than on |

*(continued)*

TABLE 8.1 *(continued)*

| Stage | Description | Example |
|---|---|---|
| | ety. There is an emphasis on procedural rules for reaching consensus because of awareness of the relativism of personal values and opinions. Aside from what society agrees on, there is the possibility of changing the law in terms of rational considerations of social utility. Outside the legal realm, free agreement and contract are the binding elements of obligation. | the right to make a large profit. Everyone has the right to get medicine if he or she needs it badly, regardless of the law against stealing. |
| Stage 6 | ***Universal ethical orientation:*** The person defines right by decisions of conscience in accord with self-chosen ethical principles that appeal to logical comprehensiveness, universality, and consistency. These principles are abstract and ethical; at heart they are universal principles of justice, of the reciprocity and equality of human rights, and of respect for the dignity of human beings as individuals. There is an orientation of letting one's conscience be a directing agent and of letting mutual respect and trust dominate interpersonal relationships. | Heinz should steal the drug, because a human life takes precedence over any other moral or legal value, whatever it is. A human life has inherent value whether or not it is valued by a particular person—Heinz's wife's life has inherent value whether or not it is valued by the druggist. |

*Source: Johnson, 1979.*

Kohlberg developed his theory by analyzing **moral dilemmas** presented to children at various age levels. The diagnosis of each child's stage is based on the child's reasons for believing rather than behaving in a certain way. A person's stage of moral reasoning cannot be determined on the basis of responses to a single dilemma, because a person may apply more advanced reasoning to some situations than to others. The following is an example of a moral dilemma (Kohlberg, 1976):

> In Europe, a woman was near death from a rare form of cancer. There was one drug that the doctors thought might save her, a form of radium that a druggist in the same town had recently discovered. The druggist was charging $2,000, ten times what the drug cost to make. The sick woman's husband, Heinz, went to everyone he knew to borrow the money, but he could only get together about half of what [the drug] cost. He told the druggist that his wife was dying and asked him to sell it cheaper or let him pay later. But the druggist said, "No." So Heinz got desperate and broke into the man's store to steal the drug for his wife. (pp. 41–42)

In Table 8.1, you will find three levels of moral reasoning. These levels represent three possible perspectives an individual can take in relation to society's moral norms: Level I, preconventional; Level II, conventional; and Level III, postconventional, or principled. A person at the preconventional level deals with a moral issue from the viewpoint of the specific interest of the individuals involved. Rather than being interested in society's laws, a person at this level is concerned with the consequences individuals would face in deciding upon a particular action. A person at the conventional level deals with a moral issue from the perception of a law-abiding citizen in society. As a result, this person is concerned with what society views as right or just. A person at the postconventional, or principled, level deals with a moral issue from a perspective beyond the given laws of that person's own society and asks: "What are the principles upon which any good society is based?"

The first level characterizes children's moral reasoning but can represent adolescent or adult reasoning as well. The second level develops during adolescence and remains as the dominant level of thinking of most adults. The third level is the rarest. It begins, if at all, during adolescence or early adulthood and represents the moral reasoning of only a few adults (Hersh, Paolitto, & Reimer, 1979).

Let us now review the six stages. Read the description in Table 8.1 of each stage and the example replies from the case of Heinz. In Stage 1, the "punishment-and-obedience orientation," moral decisions are based on whether the individual expects to be praised or punished for a given behavior. In Stage 2, the "instrumental-relativist orientation," decisions are based on whether following rules or laws brings the individual some benefit in return. In Stage 3, the "good boy, nice girl orientation," decisions are based on the approval of others and on conformity in order to please. In Stage 4, the "authority-maintaining orientation," and sometimes called the "law-and-order orientation," decisions are based on the individual's adherence to a sense of duty to follow rules for maintaining social order. In Stage 5, the "social-contract, legalistic orientation," decisions are based on standards critically examined and agreed on by the society as a whole. Stage 6, the "universal ethical orientation," represents a person who makes decisions based upon conscience, in accord with self-chosen principles. An individual in this stage believes that citizens have a right to disobey laws that deny human dignity and equality.

Remember that the particular response chosen by the student does not reveal the student's stage of moral development. It is the explanation, or reason, given for the solution that determines the identification of the stage.

It is important to realize that students can choose the same resolution for a dilemma for entirely different reasons. Suppose students were discussing how they would deal with a moral dilemma. They were asked whether they would loot a store during a riot. Four different students may state that they would not—all for different reasons! One student might refrain for fear of being shot by the police (Stage 1, "punishment-and-obedience orientation"). Another student might decide not to loot because he wanted a summer job at the store and might be afraid that the store would close down. This student is reasoning at Stage 2, "self-benefit orientation." A student at Stage 3 might be worried about how his friends would view his unlawful act ("good-boy, nice-girl orientation"), and a student at Stage 4 ("law-and-order") believes that a society cannot function effectively if individuals take advantage of social turmoil by participating in unlawful acts. All the students made a decision not to loot, but the reasons for their decision, not their decision, determine their placement at four different stages (Mattox, 1975).

Kohlberg (1976) has found that discussing one stage above a person's present level of moral reasoning is most effective in raising moral judgments. Thus, if a student is reasoning at Stage 2, hearing arguments at Stage 3 is more effective than hearing arguments at Stage 2 or Stage 4.

Numerous evaluations of moral education programs using Kohlberg's theory have indicated that such programs can be effective in promoting moral judgment (Enright, Lapsley, & Levy, 1983; Leming, 1981; Lockwood, 1978), especially if the program lasts more than a few weeks and if the intervention involves students in discussion of controversial moral dilemmas (Schlaefli, Rest, & Thoma, 1985). A question often asked is whether the training influences *moral behavior*. Unfortunately, *there is no evidence to suggest that changes produced by values clarification or Kohlberg's programs bring about subsequent changes in actual moral behavior*. Rest (1983) explains the lack of such change by pointing out that moral judgment is but one of four components influencing the production of moral behavior, as follows:

- *Moral sensitivity*—the individual realizes that a situation exists that involves a decision to act and that the action has some consequences for the welfare and interests of others.
- *Moral judgment*—the individual must make a decision that involves a course of action (this is the process that the dilemmas measure).
- *Moral motivation*—the individual must act on personal judgment.
- *Moral character*—the individual must have sufficient persistence to implement strategies to behave morally.

It is clear that most educational programs do not deal with all the necessary components. However, it is argued that if programs deal with moral sensitivity and judgment (the first two components), it may be possible to stimulate the development of the last two processes—moral motivation and character.

*Criticisms of Kohlberg's Theory.* Kohlberg's theory of moral reasoning is one of the major approaches to moral development, but he is not without his critics. Some of the major criticisms include the following:

- Kohlberg underestimates the importance of Stage 3 reasoning, the "good-boy, nice-girl" orientation. Although postconventional morality (Stages 5 and 6) is a worthwhile goal, Kohlberg has found few individuals who have reached this level. Thus a society will benefit if most of its citizens have respect for law and order. As a result, more emphasis should be placed on Stage 3 reasoning by helping children to understand the importance of rules in maintaining society.
- Kohlberg has a narrow perception of morality in emphasizing justice. He fails to recognize the role of the affective side of morality

in terms of such moral emotions as guilt, concern for others, and remorse.

- Although Kohlberg presents research in nine different cultures supporting the universality of his stages, he should not conclude that his description of moral development holds true for all people in all cultures.

- The theory places unrealistic demands on teachers. According to Kohlberg, a teacher should present a moral argument one stage above the student's present level of reasoning. This requirement produces some problems because very few people reach Stages 5 or 6. Therefore, some teachers may interact with students who reason at stages higher than their own! How will teachers help these students? Another related problem is the difficulty some teachers will have in attempting to lead a class discussion on a dilemma with students who are at different levels and responding appropriately each time at one stage higher than the students' level of reasoning (Fraenkel, 1976; Peters, 1975).

- Gilligan (1982; Gilligan & Attanucci, 1988) argues that Kohlberg's theory was developed on the basis of his investigation with males and that the description of criteria for each of the stages may be more appropriate for the development of moral reasoning in males than in females. She asserts that women follow a different path to complex moral reasoning and that their development is based, in part, on a different set of values. For example, a woman who would solve a moral dilemma based on a concern for the people involved (i.e., a care perspective or focus) might not score as high as a male who might resolve the same dilemma on the basis of a theme of universal justice. Some research findings challenge Gilligan's claims of different sequences of moral development for males and females (Gibbs, Arnold, & Burkhart, 1984; Walker, 1984). Thus, it appears that this controversy is far from being settled.

## CLASSROOM APPLICATION: LEADING A DISCUSSION ON A MORAL DILEMMA

The teacher can play an important role in the enhancement of moral reasoning by leading discussions on moral dilemmas and creating opportunities for students to think about the issues in increasingly complex ways. When students are forced to think about moral conflicts in a more complex manner than they are used to, cognitive disequilibrium results. After a time, the experience with higher-level thinking stimulates reasoning at a more advanced stage. Some helpful guidelines for the implementation of these discussions follow (Hersh, Miller, & Fielding, 1980).

Various types of instructional material can be used to raise the issue of moral dilemmas: *hypothetical situations*, like the "Heinz" case (see Hersh, Paolitto, & Reimer, 1979; Howe & Howe, 1975; Mattox, 1975); *content-specific issues* stemming from curriculum content such as America's participation in the Vietnam War or the responsibility of chemical companies to protect the environment; problems of *real or practical concern*, such as classroom situations ("Would you report a friend who was cheating on a test?"), family problems, or events in the community.

There are two phases of questioning: initial and in-depth strategies. In the initial phase of the discussion, the teacher attempts to ensure that the students understand the moral dilemma, to help students confront the various moral aspects of the issue, to elicit students' rationale for their point of view, and to encourage students to discuss their point of view with one another. The following questions can provide the framework for accomplishing these goals:

- *Highlighting the moral issue.* These questions encourage students to take a stand on the moral issue and imply questions of "should," "ought," "right," or "wrong": "Should Heinz steal the drug?" "Should a husband commit a crime in order to save the life of his wife?" "Should a person report a cheating incident to the teacher if his or her best friend is involved?"
- *Asking "why" questions.* These questions ask students to defend their position on the dilemma and stimulate interest and discussion. An important aspect of this type of question is that it gives students the opportunity to learn that their classmates may take a similar stand but for different reasons. Good examples of "why" questions are: "Why do you think your solution to the dilemma is a good one?" "Why did you reach that conclusion?"
- *Complicating the circumstances.* As the discussion develops, the teacher can add new information to complicate the original moral problem. In the Heinz dilemma, the teacher might ask: "Suppose Heinz's wife asked him to (or not to) steal the drug. Would your position be different?" The purpose of this type of question is to encourage the students to consider many aspects of an issue. Another type of complicating question is asked to prevent students from escaping the moral dilemma. When students first begin discussing moral issues, they often avoid taking a stand by trying to change the dilemma—for example, by stating that Heinz should try another drug before stealing the drug in question. This approach attempts to alter the facts of the issue and helps to resolve the dilemma by eliminating the conflict. To help students face the dilemma, the teacher might say: "But for the moment, let's assume that there is no other drug" or "Suppose there wasn't any other drug that could be used?"

After students have identified the moral dilemma and have exchanged points of view, the teacher moves into the second phase of the discussion by asking in-depth questions that encourage students to deal with different points of view. These advanced strategies include asking refining questions, highlighting contiguous-stage arguments, clarifying and summarizing, and using role-taking techniques.

Refining questions help to extend the various positions taken on the issue and can take many forms. A teacher can ask students to

- explain ambiguous terms that they use in discussion ("What kind of *trouble* would you get your friend into if you reported the cheating?").
- explore one moral issue related to the dilemma, such as authority, contract obligations, and the value of life ("Do you have any obligations to a stranger?" "What is the difference between an obligation to a member of one's family and to a stranger?").
- assume the perspective of a different person in the conflict contrary to the position the student is taking ("What do you think the teacher ought to do in a situation in which a student is cheating?" "Would your parents think you should report your friend?").
- consider what would happen if everyone followed his or her reasoning on the moral dilemma ("How could teachers run classrooms if everyone cheated on tests?" "What would happen if everyone stole from other people to save the life of someone they knew?")

A second in-depth questioning strategy is to highlight arguments at various stages of moral reasoning. For example "John, your approach to this problem is different from Peter's. Could you tell us why you think your solution was a good one? How is it different from what Peter said?" If everyone in class provides the same perspective on an issue, the teacher should pose arguments at the next higher stage: "I noticed that no one mentioned that the law states _____ based on the reasoning that _____. Does anyone have an opinion about this legal point of view?"

Another in-depth strategy involves a change in the teacher's role from that of initiating questions to clarifying and summarizing students' statements. After listening to a discussion about whether to report a friend who was cheating on a test, the teacher might state: "I hear a couple of things. Some of you are concerned that classroom rules should not be broken. Others feel that a close personal friendship is more important than any regulation. Finally, some people believe that a close friendship can still be maintained if the student were reported to the teacher."

Finally, the teacher can ask role-taking questions and use strategies designed to stimulate students to take different points of view, such as holding debates or viewing films that depict controversial issues. The teacher will find these strategies most effective when the students are asked to reason from another's point of view.

**What is the controversy concerning direct and indirect approaches to moral character development?**

*Direct Approaches to Moral Education.* A number of educators are critical of the indirect approaches to moral education because of their preoccupation with how students think about moral issues rather than how they behave ( Ryan, 1986; Wynne, 1988). The critics indicate the ineffectiveness of these approaches by pointing out that they have done little to deal with the moral problems in schools (e.g., poor discipline, vandalism, and physical abuse of students and of teachers) and society. In addition, in both values clarification and Kohlberg's theory of moral development, the teacher plays a relatively neutral role. Teachers present critical situations and serve as group facilitators but never give their opinion concerning right and wrong in what students say. Today there appears to be more concern that teachers and the schools play a more direct role in developing standards and teaching moral behavior. For example, a former secretary of education, William Bennett (1986), suggested that schools should develop discipline codes, explain to children and their parents what the schools expect from them, and enforce the rules.

Lickona (1988) provides the following advice on how teachers can be more actively involved in moral education:

- Serve as moral models and mentors for children, providing examples of respect and caring by the way they treat their children and offering corrective moral feedback when students act insensitively toward others.
- Develop a cohesive classroom community in which students know each other, care about each other, and feel part of the group.
- Hold students accountable to high standards of academic responsibility in order to teach the value of work as a way to develop oneself and contribute to the human community.
- Handle discipline in a way that develops moral reasoning and encourage students to discipline themselves and to voluntarily comply with rules.
- Provide opportunities, such as class meeting, for participatory decision making and shared responsibility.
- Teach the skills of cooperation through cooperative learning and practice in reasoned conflict resolution.
- Develop students' capacity for moral reflection through discussion and debate of moral issues drawn from the traditional subject areas.

- Use inspirational role models from current events and history to help students admire and identify with good character. (p. 9)

Wynne (1988) is especially interested in service activities. He states that it is easy to fool oneself into believing that even though students' behavior is inappropriate, their moral thinking or reasoning is good. He believes that one's character is demonstrated in one's conduct. Thus, if educators want to help students develop character, they need to organize experiences that generate good conduct. He points to the "For Character" school recognition program in Chicago as an example of what schools need to do. Students are given recognition for participating in such activities as

- tutoring peers or students in other grades
- serving as crossing guards
- taking part in dramatic, musical, or athletic activities
- raising funds for school or community
- helping on service projects with the school or community
- taking part in academic group projects
- visiting patients in hospitals
- helping care for children in nursery school or kindergarten

*A Possible Reconciliation.* Benninga (1988) believes that we can reconcile the issue of direct versus indirect approaches to moral education. He advocates that certain values should be taught in school that few individuals would question: justice, persistence, generosity, loyalty, social cooperation, and fairness. When issues arise concerning the application of these values, structured discussions would be the preferable teaching method. He uses the example of how we teach students the principle of free speech and expression as identified in the First Amendment. Yet the Supreme Court of the United States constantly hears cases by litigants who wish to redefine what free speech means. For example, the re-examination of free speech and expression by the Court in 1989 and 1990 made it legal for protestors to burn the United States flag. Benninga's point is that we can and should teach young people the important values of one's community and Western culture. However, we should deal with controversy in moral perceptions and behavior within the framework of open discussion and dialogue.

In addition to formal instruction and discussion, students can have opportunities to become involved in their community whereby they can experience the consequences of positive social behavior. Helping others can be a good place to begin.

What do think is the best way to deal with the moral education of students? Do you believe that teachers should be more actively involved in promoting community values or even the core values of Western society? Is there a danger of indoctrination? Can educators agree as to what values should be taught? Is there greater danger of doing nothing because of the fear that consensus can't be reached?

## Open Education

**How are humanistic principles and Piaget's theory of cognitive development used in the open classroom?**

The apparent success of the British primary schools and the publication of the Plowden Report (1967), a study advocating the development of the open classroom as a model for elementary education in England, have been catalysts in the spread of open education in the United States.

Advocates of *open education* claim that it is both a philosophy of education and the application of Piaget's theory of cognitive development. Because of the confusion over what exactly is involved in open education, Walberg and Thomas (1972) have reviewed relevant literature, broken it down into components, and then sought to verify their descriptions with prominent advocates of open education. They have evolved a list of eight themes, paraphrased as follows:

1. *Provisions for learning.* Manipulative materials supplied in great diversity and range. Children move freely around room. Talking encouraged. No grouping by ability using test scores.
2. *Humaneness, respect, openness, and warmth.* Use of student-made material. Teacher deals with behavior problems by communicating with child, without involving the group.
3. *Diagnosis of learning events.* Students correct their own work. Teacher observes and asks questions.
4. *Instruction.* Individualized. No texts or workbooks.
5. *Evaluation.* Teacher takes notes. Individualized. Few formal tests.
6. *Search for opportunities for professional growth.* Teacher uses assistance of someone else. Teacher works with colleague.
7. *Self-perception of teacher.* Teacher tries to keep all children within sight to monitor their work.
8. *Assumptions about children and the learning process.* Classroom climate warm and accepting. Children involved in what they are doing.

Walberg and Thomas found that open classes differ from traditional classes on five of the eight criteria: provisions, humaneness, diagnosis, instruction, and evaluation.

Barth (1971) has investigated the eighth criterion—assumptions about children and the learning process—and suggests that before jumping on the bandwagon, teachers should examine whether their assumptions are attuned to those of successful open educators in the United States and England. (Remember the importance of linking beliefs and practices, discussed in Chapter 1.) The following is a partial list of these assumptions. Read each, and determine the degree to which you agree with it.

### Learning

- Children are innately curious and will explore their environment without adult intervention.
- Children will display natural exploratory behavior if they are not threatened.

- Play is not distinguished from work as the predominant mode of learning in early childhood.
- Children will be likely to learn if they are given considerable choice in the selection of the materials they wish to work with and in the questions they wish to pursue with respect to those materials.

### Intellectual Development
- Concept formation proceeds slowly.
- Children pass through similar stages of intellectual development, each in his own way and at his own rate and in his own time.
- Verbal abstractions should follow direct experience with objects and ideas, not precede them or substitute for them.

### Evaluation
- Errors are necessarily a part of the learning process They are to be expected and even desired, for they contain information essential for further learning.
- Those qualities of a person's learning that can be carefully measured are not necessarily the most important.
- The best way of evaluating the effect of the school experience on the child is to observe the student over a long period.

### Knowledge
- Knowledge is a function of one's personal integration of experience and therefore does not fall neatly into categories or "disciplines."
- There is little or no knowledge that is essential for everyone to acquire. (pp. 97–99)

The Walberg and Thomas list of themes suggests that although open educators support students' freedom to move around the room and to select their own learning activities, teacher guidance throughout the process is in evidence. Proponents of open education present this fact to some critics who characterize open education as simply "doing your own thing."

One of the most salient features of an open classroom is the physical environment of the room, in which students work individually or in small groups. Most of the individualized instruction is provided by learning or activity centers in the classroom that allow students to explore particular subject areas, topics, skills, or interests. These centers have the advantages of posting explicit directions for proceeding on a topic without the presence of the teacher and of recording the student's participation and progress for later discussion with the teacher.

*Research on Open Education.* Evaluations of open education programs (Peterson, 1979; Giaconia & Hedges, 1982) generally show that these approaches are slightly more effective than traditional education in improving affective but not academic outcomes. In reviewing a large number of studies comparing open and traditional classrooms, Giaconia and Hedges found that open classrooms were moderately more successful in improving cooperation, creativity, achievement motivation, and independence. However, on measures of academic achievement, traditional classrooms were clearly superior.

Interestingly, Giaconia and Hedges also found that when open classes did improve affective outcomes, it was often at the expense of student progress in language, math, and reading. They also noted that certain features differentiated the more effective open education programs from the less effective, including greater emphasis on the role of the children in determining their own learning, greater use of evaluation focusing on students' specific strengths and weaknesses, more individualized instruction, and the presence of manipulative materials.

It appears that other forms of instruction that are based in part on humanistic principles (e.g., cooperative learning) have been more successful in producing academic gains as well as affective outcomes. Slavin (1988) summarizes the research on open classrooms by stating: "The experience of the open-schools movement does suggest that there are limits to self-directed learning by students, particularly when they are learning the basic skills on which so much later learning depends" (p. 303).

In a recent review of the open classroom, Rothenberg (1989) urged educators to reconsider its use. He pointed out that important cognitive and affective outcomes can be attained through the use of open classrooms and that educators should consider more *structure* in organizing open classrooms. This structure would include more frequent monitoring of student work so that basic skills are not neglected.

## Cooperative Learning

When teachers first hear the term *cooperative learning*, many different images emerge. Some might think of cooperative learning as assigning individual projects and allowing students to interact so they can check their progress or ask questions of other students; or assigning a group project with one student doing most of the work. Some might even think of cooperative learning as having students sit with each other as they do their own homework assignments. Unfortunately, the above descriptions *do not* describe cooperative learning (Johnson & Johnson, 1987).

Johnson and Johnson (1989) describe five basic elements that need to be included for a lesson to be cooperative: The first is *positive interdependence*. The students must perceive that they "sink or swim" together. This means that they must share goals, divide the tasks, share resources, information, assume responsibility for different roles, and, most important, receive rewards based on their group performance.

The second element requires *face-to-face interaction* among students so that they discuss the nature of the task, decide how they can best work together, and explain to each other how to solve problems. The importance of helping others is emphasized.

The third element is *individual accountability* for learning the assigned material. Each student must develop a sense of personal responsibility to the group. A key to success in cooperative learning is for each member to master material so that he or she can help other members of the group achieve success.

The fourth element is *collaborative skills*. Obviously, placing students in groups and telling them to work cooperatively without teaching them the necessary social skills will not lead to compatible working relationships within the group. The Classroom Application later in this chapter provides you with help in preparing students for cooperative learning. In addition, you will learn how to develop lesson plans for cooperative learning in Chapter 9.

The final element in cooperative learning is *group processing*, which occurs when groups discuss and evaluate their progress and maintain effective working relationships among members.

In cooperative learning, students work together in small (four- to-six-member) teams that remain stable in composition for many weeks. There are many ways to organize cooperative learning in classrooms. However, I shall briefly discuss four of the most widely used and researched techniques: Teams-Games-Tournaments (TGT), Student Teams-Achievement Divisions (STAD), Jigsaw, Group Investigation, and Team-Assisted Individualization (TAI).

*Teams-Games-Tournaments (TGT)*. In TGT, students of different ability, race, and gender are assigned to four- to five-member teams. After the teacher presents the material for the day, the teams complete worksheets, quiz each other, and study together in preparation for a tournament, which is usually held once each week. In the tournament, students are assigned to three-person "tournament tables," in which they compete with students of similar ability (based on the previous week's outcomes). As a result, the lowest-achieving students in each group have the same opportunity to earn points for their teams as the highest-achieving student.

The tournaments consist of students' taking turns picking cards and answering corresponding questions on the material studied during the week. At the end of the tournament, the teacher prepares a newsletter that recognizes successful teams and the top scores (similar to the results in a bowling league!). Although team membership stays the same, tournament table assignments are changed on the basis of the performance of individual students. Low achievers, who initially compete against students of similar ability, can compete against high achievers as they become more competent.

*Student Teams-Achievement Divisions (STAD)*. STAD uses the same four-to five-member teams used in TGT but replaces the tournament with 15-minute quizzes, which students take after studying with their teams. The quiz scores are translated into team scores, with top scores receiving more points than lower scores. An "improvement score" also has been used.

*Jigsaw.* In the **jigsaw method,** students are assigned to small, heterogeneous teams. The academic material is divided among the members of the team, and students study their parts or sections with members of other teams who have the same material to learn. Next, they go back to their groups and teach their sections to team members. Finally, all the group members are tested on the entire body of information. For example, suppose a teacher established an objective that required the students to learn biographical information on Martin Luther King. The teacher would divide the biographical information into four or five parts, depending on the number of students in the groups. The students would study with members of other groups who had been given the same section of the biography. Then they would go back and teach their section to the rest of their group. The goal is to have each group learn the complete biographical information. Student scores can be determined by a variety of procedures. One approach records grades for individual students only. In another approach, quiz scores are used to establish team scores.

*Group Investigation.* Group Investigation is a method of cooperative learning in which students work in small groups to complete various class projects. Each team breaks the task into subtopics, with individual students carrying out the activities needed to achieve their group goal. Each group makes a presentation about its research to the class. In group investigation, rewards or points are not given; instead, students are asked to work together to achieve group goals.

Sharon et al. (1984) describe the following six steps of the Group Investigation approach:

1. *Topic selection.* Students choose specific subtopics within a general problem area, usually delineated by the teacher. Students then organize into small two- to six-member task-oriented groups. Group composition is academically and ethnically heterogeneous.
2. *Cooperative planning.* Students and teacher plan specific learning procedures, tasks, and goals consistent with the subtopics of the problem selected in Step 1.
3. *Implementation.* Pupils carry out the plan formulated in Step 2. Learning should involve a wide variety of activities and skills and should lead students to different kinds of sources both inside and outside the school. The teacher closely follows the progress of each group and offers assistance when needed.
4. *Analysis and synthesis.* Pupils analyze and evaluate information obtained during Step 3 and plan how it can be summarized in some interesting fashion for possible display or presentation to classmates.
5. *Presentation of final product.* Some or all of the groups in the class give an interesting presentation of the topics studied in order to get classmates involved in each other's work and to achieve a broad perspective on the topic. Group presentations are coordinated by the teacher.

6. *Evaluation.* In cases where groups pursued different aspects of the same topic, pupils and teachers evaluate each group's contribution to the work of the class as a whole. Evaluation can include either individual or group assessment, or both. (pp. 4–5)

*Team-Assisted Individualization (TAI).* TAI is an excellent example of how behavioral and humanistic principles are combined to teach mathematics in a cooperative learning format (Slavin, 1985). In this approach, students are assigned to four- to-five-member, mixed-ability learning teams, as well as skill-level groups, on the basis of a placement test. Students proceed through a specific hierarchy of skills. Teachers work with the skill-level groups on different mathematics concepts and skills, after which students return to their teams and work on self-instructional materials. Group members check each other's work against answer sheets, help with difficult problems, and prepare each other for quizzes. Students who achieve mastery scores on quizzes add points to their teams' scores. At the end of each week, groups that exceed a pre-established criterion for completing units of material can earn certificates or other rewards. Students who do not achieve at a mastery level are given special help.

**How do individual differences influence group functioning?**

*Research on Cooperative Learning.* Investigations on cooperative learning have found that in most cases it has a positive effect on academic achievement. It also increases students' cooperative and altruistic behaviors and students' liking of others. In addition, it can improve race relations and

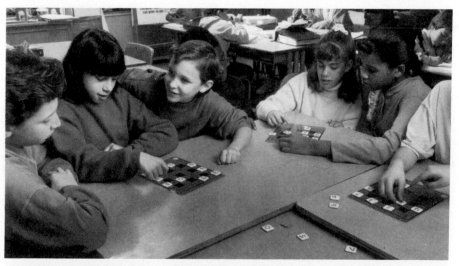

Teaching students how to learn cooperatively can improve their academic achievement, social skills, and concern for others.

the social acceptance of mainstreamed students in regular classrooms (Johnson & Johnson, 1987; Slavin, 1990). On the basis of positive research findings, it appears that cooperative learning can be an effective instructional method for attaining some of your classroom instructional objectives.

*Group Interaction.* Webb (1985; 1987) has reviewed the research on helping behaviors that contribute to successful learning in cooperative groups. She has reported that it is important to differentiate between giving help and receiving help as well as to distinguish between different kinds of help. Help that a student gives to others in his or her group can be categorized as *explanations* or as *terminal help.* Explanations consist of step-by-step descriptions of how to solve a problem or how to correct an error. An example of an explanation given during a unit on scientific notation is "Okay, look. 63,000,000 times 8,5000,000. This is 63 with 6 zeros. So in parentheses, 63 times 10 to the sixth and then times 10 to the fifth . . ." (Webb, 1982, p. 646). Terminal help, on the other hand, consists of brief responses such as "No, that's not right." or "No, I got 45,000,000." The following are findings from Webb's reviews:

- Not all kinds of help are equally effective.
- How often students give and receive help is not important for learning.
- Giving and receiving explanations are beneficial for learning.
- Giving and receiving terminal help are not beneficial for learning.
- Exchanging information is not effective for learning (e.g., "The answer to No. 4 is 36.78" or "That's not right. I got 23.5").
- Receiving no response to one's question is detrimental for learning.
- High-ability students are most likely to give explanations to others.
- Extroverted students are more successful than introverted students in obtaining explanations when they ask questions.
- Boys may be more successful than girls in obtaining help.
- Groups with only students of *medium* ability spend more time explaining, and all students participate in group discussions.
- Heterogeneous groups with a moderate range of ability demonstrate a high level of explaining.
- Groups with only low-ability or high-ability students do little explaining.
- In groups with a wide range of ability, the high-ability students often explain to the low-ability students while ignoring the middle-ability students.
- In groups with equal numbers of boys and girls, all students are able to obtain help when asked.
- In groups where boys outnumber girls or when girls outnumber boys, the boys are more successful than girls in obtaining help.
- In groups of mostly girls, the girls direct many of their questions to the boy, who is not likely to answer all their questions.

- White students tend to be more active and influential in groups than minority students.

Webb (1987) suggests that the teacher who initiates cooperative learning begin by assigning equal numbers of boys and girls to a group, forming groups in which students have "medium" ability or in which there is a moderate range of ability, and avoiding group compositions with only one male or female, or all low- or high-ability students. In addition, students need to be taught when and how to ask for help and how to give help.

Cohen (1982, 1986) has been concerned with improving group interaction in multiracial groups in which white students dominate minority students. This condition is likely to occur even when minority students have more ability than white students. Cohen contributes this behavior to status differences between the two groups of students. The white students talk more often and their suggestions are used more often by the group. In evaluations after group work, the white students are seen as having better ideas and are viewed as the leaders of the group. The problem is that students sometimes act as if race or ethnicity (and sometimes gender) are themselves indicators of competence. Unless someone shows them otherwise, they will tend to use these false indicators to guide their behavior.

While it is often difficult to change students' perceptions of each other, Cohen and her colleagues (see Cohen, 1982) have found some success by altering students' expectations about each other's competence. They gave minority students special training on some tasks and asked them to tutor white students on the task. When groups of white and minority students were formed, the white students no longer dominated the group interaction.

Cohen (1986) also thinks that providing opportunities for all group members to experience different assigned roles may help to change competence expectations held for low-status students. Students are assigned to the roles of facilitator (to see that everyone in the group gets the help she or he needs), checker (to make sure that everyone finishes his or her work), and reporter (to present what the group found during each work session). This approach led to greater interaction among students but did not eliminate the impact of all status influence in the groups.

Be aware of status differences in group interaction. If certain students believe that other students are not capable of helping them, they may not ask for assistance, offer to help them, or even work cooperatively with them. Thus, while educators are excited about the outcomes of cooperative learning, we must realize that simply placing students in groups will not lead to greater learning for all students unless we deal directly with the factors that contribute to unequal or inappropriate group interaction.

Now that I have identified the types of cooperative learning and some of the research supporting its effectiveness, it is important to discuss how

Developing a climate wherein boys and girls interact positively can make cooperative learning more successful.

you can go about *preparing* students for cooperative learning. I have spoken to many teachers who say that they have tried cooperative learning but that it did not work. After further discussion, it was apparent that their students had little experience with and preparation for group learning. Remember that students spend most of their school experiences competing with each other and often find it difficult to abandon their competitive approach to learning. The next Classroom Application section will help you to prepare students for cooperative learning.

## CLASSROOM APPLICATION: PREPARING STUDENTS FOR COOPERATIVE LEARNING

The success of cooperative learning depends a great deal on the ability of students to interact appropriately in group settings. Johnson et al. (1984) identify a number of interpersonal skills necessary for success in cooperative settings.

**Forming**

Forming skills are needed for organizing the group and for establishing minimum norms of appropriate behavior. Such skills include being able to move into and out of groups with a minimum of noise and disruption, working quietly and actively while in the group (i.e., staying on-task), encouraging everyone to participate, and interacting with group members in a courteous way. One of the most important behaviors that teachers need to stress is that put-downs are not a part of effective group functioning.

## Functioning

Functioning skills are the second level of cooperative skills. They involve the managing and implementation of the group's efforts to accomplish tasks and to maintain effective working relationships among members. Such skills include expressing support and acceptance for the contributions of group members, knowing when and how to ask for help or clarification about what is being said or done, offering to explain or clarify another student's position, and motivating the group with new ideas or suggestions when enthusiasm wanes.

## Formulating

Formulating skills are directed at helping students to understand and remember the material being studied in the group. Such skills include encouraging group members to summarize aloud what was covered, adding important information when something is left out of the summary, reviewing important information, and using learning strategies to remember important ideas.

## Fermenting

Fermenting skills are used to stimulate academic controversy so that students will rethink and challenge one another's positions, ideas, and reasoning. Examples of such skills include knowing how to criticize ideas but not people, knowing how to formulate a coherent and defensible position on an issue, and knowing how to probe for and elicit information for arriving at answers and solutions to problems. The major concern at this level is to teach the group members not to stop an investigation when the first solution to a group is presented. Sometimes the first answer or the quickest solution is not the best one. Students need to learn how to stimulate the thinking and intellectual curiosity of group members.

In review, students need to be taught *forming* skills to maintain good classroom management and to ensure that group members develop a positive attitude toward work in the group. The *functioning* skills help the students to interact effectively in the group. *Formulating* skills ensure that the highest quality thinking and decision making are made in the group. Finally, *fermenting* skills, which often are the most difficult to teach, ensure that students learn how to deal with controversy and deal openly with intellectual disagreements.

To teach these skills, Johnson et al. (1984; quoted material from p. 49) suggest the following five steps:

1. *"Ensure that students see the need for the skill."* Some teachers use bulletin boards or posters to identify important group behaviors. These behaviors can be introduced during the first few days of school, when you are introducing students to the rules and procedures in your classroom. Start with a few basic rules of group behavior and discuss their importance with your class.

2. *"Ensure that students understand what the skill is and when it should be used."* Students need to model and practice basic classroom rules (see Chapter 11). Observing appropriate group behavior and having an opportunity to practice the skills are important procedures in learning how to behave appropriately in a group.

3. *"Set up practice situations and encourage mastery of skills."* You can assign and alternate different roles to group members, such as encourager, summarizer, and elaboration seeker, and evaluate with the class how these roles were played in the group. Often students will recommend helpful tips that can be incorporated into the suggested behaviors or procedures for group interaction.

4. *"Ensure that students have the time and the needed procedures for discussing (and receiving feedback on) how well they are using the skill."* You need to help each group evaluate its functioning. One way is to develop a questionnaire with such questions as "Did you feel that you had an opportunity to contribute to the group discussion? Did the group members listen to your contribution? How effective was your group in working toward a solution to the problem?" The answers to such questions can be helpful indicators of the groups' interaction.

5. *"Ensure that the students persevere in practicing the skill until the skill seems a natural action."* Remember that it takes time to learn new skills. Some skills will be learned quickly, whereas others will need constant practice over a long period of time. When the day comes when students can move quickly into their group, begin their task, and interact effectively, you will realize that the time and energy spent teaching appropriate group behaviors and procedures was well worth it. Check the suggested readings list for additional information on working with classroom groups.

## CRITICISMS OF HUMANISTIC EDUCATION

Much of the criticism of humanistic education attacks the belief that students will learn if they are freed from teacher-directed pressure and are allowed to decide what they want to do in the classroom. Skinner (1973) feels that too many educators delude themselves about what constitutes "freedom": Students are not free simply because their teacher chooses not to exert control over their behavior. He states "They [students] then simply come under the control of other conditions, and we must look at those conditions and their effects if we are to improve teaching" (p. 13). The teacher who understands the behavioral process, says Skinner, can help students *learn* to be free and happy. This will occur because students will acquire the knowledge and the skills of productive and creative individuals.

Although a proponent of humanistic education, Kozol (1972), in his book *Free Schools,* points out that some teachers seek to *force* freedom on students. From his vantage point he sees that although conscious, or structured, teaching is not always necessary for learning, it is wrong to assume that learning is *never* the result of conscious teaching. (Carl Rogers's writings about teaching have sometimes been so interpreted.) Kozol maintains that when conscious teaching is necessary but "in the name of Joy and Freedom it is not undertaken," parents whose children fail to learn have good reasons to be disturbed with school and with teachers who have let them down.

Beane (1985/1986) identifies a number of additional criticisms of affective, or humanistic, educational programs. First, there is often an absence of clear direction or purpose. Some affective programs are based on vague goals such as "enhancing self-worth" or "developing the total individual." Investigations of affective programs indicate that there is weak support for their ability to bring about changes in attitude, self-esteem, attitude toward school (Baskin & Hess, 1980; Strein, 1988). Second, there often is a lack of thoroughness in program planning. Many programs are based on short, experiential activities that lack organization and any theoretical orientation to support the approach. As a result, many programs have little impact on students. Third, inadequate measurement and evaluation are used in affective programs. As a result, educators have less understanding of the factors that influence affective behavior and development than they do in the cognitive domain. Finally, there is an inconsistency among components of the affective school program. Many teachers attempt to develop various affective programs so that students can develop their own values and beliefs. However, when these values or beliefs conflict with institutional or community values, some teachers "end up insisting on specific conclusions through gentle coercion or systematic persuasion" (Beane, 1985/1986, p. 29).

More recent writings by the proponents of humanistic education emphasize the successes of cooperative learning and recommend more structure and specific goals for open and moral education. As a result, we may see an increased emphasis on different types of humanistic programs in the 1990s.

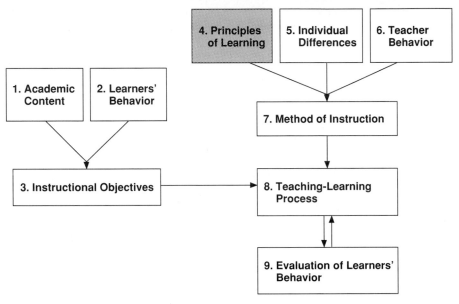

*Source: Adapted from Hunter, 1971, in Allen and Seifman.*

The instructional methods covered in Chapters 6 through 8 were organized by conceptual orientation—behaviorism, cognitivism, and humanism—to untangle better the "pure" assumptions of each theory that underlie common educational procedures. However, the classification of methods under particular theories of learning does not irrevocably wed these methods to one theory. For example, the open classroom is an instructional use of Piaget's cognitive-developmental theory and of humanistic theory. Cooperative learning uses ideas from all three theoretical positions: In cooperative learning, interpersonal relations and positive communication (humanistic goals) are given high priority. In addition, group rewards provide an incentive for group members to help each other, and individual accountability can be achieved by calculating group scores based on individual achievement (behavioral principles). Finally, group members must identify their task and select appropriate learning strategies to achieve their objectives (cognitive principles). My point is that some teaching methods can be used simultaneously for different objectives and can be claimed by more than one theoretical position.

In analyzing learning theories and instructional applications, one must be careful not to make simplistic or incorrect distinctions among them. For example, one of my students attempted to summarize the differences between humanism and behaviorism as follows: "The humanists are the 'good' guys, who are concerned about students, while the behaviorists are the 'bad' guys, who are more interested in technology and control than in understanding people." Behaviorists would take issue with this conceptualization by pointing out that they are not against a teacher's being warm and friendly and that they are strongly people-oriented. However, they do not believe that these characteristics are sufficient for effective instruction. Likewise, although humanists are less interested than behaviorists in the sequencing of content for instruction, they are not necessarily opposed to planning and using specific teaching techniques.

A great deal of research has focused on the effectiveness of various types of instruction. One of the major issues in the literature deals with the effectiveness of direct, or structured, methods of instruction versus unstructured, or open, methods. The research findings indicate that, in general, direct instruction is superior to unstructured methods for producing mastery of basic skills (Brophy, 1979; Good, 1979). However, mastering basic skills should not be the only objective in the classroom. When the educational goals are to promote cooperation, positive attitudes toward the subject area, and personal development, direct instruction may *not* be the best approach. Unstructured teaching methods can be effective in helping students to attain many educational objectives. For example, Peterson (1979) found that open teaching was somewhat more effective in developing independence and curiosity among students than was structured teaching. This does not mean that unstructured methods are the only way to attain affective goals. The research on mastery learning and other forms of individualized instruction indicate that positive affective outcomes also can be achieved through structured methods of teaching.

Humanistic psychologists are more closely aligned with cognitive psychologists in their view of the teacher as a facilitator or mediator of learning than they are with behavioral psychologists, who view the teacher more as a director or manager of learning. One of the implications of using various teaching methods is to realize that diverse teacher behaviors often are necessary to implement various methods of instruction successfully.

Teachers have different belief and value systems regarding methods of classroom organization and instruction. For example, some teachers believe that socialization outcomes are as important for younger children as are cognitive outcomes. As a result, these teachers tend to emphasize more affective outcomes and teach differently from teachers with other belief systems (Good & Brophy, 1990).

Prawat and Nickerson (1985) investigated the question whether teachers with a stronger affective orientation actually produce more or greater affective outcomes. If teachers stress interpersonal relationships, will their students develop differently from other students in classrooms in which these affective characteristics are less emphasized?

Prawat and Nickerson identified teachers to represent three different types: affective, cognitive, or mixed (a balance of cognitive and affective). They found that positive affect was *not* more evident in classrooms in which teachers placed more emphasis on affective outcomes than it was in classrooms in which teachers stressed more traditional cognitive outcomes. In fact, high-affective teachers were less successful than mixed teachers in producing affective growth. The researchers argue that valuing affect to the exclusion of cognitive goals may be counterproductive for both affective and cognitive growth. The investigation also showed that successful co-operative behavior was more likely to occur when the teacher provided direction as to the purpose and function of cooperative behavior.

In addition to the teacher's belief system, instructional objectives and information about individual differences should guide you in making decisions about methods of instruction. For example, Friedlander (1975) points out that although an unstructured environment may be beneficial for some students, it may be extremely threatening and anxiety-producing to students who have a low tolerance for ambiguity and uncertainty.

In summary, humanistic principles can make important contributions to learning in any classroom. Personally, I do not go as far as some proponents of humanistic education in the belief that all one has to do is create a humanistic climate and children will learn. The research simply does not support this contention. There are times when teacher direction is a necessary part of instruction.

## KEY POINTS

1. Humanistic educators value educational goals that help students to learn more about themselves, relate to others, and make independent decisions. They prefer learning situations that are student-centered and oriented toward discovery methods of teaching and learning.
2. Humanistic psychologists are concerned with individuals' feelings and perceptions as clues to their actions.
3. Humanistic psychologists believe that persons determine their own behavior.
4. Humanistic psychologists identify two parts in learning: the acquisition of new information and the individual's personalization of this information.
5. Combs believes that the way individuals perceive their actions is the key to understanding their behavior. In addition, the closer to themselves individuals perceive events to be, the more likely it is that they will react to those events.
6. Maslow sees a person's motivational tendency as moving toward self-actualization, or self-fulfillment. He places the satisfaction of lower-order needs such as food and safety before people's motivation to develop their individuality or to realize their potential.
7. Rogers believes that individuals have a desire to learn and are more likely to learn when they perceive that the learning is relevant to their own needs and purposes and when it is self-initiated. He points out that threat can diminish learning.
8. Rogers points out that the teacher's role as a facilitator of learning can

be enhanced if the teacher is real or genuine with students, displays trust or confidence in students' potential for self-actualization, and communicates empathic understanding.

9. Recent changes in society require that the school assume more responsibility for character development, which includes training both for citizenship and for personal adjustment.

10. An important issue in moral/character education is the effectiveness of direct and indirect approaches.

11. Values clarification aids students in examining their value system so that they can arrive at better decisions.

12. Kohlberg's stages of moral reasoning can be used to classify individuals' responses to moral dilemmas into one of six stages representing different ways of thinking about moral issues.

13. Open education gives students freedom to select their activities and encourages the teacher to act more as an assistant or facilitator of learning than as one who possesses all the knowledge.

14. Open classrooms are moderately more successful in attaining affective goals (e.g., cooperation and independence) than traditional classrooms. However, on measures of academic achievement, traditional classrooms are superior.

15. Cooperative learning can have a positive effect on student achievement and interpersonal relations.

16. Students need to be prepared to work effectively in cooperative groups.

17. The most beneficial behavior in small groups is giving and receiving explanations.

18. Teachers should consider gender, ability, and racial or ethnic differences when forming groups, since these characteristics can influence students' perceptions and behavior in the group.

## KEY TERMS

open education, p. 322
hierarchy of needs, p. 325
self-actualization, p. 326
person-centered education, p. 328
empathic understanding, p. 330
values clarification, p. 333
Kohlberg's stages of moral reasoning, p. 334
moral dilemmas, p. 336
jigsaw method, p. 348

## SUGGESTIONS FOR FURTHER READING

The following books provide detailed discussions by some of the major humanistic theorists:

Combs, A. W., & Avila, D. L. (1985). *Helping relationships: Basic concepts for the helping professions.* (3rd ed.). Boston: Allyn & Bacon.

Maslow, A. (1962). *Toward a psychology of being.* New York: Van Nostrand.

Rogers, C. R. (1983). *Freedom to learn for the 80's.* Columbus, OH: Merrill.

Simpson, E. L. (1976). *Humanistic education: An interpretation.* Cambridge, MA: Ballinger. Defines humanistic education and presents numerous examples of classroom practices.

Read the following references for specific information on the open classroom:

Blitz, B. (1973). *The open classroom: Making it work.* Boston: Allyn & Bacon.

Stephens, L. S. (1974). *The teacher's guide to open education.* New York: Holt, Rinehart and Winston.

These books are helpful in implementing cooperative learning in the classroom:

Cohen, E. G. (1986). *Designing groupwork: Strategies for the heterogeneous classroom.* New York: Teachers College Press.

Johnson, D. W., & Johnson, R. T. (1987). *Joining together: Group theory and group skills* (3rd ed.). Englewood Cliffs, NJ: Prentice-Hall. Includes exercises to develop collaborative skills among group members.

Johnson, D. W., & Johnson, R. T. (1987). *Learning together and alone: Cooperation, competition, and individualization.* (2nd ed.). Englewood Cliffs, NJ: Prentice-Hall.

Johnson, D. W., Johnson, R. T., Holubec, E. J., & Roy, P. (1986). *Circles of learning: Cooperation in the classroom* (rev. ed.). Alexandria, VA: Association for Supervision and Curriculum Development.

Johnson, R. T., Johnson, D. W., & Holubec, E. (Eds.). (1987). *Structuring cooperative learning: Lesson plans for teachers.* Edina, MN: Interaction.

Slavin, R. E. (1978). *Using student team learning.* Baltimore: Johns Hopkins University Press.

Slavin, R. E. (1990). *Cooperative learning: Theory, research, and practice.* Englewood Cliffs, NJ: Prentice-Hall.

## FOLLOW-UP ACTIVITIES

_____ 1. **Remember Your Teachers**

Select a teacher you had who used humanistic principles in interacting with students and another whose behavior tended toward the opposite continuum. How successful were they in motivating and gaining respect from students, attaining educational objectives, and encouraging independent learning?

_____ 2. **Think about the School's Role in Teaching Values**

Select one of the following statements that comes closest to your point of view, and defend the reasons why you support the statement:

    a. The schools should help students to develop their own value system through the process of continuous questioning of beliefs. Through this process, students will develop their own value system and become productive and caring citizens.

    b. Our society is based on a number of fundamental values. If we want our society to flourish, it is important that the schools teach specific values. If the schools take a position that one value is as good as another, the public will continue to witness inappropriate and destructive behavior among its citizens.

### 3. Use a Method of Cooperative Learning

Review the various methods of cooperative learning, and consult the Suggestions for Further Reading list for additional information. Describe how you can use cooperative learning for a unit of instruction lasting two weeks on some topic in your teaching specialty (see example of a lesson plan in Chapter 9).

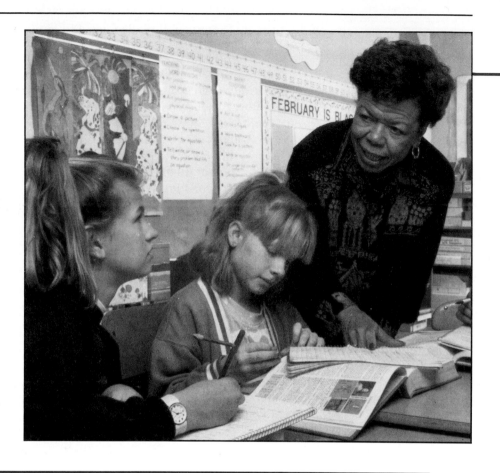

# PART THREE

# Preparing for Effective Teaching

## PART OVERVIEW

Thus far we have discussed development and individual differences, and learning and instruction. The principles of learning in Part Two of this book will be applied to help you make decisions about instructional planning (Chapter 9), motivation (Chapter 10), and classroom management and discipline (Chapter 11). As I mentioned in Chapter 1, these topics are among the major problems that arise in the classroom (Veenman, 1984). My goal in this section of the book is to help you acquire relevant *knowledge* about effective teaching strategies and develop the *competencies* to perform successfully in the classroom.

Put yourself in the role of teacher for a moment and identify some of the thoughts you may have about working with 30 or more students: "Am I sufficiently prepared for the students? Do I know what I want to teach? How should I teach the lesson? What do I do if they are not motivated to learn? What can I do to change their motivation? Will they listen to me? How should I manage the classroom? Should I act tough or be nice? How should I handle discipline problems?" These are just a few of the many concerns that a teacher could raise about classroom instruction. I am sure that you could expand this short list to include many more concerns.

As teachers gain both the knowledge and competencies to deal with instructional issues, they learn how student characteristics influence their decision making. The answers to many of these questions depend on the abilities, interests, attitudes, and goals of the students in their classes. Thus I would like you to review material on development and individual differences as you read the next three chapters.

# CHAPTER 9

## Planning for Instruction

**CLASSROOM APPLICATION: DEVELOPING A LESSON PLAN USING DISCOVERY LEARNING**
Cooperative Learning
**CLASSROOM APPLICATION: DEVELOPING A LESSON PLAN USING COOPERATIVE LEARNING**

## ORIENTATION

From time to time, you have probably gone for a drive in your car with no particular destination in mind. Sometimes you wind up in unexpected places! Taking some college courses can be a similar experience. I am sure that at times during your college career you have asked the following questions: "Where is this instructor taking me? What is this class about? What am I supposed to be learning in this class?" One important aspect of a teacher's decision making is, first, to determine what is to be learned and, then, to communicate this information to the students. To accomplish this task, the teacher must take the time to plan for instruction.

All individuals who want to become competent in their chosen field of specialization spend time planning their work-related tasks. For example, can you imagine a defense attorney beginning a trial without studying the evidence against the client or without selecting a defense strategy? Can you imagine a surgeon beginning an operation without having studied the patient's X rays? Does a football coach send a team out to play without a game plan? Competent individuals in any area realize that if they do not take the time to plan, the results will be ineffective or disastrous (Jacobsen, Eggen, & Kauchak, 1989).

Although ineffective planning in teaching does not usually lead to immediate life-and-death situations, it can ultimately lead to disastrous classroom experiences for both the teacher and the students. Effective planning in teaching involves formulating a course of action for implementing instruction over the school year, semester, month, day, and lesson (Clark & Peterson, 1985). Although planning does not always ensure success, it can help to increase the probability of success. Think about some of your present professors or the teachers you had in elementary and high school. Can you identify differences in their teaching that may have been related to their planning for class? Some instructors do get by without spending much time planning for instruction. Many of them simply follow the textbook and use as test material duplicated sheets that students complete by finding the answers to rote questions from the material in the textbook.

It is not always easy for a student to determine on a daily basis whether an instructor is prepared to teach. Some instructors learn how to "wing it," or get by when they are not prepared. For example, it is often difficult to determine whether the instructor who asks, "What do you want to talk about today?" actually has a lesson plan to teach a particular idea or simply has not prepared any lesson for the day.

After you master the material in this chapter, you will be able to:

- Write behavioral objectives using the Taxonomy of Educational Objectives.
- Construct a task analysis.
- Develop unit lesson plans.
- Develop daily lesson plans for direct instruction, cooperative learning, and discovery learning.
- Establish homework policy.

## FOCUS QUESTIONS

1. How does a teacher decide what should be taught?
2. What are the alternative approaches in writing objectives?
3. What are the advantages and disadvantages of using behavioral objectives?
4. What is the difference between the organization of the cognitive and affective domains in the Taxonomy of Educational Objectives?
5. How do a unit and a daily lesson plan relate to each other?
6. When and for what purpose would you use direct instruction, discovery learning, and cooperative learning lessons?
7. What factors should a teacher or school consider in devising guidelines for a homework policy?

## WHAT SHOULD STUDENTS LEARN IN SCHOOL?

**How does a teacher decide what should be taught?**

Before you can decide how to teach, you must determine what to teach, or the goals of instruction. Instructional goals come from several sources—the student, society, and academic discipline (Jacobsen, Eggen, & Kauchak, 1989). The student as a source of goals derives partly from the concern that the school can help the student grow emotionally, intellectually, and physically. Special attention is given to the developmental level of the student. Objectives focusing on health to help students understand their bodies and the importance of proper nutrition in the diet are an example of the school's concern for the optimal development of the student. As you learned in Chapter 8, proponents of humanistic education stress the importance of such personal and social development as self-esteem, positive attitudes toward academic tasks and school, clarification of values, and positive interaction with peers.

Another approach to determining educational goals is to examine the society in which the student lives and to see how the school can best help the student function in that society. Helping students to become better consumers by learning how to balance checkbooks and to calculate the costs of interest on loans is an example of a goal that has society as its source. Many states include in their graduation requirements a number of "survival" competencies that all students must master in addition to their basic academic requirements.

Finally, the academic disciplines can be analyzed to determine which knowledge is most important to understanding the content areas presented at various grade levels. Educators who believe that the major focus of the school's goals should derive from the disciplines emphasize a curriculum based on subject matter that has stood the test of time rather than a curriculum designed to help students adjust to society. For example, emphasis on the classic books and the history of civilization derives from a discipline or subject matter orientation to instructional goals.

Although an individual can be a proponent of one of the sources of goals, it is still possible to focus on more than one source in developing a balanced educational program. The teacher must interpret the importance of each of the sources and make decisions about the focus of instruction in the classroom. Not all educators agree as to the importance of different type of objectives.

## SPECIFICITY OF EDUCATIONAL OBJECTIVES

Learning goals are generally expressed in terms of educational objectives written at different levels of specificity for various purposes. At one level are general objectives describing long-range projections for the direction of education on a local, state, or national level. These objectives are usually formulated by special committees or commissions studying the aims and goals of education. For example, *Central Purposes of American Education* (National Education Association, 1961) included a discussion of general educational objectives, and *Academic Preparation for College* (National Education Association, 1983) identified basic competencies for various academic areas. In addition, specific objectives were included for each of the basic competencies. This list provided a useful set of criteria by which to judge various aspects of any high school curriculum. The first report outlined goals in phrases similar to the following: "to develop better citizens," "to foster creative ability," and "to promote our cultural ideals." These statements provide us with the philosophical guidance for determining the nature of the curriculum in our schools. The second report provided more specific competencies that need to be developed. These specific competencies are explicit *instructional objectives* (sometimes called *performance objectives*, or **behavioral objectives**)—precise statements of what the student will be able to *do* as a result of instruction. They are stated in terms of behaviors that can be observed and measured to determine whether the objectives have been attained. The objectives in Table 9.1 are examples.

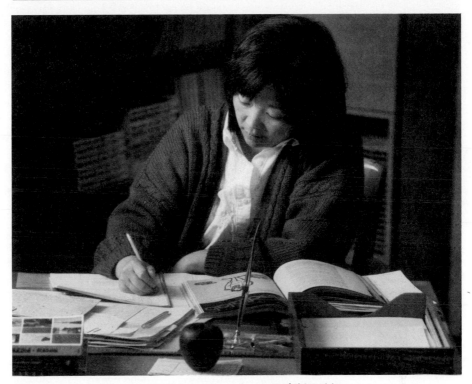

Effective planning is an essential step toward successful teaching.

Some objectives do not fit neatly into either the general or explicit instructional objective category and are placed at different levels between the two. Table 9.1 provides examples of three types and levels of objectives. It would not be difficult to add additional levels of implicit objectives to this schema.

**What are the alternative approaches in writing objectives?**

One crucial issue in instructional planning is the specificity of educational objectives—the teacher's determination of precise goals for a lesson, unit, or course. Some teachers do not feel that it is necessary to identify all outcomes of a lesson before starting to teach, or they are satisfied with general descriptions of learning outcomes (implicit objectives). At the opposite end of the continuum are teachers who believe that all outcomes must be stated in behavioral terms that identify specific performances the students are to exhibit at the end of the lesson (explicit objectives). Many educators support explicit instructional objectives because such objectives aid in teaching, learning, and evaluation (Gronlund, 1985b; Popham & Baker, 1970).

**TABLE 9.1  SEQUENTIAL EXAMPLES OF EDUCATIONAL, IMPLICIT INSTRUCTIONAL, AND EXPLICIT INSTRUCTIONAL OBJECTIVES**

| Type and Level of Objective | Examples |
| --- | --- |
| Educational Objectives | The student should be able to read well. |
| | The student should be able to spell correctly. |
| | The student should know about American history. |
| | The student should understand addition. |
| Implicit Instructional Objectives | The student will learn how to read with comprehension. |
| | The student will develop appropriate spelling skills. |
| | The student will learn about the American Revolution. |
| | The student will know how to solve addition problems. |
| Explicit Instructional (Behavioral or Performance) Objectives | Given a brief paragraph from a newspaper article, the student will be able to identify the main idea. |
| | Given a list of 20 incorrectly spelled words, the student will be able to identify and correct the misspelled words with 90% accuracy. |
| | The student will be able to list 5 American Revolutionary heroes and describe their respective roles in history. |
| | Given 10 addition problems involving pairs of 3-digit numbers, the student will be able to calculate the correct answer with 85% accuracy. |

## CLASSROOM APPLICATION: WRITING INSTRUCTIONAL OBJECTIVES

There are a number of ways to write instructional objectives. The instructional objectives in Table 9.1 include one approach, recommended by Mager (1978), that uses three major components:

1. The *behavioral term* expressing the type of task required by the student ("write," "list," "solve").
2. The *situation*, or *condition*, under which the behavior is to be performed ("given a reference manual," "without the aid of references," "without the use of tables or a slide rule").
3. The *criterion*, or *level of performance*, that will be used to evaluate the success of the performance or product ("no grammatical or spelling errors," "at least five major steps, 90%").

### The Behavioral Term

The most important component of an instructional objective is the specific term that describes the observable act the student is to perform.

This description is in the form of an action verb. Mager (1978) states that many ambiguous words used in writing objectives are open to a wide range of interpretations. Following is a list of words that express outcomes. The words in the left-hand column are ambiguous and can be interpreted in many ways; the words in the right-hand column are open to fewer interpretations.

| Ambiguous | Precise |
|---|---|
| to know | to write |
| to understand | to recite |
| to really understand | to identify |
| to appreciate | to differentiate |
| to fully appreciate | to solve |
| to grasp the significance of | to construct |
| to enjoy | to list |
| to believe | to compare |
| to have faith in | to contrast |

What do teachers mean when they state that they want students to "know" something? Do they want the students to remember certain information, to solve problems, to create new ideas? To "know" can mean many things. The same holds true for such words as "appreciate" or "grasp the significance of." How do we determine whether students appreciate or grasp the significance of some information or value? Until we describe specifically what the students will be *doing* to demonstrate that they "appreciate" or "grasp the significance of," we really do not know exactly what the student is to learn from the experience. The more we use words similar to those in the right-hand column of the foregoing list, the more we communicate to the students the exact behavior expected of them. The following statements provide concise information on student outcomes:

- The student *presents* an impromptu speech.
- The student *draws* a diagram of the combustion engine.
- The student *writes* the name of each of the states in the United States.

### The Situation, or Condition

The important aspect of this component is to describe the "givens," limitations, or restrictions that are imposed on students as they strive for the learning outcome. Following are examples of some conditions that narrow the focus of instructional objectives:

- Given a map of the United States
- Without the use of notes
- After reading Chapter 4 in the textbook
- After viewing *Hamlet*

## The Criterion, or Level of Performance

This component is a statement of the minimal level of performance that will be accepted as evidence that the learner has achieved the objective. The following are some levels of performance that further delineate an instructional objective:

- All four steps stated in the textbook
- Without an error
- At least 90% correct
- Must include three of the four reasons
- Must be correct to the nearest percentage point
- Must be completed within 30 minutes

Now try to write an instructional objective for teaching students to determine the area of a square. The exact wording will vary, but you should have written something like the following: "Given a square with the length of one side marked, the student will determine its area using the formula $A = s^2$."

Try writing another objective for teaching students the correct use of colons in writing. (Don't read on until you have written the objective.) You should have written something like the following: "Given a set of rules for the use of colons and a set of sentences that require colon insertion, the students will place each colon properly without any errors."

The following are additional examples of instructional objectives in different subject areas:

*Science*: Given a diagram of a cell, the student will be able to identify the major components of the cell and state their functions.
*Geography*: Given a map of the United States, the student will be able to locate and name each of the original thirteen colonies.
*French*: After studying Chapter 1, the student will be able to conjugate the verb *avoir*.

## An Alternative Approach to Writing Instructional Objectives

Some educators believe that it is not always necessary to describe the situation or condition for every objective, especially if a unit of instruction is based on material from a textbook. Also, sometimes the explicit statement of the criterion can be difficult to determine and often appears artificial. Gronlund (1985b) believes that the three components of behavioral objectives described in the preceding sections—situation, performance, and criterion—can result in long, cumbersome lists of objectives that restrict the freedom of teachers. Instead, Gronlund recommends that teachers should first state the general instructional objective and then clarify the objective by listing a *sample* of the specific types of student performance they are willing to accept as evidence of the attainment of that objective. The following is an example of this procedure (Gronlund, 1985b):

1. Understands the meaning of technical terms.
   1.1 Defines the term in own words.
   1.2 Identifies the meaning of the term when used in context.
   1.3 Distinguishes between terms that are similar in meaning. (p. 5)

The objective, "Given a drawing of a flower, the student will label in writing at least four of the five parts shown," can be restated as, "Identifies the parts of a given plant structure." In the restated objective, teachers would be free to use real plants, pictures, diagrams, or slides. Also, the students could respond orally, in writing, or by pointing to a specific part of the flower. Last, because the specific standard or criterion is not stated, teachers can vary the standard without rewriting the objective. Teachers may want to have different standards for different groups of children or have lower standards at the beginning of a unit and higher standards at the end of the unit. In summary, if objectives are to help teachers plan for instruction, then any system that helps teachers while reducing the amount of work needed to write objectives should be carefully considered. Take time to try different systems until you feel comfortable with some method.

## THE VALUE OF INSTRUCTIONAL OBJECTIVES

Proponents of instructional objectives believe that they enable teachers to know exactly what student behavior is desired upon the completion of a lesson. Teachers are then in a better position to select appropriate teaching methods for the designated student outcome. Knowing the type of expected outcome is important in making decisions that will help to direct students to that outcome.

Instructional objectives help teachers during evaluation, because the teachers can construct test questions directly from their objectives. Constructing tests in this manner takes the guesswork out of the evaluation process.

Finally, there is evidence to suggest that if teachers initially give students the objectives of a lesson or course, the students will spend more time focusing on the designated outcomes (Hamaker, 1986; Mayer, 1987). Hamilton (1985) reviewed studies that investigated the use of different degrees of explicit objectives as an aid to prose learning (e.g., objectives before the presentation of reading material). He found that the different forms of objective had important effects on the retention of verbal information. The implication of his findings is that it may not matter how objectives are written so long as they identify the information to be learned.

## Can Teachers Plan for Instruction without Using Objectives?

When objectives were first introduced in education, many proponents argued that *all* teaching goals should be translated into explicit objectives. In rethinking the role of objectives, some educators have raised questions about the need for precision in stating every objective. It may not be necessary to develop long lists of objectives for each unit of instruction. Gage and Berliner (1988) believe that objectives should act as a road map. They state: "And just like a road map, to be useful, need not specify every town and creek, so objectives for a unit of instruction need not specify every change in student behavior" (p. 40).

Some educators argue that the use of instructional objectives can lead to emphasizing outcomes that can be easily measured and that unanticipated outcomes in education are often the most important. The proponents of instructional objectives respond that teachers can be trained to write objectives at higher levels of thinking. In response to the issue of the importance of unanticipated outcomes, some proponents point out that they do not believe that every outcome of instruction must be specified in advance. However, the decision to spend time in unplanned activities or discussions can better be made if the teacher has some specific objectives in mind. The alternative to not having any objectives is constant wandering throughout the curriculum.

Eisner (1969), one of the critics of the behavioral objectives movement, argues for the legitimacy of what he calls **expressive objectives**. According to Eisner, an expressive objective

> identifies a situation in which children are to work; a problem in which they are to cope; a problem in which they are to engage; but it does not specify what from that encounter, situation, problem, or task they are to learn. An expressive objective provides both the teacher and the student with an invitation to explore, defer, or focus on issues that are of particular interest or import to the inquirer. (pp. 15–16)

A teacher who wants to take a class to the zoo for no purpose other than to allow the students to explore the environment knows that each student will achieve different learning outcomes from the experience. In this situation, the teacher is more concerned with an expressive objective than with an instructional objective.

There is some empirical support for Eisner's concern that activities be considered as a legitimate form of planning (see Borko & Shavelson, 1989, for a review of this literature). For example, Zahorik (1975) asked teachers to list in writing the decisions they made prior to teaching and to indicate the order in which they made them. He found that teachers made decisions about objectives, content, pupil activities, materials, diagnosis, evaluation, instruction, and organization. Most important, he found that the type of decision mentioned by the largest number of teachers (81 percent) concerned pupil activities. This was followed by content (51 percent) and learning objectives (28 percent). Other researchers (e.g., Goodlad & Klein, 1970; Peterson, Marx, & Clark, 1978) have reported similar findings. The results of these investigations indicate that many experienced teachers do not use instructional objectives in planning! Although researchers have reported planning strategies used by classroom teachers that do not involve instructional objectives (see Clark & Peterson, 1985), there is no evidence to indicate that more effective teaching results from these alternative strategies.

At this time, you may be thinking: "If many experienced teachers do not use objectives in planning, why am I reading this material?" I have three responses to this question:

**What are the advantages and disadvantages of using behavioral objectives?**

1. On the basis of research evidence, planning by objectives is one approach that can help teachers and students.
2. Although I realize that planning by objectives is not the only approach—and may not even be the best approach—educational psychologists have not adequately prescribed alternative approaches.
3. Beginning teachers need a formalized method of planning as a point of departure. They then can develop alternative strategies as they experiment with various procedures.

This is my position. You should discuss this controversial issue with other educators to gain more insight into the various points of view regarding the use of objectives. Try using them in planning lessons, and evaluate their effectiveness. Then you will be able to draw your own conclusions about their usefulness.

## DEVELOPING OBJECTIVES FOR INSTRUCTION

Before you decide what you are going to teach, you should consider three major variables—information about the major goals of the instructional program at the school, the content to be included in your course, and the entry level of your students. Most school districts publish lists of educational goals for students. These goals often are translated into more specific goals and objectives for students at different grade levels and in different courses in documents called *curriculum guides*. These guides are helpful in long-term and lesson planning. Decisions about the course content will depend on your knowledge of the subject area and the textbooks used. In addition, your colleagues can be a useful resource as you begin the process of developing your own courses.

As you are selecting major course goals and selecting content related to these goals, you must also consider the students' abilities, knowledge, and motivation. Ascertaining an individual's entry behavior and teaching that person accordingly is one of the most important factors in effective instruction. It is possible to generate lists of objectives for a course without considering what the students already know. But what good is it to develop objectives if students do not have the necessary skills or knowledge to strive for those objectives? In such situations, it is better to establish objectives at a lower level of difficulty—objectives that the students can reach within a reasonable time.

## Academic Content

*Type of Learning.* Academic content provides important raw material for developing implicit or explicit instructional objectives. There are a number of ways in which to view academic content. The first is the type of learning involved. In Chapter 7 you learned about the difference between declarative and procedural learning. Teaching a student to follow certain procedures in solving mathematical or scientific problems involves a different type of planning and instruction from teaching a student basic concepts in these academic areas.

*Level of Difficulty.* Another way to view subject matter is in terms of its level of difficulty. Students must be able to count before they can add; they must be able to add before they can multiply. Reading a paragraph depends upon reading a sentence, which depends upon understanding the meaning of words, which depends upon identifying letters. Identifying the subskills according to a hierarchy is called *task analysis*. The outline of the subskills is an important aspect of planning the order of content in a lesson because without this planned sequence the teacher may omit important knowledge and leave students confused.

R. M. (Gagné (1977, 1985) has contributed a great deal to the theory and research on task analysis. He arranges types of learning in a hierarchy of relationships based on the assumption that the higher levels of learning depend on the lower levels. Each type of learning is distinguished from the others primarily by the conditions required for the specific learning.

Gagné stresses the importance of developing a task analysis *before* beginning instruction. This prepares students for learning something new after they have acquired the necessary capabilities. Higher-order skills or capabilities, like problem solving, are more easily learned if the student has a foundation of lower, or subordinate, capabilities.

## CLASSROOM APPLICATION: COMPLETING A TASK ANALYSIS

In completing a task analysis, a teacher should ask: "What is it I want my students to do? What do they need to know to do it?" Once the terminal objective emerges, the teacher works backward to delineate which capabilities students must possess to reach the terminal objective. Remember that some students in the class will need more time on certain subskills, whereas others can skip one or more of the subskills. Take the following steps to complete a task analysis:

1. State the learning task or objective in behavioral terms.
2. Break the task down into prerequisite skills or subtasks.
3. Determine the relationship between the prerequisite skills and the logical order in which they should be learned.
4. Determine procedures for teaching each of the subtasks.
5. Provide feedback to the students about their performance as each of the subtasks and the final objective are achieved.

Let's take a concrete example to illustrate the importance of knowing the subskills involved in teaching a task: "The student will divide any real numbers (including decimal fractions) up to four digits with 90 percent accuracy when presented in the form NN.N $\overline{)ddd.d}$" (Packard, 1975, p. 224).

1. The first step is to move the decimal point to the proper place.

$$15.2 \overline{)1862.4}$$

2. Then the student estimates the first digit of the quotient and writes the number above the line and the appropriate digit.

$$152 \overline{)18624}^{\,1}$$

3. The third step is to multiply the divisor by the estimated quotient (1 x 152) and write the product below the problem, as shown here.

$$
\begin{array}{r}
1\phantom{8624} \\
152 \overline{)18624} \\
\underline{152}\phantom{624}
\end{array}
$$

4. Then the student subtracts the product from part of the quotient and enters the difference below these numbers.

$$
\begin{array}{r}
1\phantom{8624} \\
152 \overline{)18624} \\
\underline{152}\phantom{624} \\
34\phantom{624}
\end{array}
$$

5. The fifth step is to "bring down" the next digit in the number being divided.

$$
\begin{array}{r}
1\phantom{8624} \\
152 \overline{)18624} \\
\underline{152}\phantom{624} \\
342\phantom{24}
\end{array}
$$

After Step 5 the student recommences the procedure of estimating a digit of the answer and repeating the process of multiplying and subtracting until the desired degree of accuracy is reached.

This outline presumes that the student can discriminate numbers, subtract, and divide. These behaviors are part of the student's entering abilities. If they are not, they will have to be taught before the student can successfully attain the objective. Teachers often overlook important subskills in their teaching and, as a result, find that their students have difficulty meeting requirements.

In many subject areas, subskills cannot be taught at random; some of them are prerequisite to others. In the division problem, addition and subtraction must be taught before multiplication. However, teaching the student to adjust the decimal point or to bring down another number from the quotient can take place at any time because none of the other skills depends on either.

Developing a task analysis for lessons takes practice. In the process you must estimate the students' entry behavior. If you know which skills they have already mastered before instruction, you will not have to teach them these skills. Sometimes teachers find that their task analysis is not detailed enough because they erroneously assumed that students had certain entry behavior. By pretesting and making modifications in the original task analysis, they can develop a better instructional sequence. In analyzing the total task, Packard (1975) suggests, "you decide, on the basis of what you already know about the students, what skills they probably already have, categorizing these as entry or prerequisite behaviors. Then you categorize all the other component skills as intermediate objectives leading to your terminal objective" (p. 230). Another example of a task analysis is presented in Figure 9.1.

### Cautions about Using Task Analysis

Not all learning theorists believe that the foregoing approach to developing a task analysis can guide instruction in a systematic and hierarchical fashion in all subject areas. Instructional objectives in areas that are less structured, such as literature and social studies, do not lend themselves as easily to a highly structured and sequential approach to learning. Another issue revolves around the belief that learning is more likely to occur when instruction is global, or holistic, rather than reductionistic (i.e., broken down into small parts). This latter issue is an important distinction between many behavioral (Chapter 6) and cognitive (Chapter 7) approaches to instruction. There are other approaches to task analysis (e.g., Klausmeier, 1976; Merrill, 1983; Reigeluth & Stein, 1983) and sequencing of instruction (Patten, Chao, & Reigeluth, 1986) that the interested reader may want to investigate.

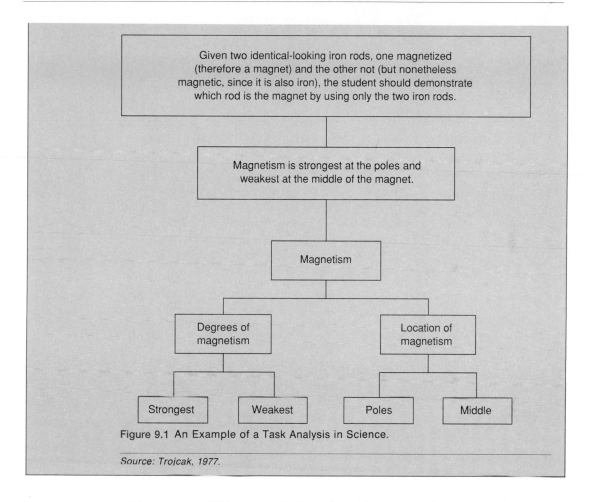

Figure 9.1 An Example of a Task Analysis in Science.

*Source: Trojcak, 1977.*

**What is the difference between the organization of the cognitive and affective domains in the Taxonomy of Educational Objectives?**

*A Taxonomy of Educational Objectives.* The second dimension of academic content is the dimension of complexity. One of the most helpful guides in selecting and defining objectives on this continuum is the **Taxonomy of Educational Objectives**, a classification system devised by Bloom and comprising two handbooks. The handbook on the **cognitive domain** (Bloom et al., 1956) classifies objectives involving intellectual tasks; the handbook on the **affective domain** (Krathwohl, Bloom, & Masia, 1964) classifies objectives involving attitudes, values, and interests. Each of the taxonomies organizes objectives into a hierarchical framework of behaviors that are more complex or internalized than the previous category (see Tables 9.2 and 9.3).

In the cognitive domain, the categories are arranged along a continuum from simple to more complex: knowledge, comprehension, application, analysis, synthesis, and evaluation. In the affective domain, the continuum is based on the degree of internalization that each behavior exhibits. That is, the classification begins with an attitude or value from the level of aware-ness, proceeding to the point at which it guides or directs a person's ac-tions: receiving, responding, valuing, organizing, and characterizing a value or value complex.

## CLASSROOM APPLICATION: USING THE TAXONOMY OF EDUCATIONAL OBJECTIVES

Tables 9.2 and 9.3 include brief definitions of each of the major categories in the cognitive and affective domains, examples of instructional objec-tives, and behavioral terms (action verbs) for writing objectives at var-ious levels of the domains. A more detailed treatment of the various categories and their subcategories appears in the taxonomy handbooks with illustrative examples and test questions.

TABLE 9.2 MAJOR CATEGORIES IN THE COGNITIVE DOMAIN OF THE TAXONOMY OF EDUCATIONAL OBJECTIVES

| Categories | Illustrative Behavioral Terms |
|---|---|
| 1. *Knowledge:* The ability to recall previously learned information. Knowledge typically in-volves the memorization of facts and is con-sidered to represent the lowest level of objec-tives in the taxonomy. *Example:* Recalling the rhyming patterns of standard sonnet forms. | *list, define, identify, recall, name, recognize* |
| 2. *Comprehension:* The ability to understand the meaning of learned information. *Example:* Interpreting the meaning of a sonnet. | *predict, interpret, explain, summa-rize, estimate, evaluate* |
| 3. *Application:* The ability to use learned infor-mation in a novel situation. *Example:* Identifying the components of a given limerick. | *demonstrate, explain, solve, calcu-late, identify, infer, use, apply* |
| 4. *Analysis:* The ability to separate material into its component parts for the purpose of under-standing its organizational structure. *Example:* Discriminating between the styles of two poets. | *distinguish, discriminate, catego-rize, outline, identify, separate* |
| 5. *Synthesis:* The ability to combine component parts into a new structure. *Example:* Composing a poem. | *create, design, organize, derive, for-mulate, compose, write* |
| 6. *Evaluation:* The ability to judge the value of ma-terial according to specified criteria. *Example:* Critiquing a poem. | *criticize, examine, judge, compare, contrast, conclude, critique* |

*Source: Bloom et al., 1956.*

TABLE 9.3 MAJOR CATEGORIES IN THE AFFECTIVE DOMAIN OF THE TAXONOMY OF EDUCATIONAL OBJECTIVES

| Categories | Illustrative Behavioral Terms |
| --- | --- |
| 1. *Receiving:* An awareness of the importance of learning combined with a willingness to concentrate on learning activities. *Example:* Observing that some people live in poverty. | *listen, ask, concentrate, observe, follow, attend, demonstrate* |
| 2. *Responding:* A willingness to participate actively in a given activity and derive satisfaction from this participation. *Example:* Volunteering to donate an old toy to a charitable organization. | *volunteer, comply, perform, answer, participate, assist, help* |
| 3. *Valuing:* The perception that an object, phenomenon, or behavior has worth. Valuing also implies a commitment to an idea or position. *Example:* Working on a food line. | *appreciate, differentiate, justify, select, share, value, invite, work* |
| 4. *Organization:* The process of integrating different values, reconciling these differences, and formulating an internally consistent value system. *Example:* Integrating personal beliefs to develop one's own value system. | *compare, combine, organize, defend, explain, synthesize, integrate, recognize* |
| 5. *Characterization by a Value or Value Complex:* The possession of a value system that governs a person's behavior. *Example:* Acting in ways consistent with one's own value system. | *act, display, perform, influence, practice, demonstrate* |

*Source: Krathwohl et al., 1964.*

An English teacher who wants to write an objective at the evaluation level of the cognitive domain can review illustrative behavioral terms for writing instructional objectives (e.g., "critique, compare, conclude"). Using this information, the teacher might write the following as a performance objective:

> After reading *Profiles in Courage*, the student will compare the political behavior of one individual in the book with one of his or her own U.S. senators.

In another situation, an elementary school teacher deplores students' intragroup hostility and wants the students to be more cooperative. The teacher would like to include this behavior in the list of instructional objectives. In Table 9.3, which summarizes the affective domain, the teacher notices the verb "help" from the behavioral terms column at the responding level of the taxonomy and writes the following instructional objective:

> After discussing the importance of cooperation in the classroom, the student will help peers having homework problems.

Notice that some behavioral terms are used at several levels of the taxonomy. The term *identifies*, for example, can be used as follows (Gronlund, 1985b):

- *Knowledge:* Identifies the correct definition of a term.
- *Application:* Identifies proper grammar usage.
- *Analysis:* Identifies the parts of a sentence. (p. 34)

The use of a particular action verb does not necessarily place the objective at a particular level of the taxonomy. Although there is some overlap in terms, many terms are more directly relevant to one category than another. Examples are "criticize" (evaluation) and "solve" (application).

One of the important uses of the taxonomy is to make the teacher aware that it is possible to write objectives for and measure more complex skills than the recall of basic facts.

Harrow (1972) has developed a separate taxonomy for the **psychomotor domain**. It is arranged from the simplest level of observable movements to the most complex. There are six levels in the taxonomy:

1. *Reflex movements.* Actions that occur in response to some stimulus without conscious awareness (e.g., blinking and stretching).
2. *Basic fundamental movements.* Basic movements developed from a combination of reflex movements (e.g., walking and jumping).
3. *Perceptual abilities.* The translation of visual stimuli into appropriate movements (e.g., following verbal instruction and jumping rope).
4. *Physical abilities.* Basic body movements and abilities that are important in the development of more highly skilled movements. These movements incorporate the following characteristics: endurance, strength, flexibility, and agility (e.g., weight lifting and basic ballet exercises).
5. *Skilled movements.* Complex body movements indicating a degree of proficiency (e.g., performing a dance or jump shot in basketball).
6. *Nondiscursive communication.* Complex movements that communicate feelings, needs, or interests to another individual (e.g., facial expressions and choreographed dance movements).

The following are examples of psychomotor objectives:

> Using correct body movements, physical education students will swim the breast stroke for 50 yards.

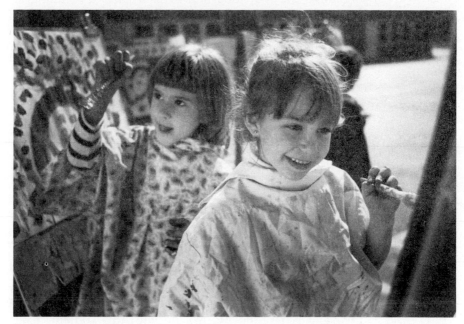

Can you identify different school activities that fall into the psychomotor domain?

Without the use of a diagram, the student will correctly assemble the biology lab equipment to demonstrate osmosis.

## PLANNING FOR INSTRUCTION

**How do a unit and a daily lesson plan relate to each other?**

Now you are ready to apply your knowledge of objectives to planning for instruction. Teacher planning serves a number of important functions, such as reducing anxiety, helping to organize time, and, most important, providing a framework for instruction and evaluation. Researchers have found that teachers' plans influence the content of instruction, the sequence of topics (Clark & Elmore, 1981; Smith & Sendelbach, 1979), and the time teachers allocate to subject matter areas. Studies of reading teachers have found that their early decisions about testing, grouping, materials, and management strongly influence the nature of their instruction (Buike, 1980; Stern & Shavelson, 1981).

During the school year teachers are engaged in various types of planning—yearly, term, unit, daily. In this chapter, I focus on unit and daily lesson planning. A daily **lesson plan** is a detailed outline of the objectives, content, procedures, and evaluation of a single instructional period. A **unit plan** is a detailed outline for a series of interrelated lesson plans on a particular topic of study lasting from two to four weeks. A good unit plan organizes the individual lesson plans into a meaningful experience (Jacobsen, Eggen, & Kauchak, 1989).

There is evidence that unit planning is viewed as being more important than daily lesson planning (Clark & Yinger, 1979). Unit planning provides a broad framework for the activities in which the teacher and students will be involved over a long period.

Jacobsen, Eggen, & Kauchak, (1989) describe how unit planning can lead to more effective lesson planning. Unit planning begins with a selection of a unit topic. This topic may come from the school district's curriculum guide for your subject area, or from the chapter topics in the textbook. Examples of unit topics for different subject areas follow:

| **Science** | **Social Studies** |
|---|---|
| Electricity | World War II |
| Solar Energy | The American Justice System |
| Scientific Inquiry | Cultural Pluralism in America |
| Astronomy | Maps |

Consider the overall goal or purpose of the unit. One way to accomplish this task is to summarize the major outcomes that you hope to accomplish. This summary statement should describe the content to be covered and what students will do with this content. Examples of such a statement follow:

> The purpose of the unit on maps is to provide students with the skills necessary to read maps for functional use. Students will be able to interpret a map key, determine direction with a compass, and compute distance using a scale of miles. Last, students will become acquainted with varied types of map from which to derive special information.

> The purpose of the unit on the newspaper is for students to learn the significance of the free press from its inception to present-day production. Through integration of the content areas, students will report for many of the paper's departments and contribute to the construction of a complete newspaper.

Having completed the statement of purpose for the unit, you are now ready to outline the major concepts, or ideas, in the unit. Outlining will help you to organize the content to be taught for proper sequencing of instruction and writing objectives. The outline also can be used to help students to understand the purpose of studying the unit. In addition, as daily lessons are presented, you can review the outline to help students to understand the relationship of a particular lesson to previous and future lessons. Figure 9.2 shows two examples of outlining the content of a unit. The first outlines a unit on maps; the second outlines a unit on the newspaper and is based on a more ambitious unit that attempts to integrate a number of content areas.

Using the outline as a planning guide, you are now ready to consider specific objectives for the unit. The task at this point of the planning process

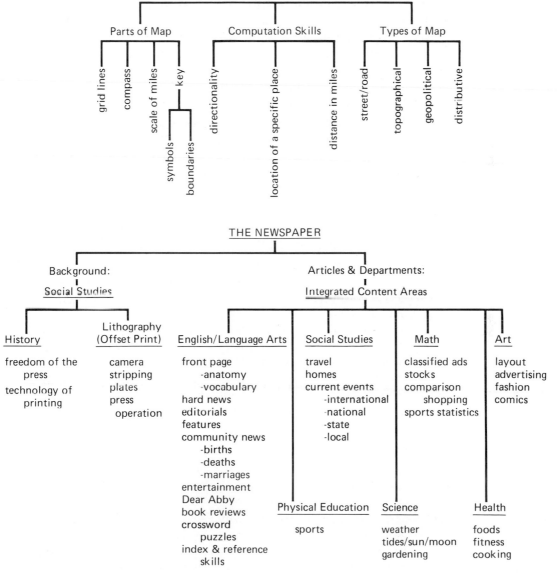

Figure 9.2 Examples of Unit Outlines.

*Source: Developed by Linda Organ.*

is to translate content topics into more specific objectives. Experienced teachers find that it is wise to limit a lesson to one, or at most two, important objectives and avoid the temptation of trying to teach too much in a short period. The danger of trying to accomplish too much is that you may end up accomplishing much less than you originally expected. The outline also will help you to decide how you will sequence your instruction. Some objectives that can be developed for the unit of maps follow:

- Students will identify the use of each part of a map by matching the term to its appropriate description.
- Using a compass, students will label the north, south, east, and west points on a map.
- Using a scale of miles, students will compute distances between points on a map.
- Students will translate written instructions consisting of key places, approximate distance, and compass readings to map directions to discover an unknown destination.

The following are some objectives that can be established for the unit on the newspaper:

- Students will write the outline of a "hard news" article using the "inverted pyramid" format.
- Students will collect the background notes on a "hard news" report by answering the five "W" questions: Who? What? Where? When? Why?
- Students will analyze the point of view of a writer by comparing "hard news" reports on three classmates who witnessed the same incident.
- Students will judge the amount of fact and opinion found in "hard news" reports by selecting and reading an article and underlying fact in blue and opinion in red.

Did you recognize how different levels of the Taxonomy of Educational Objectives were used in developing the objectives from the unit outlines?

Although your supervising teacher may require you to use a particular lesson plan format once you begin student teaching, it is important that you realize that there is no one best way to plan lessons. You need to experiment with different formats and determine the one or two that you feel most comfortable using.

## Homework

The final topic to be discussed in planning for instruction is the role of homework in a teacher's instructional program. The public's attitudes toward homework during the past century have shifted considerably along a positive-negative continuum. Earlier in the twentieth century, memori-

**What factors should a teacher or school consider in devising guidelines for a homework policy?**

zation was stressed and homework was seen as a way to discipline a child's mind. In the 1940s, the importance of problem solving was stressed in schools, with a de-emphasis on learning through drill. Homework was considered less important than developing student initiative and positive attitudes toward learning. This trend was reversed in the late 1950s after the Soviets launched the Sputnik satellite. Americans became concerned that their educational system was not preparing students for the demands of a technological society. As a result, more rigorous courses were instituted in the curriculum and homework was seen as an important way to acquire greater knowledge. By the mid-1960s, the pendulum swung again. Homework was considered to be an indicator of excessive pressure on students to achieve, and educators began questioning the value of homework. Today attitudes toward homework have shifted again toward the positive side of the continuum. The public is concerned with students' declining achievement scores (National Commission on Excellence in Education, 1983) and believes that more homework should be assigned (Cooper, 1989).

Recently, I heard two parents comparing notes regarding the schools their children were attending. One of the parents was boasting about the amount of homework his child was assigned each night. His reasoning went as follows: The amount of homework assigned is a indicator of the rigor of the school's academic program, which, in turn, will lead to higher academic achievement for his child. Based on your own experiences, what do you think about the parent's reasoning? How much time do you think children and adolescents should spend doing homework? Should young children do any homework at all?

Cooper (1989) completed a comprehensive review of the research on homework. What follows is a summary of his findings and his recommendations for establishing a homework policy. To begin, homework does have positive effects on achievement. However, the impact of homework is related to students' grade level. Homework has a strong effect on the achievement of high school students, about average for junior high students, and little or no effect for upper-level elementary school students. There were no studies investigating the impact of homework for the earliest grades. Second, homework appears to have a greater effect on learning simple tasks than complex tasks. Third, there are no consistent positive effects associated with the individualization of homework assignments. Fourth, the effects of homework tend to be similar for different types of students. Finally, since research results are mixed on parents' participation in homework, no conclusions can be reached at this time concerning the advisability of directly involving parents in their child's homework assignments.

Cooper points out that one should not conclude that for older students, the more homework, the better! For example, junior high students who spent more than 10 hours a week on homework had slightly *lower* achievement scores than students spending 5 to 10 hours on homework. Thus it seems that 1 to 2 hours a night might be the optimal amount of homework for junior high students. For high school students, homework did not have any effect until somewhere between 1 and 5 hours were completed and had an increasingly positive effect through 10 hours a week. We don't know, at this time, the peak level for which homework for high school students would have no additional benefit.

Cooper stresses that homework can serve many purposes. In the early grades, the purpose of homework often is to develop positive attitudes and study habits needed to excel in school. As a result, short and simple assignments are sufficient. Teachers should not assign homework to young children with the expectation that it will enhance achievement, nor should they expect students to teach themselves complex skills at home. In the upper grades, teachers often use homework to develop interest in a topic; more challenging assignments requiring higher-level thinking skills might best meet this purpose.

Finally, Cooper finds no evidence that any particular type of grading or evaluative comments on homework assignments has an impact on achievement. He states: "Intermittent grading and comments are no less effective than providing continuous feedback" (p. 183). In fact, he suggests that when the teacher uses homework to develop positive attitudes toward the subject matter, grading should be kept to a minimum.

Learn about the homework policy at your school. If teachers are given some responsibility in establishing their own policy, think carefully about the purpose and goals you wish to achieve by assigning homework. The guidelines in the following Classroom Application can serve a useful purpose in your decision making in this area.

## CLASSROOM APPLICATION: ESTABLISHING HOMEWORK POLICY GUIDELINES

### For Districts

Homework is a cost-effective instructional technique. It can have positive effects on achievement and character development and can serve as a vital link between the school and family.

Homework should have different purposes at different grades. For younger students it should foster positive attitudes, habits, and character traits. For older students, it should facilitate knowledge acquisition in specific topics.

Homework should be required at all grade levels, but a mixture of mandatory and voluntary homework is most beneficial.

**For Schools**

The frequency and duration of homework assignments should be further specified to reflect local school and community circumstances.

In schools where different subjects are taught by different teachers, teachers should know:

1. What days of the week are available to them for assignments
2. How much daily homework time should be spent on their subject

Administrators should:

1. Communicate the district and school homework policy to parents
2. Monitor the implementation of the policy
3. Coordinate the scheduling of homework among different subjects, if needed

Teachers should state clearly:

1. How the assignment is related to the topic under study
2. The purpose of the assignment
3. How the assignment might best be carried out
4. What the student needs to do to demonstrate that the assignment has been completed

**For Teachers**

All students in a class will be responsible for the same assignments, with only rare exceptions.

Homework will include mandatory assignments. Failure to turn in mandatory assignments will necessitate remedial activities.

Homework will also include voluntary assignments meant to meet the needs of individual students or groups of students.

All homework assignments will *not* be formally evaluated. They will be used to locate problems in student progress and to individualize instruction.

Topics will appear in assignments before and after they are covered in class, not just on the day they are discussed.

Homework will not be used to teach complex skills. It will generally focus on simple skills and material or on the integration of skills already possessed by the student.

Parents will rarely be asked to play a formal instructional role in homework. Instead, they should be asked to create a home environment that facilitates students' self-study.

---

* These guidelines are taken from Cooper, 1989, pp. 190–191.

## DEVELOPING A LESSON PLAN

After stating the instructional objective of the lesson, a basic lesson plan typically begins by identifying the content of the lesson in outline form and the instructional procedures. Whereas the content section of the lesson plan identifies what is to be taught, the instructional procedures section outlines how it will be taught. Another component is a checklist of all the materials and aids the teacher needs to teach the lesson (e.g., handouts, books, and charts). It is distressing to be in the middle of a lesson and find that you do not have important handouts or other resource material to complete the lesson. Finally, the last section of a lesson plan usually includes the evaluation procedures that describe how the teacher will assess student performance. That is, did the students master the stated objective of the lesson? Keep in mind that not all lessons require that the students demonstrate attainment of the objective on a test on the exact day that instruction is provided. The teacher may want to combine several objectives before testing students. Orlich et al. (1985) provide some good questions for teachers to consider during this stage: "Were the objectives realistic and appropriate? Did the instructional methods work? For what learners and what degree? What components of the lesson succeeded? What aspects need to be improved?" (p. 144). The answers to these questions can help the teacher to improve instruction and future planning. Planning for the evaluation of the lesson should become a part of any lesson plan.

**When and for what purpose would you use direct instruction, discovery learning, and cooperative learning lessons?**

I shall now present three different lesson plan formats based on learning principles discussed in the previous chapters: direct instruction, discovery or inquiry learning, and cooperative learning.

### Direct Instruction

During the late 1970s and early 1980s, a number of large-scale investigations found that students taught with a structured curriculum with direct or active involvement by the teacher learned more than students taught with more individualized, or discovery learning, methods. These studies were conducted at the elementary and junior high school level and focused on instruction in basic academic areas such as reading, mathematics, and English (Rosenshine, 1983).

This instruction has been called **direct instruction**, *explicit instruction*, or *active teaching*, depending on the individual researcher. This type of instruction appears to be most successful in highly structured academic areas where there is a specific body of knowledge to learn. It seems to be less relevant in more subjective areas such as identifying the moral positions of world leaders, analyzing literature, or discussing political views of senatorial candidates. In these areas, instructional objectives are less clear, the material is less structured, and the skills or knowledge does not follow in any particular order.

Rosenshine (1986) has identified the following six major teaching functions that aid the learning of explicit, well-structured content:

- *Review.* Each day, start the lesson by correcting the previous night's homework and reviewing what students have recently been taught.
- *Presentation of new material.* Tell students the goals of today's lesson. Then present new information a little at a time, modeling procedures, giving clear examples, and checking often to make sure students understand.
- *Guided practice.* Allow students to practice using the new information under the teacher's direction; ask many questions that give students abundant opportunities to correctly repeat or explain the procedure or concept that has just been taught. Student participation should be active until all students are able to respond.
- *Feedback and corrections.* During guided practice, give students a great deal of feedback. When students answer incorrectly, reteach the lesson if necessary. When students answer correctly, explain why the answer was right. It is important that feedback be immediate and thorough.
- *Independent practice.* Next, allow students to practice using the information on their own. The teacher should be available to give short answers to students' questions, and students should be permitted to help each other.
- *Weekly and monthly reviews.* At the beginning of each week, the teacher should review the previous week's lesson and at the end of the month review what students have learned during the last four weeks. It is important that students not be allowed to forget past lessons once they have moved on to new material. (p. 68)

There are several applications of direct instruction in the literature. Good, Grouws, and Ebmeier (1983) developed the *Missouri Mathematics Program,* in which teachers were trained to use effective teaching behaviors (similar to the steps identified by Rosenshine) in mathematics instruction. They found that the teachers implemented many of these behaviors in the classroom and taught differently from teachers who did not receive the training. For example, the trained teachers conducted more reviews and checked homework and student seatwork more frequently. The result was that the test scores in mathematics for the students in classes with the trained teachers were higher than for the students in classrooms with teachers who had not received any special training.

Good, Grouws, and Ebmeier prefer the term *active teaching* to *direct instruction* or *explicit teaching,* because they believe that the term identifies a wider range of teaching behaviors than is specified by the other two terms. In active teaching, students can learn independently or through direction by the teacher. Most important, instruction can become less direct as students become more mature and the instructional goals become less concerned with basic skills. Rosenshine (1986) has pointed out that direct forms of instruction can be modified to suit different students. For example, slower students need less presentation but more review and practice. Faster students benefit from more presentation and need less review and practice.

Hunter (1982) developed a direct instruction model that was evaluated over a four-year period. Students involved in the program during the four years increased their reading and mathematics achievement test scores during the first three years, but their scores declined during the last year of the program. The investigators raised a number of questions about maintaining the positive outcomes of the program after supervision from the trainers was withdrawn (Stallings & Krasavage, 1986; Stallings et al., 1986). More recently, a large-scale investigation of Hunter's model (Mandeville & Rivers, 1988/1989) in South Carolina indicated that the program failed to improve student achievement. Hunter's (1986; 1988/1989) response to the critics in both programs was that poor implementation was a factor in limiting the outcomes of the program.

## CLASSROOM APPLICATION: DEVELOPING A LESSON PLAN USING DIRECT INSTRUCTION

The following teaching processes and example of a lesson plan that uses a form of direct instruction were developed by Hunter (1982):

1. Anticipatory set
2. Instruction or providing information (which includes modeling and checking for understanding)
3. Guided practice
4. Closure (or checking for performance)
5. Independent practice

Sometimes you will use all five of these teaching processes in sequence, but it is important to notice that these processes may not be *taught* in every lesson. Instead, they should be *considered* in every lesson. Wolfe (1984) developed a training manual for teachers in which she discussed each step in detail. Figure 9.3 shows a lesson plan on maps that Linda Organ developed from the Hunter model.

### Anticipatory Set

The key question is: How do you get the students' minds ready to learn? The anticipatory set has five possible functions:

1. It can serve to focus the learner's attention on the lesson (e.g., the teacher conducts a laboratory experiment as the students enter the classroom).
2. It can relate previous learning to the present learning (e.g., the teacher asks, "Do you remember last week when we discussed

different parts of a short story? Today we're going to analyze a short story and locate those parts").

3. It can diagnose the students' skills as they relate to the lesson (e.g., "Write down three things you learned from yesterday's lesson on immigration").

4. It can let the students know what the objective is (e.g., "By the end of the period today, you're going to be able to determine the distance between two points on a map").

5. It can provide reasons why the lesson is important (e.g., "In a few weeks you're going to write a term paper. Today you're going to learn how to locate references in the library, one important skill for writing a term paper").

Keep in mind that very seldom will you include all five possible functions of an anticipatory set. You need to consider before you begin a lesson which function or functions you want to include. Your decision will be based on the difficulty of the content to be taught, the student's readiness level, and/or how motivated you feel the students are for the lesson.

## Instruction

This step in the lesson plan includes the learning activities to be experienced by the students in order to accomplish the objective. It is the manner in which you provide information or help students to achieve skills. You must consider two points in providing this information: first, determine the basic information and organize it, and second, present the basic information in its simplest and clearest form.

It is helpful for students to see examples of what the new learning looks like. This procedure is called *modeling*, a process by which a person learns from observing the behavior of another person (Chapter 6). During the modeling phase of a lesson, the teacher (or a student who can perform the task correctly) models or demonstrates the skills or process for the student. A verbal description often should accompany the model. A good example is a mathematics teacher who "talks through" each step of a problem as he solves it on the blackboard.

While you are teaching, you need to check for the students' understanding of the new skill or concept so that you can correct errors in their thinking by using a different example, providing another model, and so forth. Posing a question to the entire group and then getting responses from students of varying ability levels can be a useful approach.

The three strategies (input, modeling, and checking for understanding) are generally used throughout a lesson in a cyclical fashion. This is especially true if the objective requires considerable new information.

## Guided Practice

After the initial instruction, it is important that you monitor the students' initial practice to make certain they understand the material before turning them loose to practice. You should not simply ask, "Are there any questions?" or "Does everyone understand?" These questions are generally ineffective because students are usually uncomfortable admitting to the whole class that they do not understand something. In addition, students often *think* they understand, but when asked to demonstrate, they are unable to show their knowledge.

The key to guided practice is to obtain *overt* responses from students. Have them work a problem, show how something is done, or tell you the steps of an equation. Overt responses let you know where your students are and what they are thinking so that you can correct any problems immediately and move on.

## Closure

At some point during the lesson, you must decide if the students can meet the objectives of the lesson. Closure is a final check for understanding or performance, when you can determine the status of each student's progress toward the achievement of the instructional objectives. Closure is *not* a summary of the lesson; you do not tell the students what they have learned. Rather, it is a time when the students demonstrate to you what they have learned. Closure answers three questions regarding the achievement of the objective: Which students have reached the objective and are ready to move on and practice independently? Is more guided practice, or reteaching, necessary for some students? Should the lesson strategy be altered, or should the teacher move on to another activity?

You achieve closure in a lesson in several ways: question and answer, discussion, explanation by students regarding what they learned, and paper and pencil activities.

## Independent Practice

The last step in planning and teaching an effective lesson is called *independent practice*. After students have demonstrated that they can perform the new skills or use the new knowledge, they are ready to practice alone or with minimal supervision.

At the beginning of this Classroom Application, I mentioned that you should consider each step in every lesson but that you do not have to follow each step in every lesson. For example, if a lesson is a continuation of some class activity, it may not be necessary for you to include an anticipatory set because the students may already understand the objective and be motivated. In another situation, you might be expecting the students to discover the concept on their own with minimal guidance. In such an instance you would not present the material. Guided practice may be omitted in a class discussion in history on equal rights. If you want the students to apply what they learned during the discussion, however, you may give them an assignment on a topic that will fulfill the purpose of guided practice. You also may want to omit closure because more guided practice is necessary or because closure is not desired (as in a music appreciation lesson). Finally, independent practice may be omitted in a lesson if the students have not demonstrated a readiness to practice alone.

**TITLE OF LESSON:** USING THE SCALE OF MILES          **DATE** _____

| 1. BEHAVIORAL OBJECTIVES | 2. ANTICIPATORY SET (FOCUS) | 3. PROCEDURE FOR LESSON | 4. CHECK FOR UNDERSTANDING |
|---|---|---|---|
| **What will the learner be able to do when you are finished?**<br><br>Students will:<br><br>compute distances between points on a map using the scale of miles. | **How will you focus the learner's attention?**<br><br>Someday you will receive your license to drive a car. While driving, you're liable to become lost. If you are able to use the scale of miles on a map, you will know how far away you are from your destination. | **What will *you* do?**<br><br>Provide information:<br>a. locate key on map<br>b. interpret scale of miles (inches = miles)<br>c. demonstrate use of ruler to determine inches<br>d. demonstrate computation of inches times miles<br><br>Model: a. use of ruler<br>           b. multiplication | **How will you know if you're presenting clearly?**<br><br>a. Students will use individual maps and rulers to follow along with the teacher as she models examples.<br>b. Students will volunteer answers to each step in the teacher's sample problems. |
| 5. GUIDED PRACTICE (ACTIVITY) | 6. CLOSURE (FINAL CHECK FOR UNDERSTANDING) | 7. INDEPENDENT PRACTICE (ASSIGNMENT) | 8. COMMENTS ABOUT HOW THE LESSON WENT |
| **How will the learner practice with you there?**<br>a. give a map to each student<br>b. break class into small groups of 4 to 5 students.<br>c. have groups use the scale of miles to calculate real distances between points on the map.<br>d. after, groups explain answers to each other. | **How will you know if each student has reached the objective?**<br><br>Each student will use the scale of miles on a map to determine the total distance in miles of a journey through eight towns. | **What will the learner do for additional practice to develop speed and fluency?**<br><br>a. Every student will create an imaginary country, a map, a scale of miles, and 2 trips for his fellow students to calculate in miles.<br>b. Each student will calculate 10 trips designed by classmates. | |

Figure 9.3 An Example of a Lesson Plan Using a Form of Direct Instruction.

*Source: Wolfe, 1984.*

## Discovery Learning

The essential criterion for discovery learning is that the learner organize into final form the material to be learned. The discovery of the relevant concept or abstraction occurs during the student's involvement in a learning activity. This procedure differs from *expository teaching* (sometimes referred to as *didactic teaching*), in which the teacher explains to students all the information they must learn.

Both Piaget and Bruner (Chapter 2) are advocates of discovery learning. Bruner (1961) believes that discovery learning helps students take responsibility for their own learning, emphasizes high-level thinking, focuses on intrinsic rather than extrinsic motivation, and helps students remember important information.

Some educators use the term **inquiry learning** interchangeably with *discovery learning*, and others make a distinction between the terms. Both of these terms can be viewed on a continuum based on the amount of structure provided in the lesson. Although it is possible to provide no structure and have students discover all information totally on their own, most school programs use a form of *guided discovery*, or *guided inquiry learning*, whereby the teacher plays a role in the planning and facilitation of learning.

One distinction often made between discovery and inquiry learning is as follows: In discovery learning, the students are provided with data; with questioning by the teacher, they are expected to discover the particular principle or abstraction identified in the goal of the lesson. In inquiry learning, the goal is for students to develop strategies to manipulate and process information. Students identify problems, generate hypotheses, test the hypotheses in terms of the data, and apply their conclusions to new content or situations. The purpose of this type of instruction is to teach students process (thinking) skills that can be applied to new situations. Carin and Sund (1985) state: "Inquiry focuses upon *how* students process data (processes) rather than *what* they process (product)" (p. 102).

In many situations discovery and inquiry learning involve the same problem-solving skills. Thus I am more concerned that you be able to use an inductive method of instruction (i.e., reasoning from the particular to the general) than that you attempt to make discriminations between various forms of discovery and inquiry learning.

The evaluation of discovery learning methods discussed in Chapter 2 indicated that this method is not as effective as direct instruction in teaching basic skills. Although I would not suggest that discovery learning be used on a regular basis as the primary method of instruction, it can be used as a supplementary procedure to teach problem-solving skills, stimulate curiosity, and encourage more self-directed learning. Discovery learning techniques are most useful when students have the necessary skills and motivation to succeed.

## CLASSROOM APPLICATION: DEVELOPING A LESSON PLAN USING DISCOVERY LEARNING

The teaching methods used for discovery and inquiry learning vary greatly, depending upon the particular program developed and the content area taught. Planning for discovery and inquiry learning is an important aspect of the process. If you think all one has to do is tell students to discover something and sit back and wait for the results, you are going to be disappointed. Discovery and inquiry methods often take more time to plan than expository teaching methods.

In discovery learning, you must carefully plan the questions that should be asked in order to help students to attain the principle or abstraction being taught, order the examples in the lesson, and be sure that the reference materials and/or equipment are readily available. Otherwise, a good deal of time will be wasted.

Figure 9.4 presents a detailed example of a lesson plan for a guided discovery lesson in science. The questions on the left side of the lesson serve as a guide for planning.

There are many different forms of inquiry learning. I suggest that you begin by using the following steps in developing your own lesson plans and that you make modifications as you learn more about the strategy:

1. Identify the problem.
2. Formulate hypotheses.
3. Collect data.
4. Analyze data and form conclusions.

In planning, you can identify a problem in the particular content area you teach or capitalize on situations arising spontaneously in the class or in current events. As in discovery learning, you need to arrange opportunities for data collection and to make needed resources available. In helping the students to develop hypotheses, provide a focusing event to capture their attention. For example, in science you can set up a perplexing experiment, or in social studies you can focus on a national or international issue such as the use of atomic energy. After the students have had time to investigate the problem, you should encourage them to offer ideas about solutions. This will help students to redefine their hypotheses or develop new hypotheses. Next, the students should collect data to test their hypotheses. Depending on the complexity of the problem, time both in and out of class can be used for the activity. The final phase of inquiry learning is analysis of data, a process that involves examining hypotheses in terms of the information obtained. The students need to decide whether their hypotheses can be confirmed or whether they have to be changed or modified as a result of the avail-

**LIGHT**

**What Does a Prism Do to Light? (K–8)**

**What Do I Want Children to Discover?**

White light, when passed through a prism, disperses to form a continuous spectrum similar to a rainbow.
White light is a mixture of many colors of light.
Each color in the spectrum has a different wavelength.

**What Will I Need?**

A prism.

**What Will We Discuss?**

What is a prism?
What does a prism do?

**What Must I Know?**

This activity should be done in groups of two or more children.

**PROCESSES**

**PART I**

**What Will Children Do?**
*Hypothesizing*

**1.** Obtain a prism.
What do you think will happen to the light rays after they pass through the prism?
**2.** Place the prism in the path of a strong beam of light as indicated in the diagram.

*Observing*

What does the prism do to the light rays when they pass through it?

*Observing*

What colors do you see?

*Observing*

Which color seems to have bent the most?

*Observing*

Which color seems to have bent the least?

*Inferring*

What do you know about the way the different colors of lights are refracted (bent) by the prism?

*Inferring*

What is white light made of?

**What Must I Know?**

The children should see that white light is produced by the combination of several wavelengths of light. Draw a prism on the board and have the children show how the spectrum is formed. Their drawing should be something like the previous diagram.

Figure 9.4 Lesson Plan for Discovery Learning.

*Source: Carin and Sund, 1985.*

**PART II**

*Hypothesizing*

What do you think will happen if you look through the prism at your partner?

*Experimenting*

**1.** Look through the AB side of the prism at your partner.
**2.** Record your observations.

*Inferring*

Why is it possible to see what your partner is doing without looking directly at him or her?

*Inferring*

What happens to the light entering the prism that makes it possible for you to see your partner?

*Inferring*

What does the prism do to the light rays?

*Comparing*

What is the difference between a prism and a mirror in the way that each affects light?

**What Must I Know?**

A prism is used in expensive optical equipment instead of mirrors because prisms absorb less light. At the conclusion of this activity, place a diagram of a prism on the board and have the children draw how light passes through it. If they do not understand how a prism can be used in a periscope, draw and discuss the diagram below.

Light

**How Will Children Use or Apply What They Discover?**

**1.** What happens to X rays when they pass through a prism?
**2.** What would happen if you passed light through *two* prisms?
**3.** Why are prisms used in expensive optical equipment instead of mirrors?

Figure 9.4 *continued*

able data. Finally, the major outcome of the lesson should be the conclusions reached by the students as a result of the inquiry process (Jacobsen, Eggen, & Kauchak, 1989).

### Social Inquiry: A Classroom Example

The following teaching example illustrates the use of social inquiry in a high school classroom.* The four basic steps in the process are identified in parentheses.

> Miss West began the lesson by stating, "The influx of immigrants into Monterey Park, California, means that only approximately 23% of the people speak English as a native language. A walk through the streets of the Monterey Park business district illustrates the variety of languages spoken in the city. Does this situation present a problem to residents and visitors of Monterey Park?" (*Identify Problem*)
>
> Mary responded, "Well, if the business signs aren't in English, how will English-speaking people know what is sold in the store?"
>
> Bill added, "You just don't go into stores if you can't figure out what is being offered. Besides, it doesn't sound like there are many English-speaking people in Monterey Park."
>
> "What if there were a fire or another emergency? How would the firefighters know which business to go to?" asked Joe.
>
> Celia asked, "Do the businesses have their street numbers on the shops?"
>
> Miss West asked, "Why is that important, Celia?"
>
> Celia responded, "Well, at least a common style for displaying an address would help if you need to locate a particular business or office."
>
> "You said there are a variety of languages spoken in the city. How do people conduct business? Just because only 23% speak English as a native language doesn't mean that other people don't know English," replied Bob.
>
> "Do you want to explore that some more, Bob? What are you getting at?" asked Miss West.
>
> Bob continued, "I was just thinking what would happen if I went into a bank in Monterey Park and nobody understood me. What would I do?"
>
> Miss West commented, "Let's stop and reflect a moment. What are the issues involved here?"
>
> "Isn't the main issue whether or not English should be required to conduct business in Monterey Park?" Betty asked.
>
> "Miss West, you asked us whether or not the variety of languages spoken in Monterey Park was a problem to residents and visitors. I

---

* This example was developed by Johanna Lemlech at the University of Southern California.

don't think it is a problem unless the residents of Monterey Park see it as a problem," responded Marty.

Miss West asked, "How many agree with Marty?"

(Agreement is expressed by the students.)

Miss West continued, "Could we suggest alternative hypotheses to focus on the problem? Marty, why don't you try?"

Marty (after some thought) commented, "Some residents of Monterey Park may believe that English should be the required language of the city."

Shelly quickly added, "Yes, and some residents may believe that they have a right to speak whatever language they want to."

"Well done," Miss West replied. "Okay, now let's see what is involved in the two positions."

Marty answered, "If you believe that English should be required, then you probably believe that Congress should pass a law that English is the only language to be used in this country." (*Formulate Hypotheses*)

Terry responded, "On the other hand, if you don't want it required, then you believe that the Constitution protects your right to speak whatever language you want." (*Formulate Hypotheses*)

Miss West requested, "How many agree that the question has to do with constitutional rights? (The students appear to agree.) Is there another issue here? Are values involved?" (The students nod their heads.)

Bella asked, "Miss West, doesn't one of the values revolve around the need for people to maintain their own cultural identity?"

Miss West replied, "You may be right, Bella. Why don't we now see if we can identify the implications involved in the two positions?"

She wrote the two positions on the chalkboard and guided the students to explore the underlying assumptions and implications of the positions. When this task was completed, she told the students that she would provide them with some current newspaper articles about the language rift in Monterey Park and that they should also use their government text to gather facts to support their position. Miss West then divided the class into four teams. Two groups took the position that English should be required, and two groups took the opposite position. The students began work to gather facts and evidence to support their hypotheses. While the students worked in their groups, Miss West listened to them as they discussed the issues. Sometimes she asked the students questions in their groups to clarify specific points of view. On one occasion, she suggested that a group read the Bill of Rights. (*Collect Data*)

The students continued to work at the task as a homework assignment, and on the following day each team reported its findings. Because there is no solution to the problem, each team's conclusion was presented in the form of a statement about the issues, values, and probable consequences concerning the two different actions that could be taken. (*Analyze Data and Form Conclusions*)

## Cooperative Learning

In Chapter 8, I discussed different types of cooperative learning situations as well as factors that need to be considered when formulating groups and preparing students to work cooperatively. I have found Slavin (1990) and Johnson, Johnson, and Holubec (1987) useful references for developing lesson plans for cooperative learning. It is important to mention that your first attempt with cooperative learning may not be as successful as you would like. It takes time to prepare students to work cooperatively and for you to feel comfortable with this instructional method. Remember the research in Chapter 3 explaining that students from certain cultural groups prefer to work cooperatively than competitively. Cooperative learning can be an effective approach to dealing with the diversity of students in your classroom.

The cooperative lesson in the next Classroom Application is only one of many different ways you can organize the lesson. As you read the lesson plan, devise at least two different modifications that can be made in it.

## CLASSROOM APPLICATION: DEVELOPING A LESSON PLAN USING COOPERATIVE LEARNING

This lesson plan involves four instructional periods and is for a ninth-grade English class that is reading short stories.* Four students of different ability levels are assigned to each group. The lesson has two objectives:

- The students will identify the literary elements in a short story.
- The students will apply the literary elements to analyze a short story.

### Decisions Prior to Teaching
#### MATERIALS

1. Student-prepared flash card with literary terms (one set per student)
2. Teacher-prepared test on literary terms (one test per student)
3. Short story analysis form (one form per group)
4. Short story analysis form in four separate parts (one part to each group member)
5. Literature books (one per student)
6. Job description cards (four cards per group)

* This lesson plan was developed by Lucinda Boswell.

**STUDENT ROLES IN GROUP**

When preparing for the test on literary terms, the group divides into partners and alternates roles to quiz each other. Next, when the group analyzes the short story, each student has a separate set of literary terms to apply and become the group expert. Finally, when the group assembles the finished analysis form, each member is assigned a role:

> Recorder: Reads the answers of the group members and transcribes the answers for the group.
>
> Summarizer: Summarizes the material the group writes and puts the information in final form for presentation.
>
> Editor: Makes sure all group members complete their assignment, sees that the final analysis form is completed as required, and makes any corrections in spelling and punctuation.
>
> Researcher: Investigates the short story to settle any differences of opinion in the group on literary terms or on the correct answers for the short story analysis form. This student also acts as a liaison between the group and the teacher when assistance is needed either for content or cooperative skills.

**The Lesson**

Before the cooperative learning experience begins, the teacher discusses the following literary terms: *plot, setting, exposition, climax, resolution, theme, character, symbol, figurative language,* and *point of view.*

*Day 1.* Students are divided into study partners to review the literary terms on flash cards. A test is administered at the end of the period, with passing set at 80%. If the group meets the criterion, members receive the short story analysis form (comprising the 10 literary terms) and story assignment. If the group does not meet the criterion, members spend the rest of the period studying the literary terms and repeat the test the next day. At the end of the period, all groups receive the short story assignment to read for homework.

*Day 2.* The first 10 minutes of the period are used for retesting. Each member of the group is responsible for two or three analyses. Members take their short story analysis form and meet with students of other groups who have the same terms to analyze. Each member of the group is given a special job: recorder, summarizer, researcher, or editor.

*Day 3.* Students return to their original groups and analyze the short story according to their assigned literary terms. At the end of the period, each group will have analyzed the short story using all literary terms. The purpose of this class session is to begin preparing for an examination on the analysis of the short story.

*Day 4.* Students take a multiple-choice test on the analysis of the short story. Grades are assigned according to the composite scores of the group members.

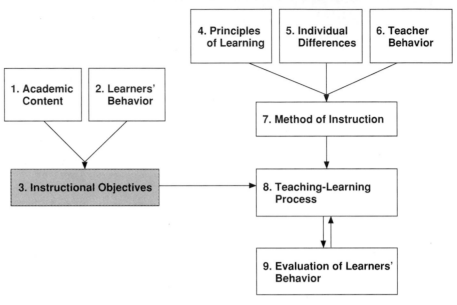

*Source: Adapted from Hunter, 1971, in Allen and Seifman.*

The teaching-learning model illustrates the importance of individual differences in planning for instruction. According to the model, you need to determine what the learners already know about the subject (box No. 1) in order to plan what you are going to teach, and you need to make instructional modifications for learners (box No. 5) in the planning and teaching of instructional lessons. In Chapter 11, I will discuss the steps that must be taken to plan for effective classroom organization and management. Unless students know and follow the rules and procedures for participating in your class, the impact of your instructional planning will be seriously diminished.

Glass, Christiansen, and Christiansen (1982) identify some decisions regarding individual differences that need to be made before and during instruction:

Goals. Will I need to adjust my instructional goals for some students? Should the students be expected to master the same skills and knowledge as their classmates, or will I need to modify my expectations of how much these students will be able to learn?

Methods. Will I need to adjust my teaching and testing methods for this student? Will the student learn as a result of the way I teach most other students, or will I need to use different methods, materials, or techniques?

There are many ways of making instructional adaptations (Glass, Christiansen, & Christiansen, 1982):

- *Delivery of instruction*. Change the methods used to teach an idea. You have learned about many instructional procedures (e.g., programmed instruction and other forms of individualized teaching, cooperative learning, and discovery learning) that may be successful for certain types of objective or for certain types of student.
- *Peers, teacher, or aide*. Change the person who actually teaches the learner. The teacher is not always the best person to teach a particular idea or review material taught earlier. Consider when a change in who presents material may facilitate learning.
- *Timing of instruction*. Change the time when certain subjects are taught. For example, moving reading instruction to early in the day, when young students are more alert, often can make a difference in students' responses to the material. Consider the effects of the sequence of various subjects.
- *The instructional setting*. Changing seating arrangements or eliminating classroom distractions can make a difference in attentiveness. Consider the size of the group. Sometimes a small-group or independent learning situation can be more effective for a particular student than whole-group instruction.

The following are some guidelines for decision making when you are considering how you might plan for adaptations for students with learning problems (Glass, Christiansen, & Christiansen, 1982):

- Review the assessment data collected on the student, particularly observations of the student's performance in the classroom and preferred learning styles.
- Establish learning goal(s) or objectives for the student.
- Review the content to be taught, noting the methods to be used with the class as a whole.
- Select the adaptation that varies the least from the typical methods used for the content to be presented.
- Evaluate the adaptation, based on the student's needs. If it seems appropriate, try it. If not, select the next adaptation and evaluate its potential for success. Continue this process until the adaptation is selected that meets the student's needs. (p. 255)

This type of decision making is designed to enable you to make the least amount of change necessary to facilitate the student's learning.

Specific types of modification for individual students can be planned (Roffman, 1983). For example, the student who is easily distracted can be placed in a seat where the potential for distraction is reduced. Also, you can provide outlets for the student's restless behavior. If a student's auditory discrimination is weak (i.e., if the student has difficulty interpreting or organizing data that are heard), you might provide outlines of lectures and use tables and graphs to reinforce concepts. In addition, you can provide extra explanations and supplemental visual work (e.g., write out new vocabulary and technical terms on the chalkboard so that the student can see the material). If students have problems with recalling material, you might give them extra time, have them write down important information, present key points of a lecture at the beginning, and/or summarize key points at the end of a lecture. These adaptations involve changes in teaching methodologies, but they are less likely to occur if you have planned ahead for their prevention. As you learn more about the students in your class, you will be able to anticipate the types of modification that need to be made during the teaching-learning process.

## KEY POINTS

1. Educators disagree about what students should learn in school.
2. Instructional goals come from many sources: the student, society, and academic discipline.
3. Learning goals are expressed in terms of educational objectives that are written at different levels of specificity.
4. An explicit instructional or behavioral objective is a precise statement of what a student will be able to do as a result of instruction.
5. There are several ways to write behavioral objectives. One approach includes a *behavioral term* that expresses the type of task required of the student, the *situation*, or *condition*, under which the behavior is to be performed, and the *criterion*, or *level of performance*, that will be used to evaluate the success of the performance or product. Another approach uses only the behavioral term.
6. Not all educators agree on the need to state goals explicitly before instruction.
7. There is some concern that explicit objectives may dehumanize the educational process and force teachers to emphasize experiences that are easiest to measure.
8. Knowledge of objectives can help the teacher to plan appropriate instructional procedures and methods.
9. Teachers' plans influence their classroom behavior.
10. In planning lessons, teachers should consider the major goals of the instructional program at the school, the content of the course, and the students' present knowledge.
11. Academic content can be assessed by the type of learning, the degree of difficulty, and the level of complexity.
12. Teacher-made tests help the teacher to determine the students' present knowledge. The Taxonomy of Educational Objectives helps to identify objectives at different levels of complexity.
13. A good unit plan can organize daily lesson plans.
14. There is no one best way to plan lessons.

15. A teacher needs to consider adaptations for individual students in planning lessons.
16. An evaluation component is an important part of any lesson plan.
17. A teacher needs to carefully consider the amount of homework assigned. In some situations, too much homework can have a negative impact on both academic achievement and attitude toward learning.
18. It is not necessary to grade all homework assignments.
19. Direct instruction tends to be most successful in highly structured subjects in which there is a specific body of knowledge to learn.
20. Although there are various applications of direct instruction in education, the following teaching functions are included in most programs: review, presentation of new material, guided practice, feedback and corrections, independent practice, and weekly and monthly reviews. The amount of time or emphasis on each function can vary, depending on the characteristics of the students.
21. Students tend to learn more and to reach objectives in basic skills when taught with a structured curriculum with direct or active involvement by the teacher.
22. Discovery learning can be used occasionally to change the format of classroom instruction, motivate students, and focus on higher-level thinking skills.
23. Cooperative learning is effective in achieving both cognitive and affective objectives.

## KEY TERMS

behavioral objectives, p. 368
expressive objectives, p. 374
Taxonomy of Educational Objectives, p. 379
cognitive domain, p. 379
affective domain, p. 379
psychomotor domain, p. 382
lesson plan, p. 383
unit plan, p. 383
direct instruction, p. 390
inquiry learning, p. 396

## SUGGESTIONS FOR FURTHER READING

The following books provide an excellent discussion of planning for instruction as well as different methods of teaching:

Borich, G. D. (1988). *Effective teaching methods*. Columbus, OH: Merrill.

Davis, G. A., & Thomas, M. A. (1989). *Effective schools and effective teachers*. Needham Heights, MA: Allyn & Bacon.

Dick, W., & Reiser, R. A. (1989). *Planning effective instruction*. Englewood Cliffs, NJ: Prentice-Hall.

Jacobsen, D., Eggen, P., & Kauchak, D. (1989). *Methods for teaching: A skills approach* (3rd ed.). Columbus, OH: Merrill.

Kauchak, D. P., & Eggen, P. D. (1989). *Learning and teaching: Research-based methods*. Needham Heights, MA: Allyn & Bacon.

Orlich, D. C., Harder, R. J., Callahan, R. C., Kravas, C. H., Kauchak, D. P., Pendergrass, R. A., & Keogh, A. J. (1985). *Teaching strategies: A guide to better instruction* (2nd ed.). Lexington, MA: Heath.

Excellent sources for writing instructional objectives:

Gronlund, N. E. (1985). *Stating objectives for classroom instruction* (3rd ed.). New York: Macmillan.

Mager, R. F. (1978). *Preparing instructional objectives*. Belmont, CA: Fearon.

A position paper by one of the leading critics of behavioral objectives:

Eisner, E. W. (1967). Educational objectives: Help or hindrance? *School Review, 75,* 250–260.

References on different teaching methodologies:

Carin, A. A., & Sund, R. B. (1989). *Teaching science through discovery* (6th ed.). Columbus, OH: Merrill. An excellent source for examples on discovery learning lessons.

Good, T. L., Grouws, D., & Ebmeier, H. (1983). *Active mathematics teaching*. White Plains, NY: Longman. A description of a successful inservice training program using a structured method of teaching.

Rosenshine, B.V. (1986). Synthesis of research on explicit teaching. *Educational Leadership, 43,* 60–69. A good review of literature on the effectiveness of structured (explicit) teaching.

## FOLLOW-UP ACTIVITIES

### 1. Rank the Goals of Education

In 1973 Spears undertook a survey of American educators to determine how they would rank-order the importance of 18 educational goals. The ranking, from most to least important, is listed below:

- Develop skills in reading, writing, speaking, and listening
- Develop pride in work and a feeling of self-worth
- Develop good character and self-respect
- Develop a desire for learning, now and in the future
- Learn to respect and get along with people with whom we work and live
- Learn how to examine and use information
- Gain a general education
- Learn how to be a good citizen

- Learn about and try to understand the changes that take place in the world
- Understand and practice democratic ideas and ideals
- Learn how to respect and get along with people who think, dress, and act differently
- Understand and practice the skills of family living
- Gain information needed to make job selections
- Learn how to be a good manager of money, property, and resources
- Practice and understand the ideas of health and safety
- Develop skills to enter a specific field of work
- Learn how to use leisure time
- Appreciate culture and beauty in the world (pp. 31–32)

Would you have ranked these goals in about the same order today? Notice that subject matter skills headed the list and that appreciation of beauty and culture ranked least in importance. Rank the goals yourself on the basis of what you hope to gain from your college education, and compare your list with those of other students in your class.

## 2. Justify Your Own Subject Matter

Suppose a student asked you on the first day of class, "Why do I have to take this course?" Generate a list of reasons to support the existence of your subject area in the school curriculum.

## 3. Interview Teachers Regarding Their Use of Objectives

Interview teachers and ask them whether they use instructional objectives and to what degree of specificity. What reasons do they give for and against developing explicit objectives?

## 4. Write Behavioral Objectives

Select a topic in your teaching field and write an objective for each level of the Taxonomy of Educational Objectives in both the cognitive and affective domains.

### Cognitive

- Knowledge
- Comprehension
- Application
- Analysis
- Synthesis
- Evaluation

### Affective

- Receiving
- Responding
- Valuing
- Organization
- Characterization by a value

_____ 5. Complete a Task Analysis

In this activity you will have a chance to apply what you have learned in developing a task analysis for a small instructional unit. The activity involves the following basic steps: choosing a task, specifying the entry behavior (skills a student has already mastered before instruction), defining the prerequisite skills (all skills and behaviors that must be mastered prior to attaining the terminal objective), and determining the order in which the skills must be taught. Choose a task in your field of specialization that is relatively small and simple. Your instructor may want to approve Part One of the activity before allowing you to proceed to Part Two.

**Part One: Task Analysis Activity**

    a. What is the task you are going to analyze?
    b. What is the makeup of the student population you would teach the task to? Identify the grade level, age, and possible background of the students.
    c. Specify the task as a behavioral objective
    d. What are the entry behaviors for this task?

**Part Two: Task Analysis Activity**

    a. What are the prerequisite skills?
    b. What are the relationships between the prerequisite skills?
    c. Diagram your task analysis using the format shown in Figure 9.2.

_____ 6. Develop a Lesson Plan

Use any of the lesson plan formats discussed in the chapter or use one given to you by your instructor to develop a lesson plan on a topic in your teaching specialty.

# CHAPTER 10

# Motivation

## ORIENTATION

Teachers experience many different motivational problems in the class-room. Some students are more concerned with avoiding failure than trying to learn; others don't believe anything they do will lead to success; some students are so anxious that they can't concentrate on tasks; and other students have the ability to succeed but don't contribute in class because they lack self-confidence in their ability. Motivational theory and research can be used to help teachers understand the different factors influencing achievement behavior in the classroom.

Two orientations have dominated teachers' thinking about motivation. The first is the behavioral approach, which views motivation in terms of intensity and duration of behavior. The student who works harder and longer on a task is considered to be more motivated than the student who fails to expend similar energy and persistence. I have provided extensive coverage of this approach in the discussion of operant conditioning (Chapter 6). You will learn more about behavioral approaches to classroom management and discipline in Chapter 11. Finding appropriate incentives or reinforcers to maintain task behavior is an important aspect of this approach.

The second orientation comes from the work by Atkinson (1964) and McClelland (1965), who view motivation as an unconscious drive or need that is socialized early in a child's life. This view closely aligns motivation with the study of personality. For a teacher following this perspective, responsibility for increased academic involvement rests primarily on the students. If students are not motivated to achieve, teachers are limited in what they can do to change students' achievement motivation, since it is strongly influenced by child-rearing experiences. It is not uncommon to hear teachers complain about students' family backgrounds and lament: "I don't know how to turn this student on!"

Maehr (1978) points out the problem with this perspective in attempting to enhance student motivation in the classroom: "If one assumes that motivational change only comes through personality change, one inevitably accepts a certain fatalistic outlook as a teacher. How many personality changes can a teacher—or even the best special education program—affect in a given year?" (pp. 223–224).

In this chapter, I will introduce developments in the cognitive approach to motivation (see Ames & Ames, 1984, 1990). In this approach, the teacher is concerned with cognitive-mediational processes (e.g., the personal explanations for success and failure and informational processing that occur in instructional settings). As a result, motivation is reflected in how students think about themselves, the task, and their performance: "How well have I done in the past?" "How am I doing now?" "How are others doing?" The perspective of this approach is to understand *why* students choose to engage in academic tasks rather than what they do or how long they spend doing so.

In Chapter 1, I emphasized the importance of teacher beliefs in influencing classroom decisions. How teachers view motivation will influence their perceptions of what they can do or should do to establish a classroom environment that will enhance student motivation. The cognitive view of motivation provides important insights for understanding, diagnosing, and remediating motivational deficiencies. Thus, I believe that if teachers realize that student motivation is influenced to a great extent by students' self-perceptions that are changeable rather than personality characteristics that are less likely to be changed, teachers will assume more responsibility for the way students behave. The result can be increased motivation to learn and academic achievement.

The theme of this chapter is that teachers do not have to wait for students to become motivated to learn. They have the ability to influence the type of motivation displayed in the classroom through a variety of teaching decisions. Table 10.1 identifies some factors that contribute to a negative motivation pattern according to four variables identified in the teaching-learning model: student characteristics, teacher behavior, instructional procedures (including goals and tasks), and evaluation processes. Although the factors are listed under separate headings, they interact with each other to influence student behavior. These variables will serve as the basis for organizing the theory and research in the chapter.

By the time you master the material in this chapter, you will be able to :

- Identify how student characteristics, teacher behavior, instructional procedures, and evaluation interact to affect motivation for learning.

TABLE 10.1 **FACTORS THAT CONTRIBUTE TO A NEGATIVE MOTIVATION PATTERN**

**Student**
  Poor self-concept of ability
  Learned helplessness
  Low self-efficacy
**Teacher**
  Communication of low expectations
  Low sense of efficacy leading to less effective instruction
**Instructional Procedures**
  Competition and social comparison
  Emphasis on performance rather than mastery goals
  Emphasis on extrinsic rather than intrinsic motivation
  Poor presentation of tasks
  Little task selection by students
  Unidimensional classroom
**Evaluation**
  Public evaluation producing achievement anxiety
  Emphasis on ability instead of effort
  Emphasis on grades

*Source: Based in part on Ames and Ames, 1990.*

- Make modifications in the teaching-learning process to enhance student motivation for learning.

1. Why do students interpret success and failure differently?
2. How do reinforcement and cognitive theories of motivation differ?
3. How are emotions related to causal explanations of success and failure?
4. How can causal attributions of students and teachers conflict?
5. Why are some students motivated to avoid failure?
6. How can teacher expectations influence student behavior?
7. How can the improper use of praise have a negative impact on students?
8. How can teacher efficacy impact student behavior?
9. How does the classroom climate influence student motivation?
10. What are the consequences of the development of intrinsic or extrinsic motivation?
11. How do different goal structures influence self-perceptions of ability?
12. How does anxiety influence student achievement?
13. What can teachers do to reduce anxiety in the classroom?

## STUDENT CHARACTERISTICS

We begin our study of motivation by exploring different theories and constructs that explain how various student characteristics can lead to different types of motivation.

### Locus of Control

Some students blame someone or something else for their poor performance: a poor test, a confusing book, or an incoherent teacher. These students believe external aspects of their environment wield control over their downfall (or over their success). They see themselves powerless to counteract this trend. Psychologists classify such personality dispositions under one aspect of the construct **locus of control**, which pertains to how individuals perceive the link between their behavior and its consequences and whether they accept responsibility for their actions.

Much of the conceptualization and research in this area stems from the social-learning theory of Rotter (1966), who views locus of control as having two dimensions—**external locus of control** and **internal locus of control.** An "external" person perceives having little control over fate and fails to perceive a cause-and-effect relationship between actions and their consequences. An "internal" person holds the reins of fate securely and understands that effort and reward are correlated.

The students' orientation is extremely important. If they do not anticipate teachers' approval as a response to their efforts, they will be less disposed to strive for success. Children will work harder at tasks if they believe they (rather than chance or the teacher) are responsible for the success they achieve (Lefcourt, 1966; Rotter, 1966). As they work harder and achieve success, they acquire better self-concepts of their ability.

There is some evidence that parental behavior is related to the development of control in their children. In several studies (Davis & Phares, 1969; Katkovsky, Crandall, & Good, 1967), it was found that parents who were identified as "warm," "encouraging," and "approving" and who expected children to be independent at an early age produced youngsters who developed a more internal locus of control than those children whose parents were identified as "dominant," "rejecting," and "critical." It appears that the parental factor leading to an internal orientation is similar to the factors leading to the development of positive self-concept and high self-esteem.

Previous research indicated that the sense of internal control is stronger in white children than in blacks, and stronger in the middle-class than in the low-SES population (Battle & Rotter, 1963; Crandall, Katkovsky, & Crandall, 1965). Some minority group children do not experience a sense of control over their environment. This finding is not surprising because many minority children have come up against barriers to their efforts to influence their environment. Later research (e.g., Graham & Long, 1986; Willig et al., 1983) failed to find differences between blacks and whites in their causal preferences.

The more individuals find that they cannot control the sources from which important events in their lives spring, the more external a sense of control they develop. Coleman et al. (1966) found that belief in internal control was the most important indicator of school achievement for black students. Black children who exhibited a sense of internal control enjoyed considerably higher achievement than those who exhibited a sense of external control. The same result occurs in white populations. Coleman also found that the extent of desegregation in the school affected the sense of control. As the proportion of white students in the school increased, black students' sense of control grew stronger.

A considerable amount of research distinguishes between externals and internals (Lefcourt, 1982; Strickland, 1989). Externals score higher than internals on measures of anxiety, suspicion of others, and hostility. Internals typically perceive themselves to be effective, assertive, and independent. Internals spend more time in intellectual activities and academic pursuits and exhibit more achievement motivation They investigate and plan for college and spend more time doing homework.

## Weiner's Theory of Attribution

One of the early theories of achievement motivation was developed in the 1950s and 1960s by David McClelland (1965) and John Atkinson (1964) and focused on motivation as a learned behavior. According to the theory, achievement behavior is based on the resolution of two competing needs—the need to achieve versus the need to avoid failure. Some students work hard for success without seriously worrying about the possibility of failure; other students think less about succeeding than about avoiding failure. Atkinson and Feather (1966) found that persons in whom motivations to achieve are stronger than motivations to avoid failure set goals of intermediate difficulty, whereas persons with the opposite motivational tendency avoid tasks of intermediate difficulty and prefer easier to more difficult tasks in which their efforts are neither doomed to failure nor guaranteed success. Avoiders of failure like very easy or difficult tasks because they are certain of succeeding at an easy task and they can rationalize failing a difficult task—either way they can't lose!

The factor that determines whether children develop the need to achieve or avoid failure is the types of experience in the home. Certain child-rearing practices are believed to contribute to greater achievement striving. In particular, parents who provide opportunities for children to explore their environment, accept their children's strengths and weaknesses, and offer clear guidelines for appropriate and inappropriate behavior are likely to have children who will attempt success. In addition, these children have parents who reward performance when they are successful and are neutral toward performance that falls short of their expectations. The opposite pattern occurs for parents of failure-avoiding children: They punish their children's failures but say little when they are successful (Rosen & D'Andrade, 1959; Winterbottom, 1953).

In the early 1970s, Bernard Weiner and his associates (Weiner, 1972; Weiner et al., 1971) proposed a reinterpretation of Atkinson's theory. Weiner's research has shown that individuals' beliefs about the causes of their successes and failures are important in understanding achievement-related behavior. He has proposed an attributional model to explain achievement that includes the locus of control dimension. An **attribution** is the inferences that an observer makes about the causes of behavior. Weiner's model deals with four major perceived causes of success and failure in achievement situations: *ability, effort, task difficulty,* and *luck.*

Table 10.2 shows that the attributions can be classified into two dimensions—stability and locus of control. Two of these attributions (ability and task difficulty) are stable in nature, whereas the others (luck and effort) change. This means that if a person is asked to repeat the same task, it is likely that the perception of ability and the difficulty of the task would remain the same. However, the perception of the role of luck and effort is likely to change from one time to another. The other dimension—locus of control—refers to whether a person's achievements are seen as being

TABLE 10.2 DETERMINANTS OF ACHIEVEMENT BEHAVIOR

| Locus of Control Factors | Success or Failure Attributed to Stability Factors | |
|---|---|---|
| | Stable | Unstable |
| Internal | Ability | Effort |
| External | Task difficulty | Luck |

**Why do students interpret success and failure differently?**

under the person's own control (ability or effort) or are seen as being caused by forces external to the person (task difficulty and luck).

Let's look at some examples to understand how individuals assign causes to their performance and how these explanations affect subsequent achievement. Consider two students who have received a high score on an English test. The first student attributes success to superior ability, whereas the second student attributes success to luck. For the first student, success will likely increase self-confidence, since he attributed success to his own skills. For the second student, however, the impact of success will be less meaningful, since he takes no credit for it.

Attributions also affect future expectations in failure conditions. A person who fails an English test and attributes the failure to lack of effort will likely believe that he could do better next time if he tries harder, but the person who views failure as being the result of a lack of ability will hold less hope for doing better in the future. For this reason, Weiner believes that the stability dimension (ability and task difficulty) is more predictive of future performance than the locus of control dimension (effort and luck).

Covington and Beery (1976) discuss attributions among success-oriented and failure-avoiding students. Success-oriented students tend to believe that they can handle most academic challenges. As a result, their ability is not viewed as an important issue in learning. Therefore, these students view success and failure as related to the quality of their efforts. The research clearly points out that success-oriented students tend to attribute success to ability and effort and failure to lack of proper effort (see Bar-Tal, 1978). These explanations are helpful to the individual because success inspires further confidence as a sign of one's ability to do well, whereas failure signals the need to try harder. The success-oriented individual is not threatened by failure when it does occur, because it doesn't reflect on the individual's ability. This explanation also helps to explain why failure can be used to motivate already successful students.

Failure-avoiding students generally have a different set of attributions. They tend to attribute their failures to a lack of ability and attribute their successes to external factors such as luck or an easy task (Weiner & Kukla, 1970). It is difficult to imagine a more distressing situation—the students blame themselves for failure but take little or no credit for success. They feel that they have little control over their academic destiny so they minimize pain by trying to avoid failure.

If success is so important to a positive self-esteem, why do these students fail to take responsibility for their success? Covington and Beery (1976) believe that success implies an obligation to do well the next time. Students who find it difficult to live up to this expectation believe that success is not of their own making. Aronson and Carlsmith (1962) found that such individuals sometimes sabotage their own effort when they find themselves in danger of succeeding!

Some of the more severely failure-oriented students develop **learned helplessness**, a situation in which an individual learns over time that he or she has no control over the outcome of events. The individual sees no relation between effort and the attainment of goals (Abramson, Seligman, & Teasdale, 1978). These students need considerable attention by teachers if they are going to work toward the attainment of educational goals.

The attribution literature suggests that it is incorrect to assume that low-achieving students are always unmotivated. On the contrary, they appear to be extremely motivated—to avoid failure, rather than to succeed. Teachers need to spend more time learning about their students' beliefs about the causes of their success and failure. One important goal is to establish classroom conditions in which students learn that proper effort leads to success. A number of reattribution training programs have been successful in altering individuals' perceived causes of failure. For example, Andrews and Debus (1978) demonstrated that a program of systematic reinforcement can get students to attribute their problems to their own lack of effort. Another goal must be to provide students with short-term goals and strategies so that they acquire the skills to reach the goals. Emphasizing effort without providing the competencies and skills to achieve will do little to help students.

**How do reinforcement and cognitive theories of motivation differ?**

There are some other considerations about the emphasis on effort you need to consider. First, some students may already believe that they are working as hard as they can. If you convince these students that poor effort is the primary cause of their academic problems, they may decrease their sense of efficacy regarding the task. Their reasoning may be as follows: If I try hard and still can't solve the problems, then I must lack ability. Second, if you continually emphasize the importance of sustaining a maximal effort on tasks, some students may conclude that they don't want to work so hard to succeed (Ames, 1990). The implication is that you need to (1) know how your students attribute the causes for their successes and failures, and (2) encourage both reasonable effort attributions and the use of appropriate learning strategies so that students can learn more effectively and efficiently.

The next two theories focus on students' perceptions of their ability—perceptions that play an important role in their achievement behavior.

## Covington's Self-Worth Theory

The self-worth theory of achievement motivation (Covington, 1984; Covington & Beery, 1976) incorporates a motivational component with the causal perceptions of success and failure. According to self-worth theory,

**How are emotions related to causal explanations of success and failure?**

**How can causal attributions of students and teachers conflict?**

an individual learns that in our society one is valued because of one's accomplishments. The key factor to achievement motivation can be explained by how a person attempts to maintain positive ability perceptions that are the basis of self-worth.

If a person fails at a task, the feedback evokes the possibility of a lack of ability. In addition, failure creates feelings of unworthiness and self-rejection. As a result, when individuals are faced with the possibility of failure, they will avoid the situation or develop strategies to protect any inferences as to the lack of ability.

A problem that teachers must deal with is that children's perceptions of their academic abilities decline as they proceed through school (Nicholls, 1984). When children first enter school, they believe that effort is the most important student attribute. In fact, young children generally believe that students who work hard are brighter than those who do not try (i.e., ability and effort are perceived as synonymous). Second, they believe that if they work harder they can actually cause an increase in ability. By working hard they can please their teacher and develop the positive image of a "good" student (Covington, 1984). The results of such perceptions are that young children do not feel bad when they fail.

By ages 11 and 12, students have considerably lower self-perceptions of competence. As students get older and perceive the social comparison in the classroom (e.g., grades, ability grouping), their sense of worth begins to depend on doing better than someone else. The consequence of social comparison information for most students leads to the realization that effort does not compensate entirely for ability. Ames and Felker (1979) have shown that competition tends to magnify the positive affect associated with success (pride) and the negative affect associated with failure (shame or guilt).

Another factor related to changes in self-perceptions is that while young children believe that trying hard leads to improvement in ability, trying hard takes on negative characteristics for older children (by age 12). As these children make greater distinctions between effort and ability, they come to realize that success with a good deal of effort indicates lower ability. As a result, high effort becomes an indicator of low ability (Paris & Byrnes, 1989).

Holt (1982) provides a good example to illustrate how evaluation by others influences our behavior. The next time you are around an infant, observe its motivation in trying to succeed at a new task. The infant is like a scientist, always observing and experimenting. Even when the infant fails, it continues to try to make sense out of its environment. An infant does not react to failure as does a child or adolescent. "She has not yet been made to feel that failure is shame, disgrace, a crime. Unlike her elders, she is not concerned with protecting herself against everything that is not easy and familiar; she reaches out to experience, she embraces life" (Holt, 1982, p. 112).

If we examine the role of effort from both teachers' and students' perspectives, we will find that in some cases teachers and students operate at cross-purposes. Although teachers highly value achievement, they often reward (or punish) some students more than others for exactly the same level of performance. Students who are perceived as having expended effort (regardless of their ability) tend to be rewarded more and punished less than students who do not try (Weiner & Kukla, 1970).

However, Covington and Omelich (1979) found that students experienced greatest shame with a combination of high effort and failure and least shame with low effort and failure. This research helps to explain why failure-avoiding students often do not try! Expending effort and still failing poses a serious threat to one's self-esteem. If one does not try but fails, one can always rationalize that success could have been achieved through proper effort, thus maintaining a reasonable level of self-esteem. Teachers, however, tend to reinforce students who demonstrate effort and punish those who do not. Understanding the perspectives of both the teacher and the student helps to see how effort can become a "double-edged sword" for many students. They must walk the tightrope between the threatening extremes of high effort and no effort at all. They must demonstrate some effort to avoid negative sanctions from their teachers but not enough to risk shame if they should try hard and fail. Some students use excuses in maintaining a balance between these extremes. A popular tactic is to try hard but to use excuses (external factors) to explain why trying did not help. Such behavior avoids any inference as to low ability (Covington & Omelich, 1979). Covington (1983) summarizes the safe strategy of many students: "Try, or at least appear to try, but not too energetically and with excuses always at hand" (p. 149).

I can remember a friend in college who was a bright but anxious student. He always told everyone that he didn't plan to study much before an exam. Everyone was impressed by the success he gained with little apparent effort. It was not until years later that I learned that he had always found time to study regularly during the term. If he did not do well on an exam, he always had his previously announced excuse that he had not crammed for the exam!

*Strategies for Avoiding Failure.* What strategies have you used to protect yourself from the possibilities of failure? Have you ever raised your hand early in a class period to answer a question, knowing that the instructor might not call on you later? Have you remained silent when asked a question by an instructor, hoping that if you paused long enough, the instructor would rephrase the question once or twice until either the answer was given to you or someone else was called on? Have you ever entered a class when you had read only part of the assignment and raised a question early in the discussion, hoping that the instructor would not call on you again? If you stop to think about it, you will be able to recall numerous incidents of classroom strategies that you used to protect yourself from failing.

I can identify with the following situation, and it may be uncomfortably familiar to you, too: A common practice in language classes is to require students to take turns translating sentences into English. As the instructor moves down the row asking one student after another to translate, anxious students are not paying attention to each translation. Instead, they are counting down the row to locate the sentence they will have to translate and begin covertly practicing the task. During this time they have missed the translations of all the previous sentences. Learning all the sentences is vital to the content of the particular lesson, but some students are more motivated to avoid failure than to learn the lesson.

Here is another example from elementary school: A student knows that the teacher does not collect seatwork, or if the teacher does collect it, it will not be corrected. If the assignment requires yes-no answers, multiple-choice, or $>$, $<$, $=$ equations, the student need only pattern answers so that they look legitimate. The assignment gets "done," and the student is not hassled by the teacher to keep busy. Unfortunately, nothing is learned but how to avoid completing an assignment.

**Why are some students motivated to avoid failure?**

During the past few years, I have asked college students to provide examples of strategies they have used to avoid failure or to reduce personal responsibility for their achievement. The following are some samples:

- Fail to show up for class when you're not prepared.
- If you fail to complete your assignment, tell the instructor at the *beginning* of the class that you left the assignment at home and will bring it in the next day. The instructor will be impressed with your honesty and usually will allow you the extra day.
- Remain anonymous to the instructor and class to avoid getting involved, and thus avoid the responsibility of participation.
- To avoid being called on, look at the instructor, then look down at your open book and flip through the pages as if you're looking for something. The instructor thinks you're looking for the answer, so he won't call on you.
- Study everything else but what you are supposed to study. When you run out of time, you can rationalize, "But I studied as much as I could. I really tried, but I just didn't have enough time."
- Take your notes and books wherever you go (i.e., beach, meals, home). This lessens the guilt of wasting time.
- If you have no idea as to what is going on in class, and the big final is coming up, call for a study session and make sure all the smart people are present so they can "share their knowledge."

Do public school teachers and college instructors contribute to failure-avoiding strategies? If so, in what way? Discuss your opinions (diplomatically, of course!) with your instructor.

## Self-Efficacy

*Self-efficacy* is an individual's evaluation that he or she has specific performance capabilities on a particular type of task (Bandura, 1982). Efficacy perceptions are different from locus of control or outcome expectations. It is possible for a person to believe that a successful performance will lead to a desired outcome—that is, a good term paper will lead to a high grade (locus of control). Yet the person might not believe that he or she has the necessary knowledge or skill to perform well (self-efficacy). Thus self-efficacy is a judgment about and one's confidence in his or her ability to achieve a particular task.

Attribution beliefs can influence self-efficacy. For example, students who attribute academic problems to low ability are likely to have a low sense of efficacy and not try very hard to succeed. However, self-efficacy theorists argue that efficacy judgments, rather than attributions, are the major determiners of achievement behavior and affect (Ames, 1987).

Think about your beliefs and behavior regarding an assignment in a particular course that you believed you could complete and another assignment in which you doubted your competency. You may have procrastinated or attempted to avoid the task that you believed exceeded your abilities and might result in low sense of efficacy. On the other hand, when you believed you had the skill to master tasks, you were probably eager to get started, worked hard, and gained further confidence in your ability when the task was successfully completed.

Perceived efficacy can influence motivation. Students with a high sense of efficacy are more likely to choose difficult tasks, expend greater effort, persist longer, apply appropriate problem-solving strategies on tasks, and have less fear and anxiety regarding tasks than students with a low sense of efficacy for a task (Schunk, 1989). An investigation by Collins (1982) illustrates how self-efficacy beliefs impact achievement behavior. Collins selected students who were high, average, and low in mathematical ability and identified those students who had high and low mathematical self-efficacy. He found that within each ability group, those students who had high efficacy solved more problems correctly and were willing to redo problems they missed than students low in self-efficacy. Self-efficacy was more predictive of achievement behavior than the students' actual ability levels.

## TEACHER BEHAVIOR

Can a teacher's behavior toward a student influence his or her motivation? We know that teachers don't treat all students the same and that certain treatment may limit students' opportunities in the classroom. The result may be lowered academic performance.

### Teachers' Expectations as Self-Fulfilling Prophecies

Teachers often have different interaction with different types of students. In some instances, these differences affect **teacher expectations** (i.e., beliefs about students' present and future achievement and behavior). These expectations can lead to self-fulfilling prophecies, a process in which teacher expectations determine the ways students are treated. Over time, the expectations influence how the students behave in the classroom and how much they learn. Race, social class, and personality are most likely to be related to teacher expectancies (Dusek & Joseph, 1985). That is to say, some teachers tend to have greater expectancies for success for white than for black and other minority students, and for high than for low-socioeconomic status students, and prefer more conforming and docile students to independent and assertive students.

Rosenthal and Jacobson's (1968) *Pygmalion in the Classroom* stimulated a great deal of interest and controversy about teacher expectations. In their study, Rosenthal and Jackson administered a nonverbal intelligence test to all children in an elementary school. The test was disguised as one designed to predict academic "blooming," or intellectual gain, during the school year. Rosenthal and Jacobson provided each teacher with the names of children in the class who had encouraging scores on the test of intellectual blooming. Actually, these children were selected randomly from the teachers' class lists, not on the basis of any test. There was no real reason to expect unusual gain from the children on the investigators' list. Eight months later, all children in the school were re-examined with the same IQ test, and the designated "bloomers" *did* demonstrate significant intellectual growth. The effects showed up more strongly in the first two grades.

Many subsequent studies attempting to induce similar teacher expectations failed to show any impact on student behavior (e.g., Claiborn, 1969; Fleming & Anttonen, 1971). Although the findings of *Pygmalion in the Classroom* have been widely publicized and discussed, many individuals have criticized the methodology of the study (see Rosenthal, 1985, for a review of these criticisms). Good and Brophy (1987) have pointed out that studies attempting to induce teacher expectations by providing teachers with phony information have generally not yielded significant results. However, naturalistic studies (observing actual teacher behavior in the classroom) do show the effects of expectancy.

**How can teacher expectations influence student behavior?**

Good and Brophy (1978) present a model to explain how teachers' naturalistic expectations for students can lead to differential patterns of teacher-student interaction, as follows:

1. The teacher expects specific behavior and achievement from particular students.
2. Because of these different expectations, the teacher behaves differently toward the different students.
3. This teacher treatment tells each student what behavior and achievement the teacher expects from him and affects his self-concept, achievement motivation, and level of aspiration.
4. If this teacher treatment is consistent over time, and if the student does not actively resist or change it in some way, it will tend to shape his achievement and behavior. High-expectation students

will be led to achieve at high levels, while the achievement of low-expectation students will decline.

5. With time, the student's achievement and behavior will conform more and more closely to that originally expected of him. (p. 12)

This model charts a course for teacher expectations to be self-fulfilling They must be translated into behavior that will communicate the expectations to the student and shape behavior in the expected direction. This process does not always happen, because the teacher may either not form a concise expectation about a student or may continually change those expectations. Even when a teacher does have a consistent expectation for a particular student, if that expectation is not communicated to the student, the expectations cannot be self-fulfilling. In still another situation, students who reject teachers' conception of themselves will act in ways that force the teachers to change their behavior toward them. Teacher expectations about students have no direct impact on their behavior unless the expectations are communicated to students and ultimately shape their behavior.

Individual differences of students influence the effects of teacher expectations. For example, students who are more sensitive to subtle communication cues, more dependent or "other-directed," heavily dependent upon the teacher for information, and more disruptive, are more susceptible to expectation effects than other students (Brophy, 1985a).

Brophy (1985a) has summarized the research on how teachers may behave differentially toward students in the class:

1. Wait less time for lows [low-expectation students] to answer.
2. Give lows the answer or call on someone else rather than trying to improve lows' responses by giving clues or repeating or rephrasing the question.
3. Inappropriate reinforcement rewarding inappropriate behavior or incorrect answers by lows.
4. Criticizing lows more often for failure.
5. Praising lows less frequently than highs for success.
6. Failure to give feedback to the public responses of lows.
7. Generally paying less attention to lows or interacting with them less frequently.
8. Calling on lows less often to respond to questions.
9. Seating lows farther away from the teacher.
10. Demanding less from lows.
11. General differences in type and initiation of individualized interactions with students; teachers interact with lows more privately than publicly and monitor and structure their activities more closely.
12. Differential administration or grading of tests or assignments, in which highs but not lows are given the benefit of the doubt in borderline cases.
13. Less friendly interaction with lows including less smiling and other nonverbal indicators of support.
14. Briefer and less informative feedback to the questions of lows. (pp. 309–310)

In reviewing the research on teacher-student interaction relating to teacher expectation for student achievement, Brophy (1985a) points out that high achievers are likely to be more responsive in class, to complete their assignments, and to cooperate more with their teacher than are low achievers. Because teacher expectations are generally accurate, the high-expectation students in a classroom *are* actually the high achievers and the low-expectation students *are* actually the low achievers. Brophy points out that one should not judge all differences in interaction between high and low achievers as a result of teacher expectations. A similar conclusion was observed earlier in terms of teacher interaction with male and female students (see Chapter 4).

Can you think of incidents in your schooling when teacher expectations led to self-fulfilling prophecies? Identify the behaviors under each of the following categories: How were they formed? How were they communicated? What type of behavior was exhibited?

The important aspect of teachers' expectations is that they are major factors in the development of children's expectations for their own learning. Students can accurately report differences in the ways in which teachers work with high and low achievers. Even more important, teacher practices provide clues about student ability. For example, children read clues about their relative smartness in the differentiation of the following (Weinstein, 1989):

- assignments of tasks to students ("one person will be doing harder work")
- patterns used to group students ("I wanted Miss _____ to put me in a smarter group")
- motivational strategies used for instruction (highs could "read any book they want," lows "can't choose what they read because they need it")
- responsibilities given to learners ("the way you know a person is smart, Miss _____ always picks them to go different places")
- quality of teacher-student relationships ("you can really tell just by the way she treats people who are doing well") (p. 203)

## Appropriate Teacher Expectations

Now that you know that *some* teachers have low expectations for particular students, you may conclude that the best strategy is that a teacher should have no expectations or only positive expectations for student behavior and performance. Good and Brophy (1990) argue that neither of these solutions is a viable alternative. First, expectations cannot be suppressed or avoided. We all develop expectations from our interaction with individuals that tend to stay with us. Even if teachers attempted to avoid other sources of information about their students, they would still develop expectations. Moreover, it probably would be worse to avoid information that could help in planning more effective instructional programs. Second, although it is important for teachers to believe that all students can achieve,

**How can the improper use of praise have a negative impact on students?**

this attitude must not be carried to the point of distorting reality by setting unrealistically high standards that some students cannot reach. This strategy can lead to student frustration and failure.

Teachers also need to reconsider the common strategy of finding opportunities to constantly praise students for all types of behavior and academic performance. You may be thinking: "What's wrong with praising students? Isn't this a good way to communicate high expectations and reinforce good behavior at the same time?" Brophy (1981) has pointed out how the incorrect use of praise can undermine achievement behavior. First, when teachers try to find something good in the work of low-achieving students to encourage them, the praise is often for some irrelevant or unimportant aspect of completing the task. For example, if the task is to complete math problems, commenting on a student's neat homework paper is not likely to have the positive effect on the student that the teacher intended. What happens is that the student often discounts the praise. What's worse is that the student often interprets the praise to be unrelated to effort or performance, but as evidence of lack of ability. The result is a negative effect on self-confidence. The student may be thinking the following about the teacher: "He must really think I'm dumb, if he praised me for that" or "How could she say that paper looks good? I know it's lousy."

The effect of praise also must be considered in terms of the students' stage of development. For young students who view effort and ability similarly, praise can enhance their perceptions of their competence. However, praising older students who view ability and effort differently, praising their effort may be interpreted as having low expectation for their ability (Ames, 1990).

Brophy (1981) provides guidelines for the effective use of praise. Included in his advice is praising genuine progress or accomplishment, making it contingent upon objective accomplishment, specifying the reasons why it is given, making it private (so as not to embarrass the student), and attributing success to effort and ability.

Good and Brophy (1990) suggest that teachers need to develop appropriate expectations by establishing goals *and* moving students along at a pace that they can handle. It is important that teachers monitor their treatment of individual students to ensure that they do not act in a detrimental manner toward certain students and that they change their response as the student changes. As Brophy (1985b) states: "The probability of self-fulfilling prophecy effects does not depend so much on the initial accuracy of expectations as on the degree of rigidity with which they are held and the degree to which they are taken into account in planning and decision making about instruction" (p. 179). In summary, according to Good and Brophy (1987), teachers can deal with expectations

by keeping a general focus on instruction as their main task, and by training themselves to observe students systematically with an eye toward their present progress and needs, teachers can maintain a generally appropriate orientation to the classroom. They can reinforce this by learning to recognize and evaluate the attitudes and expectations that they form spontaneously in daily interaction with students. This will enable them to correct inaccuracies and to use accurate information in planning individualized treatment. (p. 161)

## Teachers' Sense of Efficacy

**How can teacher efficacy impact student behavior?**

It appears that high expectations for student achievement are related to a pattern of attitudes, beliefs, and behaviors that identify teachers and schools that maximize gains in student achievement (Brophy & Evertson, 1976). For example, Brookover et al. (1978) investigated variables in school climate that influenced achievement and found that teachers in high-achieving schools spent more time on instruction and demonstrated greater concern for and commitment to their students' achievement.

Recently, researchers have been interested in the construct **teacher efficacy**, teachers' belief in their own ability to affect student learning (Ashton & Webb, 1986; Gibson & Dembo, 1984). A number of investigations have indicated that teachers who have a greater sense of efficacy produce higher achievement gains in their students. The measure of teacher efficacy was originally determined by teachers' responses on a scale from 1 (strongly disagreed) to 7 (strongly agreed) to two items: (1) "When it comes right down to it, a teacher really can't do much because most of a student's motivation and performance depends on his or her home environment," and (2) "If I really try hard, I can get through to even the most difficult or unmotivated students."

What causes differences in teachers' sense of efficacy? Dembo and Gibson (1985) believe that it results primarily from environmental factors. For example, teachers who are properly trained to deal with the diversity of students found in the classroom, who are supported by their principals, who develop collegial relations with their fellow teachers, and who work cooperatively with parents are more likely to develop the belief that they can solve teaching problems and help students to learn. Unfortunately, there are teachers with a low sense of efficacy who do not have these positive experiences. As a result, they are less likely to believe that they can help certain students to learn.

I believe that research in the area of teacher efficacy raises important concerns about the professional development of teachers. The most important question is: How can teachers maintain their enthusiasm for teaching during the difficult early years of teaching? Reread the "Diary of a Beginning Teacher" in Chapter 1 and notice the frustration expressed by the teacher. Regardless of whether or not additional inservice training and other support are provided at your school, you need to take responsibility for your own career development. Find someone in the school with whom you can relate to, ask questions, share ideas with other teachers, and seek ways to involve parents in some of the activities of the class. One of the most important factors relating to a low sense of efficacy in teaching is isolation and the feeling that you are the only one facing teaching problems. The fact is that many teachers have problems, but most do not talk about them to other teachers. Don't judge yourself too harshly as you begin to practice the methods and techniques you learned during your teacher education.

# INSTRUCTIONAL PROCEDURES

An important factor influencing student motivation is the many decisions teachers make about how the classroom is organized for instruction. These decisions influence student perceptions that will affect their achievement behavior. This section focuses on the interaction of teacher behavior and instructional processes.

## Classroom Climate

**How does the classroom climate influence student motivation?**

In Chapter 9, I discussed how teachers can formulate goals or objectives for instruction. Teachers also structure activities and reward students in ways that influence students' personal learning goals or intentions for performing a task.

Two different goal orientations have been identified by researchers— mastery (or learning) and performance (Dweck, 1985). A *mastery goal* is oriented toward learning as much as possible for the purpose of self-improvement, irrespective of the performance of others. A *performance goal* focuses on social comparison and competition, with the main purpose of outperforming others on the task. Different teachers establish different types of learning climates in their classrooms. Table 10.3 identifies the distinctions between these goals.

**TABLE 10.3 ACHIEVEMENT GOAL ANALYSIS OF CLASSROOM CLIMATE**

| Climate Dimensions | Mastery Goal | Performance Goal |
| --- | --- | --- |
| Success defined as . . . | Improvement, progress | High grades, high normative performance |
| Value placed on . . . | Effort/learning | Normatively high ability |
| Reasons for satisfaction . . . | Working hard, challenge | Doing better than others |
| Teacher oriented toward . . . | How students are learning | How students are performing |
| View of errors/mistakes . . . | Part of learning | Anxiety-eliciting |
| Focus of attention . . . | Process of learning | Own performance relative to others' |
| Reasons for effort . . . | Learning something new | High grades, performing better than others |
| Evaluation criteria . . . | Absolute, progress | Normative |

*Source: Ames and Archer, 1988.*

At different times both goals are pursued by students. However, there are times when students make choices as to which goal to pursue. An important factor influencing their choice is situation variables. For example, if evaluation is emphasized, students will be less interested in mastery and will pursue performance goals (i.e., they will select tasks to demonstrate their high ability or conceal low ability). If the value of the skill rather than evaluation is emphasized, students tend to choose the mastery goal—that is, select a task that maximizes learning, even though it may involve risks and possible confusion (Elliott & Dweck, 1981).

Different classroom environments can also affect students' use of learning strategies. Ames and Archer (1988) found that students who perceive their classroom as emphasizing mastery rather than performance goals were more likely to use effective learning strategies. This is an important finding for two reasons. First, students may acquire many different learning strategies, but never choose to use them unless they are motivated to do so. Second, one factor determining students' motivation to use strategies is their perceptions of the classroom climate. Thus teachers should be alert to the fact that they must establish classroom environments that support the use of the learning strategies they are teaching.

Another distinction in classroom climates that can have an affect on student perception of abilities is the unidimensional-multidimensional classification. Rosenholtz and Simpson (1984) found that some teachers develop a unidimensional classroom, which has a single standard for success. These teachers constantly reinforce the notion that some students are smarter than others, and they behave in ways that support this belief (e.g., constantly talking about the "top" or "smarter" students). Other teachers develop a multidimensional classroom, in which they communicate to their students how much everyone in the class is learning and that there are many ways to succeed. In addition, these teachers point out that all students have different strengths and weaknesses. Can you provide examples of these climates from your own school experiences? What influence did such climates have on the motivation of different students in the class?

## Task

Maehr (1984) believes that the key factor determining whether individuals will become involved in a particular activity depends on what the activity means to them. Two variables that affect meaning are *social expectations* and *task design*. For example, individuals who are assigned a leadership role or who are given higher status are likely also to exhibit higher performance levels. In an investigation that has important implications for teachers, Zander and Forward (1968) placed students motivated toward low and high achievement in groups in which the leader and follower roles were rotated. When in the leadership role, the low-motivated students exhibited the same achievement patterns as the high-motivated students. The temporary assignment of social role elicited the same behavioral patterns exhibited by the high-motivated students in the leadership role. The results of this research suggest that a part of one's achievement motivation may be related to one's perceived role as a class clown, a low achiever, or a lazy student and to the expectations that follow the role. As a result, the teacher should attempt to modify or change students' expectations by placing them in situations requiring different types of behavior (e.g., giving them responsibility for completing an important task for the class such as finding an appropriate location for an event, chairing a committee, leading a group discussion, or explaining how to solve a problem). The result of such action by the teacher communicates to the students that the teacher expects successful completion of the task. Giving responsibility to students who are viewed as being unmotivated by other teachers and peers may be the first step in breaking the negative self-fulfilling prophecy they have experienced for many years.

Another characteristic of a teaching-learning situation is the task itself. Maehr points out that several features of the task may affect the meaning that the task will have for the student. Some tasks by their very nature are more interesting and inherently motivating than others. For example, finding a solution to an ambiguous physical event in science may be more motivating than memorizing the chart of physical elements or balancing chemical equations.

Teachers need to think about how they present assignments and whether the assignments challenge students to become involved in the subject matter. Brophy et al. (1983) found that students were less likely to become involved in a task when the teacher introduced it in a negative fashion (i.e., suggesting the task was boring or pointless, or that they would find it difficult or frustrating). You can probably remember the attitudes of students in a class when a teacher said something like "I really don't want to teach this, but the school district requires it," or "This section is the least interesting of the course."

## Intrinsic versus Extrinsic Motivation

**What are the consequences of the development of intrinsic or extrinsic motivation?**

Another factor under the control of the teacher is the extent to which intrinsic or extrinsic motivation is emphasized. **Intrinsic motivation** is influenced by personal factors such as satisfaction or enjoyment. **Extrinsic motivation** is influenced by external events such as grades, points, or money. Behavioral psychologists tend to emphasize the importance of extrinsic motivation, whereas cognitive and humanistic psychologists tend to favor intrinsic motivation.

A teacher's beliefs regarding how motivation should be viewed can influence the classroom organization. If you believe that students have little inclination to learn in school and need to be encouraged to learn through external incentives, you are more likely to be influenced by procedures that emphasize more teacher control over learning activities. If you believe that children are naturally curious and that learning is a process of self-discovery such that motivation comes from within the person, you are likely to establish a different type of classroom situation. You do not have to take a position at either extreme. Some educators believe that intrinsic motivation can be used to guide much of classroom learning and that students may need some external incentives to learn material they are less interested in.

An important issue regarding intrinsic versus extrinsic motivation is how teachers can maintain student involvement in learning activities that are not very interesting or exciting to students, without alienating them from learning, or having a negative affect on their self-concepts or independence (Ryan, Connell, & Deci, 1985). This issue is especially important because there appears to be a steady decrease in students' intrinsic motivation for learning as they progress through school (DeCharms, 1981; Harter, 1981).

The way a teacher organizes the classroom environment can have considerable impact on students' motivation and their view of themselves. Two investigations reported by Ryan, Connell, and Deci (1985) further illustrate this point.

Deci, Nezlek, and Sheinman (1981) investigated the relationship between a teacher's orientation to students' intrinsic motivation and self-esteem. They identified autonomy- and control-oriented teachers. *Autonomy-oriented teachers* are likely to support students in solving their own problems and pursuing their own interests. *Control-oriented teachers* are likely to motivate students with rewards and to use subtle control procedures. The researchers found that students' motivation and perceived competence were strongly related to the orientation of the teachers. In particular, belief in one's ability to achieve and in one's self-worth was greater in classrooms of autonomy-oriented teachers than in classrooms of control-oriented teachers.

In another investigation, Ryan and Grolnick (1984) determined the extent to which students viewed their classrooms to be autonomy-oriented versus control-oriented. The data indicated that students who perceived their classrooms as being more autonomy-oriented were higher on intrinsic motivation and perceived cognitive competence, and reported higher levels of self-esteem than did the students who perceived their classrooms as being more control-oriented.

Researchers also have found that teachers can undermine intrinsic motivation and learning by too much emphasis on external rewards or incentives (see Lepper & Hodell, 1989, for a detailed discussion of this literature). It appears that when students already enjoy an activity and receive rewards for participating in the activity, they will be less likely to return to the activity than students with the same interest who didn't receive any rewards for participation.

This result seems contrary to what you have already learned about reinforcement theory. Could it be that too much reward is not good? Let's look at one explanation of this phenomenon: When students receive a reward for doing something, they attribute the reward as the reason for engaging in the activity, even if, without the reward, they would have been intrinsically motivated to complete the task. Once they perceive the extrinsic reward as the reason for participating in the activity, they will engage in the activity only if the reward is given. Another way of explaining this result is that the students discount their initial interest in the task as the reason for doing the task. Instead, the more powerful extrinsic reward is perceived to be the cause (Stipek, 1988).

This research doesn't suggest that rewards are bad or that teachers should not reinforce students. You need to differentiate between using rewards to involve students in activities that they don't want to pursue (such as completing homework assignments) and using rewards in situations in which students already enjoy the assigned activity. Don't worry about undermining intrinsic motivation in the former case; it is only when the activity may be interesting or enjoyable that you need to omit or reduce the use of rewards for students. Stipek (1988) suggests: "When extrinsic rewards are used to prod students into initially engaging in a task, every effort should be made to shift students' attention away from the extrinsic reward and toward the importance of the task and the feelings of competence that derive from mastery" (p. 67).

## Continuing Motivation

Maehr (1976) has cautioned teachers to be concerned about students' **continuing motivation**—that is, the tendency to return to and to continue working on tasks away from the classroom without the supervision or control of the teacher. These questions pertain to continuing motivation: Will students read during vacations? Will students visit scientific exhibits and museums? Will students follow current events? Will young adults vote? The point is that although teachers have power and control over students while they are in the classroom and can make them follow directions and complete academic tasks, some of the methods they use to attain these short-term objectives (e.g., punishment, threats, and criticism) may be detrimental to the students' continuing motivation in the subject area. Inappropriate classroom experiences can make today's highly motivated students tomorrow's unmotivated students. Pascarella et al. (1981) found that although teacher control was positively related to science achievement in high school, it was negatively related to a number of behavioral indicators of continuing motivation.

Finally, an important motivational factor is the degree of freedom in selecting the task or assignment. In general, giving students some options as to the type of assignment they can complete is related to continuing motivation. Maehr (1984) believes that a choice of assignments can affect the meaning or purpose of the task and result in greater personal investment. However, if the teacher strongly emphasizes social comparison, student choices may be based on ability to complete the selected task successfully (i.e., to protect their perceptions of ability) rather than on their interest in the task (Ames, 1990).

## Goal Structure

Another approach to understanding the context of learning is the type of **goal structure** a teacher establishes for various learning activities. A goal structure determines the way in which students will relate to one another and to the teacher while working toward instructional goals (Johnson & Johnson, 1987). There are three types of goal structures:

- *Cooperative*—students work together to accomplish shared goals
- *Competitive*—students work against each other to achieve goals that only a few students can attain.
- *Individualistic*—one student's achievement of the goal is unrelated to other students' achievement of the goal.

An example of each of these goal structures includes students working together to survey political attitudes in the community (cooperative), students completing individual projects in science that will be graded on a curve (competitive), and students working individually on specific areas of weakness in mathematics, with their grade to be based on their own progress (individualistic).

Each type of goal structure promotes a different pattern of interaction among students, thus creating a different learning climate. In addition, different types of motivation are elicited under each learning condition. A cooperative goal structure promotes positive interpersonal relations such as trust, acceptance, sharing, and helping. A competitive goal structure promotes little trust and acceptance and often generates more attempts to mislead and obstruct others. An individualistic goal structure promotes interaction with the teacher rather than with peers and minimizes positive affective outcomes.

All three goal structures are effective under certain conditions and are relevant to specific goals and objectives of a lesson. Knowing when to use cooperative, competitive, and individualistic learning is an important instructional decision that the teacher must make.

Johnson and Johnson (1987) believe that cooperative settings are more likely to produce higher levels of motivation to learn because the interaction patterns encourage and support one's efforts to achieve. They present evidence to show more cross-ethnic and cross-handicap helping and tutoring in cooperative than in competitive or individualistic learning situations.

*Altering Motivation through Changes in Methods of Instruction.* Ames and Ames (1984) have studied how goal structures affect types of motivation. They point out that a student's attributions (e.g., "I did well because I am smart," or "If I work harder, I can succeed") may be influenced by classroom learning settings as well as performance history. Table 10.4 outlines

TABLE 10.4 **MOTIVATIONAL PROCESSES WITHIN THREE GOAL STRUCTURES**

| Goal Structure | Salient Performance Information | Attributional Focus |
|---|---|---|
| Competitive | Other's performance relative to own | Ability |
| Cooperative | Group performance | Effort |
| Individualistic | Own performance change/improvement over time | Effort |

*Source: Ames and Ames, 1984.*

**How do different goal structures influence self-perceptions of ability?**

the motivational systems that relate to competitive, cooperative, and individualistic goal structures in terms of salient performance information and attributional focus.

A competitive setting promotes a situation in which personal satisfaction depends on whether a student has won or lost. Self-assessment of *ability* based on social comparison information is the major attributional focus. Students evaluate their ability as high after success and as low after failure. If one is a low achiever, it is difficult to feel good about one's self or one's performance if the basis of comparison is the performance of others in the class.

A cooperative setting elicits a concern for responsibility to the group, with a focus on group performance information and the degree to which *effort* was related to both individual and group performance. Although success and failure are still key factors influencing personal satisfaction and perception of ability, an important finding is that successful cooperative groups can alleviate the negative self-evaluation that many low achievers exhibit (Ames, 1981). The implication is that the teacher, by using cooperative groups, may be able to insulate the low-achieving students from the negative effects of failure on self-esteem. This condition is likely to occur because of the focus on effort and group outcomes in addition to personal achievement.

Finally, a noncompetitive-individualistic structure elicits a mastery orientation in which *effort* attributions prevail and personal performance over a series of assignments becomes salient. When low-achieving students can judge their progress according to individual improvement rather than by the performance of others, the students are more likely to believe that trying can pay off, and the students will feel better about their performance. However, if individuals work independently but their performance is compared to that of others in the class, the situation is similar to interpersonal competition.

Ames and Ames (1981) illustrated how various goal structures influence the way students attend to sources of information. They found that in competitive structures, students were less concerned about their previous performance. Instead, they judged themselves and based their feelings of satisfaction only on whether they won or lost. By contrast, in individualized settings, the past performance information influenced students' affective reactions. Students whose past performance was good seemed less negatively affected by a failure in individual settings than those who had a history of failure. A significant implication for the teacher is to realize that, in competition, the low-achieving students are less likely to be influenced by the teacher who points out how much progress was made over the week or semester. The students are primarily concerned about whether they have been successful on the present task.

An important aspect of competitive goal structures is that rewards are often limited to the students who do the best or to the highest performers. As a result, less capable students find it difficult to obtain recognition for their achievements (Ames & Ames, 1990).

Goal structures also appear to affect how teachers perceive and evaluate students (Ames & Ames, 1984). There is some evidence that competitive settings may cause teachers to view students in more dichotomized ways (e.g., able versus unable, or successful versus unsuccessful). In a cooperative setting, a teacher may place more emphasis on effort and try to help more students in the class.

In conclusion, different goal structures lead to different types of motivation because each structure promotes a different value orientation. It is important for teachers to realize how instructional procedures can affect their own behavior and to understand why students attend to certain sources of performance information and not others in judging their academic success.

I have been critical of competition in this section because of its overuse in the classroom. There are situations in which a limited amount of competition can be effective (e.g., motivating a group of bored students to complete an assignment, or motivating a group of learners of similar ability to work harder). However, the evidence is clear that the extensive use of competition does not produce many of the intended motivational effects for which it is used.

## EVALUATION AND ACHIEVEMENT ANXIETY

**How does anxiety influence student achievement?**

The type of and frequency of evaluation in the classroom can have important implications for student motivation (Ames & Ames, 1990). Some teachers employ evaluation procedures that have questionable impact on student motivation. For example, many teachers use public display of students' assignments and tests as a motivational strategy. This display may be in the form of charts and graphs to show where students stand in relation to each other. Do you think that low-achieving students are motivated by such a procedure? Do they spend time reviewing these charts or graphs?

Some teachers have too much evaluation in that almost every activity and performance is related to a grade. The fear is that unless an activity is graded, the students will not complete it. If a teacher's goal is to increase intrinsic motivation, excessive grading is not the answer. Teachers must consider the extent to which their grading and evaluation procedures encourage completion of the task rather than an increase in student knowledge and motivation to learn.

Researchers have indicated that for some students small amounts of anxiety can facilitate learning (Sieber, O'Neil, & Tobias, 1977). If you feel confident and prepared for an examination, a little anxiety can serve as motivation to excel. However, if you have a high level of anxiety, it can be detrimental in achievement settings (Stipek, 1988).

The type and degree of anxiety differ widely among students. For some, anxiety is a generalized fear of the total school situation and, for others, a fear of specific aspects of the school environment such as teachers, peers, particular subject areas, or tests. In extreme cases (as in school phobias), the fear is so great that the child may refuse to go to school.

Some school subjects evoke more anxiety than others. For example, Tobias (1980) has written about math anxiety, pointing out that "math-anxious" and "math-avoiding" individuals do not trust their problem-solving abilities and experience a high level of stress when asked to use them. These anxious feelings about math can lead to lower grades and to the avoidance of math and math courses (Hackett, 1985; Hutton & Levitt, 1987). The sources of anxiety in math classes stem from time pressures to complete

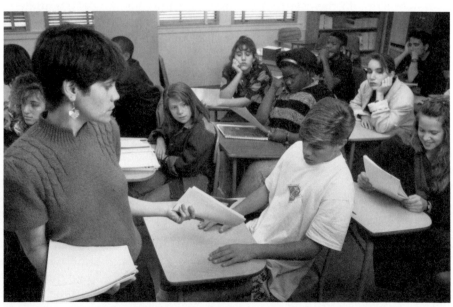

There are many anxiety-producing situations in a classroom. Can you relate to the student in this photo?

work, humiliation at being called on to perform in front of the class (remember the feeling when you were asked to put a homework problem on the board and were not prepared), and emphasis on right answers.

## Classroom Behavior of Anxious Students

Several behaviors of highly anxious students in learning situations account for their low performance levels (Hill & Wigfield, 1984). First, highly anxious students have a tendency to avoid failure because they fear negative evaluation. As a result, they will attempt to avoid evaluative situations and choose, persist, and perform more successfully on easy tasks in which success is more certain. They also are likely to become involved in failure-avoiding strategies. Second, highly anxious students do not attend to tasks in sufficient detail because they are overly preoccupied with negative self-references or worry. As the teacher is presenting information on a topic, the highly anxious student is likely to be thinking about inadequacies that may make it hard to attempt to learn the material. Third, highly anxious students have difficulty when instructional methods require them to rely on short-term memory or when they are asked to perform quickly. Finally, highly anxious students have difficulty learning material that is not well organized. They tend to perform better when the teacher structures the material for them. Instructional methods such as independent study or inquiry techniques and other nondirective procedures often are less successful for highly anxious students.

Anxiety has a number of additional consequences that can cause the student to have social as well as academic problems. Many highly anxious students have lower self-concepts, blame themselves for their failures, and daydream extensively. During adolescence, anxiety can lead to feelings of inadequacy that are associated with hostility toward school (Phillips, Hindsman, & McGuire, 1960).

## Causes of Anxiety

Why do students become anxious? Two sets of factors contribute: factors that are immediately and directly responsible for anxiety reactions and factors that have had an impact during the child's early years of life and whose effects spread throughout life (Phillips, Martin, & Meyers, 1972). The first set of factors relates to such stress conditions in the environment as an ambiguous threat (e.g., the child who anticipates a new class in September), a situational constraint, and a feeling of inability to cope. The second set of factors is indirect and includes unpleasant preschool and elementary school experiences, racial-ethnic minority status and/or lower social-class status, a nonsupportive parent-child relationship, and gender.

In a study of factors influencing anxiety in school, Phillips (1978) reported students' concerns about the difficulty of doing as well as the teacher expected them to do, the competitiveness underlying much of school work, the desire for the teacher to slow down until they understood what he or she was saying, fear of making a mistake while reciting in front of the class, and meeting parents' expectations for a good report card.

Sarason et al. (1960) undertook an extensive study on school anxiety and test situations and provided a good deal of information about both the direct and indirect antecedents of anxiety. First, they found that bright children, as well as average and slow children, are often anxious about tests and classroom performance. Second, they attributed a major role to parental attitudes in the initial formation of anxiety in children. Mothers of highly anxious children probably have conflicts about their own adequacy and depend on the opinions of others. They consistently make demands on their children that the children feel are difficult to meet and that lead to failure and the development of a poor self-image. When the children begin school, they transfer their anticipation of negative evaluation from their parents to their teachers and become anxious when their teachers present them with any type of test.

Last, the researchers found girls to be more anxious than boys. They attributed this difference between the sexes to the boys' defensiveness about admitting anxiety. In boys, such admission is not culturally accepted; it is unmasculine. However, whether or not girls admit to anxiety feelings, their femininity is not called into question.

Hill and Wigfield (1984) believe that test anxiety begins for many children during the preschool or elementary years when parents begin to make unrealistic demands or have too high expectations for their children's performance. When parents react negatively to poor performance, the children become more fearful of evaluation in test situations and become overly concerned about their parents' reactions to their future performance. As children become more aware of comparative standards and are better able to judge their ability throughout elementary school and junior high school, they develop even more anxiety in evaluative situations.

## Identifying Anxious Children

Anxiety levels can be inferred in a variety of ways. One of the easiest ways is to elicit the child's feelings about a particular situation or task.[1] There are also psychological indicators, such as severe headaches or stomach disorders that have no physical cause. Nail biting, sweating, irregularity in speech or motor coordination, restlessness, and general distraction are also warning signs for the teacher.

---

[1] Although this procedure may seem too obvious to mention, I have witnessed many teachers begin their problem solving by calling in specialists to initiate personality assessments of the child without first discussing the behavior problem with the parent or child. A good rule to follow when confronted with any serious behavior problem is first to talk to the child about the behavior. You may be surprised by the amount of information that you can learn. Also check the student's health records for physical clues to the behavior—for example, poor vision or hearing. When these avenues have been exhausted and the problem still persists, call on a professional to assist you.

Tests can be used to identify anxious students. One of the most widely used is the Test Anxiety Scale for Children (TASC), which contains 30 questions about test situations to which the student answers "yes" or "no." Some sample questions are "Do you worry a lot before you take a test?" and "Do you think you worry more about school than other children?" More recently, Harnisch, Hill, and Fyans (1980) have developed a 7-item instrument called the Test Comfort Index, which focuses on questions such as asking students if they are relaxed in the test situation. This instrument takes about five minutes to administer and has been used successfully in large-scale testing programs.

## Dealing with Anxious Students in the Classroom

**What can teachers do to reduce anxiety in the classroom?**

Children want to succeed in school, but sometimes stress and anxiety are so intense that they interfere with academic performance. If students respect their teachers highly and want to be liked by them, they must be reassured that they are capable and that a teacher will still like and accept them regardless of their academic performance. Sometimes teachers find this a burden because they have negative reactions to highly anxious students. Teachers should not compare such students with students who are succeeding or question them rigorously in front of the class to find out the nature of their difficulties or simply tell them, "You'll do better next time." The teacher should help these students to improve. Ignoring students' performance is not the answer either, because anxious students' dependency needs are great. Perhaps the worst thing teachers can do is simply to neglect these students; such behavior reinforces their ideas that their poor performance affects teachers' attitudes toward them (Sarason et al., 1960).

Anxious students perform better in more structured learning situations (Gaudry & Spielberger, 1971). Certain students who prefer and excel in highly structured classrooms tend to be personally insecure and fear failure; if they know exactly what is expected of them, they can control their anxiety to some degree. This precludes independent study, discussion groups, and other types of student-directed learning activities as wise learning strategies for anxious students.

Anxious students have trouble memorizing information as well as retrieving information that has been previously learned. Therefore, diagrams, outlines, and other methods for organizing information can be helpful to these students. An occasional open-book test also can help to reduce anxiety. As anxious persons experience success in the less threatening open-book situation, they often become better able to handle evaluation of other kinds with less anxiety.

*Test Anxiety.* Test anxiety is a specific form of anxiety about academic and ability evaluation. Hill and Wigfield (1984) state: "Test anxiety is one of the most important aspects of negative motivation and has direct debilitating effects on school performance" (p. 106). Educators are especially concerned about this type of anxiety because it increases through the elementary grades to high school and becomes more strongly (i.e., negatively) related to indexes of intellectual and academic performance (Hembree, 1988; Wigfield & Eccles, 1989). As students proceed through school, the higher their anxiety is, the more likely it is that they will have lower achievement. There is also a negative correlation between anxiety and intelligence test scores: the higher the test anxiety, the lower the IQ score. To the argument that people with high anxiety are also less intelligent, and as a result, score lower on IQ tests, Gaudry and Spielberger (1971) respond: Highly anxious students perform as well as students with low anxiety on nonstressful and more structured tasks. Other researchers have found a more plausible explanation. Highly anxious students react to a normal intelligence test situation as they would to any regular examination seen as a stressful situation, but when intelligence tests or learning tasks are presented under "nontest" situations, highly anxious students perform as well as or better than students with low anxiety (Sarason et al., 1960; Wrightsman, 1962). More will be said in the next section about factors that reduce the effects of anxiety in test situations.

*Dealing with Test Anxiety.* Hill and Wigfield (1984) suggest a number of interventions that can be implemented in a school to improve the performance of highly anxious students. First, begin at the elementary school level by changing report cards from the traditional A-B-C-D-F grades to a form that reports a student's achievement, effort (remember what we learned about the impact of stable [ability] attributions in terms of future performance), and strengths and weaknesses (see Chapter 13 for more information on grading and reporting systems). Letter grades can promote excessive competition among students as they compare grades among themselves. Parents as well often view children's report card grades in a comparative manner, wanting their children to perform at a higher level than other students in the class. If most parents want their children to be in the top quarter of their class, many children are going to feel unsuccessful. Reducing the focus on comparative ability but still reporting student progress may have important effects on reducing anxiety among students.

Second, there is evidence to indicate that the achievement test scores of highly anxious students are similar to scores of low-anxiety students when the testing procedures are changed. Two major factors are a change in time limits and modification of instructions (e.g., telling them not to worry about difficult items and to do their best). An important implication of the investigations in this area is that current testing programs may be underestimating the achievement and ability of highly anxious students. Hill and Wigfield (1984) suggest that school districts should consider giving certain tests in standard as well as in optimizing ways. Teachers also need to consider how they present regular classroom tests to students and whether they are allowing sufficient time for highly anxious students to complete the test.

Finally, classroom programs can be implemented to teach students how to deal with test situations. Special attention can be given to students who are identified as being anxious about testing and who do poorly in evaluative settings. Some guidelines for establishing a program that teaches test-taking skills are included in the Classroom Application "Teaching Test-Taking Skills," in Chapter 12.

In trying to help the low-achieving, anxious student, we should not forget the influence of the child's parents. Some psychologists believe that parents (particularly the mother) initially contribute to the student's anxiety. Brookover, Patterson, and Thomas (1965) initiated a successful program to raise the academic achievement of underachieving junior high pupils by enhancing their self-evaluations and expectations. Over 90% of the pupils valued their parents' opinion of their ability over the opinion of friends and teachers. As a result of this finding, Brookover, Patterson, and Thomas set up a series of discussions over a period of one year to inform parents about ways they could encourage the self-concept and academic ability of their children. By the end of the ninth grade, the pupils whose parents were in the program significantly improved their grade-point averages and self-concepts. These pupils were pleased to perceive that their parents also had higher expectations for their ability.

This program has important implications for dealing with parents. In too many situations, parents are contacted by the school only when their children are in some difficulty. The one-sided negative input lowers parental concepts of their children's potential, which in turn has detrimental effects on their children. Teachers need to communicate positive information to parents and work more closely with them as they attempt to help their children.

The following Classroom Application reviews some important factors in motivating students.

## CLASSROOM APPLICATION: MOTIVATING STUDENTS

**Curiosity**

Provoke curiosity in students before stating a topic by pointing up a problem or conflict, or giving a pretest to make them realize what they don't know about the topic. Arouse surprise and a feeling of contradiction in students by presenting a phenomenon that violates their expectations or runs counter to their experience and former training—for instance, plants that live without sunlight or chlorophyll (fungi). Arouse doubt, uncertainty, bafflement by giving students a problem with no indications for its solution—for example, how to find one's position (latitude and longitude) in the middle of the desert.

## Attention

Arouse attention in students by starting a class with something novel, different, unusual, such as a brainstorming demonstration or a copy of an old newspaper in history. Maintain attention and interest through variety and change; never start a class the same way day after day.

## Level of Aspiration

Provide for different levels of aspiration among students by encouraging them to strive for levels of performance in keeping with their abilities and by having differentiated materials, activities, and projects available for students of different ability and aspiration levels. Independent study programs are a good example of such an approach.

With individual ability levels in mind, set standards and provide tasks of intermediate difficulty that are within the reach of students but still offer some challenge. Provide easier tasks for students who are discouraged because of low or failing grades. Mastering easier tasks will help them set realistic—and gradually higher—levels of aspiration for their work.

## Promote Beliefs in Competence

On occasion, try to increase the basic achievement motivation of some students through talking with them, having them read about highly motivated persons, putting them in with a group of highly motivated students, and so forth. Make students aware of their successes and the satisfaction they bring through comments such as "You really did well in that," "Didn't it feel good to get so many right?" Try to divert students' attention away from their failures by not threatening or punishing them or dwelling on their errors.

## Reinforcement

Use praise and encouragement appropriately, particularly for average and slower students and those who are more introverted and lack self-assurance. Give personal, encouraging comments on tests and other work rather than just a grade. Inform students regularly on how they are doing in a course, the sooner after a test or assignment the better.

## Reduce Social Comparison and Competition in the Classroom

Social comparison can be reduced by having students work toward individually prescribed or group goals. Limit the use of charts, posting grades, public pronouncements of high and low scores, and other strategies that lead to excessive emphasis on comparing successful and unsuccessful students. Competition should be geared to the ability levels of the students so that all have a chance to succeed, and [students] should focus on their own past performance as they set new goals for themselves, rather than on what others are doing or have done.

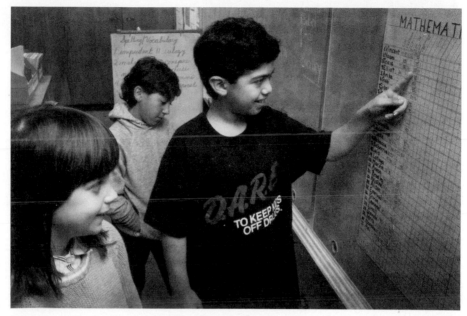

Classroom charts and graphs identifying student progress do not motivate all students to excel.

### Encourage Students' Effort Attributions

Students should be given individual feedback when they fail and shown concrete steps they can take to improve. Teachers can model how success is attributed to effort by describing personal experiences in which they accomplished tasks by trying hard to succeed. Students might read stories and biographies describing individuals who have accomplished goals through effort and discuss individually or in groups the reasons why people succeed or fail. The discussion should focus on how attitudes, interests, and efforts are related to succeeding. Along with emphasis on the importance of effort, teach students the necessary learning strategies so they have the competencies and skills to succeed.

### Increase Students' Involvement in Learning

Students should be given opportunities to select activities, assignments, due dates, and those with whom they want to work, as well as their own methods and pace of learning. They can be involved in relating the curriculum material to their own experiences and problems. It is important that students perceive choices as equally attractive and difficult so they don't select simple tasks just to succeed. Involvement in learning also can be enhanced through games, small-group teaching, cooperative learning, and class discussions.

### Reduce Anxiety in Achievement Situations

Students must have sufficient time to complete assignments, tests, and other work so they do not worry about them. Clearly identify what is expected in assignments and help students develop a plan to accomplish tasks. Use relaxation training and teach test-taking skills (Chapter 12) when needed.

### Provide for Students' Affiliation Needs

Varied procedures should be used for grouping students according to shared interest, similar ability levels, friendship patterns, and at random, for example. They should have time to talk to each other about personal affairs as well as academic tasks. Games or activities that require team effort also help students satisfy their needs for affiliation and belonging.

---

\* Material in this Classroom Application is quoted in part from Gorman (1974, pp. 127–128), Hudgins et al. (1983, pp. 424–427), and Ames and Ames (1990).

---

**THINKING ABOUT THE TEACHING-LEARNING MODEL**

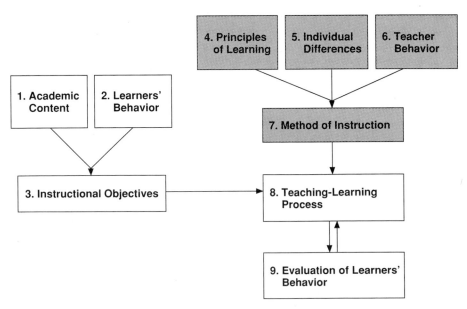

*Source: Adapted from Hunter, 1971, in Allen and Seifman.*

This chapter has focused on the importance of student perceptions in understanding achievement-related behaviors. The interaction of individual differences (box No. 5), principles of learning (box No. 4), teacher behavior (box No. 6), and methods of instruction (box No. 7) can be viewed from a number of perspectives. Most important, teachers must understand the link between metacognitive knowledge and motivational-attitudinal factors, since each component influences the other.

The motivational factors that are related to using learning strategies (Chapter 7) include positive self esteem, an internal locus of control, and a positive attributional belief about success and failure (aspects of what is called the self-system). Students with positive self-systems are more likely to attempt strategies to help them learn more effectively. However, students with dysfunctional self-systems (i.e., they perceive they have little control over the factors determining their success, lack confidence in their abilities, and/or have a low self-esteem) are less likely to use strategies. When students are successful in the use of the strategies, they feel better about their abilities, are more likely to attribute effort as an important cause of their success, and are likely to use learning strategies in the future (Borkowski et al., 1990).

Borkowski et al. point out why metacognitive skills and motivation are equally important:

> Although the self system provides the necessary motivation and affective states to foster children's progress towards self-determination, it is the metacognitive system which provides the means to reach that goal. In order for the metacognitive system to work, children must have adequate information about both general and specific strategy knowledge—about why, when, and how to use strategies. Effort-related attributions are of little use to a child who does not have the necessary accompanying specific strategic knowledge. Such children will end up "spinning their wheels," for instance, having high motivation and energy to use appropriate strategies but not knowing how to select the one to employ for a particular task. Hence, intervention programs must focus on the development of both the self and the metacognitive systems in order to maximize children's academic performance. (p. 19)

Learning disabled students need to be taught effective strategies to help them in school, but they are likely to have dysfunctional self-systems that lead, for some students, to a learned helplessness. The result is not only a decline in motivation; they are also discouraged from engaging in task analysis, task persistence, and task selection (Short & Weissberg-Benchell, 1989). This is why low-achieving or learning disabled students often can't tell the teacher what they don't understand—they are unable to distinguish what they know from what they don't know and they are unable to plan an effective study strategy. Thus, telling these students to study longer or harder is not useful advice. Review the work of Schumacker et al. (1983, 1986) identified in Chapter 5 for teaching learning strategies to learning disabled students.

The final point I would like to make about teaching low-achieving and learning disabled students relates to the impact of teacher behavior with methods of instruction. Most teachers use highly organized and structured approaches (such as direct instruction) to help low-achieving students acquire basic skills and strategies for learning. While students initially benefit from this approach, they need more opportunity for self-structuring and self-monitoring to use their newly acquired metacognitive skills. Thus teachers who maintain tight control over the students by offering help all the time when problems are confronted may be inadvertently training their students to be dependent on them. Therefore, it is important to gradually allow students more responsibility for their own learning (Ellis, 1986).

## KEY POINTS

1. Teachers can make instructional decisions that can enhance student motivation.
2. Locus of control pertains to how individuals perceive the link between their behavior and its consequences and whether or not they accept responsibility for their actions.
3. Child-rearing practices that focus on raising an independent child are associated with the presence of high achievement motivation in children.
4. Student self-perceptions influence their achievement behavior.
5. An individual's beliefs (attributions) about the causes of success and failure are important in understanding achievement-related behaviors.
6. The attributions of success-oriented and failure-avoiding students differ.
7. Many students develop strategies to avoid failure to protect their sense of worth.
8. Learned-helpless students don't see any relation between effort and achievement outcomes.
9. Teachers can enhance student motivation and academic achievement by encouraging greater effort while teaching them strategies for learning more effectively.
10. Teachers' expectations can lead to self-fulfilling prophecies in students.
11. Teachers need to set appropriate or realistic expectations for their students.
12. Teacher expectations can determine how much students learn.
13. Teachers need to develop appropriate or realistic levels of expectations rather than believe that they should have no expectations or only high expectations for student behavior and performance.
14. Praise can be used ineffectively in the classroom.
15. Teachers vary in their sense of efficacy—the belief that they can help

any students learn. The development of a high sense of efficacy appears to be related to environmental factors such as effective teacher training and positive collegial and parent-teacher relations.

16. The classroom climate can influence whether students choose to use effective learning strategies and are able to receive recognition for their abilities.
17. Students' perception of a task can influence the extent to which students become involved in it.
18. Student motivation can be influenced by the manner in which teachers introduce assignments.
19. Teachers' classroom practices can determine the extent to which intrinsic or extrinsic motivation is developed.
20. Certain control measures that are effective in maintaining students' present performance may contribute negatively to their continuing motivation.
21. Different goal structures produce different types of motivational systems.
22. Some teachers overuse competitive goal structures.
23. High anxiety has a debilitating effect on academic performances that require difficult tasks.
24. High anxiety often is associated with low self-concept and low academic performance.

## KEY TERMS

locus of control, p. 414
external locus of control, p. 414
internal locus of control, p. 414
attribution, p. 416
learned helplessness, p. 418
teacher expectations, p. 422
teacher efficacy, p. 427
intrinsic motivation, p. 430
extrinsic motivation, p. 430
continuing motivation, p. 432
goal structure, p. 433

## SUGGESTIONS FOR FURTHER READING

Dusek, J. (Ed.) (1985). *Teacher expectancies*. Hillsdale, NJ: Erlbaum. An excellent source of research findings in teacher expectations.

Nicholls, J. G. (1989). *The competitive ethos and democratic education*. Cambridge, MA: Harvard University Press. A discussion of the impact of competition on students.

The following four books provide the most comprehensive review of theory and research available regarding motivation in education:

Ames, C., & Ames, R. (Eds.). (1984). *Research on motivation in education: Vol. 1. Student motivation*. Orlando, FL: Academic Press.

Ames, C., & Ames, R. (Eds.). (1985). *Research on motivation in education: Vol. 2. The classroom milieu*. Orlando, FL: Academic Press.

Ames, C., & Ames, R. (Eds). (1989). *Research on motivation in education: Vol. 3. Goals and cognitions*. San Diego: Academic Press.

Stipek, D. J. (1988). *Motivation to learn: From theory to practice*. Englewood Cliffs, NJ: Prentice-Hall. A concise book on motivational problems in education.

## FOLLOW-UP ACTIVITIES

### _____ 1. Remember Your Teachers

Students have diverse experiences with teachers during their school career. They remember some teachers with excitement and fondness and others with resentment and hate. Think about the teachers who had the greatest impact on you (either positive or negative), and examine their behavior. Tell your class or group about these teachers.

### _____ 2. Consider Factors That Influence Student Motivation

Many factors influence the level and kind of motivation exhibited by students in class. From your own experience in school and/or your observations in classrooms, identify factors that enhance or inhibit student motivation in school in each of the following categories:

a. The nature of the learning task
b. The characteristics of the individual learner
c. The classroom environment
d. The behavior of the teacher
e. The grading or evaluation procedures used in class

### _____ 3. Think about Student Characteristics

The following is a list of student characteristics you may find in your classroom. *Check* each characteristic or behavior that you would encourage. *Mark two checks* beside each characteristic or behavior that you would strongly encourage. *Place an x* by each characteristic or behavior that you would *discourage*. Discuss the reasons for your selections (adapted from Torrance, 1970, p. 115).

| | |
|---|---|
| _____ adventurous, testing limits | _____ obedient |
| _____ affectionate, loving | _____ persistent |
| _____ preoccupied with tasks | _____ quiet, not talkative |
| _____ competitive, trying to win | _____ self-assertive |

_____ conforming
_____ critical of others
_____ energetic
_____ fearful

_____ sense of humor
_____ talkative
_____ timid
_____ willing to take risks

_____ 4. **Observe a Classroom**

Focus on a few students (perhaps two high achievers and two low achievers) and keep a record of their interaction with the teacher and their participation in the class. It might be interesting to include in your report the following type of information (Good & Brophy, 1984):

1. How often do low, middle, and high achievers raise their hands?
2. Do all students approach the teacher to receive help, or do some students seldom approach the teacher?
3. How long does the reading group last for each group of achievers?
4. Are the students involved in their work? How long do they work independently at their desks?
5. How often are students in different groups praised? (p. 69)

_____ 5. **Explore Anxiety-Producing Situations in School**

The term _school anxiety_ covers anxiety stemming from all situations in school-peer relations, authority relations, test situations, and other in-school, anxiety arousing transactions. Discuss your school experiences and identify situations that you found anxiety-producing.

The following are common thoughts and worries expressed by individuals who have test anxiety (Smith, 1982, p. 179). Check those with which you can identify the most, and then add additional thoughts you have experienced. Compare your thoughts with those of other students in your class.

a. Worry about Performance
_____ I should have reviewed more. I'll never get through.
_____ My mind is blank, I'll never get the answer. I must really be stupid.
_____ I can't remember a thing. This always happens to me.
_____ I knew this stuff yesterday. What is wrong with me?
_____
_____

b. Worry about Bodily Reactions
_____ I'm sick. I'll never get through.
_____ I'm sweating all over—it's really hot in here.
_____ My stomach is going crazy, churning and jumping all over.
_____ Here it comes—I'm getting really tense again. Normal people just don't get like this.
_____
_____

c. Worry about How Others Are Doing
   \_\_\_\_\_ I know everyone's doing better than I am.
   \_\_\_\_\_ I must be the dumbest one in the group.
   \_\_\_\_\_ I am going to be the last one done again. I must really be stupid.
   \_\_\_\_\_ No one else seems to be having trouble. Am I the only one?
   \_\_\_\_\_
   \_\_\_\_\_

d. Worry about the Possible Negative Consequences
   \_\_\_\_\_ If I fail this test, I'll never get into the program.
   \_\_\_\_\_ I'll never graduate.
   \_\_\_\_\_ I'll think less of myself.
   \_\_\_\_\_ I'll be embarrassed.
   \_\_\_\_\_
   \_\_\_\_\_

# CHAPTER 11

# Classroom Management and Discipline

Behavioral Approaches to Classroom Management: Arranging
Consequences That Decrease Behavior
A Humanistic Approach—Teacher Effectiveness Training (T.E.T.)
An Interactionist Approach—Glasser's Reality Therapy
Reality Therapy in the Classroom
**CLASSROOM APPLICATION: CONDUCTING CLASSROOM
MEETINGS**

## ORIENTATION

**Classroom management** and **discipline** are important components of effective teaching. In fact, these areas consistently rank at or near the top of the list of teacher concerns. *Classroom management*, a broader term than that of discipline, refers to the teacher behaviors and activities that encourage learning in the classroom. The term *discipline* is used to indicate the degree to which students behave appropriately, are involved in classroom activities, and are task-oriented (Emmer, 1987). Thus one aspect of classroom management is discipline; other aspects of management are related to instructional organization, teacher behavior, and classroom organizational patterns (e.g., how the teacher structures the classroom in terms of individualistic, competitive, and cooperative learning activities) (Jacobsen, Eggen, & Kauchak, 1989).

It is important to realize that there are many different reasons for discipline problems. Teachers must be able to analyze situations and determine what steps need to be taken to solve problems that interfere with classroom instruction. Keep in mind that the difficulty is not always with the students; teachers may also aggravate the situation through inconsistent management techniques, inappropriate reinforcement, poor instruction, overreliance on punishment, inappropriate expectations for students, insensitivity to student's legitimate concerns, and/or unwillingness to try new strategies to solve teaching problems (Kauffman, Pullen, & Akers, 1986).

The extensive research on classroom management indicates that the key to successful management is not in what teachers do *after* misbehavior but what they do to *avoid* misbehavior and *prevent* it from occurring in the first place (Brophy & Evertson, 1976; Kounin, 1970). The differences between successful and unsuccessful classroom managers are related to the preparation for instruction and to the techniques of group management used by the successful teachers to prevent inattention and boredom.

This chapter is organized in two major sections—developing a management plan to prevent problems and dealing with problems once they occur. The recommended intervention procedures identified in the second section also could be used as part of a prevention strategy. These two aspects of classroom management are described below:

- *Developing a management plan and implementing effective instructional strategies*. This is the time before and at the beginning of school when the teacher makes his or her most important decisions about how the class will be organized and run. The main purpose here is to reduce the probability of problems occurring in the first place. Classroom rules are established and the students soon determine whether or not the teacher means what he or she says. The teacher's instructional organization and teaching strategies play an important role in increasing learning and minimizing disruptions that interfere with learning. For example, many discipline problems occur when students don't understand the assignment, don't know what to do when they finish their work, have to wait for long periods of time for direction, and are not supervised carefully during seatwork. Researchers have found a positive relationship between effective managers and effective instructors (Brophy, 1979; Emmer, Evertson, & Anderson, 1980; Evertson & Emmer, 1982a). Because good management leads to the increase of time that students can spend on academic activities, the students will cover more work and generally perform better on academic tasks.

• *Dealing with management problems.* This is the time when the teacher has developed rules and implemented basic classroom instructional procedures, but still experiences problems. Various intervention strategies need to be used with the entire class or with particular students to maintain learning in the classroom.

As you read this chapter you will see how behavioral and humanistic theories of learning and motivation can be applied to classroom management and discipline.

After you master the material in this chapter, you will be able to:

• Establish a management system for a classroom.
• Use teacher behaviors that lead to greater student involvement in tasks.
• Use behavioral techniques to modify behavior.
• Teach students appropriate social skills.
• Use I-messages and active listening responses to improve communication.
• Conduct classroom meetings.

## FOCUS QUESTIONS

1. What are the major planning, managing, and implementation behaviors involved in a management plan?
2. How can teachers develop credibility for the importance of the rules and procedures they establish?
3. How does assertive discipline differ from Evertson and Emmer's recommendations for classroom management?
4. What type of instructional behaviors lead to effective classroom management?

5. Why is time-on-task an important component of effective management?
6. How can teachers make seatwork more productive?
7. What factors should be considered in determining the use of contingency contracting, group-based contingencies, and home-based contingencies?
8. How are different learning principles used in teaching social skills?
9. What are the advantages and disadvantages in the use of punishment to control or modify classroom behavior?
10. When should a teacher use I-messages and active listening?
11. How does Reality Therapy incorporate both behavioral and humanistic principles?

## DEVELOPING A MANAGEMENT PLAN

Evertson and Emmer (1982a) recommend three major phases in the development of an effective management system: planning before the year begins, managing during the first few weeks, and developing important behaviors needed to implement and maintain the system for the year.

### Planning before the Year Begins

*The Physical Environment.* Arranging the physical environment of the classroom is a good starting point for classroom management. Some important questions include: How are the desks to be arranged? Where should the teacher's desk be located? Where is the pencil sharpener and the water fountain, and how does their location affect the students in the class? Where will I meet reading groups? Where can students work cooperatively?

**What are the major planning, managing, and implementation behaviors involved in a management plan?**

Remember that you and your students will be working in the classroom environment for long periods of time. Your task is to provide the best environment to permit orderly movement, reduce distractions, and make the best use of available space. Evertson et al. (1989) recommend four keys to good room arrangement:

- Keep high traffic areas free of congestion.
- Be sure students can be easily seen by the teacher.
- Keep frequently used teaching materials and student supplies readily accessible.
- Be certain students can easily see instructional presentations and displays. (pp. 4–5 )

Once the classroom environment is arranged, you can shift your attention to other aspects of classroom management.

The planning phase for establishing guidelines for appropriate student behavior consists of three steps: (1) determining expected student behaviors, (2) translating expectations into procedures and rules, and (3) identifying consequences.

*Step 1: Determining Expected Student Behaviors.* The important aspect of this step is to determine how you want to run your classroom. You must be thinking about expectations *before* you enter the classroom. Take notes of effective classroom procedures that you observe in other classrooms and during your student teaching experiences so that you will be in a better position to make these decisions.

Keep in mind that rules need to be established for the diversity of activities found in the classroom (e.g., seatwork, small-group discussions, whole-class instruction, and independent projects). These situations call for different student behaviors. For example, knowing that they are expected to listen quietly while the teacher presents information does not guide students to the appropriate behaviors for small-group discussions. You must also consider the optimal use of available space, traffic patterns, equipment storage, and routine procedures such as handing in papers.

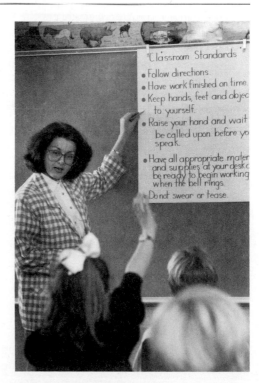

Establishing classroom rules during the first few weeks of school and teaching students to follow them can lead to fewer discipline problems during the school year.

*Step 2: Translating Expectations into Procedures and Rules.* After you have identified your expectations, you must translate them into specific procedures and rules. Following are some basic rules that you can modify for different grade levels (Mayer et al., 1983):

- Raise your hand before asking questions.
- Listen carefully to teachers' instructions.
- Follow directions.
- Cooperate with your classmates.
- Work on assigned tasks.
- Complete assignments on time.
- Treat others as you would like to be treated.
- Bring books, pencil, and paper.
- Be in your seat before the tardy bell rings.
- Keep your hands, feet, and objects to yourself. (p. 23)

Keep the rules simple and concise so that there is no misunderstanding about what you expect.

*Step 3: Identifying Consequences.* The purpose of this step is to discuss with students the consequences of following or neglecting classroom rules and procedures. You have learned in Chapter 6 that behavior followed by positive consequences is likely to be repeated. It is important that you reinforce students for behaving appropriately. In addition, various incentive systems can be used, such as awarding "happy faces," certificates, and honors for elementary school children and free time and special privileges for secondary students.

You also need to determine what you are going to do, without being punitive or authoritarian, when rules are violated. Some commonly used penalties include detention, demerits, and withholding privileges. The key is to develop an effective reinforcement system for appropriate behavior so that punishment can be limited.

## Activities at the Beginning of the School Year

The beginning of the school year is important because the teacher formulates the basic system of rules and procedures and students develop expectations about their behavior in the class. Evertson and Emmer (1982b) suggest the following procedures for the first few weeks of school:

- Set aside some time during the first day or first class meeting for a discussion of rules.
- Teach classroom procedures as systematically as any other learning objective.
- Teach procedures as they are needed by students to help them deal with specific aspects of the classroom routine.
- Involve children in easy tasks and promote a high rate of success for the first few days of school.

- Use only those activities and formats that have a whole-group focus or that require simple procedures, at least for the first several days.
- Don't assume students know how to perform a procedure after one trial. In other words, the fact that you explain something once does not mean that the students understand what you want them to do, or if they understand what you said, that they can do it. Ask the students to perform the task or procedures.

Several investigations indicate that the first few weeks of the school year are important in determining how the students in the classroom will interact with one another and with the teacher for the rest of the year. Emmer, Evertson, and Anderson (1980) studied third-grade teachers from the beginning of school to the end of the year. They identified teachers who had comparable classes at the beginning of the year but differed in their management effectiveness during the year. Table 11.1 summarizes the mean (arithmetic average) behavioral ratings for the more effective and less effective managers in the group on a number of important instructional behaviors.

The researchers found differences between more effective and less effective managers beginning on the first day of school. The more effective teachers were well prepared for students, had name tags, explained some basic rules, had activities for the students to keep them occupied when the teachers were distracted by administrative tasks. The less effective managers started the first day in a less organized fashion, with no clear rules or name tags for students, and the students wasted a great deal of time waiting for directions.

**TABLE 11.1 RATINGS OF BEHAVIORS FOR MORE EFFECTIVE AND LESS EFFECTIVE MANAGERS**

| | Mean | |
|---|---|---|
| Variable | More Effective Managers | Less Effective Managers |
| Variety of rewards | 4.3 | 3.1 |
| Signals appropriate behavior | 5.4 | 3.8 |
| Eye contact | 6.1 | 4.9 |
| States desired attitudes | 5.5 | 3.9 |
| Describes objectives clearly | 5.1 | 3.1 |
| Materials are ready | 6.2 | 4.4 |
| Clear directions | 5.2 | 3.8 |
| Clear presentation | 5.8 | 4.1 |
| High degree of student success | 5.5 | 3.9 |
| Content related to pupil interest | 5.2 | 3.6 |
| Teacher listening skills | 5.4 | 3.8 |
| Teacher expression of feelings | 5.0 | 3.2 |

*Note: The scales range from 1 to 7. 1 represents little or no evidence of the rated characteristics or behavior; 7 indicates relatively high amounts or frequent occurrences.*
*Source: Adapted from Emmer, Evertson, and Anderson, 1980.*

More effective managers did not take any previous knowledge for granted. They began the year by establishing rules and procedures and actually taught "minilessons" on these rules and routines. They explained, posted, and discussed the rationale for each rule (e.g., "If I am trying to help someone and you interrupt me, it will take me longer to help the student," or "If everyone talked at once, I wouldn't be able to hear anyone"). More effective managers also drilled students in the rules and routines and monitored the extent to which they followed them. In some cases, the teachers themselves modeled proper behaviors or asked certain students to demonstrate them (e.g., cleaning up one's desk before leaving the room, or placing equipment in its proper place). Less effective managers also had rules, but their rules often were vague (e.g., "Be in the right place at the right time") and were introduced casually without discussion.

More effective managers also dealt with problems immediately by not ignoring deviations from classroom rules and procedures. They assumed that students would complete assignments, and they held the students accountable for work. Most important, students learned what to do when they finished assignments, and they moved directly to the next activity. The less effective managers were poor monitors of their classes, allowed inappropriate behavior to occur, and failed to admonish those students who were not following the rules and procedures.

The more effective managers gave clearer directions and had better instructional procedures to organize their time, deal with transitions from one activity to another, and provide feedback to students. Less effective managers had more disorganized classrooms, in which students did not work on academic material for long periods, were often confused about their directions, and didn't know what to do after they completed assignments.

Finally, the more effective managers appeared to have a better understanding of student needs and concerns than did the less effective managers. As a result, they were more likely to know when to modify instructional activities, planned better, and used more interesting material.

A second investigation was conducted at the junior high level in seventh- and eighth-grade mathematics and English classes (Evertson & Emmer, 1982a). Most of the characteristics differentiating more effective from less effective managers at the elementary school level were similar for their counterparts at the junior high school level. However, the junior high teachers did not have to spend as much time explaining rules and routines. It was important for the junior high teachers to develop expectations and procedures about academic work (e.g., monitoring completion of assignments and keeping track of student progress).

## Maintaining an Effective Management System throughout the Year

As soon as you have established your rules and procedures, it is important that you carefully *monitor* student behavior to determine whether the rules and procedures are being followed. The purpose of this monitoring is to

**How can teachers develop credibility for the importance of the rules and procedures they establish?**

detect inappropriate behavior before it becomes a major problem and to clarify any misunderstanding students may have about what you expect. Many teachers have to practice their monitoring skills to become effective. This means that as you work with a small group of students, you need to look up occasionally and scan the classroom or move around the room to check students' work.

Monitoring early in the year is especially important to determine whether the amount and difficulty of homework and other assignments are appropriate to the ability levels of the students in the class. If certain students are having difficulty, you can decide whether changes in instructional approaches are needed.

Another aspect of maintaining a good management system is *managing inappropriate behavior*. You may do an excellent job of presenting the rules and procedures, but if inappropriate behavior is not called to the attention of students, you can expect trouble. For example, once students begin missing assignments, they are likely to develop a pattern of behavior that is difficult to change for the remainder of the year.

Evertson and Emmer (1982b) report that effective managers in their study used direct and simple methods to deal with failure to follow rules. They made clear requests regarding the behavior they expected and avoided overreaction and emotionality, using the following procedures:

- Ask the student to stop the inappropriate behavior. The teacher maintains contact with the child until the appropriate behavior is correctly performed.
- Make eye-contact with the student until appropriate behavior returns. This is suitable when the teacher is certain the student knows what the correct procedure is.
- Restate or remind the student of the correct rule or procedure.
- Ask the student to identify the correct procedure. Give feedback if the student does not understand it.
- Impose the consequence or penalty of the rule or procedure violation. Usually, the consequence for violating a procedure is simply to perform the procedure until it is correctly done. When the student understands the procedure and is not complying in order to receive attention or for other inappropriate reasons, the teacher can use a mild penalty, such as withholding a privilege.
- Change the activity. Frequently, off-task behavior occurs when students are engaged too long in repetitive, boring tasks or in aimless recitations. Injecting variety in seatwork, refocusing discussion, or changing the activity to one requiring another type of student response is appropriate when off-task behavior spreads widely throughout a class. (p. 27)

The final aspect of Evertson and Emmer's approach to formulating an effective management system is *developing student accountability*. This phase involves several important behaviors:

- *Clarity of work assignments*, covering such details as completeness, due dates, and procedures for makeup work

- *Communicating assignments* so that every student knows exactly what to do and how assignments will be graded
- *Monitoring student work* during class by moving around the room and systematically checking each student's progress
- *Checking work* to provide feedback for assignments
- *Giving feedback to students* by returning assignments as soon as possible, meeting with them to review progress, and/or allowing them to keep a record of their own work in each grading period

The primary purpose of accountability is to communicate to students that you really mean what you say and that you are implementing the procedures you established on the first day of class. It does not take students long to determine inconsistency between what a teacher says and does. Think of some of your own instructors who began the first day of class discussing how the course would be taught and what was expected of the students. Did the instructors follow through? How did students respond? Sharing some of these experiences with other students in your class would be helpful in understanding the importance of establishing accountability.

## Assertive Discipline

**How does assertive discipline differ from Evertson and Emmer's recommendations for classroom management?**

One of the most popular and controversial methods of classroom management is **assertive discipline**. Thousands of teachers are trained in this method throughout the country each year. Assertive discipline, developed by Canter (1976), emphasizes teachers' rights to an orderly classroom and identifies procedures that they can take to ensure these rights. Assertive discipline encourages teachers to expect students to behave appropriately; to use an assertive response style—for example, "Don't answer questions unless you raise your hand and I call on you," rather than "You are constantly answering questions without raising your hand" (nonassertive style) or "Learn the rules or you're going out of here" (hostile response style); to set limits (i.e., tell students what behaviors you want and need from them); and to follow through on limits (i.e., tell students the positive consequences that will result from appropriate behavior and the negative consequences when they fail to comply).

Assertive discipline is a more "take charge" approach than recommended by Evertson and Emmer (1982b). Canter (1976) suggests the following for the beginning of the school year:

- Decide on behaviors you want from students, together with the positive and negative consequences.
- Take your list to the principal for approval and support.
- At the first meeting with new students, discuss the behavior, consequences, and methods to follow through you intend to use. Keep the list of behaviors (rules) to six or less.
- Stress that no student will be allowed to break the rules. Tell the

students exactly what will happen each time a rule is broken (first, second, third offense, etc.).
- Ask the students to write the behaviors and consequences on a sheet of paper, take the plan home, have their parents read and sign it, and return it the next day.
- Emphasize repeatedly that these rules will help the class toward its responsibility of learning and behaving acceptably.
- Ask students to repeat orally what is expected and what will happen for compliance and for violations.
- Prepare a short letter concerning the plan to go home to parents, indicating your need for their support and your pleasure in collaborating with them toward the benefit of their child.
- Implement the assertive discipline plan immediately. (pp. 136–139)

There are teachers who strongly believe that this program is an excellent approach to preventing and solving discipline problems; there are others who find fault with it. Among the complaints is that it doesn't encourage personal responsibility by helping students learn self-discipline, and it is too harsh and demeaning to older students.

Curwin and Mendler (1989) believe that an effective discipline program should emphasize respect and responsibility while attempting to improve behavior:

> We see assertive discipline as little more than an attractive, well-marketed behavior modification program in which one person (teacher or administrator) has all the power to define the rules while offering group and individual rewards for compliance and administering punishments through public disclosure. There is no systematic means by which students are allowed any input into the process. Nowhere are they viewed as capable critical thinkers or decision makers. . . . His [Canter] program implicitly sees students as the cause of all problems, so there are no demands on anybody else in the system to change. (p. 83)

Recently, Render, Padilla, and Frank (1989a, 1989b) have presented critical reviews of assertive discipline emphasizing that the research does not support the claim by Cantor that it will greatly reduce discipline problems. In a response to this criticism, McCormack (1989) argues that no other discipline program is better researched than assertive discipline; and Canter (1989) defends his program by stating that it is a proven method of classroom management.

I recommend that you read the references cited in the previous paragraph. They bring up important issues pertaining to how research in education should be conducted to resolve issues and forcing teachers to consider where they stand on the continuum between obedience to authority and teaching personal responsibility (Curwin & Mendler, 1988). Is there a middle ground? Is it essential first to establish obedience and respect before one can teach personal responsibility? Is student input in establishing rules a necessary step in teaching personal responsibility? In Chapter 8 you read about values clarification. Here's an excellent opportunity to clarify your own values!

## KEY INSTRUCTIONAL STRATEGIES

**What type of instructional behaviors lead to effective classroom management?**

In the orientation to this chapter, I pointed out that the differences between successful and unsuccessful classroom managers are related to the planning and preparation for instruction and to the techniques of group management used by the successful teachers to prevent inattention and boredom.

The major instructional behaviors used by effective classroom managers that were identified by Kounin (1970) and supported by research by Brophy and Evertson (1976) and Anderson, Evertson, and Brophy (1979) include the following.

### With-it-ness

**With-it-ness** refers to teachers' ability to communicate, by their actual behavior, that they know what the students are doing. Students often refer to these teachers as "having eyes in the back of their head." The *with-it* teachers were quick in reacting to possible problems in the classroom, whereas the less successful managers often made mistakes that led to disruptions. Examples include waiting too long to respond to misbehavior, thereby causing a minor problem to turn into a major one; blaming the wrong individuals for misbehavior; and overreacting by shouting or screaming, when the situation called for a lesser response. The major advantage of with-it-ness is the ability to respond to potential problems before they become serious. When students realize that the teacher knows what is going on, they are less likely to become involved in unproductive classroom behavior.

### Overlapping

**Overlapping** refers to teachers' ability to deal with two matters at the same time and to make transitions between different kinds of activity smoothly without having to stop and break the pace of classroom activities. A good example of overlapping occurs when two students are talking to each other while the teacher is presenting a lesson. Rather than call attention to the students, the teacher walks slowly toward them while continuing the presentation. The students would most likely stop talking, and the teacher would continue the lesson uninterrupted. Think of examples of situations in which overlapping did *not* take place because the teachers you observed handled the matter inappropriately.

## Signal Continuity and Momentum in Lessons

Lessons of successful teachers proceeded smoothly and at a good pace. In addition, they wasted little time moving from one activity to another, and students were given a *signal* as to what they should attend to. The lessons of unsuccessful teachers lacked cohesiveness and **signal continuity**. Kounin found that student inattentiveness and misbehavior often were linked to discontinuity in a lesson, which in turn was linked to inadequate teacher preparation. Classroom discipline problems increased when the teachers began to wander for no apparent reason, repeat and review material that was understood, pause to think about their next move, prepare materials, or interrupt the lesson to deal with other concerns that could have been postponed (e.g., writing a note to the principal or reminding a student to complete a chore in the middle of an algebra lesson).

## Variety and Challenge in Seatwork

Kounin also found that students' involvement in seatwork was related to the challenge and variety that the work provided. They became bored with busywork. The implication is that if students are expected to work diligently at independent work for long periods, the work should be at an appropriate level of difficulty and provide interest and variety. However, take some caution in applying this information. The research indicates that learning is increased when students experience a high level of success in completing tasks (e.g., 80–90%). The teacher must balance the degree of challenge with the probability of success, because variety and challenge with *low* levels of success will lead to less learning.

In summary, teachers who produce substantial achievement gains in their students tend to behave in the following ways (Brophy & Evertson, 1976):

- They prevent most potential problems from occurring.
- They move activities along at a good pace without confusion or loss of focus.
- They provide seatwork that is at the right level of difficulty for students and is interesting enough to hold their attention.
- They monitor the entire class continuously and can do two or more things simultaneously without having to break the flow of classroom events.

## INSTRUCTIONAL ORGANIZATION

Well-managed classrooms facilitate more learning and higher rates of student achievement than do poorly managed classrooms. One of the major reasons for this finding is that more effective managers are better users of instructional time.

## Use of Time

In a typical elementary school classroom, the daily activities can be divided into three major parts: academic activities (e.g., reading, mathematics, science, and social studies), nonacademic activities (e.g., music, art, storytime, sharing), and noninstructional activities (e.g., transitions, waiting between activities, class business). The Beginning Teacher Evaluation Study (BTES) reported that at the fifth-grade level, the average amount of time spent in academic, nonacademic, and noninstructional activities was 60%, 23%, and 17%, respectively (Rosenshine, 1980). Individual teachers vary greatly in the time used for different activities and subjects, and as a result, students in some classes have much more opportunity to learn subject matter than do others.

Educators are interested in many different aspects of time—the length of the school year, the number of days a student attends school in a given year, or even the length of the school day. Researchers have identified that the more time a student spends actually engaged in an academic task, the higher the student's achievement (Fisher & Berliner, 1985). Educational researchers call this type of time *engaged time*, or **time-on-task**.

Three types of instructional time need to be differentiated. **Allocated time** is the time that a teacher designates for a particular learning task. *Engaged time*, a subset of allocated time, refers to the time students are actually involved in the task. Finally, a student can be successful at different rates—high, middle, and low. Thus **academic learning time (ALT)**, a subset of engaged time, is the amount of time a student spends on academic tasks while performing at a high rate of success. Researchers have determined that the more a measure relates to the quality of a student's classroom time, such as engaged time or academic learning time, the more the measure is related to achievement. The amount of time scheduled for instruction is not as crucial as how well the students are engaged in the particular lesson and their rate of success.

Table 11.2 depicts three hypothetical elementary school classrooms in terms of the use of time. The averages were obtained from data reported in a number of investigations (Caldwell, Huitt, & Graeber, 1982). Look at the average situation, in which the length of the school day is about five hours. The total allocated time for basic skills is 165 minutes a day. Sixty % (99 of the allocated 165 minutes) of the instructional time is spent actively working, or engaged, in a subject area (engagement rate). The percentage of academic learning time is 50%, meaning that half of the engaged time is spent at a high level of success.

The school day is 4½ hours and 5½ hours, respectively, for the low-average and high-average classrooms. Compare the differences in time use. What is striking about the data is that the daily average for academic learning time ranges from a low average of 16 minutes a day to a high average of 111 minutes a day. This means that the students in the high-

TABLE 11.2 COMPARISONS OF TIME AVAILABLE FOR SCHOOLING ACROSS VARIOUS SITUATIONS

| | Low Average (Daily) | Average (Daily) | High Average (Daily) |
|---|---|---|---|
| Allocated time | | | |
| Reading/language arts | 90 min. | 120 min. | 150 min. |
| Mathematics | 30 min. | 45 min. | 60 min. |
| Basic skills total | 120 min | 165 min. | 210 min. |
| Engagement rate (% Student engaged time) | 45 | 60 | 75 |
| Reading/language arts | 41 min. | 72 min. | 113 min. |
| Mathematics | 14 min. | 27 min. | 45 min. |
| Basic skills total | 55 min. | 99 min. | 158 min. |
| Academic learning time (%) | 30 | 50 | 70 |
| Reading/language arts | 12 min. | 36 min. | 79 min. |
| Mathematics | 4 min. | 14 min. | 32 min. |
| Basic skills total | 16 min. | 50 min. | 111 min. |

Source: Caldwell, Huitt, and Graeber, 1982.

average class spend twice as much academic learning time as in the average class and almost seven times as much as in the low-average class. Furthermore, because these data were generated for average situations, there are classrooms in which the daily academic learning time for basic skills is *less* than 16 minutes a day! Also notice that the time spent on mathematics is considerably less than the time spent on reading and language arts. You can begin to understand why engaged time and academic learning time are related to school achievement. If students are working at a high success rate in mathematics for *4 minutes or less* a day, how can they possibly cover the content of the course during the year?

It is important for teachers to evaluate the amount of time allocated to different subject areas to ensure that all content areas receive the recommended instructional time during the year. In addition, improvements should be made in the use of time. I am not saying that students must be kept busy every single minute during the day. Time spent in transition from one activity to the next, daydreaming, socializing, working on special assignments, and experiences out of the classroom are a normal part of classroom life. But if these activities take up too much time, they can interfere with learning. Consider for a moment that an improvement of engaged time of 10 minutes a day translates into 50 minutes a week, and 1,500 minutes a year (based on a 150-day school year). Much of this improvement can be made by more effective management procedures such as starting class on time and avoiding early finishes, developing routines to handle classroom procedures and interruptions, and minimizing time spent on discipline.

## Seatwork

**How can teachers make seatwork more productive?**

One aspect of school that most students remember is the hours spent doing seatwork at one's desk. At times, the work was interesting and useful, but sometimes it was redundant and boring. In fact, very often you probably didn't even know why you were doing the work.

In order to deal with the individual differences in the classroom, teachers work with small groups of students while giving independent seatwork to the remaining students in the class. In some classes students spend up to 70 percent of their time doing independent work (Fisher et al., 1978). If students do not use this time effectively, they will waste a large amount of the instructional time available to them. In addition, confusion during seatwork can disrupt the class and limit the effectiveness of the teacher who is working with other students in the classroom.

Data from the Beginning Teacher Evaluation Study (BTES) indicated that students are less likely to be on-task doing seatwork than when they are working with their teacher. In mathematics, increased seatwork was negatively related to engagement, which means that the more time spent doing seatwork, the less students were engaged in their work. Recommendations from this study were that teachers should keep seatwork time as low as possible and increase students' substantive interaction with the teacher or aide during seatwork (e.g., by having students ask them more questions about their seatwork) (Rosenshine, 1980).

Anderson et al. (1984) have investigated student behavior during seatwork assignments and gathered important information on how students think about what is occurring in the classroom and how teachers affect student's learning in the classroom. Low achievers often did not have the skills to complete their assignments independently. As a result, they developed strategies to complete their assignments that did not contribute to their knowledge of the subject matter. Students obtained "correct" answers without practicing the skill or concept that was the basis of the lesson. The students' behavior was similar to behavior observed by Holt (1982)—children often perceive the main purpose of school as getting daily tasks done, or at least out of the way, with a minimum of effort and unpleasantness. Whether they learn something during this process appears to be a secondary concern of these students.

Anderson et al. (1984) found differences in the way high achievers and low achievers approached seatwork. The high achievers expected the work to make sense to them and asked questions when they did not understand something, or they developed useful strategies for solving the problems themselves. The low achievers, however, were more likely to develop strategies merely to complete the assignment and did not ask questions when they failed to understand. The researchers suggested that low achievers were so used to classroom learning not making sense to them that they thought that not understanding something was "business as usual." The following (Anderson et al., 1984) are two examples of in-effective seatwork strategy:

> Randy could not read some of the words on the board assignment. Even when he did read some, he tried to decide on a word to go in the blank as soon as he came to the blank in the sentence, even if it was the second or third word. That is, he did not read the entire sentence to provide a context for the choice. When he did not figure out the answer immedi-ately, he asked another child for the answer. In this manner, he often received most of the answers from others and completed his assignment without learning to read the new vocabulary words (ostensibly the pur-pose of the task). (p. 18)

> Beth, unable to read enough of the Weekly Reader articles to answer the questions, simply copied the questions and wrote answers that seemed logical to her, without consulting the articles. In the one instance when she did look, she searched for a number word to answer "How many legs does a grasshopper have?" She came to the phrase "five eyes" in the article and copied the number five. (p. 19)

Do you have any favorite seatwork strategies you can recall from your grade school days?

## CLASSROOM APPLICATION: IMPROVING INSTRUCTIONAL ORGANIZATION

Effective classroom management can lead to greater student learning. The paragraphs that follow contain suggestions for making seatwork more effective and are adapted from Anderson et al. (1984).

### Selection of Seatwork Assignments

In addition to selecting content that is at the correct level of difficulty, it is important that you diagnose the assignments to determine possible problems that students may have in completing the work. In this way, you will be able to point out strategies before the students begin and are more likely to determine the nature of the problems during the com-pletion of the assignment.

### Presenting Seatwork Assignments

Remind the students before they start the assignment why they are doing it (e.g., "This will help you prepare for adding fractions") and the strategy that they should use to solve the task. You may even "think aloud" while solving one or two problems on the board to demonstrate them.

TABLE 11.3 INSTRUCTIONAL ORGANIZATION

Competencies

Allocated Time

| | |
|---|---|
| 1.1 | Maximizes time in instruction by continually scheduling students in direct instruction (e.g., interacts with 70% or more of the students per hour). |
| 1.2 | Minimizes time in noninstructional activities (e.g., spends 80% or more of class time in instructional activities). |
| 1.3 | Keeps transition time between lessons short (e.g., no more than 3 minutes between change of students and activity; no more than 30 seconds when a change of activity only.) |
| 1.4 | Establishes procedures for lessons that signal a clear beginning and end. |
| 1.5 | Gains all students' attention at the beginning of the lesson, and maintains student attention during lesson at 90% level. |
| 1.6 | Prepares students for transitions in advance by stating behavioral expectations and informing students that lesson is drawing to a close. |

Engaged Time

| | |
|---|---|
| 2.1 | Maintains students' attention during seatwork at 80% levels or higher. |
| 2.2 | Monitors seatwork students continuously through eye scanning. |
| 2.3 | Circulates among seatwork students between lessons to assist students and to monitor progress. |
| 2.4 | Maintains seatwork accuracy at 90% level or higher. |
| 2.5 | Tells rationale for seatwork, and communicates the importance of the assignment. |
| 2.6 | Provides active forms of seatwork practice clearly related to academic goals. |
| 2.7 | Sets seatwork and assignment standards (neatness, accuracy, due dates). |
| 2.8 | Uses tutoring (e.g., peer; volunteers; aides) and other specialized instructional technology to increase opportunity for active academic responding during seatwork. |
| 2.9 | Establishes procedures for early finishers, students who are stalled, and those seeking help. |
| 2.10 | Schedules time to review seatwork. |
| 2.11 | Requires that students correct work and make up missed or unfinished work. |
| 2.12 | Gives informative feedback to students in making written or verbal corrections. |

*Source: Englert, 1984.*

## Monitoring Assignments

Circulate around the room to see how students are doing before beginning a lesson with another group. If a pattern of errors is noted, you can give a quick explanation, change the assignment, or ask the students to wait until you can give them more attention. Second, occasionally ask the students to explain how they obtained certain answers (both correct and incorrect). This forces the students to think about the strategies they use to solve problems and demonstrates to the students that obtaining right answers is not the only goal of education. Third, establish a system through which students can receive help when they have problems. Some teachers set up a buddy system so that students can help each other; other teachers use a system whereby students with a problem place a "help card" at their desk and wait for help from the teacher.

### Evaluating Seatwork

Teachers need to develop routines for checking seatwork. Some teachers check it immediately after it is completed, and others check it the next day. The important point is that if teachers expect students to take seatwork seriously, they must provide students with feedback. If not, strategies for completing seatwork without real understanding will surely increase.

I have heard many students state: "Why should I spend a lot of time on this assignment? The teacher never corrects it, anyway!" One of the problems that I faced as a beginning math teacher is that I would spend hours correcting papers only to see the students throw them in the wastebasket without even looking at them. I mentioned this situation to an experienced teacher, who suggested that the next day I walk around the class and ask the students to explain why the problems were marked wrong. After continuing this monitoring a few days, I noticed that the students began analyzing their papers in preparation for my visit to their desks. This advice went a long way in making my first year of teaching more effective.

Table 11.3 includes a list of teacher behaviors related to instructional organization that can improve a teacher's use of time and make seatwork more effective. You can use this list to help you plan for instruction and evaluate your performance.

## DEALING WITH MANAGEMENT PROBLEMS

There are a number of approaches to classroom management from which teachers can choose. Each of these approaches views the role of the teacher in a different manner and has different beliefs about students. The behavioral approach is based on the assumption that children's behavior is a product of their reinforcement history. The teacher's role is to establish rules and procedures, communicate them to students, and implement rewards and punishment according to how well students comply with the rules. The humanistic approach is based on the notion that students, in general, want to behave appropriately, but sometimes they don't understand the causes or consequences of misbehavior. The teacher's role is to develop a strong, trusting relationship, and encourage good communication in the classroom so that students can learn to solve problems more effectively. Finally, an approach that is based on both behavioral and humanistic notions (what Glickman & Wolfgang, 1979, call the *interactionist* approach) holds that a student is influenced by both personal and environmental factors. The teacher's role is to help students understand their own behavior and its consequences. This position is intermediate to the behavioral and humanistic positions in that it stresses the importance of students' rational decision making while creating a important role for the teacher in *collaboratively* establishing rules and confronting students when they deviate from them (Jacobsen, Eggen, & Kauchak, 1989).

## Behavioral Approaches to Classroom Management: Arranging Consequences That Increase Behavior

**What factors should be considered in determining the use of contingency contracting, group-based contingencies, and home-based contingencies?**

*Token Economy.* Many students can't function successfully in the classroom if they must wait for an extended period of time for reinforcement. In addition, for many students, social reinforcers (e.g., a smile or the statement "good work") alone are not sufficient to maintain proper classroom behavior. In these cases, the use of a **token economy** has proved to be a good method of behavior change intervention (Walker & Shea, 1988).

As mentioned earlier, tokens can be points, stars, stickers, or other objects that usually are valueless to students. Their value becomes apparent when they are exchanged for a variety of rewards such as free time, a magazine to read, the chance to be first in line for lunch, a candy bar, and so forth. This system allows teachers to provide immediate reinforcement for appropriate behavior and is especially useful when teachers are attempting to provide reinforcers to many students at once. Some teachers use an additional component called **response cost**, a system in which tokens are removed for specific inappropriate behaviors.

The following is an example of a token economy, introduced in an elementary classroom, that increased the number of completed assignments (McLaughlin & Malaby, 1972): The teacher used points as tokens and gave each student a special form to record the points; the form included the various behaviors that earned points. The behaviors were typed on the left side of the page with enough squares after each item so that students could record their earned points for each assignment and for their social behavior.

Nineteen different behaviors were identified. They included assignment completion, appropriate noon hour behavior, listening, studying, writing neatly, and so forth. In addition, a response cost component was used, in which failing to complete work, chewing gum, eating candy, and cheating resulted in losing points.

The teacher had a meeting with the students to develop a list of activities that they enjoyed. From this list, they ranked the different activities in terms of their preference. Twelve activities were listed on a bulletin board, with the price of each listed beside each activity. These activities included playing with classroom pets, sharpening pencils, writing on the board, playing games, and so on.

During the first token economy condition, the students earned points each day of the week, and these were exchanged each Friday. This procedure was changed later to a variable number of school days. On the day before the exchanging of points for activities, the teacher collected all the point charts, and a student in the room summed the points for other students. The students' totals for academic and social behavior were compared with the teacher's records to ensure accurate self-monitoring of points earned and lost. A student who failed to self-record enough points was given the missing points. If a student recorded more points than earned, then the student lost the opportunity to exchange points for that week.

Walker and Shea (1988) recommend the following guidelines to be applied when establishing a token economy for the classroom:

- Identify the desired classroom behaviors.
- Discuss these behaviors (in positive terms) with the students and explain exactly how the program will operate.
- Post the rules and review them often. Begin by including just a few basic rules. You can use more complex regulations after the system is operating smoothly.
- Select an appropriate token. (One of the easiest methods is to give each student a card numbered 1 to 100 or strips of colored paper.) Beware of the problem in using objects such as marbles that can be distracting if they are dropped on the floor.
- Establish reinforcers for which tokens can be exchanged.
- Develop a reward menu and post it in the classroom (e.g., reading a magazine for 15 minutes is worth 20 points, getting free time for 10 minutes is worth 15 points).
- Implement the token economy program.
- Provide immediate reinforcement for proper behavior. Many systems don't succeed because teachers fail to dispense the tokens at the appropriate time.
- Gradually change from a continuous to a variable schedule of reinforcement.
- Provide time for the students to exchange tokens for rewards.
- Revise the reward menu frequently so that the students do not get bored with the same activities or privileges.

*Contingency Contracting.* In Chapter 6, I discussed Premack's (1959) principle that a high-probability response can be used to reinforce a low-probability response. Parents often use Premack's principle effectively: "Eat your vegetables and you can have dessert" or "Clean your room and you can use the car to drive to the beach." Teachers have found that **contingency contracting** is another way to systematize and individualize the use of reinforcement in responding to a student's interests, needs, and abilities. *Contracting* is a procedure whereby the contingencies for reinforcement are placed into a verbal or written statement. Although the wording can differ for various students, all contracts contain some form of the basic: "If . . ., then . . ." statement (Alberto & Traotman, 1990). Figure 11.1 illustrates a sample contract.

In developing contracts with students, remember to involve the student in developing the contract, including the reinforcers; make the contract clear, and fair for both the student and the teacher (i.e., the reinforcement should be in proportion to the amount of behavior required), make the contract emphasize and reinforce accomplishments rather than obedience; and, finally, reinforce the desired behavior after it occurs (Homme et al., 1979).

*Group-Based Contingencies.* A **group contingency** is a standard of behavior that specifies how a consequence is applied to a group. For example, it is often easier for teachers to establish a group contingency program when they have trouble instructing the class because of continuous noise rather than attempt to change the behavior of each student separately. Another factor is that when many students are misbehaving at the same time, it is often difficult to monitor each individual student to determine who is engaging in the misbehavior and who should receive reinforcement for appropriate behavior. In applying a group contingency, the teacher might identify an activity as a reinforcer if the noise level is reduced. If the noise level increases, the whole class would miss the activity.

Group contingencies are most appropriate when peer reinforcement

---

Date _____

## Contract

This is an agreement between _____ and _____
                                                Student                    Teacher

beginning on _____ and ending on _____. It will be

reviewed on _____.

The terms of the agreement are:

Student will _____

Teacher will _____

If the student completes the requirements of this agreement, then he or she

will receive the established reward from the teacher.

Student's signature _____

Teacher's signature _____

---

Figure 11.1 A Sample Student-Teacher Contract

is a factor is maintaining misbehavior, such as laughing at funny noises or engaging in pranks to defy the teacher for the benefit of other students. These attention-based behavior problems often are reinforced by other students in the class. Once the attention stops, the problems stop (Jenson, Sloane, & Young, 1988).

One variation of group contingencies is the "good behavior game" (Barrish, Saunders, & Wolf, 1969, in which the teacher divides the class into two teams and each team receives marks on the chalkboard each time one of its members exhibits misbehavior (e.g., talked out or got out of her seat, or moved his desk without permission). *Both* teams are winners if they receive five or fewer marks on the board over a specified period of time. If one team has more than five marks and the other team has fewer, the team with the fewer marks is the winner. In the situation, both teams can win or lose, or one team can win and the other lose.

The use of peer influence in maintaining discipline in the classroom can have powerful effects. Therefore, you should use caution to avoid negative side effects such as students threatening their teammates to "shape them up." Another caution is the possibility that one student might find it reinforcing to sabotage the team's efforts by misbehaving (Barrish, Saunders, & Wolf, 1969). In this situation, the student should be removed from the team and placed in a one-person team.

*Home-Based Contingencies.* Another effective behavior change program is to allow the student's behavior in the classroom to earn reinforcers provided by the parents at home. The student is reinforced for school performance but receives the reward at home. The teacher needs to meet with the student's parents and discuss the nature of the misbehavior and establish the guidelines for the programs. Parent-teacher cooperation often can make a program more consistent and lead to greater effectiveness. In addition, parents often can provide a greater variety of reinforcers than teachers have at their disposal in the classroom (Kelley & Carper, 1988).

While teaching junior high school mathematics, I worked with the parents of a student who never completed any homework assignments. We met and agreed upon a program whereby I would notify them each day if their child completed her homework. They agreed to purchase a ticket to a concert she wanted to attend if she handed in 90% of the assignments during the month.

If parents are to help the teacher reinforce appropriate academic behaviors, parents must be provided with sufficient information concerning their children's behavior so that effective consequences can be delivered at home (Kelley & Carper, 1988). One way to provide such information is through school-home notes (see Figure 11.2). Many parents never hear from a teacher unless their children have a problem. Many principals encourage teachers to call one or two parents a week or send them a note telling them the *good* behavior their children or adolescents have displayed. If you develop a positive relationship with parents, it is easier to work with them when problems develop.

```
┌─────────────────────────────────────────────────────────────┐
│                                                               │
│   Name _____        Date _____    │
│                                                               │
│   Subject _____                            │
│                                                               │
│   Was prepared for class    yes  no  NA                       │
│   Used class time well      yes  no  NA    Homework assignment│
│   Participated in class     yes  no  NA                       │
│   Handed in homework        yes  no  NA                       │
│                                                               │
│   Homework grade    F  D  C  B  A  NA                         │
│   Test grade        F  D  C  B  A  NA   Teacher's initials ___ │
│                                                               │
│   Comments                                                    │
│                                                               │
│                                                               │
└─────────────────────────────────────────────────────────────┘
```

Figure 11.2 Sample School-home Note.

*Source: Kelley and Carper, 1988.*

**How are different learning principles used in teaching social skills?**

*Social Skills Training.* Many students behave inappropriately in the classroom because they lack the appropriate social skills. Social skills can be described as being either *task-related* or *person-related*. The former include such behaviors as attending, displaying task persistence, and complying with teacher requests, and the latter include helping and sharing, greeting others, and moderating one's aggressive behavior (Hops & Cobb, 1973). There is evidence that poor social behavior in school can adversely affect students' academic achievement and later psychological adjustment (Gresham,1988b).

A number of strategies for training students in social skills have been developed. They are designed to teach students better interpersonal behavior and skills for functioning more successfully in the classroom. The strategies use a variety of techniques derived from behavioral psychology, many of which have already been discussed in previous chapters in this book. The following strategies are most often used in training in social skills:

- Having students *model* such exemplary behavior of others as self-control, sharing, and cooperation
- Giving students the opportunity to practice, or *role-play*, appropriate behaviors
- Using *positive reinforcement* to teach new social skills and/or to maintain the frequency of previously acquired skills
- Using *cognitive behavior modification* such as self-instructional training to emphasize the development of specific thinking skills (self-statements) to guide one's behavior in social situations

Another cognitive technique teaches students to recognize problem situations and to stop and think before acting. In essence, students are taught to interrupt their habitual nonproductive, or self-defeating, thought patterns and instead engage in more positive and productive thought processes that will guide them through problem situations (Bash & Camp, 1980) (e.g., "What is the problem?" "What is my plan?" "Am I using my plan?" and "How did I do?").

Keep a few ideas in mind before beginning training in social skills in the classroom. First, select for training only the social skills that are considered significant in the students' natural environment. This will help to ensure that the new behavior will be appreciated by others (especially parents) and, thus, reinforced. Second, make sure you select a training method that matches the students' level of functioning or ability. For example, don't require very young children to engage in detailed self-statements regarding their social behavior. Finally, when you teach a student a new skill, such as waiting for a turn, you want the student to be able to behave appropriately in a variety of settings (e.g., classroom, playground, and home) and with various people (e.g., teachers, peers, and parents). As a result, plan for the practice of the skill in several situations and with various people to ensure generalization of the trained skill. This issue is a major concern in all programs of behavior modification.

The next classroom application involves a five-step social-skills training program developed by McGinnis et al. (1984) for elementary school children, called *skill streaming*. A similar program is available for adolescents (Goldstein et al., 1980).

## CLASSROOM APPLICATION: IMPROVING STUDENTS' SOCIAL SKILLS

The five steps in the skill-streaming program for improving social behavior are as follows (McGinnis et al., 1984):

1. Modeling
2. Role playing
3. Performance feedback
4. Practice
5. Reinforcement

As an example, let's see how each of these steps is used to teach the skill "Dealing with Your Anger."

**Modeling**

The first step in teaching students how to deal with anger is to model this skill for them. To do this, you must first task-analyze the skill into specific behavioral steps. For example, try the following steps:

1. Stop and count to 10.
2. Think about your choices: I can tell the person why I'm angry, I can walk away, or I can try to relax.
3. Act out your best choice.

Then demonstrate each of these steps as it would be performed in a real-life situation. As you model, verbalize the skill steps. Verbalizing aids learning and helps to increase the effectiveness of the modeling display by demonstrating the cognitive process underlying the skill.

It is sometimes helpful to model more than one example of the skill so that the students can see how it is used in different situations. You might, for example, model controlling anger with a teacher, a parent, and a peer. It is also helpful to use more than one model and to select models who are like the student in important ways (same age, sex, SES, etc.).

## Role Playing

After you have modeled the skill steps, the students should practice the demonstrated behaviors. This is best accomplished by having the students role-play a situation relevant to the use of the skill. For example, they could role-play controlling anger if they lose a game or get hit with a ball. To add realism to the role play, students can choose role-playing partners who closely resemble someone they have previously encountered in anger-provoking situations.

While they are role playing, encourage the students to verbalize the skill steps. This aids in controlling impulsivity and in organizing skill steps in sequence.

To facilitate generalization of the new skill, have the students role-play various situations (e.g., getting angry in class, out on the playground, and at home), and with a variety of different partners (e.g., other peers, teachers, the bus driver).

## Feedback

When the students have finished role playing, it is important that you give them feedback about their performance. Feedback should be quite specific, focusing first on the accuracy of the performance (Were all the steps enacted, or were some omitted?), and then on the quality of the performance (Were the students enthusiastic? Was their body language appropriate for their roles?). If a student skipped a step or otherwise performed poorly, show what to do by reteaching or prompting. Always follow your negative comments by constructive suggestions on how to improve.

Be sure to praise or otherwise reinforce students following a good performance. This engenders feelings of success in the students and gives them confidence to perform the skill in a real situation. However, try to avoid giving reinforcement if the students significantly depart from their prescribed roles. McGinnis et al. (1984) suggest that in these instances a poor performance can be praised as "a good try" and then corrective feedback, reteaching, or direct guidance given so that the students know how to perform the skill successfully.

## Practice

Once the students know how to perform a new skill successfully, they should have opportunities to practice the skill in other settings. You can accomplish this in a variety of ways. For example, the teacher can enlist the services of an informed collaborator (someone outside the training setting) who is willing to practice with the students. A fellow teacher or an older student could be a good choice. Practicing with other people helps the children hone their skills and aids in the generalization of new behaviors.

Social skills learned in school can also be practiced at home. McGinnis, Sauerbry, and Nichols (1985) suggest the use of "homework" assignments that require students to select particular skills for home practice. Practice results, which are recorded by the students on a homework sheet, are later evaluated by students and teacher.

Another technique for practicing skills comes from the work of McGinnis et al. (1984). This technique, called "Red Flag," involves testing students on skill use in "set-up" situations. For example, for the skill of dealing with anger, students may be told that they will be provoked by the teacher sometime during the day (the exact time is not given). When this happens, the students should try to remember to respond appropriately. When the teacher has provoked the students and they have responded, the teacher calls, "Red Flag." The students' responses are then mutually evaluated by student and teacher.

Regardless of how a student practices, it is important to keep in mind that practice makes perfect only if the student practices correctly. Incorrect responses are difficult to remediate once they become part of a student's behavioral repertoire, and thus one cannot overemphasize the need to carefully monitor each step in the acquisition of a new behavior.

## Reinforcement

Reinforcement, the final component in the social skills training program of McGinnis et al. (1984), helps in maintaining and generalizing newly trained skills. Once a skill such as dealing with anger is learned, encourage the students to use it whenever appropriate. One way to do this, at least initially, is to reward the students each time the skill is performed. Rewards can be either tangible (such as prizes, food, or privileges) or of a social nature (e.g., praise, positive attention, smiles). The type of reward should depend on the age of the students, their level of maturity, and so on. As the students become more proficient in using the skills, reinforcement can be "thinned" or reduced to a level that is comparable to its occurrence in the natural environment.

> A primary goal in training is to get the students eventually to rein-
> force themselves for appropriate behavior. Self-reinforcement can be
> encouraged by teaching students to make positive self-statements and
> to reward themselves for a job well done. It is important, however, that
> the students learn to evaluate their behavior accurately so that they do
> not reward themselves for poor or inappropriate responses.

## Behavioral Approaches to Classroom Management: Arranging Consequences That Decrease Behavior

In Chapter 6 you learned about extinction as a method for decreasing behavior. It is based on the principle that if a reinforcer is removed, the
probability of recurrence of the behavior is decreased. Other methods of
decreasing and eliminating behavior are reinforcement of incompatible behavior, stimulus control techniques, and punishment (including the use
of time-out).

*Reinforcing Incompatible Behaviors.* The key to changing undesirable behavior is the successful strengthening of desirable behavior that will compete with and eventually replace undesirable patterns of behavior. Reinforcing a student for cooperating with the teacher is incompatible with
sitting passively; working at one's desk is incompatible with wandering
around the room. Gardner (1974) states:

> It is easy to punish inappropriate behavior as it occurs; it is more difficult
> to identify and to provide systematic reinforcement for appropriate com-
> peting modes of responding. The major question should be "what should
> the child be doing at the time he is behaving inappropriately?" Once this
> is established and demonstrated to the child, such behaviors or reason-
> able alternatives can more easily be strengthened through reinforcement.
> (p. 136)

Becker et al. (1967) demonstrated that selective reinforcement of desired behaviors can replace a variety of undesirable ones. A group of children attending elementary school exhibited a high degree of undesirable
behaviors—pulling hair, ignoring the teacher's requests, fighting, and
walking around the room. After explaining the classroom rules to the children, the teacher ignored the inappropriate behavior but praised any behavior that enhanced learning. In a short time the social reinforcement for
appropriate behavior led to a significant reduction in the behaviors that
were incompatible with effective classroom learning.

*Changing the Stimulus Environment.* Some behavior can be controlled by
changing the stimulus condition that influences the behavior. If a student
is distracted by the noise outside the classroom, shutting the window may

alleviate the distraction. If a difficult task is frustrating to a student, the teacher may want to replace the task with a less difficult one.

Instead of changing the stimulus conditions influencing inappropriate behavior, the teacher may find it helpful to present cues that inhibit problem behaviors. When two students are not working, the teacher may sit down by the students or walk by them.

Last, the teacher can prompt desired behavior that competes with problem behavior. The student who finishes work and gets into mischief can be asked to help pass out some material to the rest of the class.

Each of these procedures can prevent the occurrence of inappropriate behavior and provide the teacher with an opportunity to prompt desirable behaviors that can be reinforced.

**What are the advantages and disadvantages in the use of punishment to control or modify classroom behavior?**

*Using Punishment.* The last procedure used to weaken behavior is punishment. There are two basic forms of punishment: the presentation of a distressing stimulus (being yelled at, ridiculed, or threatened) and the withdrawal of a positive reinforcer (taking away a magazine or preventing a child from playing with peers).

Most of us have witnessed teachers who spend considerable time yelling at students, but rarely get students to maintain appropriate behaviors for very long. You might wonder why some teachers continue to nag, yell, and scream. One reason is that they have probably been reinforced for this behavior! Let's look at how this might work in getting students to stay in their seats. When the teacher sees a student out of his seat, she begins the tirade: "Get back in your seat. How may times . . . blah . . . blah . . . blah . . . !" The student returns to his seat; the teacher has been reinforced. This behavior sequence leads to an increase in yelling and a decrease in ignoring out-of-seat behavior. Soon the process recommences. The teacher often feels bad about yelling so much but learns that yelling suppresses behavior—albeit only for a while (Poteet, 1973).

Psychologists have found that punishment does not eliminate behavior; it merely suppresses it (Cooper, Heron & Heward, 1987). Clarizio (1980) points out that "punishment simply serves notice to stop inappropriate behaviors. It does not indicate to the student what behaviors are appropriate in the situation" (p. 133). He believes that positive reinforcement should be used with punishment so that desirable behavior can be developed to replace the unacceptable behavior. Earlier in the chapter you read about how important it is to teach students' appropriate behavior beginning the first day of school.

Sometimes a teacher's behavior instills undesirable behavior in students, unbeknownst to the teacher. In an interesting study, Madsen et al. (1968) found that the more frequently teachers asked young children to sit down after getting out of their seats at inappropriate times, the more frequently they stood up. It appeared that although the teachers intended their remarks as only mild reprimands, their social attention was reinforcing to the students. The undesired behavior increased rather than decreased.

There is evidence to suggest that punishment administered immediately upon the child's initiation of inappropriate behavior is more effective than deferred punishment (Walters, Parke, & Cane, 1965). Once the child has completed the misbehavior, self-reward or peer reward maintains the behavior and to some extent counteracts the inhibiting effects of punishment. In other words, the child has already accomplished what was intended! As a child, you may have heard a baby-sitter say something like, "Just wait until your parents come home!" This threat probably didn't change your behavior much while the baby-sitter was there, but you probably did learn one thing—to avoid your parents' return.

There are some other effects of punishment of which the teacher should be aware. First, the person undergoing constant punishment learns to avoid situations. The student may not want to attend class, or, if physical escape is impossible, may psychologically escape by not listening in class. Second, punishment can produce fear or anxiety so that the teacher, the classroom, or educational materials can become aversive (negative) stimuli because of their association with unpleasant consequences. The anxiety response occurs through the process of classical conditioning. Last, punishment does not direct the student to alternative behavior.

*Time-out.* Many teachers prefer the withdrawal of a positive reinforcer, used under the proper conditions, as a more effective use of punishment. One technique in this category is *time-out*, a procedure that temporarily removes the child from a reinforcing situation and places him or her in a location where the reinforcement is minimal or unlikely to occur.

There are three types of time-out procedures that can be used in the classroom (Lewellen, 1980): *observational time-out* is a procedure in which students are removed from a reinforcing situation by being placed on the outer perimeter of the activity, asked to place their heads down on their desks, and/or having all materials taken from them. Sometimes they are asked to observe the appropriate behaviors of the rest of the students in class. *Exclusion* is a procedure in which the students are not allowed to observe the activities of the group and are placed in a location in the room where there is little interest such as behind a cabinet or bookcase. Finally, *seclusion* is a procedure whereby the students leave the classroom and go to a special "time-out room."

Sometimes teachers use time-out ineffectively because the experience actually ends up as reinforcing rather than nonreinforcing to the student. I can remember a situation in high school in which the teacher placed a student behind a large bookcase in the back of the classroom. As the teacher presented his lesson, the student kept peeking from behind the bookcase and making funny faces. The rest of the students in the class started laughing and no longer attended to their work. A good time was had by all! Unfortunately, the student was reinforced (by receiving attention from his classmates) for his inappropriate behavior.

There are some important guidelines to use for time-out procedures. First, check to see whether your school has policies regarding the use of

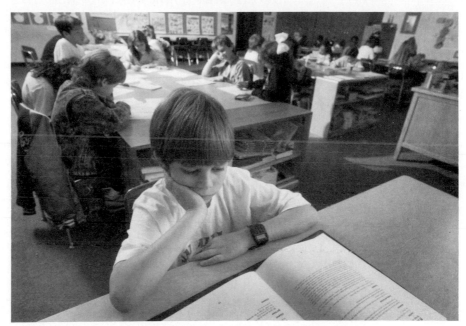

Placing a student who does not follow classroom rules in time-out can be an effective method of behavior modification.

time-out and follow the policies in developing your own procedures. The courts have reviewed time-out procedures and have emphasized that "exclusion should be from privileges and not from substantive rights" (Wherry, 1983, p. 49). This means a teacher cannot bar a student from access to water or the bathroom. Second, use the procedure only for changing behaviors that are clearly intolerable. Third, make sure the time-out area is safe and easily supervised. Fourth, identify the behaviors that will result in time-out and determine how long the time-out period will be. (Many teachers use a timer so they don't forget about the student.) Fifth, when the misbehavior occurs, calmly identify it and tell the student to go to time-out for a designated number of minutes. Don't make any other comments and ignore pleas for how the behavior will never happen again. In some cases, you may have to escort the student to the time-out area.

*Criticisms of Behavioral Approaches.* Cote (1973) has raised a number of issues regarding the use of behavior modification techniques in the schools. First, he questions how a teacher can reconcile the objective—the development of creative, free, and open individuals—with a program that controls and manipulates behavior. Behavior modification can create, maintain, or eliminate almost any behavior. However, in the process students lose control over their own behavior. It is the teacher who has the control, and it can be misused! Second, behavior modification is used when students' motivation and achievement are low or when classroom behavior is inappropriate. But are the students telling us something about themselves, the teacher, or the classroom environment when they behave in ways that call for the use of behavior modification? Perhaps we should spend more time attempting to diagnose the problem than quickly deciding that the students' behavior must be changed to fit the environment. Cote states:

> The child may be acting more like an accurate weather vane than a troublesome pupil. He may be telling us that something is radically wrong with the way we are trying to educate him. . . . Is it moral to use a system of control to adjust a child to a learning environment that his behavior tells us does not work? Should we change the environment instead of changing the child? (p. 278)

Behavior modification was never intended to force students to adapt to a boring or dull classroom environment. A danger is that it may take the pressure off the teacher to develop a more stimulating environment and an improved teacher-student relationship.

In response to the critics of behavior modification, its proponents are sensitive about any criticisms concerning the blocking of students' creativity or creating a mechanistic or dull environment. For example, Givner and Graubard (1974) respond that creativity can come about only when the foundation has been laid. That is, students cannot be creative if they do not have the basic skills to be creative with. If they are given these skills and the ability to interact with individuals in one's environment, students can create new ideas and behaviors. Nolan (1974) identifies four strengths of behavior modification:

1. It extends the system of rewards to those who rarely, if ever, receive them.
2. It removes the punitive aspects from the educational process.
3. It systematizes what we have always done so that we do it more effectively.
4. It demands better teaching by forcing the teacher to analyze carefully the learning behavior of each student. (p. 337)

You have been presented with the major arguments on both sides of the issue. What are your beliefs about behavior modification? Would you use it? Why or why not? If so, under what circumstances would you use behavior modification?

In closing this section, I must emphasize that behavioral procedures can have powerful effects on student behavior. Attention must be given to ethical and legal issues involved in any procedure you use (Corrao & Melton, 1988; Jenson, Sloane, & Young, 1988). Don't hesitate to ask your principal or school psychologist for help in initiating a behaviorial change program.

## A Humanistic Approach—Teacher Effectiveness Training (T.E.T.)

**When should a teacher use I-messages and active listening?**

Thomas Gordon (1974) has used Carl Rogers's ideas concerning human relationships in developing Teacher Effectiveness Training (T.E.T.), a method of interaction that seeks to enhance the teacher-student relationship through the development of effective communication skills. T.E.T. provides a model for establishing open and honest communication in the classroom and for resolving teacher-student conflicts in a way that is mutually beneficial and democratic.

*Active Listening.* A primary goal of T.E.T. is to improve the quality of communication between teachers and students. One way this can be done, says Gordon, is for teachers to practice **active listening** with their students. This requires the teacher to summarize or paraphrase what the student has said so that the student feels understood and encouraged to communicate more honestly and directly. According to Gordon, active listening helps students to express feelings, solve problems, and develop trust in the teacher.

The following examples from Gordon's book *T.E.T.: Teacher Effectiveness Training* demonstrate how active listening is done:

1. Student: Sally tore up my drawing. (*Sobs*)
   Teacher: You're disappointed at losing your drawing and angry at Sally for tearing it up.
   Student: Yeah. Now I'll have to do it over!
2. Student: Richard always cheats. I'm not going to play with him anymore.
   Teacher: You hate the way Richard treats you so much that you're going to quit playing with him.
   Student: Yes, I'll play with Tommy and David instead.
3. Student: This school sure isn't as good as my last one. The kids there were friendly.
   Teacher: You feel pretty left-out here.
   Student: I sure do. (p. 70)

As you can see from these examples, the teacher reflects back the meaning of the student's message in a clear and objective way. The teacher focuses on the student's feelings and avoids giving advice. This helps to confirm and validate the student's feelings, as well as to set the stage for problem solving by getting the student to talk it out.

Gordon believes that active listening is effective because it avoids the blocks that interfere with or stop the two-way process of communication. Such blocks include ordering, threatening, moralizing, lecturing, judging, labeling, sympathizing, questioning, being sarcastic, and the like. According to Gordon, such blocks often lead to negative student reactions (resentment, defensiveness, anger, etc.), which can impair teacher-student communication and result in classroom management problems.

Teachers who develop good listening skills often find that students want to share concerns with them.

*Problem Solving.* In addition to the goal of improving communication, T.E.T. attempts to help teachers solve classroom problems more effectively. Basic to T.E.T.'s problem-solving approach is the idea of problem ownership. Problems can be owned either by the teacher or the student. According to Gordon, the concept of ownership is important because it helps to determine how problems will be solved. For a student-owned problem, the approach is to use active listening, and for a teacher-owned problem, the approach is to use **"I-messages"** and/or the "no-lose" method of conflict resolution.

Before we consider each of these approaches, let's take a closer look at what Gordon means by problem ownership.

*Who Owns the Problem?* Gordon describes the difference between student-owned and teacher-owned problems in terms of tangible and concrete effects. When the problem has a real, direct, and undesirable effect on the teacher, it is the teacher's problem; when the problem has a real, direct, and undesirable effect on the student, it is the student's problem.

Gordon says that teachers can distinguish their problems from those of their students by asking themselves such questions as "Am I being interfered with, damaged, hurt, or impaired by the student's behavior in some way? Or am I feeling unaccepting merely because I'd like the student to act differently, not have a problem, feel the way I think the student should?'' If the teacher answers yes to the first question, the problem belongs to the teacher. If the answer is yes to the second question, the problem belongs to the student.

Brophy and Rohrkemper (1981) investigated the ways in which elementary teachers viewed 12 problem behaviors such as underachievement, hostility, defiance, hyperactivity, rejection by peers, and shyness and withdrawal. The researchers classified the problems according to Gordon's perspective:

- Teacher-owned problems: The students' behavior interferes with the teacher's needs or plans (e.g., defiance).
- Student-owned problems: The students' needs or plans are frustrated by individuals other than the teacher (e.g., rejection by peers).
- Shared problems: The students' behavior does not directly affect the teacher but has an impact on general classroom management and control (e.g., hyperactivity).

The researchers found that teachers who perceived students as presenting teacher-owned problems viewed the students as acting intentionally and, as a result, blamed the students for their misbehavior. The students demonstrating student-owned problems, in contrast, were viewed as victims of circumstances beyond their control. Teachers were pessimistic about their ability to deal with students who presented teacher-owned problems. As a result, they made no major attempts to modify the students' behavior. They were, however, more motivated to modify the behavior of students who were seen as having student-owned problems.

*What Teachers Can Do to Help Students with Problems.* Gordon (1974) suggests a number of strategies for helping students who have problems. The most basic is simply to listen. Gordon states that saying nothing is actually a form of communication "Silence—'passive listening'—is a powerful nonverbal message that can make a student feel genuinely accepted and encourage him to share more and more with you" (p. 61). In conjunction with passive listening, Gordon also suggests using "acknowledgment responses"—nonverbal and verbal cues that signal to the student that you are truly attentive. Smiling, nodding, saying, "Uh-huh," or "Oh," or "I see" are examples of responses that tell the student that you are really attuned to what he or she is saying.

On those occasions when students are reluctant, shy, or hesitant to speak, teachers can use another strategy that Gordon calls "door openers" or "reopeners." These are messages that take the form of nonevaluative questions and statements that are intended to encourage students to talk more openly and honestly about their concerns and feelings. Some examples include: "What you're saying sounds serious, tell me more," "Why don't we talk a while?" "You seem upset," or "What you say is interesting. I'd like to hear more about it."

*What Teachers Can Do to Help Themselves.* When problems belong to the teacher—that is, when student behaviors are interfering with the teacher's needs—a strategy called "I-messages" can be used. Gordon describes I-messages as statements made by the teacher to the student that clearly describe the student's troublesome behavior and how it is negatively affecting the teacher. Gordon states that I-messages are effective because they have a high probability of changing the student's undesirable behavior, are only minimally negative, and do not impair the teacher-student relationship. I-messages place the responsibility for the student's behavior with the student. I-messages tell students that their behavior is having a direct, adverse effect on the teacher. Gordon claims that when students realize that their behavior is causing the teacher a genuine problem, they will be motivated to change.

Effective I-messages have three components:

1. A nonblaming, nonjudgmental description of the student's behavior;
2. A description of the tangible, or concrete, effect the behavior is having on the teacher; and
3. A description of how this behavior is making the teacher feel.

Each of these components can be seen in the following example of an effective I-message: "When you leave the room without my permission, I have to waste a lot of time looking for you, and this makes me feel frustrated and angry."

As you can see, this I-message has clearly described the student's behavior (leaving the room without permission), its effect on the teacher (wastes her time), and how it makes the teacher feel (frustrated and angry). Because this type of message focuses on the teacher's feelings, it is far less likely to generate negative student responses, like anger or resentment, than would a *you-message*: "You are always leaving the room without my permission. When will you grow up?" Unlike the I-message, the you-message is almost always interpreted by students as an evaluation of how bad they are. Gordon maintains that you-messages have a detrimental effect on the student's self-esteem, make students feel inferior and inadequate, and often carry the hidden message "There's something wrong with you, or you wouldn't be causing me this problem!" I-messages, on the other hand, are noncritical statements about the effects of the student's behavior on the teacher. The negative impact of the you-message is thus avoided, and students are more likely to feel motivated to be considerate and helpful.

*Resolving Conflict.* There are times when it is not possible to solve classroom problems by using such strategies as active listening or I-messages. Such times usually occur when teachers and students interfere with the fulfillment of each other's needs. In these situations, *both* teachers and students are said to own the problem. For example:

Teacher: Tom, you're late for class again! Each time this happens I have to repeat the instructions for the day's activities for you personally. I'm getting tired of having to do that.

Student: Well, it's not my fault. I have morning basketball practice, and the coach keeps us until the last minute.

It is apparent from this dialogue that the needs of the teacher and student are in conflict. When conflicts occur in the classroom, they are usually resolved, according to Gordon, by one of two power-based methods. In Method I, the teacher uses power and authority to override the student's needs; the teacher wins and the student loses. In Method II, the teacher defers to the student's needs, with the student winning and the teacher losing. Here are examples of each method applied to the conflict just described.

**Method I: (Teacher wins, student loses)**

Teacher: Tom, you're late for class again! I've had it. Either you get here on time, or you're out of the class. And that's final!

**Method II: (Student wins, teacher loses)**

Teacher: Tom, I sure wish you would get here on time. It makes it easier for me when I don't have to repeat everything you've missed.

Student: With basketball practice, I just can't. If you keep hassling me, I'll drop your class.

Teacher: Okay, okay. Don't get so upset. Just try to get here on time.

Note that in each case power is used to resolve the conflict and that one of the parties is forced to give in to the other. This generates feelings of anger and resentment in the loser, and, in the case of the student, precludes the development of self-control and personal problem-solving skills.

As an alternative to these win-lose methods of conflict resolution, Gordon offers Method III, a no-lose approach in which teacher and student cooperatively achieve a solution to their problem without the use of power or threat. Method III is based on a scientific model of problem solving and includes the following steps:

1. Defining the problem
2. Generating possible solutions
3. Evaluating the solutions
4. Deciding which solution is best
5. Determining how to implement the decision
6. Assessing how well the solution solved the problem

Earlier we saw how Tom's problem of arriving late to class was "resolved'' by Methods I and II. Let's now see how this same problem is handled with Method III.

> Teacher: Tom, when you get to class late, I have to waste a lot of time repeating instructions for you, and this makes me feel frustrated and upset. (*I-message*)
>
> Student: It's not my fault, Mr. Smith. I have morning basketball practice, and the coach won't let us go until the last minute.
>
> Teacher: I understand. You feel that you have to stay until the last minute so you won't get into trouble with the coach. (*Active listening*).
>
> Student: Yeah, that's it.
>
> Teacher: Maybe it would help if I talked to him.
>
> Student: No, it won't help. Other kids have tried. If you're gonna play basketball, you've got to stay for the whole practice period. I think your class is important, but I can't cross the coach.
>
> Teacher: Well, we do have a problem. I need you to get here on time. There's no doubt about that. Got any ideas about how we might figure out a way to make us both happy?
>
> Student: Well, maybe what I could do is have Gabriel write out the instructions for me, and when I come in I could look them over quietly. That way, I'd know what was going on, and I wouldn't have to bother anybody.
>
> Teacher: Sounds good to me. I'll make sure that Gabriel has time to write the instructions down if he's willing.
>
> Student: Thanks, Mr. Smith.

It is apparent that in Method III cooperation and not power was the basis of resolving the problem. A solution was achieved with neither the teacher nor the student losing, and no resentment was generated, as in Methods I and II. Other advantages of Method III, as noted by Gordon, are that it increases student motivation to carry out solutions; it enhances feelings of mutual respect, caring, and trust; and, because students are a part of the problem-solving process, greater student responsibility and maturity are fostered.

## An Interactionist Approach—Glasser's Reality Therapy

**How does Reality Therapy incorporate both behavioral and humanistic principles?**

William Glasser, a psychiatrist, has developed a model of classroom management that stresses social interdependence and the meeting of needs in a socially responsible and realistic way. His model is based on **Reality Therapy (RT)**, a counseling approach that evolved from his work with delinquent adolescents. The basic principle of RT is that human problems arise when the primary needs of love and worth go unfulfilled. This need deficiency results in disruptive behaviors that tend to alienate individuals from the reality of the world around them. The primary goal of RT is to help individuals meet their needs within the context of the real world in ways that are responsible and sensitive to the needs of others (Glasser, 1965).

## Reality Therapy in the Classroom

Following are some strategies from RT for communicating with students and assisting them in meeting individual goals.

*Agreeing on Rules.* Rules are an essential part of Glasser's system. The rules need to be reasonable, enforceable, and either cooperatively developed or at least agreed to. The rules for behaving should be characterized by small manageable steps and goals that can be easily attained. A student who has mutually agreed to rules and then chooses to misbehave also has chosen to receive a consequence.

*Focusing on Current Behavior.* Glasser (1972) has observed that "people often avoid facing their present behavior by emphasizing how they feel rather than what they are doing" (p. 114). It is important, therefore, that teachers help students to focus their attention on behavior. Although feelings are important, in problematical situations it is behavior that must be changed.

*Commitment.* Once plans are developed, the students need to make a firm commitment to carrying them out. This commitment can be either verbal or written. If written, it should include a list of specific actions or behaviors to be performed. In this way, the students' progress in carrying out the plan can be more clearly evaluated.

*Using Directive Statements.* When a child misbehaves, the teacher confronts the student with directive statements such as, "Susan, if you are going to talk, you must raise your hand." The teacher needs to tell the student to stop the wrong behavior and to act correctly and responsibly.

*Accept No Excuses.* No excuses are accepted by the teacher for a student's failure to abide by the plan. In accepting excuses, the teacher weakens the student's commitment to the plan and gives the student a way out. When failure does occur, the student should be encouraged to try again. If necessary, small modifications to the plan can be made but only if they do not compromise the overall goal of improving the student's behavior.

*Evaluating Behavior.* Students are more motivated to improve when they understand the effects of their self-defeating and irresponsible behavior on others. In this regard, the teacher can help students to accept responsibility for their actions by getting the students to examine their behavior and its effect on others in the classroom.

*Providing Consequences.* A student needs to have logical consequences follow his or her behavior, whether that behavior is positive or negative. The student is encouraged to determine what those privileges or negative results should be. A student who continues to misbehave or refuses to work out the problem should be isolated within the room (see discussion of time-out earlier in the chapter).

*No Punishment.* In Reality Therapy, punishment is seen as reinforcing feelings of failure and should be avoided. If students fail, it is more valuable to let them experience the natural consequence of their failure rather than to punish them for it. With repeated failure, it may be necessary to re-examine the plan; it may be beyond the ability of the students to fulfill its requirement.

More recently, Glasser (1985) has developed a new therapeutic approach with implications for school discipline that is called *control theory*. Control theory suggests that students will follow rules and work hard in school to the extent that their needs to belong, to be free, to gain power, and to have fun are satisfied. Glasser's emphasis now appears to be more on the schools meeting student needs than helping students deal with the conditions that they encounter in school (Charles, 1989). These needs can be satisfied through such activities as classroom discussions, school-supervised work opportunities in the community, student-directed learning, and cooperative learning in academic areas. Glasser believes that when control theory is practiced in school, externally imposed behavioral programs of discipline will no longer be necessary; students will be motivated to control themselves.

Glasser's (1990) newer views on discipline have been influenced by his work in secondary schools. He maintains that "no more than half of our secondary school students are willing to make an effort to learn, and therefore cannot be taught" (p. 3) and despite the best efforts of teachers, "we have gone as far as we can go with the traditional structure of our secondary schools" (p. 6).

Recently, Glasser (1990) has used control theory to describe a new management system to make schools more successful. He describes the typical school administration as "boss management"—an adversarial relationship between teachers and students occurring when the teacher attempts to use coercion to make students work harder. The result is that "the child learns less and resists more; the teacher coerces more and teaches less" (p. 431). Glasser would like administrators and teachers to adopt "lead management" methods that are noncoercive and that are based on the assumption that motivation comes from within ourselves (a major premise of humanistic psychology). In order to become harder-working, Glasser suggests, students need to believe that there is value in what they are being asked to do, they need to be encouraged to set their own standards for quality, and they need to be given more encouragement to succeed.

Charles (1989) doesn't see Glasser's recent work as inconsistent with his early work on Reality Therapy. Glasser would have teachers attempt to develop classroom rules, procedures, and instructional methods sensitive to student needs. This approach would help a large percentage of students succeed in school, but there would still be some behavioral problems. Glasser's earlier suggestions for dealing with misbehavior would be used as an intervention strategy for controlling and improving student behavior.

As you can see, Glasser's humanistic approach to classroom management and instruction is in sharp contrast to assertive discipline. He would encourage teachers to organize the classroom to meet students' needs rather than teachers' needs! Is this a realistic approach? Do you agree with his position that few students are doing high-quality work in their regular academic classes? Do teachers need to re-evaluate the ways they attempt to motivate students? What's your position on this issue?

## CLASSROOM APPLICATION: CONDUCTING CLASSROOM MEETINGS

The application of RT to problems of classroom management centers on creating an atmosphere of mutual caring and involvement among students and teachers. When students feel connected to what is going on in the classroom, they are more likely to engage in responsible behavior and to develop feelings of importance and self-worth. One of the ways in which teachers can make students feel more involved is to conduct classroom meetings. Glasser (1969) defines these sessions as "meetings in which the teacher leads a whole class in a non-judgmental discussion about what is important and relevant to them" (p. 122). Glasser describes three types of meeting:

1. The "social-problem-solving meeting," which is intended to help students solve individual and group problems of the class and school (e.g., "How are we going to share time on the classroom computer?" or "How can we help Bill and John to stop fighting?")
2. The "open-ended meeting," which is concerned with stimulating student thinking on questions related to their lives or to the classroom curriculum (e.g., "What does it feel like to be blind?" or "What is friendship?")
3. The "educational-diagnostic meeting," which is designed to help the teachers evaluate student understanding of school curriculum or the effectiveness of their own teaching strategies (e.g., "What is the Constitution?" or "Does everyone feel comfortable taking just one practice test before the final?")

To conduct a classroom meeting, Glasser (1969) recommends the following strategies:

- Meetings should be held with the teacher and students seated in a circle.
- The duration of the meetings should be short for primary grade children (about 10 to 30 minutes), and longer for upper grade children (30 to 45 minutes). Most important, meetings should be held regularly—every day or, at least, every other day.
- The teacher should begin with open-ended meetings because these are the easiest to conduct and the best for acquainting students with the concept of class meetings.
- The teacher should begin by introducing a topic or problem, or by asking students to identify a subject of interest to them.
- In order to encourage a free exchange of ideas, the teacher should tell the students that there are no right or wrong answers. The purpose of the meeting is to allow all students to express their opinions, feelings, and ideas in a nonthreatening environment.
- It is important for the teacher to be nonjudgmental in reactions to the students in the group. The teacher's primary role is to guide the discussion, keeping students on track and encouraging everyone to participate.
- Any problem that is relevant to the group or to an individual in the group is open for discussion. The goal of the discussion should always be directed toward solving the problem in a positive way. Punishment or fault finding is avoided in seeking a solution. Also, the students' attention is kept focused on the present state of the problem. Students should not dwell on the past; this is unprofitable and wastes time.
- Students' reactions and comments can be periodically paraphrased or summarized by the teacher. This helps students to feel that they are being listened to, and it keeps the discussion focused on the topic or problem at hand.
- The teacher should not expect to solve problems in a single class meeting. Some problems are quite complex, especially those that affect large groups of students, and may require several meetings before a satisfactory solution is achieved. Also, it may be necessary to hold further meetings if the solution chosen fails to work.

Glasser notes that classroom meetings can provide an effective format for resolving problems of the individual student or the whole class and for getting students to participate cooperatively in group activities. Holding meetings on a regular basis, he says, encourages students to become more involved with one another, their teacher, and their school. Moreover, responding in a group helps students to gain self-confidence by giving them the opportunity to express their ideas and opinions in front of others.

See Palomares and Ball (1974) and Fearn and McCabe (1975) for further information about conducting group discussions with students.

## THINKING ABOUT THE TEACHING-LEARNING MODEL

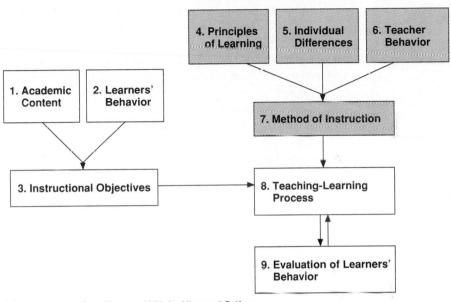

Source: Adapted from Hunter, 1971, in Allen and Seifman.

Classroom management provides a good example of the influence of many variables in the teaching-learning process. You learned that well-organized and well-managed classrooms provide students with more opportunities to learn. However, the teacher behaviors that lead to well-organized and well-managed classrooms are *not* authoritarian or harsh. Successful teachers tend to be businesslike, yet they develop a warm and accepting classroom climate. I mention this because sometimes beginning teachers believe that the only way to manage a classroom effectively is to be dogmatic or authoritarian.

Some teachers are disappointed when they find it difficult to model a respected teacher's management style. While you can learn a great deal from observing good teachers, you need to realize that you have to find a style that is comfortable for you. The debate over the use of assertive discipline is a good example of a management issue that should consider the personality of the individual teacher. The answer to the question: "How assertive should a teacher be?" depends to a great extent on the characteristics of the individual teacher. The advantage of observational experiences and student teaching is that one has the opportunity to practice and evaluate different management styles.

The research on motivation has some important implications for teachers as they consider different management styles. For example, management style can influence continuing motivation or whether students are more likely to develop extrinsic or intrinsic motivation. If the teacher's primary goal is to keep students quiet, they may use control techniques that get the job done but have negative consequences on students' attitudes toward learning. Returning again to the debate concerning assertive discipline and the issue of whose needs should be emphasized: the student or teacher. I think the answer must be both! Teachers should work toward the development of classroom environments in which they can function effectively while at the same time enhancing student motivation and achievement.

In the previous chapter, I discussed teacher efficacy and expectations and their impact on student behavior and achievement. Teachers who have high expectations for student achievement expect their students to master the curriculum, and they allocate most of their classroom time to the attainment of academic objectives. In contrast, if teachers do not believe that their students can learn the material in a course, the classroom focus will have less emphasis on mastery of academic material. If students perceive that little academic work is expected from them, the consequent behavior (e.g., talking, daydreaming, getting out of one's seat) can lead to considerable discipline problems. Therefore, it is important for the teacher to assess how his or her behavior influences student responses in the classroom.

Finally, it is important that teachers determine what characteristics they like and dislike about students so that they are more aware of the possibility of differential behavior toward the students. What types of student do teachers favor? Feshbach (1969) studied female student teachers' preferences for particular kinds of pupil. She asked her student teachers to read stories about elementary students engaged in routine classroom activities and to rate each child in the stories according to the child's probable popularity among peers, intelligence, grades, generosity, and whether or not the student teachers would prefer the child as a student in their class. Student teachers preferred rigid, conforming, and orderly students. Next in popularity were dependent, passive, and acquiescent students, followed by flexible, nonconforming, and untidy students. The student teachers least preferred the independent, active, and assertive students.

Teacher attitudes are strongly influenced by the degree to which students conform to expected or appropriate attitudes and behavior. Because teachers are expected to maintain order and implement the curriculum, a more passive or receptive learner role generally is preferred by the teacher. For this reason, orderly, passive, obedient, and patient students are more likely to be preferred by teachers than students who assume a more active role by demonstrating curiosity, independence, and probing and exploring behavior—the very behaviors that educators state they want to develop! Because the conventional female role is more likely to be compatible with the receptive student role and the conventional male role to be compatible with the active student role, one can understand why males may have more difficulty than females in certain classrooms (Kedar-Voivodas, 1983). The teacher's challenge is to maintain order and discipline but still develop characteristics of the active student role in both males and females.

## KEY POINTS

1. Effective classroom managers also tend to be effective instructors.
2. The key to classroom management is the ability to prevent misbehavior from occurring.
3. Effective classroom managers prevent problems from occurring by using the following behaviors: with-it-ness, overlapping, signal continuity and momentum in lessons, and variety and challenge in seatwork. They teach students appropriate behavior based on specific rules taught the first weeks of school and hold students accountable for following the rules and procedures by carefully monitoring their behavior.
4. Assertive discipline is a "take-charge" approach to discipline that emphasizes the importance of teacher rights to an orderly classroom.
5. An important issue in establishing a management system is the procedure for teaching students to abide by the rules established by the teacher and teaching personal responsibility.
6. In general, the more time a student spends actually engaged in an academic task, the higher the student's achievement.
7. Classrooms vary in the extent to which students are engaged in instruction.
8. Teachers can influence students' engagement in instruction by the way they organize and manage the classroom.
9. In general, the more time students spend doing seatwork, the less they are engaged in instruction. The fact that teachers cannot easily monitor seatwork contributes to this outcome.
10. High and low achievers approach seatwork differently. High achievers expect the work to make sense to them, ask questions, and are more likely to benefit from their seatwork. Low achievers are more likely to develop strategies to complete their assignments and are less likely to ask questions when they do not understand something.
11. Behavioral approaches to classroom management emphasize the establishment of rules and the implementation of rewards and punishment according to how well students comply with the rules. Behavioral techniques used to increase appropriate behavior include token economy, contingency contracting, group-based contingencies, home-based contingencies, and social skills training. Behavioral techniques used to decrease behavior include reinforcing incompatible behavior, changing the stimulus environment, and time-out.

12. Some educators question the use of behavioral techniques on ethical grounds, whereas others defend their use because such procedures provide students with greater opportunities to succeed in the classroom.
13. Gordon believes that active listening and the use of I-messages can improve teacher-student communication.
14. Glasser states that when students feel more connected to what is going on in the classroom, they are more likely to engage in responsible behavior and develop feelings of importance and self-worth. He recommends that teachers conduct classroom meetings on a regular basis as a means of accomplishing this goal.

## KEY TERMS

classroom management, p. 452
discipline, p. 452
assertive discipline, p. 460
with-it-ness, p. 462
overlapping, p. 462
signal continuity, p. 463
time-on-task, p. 464
allocated time, p. 464
academic learning time (ALT), p. 464
token economy, p. 470
response cost, p. 470
contingency contracting, p. 471
group contingency, p. 472
active listening, p. 483
I-messages, p. 484
Reality Therapy (RT), p. 488

## SUGGESTIONS FOR FURTHER READING

Cangelosi, J. S. (1988). *Classroom management strategies*. White Plains, NY: Longman. Includes numerous classroom experiences to illustrate how problems can be resolved.

Charles, C. M. (1989). *Building classroom discipline: From models to practice*. (3rd ed.). White Plains, NY: Longman. A good review of the different approaches to discipline.

Duke, D. L., & Meckel, A. (1984). *Teacher's guide to classroom management*. New York: Random House. Provides helpful ideas for handling behavior problems.

Fisher, C. W., & Berliner, D. C. (Eds.). (1985). *Perspectives on instructional time*. White Plains, NY: Longman. Reviews the research on time and learning.

Johns, F. A., MacNaughton, R. H., & Karabinus, N. G. (1989). *School discipline guidebook: Theory into practice*. Needham Heights, MA: Allyn & Bacon. Some good practical advice for teachers.

The following two books provide a comprehensive discussion of preparing a management program for the classroom:

Emmer, E. T., et al. (1989). *Classroom management for secondary teachers* (2nd ed.). Englewood Cliffs, NJ: Prentice-Hall.
Evertson, C. M., et al. (1989). *Classroom management for elementary teachers* (2nd. ed.). Englewood Cliffs, NJ: Prentice-Hall.

To read more about the approaches discussed in this chapter:

Canter, L. (1976). *Assertive discipline: A take-charge approach for today's educator*. Seal Beach, CA: Canter and Associates.
Glasser, W. G. (1965). *Reality therapy: A new approach to psychiatry*. New York: Harper & Row.
Glasser, W. G. (1969). *Schools without failure*. New York: Harper & Row.
Glasser, W. G. (1985). *Control theory*. New York: Harper & Row.
Gordon, T. (1974). *T.E.T.: Teacher effectiveness training*. White Plains, NY: Longman.
Martin, G., & Pear, J. (1988). *Behavior modification: What it is and how to do it* (3rd ed.). Englewood Cliffs, NJ: Prentice-Hall.
Walker, J. E., & Shea, T. (1988). *Behavior management: A practical approach for educators*. (4th ed.). Columbus, OH: Merrill.

## FOLLOW-UP ACTIVITIES

### 1. Think about the Discipline Problems of Past Teachers

All of us have been in classes in which teachers had problems managing and disciplining students. Identify specific problems some of your past teachers had and describe what steps could have been taken to improve their management skills.

### 2. Deal with Common Teaching Problems

The following is a list of some common student behaviors that cause management problems for teachers:

    a. Failing to attend school or class
    b. Failing to complete assignments on time
    c. Fighting with other students
    d. Showing disrespect for other students
    e. Annoying other students after their own work is completed

Describe how you might deal with these problems. Then return to this exercise after reading Chapters 8 through 11 and add additional insights gained from material in the book.

_____ 3. Debate the Use of Reinforcement Systems

Is the use of systematic reinforcement and token economies a form of bribery? Select one of the following statements that comes closest to your point of view, and defend the reasons why you support the statement:

a. Students should not be "paid off" for something that they should do naturally. The problem with society today is that individuals are not developing self-initiative because they expect someone to give them something for acting responsibly.

b. Bribery is an incentive for someone to participate in illegal or immoral behavior. Reinforcement in school is used to encourage positive, not negative, behavior. Also, bribery offers an incentive at the time that students are not performing, to get them to perform. Reinforcement programs specify the rules for earning tokens and obtaining privileges *before* the program starts. Thus, reinforcement is not bribery (Jensen, Sloane, & Young, 1988).

_____ 4. Observe a Teacher's Management Skills

Make arrangements to visit a class to observe a teacher's instructional organization and management skills. Use the organizational skills given in Table 11.3 to rate the teacher's degree of effectiveness on a scale from 1 (very effective) to 10 (very ineffective). Are students engaged in academic instruction? How is teacher behavior related to the students' engagement rates? What are the teacher's strengths and weaknesses? Write a brief description of the teacher's behavior, and discuss why you rated the teacher as you did.

_____ 5. Teach a Social Skill

Using the information on teaching social skills in this chapter, describe how you would train a student in one of the following social skills:

a. Waiting your turn
b. Making friends
c. Asking for help
d. Interviewing for a part-time job

_____ 6. Experiment with Behavior Modification

If you have the opportunity to work with students on an individual or group basis, you might try to use behavior modification. Review the principles of learning and basic techniques covered in Chapters 6 and 11 before you begin. First, state operationally the behavior to be changed. Next, obtain an operant level of this behavior. Then write a procedure for changing the behavior. Try out your plan, and maintain records of the reinforced behavior to keep track of whether or not strength or frequency of response has increased. Evaluate the effectiveness of your behavior modification program. Use the following checklist as a step-by-step plan:

- Description of behavior to be changed
- Operant level of behavior (use a graph to chart behavior over a period of time)
- Procedure used to change behavior
- What happened when you tried out procedure (plot behavior on the graph used in the second step)
- Evaluation of behavior modification program

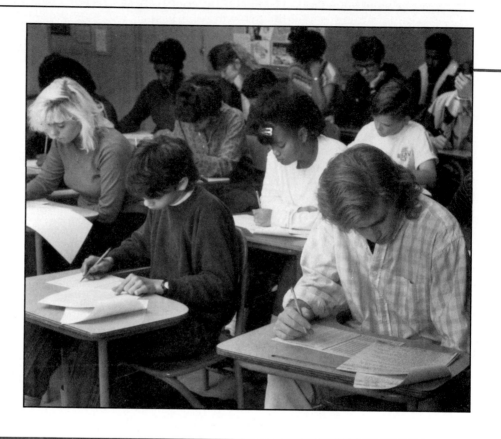

# P A R T   F O U R

# Measurement and Evaluation

## PART OVERVIEW

The evaluation of student performance is an important responsibility of both school and teacher. The public is so concerned about the quality of education today that statewide testing results by school and by grade are published in local newspapers in many communities. These scores are used by the public to determine how successful the school has been in educating students. Although scores are important, measurement and evaluation involves much more than giving achievement tests to determine competency in different subject areas. Teachers use a variety of measurement procedures, both formal and informal, to make instructional decisions on a daily basis.

Throughout the next two chapters the terms **test**, **measurement**, and **evaluation** will be used repeatedly. A *test* is a measure containing a series of questions, each of which has a certain correct answer. *Measurement* is a broader concept because educators and psychologists can measure characteristics in ways other than by testing (e.g., using observation and rating scales). Measurement is the process of assigning numbers to behavior according to certain rules or specifications in order to determine differences among individuals on the behavioral characteristics being measured. Finally, *evaluation* is the process of obtaining information to form judgments so that educational decisions can be made. Evaluation is the most comprehensive of the three terms and always includes value judgments regarding the desirability of the data collected.

It is important that the teacher consider how classroom evaluation practices influence students (Crooks, 1988). For example, the cognitive level of teacher questions or test items influences the student's level of thinking and methods of studying. Do you study the same for an instructor who focuses on memory level information as compared to the instructor who requires you to analyze and synthesize information? Have you considered how different evaluation procedures motivate students differently? Think about these issues as you read the next two chapters.

# CHAPTER 12

## Standardized and Teacher-Made Measurement Instruments

ʎ ### ORIENTATION

Teachers are faced with a variety of measurement and evaluation decisions. Gronlund (1985a) provides examples of the types of instructional decisions teachers face and the type of evaluation information (in parentheses) that might be helpful in answering the questions:

1. How realistic are my teaching plans for this particular group of pupils? (scholastic aptitude tests, past records of achievement)
2. Should students be grouped for more effective learning? (range of scholastic aptitude and achievement scores, past records of achievement)
3. To what extent are the pupils ready for the next learning ex-

perience? (readiness tests, pretests of needed skills, past records of achievement)

4. To what extent are pupils attaining the course's minimum essentials? (mastery tests, observation)
5. To what extent are pupils progressing beyond the minimum essentials? (periodic quizzes, general achievement tests, observation)
6. At what point would a review be most helpful? (periodic quizzes, observation)
7. What type of learning difficulties are the pupils encountering? (diagnostic tests, observation, pupil conferences)
8. Which pupils should be referred for counseling, special classes, or remedial programs? (scholastic aptitude tests, achievement tests, diagnostic tests, observation)
9. Which school mark should be assigned to each pupil? (review of all evaluation data)
10. How effective was my teaching? (achievement tests, pupils' ratings, supervisors' ratings) (p. 4)

These questions are not meant to be an all-inclusive list of evaluation issues that teachers encounter during the year. However, the questions do cover a broad range of concerns that need to be addressed during the instructional process. They can be helpful for you to keep in mind as you read the next two chapters. Also, remember that these questions do not occur in any particular order but are interrelated in the teaching-learning process.

Before going further in this chapter, let us think about possible student perspectives on the measurement and evaluation process. When students hear the term *evaluation*, the first thought that they often have concerns tests and/or grades. By the time students reach college, they will have taken hundreds of examinations—some welcomed, some feared. Unfortunately, most of us probably remember more of the anxiety engendered by examinations than we do the joys. Can you remember how you felt as a young child waiting for the teacher to return a test or homework assignment? What about the sleepless night before an important examination in college or the wait for a postcard reporting a final grade?

Students usually do not understand why they have to be involved in so much testing. It is often useful to take the time to explain the purpose of measurement activities so that students better understand how you will use the information. Finally, consider how your policies and procedures regarding measurement and evaluation may influence students' achievement, motivation, and classroom behavior.

After you master the material presented in this chapter, you will be able to:

- Identify the characteristics of good tests.
- Evaluate different standardized tests.
- Teach test-taking skills.

- Write test questions.
- Write survey questions measuring affective outcomes.
- Use item analysis to improve test questions.

1. What are the different uses of evaluation?
2. What is the difference between norm-referenced and criterion-referenced measurement?
3. Why are both validity and reliability constructs necessary in evaluating tests?
4. Under what conditions would a test maker be concerned with each of the following types of validity: content, criterion-related, and construct validity?
5. What is the difference between criterion-related validity and criterion-referenced measurement?
6. Why are different types of reliability used in measurement?
7. What factors need to be considered in selecting standardized tests?
8. What are the strengths and weaknesses of minimum competency testing for students and teachers?
9. What are the strengths and weaknesses of standardized testing?
10. How do standardized tests differ from teacher-made tests?
11. When would you use the following type of tests: multiple choice, matching, completion, and true-false?
12. What are the advantages and disadvantages of essay and objective tests?
13. How does an item analysis help teachers improve the quality of their tests?

## THE USE OF EVALUATION IN CLASSROOM INSTRUCTION

**What are the different uses of evaluation?**

In Chapter 1, I stated that teachers are involved in evaluation throughout the teaching-learning process. The examples of instructional decisions identified in the preceding section illustrate this involvement: Teachers must make some decisions before beginning instruction (e.g., How realistic are my teaching plans for this particular group of pupils?); other decisions, during instruction (e.g., To what extent are the pupils progressing beyond the minimum essentials?); and still others, after instruction (e.g., Which school mark should be assigned to each pupil?).

Airasian and Madaus (1972) developed a classification system for describing evaluation procedures for various instructional purposes that helps to organize the types of question that concern teachers in planning, implementing, and evaluating the outcomes of instruction. The system includes four functions of evaluation—*placement* (to determine student performance at the beginning of instruction), *formative* (to monitor learning progress during instruction), *diagnostic* (to diagnose learning difficulties during instruction), and *summative* (to evaluate achievement at the end of instruction). I first introduced formative and summative evaluation in Chapter 6 when describing mastery learning. Gronlund (1985a) provides a summary of each type of evaluation.

## Placement Evaluation

**Placement evaluation** is concerned with the student's entry behavior before the beginning of instruction. A number of important questions need to be answered at this stage of instruction: Does the student have the needed knowledge and skills to begin instruction? Has the student already mastered the objectives of the particular lesson or unit? Does the student's ability, learning style, attitude, or interest indicate that the child would benefit from a particular method of instruction? To answer these questions, teachers use a variety of instruments such as readiness tests, aptitude tests, pretests on course objectives, and observational techniques. In summary, placement evaluation concerns relate to placing students in the proper position in the instructional sequence and providing the most beneficial method of instruction for each student.

## Formative Evaluation

**Formative evaluation** is used to provide ongoing feedback to the teacher and student regarding success and failure during insrtuction. This feedback is helpful in deciding whether changes in subsequent learning experiences are needed and in determining specific learning errors that need correction. Formative evaluation depends on the development of specific tests to measure the particular aspect of instruction that is covered. For example, if the teacher spends two weeks covering World War I in a history class, it may be useful to determine students' knowledge after the first week in order to decide what should be reviewed and how the second week of instruction should be approached. In this case, a specially designed test on the material in the first week is necessary to provide the information. Observational methods, in addition to paper and pencil tests, are often useful in monitoring student progress.

## Diagnostic Evaluation

**Diagnostic evaluation** is used when formative evaluation does not answer all the questions regarding problems students have with certain instructional objectives. For example, why is it that Steve cannot divide by two digits? Why does Susan confuse certain letters in reading? Diagnostic evaluation searches for the underlying causes of learning problems in order to

Teachers evaluate student progress so that they can make more effective instructional decisions.

formulate a specific plan for remedial action. It involves special diagnostic instruments as well as observational techniques.

## Summative Evaluation

**Summative evaluation** generally comes at the end of instruction to determine how well students have attained the instructional objectives, to provide information to grade students, and/or to evaluate teacher effectiveness. This type of evaluation usually includes achievement tests, rating scales, and evaluations of student products. Some educators believe that teachers overemphasize this category of evaluation while neglecting the other three categories in improving student achievement. It is important to remember that giving students grades is only a small part of the measurement and evaluation process.

## JUDGING STUDENT LEARNING: NORM-REFERENCED AND CRITERION-REFERENCED MEASUREMENT

In evaluating achievement, you can interpret student learning in one or both of two ways: (1) in terms of performance relative to a group, or (2) in terms of performance relative to a behavioral criterion of proficiency.

**What is the difference between norm-refer-enced and criterion-referenced measurement?**

The first method is called **norm-referenced measurement**; the second, **criterion-referenced measurement**.

*Norm-referenced measurement* is the most common method of testing used by teachers and thus receives the most attention in this book. Students' scores on most tests reflect their performance as compared to that of their classmates. Grading on a curve is an example of norm-referenced measurement.

In recent years, *criterion-referenced measurement* has gained in use. With this method, the performance of a student is measured in terms of the learning outcomes or objectives of the course. The statement "Lisa did better than 80% of the students on a test of biological terminology" is a norm-referenced measurement. In criterion-referenced measurement, we might say that Lisa correctly answered 80% of the items on a test of biological terminology. *Eighty percent* means something quite different in the two situations.

In criterion-referenced testing, the teacher concentrates on a limited number of specific objectives. Explicit instructional objectives are necessary because each test item must correspond to a particular objective or criterion. The following objectives and corresponding test items reflect this relationship:

**Objective**

A. Discriminates between +, −, =, ×

B. Names the instrument used for measuring each weather unit.

**Sample Test Item**

A. Draw a circle around the sign that means "to add": + − = ×

B. The instrument used to measure the amount of precipitation in a city is called a (an) _____.

In criterion-referenced measurement, the teacher is primarily concerned with how many items in a set of specific objectives a particular student has mastered. In norm-referenced measurement, the test items are written to reflect the objectives and content in a more diffuse manner and result in a large spread of scores, which is necessary to rank students reliably in order of achievement. Criterion-referenced measurement does not aim for a wide range of scores because the purpose is to have all students master the objectives.

The actual construction of norm-referenced and criterion-referenced tests is similar, both essay and objective items being used. The difference lies in the purpose of the tests.

Criterion-referenced testing tends to be used more in mastery learning programs (discussed in Chapter 6) when the instructional intent is to raise almost all students to a specified level of achievement. Presently, classroom instruction uses this testing to greatest advantage when the learning outcomes are cumulative and progressively more complex, as in mathematics, reading, and foreign languages, and when minimum levels of mastery can be established. When the subject matter is not cumulative, when the student does not need to reach some specified level of competency, and when tests measure success in comparative steps, norm-referenced testing is preferred.

## CHARACTERISTICS OF A GOOD TEST

Anyone can develop an instrument and state that it serves a specific function or purpose. For example, we often find pamphlets in drugstores describing how for a small fee individuals can determine their personality profiles by completing a brief questionnaire. In most cases, these questionnaires cannot accurately measure personality or any other trait. Fortunately, evaluation specialists have developed specific criteria for judging the quality of various measurement instruments. Test specialists are expected to provide detailed information concerning these criteria. Two of the most important criteria for evaluating instruments are **validity** and **reliability**. Each criterion is discussed in terms of norm-referenced measurement.

### Validity

Test *validity* refers to the appropriateness of the interpretation of the test scores with regard to a particular use. For example, if a test is to be used to measure reading comprehension, it should measure reading comprehension and not measure other irrelevant factors not associated with comprehension. The more a test can be shown to accomplish this goal, the more valid is the test.

It is important to realize that validity refers to the appropriate use of test scores and *not* to the test itself. Also, validity is a matter of degree because validity does not exist as an all-or-none characteristic. Finally, validity is specific to some particular use because a test is not valid for all purposes (Gronlund, 1985a). For example, a mathematics test may have high validity for measuring mathematical reasoning but have low validity for measuring computational skills.

In the past, validity was separated into three types—content, criterion-related, and construct. However, the most recent revision of the *Standards for Educational and Psychological Testing* (1985) takes the position that validity is *unitary* and that each of what used to be considered as separate types of validity should be thought of as approaches to establishing validity. Messick (1981) points out that this change was made because the notion of separate types of validity gives the impression that the types are equal and that any one type could be used by test developers to establish validity.

**Content validity** aims for an adequate sampling of a specified universe of content. In constructing a test, the teacher should include test items that sufficiently represent the instructional objectives of the unit and the subject matter. Many students, after analyzing the test questions in their courses,

Under what conditions would a test maker be concerned with each of the following types of validity: content, criterion-related, and construct validity?

What is the difference between criterion-related validity and criterion-referenced measurement?

often remark that some material was not even tested on the examination. Such a test may have low content validity. Later in this chapter, some guidelines to help you ensure content validity when constructing your own tests will be identified.

**Criterion-related validity** is concerned with two questions: How well does the test judge present ability? How well does the test judge future ability? Let us take two examples of tests: A typing test determines an applicant's ability as a secretary; the Scholastic Aptitude Test (SAT) predicts a student's future academic performance in college. In the first example, we want to estimate present ability, and we obtain the relationship between the test score and present performance at the same time. A high correlation in this case would indicate that the typing test is a good indicator of typing skills on the job. This type of criterion-related validity is often called *concurrent validity*. In the second example, we are interested in prediction, and we extend the criterion related to the test scores over a period of time (usually a student's grade-point average during the first semester in college). This type of criterion-related validity is called *predictive validity*. Time is the variable in the two types of criterion-related validity. The typical procedure for reporting criterion-related validity is by the use of a *validity coefficient*, which reveals the correlation, or relationship, between the test and the criterion. Although the criterion could be another test, it usually is some other type of performance indicator.

The third approach to validity is **construct validity**. Psychologists develop tests to measure traits and abilities such as intelligence, anxiety, creativity, and social adjustment. These traits are also called *constructs*. The tests determine the "amount" of the trait or construct a person possesses.

Although a test may exhibit more than one approach to validity, some tests are constructed with one major source of validity in mind. Content validity is an earmark of teacher-made tests and standardized achievement tests. Criterion-related validity is the main factor in the scholastic aptitude tests used to predict school or college success. Construct validity justifies the use of a test for measuring specific psychological traits or abilities.

## Reliability

Why are different types of reliability used in measurement?

*Reliability* is a qualitative judgment about the *consistency* of test scores or other evaluation results from one measure to another. It is difficult to make good judgments on the basis of unreliable test scores. The methods available for determining reliability are evidence of the recognition that there are different types of consistency. Two important kinds of reliability are consistency over time and consistency over different forms of an evaluation instrument.

Consistency over time is often referred to as **test-retest reliability**. In this procedure, individuals take the same test at two different times, and the results of the tests are compared by using a correlation coefficient. If the results are stable—students who score high on the first administration score high on the second administration, and low achievers score low both times—this consistency will be indicated by a high correlation coefficient (see Figure 12.1).

Consistency over different but **equivalent forms** of the *same* test is determined by administering these forms to the same students in close succession and then correlating the resulting scores. The correlation coefficient so obtained provides a measure of equivalence indicating the degree to which the two forms of the test measure the same aspects of student behavior. A high correlation coefficient would indicate that either test could be used to measure students' knowledge of the material. A low correlation coefficient would indicate that the two forms of the test *do not* measure the same material or that they differ in the degree of difficulty. This type of reliability is important when using different forms of a test to measure the growth of students over a period. For example, students can be given form *A* of an achievement test in September and form *B* at the end of the year. If a history teacher has many sections of the same class, the teacher may want to use two forms of the same test. However, unless the two tests

---

Formula:    $r = \dfrac{N\Sigma xy - \Sigma x \Sigma y}{\sqrt{\{N\Sigma x^2 - (\Sigma x)^2\}\{N\Sigma y^2 - (\Sigma y)^2\}}}$

$N$ = number of scores
$r$ = product-moment correlation coefficient
$\Sigma xy$ = the sum of each person's $x$ score multiplied by his or her $y$ score
$\Sigma x \Sigma y$ = the sum of all the $x$ scores multiplied by the sum of all $y$ scores
$\Sigma x^2$ = the square of each $x$ score, subsequently added together
$(\Sigma x)^2$ = the sum of all the $x$ scores, subsequently squared
$\Sigma y^2$ = the square of each $y$ score, subsequently added together
$(\Sigma y^2)$ = the sum of all the $y$ scores, subsequently squared

Problem: Compute the product-moment correlation for the same arithmetic test given at two different times for 4 children.

| $x$ (first time) | $y$ (second time) |
|---|---|
| 2 | 1 |
| 4 | 2 |
| 6 | 4 |
| 8 | 3 |

Step 1:  Add all the scores for $x$; add all the scores for $y$.
Determine that $\Sigma x = 20$; $\Sigma y = 10$.
Step 2:  Square all $x$ scores and add the products; square all $y$ scores and add the products. Determine that $\Sigma x^2 = 120$; $\Sigma y^2 = 30$.
Step 3:  Multiply $x$ by $y$ for each child; add these to determine that $\Sigma xy = 58$.
Step 4:  Substitute numbers in the formula and perform the indicated operations.

$r = \dfrac{4(58) - (20)(10)}{\sqrt{\{(4 \times 120) - (20)^2\}\{4 \times 30 - (10)^2\}}}$

$r = \dfrac{232 - 200}{\sqrt{(480 - 400)(120 - 100)}} = \dfrac{32}{\sqrt{1600}} = \dfrac{32}{40} = .8$

Figure 12.1 Computational Guide for Correlation.

cover the same material with a similar level of difficulty, the procedure will be unfair to some students. The teacher should evaluate the equivalent form reliability of the tests before using them.

A third type of reliability is called **split-half**, a measure of the internal consistency of the test. It is similar to the equivalent forms method. In the split-half method the two equivalent forms are contained in the same test. Thus, instead of two different tests, only one test is administered. Suppose a teacher has a 100-item multiple-choice test. After the test is completed, he divides the test into two 50 item tests and gives each student a score on the odd items and another score on the even items. The assumption is that students should score about the same on the odd and even items of the test. The final steps involve correlating the odd and even items and using a special formula to estimate the reliability of a test only half as long as the original (50 items instead of 100 items). The interested reader can refer to the readings at the end of the chapter to learn more about this method of estimating reliability.

In general, teachers can improve the reliability of their tests by (1) including items that discriminate among students, so that almost no one gets all the items correct or incorrect (reliability is higher when the items are of medium difficulty because the scores are spread out over a greater range), (2) using objective scoring procedures , and (3) including a sufficient number of test items. In general, a longer test is more reliable than a shorter one. This is why test specialists recommend that multiple-choice tests include at least 35 to 40 items.

In thinking about reliability and validity, remember that a test can be reliable without being valid. A valid test must be reliable. For example, your instructor could give a spelling test for the final examination in this course. The instructor could show that the test produces relatively consistent scores on test-retest reliability. However, does the test measure knowledge of educational psychology? Is the test valid? Obviously not! If you can determine that a test has a high degree of validity, then you can be assured of a reasonable level of reliability.

We are now ready to explore the types of measurement instrument used by teachers in making placement, formative, diagnostic, and summative evaluations. Remember, no matter what the function or purpose is of the instrument being used, the goal is to select or develop the most valid and reliable instruments possible.

## STANDARDIZED TESTS

**What factors need to be considered in selecting standardized tests?**

One way to improve the validity and reliability of tests is to construct the test adequately and to make the test situation as similar as possible for all students. This process is called standardization. **Standardized tests** include the following characteristics:

- They are commercially constructed by measurement experts who have carefully prepared and studied all test items.
- They measure various aspects of human behavior under uniform procedures.
- They include a fixed set of questions with the same directions, timing, constraints, and scoring procedures.

Test publishers provide a reference, or *norm*, group of students who have already taken the test so that teachers can compare their students' performances with those of other students in the state or nation. Thus test **norms** provide a standard for comparing an individual's relative level of performance on a specific test. Test norms usually are provided in tables in the test manual.

Norms are established as part of the standardization process by administering the test to representative groups of students for whom the test was constructed. For example, if a test is designed to measure the arithmetic achievement of seventh and eighth graders, the test specialists would obtain scores of representative seventh and eighth graders from many regions and schools throughout the country. The size and sampling procedures for selecting schools and students differ from one test to another. As a result, it is important for the educational committee responsible for selecting tests in a school district to evaluate the appropriateness of the norm or comparison group provided by the test publishers before selecting a test. In some situations, a test may have a norm group (e.g., students in urban areas) with which it would be inappropriate to compare the performance of students in another group (e.g., students in a rural school). Most test publishers who distribute achievement tests nationally undertake large-scale norming procedures that involve representative groups from all geographical regions of the country and from schools of different sizes and cultural and ethnic composition.

The two types of standardized test most used in school evaluation programs are the **aptitude test** and the **achievement test**. An aptitude test measures a student's potential for success in learning. Individual intelligence tests and group scholastic aptitude tests are the most widely used aptitude tests. They are useful in comparing a students' actual achievement, in the form of school grades, with their potential achievement. The results of an aptitude test often indicate that a student has the potential to attain a higher achievement level than is presently being achieved. Aptitude tests are often used in placement evaluation.

An achievement test measures how much of the academic content a student has learned in a particular grade level or course. Various forms of achievement tests are used in placement evaluation (to determine whether students have the needed knowledge to begin instruction), in diagnostic evaluation (to determine the underlying causes of learning problems), and in summative evaluation (to determine how well students have attained the instructional objectives). A school district can evaluate its instructional program by comparing students' achievement test results with those of other students in the state or nation. For example, if the students in a particular high school score consistently lower than the norm in mathematics, the school district should evaluate its curriculum and instructional methods.

Other standardized tests used to a lesser extent in school are interest, attitude, and personality inventories. Guidance counselors use interest inventories to help them in vocational counseling. Attitude and personality inventories identify factors that may influence study habits, motivation, and adjustment in school, and they can be helpful in furthering teachers' and counselors' understanding of their students.

Because most of the standardized tests used in school are aptitude and achievement tests, this chapter focuses on them. If you are interested in learning more about other types of test, see the list of suggested readings at the end of this chapter for basic textbooks on measurement and evaluation that include discussions on a wide variety of standardized tests.

## APTITUDE TESTS

In Chapter 2, I introduced individual intelligence tests as one method of assessing aptitude. Most of the testing in school is done on a group basis. *Scholastic aptitude tests*, like achievement tests, are usually administered to a large number of students at one time by persons with relatively little training in test administration. These aptitude tests attempt to predict school success. The names of group tests often cause confusion over what they measure. Do not make a decision to use a test on its name alone, for it may turn out to measure something entirely different from what you intended it to.

The use of group tests above the first two to three grades requires that the students be able to read the questions and the choice of responses, and indicate their responses on a special answer sheet provided. School officials need to make decisions about the appropriateness of the test format, types of test items, and their level of difficulty for various ages and grade levels.

Some group aptitude tests provide a single score similar to that of the Stanford-Binet, whereas others provide two or more scores based on separate types of mental ability. Examples of single-score tests are the Henmon-Nelson Tests of Mental Ability (grades 3–12) and the Otis-Lennon Mental Ability Test (grades K–12). Tests representative of a two-factor approach are the California Test of Mental Maturity (CTMM) (grades K–16) and the Kuhlman-Anderson Measure of Academic Potential (grades K–12).

Although group tests are economical and easy to administer, they have some disadvantages. First, the uninterested and unmotivated student may score lower on a group test than on an individually administered test because there is no individual examiner to focus specifically on that student's responses. Second, group tests rely heavily on paper and pencil items and emphasize speed, verbal ability, and reading comprehension to a much greater extent than do individual tests. Last, the scoring is completely objective and allows no room for judgment of test-taking behavior. It is not uncommon for a teacher to ask for the administration of an individual intelligence test when information about a student appears to be inconsistent with the group test result.

## ACHIEVEMENT TESTS

The measurement of educational achievement is an important part of developing effective educational programs because not all methods and procedures are uniformly successful. As a result, students, teachers, parents, and school officials need to know how successful their efforts have been, so that decisions can be made regarding which practices to continue and which to change. Two types of achievement test provide information about student progress—*standardized* and **teacher-made tests**.

Standardized achievement tests are constructed by test publishers for wide distribution in schools throughout the country. As a result, the content coverage must be broad enough to include the basic content taught in many schools. As mentioned earlier, scores are interpreted with reference to how well a given student achieved in comparison with a state or national sample of students at the same age or grade level. Teacher-made achievement tests are constructed by the classroom teacher, or sometimes by several teachers, to measure the specific curriculum of a particular course in a particular school. Scores are interpreted with reference to a student's classmates. I first focus on standardized achievement tests and discuss teacher-made tests later in the chapter.

### Standardized Achievement Tests

The standardized achievement test can be classified by content area and function (Brown, 1983). Some achievement tests measure knowledge of arithmetic; others, history, physics, and other school subjects. Many achievement tests are batteries, measuring many content areas rather than only one area. The teacher can then compare test scores on the separate subtests to determine the relative strengths and weaknesses of students in the areas covered by the test.

Elementary school achievement tests focus on the basic skills taught in school: reading, language, mathematics, and study skills. Some tests also include measures of achievement in social studies and science. High school curricula vary more than do elementary school curricula, and, as a result, it is more difficult to develop achievement test batteries that have high content validity in all high schools. Therefore, in addition to using test batteries, high school teachers can select separate tests from specific content-oriented tests to measure achievement in English, social studies, science, or mathematics. Another approach is to use tests that measure general educational development and do not depend on any particular courses for their questions. One such test battery is the Sequential Tests of Educational Progress (STEP II). The unique aspect of this test is that it emphasizes application, interpretation, and evaluation of academic content to a greater extent than do tests that measure basic skills. Because the questions are not derived from specific course content, this test provides a fairer measure of achievement for students with different educational experiences.

Select your achievement tests with care. First, although the tests have similar titles, they often differ in how much emphasis they place on the various skills measured. For example, the specific arithmetic skills tested on two achievement tests may differ. One might emphasize computational skills and the other, problem-solving abilities. Second, standardized achievement tests measure only a portion of the knowledge and skills taught in school, so be sure to choose the most appropriate test for your school's curriculum.

You can locate information about any standardized test from *Tests in Print* (Mitchell, 1983) and *Mental Measurements Yearbooks* (Mitchell, 1985). The latter provides reviews of tests by measurement experts. You can order specimen sets of the examinations that appear in the above sources from test publishers. These sets include a copy of the actual examination booklet and test manuals that evaluate the validity and reliability of the test. Check the test items against the course content in the areas to be tested to determine whether the test adequately measures the objectives of the school.

The following are some achievement test batteries commonly used in schools:

- California Achievement Tests (grades K–12)
- Iowa Tests of Basic Skills (grades K–9)
- Comprehensive Tests of Basic Skills (grades K–12)
- Metropolitan Achievement Tests (grades K–12)
- SRA Achievement Series (grades K–12)
- Stanford Achievement Tests (grades 1–12)

A number of special types of achievement test are particularly useful in making placement and diagnostic evaluations. These instruments include the diagnostic, readiness, and individual achievement tests.

*Diagnostic Tests.* A special type of achievement test used in schools is the diagnostic test, which is designed to assess those skills and abilities that are important in learning a particular subject, usually reading or mathematics. The Durrell Analysis of Reading Difficulty, for example, covers student performance in silent and oral reading, listening, comprehension, word analysis, phonetics, pronunciation, writing, and spelling. The teacher can recommend remedial instruction to overcome the learning problems identified by the test.

There are two important differences between a diagnostic test and a general achievement test. First, the diagnostic test analyzes knowledge in a single subject area in depth, whereas the general achievement test collects information on the distribution of knowledge across many subject areas. Second, the diagnostic test includes a larger proportion of items that are relatively easy to answer, the better to assess below-average performance, whereas the achievement test includes a wider range of items from very easy to very difficult, the better to assess a greater ability span for different grade levels.

*Readiness Tests.* Sometimes teachers need to know whether students are ready for certain learning tasks. Reading readiness tests are most commonly used in elementary school, but other types of test are also used. The reading readiness tests are used to determine whether the student has the necessary knowledge and skills to begin reading. They measure such skills as visual discrimination (identifying similarities and differences in words, letters, pictures), auditory discrimination (identifying similarities and differences in spoken words and sounds), and verbal comprehension. Other readiness tests measure basic concepts and skills that are important for school success. One example is the Boehm Test of Basic Concepts, which measures whether the student has learned concepts (e.g., biggest, nearest, several) needed to understand oral communication (Gronlund, 1985a).

*Individual Achievement Tests.* Individual achievement tests are used to identify students who may have learning disabilities. Individual achievement tests are more likely to determine the cause of a student's difficulty because the examiner can observe the student's attention, motivation, understanding of directions, and other factors that cannot be identified on a group achievement test. In the assessment of the learning problem discussed in Chapter 5, the Basic Achievement Skills Individual Screener (BASIS), an individual achievement test, was used by the special education teacher to understand the nature of Billy Field's problem. Other widely used individual achievement tests include the following:

- Peabody Individual Achievement Test (grades 1–12)
- Key Math Diagnostic Arithmetic Test (K–adult)
- Woodcock Reading Mastery Tests (K–grade 12)

# SPECIAL ACHIEVEMENT TESTING PROGRAMS

A number of large-scale testing programs have important implications for judging both student and teacher competence. As you read about these testing programs, identify your position as to the usefulness of the programs in terms of improving the quality of instruction in schools.

## National Assessment of Educational Progress

The National Assessment of Educational Progress is a nationwide testing program designed to report to the public and educational policymakers the educational achievement of children and young adults in the United States. This testing program involves approximately 1,500 schools representing the diversity of the school population. Student names are not identified on the tests, and no reports are available for school districts or for states. The purpose of the program is not to measure individuals or schools but to report the level of achievement attained by various groups and the nature of changes in achievement over time.

Student achievement is monitored in the following areas: reading and literature, writing, mathematics, science, social studies and citizenship, art, music, and career and occupational development. Each area is assessed every four to eight years through representative sampling of students at ages 9, 13, 17, and of young adults from 26 to 35 years of age. The results of the testing are reported separately by test item. National results are reported for each age group by religion, sex, race, size and type of community, and level of parent education.

Data from this testing program are useful in determining such questions as: What is the current level of academic achievement? What percentage of students can perform certain arithmetic computations? Does the assessment indicate that student performance is increasing or decreasing compared to previous assessments in the area(s)? How do rural and urban youth perform in relation to the rest of the nation? What are the differences among various groups over time? For example, have females increased their mathematical ability since the previous assessment?

## Minimum Competency Testing for Students

Public schools have been criticized because of declining test scores and because students are often passed each year to the next grade without regard to their level of academic achievement. Such a promotion policy results in many students graduating from high school unable to read and deficient in the basic skills necessary for survival in society.

To rectify this problem, many states have passed laws to mandate the establishment of **minimum competency testing** for elementary and secondary school students (see Jaeger, 1989, for a comprehensive review of the issues involved in minimum competency testing). The minimum standards are determined by local school districts, or they are established on a statewide basis. The standards are measured by tests given at various grade levels, and the tests must be passed by the time the student expects to graduate. Early testing allows those students who fail one or more parts of the tests to receive remedial instruction designed to help them pass the tests before the completion of the twelfth grade. A student who continues to fail the tests is usually given a "certificate of attendance" rather than a diploma.

Each state has its own regulations and procedures to determine how the testing program should operate. Some states focus primarily on basic skills in reading, writing, and arithmetic. Other states incorporate a combination of basic academic skills with "survival skills" such as consumer knowledge, oral communication, and governmental processes. In addition, the setting of standards, the grade levels assessed, and the types of testing instrument used vary widely among the states. You should find out if your state has a minimum competency testing program and how the program operates.

Included in the many issues concerning minimum competency testing programs that need to be resolved are the definition of competencies, the specification of minimal competency, and the testing of minimum competence (Haney & Madaus, 1978). Not everyone agrees on the identification of "life skills," "essential skills," or "survival skills" that should be required in education. Are the "essential skills" for a baker, a lawyer, and a salesperson the same? Perhaps skills taught in preparation for passing a test will be of little value later on. Futhermore, not everyone agrees on the appropriate cutoff levels for minimum competency. Haney and Madaus state: "In practice, the setting of minimum scores seems to be the result of compromise between judgments of what minimums seem plausible to expect and judgments about what proportions of failure seem politically tolerable" (p. 468). Larkins (1981) more critically states: "Improving the percentage of high school seniors who can pass a sixth-grade standardized reading test is not likely to halt the flight of parents who seek quality education in the form of a strong college preparatory program" (p. 136).

Testing for minimal competency raises many additional issues: Are the tests measuring what students have been taught? This is an especially important concern in states requiring one test for all students in the state. In Florida, a court order prohibited the use of its mandatory literacy test (which is what they call it) before it was to go into effect in 1979. The test was challenged by a suit brought by a group of parents whose children failed the test. In *Debra P. v. Turlington*, a federal judge ruled that there must be a sufficient amount of time before the test is announced and the date when diplomas are actually denied in order to allow students the opportunity to take remedial courses. An appeals court upheld the judge and issued an additional requirement that the state must show that the test is related to what is taught in the school curriculum (content validity).

In 1983, the court was satisfied that all the conditions had been met by Florida and allowed students who did not pass the test to be denied diplomas (Brown, 1983).

Other issues that are still being resolved by the states are the following: What type of remedial instruction is most appropriate for students failing the tests? How can fairness to minority-group members and handicapped students be ensured? How do we know what the testing program itself is contributing to student learning?

Not all educators believe that minimum competency tests are the panacea for improving school achievement. Larkins (1981) raises a number of concerns about minimum competency programs. First, the standards often are set very low. When improvement is noted, it is difficult to determine whether it has been caused by increased knowledge or instructors teaching to the test. Second, the testing programs do not address the problems with education. Larkins believes that the focus on rote learning and the overemphasis on ditto sheets to keep students busy at their desks are problems that are not being addressed. Third, there is danger that teachers will emphasize basic skills at the expense of the higher levels of learning because the higher levels are not emphasized on tests. In fact, Madaus (1981) presents evidence that the decline in Scholastic Aptitude Test (SAT) scores reflects a decline in higher-level cognitive skills, not in basic skills. Fourth, the minimum competency tests will drive from school students who need to be there. If students are not promoted and are placed in grades where the disparity in ages between children becomes too great, the students who are not promoted will drop out of school rather than remain for continual remediation.

Although it is still too early to determine the merits of minimum competency programs, we have seen a movement by the states to increase the number of days in the school year as well as the number of credits required for graduation. This program represents an important development in education. It will be interesting to follow its progress to determine the extent to which issues are resolved and competency testing becomes widely accepted by legislators, parents, teachers, and students.

## Minimum Competency Testing for Teachers

While the debate over minimum competency testing for students was occurring, attention moved to the ability of teachers to provide the quality of instruction needed to improve student achievement. Teacher selection and training have come under severe criticism that has focused on the fact that many individuals entering the teaching profession have low or marginal academic ability as measured by such tests as the Graduate Record Examination (GRE). Standards for entering and graduating from accredited teacher education programs are too low, and state certification and school selection processes are inadequate. As a result, many teachers have entered the profession having neither gained nor demonstrated teaching competency and knowledge of basic academic skills (Hathaway, 1980).

To combat this problem, every state except Alaska and Iowa has passed laws requiring competency or literacy tests for prospective teachers in such areas as reading, writing, language, and mathematics as a requirement for certification (Rudner, 1988). Some states assess actual teaching performance as well. The argument often made by proponents of teacher competency tests is that if attorneys, real estate agents, and barbers have to take tests to obtain a license, why should teachers not be required to do the same? Most important, proponents believe that the testing will lead to the improvement of education as a profession.

Although the testing programs have focused on new teachers entering the profession, Arkansas and Texas went a step further and required experienced teachers to take tests for recertification. These teachers were given other opportunities to pass the test if they failed it the first time. As you might expect, testing new teachers has been more widely accepted in the profession than has testing experienced teachers. Teachers in Arkansas and Texas were critical of the law requiring recertification, arguing that it was demeaning to require experienced teachers to take the tests.

A number of arguments are made against competency testing for teachers. In a strong indictment of teacher competency testing, Cole (1979) states:

> Minimum competency testing is a hollow means of judging the efficacy of teachers. It can only whittle away at the edges of the problem; it has no power to cure, because it treats symptoms rather than causes. The heart of the problem perceived by the public lies deep within the structure of the education system. . . . competency testing is nothing more than a search for victims, off on a false scent. The time for assurances of competence is at the beginning of the [teacher] educative process, not simply as a belated quality check at the end. (p. 23)

In addition to the argument that the tests will not necessarily improve the quality of teaching, criticisms of testing teachers generally fall into two major areas: The tests are not valid, and the standards are not high enough. The validity argument stems from the fact that the tests generally measure not classroom teaching ability but basic academic skills, which don't predict on-the-job success. In the few states that include some measure of actual teaching ability, there are also questions whether these assessments can predict teacher effectiveness. If they cannot, the tests will do little to weed out inferior teachers. Finally, a good test performance on basic skills does not assure that a teacher is proficient in teaching advanced mathematics or English classes.

The proponents of competency testing for teachers reply to the foregoing arguments by saying that it is not the whole answer to improving the quality of education but that it can be *part* of the solution. The rest of the solution involves attracting more competent individuals to the profes-

**What are the strengths and weaknesses of minimum competency testing for students and teachers?**

sion, screening prospective teachers better, providing more effective teacher education, and instituting effective staff development programs in schools (Hathaway, 1980).

What is your opinion of the competency testing movement in education? Should both teachers and students be involved? Will these tests lead to improved education? Are there alternatives?

## PREPARING STUDENTS FOR TESTS

One of the major controversies in the area of testing is the effect on test scores of coaching in test-taking skills, or **test-wiseness training**. Test wiseness is defined (Millman, Bishop, & Ebel, 1965) as "a set of cognitive skills that one may employ on a myriad of tests regardless of the nature of the tests or subject content" (p. 707). Test-wiseness training teaches students general test-taking skills regarding time management, techniques to avoid errors, and guessing strategies—information that is independent of any particular content preparation.

The term **coaching** as it relates to test preparation refers to training to increase scores on specific tests. Classes that prepare students for the Scholastic Aptitude Tests (SAT) are involved in coaching to improve test scores. Although test-wiseness training and coaching have a different focus, there is some overlap of their goals. For example, certain general test-taking skills are taught in preparation for specific tests like the SAT. In addition, specific content areas can be introduced in test-wiseness training programs.

Although there is evidence that certain types of coaching can increase test scores (see Bond, 1989; Messick & Jungeblut, 1981; Messick, 1982), a number of questions remain. How much coaching? What kinds of coaching? How much improvement? Because programs vary greatly, it is important to identify the particular programs evaluated before reaching any conclusions about their effectiveness. Researchers have learned that the greatest change in test scores has been found with more intensive training programs in terms of the number of sessions and the degree to which the programs focus on broad cognitive skills (Bangert-Drowns, Kulik, & Kulik, 1983; Messick & Jungeblut, 1981). Also, certain types of test are more responsive to coaching than are others. For example, coaching is more likely to raise test scores on the mathematics section of the SAT than on the verbal section. Finally, is the improvement worth the effort, time, and money? Students do benefit slightly from coaching, particularly if they are not familiar with the testing procedures. However, there are few students with mediocre ability who, as a result of their coaching experience alone, score high enough to get accepted into a program of study.

The results of investigations into training in test-taking skills, or test-wiseness, are similar. The training can produce a small but significant effect on academic achievement, and the longer the program, the greater the effect. Programs lasting from five to seven weeks yielded greater gains (Samson, 1985; Sarnacki, 1979).

## CLASSROOM APPLICATION: TEACHING TEST-TAKING SKILLS

I am including general guidelines for teaching test-taking skills. The first two sections, on motivation, are quoted from Hill and Wigfield (1984, p. 123), and the remaining guidelines are quoted from a program developed by Urman (1982, pp. 111–115). The guidelines include anxiety reduction and an attributional focus on effort rather than on ability (Chapter 10). More advanced principles covering deductive reasoning strategies and procedures for recognizing and making use of any consistent idiosyncrasies of the test constructor (e.g., the correct option is consistently longer than the incorrect options) can be found in Millman, Bishop, and Ebel (1965) and Sarnacki (1979).

You may want to include additional information depending on the grade level and subject specialty. For example, provide practice in certain computational problems in math, demonstrate how to identify main ideas in a reading comprehension passage, and give tips for using correct grammar in sentences. After students take tests, you can ask for recommendations from them that can be added to the guidelines for improving test-taking skills. Such a discussion can be useful in focusing on specific student concerns.

**Positive Motivation: Doing Your Best**

1. All I ask is that you do your best. I will be really pleased if you try to do your best.
2. Before we begin, remember to listen carefully to me, be quiet, take a deep breath, and feel relaxed.

**Positive Motivation: Expectancy Reassurance**

1. Some tests have some very hard problems. Don't worry if you can't do some problems.
2. If you work hard but don't finish a test, don't worry about it! The most important thing to me is that you try hard and do as well as you can. I know you'll do a good job if you try!

**Use Your Time Carefully**

1. Always know how much *time* you have for the test.
2. During the test, *do not* watch the clock, but check it every once in a while so that you will know how much time is left.
3. When you begin the test
   a. Answer the questions you know first.

b. Do not spend too much time on hard questions. Try not to get upset when you cannot answer a hard question.

c. Skip hard questions and go back to them at the end of the test.

d. Mark *every question* on the test booklet that you skip so that you can come back to it later. Remember: *Do not* mark on the answer sheet.

4 When you have answered all the questions, go back and check your work.

5. Do not leave any questions blank.

**Answer Every Question**

1. If you do *not* know the answer to a question, read the question again.

2. Read each of the answers.

3. Mark the best answer only after you have read all the answers.

4. If you cannot figure out the answer to a question, *guess.*

5. Be sure you mark *one answer for each question. Do not leave a question blank.*

**When Should You Change an Answer?**

1. When you make a mistake marking the answer sheet.

2. When you think another answer is better. A few minutes after you start taking a test, you sometimes get into the swing of the test and see things in the questions that you did not notice at first. After you finish the test and start going back over the questions, if a different answer seems better, you should *change your answer.*

# CRITICISMS OF STANDARDIZED TESTING

**What are the strengths and weaknesses of standardized testing?**

Not all educators are pleased with the extensive use of standardized testing in our nation's schools. Issues of validity and misuse of test results are most frequently raised. Following is a brief discussion of the major criticisms of standardized testing (Holmen & Docter, 1974; Strenio, 1981), followed by responses by advocates of the proper use of standardized testing.

## The Gatekeeper Function

*Criticisms.* One of the major criticisms of tests is that they are designed to measure differences among individuals to determine who receives and who is denied certain rewards and privileges. For example, students are placed in classes for the gifted, gain admission to college, or are admitted to advanced graduate study on the basis of their test scores. The important question is whether tests are the kind of gatekeepers we want in society. Do educators and employers rely too much on tests, which can be unreliable predictors of future performance? Are there alternatives? Should we rely more on individuals' actual performance rather than on their test performance?

*Response.* Tests also open the gates for some students whose academic records and/or socioeconomic status would not permit them to attend college or enter a special program. For example, a high SAT score may be the deciding factor in admitting a student into a particular college or helping a student to receive financial aid. In other situations, tests may identify special ability or talents that encourage students to enter fields they had never before thought about.

## Harmful Effects on Cognitive Styles

*Criticisms.* Some educators believe that the widespread use of the single-answer test item influences students' style of thinking. More specifically, the concern is that many students may believe that all issues or questions can be resolved by finding the *one* right answer.

*Response.* Well-constructed tests can measure higher-level cognitive skills and can enhance students' thinking.

## Effect on Curricula and Change

*Criticisms.* Some educators argue that when teachers learn how and what their students will be tested on, they are less likely to cover some important material because they do not believe it will be on the test. In addition, they may be less likely to try new methods of teaching or new resource materials if they believe that students' test results may be affected adversely.

*Response.* By knowing the general content of a standardized test given at the end of a course, a teacher is likely to cover more instructional objectives and help students to attain a higher level of mastery of content than they would if no standardized test were given.

## Students' Self-Concept and Level of Aspiration

*Criticisms.* As you have learned from reading Chapter 10, students make social comparisons to judge their own adequacy and self-worth. Students may come to believe early in their educational careers that they are less capable than their classmates and stop trying to achieve. Many parents have been misinformed by guidance counselors who have told them that their child or adolescent was not "college material"—information that may become a self-fulfilling prophecy.

*Response.* Although some students' self-concepts are negatively influenced by standardized testing, many students are positively influenced by learning that their academic efforts have paid off. With better training, teachers and counselors are less likely to provide parents and students with inaccurate information about test results.

## Selection of Homogeneous Educational Groups

*Criticisms.* Many schools use test results to assign students to classes based on estimates of learning ability. It has been argued that many students have not learned the necessary test-taking skills, and as a result their ability is underestimated by the tests. The fact that students are assigned to different levels, or tracks, in school often influences the type of education they receive in terms of course content, quality of teachers, and expectations for achievement. Finally, students who score low on standardized tests are likely to be placed with other low-scoring students in homogeneous classes, whereas in heterogeneous classes there is a mix of ability levels. There is some indication that homogeneous grouping does more harm than good for low achievers. Brookover and his colleagues (1982) have reported that more effective schools use *fewer* forms of stratification of students (e.g., tracking by type of educational program and ability grouping) than do less effective schools. Why do you think the amount of stratification in a school would be related to school achievement? Could stratification be related to expectations for student performance? Do teachers treat all ability levels the same? What have you learned in previous chapters that can help you to understand this finding?

*Response.* Decisions about class or group placement of students should not be made on the basis of any single measurement. Course grades, test scores, work habits, and teacher comments are some of the major sources of information that should be used to make educational decisions. In some situations, standardized tests may indicate that a student has mastered more content than indicated by teacher grades, thus preventing inappropriate placement.

## Invasion of Privacy

*Criticisms.* Some test critics believe that although the school has a right to measure achievement, it should not be giving intelligence, personality, and other nonacademic tests. They also say that test results should not be available to individuals other than the students' parents.

*Response.* Nonacademic tests are not usually given to students unless recommended by a counselor or school psychologist after consultation with a parent. Privacy laws (e.g., the Family Educational Rights and Privacy Act of 1974, commonly known as the Buckley Amendment) attempt to reduce the possibility that anyone will receive test information concerning a student without permission.

## TEACHER-MADE TESTS

How do stan-
dardized tests
differ from
teacher-made
tests?

Although standardized tests play an important role in measurement and evaluation in education, most tests used in school are developed by classroom teachers. Standardized tests seldom fit the specific content and objectives of a given course. If Mr. Jones wants to measure student learning at the end of a unit on the Civil War, for instance, he will have to construct his own test.

Standardized tests are useful for determining how local achievement compares with national norms; the teacher-made test is useful for measuring individual classroom instruction. Table 12.1 presents the comparative advantages of teacher-made and standardized tests of achievement.

Teacher-made achievement tests are usually divided into two categories:

1. Objective tests, which are highly structured and limit the type of response a student can make. The answer key designates a response as either correct or incorrect. These tests include multiple-choice, completion, matching, and true-false items.

TABLE 12.1 COMPARISIONS BETWEEN TEACHER-MADE AND STANDARDIZED ACHIEVEMENT TESTS

| Characteristic | Teacher-Made Achievement Tests | Standardized Achievement Tests |
| --- | --- | --- |
| Directions for administration and scoring | Usually no uniform directions specified | Specific instructions standardize administration and scoring procedures |
| Sampling of content | Both content and sampling are determined by classroom teacher | Content determined by curriculum and subject matter experts; involves extensive investigations of existing syllabi, textbooks, and programs; sampling of content done systematically |
| Construction | May be hurried and haphazard; often no test blueprints, item tryouts, item analysis or revision; quality of test may be quite poor | Uses meticulous construction procedures that include constructing objectives and test blueprints, employing item tryouts, item analysis, and item revisions |
| Norms | Only local classroom norms are available | In addition to local norms, standardized tests typically make available national, school distict, and school building norms |
| Purposes and use | Best suited for measuring particular objectives set by teacher and for intraclass comparisons | Best suited for measuring broader curriculum objectives and for interclass, school, and national comparisons |

*Source: Mehrens and Lehmann, 1984.*

2. Subjective, or essay, tests, which allow students to impose their own organization on the material and present it in their own words. In scoring an essay test, the teacher must make qualitative decisions about how close a student's answer is to the model answer.

There are no definite rules for using an objective or subjective test other than the considerations of what the teacher wants to measure and the available time for the task. Many teachers use combinations of the two types of test, since each has its merits and limitations. A comparison of essay and objective tests appears in Table 12.2. The research over the past five decades indicates that if the cognitive level of test questions is similar, telling students that the test will comprise objective or essay questions has

---

**TABLE 12.2 COMPARISONS BETWEEN ESSAY AND OBJECTIVE TESTS**

|  | Essay | Objective |
|---|---|---|
| *Abilities Measured* | Requires the student to express himself in his own words, using information from his own background and knowledge. | Requires the student to select correct answers from given options, or to supply an answer limited to one word or phrase. |
|  | Can tap high levels of reasoning such as required in inference, organization of ideas, comparison, and contrast. | Can also tap high levels of reasoning such as required in inference, organization of ideas, comparison, and contrast. |
|  | Does not measure purely factual information efficiently. | Measures knowledge of facts efficiently. |
| *Scope* | Covers only a limited field of knowledge in any one test. Essay questions take so long to answer that relatively few can be answered in a given period of time. Also, the student who is especially fluent can often avoid discussing points of which he is unsure. | Covers a broad field of knowledge in one test. Since objective questions may be answered quickly, one test may contain many questions. A broad coverage helps provide reliable measurement. |
| *Incentive to Pupils* | Encourages pupils to learn how to organize their own ideas and express them effectively. | Encourages pupils to build up a broad background of knowledge and abilities. |
| *Ease of Preparation* | Requires writing only a few questions for a test. Tasks must be clearly defined, general enough to offer some leeway, specific enough to set limits. | Requires writing many questions for a test. Wording must avoid ambiguities and "giveaways." Distractors should embody most likely misconceptions. |
| *Scoring* | Usually very time-consuming to score. | Can be scored quickly. |
|  | Permits teachers to comment directly on the reasoning processes of individual pupils. However, an answer may be scored differently by different teachers or by the same teacher at different times. | Answer generally scored only right or wrong, but scoring is very accurate and consistent. |

*Source: Educational Testing Service, 1959, 1961, 1973.*

no effect on their achievement (Crooks, 1988). Thus students who believe that the type of test question is an important factor in their performance need to be told that their studying behavior is a far more critical factor affecting their performance.

Taking time to plan a test pays dividends in a more reliable and valid measurement instrument. Too often, teachers compose tests at the last minute without giving careful consideration even to the purpose of the examination. Ms. Smith, an American history teacher, announces on Monday a test for Wednesday. After school she skims through the textbook and her lecture notes for information for the examination. She writes test items until satisfied that she has a sufficient number for the test.

Ms. Smith's strategy raises a number of questions. First, does she know what learning outcomes she is measuring? If she spent most of the class time on the *analysis* of political parties' influence on foreign policy, her examination should emphasize this learning outcome and not the *recall* of factual material about the parties. Second, did she adequately cover the content of the entire unit? Perhaps she completed her test items before reaching the last chapter in the book and failed to include any questions from an important section of the material. The first question asks the teacher to think about the cognitive level of the test item. The second question shows concern for adequate coverage of the material. Taken together, the answers to these questions evaluate the content validity of the measuring instrument.

Think about the tests you have taken during your school experience. Can you identify situations in which important lecture information or required readings were not even included in the examination? What about the level of questions? Have you taken examinations that asked for an almost total regurgitation of factual material? Make a list of some characteristics of teacher-made tests that have irritated you at some time during your academic career. Maybe your instructor would like to see your list!

## PLANNING THE TEST

Before beginning to write any test items, the teacher should perform three tasks. These steps can alleviate many problems in the nature and scope of the examination.

1. *Identify the learning outcomes to be measured by the test.* Here is where instructional objectives and the *Taxonomy of Educational Objectives* (Bloom et al., 1956) come in handy. If you have written your objectives before instruction, you should have little difficulty in completing this planning phase. If you had no specified objectives for the unit, this initial step will require more time and effort.
2. *Outline the subject matter to be measured by the test* to ensure that you identify all important content.

3. *Prepare a test plan or* **table of specifications**. A table of specifications is a two-dimensional table on which the learning outcomes are listed along one side and the subject matter topics along the other side. The intersecting cells in the table allow the teacher to fill in the proportion of test items devoted to each learning outcome and each subject matter topic. An example of a table of specifications for a short unit on test construction is given in Table 12.3.

As the teacher writes a test item, he or she makes a tally in the corresponding cell in the table. This procedure directs the teacher's attention to the assessment of instructional outcomes other than those at the knowledge level and ensures that test items are drawn from the different topics or readings in the unit. By examining the table, the teacher can easily determine whether the items adequately measure the nature of the instruction as well as the emphasis or weight given to each learning outcome and topic.

**When would you use the following type of tests: multiple choice, matching, completion, and true false?**

Regardless of the type of test items written for an examination, the following general guidelines for writing tests are always applicable (Chase, 1974):

- Avoid replication of the textbook in writing test items.
- Begin writing items well in advance of the test, and allow time for test revision.
- Avoid trick items and procedures.
- Make sure the directions are clear.

TABLE 12.3 **A TEST PLAN FOR A UNIT ON TEST CONSTRUCTION**

| Learning Outcomes | Topics | | |
|---|---|---|---|
| | Characteristics of a Good Test | Planning a Test | Writing Test Items |
| Evaluation | | | |
| Synthesis | | | |
| Analysis | | | |
| Application | | | |
| Comprehension | | | |
| Knowledge | | | |

The last two guidelines are especially important. Some teachers forget that the purpose of examinations is to assess students and not to outwit them.

## CLASSROOM APPLICATION: WRITING TEST QUESTIONS

We now examine commonly used types of objective test items—multiple choice, matching, completion, and true-false—and then go on to essay items. You will learn about the physical makeup of these items and how to write your own, as well as the pros and cons about their use.

### Multiple-Choice Items

The multiple-choice item contains a *stem*, which identifies a problem situation, and several *alternatives*, or *options*, which provide possible solutions to the problem. The alternatives include a correct answer and several plausible wrong answers, or distractors. The stem may be stated as a direct question or an incomplete statement. The student's task is to select the correct (or best) response from the list of alternatives. The following are examples of multiple-choice items with the two types of stem:

#### QUESTION VARIETY

Stem: What is the most important type of validity in teacher-made tests?

Responses: A. predictive
B. content
C. construct
D. concurrent

#### INCOMPLETE STATEMENT VARIETY

Stem: The arithmetic average is the same as the

Responses: A. median
B. mode
C. mean
D. variance

Some items are more easily written in one format than in the other. The question format is generally easier to write and encourages the item writer to pose a clear problem, but it often results in a longer stem.

Most multiple-choice items offer four or five choices to reduce the student's chances of obtaining a correct response by guessing. There is no reason for all items on the test to include the same number of alternatives; some items generate more plausible distractors than others.

The quality of a multiple-choice item is a combination of the clarity of the stem and the skill with which the various alternatives are written. Here are some suggestions for writing multiple-choice items.

1. Make all alternative responses grammatically consistent with the stem and parallel in form. Suppose the test item presented earlier was written as follows:

   The type of validity of major concern in teacher-made tests is
      1. predictive and concurrent
      <u>2.</u> content
      3. construct and content
      4. predictive and construct

   Since the item asks for *type*, a student could eliminate alternatives 1, 3, and 4 because they include more than one type.

2. Avoid making the correct response consistently longer or shorter than the others.
3. Underline negative wording whenever it is used in the stem of an item.
4. Avoid overuse of the alternatives "all of the above" and "none of the above."
5. Vary the position of the correct answer in a random manner.
6. Make certain each item is independent of the other items in the test.

The multiple-choice item has numerous merits. First, it can measure objectives from the entry knowledge level to the most complex level. Second, the teacher can sample a great deal of information in a relatively short time. Third, scoring is completely objective; the correct answer is not open to interpretation. Last, as I have already stated, the four or five choices reduce the possibility of obtaining a correct answer through guessing.

The main problems with multiple-choice items are the difficulty of writing test items, the overemphasis on lower cognitive skills by some teachers, and student complaints that there is often more than one defensible "correct" answer. You can remedy the latter two problems by writing items carefully.

Students often discuss the advisability of changing answers on multiple-choice tests. Students commonly believe that they should stick with their first answer. However, research evidence does not support this position. The research studies on this issue find that students who change their responses to test items raise their scores (Lynch & Smith, 1972; Reiling & Taylor, 1972). One explanation for this finding is that students taking examinations are aided by information from other test items as they go along, so that careful reconsideration can result in a correct response. Does this finding appear inconsistent with your own experience?

Lynch and Smith (1972) think that when students go over a corrected examination, they are more concerned with why they got a ques-

---

tion wrong than with why they got certain questions right. They are more likely to notice right-to-wrong changes and conclude that changing responses lowers test scores. Thus many students do not change responses. A good rule to follow if you understand a question better or recall additional information is: Change your answer!

## Matching Items

The matching item is a modification of the multiple-choice form. A series of stems appears in one column and the responses in another. The student must select the option that is correctly associated with the stem. The following is an example of such an item:

In the left-hand column are terms associated with different psychologists and educators. For each term, choose a name from the right-hand column, and place the letter identifying it on the line preceding the number of the term.

|  |  |
|---|---|
| _____ 1. self-actualization | a) Binet |
| _____ 2. mastery learning | b) Bloom |
| _____ 3. operant conditioning | c) Gagné |
| _____ 4. assimilation | d) Maslow |
| _____ 5. learning hierarchy | e) Piaget |
|  | f) Skinner |

Some suggestions for constructing matching test items follow:

1. Include only homogeneous material in each matching exercise.
2. Indicate clearly the basis on which the matching is to be done.
3. The questions should contain at least 5 and not more than 15 items.
4. The items in the response column should be arranged in systematic order. Dates should be in chronological order, whereas names of people, terms, and so on should be in alphabetical order. This reduces the amount of time needed to search for the correct response.
5. All the items should be on a single page.

The matching item is most appropriate for assessing associations. It is not readily adaptable for measuring complex levels of learning.

## Completion Items

A completion, or fill-in-the-blank, item confronts the students with a statement for which they must supply a missing word or phrase. This type of item emphasizes *recall* of previously learned material rather than recognition.

The Stanford-Binet is an example of a(n) _____ test.

The following are some suggestions for construction of completion items:

1. Omit key words and phrases rather than trivial details.
2. Avoid overmutilated statements, such as The _____ and _____ were _____ in World War II.
3. If possible, items should require a single-word answer.
4. Avoid lifting statements directly from the text.
5. Make the blanks of uniform length.
6. Avoid grammatical clues to the expected answer.
7. Arrange the test with the answers in a column for easier scoring.
8. Prepare a scoring key that contains all acceptable answers.

The completion item is relatively easy to construct. It requires recall of information, so it reduces the possibility of guessing the correct answer from the correct response.

The completion item has its limits. Scoring completion items is difficult because constructing them for only one answer is difficult. Second, answers are restricted to a few words, and the items tend to measure recall of specific facts rather than more complex learning outcomes.

## True-False Items

The true-false item is a declarative sentence that the test taker must decide is correct (true) or incorrect (false).

T F    A table of specifications is used to plan for teacher-made tests.

The following are some suggestions for constructing true-false items:

1. Include only one central idea in each statement.
2. Word the statement so precisely that it is unequivocally true or false.
3. Keep the statements short, and use simple language.
4. Use negative statements sparingly and avoid double negatives.
5. Avoid use of specific determiners such as "always," "never," and "seldom."
6. Attribute statements of opinion to a source.
7. Avoid a disproportionate number of either true or false statements.
8. Explain the desired method of marking before the students begin the test. You may have them write out the words "true" or "false" or circle the correct letter.

The advantage of the true-false item is that it tends to be brief. The teacher can ask questions covering a great deal of material and can score the items in a short time. Because true-false items emphasize memorizing facts and are open to guesswork, they have their limits, too.

## Essay Questions

What are the advantages and disadvantages of essay and objective tests?

Essay questions are used to their best advantage in measuring higher-order mental processes—application, analysis, synthesis, and evaluation—and should not be used to measure knowledge of facts or principles. They provide an opportunity for students to use their own words, style, and organization in dealing with the subject matter of a course.

Teachers should be aware of at least three limitations of essay questions. First is the problem of content validity. An adequate sampling of the content and objectives of a unit or course by essay questions is impossible. These questions take more time to answer than do objective items, limiting the number of questions that can be asked and thus limiting the content coverage of the examination.

Second, subjective scoring makes essay test results lower in reliability than objective tests, which use more precise scoring. A number of extraneous factors can influence a teacher's scoring of an essay question. Handwriting, the use of pen rather than pencil, and spelling and grammatical errors will probably disincline the teacher toward the student. A halo effect (or its opposite), which occurs when a teacher's general impression of the student affects the evaluation of the paper, is an unfortunate possibility. This effect can be either positive or negative.

Last, although essay questions take less time to write than objective questions, this gain is lost in the scoring. For this reason, teachers with large classes often limit essay testing to very specific objectives.

Some suggestions for constructing essay questions follow:

1. Use essay items to measure complex learning outcomes only.
2. Relate the questions as directly as possible to the learning outcomes being measured. Gorman (1974) suggests some key words that relate to specific types of learning you may wish to measure.

| | |
|---|---|
| words | define, what is the meaning |
| facts | state, identify, describe |
| concepts | explain, distinguish between |
| relations | explain giving reasons, examples |
| structures | explain the interrelationships, show how it is organized |
| comprehension | give the meaning, summarize |
| creativity | write a theme, develop a plan, suggest |
| problem solving | what was the cause |
| analysis | compare, contrast, distinguish |
| critical thinking | criticize (on the basis of . . .), evaluate |
| application, transfer | (given an example or case) explain in terms of . . . (p. 422) |

3. Formulate questions that present a clear, definite task to the students. For example, look at the following questions: a. Discuss essay tests. b. Discuss the merits and limitations of essay tests. The first question is too general because it allows the students to write whatever they want. The second question focuses specifically on the particular response requested of the students.
4. Provide ample time for answering, and give suggested time limits for each question.

Because subjectivity in scoring is one of the major limitations of the essay question, the following guidelines for uniform standards in scoring are suggested to reduce (although not totally alleviate) this problem (Gronlund, 1985a):

1. *Prepare in advance a model answer and the number of credit points allowed for each question.* You have now set a standard against which all students will be judged. By determining the number of points for each question, you can further subdivide the points for various parts of the answer.
2. *Grade all papers without knowledge of the "author."* This procedure attempts to counteract the halo effect (or its opposite). You can implement it in two ways. One method is to ask the students to write their name on the back of the examination booklet so that you will not know which student you are evaluating. A second method is to pass a sheet of paper containing a series of numbers and ask the students to write their names on the sheet opposite one of the numbers. The students place their number instead of their name on the examination booklet. After all the students have signed the sheet, take it and file it until all the examinations are scored. Only then are the students' names matched with their numbers for recording the grades. Of course, if a teacher is familiar with the handwriting of the students, these procedures would not reduce the halo effect.
3. *Grade only one question at a time for all papers.* By grading the first question for all students before moving on to the next question, you are more likely to use the same standard for every student. When you switch from one model answer to another in grading each question in one paper, you will probably modify the standard. This question-by-question procedure can also limit the halo effect. Suppose a student does poorly on the first three questions of an examination but does very well on the fourth question. If you had graded each student's complete paper, you might be prejudiced by the student's poor start. Your expectations would preclude your adequately crediting the student's response to question 4.

4. *Write comments as well as grades on the paper.* Students frequently hear that examinations are learning experiences. If this is to be true, you should briefly explain deficiencies in the students' responses for their benefit. Students also like to be praised for their good work. If they receive only criticism, they might develop anxiety about writing. Can you remember any personal experiences, bad or good, with teacher evaluations of your essays or term papers?

## MEASURING AFFECTIVE OUTCOMES

When teachers need to measure the outcomes of affective objectives or to learn more about the personal concerns of their students, they can construct their own surveys. Open-ended questions and questionnaires are useful formats for eliciting such information.

### Open-Ended Questions

Open-ended or incomplete sentences require students to complete a statement in any way they choose, thereby revealing what feelings and attitudes the topics arouse in them. The following examples illustrate stimuli that will evoke student reponses:

- My teacher . . .
- What I want most . . .
- I am happiest when . . .
- The thing I like most about this class . . .
- The thing I like least about this class . . .
- Other boys (girls) . . .

### Questionnaires

Questionnaires can be designed to obtain a wide variety of responses regarding student problems, attitudes, and interests. The following are some of the forms questionnaires can take:

A. On the next social studies unit
   1. I want to work alone.
   2. I want to work with one or two friends.
   3. I want to work with a group.

B. Forty minutes of science is
   1. too much.
   2. about right.
   3. not enough.

|  | Always | Sometimes | Never |
|---|---|---|---|

C. Does the teacher give you enough time to finish tests?
   Does the teacher listen to you when you have a problem?
   Does time go quickly in this class?

D. For each activity listed below, circle the choice that best represents how you feel about the activity in question. SL means "strongly like"; L means "like"; I means "indifferent to"; D means "dislike"; and SD means "strongly dislike."
   1. Spending time in a library
   SL  L  I  D  SD
   2. Listening to the top musical hits of the week
   SL  L  I  D  SD

## IMPROVING TEST QUALITY THROUGH ITEM ANALYSIS

**How does an item analysis help teachers improve the quality of their tests?**

After giving and scoring a test, it is important to determine which items need improvements and which should be omitted from future tests. **Item analysis** is a method of examining the students' responses to each test item to judge the quality of the test. Both *difficulty* and *discrimination* of a given item can be determined. A test item is considered to be good if it is neither too difficult nor too easy, and if it discriminates between the high and low scorers on the test. Item analysis can be applied to any type of test item. We focus here, however, on multiple-choice tests because of the wide use of item analysis of these types of question.

Let's look at two hypothetical items on a test (the asterisks identify the correct answers) to understand how to analyze items. In classes of 25 to 38 students, identify the 10 highest scorers and the 10 lowest scorers, about one-third of the class group (Gage & Berliner, 1988). Prepare their distribution of choices for items as shown below:

| **Item 1** | | **A** | **B** | **C** | **D\*** |
|---|---|---|---|---|---|
| | High Scores | 1 | 1 | 2 | 6 |
| | Low Scores | 2 | 2 | 3 | 3 |
| **Item 2** | | **A\*** | **B** | **C** | **D** |
| | High Scores | 2 | 6 | 2 | 0 |
| | Low Scores | 4 | 3 | 3 | 0 |

## Index of Item Difficulty

Find the number of students who answered the item correctly, and divide by the total number of students tested. Thus,

$$\text{Difficulty} = \frac{R}{T}$$

$$\text{where } \frac{R}{T} = \frac{\text{number of students who answered items correctly}}{\text{total number of students tested}}$$

If all students answered an item correctly, the difficulty level would be 1.00. If half the students answered correctly, the difficulty level would be .5. If no students answered correctly, the difficulty level would be .00. An attempt should be made to write questions that are neither too difficult nor too easy. In general, test items with difficulty levels between .25 to .75 will generate a wide distribution of scores. For item 1, the **index of difficulty** is

$$\frac{R}{T} = \frac{9}{2} = .45$$

For item 2, it is

$$\frac{R}{T} = \frac{6}{20} = .3$$

## Index of Item Discrimination

A good item should discriminate between students who know the information and those who do not. The **index of item discrimination** can be determined by subtracting the proportion of correct answers among low scorers from the proportion of correct answers among high scorers for that item. (The proportion is determined by dividing the number of correct responses by the total number of responses.) Thus

$$\text{discrimination} = \text{proportion of high scorers who were correct} - \text{proportion of low scorers who were correct}$$

For item 1, the discrimination index is .3 (.6 − .3 = .3); for item 2, the index is −.2 (.2 − .4 = −.2). In an extreme case, if all the high scorers answered the item correctly and all the low scorers answered the item incorrectly, the discrimination index would be 1.00 (1.00 − .00 = 1.00). This is maximum item discrimination. An index of zero (or even a negative index) indicates that the item does not discriminate well between the high and low scorers. As a general rule, a discrimination index below .3 suggests that the item needs improvement. Notice that item 2 produced a negative index—more low-scoring than high-scoring students got the item correct.

After completing an item analysis, the teacher should discuss the "bad" items with the class. The students may be able to suggest reasons why an item was too easy or too hard, or nondiscriminating. Some typical student complaints about test items are that they can be interpreted in more than one way, they have been miskeyed, they ask for information not covered in class or found in the text book, or they measure trivia (Tenbrink, 1974).

By reviewing the distribution of choices for questions like item 2, more specific information can be obtained. Why did six high scorers select choice B? Did they think that response A was too obvious and figured out some interpretation of response B that they could defend as the right answer? If so, discussion should reveal what interpretation they gave to response B, and it can be modified so that similar confusion will not exist in the future. At the same time, response D might be made more plausible but still wrong, because in the present form no one chose the response.

### THINKING ABOUT THE TEACHING-LEARNING MODEL

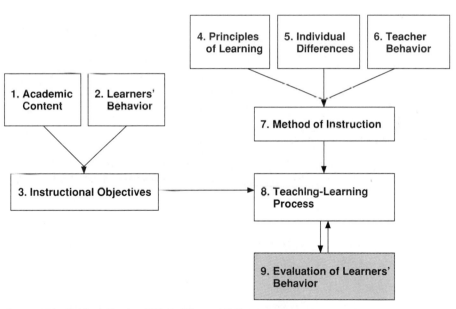

Source: Adapted from Hunter, 1971, in Allen and Seifman.

This chapter has focused on the role of standardized and teacher-made tests in providing information for instructional decisions. This may be a good time to review some of the other measurement procedures and instruments that can be useful during the teaching-learning process.

The importance of careful observation of student behavior was discussed in Chapter 1. Daily observation and direct interaction with students often will provide you with more information than can be obtained from any paper and pencil instrument. Don't underestimate your role in data collection.

In addition to measuring academic competencies, knowledge of other student differences such as cognitive styles, level of cognitive development, anxiety, and achievement motivation can help you to determine what modifications (box No. 5 in model) are needed for individual learners in the classroom. For example, on the basis of your knowledge of student characteristics, your modifications may involve a change in goal structures, a change in behavior toward certain students, or the need to use different instructional methods with specific students. These decisions are part of diagnostic and formative evaluation procedures.

At the end of a unit or semester, you will need to determine what your students have learned (box No. 9) (summative evaluation). However, you also need to determine what *you* learned about your teaching methods. Some of the more important questions you need to consider include the following:

- Did I assess the students' initial academic ability and knowledge accurately?
- Were the objectives at the proper level of difficulty?
- Did I violate any principles of learning?
- Were the instructional methods appropriate for the objectives and characteristics of the students?
- What would I do differently next time?

Finally, do not forget the importance of teacher expectations in evaluating all data concerning student behavior. Test data may be validly and reliably obtained but interpreted in a biased manner. As mentioned in the introduction to Part 4, measurement and evaluation are two separate functions.

## KEY POINTS

1. Evaluation is used for various purposes—*placement* (to determine where students should be placed in the proper sequence of instruction), *formative* (to determine student performance during instruction), *diagnostic* (to diagnose learning difficulties during instruction), and *summative* (to evaluate achievement at the end of instruction).
2. Norm-referenced measurement interprets student performance relative to a group.
3. Criterion-referenced measurement interprets student performance with respect to a specified behavioral criterion of proficiency.
4. Validity and reliability are two important criteria for evaluating the quality of tests.
5. Validity refers to the appropriateness of the interpretation of the test scores with regard to a particular use. A test may be valid for one purpose but not for another. Several approaches are taken to establish

validity—content, criterion-related, and construct. Validity is a matter of degree and should not be considered as an all-or-none characteristic.

6. Reliability refers to the consistency of test scores or other evaluation results from one measure to another. Because there are different types of consistency, different indicators of reliability are used (e.g., test-retest, equivalent form, and split-half).

7. Standardized tests are commercially prepared by measurement experts, and they measure behavior under uniform procedures.

8. Achievement tests measure a student's knowledge in a particular academic area at some point. Diagnostic and readiness tests are special types of achievement tests.

9. Aptitude tests predict the student's probability of success in various educational programs.

10. Scholastic aptitude tests are group tests for measuring academic potential.

11. Information on standardized tests can be located in *Tests in Print* and *Mental Measurements Yearbooks*.

12. Minimum competency testing is a procedure in which students and teachers must demonstrate mastery of specific skills.

13. Training in test-taking skills can help students to perform more effectively in testing situations.

14. Many educators criticize standardized tests. These criticisms pertain to both the validity and use of the tests.

15. The main advantage of teacher-made classroom tests over standardized tests is their greater relevance to the local curriculum.

16. The development of a table of specifications (a two-way grid integrating content and behavioral outcomes) can make test development easier for the teacher and ensure greater content validity.

17. The multiple-choice test can be used to measure objectives at all levels of complexity.

18. Essay tests are most appropriate for measuring the higher-order mental processes of application, analysis, synthesis, and evaluation.

19. Item analysis is a method of examining students' responses to test items to judge the quality of the test.

## KEY TERMS

test, p. 501
measurement, p. 501
evaluation, p. 501
placement evaluation, p. 507
formative evaluation, p. 507
diagnostic evaluation, p. 507
summative evaluation, p. 508
norm-referenced measurement, p. 509
criterion-referenced measurement, p. 509

## SUGGESTIONS FOR FURTHER READING

The following references are critical of the use of testing:

Block, N. J., & Dworkin, G. (Eds.) (1976). *The IQ controversy*. New York: Pantheon.
Cohen, A. S. (1988). *Tests: Marked for life?* New York: Scholastic.
Hoffmann, B. (1962). *The tyranny of testing*. New York: Collier.
Houts, P. (Ed.) (1977). *The myth of measurability*. New York: Hart.
Strenio, A. J., Jr. (1981). *The testing trap*. New York: Rawson, Wade.

For a comprehensive review of the minimum competency testing movement in the United States and a discussion of the legal and policy issues,
see the following:

Jaeger, R. M. (1989). *Certification of student competence*. In R. L. Linn (Ed.), Educational measurement (3rd ed.). New York: Macmillan.
Jaeger, R. M., & Tittle, C. K. (Eds.). (1980). *Minimum competency and achievement
testing: Motives, models, measures, and consequences*. Berkeley, CA: McCutchan.

The following are basic tests and measurement books:

Brown, F. G. (1983). *Principles of educational and psychological testing* (3rd ed.). New
York: Holt, Rinehart and Winston.
Cangelosi, J. S. (1990). *Designing tests for evaluating student achievement*. White Plains,
NY: Longman.
Ebel, R. L., & Frisbie, D. A. (1986). *Essentials of educational measurement* (4th ed.).
Englewood Cliffs, NJ: Prentice-Hall.
Gronlund, N. E. (1988). *How to construct achievement tests* (4th ed.). Englewood Cliffs,
NJ: Prentice-Hall.

Mehrens, W. A., & Lehmann, I. J. (1987). *Using standardized tests in education* (4th ed.). White Plains, NY: Longman.

Sax, G. (1989). *Principles of educational and psychological measurement and evaluation.* (3rd ed.). Belmont, CA: Wadsworth.

## FOLLOW-UP ACTIVITIES

### 1. Identify Your Position on Standardized Testing

Which of the following statements comes closest to representing your position on standardized testing? Defend the reasons for your selection.

a. Standardized tests serve an important function by helping the school and teacher assess a student's achievement level, assisting in academic and vocational guidance, and determining placement in appropriate classes. Without these tests, teachers and administrators would make greater errors in their decisions.

b. Schools spend too much time testing students. Most tests have little impact on student learning and should be abolished. Better decisions can be made without these tests.

### 2. Evaluate Teacher-Made Tests

What types of teacher-made tests have given you the greatest aggravation in the past? Why? Obtain a copy of a teacher-made test and analyze it for examples of faulty test construction. If you cannot obtain a copy of a test, report on faulty items in a test you have recently taken. Discuss the modifications you would make in the items.

### 3. Evaluate Teacher-Made Tests

Obtain a copy of a teacher-made test, and classify each question according to the *Taxonomy of Educational Objectives: Cognitive Domain* (Bloom et al., 1956). Does one type of thinking dominate the test?

### 4. Write Exam Questions

Write 10 exam questions on material covered in Chapter 12. Adapt your questions to true-false, completion, four-item multiple-choice, matching, or short-answer formats. Ask a member of your class to answer the test items. Provide your classmate with the correct answers, and allow the person to critique the quality of your test.

### 5. Use the *Mental Measurements Yearbooks*

Select two or three standardized tests that a school district could use for a subject area or grade level of interest to you. Use the *Mental Measurements Yearbooks* (Mitchell, 1985) to report on the merits and limitations of each test.

# CHAPTER 13

## Analyzing Test Scores and Reporting Student Progress

The Cumulative Record

      CLASSROOM APPLICATION: ANALYZING CUMULATIVE
      RECORDS

Grading and Reporting Student Progress

      Basing Grades on the Normal Distribution
      The Inspection Method
      Basing Grades on Predetermined Levels of Achievement
      The Contract System
      Behavioral Mastery Reports
      Pass-Fail Grading
      Parent-Teacher Conferences
      CLASSROOM APPLICATION: PREPARING AND CONDUCTING
      PARENT CONFERENCES

Grades: Help or Hindrance?

Promotion and Retention of Students

## ORIENTATION

Now that you are aware of the various tests used in school, you need to know how to interpret and report test results to students and parents and to make instructional decisions based on the information you collect. In Chapter 1, you learned that beginning teachers find that assessing students' work and establishing relationships with parents are two of the major challenges they face in teaching. My goal in this chapter is to limit the possibility that these tasks will cause you any grief! I believe that lack of information is one of the primary reasons teachers have problems relating to the interpretation of test scores. Another important variable is the emotional factor involved in discussing academic problems with students and parents. You need to understand the parents' point of view and behave in ways that will encourage parents to work with you rather than against you. The more prepared and knowledgeable you are about measurement and evaluation issues, and the more you use good communication skills, the less likely you are to have problems with parents.

By the time you master the material in this chapter, you will be able to:

- Read and interpret standardized test scores.
- Analyze cumulative records.
- Prepare for and conduct parent conferences.
- Select methods of grading and reporting student progress.

1. What is the difference between the mean, median, and mode?
2. Why is the standard deviation necessary in interpreting test scores?
3. What is the difference between a standard score and a grade-equivalent score?
4. How is the standard error of measurement used in analyzing test scores?
5. What is the difference between norm-referenced and criterion-referenced measurement?
6. What are the advantages and disadvantages of the following types of grading system: contracts, behavioral mastery reports, pass-fail, and parent-teacher conferences?
7. What are the factors that should be considered in promotion and retention decisions?

## FREQUENCY DISTRIBUTION

Suppose you correct a test taken by 35 students and put the scores in your roll book. The highest possible score is 80. The next day you hand out the corrected papers. As students receive their papers, they begin to compare scores because they have no idea how well they did in comparison with others in the class. One student received a 65 on the exam. If the test was hard, a 65 could be a good score, but if the test was easy, a 65 could be a bad score. You cannot easily provide more information for the students as you look at the scores in your grade book, listed alphabetically by student.

You can, however, develop a table that summarizes the frequency with which each score occurs. This table is called a **frequency distribution** of test scores. Using this table, you and your students can get a better picture of how well the class achieved on the test. Table 13.1 is an example of a frequency distribution for 35 students on an 80-item exam. It is an improvement over a disorganized list of scores. You can summarize the scores in greater detail by developing a *grouped* frequency distribution. In this distribution, you provide intervals of 5 or 10 points and determine the frequency of scores in the assigned intervals. For example, 12 students scored between 70 and 79, and 9 students scored between 60 and 69.

## MEASURES OF CENTRAL TENDENCY

What is the
difference
between the
mean, median,
and mode?

As part of the analysis of a distribution of scores, we often need to calculate various measures of the average, or typical, performance of the group as a whole. These calculations are called **measures of central tendency**, the most familiar of these being the **mean**, the **median**, and the **mode**. Let's

TABLE 13.1 **FREQUENCY DISTRIBUTION OF TEST SCORES**

| Test Score | Frequency | Test Score | Frequency | Test Score | Frequency | Test Score | Frequency |
|---|---|---|---|---|---|---|---|
| 78 | 1 | 68 | 0 | 58 | 0 | 48 | 1 |
| 77 | 0 | 67 | 2 | 57 | 0 | 47 | 0 |
| 76 | 2 | 66 | 3 | 56 | 2 | 46 | 0 |
| 75 | 2 | 65 | 0 | 55 | 2 | 45 | 0 |
| 74 | 0 | 64 | 1 | 54 | 0 | 44 | 0 |
| 73 | 2 | 63 | 0 | 53 | 0 | 43 | 0 |
| 72 | 0 | 62 | 3 | 52 | 1 | 42 | 0 |
| 71 | 3 | 61 | 1 | 51 | 1 | 41 | 2 |
| 70 | 4 | 60 | 0 | 50 | 0 | | |
| 69 | 0 | 59 | 2 | 49 | 0 | | |

use the following small distribution of scores to determine the three measures: 8, 10, 12, 13, 16, 16, 23.

## Mean

The *mean* is the arithmetic average of a set of scores, the result of adding the scores and dividing this sum by the number of scores.

$$\text{Mean} = \frac{\Sigma X}{N} = \frac{98}{7} = 14$$

The symbol $\Sigma$ signifies "sum" whatever follows. The letter $X$ stands for any score value, and $N$ equals the number of scores. The symbol $M$ or $X$ is often used to denote the mean.

## Median

The *median* is another measure of central tendency representing the middle score in a distribution. The median in the foregoing sample distribution is 13. In a distribution with an even number of scores (8, 10, 20, 32), there are two middle values; in this case, the median is the mean of the two middle scores ([10 + 20] ÷ 2 = 15).

## Mode

The third measure of central tendency is the *mode*, the score with the highest frequency of occurrence. The mode in the sample distribution is 16. When a distribution has two most frequently occurring scores, it is a *bimodal* distribution.

All three of these measures provide an indication of the central tendency, but their usefulness often hinges on the character of the score distribution. The mean generally gives the best average of test scores. However, when there are extreme scores at one end of the distribution, the median can better describe the average. Look at the following distribution of scores: 90, 43, 40, 30, 22. The mean is 45 and the median is 40. Four of the five scores are less than the mean because of the one extreme score. In this case, the mean gives a less accurate impression of the actual central tendency of scores than does the median. The mode is not used as often as the mean and median, but it is appropriate when there are many identical scores.

## VARIABILITY

Although the measures of central tendency provide helpful information for interpreting test scores, they don't take into consideration an important characteristic of test scores. Look closely at the following distribution:

|  | Group A | Group B |  |
|---|---|---|---|
| Mean = 100 | 96 | 82 | Mean = 100 |
| Median = 100 | 98 | 90 | Median = 100 |
|  | 100 | 100 |  |
|  | 102 | 110 |  |
|  | 104 | 118 |  |

Although the two distributions exhibit the same mean and median, the **variability**, or dispersion, of the scores differs. One indicator of the variability is the **range of scores**. In group A, the range is 8 (104 − 96); the range for group B is 36 (118 − 82).

### Standard Deviation

**Why is the standard deviation necessary in interpreting test scores?**

The range tells us the variability between the highest and lowest scores in a distribution, but it doesn't tell us anything about the variability between the mean and the rest of the distribution. For this reason, the **standard deviation** is the most important measure of variability because it provides a measure of how dispersed, or spread out, the scores are around the mean. The more spread out from the mean, the larger the standard deviation. The more scores clustering around the mean, the smaller the standard deviation. The standard deviation for the scores in group A and group B are 2.8 and 13.0, respectively. This statistic is important in understanding scores in a normal curve (discussed later in this chapter).

The formula for determining the standard deviation is

$$s = \sqrt{\frac{\Sigma (X - M)^2}{N}}$$

It reads like this: "The standard deviation is equal to the square root of the sum of the squared deviation from the mean divided by the number of scores." Figure 13.1 provides a step-by-step illustration for computing the standard deviation.

$s$ = standard deviation of a set of scores
$\Sigma$ = the sum of
$X$ = one score
$M$ = the mean of a set of scores
$N$ = the number of students with scores
$\sqrt{\ }$ = the square root of

Problem: Compute the standard deviation of the following sources: 4, 6, 8, 14.
Step 1: Prepare four columns of figures as follows: $X$, $M$, $(X - M)$, and $(X - M)^2$
Step 2: List tho scores under Column $X$, and determine $M$. ($M = 8$)
Step 3: Substract the mean from each score to obtain figures for column $(X - M)$ as
follows:

| $X$ | $M$ | $(X - M)$ | $(X - M)^2$ |
|-----|-----|-----------|-------------|
| 4 | 8 | $-4$ | 16 |
| 6 | 8 | $-2$ | 4 |
| 8 | 8 | 0 | 0 |
| 14 | 8 | 6 | 36 |

Step 4: Square each of the differences in column $(X - M)$ to obtain the figure in column
$(X - M)^2$ as shown above.
Step 5: Add column $(X - M)^2$ to obtain $(X - M)^2 = 56$.
Step 6: Substitute the numbers in the formula as follows:

$$s = \sqrt{\frac{56}{4}} = \sqrt{14}$$

Step 7: Find the square root of 14:

$$s = \sqrt{14} = 3.74$$

Figure 13.1 Computational Guide for Standard Deviation.

## INTERPRETING TEST SCORES

The number of items answered correctly on a test is the **raw score**. If a test
has a number of subtests, each subtest engenders a separate raw score.
The teacher cannot interpret the meaning of these scores or compare them
with other scores if all they represent is the number of correct items. Suppose both Vivian and Doreen answer correctly 23 items on their French
and Spanish examinations, respectively. Who performed better? First, we
don't know the number of items on each test. Second, if we are to evaluate
Vivian's and Doreen's performance relative to other students, we do not
know how they performed in relation to other students.

To simplify the interpretation of test scores, test makers provide ways
to make comparisons among test scores by converting raw scores to **derived
scores**. The derived scores most frequently used in schools are the **percentile rank**, **grade-equivalent score**, and **standard score**.

One of the easiest ways to compare an individual's score with others
in a group is to rank all the scores. The disadvantage of this method is
that it does not make distinctions between the size of groups. A rank of

14 in a group of 14 is quite different from a rank of 14 in a group of 40. In the first case, the rank is the lowest in the group, whereas in the second it is considerably higher.

## Percentile Rank

One way to alleviate the problem is to use a *percentile rank*. A percentile rank indicates a person's group rank in terms of the percentage of individuals at or below that person's score. If Bob's score on a science test gives him a rank of 10 in a class of 40, we can say that three-fourths, or 75%, of the class made a lower score than Bob on the science test. Thus, 75 is his percentile rank. Another way of stating his performance is that he scored at the 75th percentile. By using a percentile rank, the position of individuals in groups of unequal size can be compared.

The beginning student in measurement often confuses percentile ranks with the percentage of correct items on the test. These are two entirely different scores. Getting 85% of the items correct on an easy test may place a student at the 50th percentile. On a more difficult test, getting 85% of the items correct may place the student at the 95th percentile.

Another precaution to take with percentile ranks is not to average or add them, because they do not form equal intervals at all points along the scale. In most distributions, the distance between percentiles is less near the middle and greater at its extremes. More people tend to score in the middle range of a test. Therefore, in terms of actual points scored on a given test, a difference of 4 percentile ranks at the upper extreme—say, percentile 90 to 94—may mean a difference of 15 points on the test. On the other hand, a difference of 4 percentile ranks near the center of a distribution—say, percentile 50 to 54—may mean a difference of only 2 or 3 points.

## Grade-Equivalent Score

Another type of derived score is the *grade-equivalent score*. Grade equivalents indicate the average performance of students at different grade levels. A table for grade-equivalent scores is included in the test manual for most standardized achievement tests. If a score of 60 on a reading test has a grade equivalent of 4.9 (read "4 years, 9 months"), 60 would be the average score of students in the ninth month of the fourth grade. Because the school year is comprised of 10 months, grade-equivalent scores range from .0 to .9. At certain points along the scale, raw scores corresponding to grade equivalents are estimated or extrapolated rather than determined by measurement. This procedure can lead to a misinterpretation of the meaning of the scores.

Grade-equivalent scores have been popular in the elementary grades because of their apparent ease of interpretation. If a sixth-grade student takes a test in September (6.0) and scores 6.3, it is obvious that the student has scored higher than the average student in the first month of the sixth grade. The student's score is the average score obtained by students in the third month of the sixth grade.

Test specialists have been concerned about the misinterpretations to which grade-equivalent scores are often subject. The units are not equal along the scale, so an increase from 5.5 to 5.6 may very well require more items correct than an increase from 5.8 to 5.9. A second circumstance open to misinterpretation occurs when a student scores two or more grade levels above the grade level. Can a fourth grader who receives a grade-equivalent score of 6.8 on a mathematics examination do sixth-grade mathematics? Not necessarily, for the student may have received a high grade-equivalent score by successfully completing the easier test items more quickly and accurately than the average fourth-grade student. As a result, the grade-equivalent score of 6.8 may indicate nothing more than a mastery of skills taught in the first four grades. The important point to remember is that a grade equivalent score is not related to a student's actual ability to perform successfully at any given grade level (Gronlund, 1985a).

## Standard Score

*What is the difference between a standard score and a grade-equivalent score?*

Another way to interpret raw scores is by the use of a *standard score*, expressed in terms of standard deviation units. These scores indicate how far from the mean of the distribution a given score appears. A big plus in their favor is that they are based on equal units of measurement throughout the distribution. As a result, you can average standard scores.

A typical type of standard score is the **z score**. This score represents the number of standard deviation units a raw score is from the mean. It is based on a mean of 0 and a standard deviation of 1. A negative z score indicates that a student scored below the mean. For example, if Debbie made a raw score of 27 in a distribution with a mean of 30 and a standard deviation of 5, her z score would be $-.6$. She is 3 raw-score points, or $-.6$ standard deviations, below the mean. Mathematically, a z score is defined as follows:

$$z = \frac{X - M}{s} = \frac{27 - 30}{5} = \frac{-3}{5} = -.6$$

If Debbie had a score equal to the mean, her z score would be zero:

$$z = \frac{30 - 30}{5} = \frac{0}{5} = 0$$

Because many individuals find negative numbers and decimals troublesome to work with, test publishers often convert the z score to a **T score**. This is done by multiplying by 10 and adding 50:

$$T = \left(\frac{X - M}{s}\right) \times (10 + 50), \text{ or, } T = 10z + 50$$

By multiplying each z by 10, you eliminate the decimal; by adding 50 points to the product, you eliminate the negatives. The T score scale has a mean of 50 and a standard deviation of 10.

Another of the common standard scores are the College Examination Board (SAT) scores. On this scale, z scores are multiplied by 100, and 500 points are added to the product. Thus, a z score of 0 (mean) is equivalent to 500, and a z score of −1 is equivalent to 400.

Many intelligence tests convert raw scores to **deviation IQ** scores, another type of standard score. Deviation IQs have a mean of 100 and standard deviations of 15 or 16 (depending on the particular test). As a result, a deviation IQ of 130 always represents a score falling 2 standard deviations from the mean (assuming $s = 15$).

To understand the relationship between the various derived scores discussed in this section, examine the normal distribution and related scales in Figure 13.2. In a normal distribution, for example, a z score of −1 is the same as a T score of 40 or a percentile rank of 16.

## NORMAL DISTRIBUTION

A **normal distribution (curve)** is a mathematical model that represents the way in which many human characteristics are distributed. It is bell-shaped, symmetrical, and the mean, median, and mode all fall at the same point.

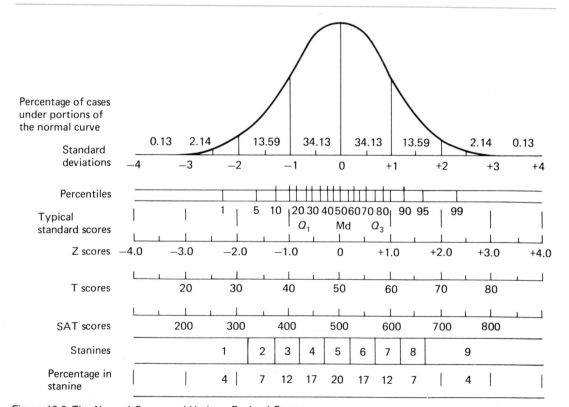

Figure 13.2 The Normal Curve and Various Derived Scores.

Because of this precise definition, it is possible to determine the proportion of scores falling under any area of the curve.

Several features of the normal curve are of special interest in interpreting scores. For example, approximately 34% of the scores fall 1 standard deviation above and below the mean. This means that approximately 68% of normally distributed scores are within 1 standard deviation of the mean. Approximately 14% of the scores fall between 1 and 2 standard deviations above and below the mean; approximately 2% of the scores fall between 2 and 3 standard deviations above and below the mean.

By identifying how far a score is from the mean in a normal distribution, you can determine the percentage of scores above or below any given score. A student who receives a 600 on the Scholastic Aptitude Test (SAT) is 1 standard deviation above the mean ($M = 500$). Therefore, the student scored higher than approximately 84% of all students taking the test. In other words, a SAT score of 600 is equivalent to a percentile rank of 84.

Many school districts report test scores by **stanines**. This type of scale divides the normal curve into nine parts. Scores are expressed along a scale ranging from 1 (low) to 9 (high), with 5 representing the average performance for students in the reference group. The percentage of students at each stanine level is shown below.

| Stanine | 1 | 2 | 3 | 4 | 5 | 6 | 7 | 8 | 9 |
|---------|---|---|----|----|----|----|----|---|---|
| Percentage | 4 | 7 | 12 | 17 | 20 | 17 | 12 | 7 | 4 |

A stanine represents a percentage of scores; it is not a point. Therefore, in a given distribution of scores, the lowest 4% receives a stanine of 1, the next highest, 7%, a stanine of 2, and so on until the highest 4% receives a stanine of 9.

Standardized tests have tables that convert raw scores to derived scores. The teacher must record these scores on a profile sheet for each student and interpret their meaning. In many instances, a profile sheet similar to the one presented later, in Figure 13.4, is provided for the teacher.

## STANDARD ERROR OF MEASUREMENT

**How is the standard error of measurement used in analyzing test scores?**

It would suit everyone if a test score were a precise measure of a student's true ability or achievement. Unfortunately, even the best tests have some degree of error in the scores they produce. As a result, measurement experts believe that it is often desirable to record a test score as a band or interval rather than as a single point or score.

Most standardized test manuals report the **standard error of measurement** of a particular test. This statistic is an estimate of the amount of error in a test score. Suppose the standard error of measurement of a test is 4. If a student who makes a raw score of 40 on the test takes the test many times, about two-thirds of the student's scores will fall between 36 and 44 (40 ± 4). The interested reader can find more information about this statistic in any basic measurement book (see the Suggestions for Further Reading in Chapter 12).

The standard error of measurement keeps us aware of the inaccuracy of test scores and helps us to compare students. A principal who decides to offer a special class for bright students might use an aptitude test to select the composition of the class. Suppose the standard error of measurement of this test is 5. The principal decides that all students who score 70 or above on the test can select the course. Mary scores 68 and wants to take the course. On the basis of her academic record, she appears to be someone who could benefit from such a course. Because the standard error of measurement of the aptitude test is 5, Mary's actual ability is probably between 63 and 73 (68 ± 5). Thus it would be quite possible for Mary to obtain a score above the cutoff score if she was tested again. There is strong support for including Mary in the class. This example illustrates the importance of considering test scores as intervals rather than as static scores.

## CLASSROOM APPLICATION: INTERPRETING STANDARDIZED TEST SCORES

Now that you know about the types of test score used in reporting test results, I want to show you how these scores are used in interpreting actual results of achievement tests. Each test company provides various options for reporting test results to school districts. The most common reports are pupil and class profiles that identify scores by subtests and national norms for determining how well the student or class has achieved on the test in comparison with other students in the nation who have taken the test. Narrative reports that describe student performance in words, not numbers, also can be sent to parents to better communicate the meaning of the test results. Additional information that is usually available includes individual and group skill analyses, in which scores are provided for various subskills such as word study skills, reading comprehension, spelling, science, and so forth. This information can be useful in determining the specific strengths and weaknesses of students in the class. In addition, pupil and group item analyses data can be provided so that the teacher can focus more specifically on particular questions that were answered correctly or incorrectly. School committees that decide which test will be used in the district take into consideration the scoring and reporting systems of the published tests.

Figures 13.3 and 13.4 present two forms that are used by the Psychological Corporation to report the results of the Stanford Achievement Tests. This company provides more than 15 different reports of test results. Figure 13.3 shows a ranked list of three scores with five different types of information on the fourth-grade students in Ms. Wellens class

# Stanford ACHIEVEMENT TEST

RANKED LISTS OF THREE SCORES
FOR MS WELLENS  GRADE 4

SYSTEM NEWTON PUBLIC SCHOOLS   SCHOOL LAKESIDE ELEMENTARY   TEST DATE 10 14 82   STANFORD NORMS GR 41

**A** LISTS ARE RANKED LOW TO HIGH

## READING COMPREHENSION

| | STUDENT NAME | RAW SCORE | NAT'L PR S | NAT'L NCE |
|---|---|---|---|---|
| 1 | GROVER MATT A | 25 | 11 3 | 24 2 |
| 2 | WANG CINDY S | 29 | 16 3 | 29 1 |
| 3 | RAYMOND VAL H | 33 | 22 3 | 33 7 |
| 4 | BURNS THELMA G | 35 | 24 4 | 35 1 |
| 5 | GORDON MIKE O | 36 | 26 4 | 36 5 |
| 6 | HALL GLENDA T | 39 | 30 4 | 39 0 |
| 7 | WHITTIER JODI A | 41 | 34 4 | 41 3 |
| 8 | PALACE BETH B | 42 | 36 4 | 42 5 |
| 9 | CRAIG ROBIN R | 43 | 38 4 | 43 6 |
| 10 | SANTOS JOSE | 44 | 40 5 | 44 7 |
| 11 | PETERS CARL E | 45 | 42 5 | 45 8 |
| 11 | FARLEY ANDREA P | 45 | 42 5 | 45 8 |
| 13 | COHAN JEAN K | 47 | 46 5 | 47 9 |
| 14 | JENNINGS BARBIE M | 48 | 48 5 | 48 9 |
| 15 | WILSON ELMER N | 49 | 50 5 | 50 0 |
| 15 | BALLARD CHUCK C | 49 | 50 5 | 50 0 |
| 17 | RIVARA SIMON R | 50 | 52 5 | 51 1 |
| 17 | MILLER PAUL | 50 | 52 5 | 51 1 |
| 19 | LONG PHIL V | 52 | 55 5 | 52 1 |
| 20 | GLADSTONE IRWIN V | 52 | 56 5 | 53 2 |
| 21 | GOLDMAN ELLEN S | 55 | 62 6 | 56 4 |
| 21 | CHANG MARY F | 55 | 62 6 | 56 4 |
| 23 | STEVENS CAROL B | 57 | 66 6 | 58 7 |
| 24 | PARIS STEVEN D | 58 | 70 6 | 61 0 |
| 24 | BLACKMAN DENNIS L | 58 | 70 6 | 61 0 |

**D** SUMMARY

| | RAW SCORE | NAT'L NCE |
|---|---|---|
| NUMBER OF STUDENTS | 25 | 25 |
| MEAN | 45 4 | 46 36 |
| STANDARD DEVIATION | 8 7 | 9 43 |

NATIONAL PR SUMMARY

| | N | % |
|---|---|---|
| PR SCORES OF 76-99 | 0 | 0% |
| 51-75 | 9 | 36% |
| 26-50 | 12 | 48% |
| 1-25 | 4 | 16% |
| TOTAL | 25 | |

**B** MATH COMPUTATION

| | STUDENT NAME | RAW SCORE | NAT'L PR S | NAT'L NCE |
|---|---|---|---|---|
| 1 | SANTOS JOSE P | 15 | 26 4 | 36 5 |
| 1 | GORDON MIKE O | 15 | 26 4 | 36 5 |
| 3 | BURNS THELMA H | 15 | 26 4 | 36 5 |
| 4 | CRAIG ROBIN N | 17 | 36 4 | 44 4 |
| 5 | GOLDMAN ELLEN S | 18 | 40 5 | 44 7 |
| 6 | STEVENS CAROL F | 19 | 46 5 | 47 9 |
| 7 | COHAN JEAN K | 19 | 46 5 | 47 9 |
| 8 | FARLEY ANDREA C | 20 | 50 5 | 50 0 |
| 8 | BALLARD CHUCK S | 20 | 50 5 | 50 0 |
| 10 | WANG | 21 | 56 5 | 53 2 |
| 10 | PALACE BETH B | 21 | 56 5 | 53 2 |
| 12 | PETERS CARL H | 24 | 62 6 | 56 4 |
| 13 | RAYMOND VAL N | 24 | 66 6 | 58 7 |
| 14 | LONG PHIL | 24 | 72 6 | 62 3 |
| 14 | CHANG | 24 | 72 6 | 62 3 |
| 16 | RIVARA SIMON J | 25 | 76 6 | 64 9 |
| 17 | BLACKMAN DENNIS R | 27 | 78 7 | 68 7 |
| 17 | MILLER PAUL | 27 | 80 7 | 77 0 |
| 19 | GLADSTONE IRWIN V | 30 | 90 8 | 77 0 |
| 20 | GROVER MATT A | 31 | 92 8 | 79 6 |
| 21 | HALL GLENDA T | 32 | 94 8 | 82 7 |
| 22 | WHITTIER JODI A | 33 | 96 9 | 86 9 |
| 23 | WILSON ELMER D | 34 | 98 9 | 93 3 |
| 24 | PARIS STEVEN | 35 | 99 9 | 99 0 |
| 24 | JENNINGS BARBIE N | 35 | 99 9 | 99 0 |

SUMMARY

| | RAW SCORE | NAT'L NCE |
|---|---|---|
| NUMBER OF STUDENTS | 25 | 25 |
| MEAN | 24 0 | 62 26 |
| STANDARD DEVIATION | 6 4 | 18 86 |

NATIONAL PR SUMMARY

| | N | % |
|---|---|---|
| PR SCORES OF 76-99 | 10 | 40% |
| 51-75 | 6 | 24% |
| 26-50 | 9 | 36% |
| 1-25 | 0 | 0% |
| TOTAL | 25 | |

## LANGUAGE

| | STUDENT NAME | RAW SCORE | NAT'L PR S | NAT'L NCE |
|---|---|---|---|---|
| 1 | SANTOS JOSE P | 12 | 20 3 | 32 3 |
| 2 | PARIS STEVEN D | 15 | 28 4 | 37 7 |
| 3 | WANG CINDY B | 16 | 30 4 | 39 0 |
| 4 | PALACE BETH B | 28 | 36 4 | 42 5 |
| 4 | BURNS THELMA G | 28 | 36 4 | 42 5 |
| 6 | JENNINGS BARBIE M | 29 | 38 4 | 43 6 |
| 6 | GROVER MATT A | 29 | 38 4 | 43 6 |
| 8 | RAYMOND VAL H | 30 | 40 5 | 44 7 |
| 9 | HALL GLENDA T | 31 | 42 5 | 45 8 |
| 10 | GORDON MIKE O | 32 | 46 5 | 47 9 |
| 11 | RIVARA SIMON J | 33 | 48 5 | 48 9 |
| 12 | PETERS CARL E | 34 | 50 5 | 50 0 |
| 13 | WILSON ELMER K | 35 | 54 5 | 52 1 |
| 13 | COHAN JEAN N | 35 | 54 5 | 52 1 |
| 15 | LONG PHIL | 36 | 58 5 | 54 2 |
| 15 | CRAIG ROBIN R | 36 | 58 5 | 54 2 |
| 17 | MILLER PAUL C | 37 | 60 6 | 55 3 |
| 17 | BALLARD CHUCK | 37 | 60 6 | 55 3 |
| 19 | GLADSTONE IRWIN V | 38 | 64 6 | 57 5 |
| 20 | WHITTIER JODI A | 39 | 66 6 | 58 7 |
| 20 | STEVENS CAROL F | 39 | 66 6 | 58 7 |
| 22 | FARLEY ANDREA P | 40 | 70 6 | 61 0 |
| 22 | BLACKMAN DENNIS L | 40 | 70 6 | 61 0 |
| 24 | GOLDMAN ELLEN S | 42 | 76 6 | 64 9 |
| 24 | CHANG MARY B | 42 | 76 6 | 64 9 |

**E** SUMMARY

| | RAW SCORE | NAT'L NCE |
|---|---|---|
| NUMBER OF STUDENTS | 25 | 25 |
| MEAN | 33 7 | 50 74 |
| STANDARD DEVIATION | 5 4 | 8 51 |

NATIONAL PR SUMMARY

| | N | % |
|---|---|---|
| PR SCORES OF 76-99 | 2 | 8% |
| 51-75 | 11 | 44% |
| 26-50 | 11 | 44% |
| 1-25 | 1 | 4% |
| TOTAL | 25 | |

NUMBER OF STUDENTS RANKED IS 25
SCALED SCORE WAS USED FOR RANKING

STANFORD LEVEL/FORM  Primary 3/E

See back for aids for interpretation.

PROCESS NO 085-1542-001   COPY 1

DATA SERVICES DIVISION   THE PSYCHOLOGICAL CORPORATION   HARCOURT BRACE JOVANOVICH, PUBLISHERS

Figure 13.3 Stanford Achievement Test. Ranked Lists of Scores.  Source: Stanford Achievement Tests, 1982.

557

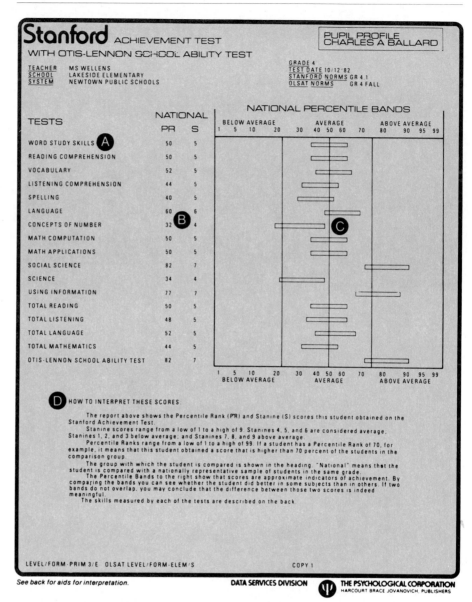

**Figure 13.4** Stanford Achievement Tests, Pupil Profile.

*Source: Stanford Achievement Tests, 1982.*

(marked *A* through *E*) on the form: *A*—students are ranked from low to high so that administrators of funded programs can easily determine who is eligible for gifted or remedial programs. *B*—three test results are listed for each student: reading comprehension, math computation, and language. *C*—four scores are reported for each student: the raw scores, national percentile ranks (PR), stanines (S), and normal curve equivalents (NCE), which are used by the U.S. Office of Education for the evaluation of federally funded programs. The NCE is a standard score with a mean of 50 and a standard deviation of 21.06. D—the number of students tested and the summary statistics for the group. E—the number, or percentage, of students in each percentile-rank quarter.

Let's look at the results for Ms. Wellens's class in reading comprehension. Twenty-five students were ranked. They attained an average of 45.4 on the test (based on the number of items on the test). The percentile-rank information tells us that only 9 students scored in the top 50% of students taking the exam in the nation, and 16 students scored in the bottom 50% of the normative group. The lowest student in reading comprehension was Matt Grover, who received a percentile rank of 11 and a stanine of 3; the highest score was attained by Dennis Blackman, who received a percentile rank of 70 and a stanine of 6. Matt scored higher than 11% of the students taking the test, and Dennis scored higher than 70% of the students taking the test.

Figure 13.4 shows the pupil profile report, including four types of information (marked A through D) that can be sent to parents with a printed narrative report from the test company. The following types of information are provided: A—the names of subtests and totals; B—national percentile ranks and stanine; C—national percentile bands spanning ±1 standard error of measurement; and D—explanation and interpretation of scores. Notice how the pictorial representation of Charles Ballard's test performance provides an easy reference to understand his achievement. His weakest areas are concepts of number and science, and his strongest areas are social science and using information. The Otis-Lennon School Ability Test is a scholastic aptitude test that allows the teacher to compare a measure of a student's potential to achieve in school with his or her actual achievement test results.

## THE CUMULATIVE RECORD

A **cumulative record** is a file on a student that includes such information as family data, health information, academic grades, standardized test results, attendance, and teacher comments. The exact form and the information included vary from one school district to the next. If a student has had an assessment by a school psychologist, a separate file reporting the results of the evaluation usually is kept in the psychological services office with a notation in the cumulative record as to when the assessment was made. The classroom teacher can ask for a consultation with the school psychologist to discuss the results of the assessment.

There is some controversy regarding the use of information in students' cumulative records. A major concern is that the information can lead a teacher to develop expectations about certain students before meeting them. The teacher may then act in ways that produce a self-fulfilling prophecy (Dusek & Joseph, 1985). For example, comments by previous teachers regarding attentiveness, obedience, industriousness, and work habits can have a strong impact on expectancies (Willis, 1972). On the other hand, an expert teacher who knows how to evaluate the information in a cumulative record may gain enough insight into a student's problem so that a more effective educational program can be developed.

My personal position on this issue is that teachers need to be aware of the danger of formulating expectations based on the opinions of others. Thus I am not in favor of reviewing cumulative records until after a teacher has worked with students in class for a few weeks, unless it appears to a teacher that a student has an obvious problem that needs immediate attention. I believe that if teachers are trained to evaluate and use the information in the cumulative record, they can gain insight into problems and make changes in the ways they interact with certain students.

## CLASSROOM APPLICATION: ANALYZING CUMULATIVE RECORDS

The following information (Roffman, 1983) will help you evaluate the information found in a cumulative record.

### Family History

The size of the family, the number of siblings living in the home, how far the student has to travel to school, and the number of changes in schools since kindergarten can provide important insight into the student's behavior. For example, if there has been some trauma in the family, such as the death of a parent or a divorce, you might check the student's grades over the years to see whether academic performance slipped during this period and whether the student recovered. A student who has attended several schools in a short time may have missed academic content and thus may not have adequate preparation for the present grade. Does the student have to travel far to get to school? If the student is tired, you may want to check with the parents to find out when the student goes to bed at night.

### Medical History

Note whether the student has any hearing, vision, or severe health problems. This information could determine classroom seating or the type of physical activity allowed in school. In most cases, you would be notified by the school nurse or psychologist if a child had a severe health problem. You may not be notified about minor health problems, however. For example, many students refuse to wear their eyeglasses in class, and, as a result, they cannot see the chalkboard. If the medical history identifies the fact that a child needs to wear eyeglasses, you can then take steps to deal with the situation.

### Yearly Attendance Record

Check the student's attendance record over the years. Notice the number of absences, the time of the year they occurred (if available), and the resulting academic achievement. Winter absences may indicate certain respiratory infections and possibly a subsequent hearing loss. Extended absences in the early grades might have caused a student to miss important basic skills and so be affecting present performance. Chronic absences over several years may suggest serious health problems or lack of parental support for ensuring that the student attend school. When there is a constant attendance problem that is not verified or health-related, you should notify the school agency responsible for home visitations to ensure student attendance at school.

### School Grades

Look for patterns of strengths and weaknesses in various academic areas. Did an academic problem begin from grade 1? Did a problem emerge in junior high school? Could the problem be developmental? For example, perhaps the student has not been prepared to do formal reasoning in algebra. Could biological and social changes at puberty have an impact on the student's adjustment to a new school?

### Individual and Group Testing Results

School districts have schedules for certain testing to be done. In addition, special tests may be given to a student to diagnose academic problems. In the preceding Classroom Application, I discussed how to interpret standardized test scores. The following are some additional questions you should be concerned about. Notice the dates for each evaluation, and determine whether you may need to request any special testing. What information do the tests provide? If an individual intelligence assessment or group scholastic aptitude test was given, does the student score differently in the verbal and mathematical areas? Do these scores correlate with grades given in various subject areas? Does the student need special attention in one area? Ask the school counselor or special education teacher to review the meaning of the test scores with you. The information presented earlier in the chapter will help you to read the manual.

### Teachers' Comments

Teachers are asked from kindergarten on to write a brief evaluation regarding a student's progress or any problems encountered during the school year. Be as concise and objective as possible when you write comments about students and describe their behavior. Remember that other professionals will read your comments and will not know your frame of mind when you made your observations. Does a pattern emerge in the teachers' comments? Be aware of a teacher writing "ditto" to the comments made by a previous teacher. This response *may not* indicate a recurring problem, only that the particular teacher did not put any effort into completing the comments on the cumulative record. Is a problem noted in an early grade that appears to persist with nothing having been done to alleviate it? The following is an example of comments from an actual cumulative record by different teachers who failed to recognize that the student might have a learning disability. This student had problems in the first grade that required special attention. However, he did not receive any special education until the ninth grade, after receiving unsatisfactory evaluation in work habits and D's and C's in his academic subjects in the seventh and eighth grades. His cumulative record indicated an IQ of 110.

- *Kindergarten.* "Sufficient growth in areas of cognitive and affective domain; uses materials in a creative manner."
- *First grade.* "Academically capable but has an extremely short attention span."
- *Second grade.* "Very poor work habits, extremely poor handwriting; has difficulty understanding presented material."
- *Third grade.* "Very poor cursive writing; avid reader; poor work habits; must be helped to adhere to room standards. At times capable if he can be motivated to follow and listen."
- *Fourth grade.* "Has learned to sit for longer periods of time. Restless; needs constant supervision. Poor writing skills; avid reader."
- *Fifth grade.* "Has made progress; still rushes through work."

In summary, the cumulative record contains a great deal of information that can help you to learn more about individual students. Do not hesitate to ask more experienced teachers, the school counselor, or the psychologist for help in evaluating any information in the file. Last, be careful in drawing conclusions about cause-and-effect relationships when you come across certain data. Consider possible alternative explanations for behavior before reaching conclusions about student behavior.

## GRADING AND REPORTING STUDENT PROGRESS

Various methods are used to grade students and report their progress, including letter grades based on comparative and absolute standards, behavioral mastery reports, pass-fail, and parent-teacher conferences. Many schools use combinations of methods, such as letter grades and parent-teacher conferences. This section presents material on the advantages and limitations of these procedures.

## Basing Grades on the Normal Distribution

**What is the difference between norm referenced and criterion-referenced measurement?**

In **norm-referenced evaluation**, grades are assigned for different levels of achievement. A certain percentage of students get A's, B's, C's, D's, and F's. Letter grades are easily understood by parents and students and are convenient in maintaining school records. These advantages aside, the meaning of letter grades varies from teacher to teacher, and the grades do not indicate a student's learning strengths and weaknesses.

The most rigid form of letter-grade evaluation is grading on the curve. In this procedure the grades are arranged to approximate the shape of a normal distribution. The largest proportion of students receive C grades, and the percentage of A and B grades is matched by an equivalent percentage of D and F grades. When a teacher grades on a curve, the percentage of students receiving each grade is predetermined. The grading is based on the assumption that the students in a typical class will fall into a normal distribution on achievement because they are normally distributed on aptitude.

The assumptions underlying the letter-grading system have been abundantly criticized. The size of many classroom groups is often too small to expect a normal distribution, and teachers' achievement tests seldom yield normally distributed scores. The homogeneous grouping system, used in many schools, of placing students with similar abilities in classes negates the assumption of normal distribution from the beginning (Terwilliger, 1971). Finally, even if students were normally distributed in terms of aptitude, would achievement be distributed in the same way? We discussed earlier the notion of mastery learning, which attempts to ensure that almost all students can master the material in a given course. You should think carefully about these criticisms before grading on the curve.

## The Inspection Method

Smith and Adams (1972) support a visual inspection method of grading. With this method, the teacher grades students on a norm-referenced system but experiences greater flexibility in the percentages of letter grades assigned.

The procedure is quite simple. After the scores have been obtained, the teacher establishes a frequency distribution (see Figure 13.5). The following are guidelines for determining letter grades:

1. The large group of scores around the median should be assigned C.
2. The lines drawn at $Q_1$ and $Q_3$, the 25th and 75th percentiles, can be used to indicate the limits of the C group.

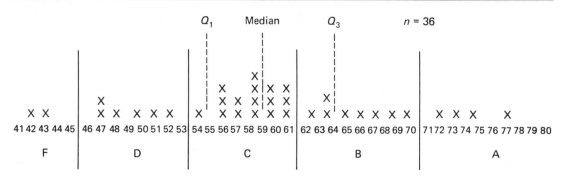

Figure 13.5 Grades Assigned by Visual Inspection of Scores.

*Source: Smith and Adams, 1972.*

3. The groups just above and below the C group are assigned B and D, respectively. The groups at either extreme are assigned A or F.

If the test is too easy or too difficult, the scores will pile up at one end of the distribution, making a clear separation of achievement levels difficult. If everyone does well, there may be no need to assign F's. In other distributions, no one may do well enough to receive an A. In distributions with gaps above or below the median, the teacher may not assign any B's or D's. A teacher must be cautious in using this approach because it is subjective and inexact; grades often don't mean the same thing, since the gaps appear by chance.

*Combining Data in Assigning Grades.* When you are faced with the task of combining scores from tests, papers, and projects for a final letter grade, it is important that you realize that each component carries different weight. This is true even if the assignments and tests have the same number of points. Let's assume that an instructor gives a midterm and final worth 50 points each and says to the class that each exam is worth 50% of the final grade. At the end of the semester, the instructor adds the total number of points, ranks the students from highest to lowest, and assigns the final grade.

The procedure I have just described is accurate *only* if the standard deviations, or variability, of the two exams are approximately equal. For example, if Set of Scores A is twice as variable as Set of Scores B, then A is likely to be twice the weight of B when they are totaled. Suppose the range of scores on the midterm was 20 to 45, with most of the scores being spread along the distribution, and the range of the scores on the final was 40 to 50, with most of the scores being between 40 and 45. If the total points for the two tests are to be summed, which test carries the greater weight? If you said the midterm, you would be correct. Because most of the scores on the final are clustered together, the lowest student (40) is only 10 points from the highest student (50). However, on the midterm, the difference between the highest and lowest is 25 points. You also know that the scores are spread out, so it is more difficult to make up lost ground on the final because of the lack of variability of the examination. If the number of points on each exam differs, as in most test situations, the possibility of even greater variability is apparent.

Gronlund (1985a) recommends that the teacher determine the range of scores as an estimate of score variability and equate the set of scores. For example, if the range of scores on midterm and final examinations were 80 to 100 and 10 to 50, respectively, the range for the midterm is 20 (100 − 80) and for the final 40 (50 − 10). The teacher then multiplies each midterm examination score by 2 to obtain the equal weight.

This procedure provides a fairly accurate measure of the variability, or standard deviation, if the scores extend across the whole range of scores. If students score along a small part of the range, the difference between the highest and lowest scores (range) can be a poor estimate of the variability of the scores. For this reason, measurement experts find that the most accurate procedure for weighting scores is to compute the actual standard deviation for each test or paper and then change all the scores to a standard score, perhaps a T score. The scores are then based on the same scale. A teacher has five components of a final grade and wants to weight them as follows: Unit test I—20%; Unit test II—20%; final—30%; paper—10%; term project—20%. The T scores for each component would be multiplied by 2, 2, 3, 1, and 2, respectively, to complete the desired weighting. More detailed information on this procedure can be found in Terwilliger (1971) and most basic texts in measurement.

One final note regarding grading and combining scores: It is not a good procedure to convert test scores to letter grades and then reconvert the grades to numbers (A = 3, B = 2, and so forth) for the purpose of determining a final grade. The problem with this procedure is that information is lost because the same grade is given whether a student is at the top or bottom of a grade range in the reconversion process. A better procedure is to record the test score directly and use the weighting procedure at the end of the semester (Ebel & Frisbie, 1986).

## Basing Grades on Predetermined Levels of Achievement

Sometimes grades are assigned on the basis of predetermined levels of achievement, such as the following:

$$A = 90–100\%$$
$$B = 80–89\%$$
$$C = 70–79\%$$
$$D = 60–69\%$$
$$F = \text{below } 60\%$$

With this system the student receives a grade based on the percentage of questions answered correctly. There are no limitations on the percentage of letter grades given. At first glance, this system of grading appears fair: No student receives a low grade just because that person is at the bottom of the class distribution. The drawback lies with the teacher, who through the difficulty of the tests can control the percentage of students receiving high or low grades. If scores are too high, the teacher may begin to grade a little tougher to bring them down. If they are too low, the teacher may grade a little easier.

## The Contract System

**What are the advantages and disadvantages of the following types of grading system: contracts, behavioral mastery reports, pass-fail, and parent-teacher conferences?**

A system of grading that is most appropriate at the junior high and high school levels is to establish individualized contracts with students allowing them to determine how much effort they wish to expend on school tasks. This is done by promising specific grades when certain levels of accomplishments are achieved. For example, a teacher might require a 90% on tests and a paper for an A; 85% on tests without a paper would earn a B, and 80% on tests for a C, and so on. Standards can be adjusted according to the ability and interests of the students and the expectations of the teacher. Make up assignments and extra-credit assignments can be added to the contract so that students can improve their grades by doing extra work. Attendance requirements also can be included in the contract.

The advantage of this system is that students know exactly what is expected of them in order to achieve specific grades. In addition, it can reduce anxiety because students know their performance level and what can be done to increase their grades. It is important that the teacher establish standards that differentiate acceptable from unacceptable work in evaluating student papers and projects. Sometimes there is difficulty judging the appropriate performance level of a class by establishing a system in which it is too difficult or too easy to obtain an A or B. Don't hesitate to modify your standards if you find that they are unfair or inappropriate for the students in your class.

## Behavioral Mastery Reports

Dissatisfaction with traditional grading and reporting systems has led to the development of **behavioral mastery reports**. These reports consist of a list of behavioral objectives with indications of the extent to which the student has met or mastered each objective. Figure 13.6 is a report card with such a list of objectives.

A behavioral report permits a degree of communication to the parents not possible with other systems. By specifically identifying those skills and abilities the student has attained, the report puts the parents in a better position to judge the quality of their child's education.

The use of this approach drives home its limitations. In highly structured subjects like mathematics, it is possible to identify and report student

| Grade Two | |
|---|---|
| *Skill* | *Date* |
| *Concepts* | |
| Understands commutative property of addition (e.g., 4 + 3 = 3 + 4) | _____ |
| Understands place value (e.g., 27 = 2 tens + 7 ones) | _____ |
| *Addition* | |
| Supplies missing addend under 10 (e.g., 3 + ? = 5) | _____ |
| Adds three single-digit numbers | _____ |
| Knows combinations 10 through 19 | _____ |
| Adds two 2-digit numbers without carrying | _____ |
| Adds two 2-digit numbers with carrying | _____ |
| *Subtraction* | |
| Knows combinations through 9 | _____ |
| Supplies missing subtrahend—under 10 (e.g., 6 − ? = 1) | _____ |
| Supplies missing minuend—under 10 (e.g., ? − 3 = 4) | _____ |
| Knows combinations 10 through 19 | _____ |
| Subtracts two 2-digit numbers without borrowing | _____ |
| *Measurement* | |
| Reads and draws clocks (up to quarter hour) | _____ |
| Understands dollar value of money (coins up to $1.00 total) | _____ |
| *Geometry* | |
| Understands symmetry | _____ |
| Recognizes congruent plan figures—that is, figures which are identical except for orientation | _____ |
| *Graph Reading* | |
| Knows how to construct simple graphs | _____ |
| Knows how to read simple graphs | _____ |

Figure 13.6 Report Card Based on a System of Criterion-Referenced Measurement.

*Source: Millman, 1970.*

progress in a specific domain of learning outcomes; in loosely defined subjects like social studies, the domain of learning outcomes is difficult to assess and there is no clear hierarchical structure. A second deficiency in behavioral mastery reports is the problem of identifying all instructional objectives in terms of specific student outcomes. Third, it is difficult to specify meaningful standards of performance for many objectives: What is mastery? How does one establish a minimal level of competency (Gronlund, 1974a)?

## Pass-Fail Grading

Pass-fail grading removes the competitive pressures of letter grading and permits students to explore new subject areas without fear of receiving low grades. In some pass-fail procedures, the instructor does not know who in the course is on the pass-fail basis and who is in on a regular grading system. The instructor submits letter grades for all students to the registrar, who then converts all passing grades to P for the pass-fail students.

This system is limited in that it provides little information about student learning. In addition, students may not do assigned readings or may do just enough to get by in lieu of attempting to attain a high level of competency in the course. Finally, there is no evidence that students are more motivated to learn under this system of grading.

## Parent-Teacher Conferences

The parent-teacher conference is most effective for reporting student progress at the elementary school level and for dealing with special problems at the secondary level. It improves the teacher's communication with parents and can provide the teacher with a source of more detailed information about the student. The limitations of the parent-teacher conference are the amount of time needed to conduct the interviews and the special counseling skills required for communicating productively with the parent.

## CLASSROOM APPLICATION: PREPARING AND CONDUCTING PARENT CONFERENCES

Teachers often find meetings with parents uncomfortable, especially if they have to report unpleasant information about students. Yet an effective conference can provide parents with the information needed to help their child function more effectively in school and to help them work more closely with the classroom teacher. Thus, in the long run, dealing with learning problems in a direct manner can benefit the teacher as much as students and parents.

Conferences with parents are more likely to be successful if teachers adequately prepare for the conference and use effective communication techniques during the conference. The following guidelines should be helpful in making parent-teacher conferences more productive (Gronlund, 1974a).

### Planning the Conference

1. *Send adequate advance notice of the need for a conference with some options on time and date.* Remember that parents have many demands in their lives and may not be available when you want

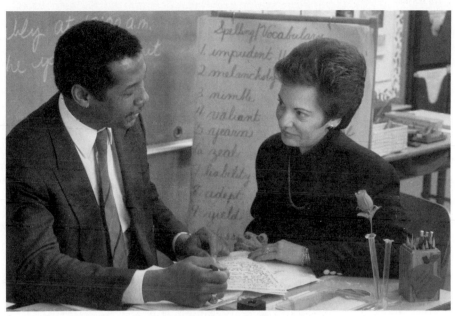

Parent-teacher conferences can be a good method for reporting student progress and working with parents to develop a plan of action to help students achieve at higher levels.

them. Do not jump to the conclusion that they are not interested in their child if they cannot come to the meetings at the time you suggest.

2. *State the purpose of the conference when contacting the parents.* Making such a statement can help to relieve anxiety and give parents an opportunity to think about issues that might be discussed at the conference.

3. *Review the student's records and collect all relevant information related to the purpose of the conference.* Take notes from the student's cumulative record regarding past performance and adjustment in school. Identify the student's strengths and weaknesses.

4. *Provide a folder of the student's present work.* This folder should include tests, completed assignments, and any other information that will give the parents a clearer understanding of their child's achievement.

5. *Make a tentative list of questions to ask the parents.* Because the purpose of a conference is to provide information for both the teacher and the parents, it is important that the teacher ask questions that will offer insight into the student's attitudes, interests, and general development.

6. *Anticipate parents' questions during the conference.* Although it is impossible to anticipate parental reactions to the conference, there may be particular issues that you can expect to be high on the parents' list of questions. For example, if a child has had social behavior problems, the parents may want to know if the child has friends in class, whether any students are annoying the child, and how they might deal with the child's behavior at home. You may not have all the answers to these questions, but you should be able to refer parents to other school personnel or resource materials that would be helpful.

7. *Select a suitable site for the conference.* In most situations the conference will be held in your classroom. To ensure that you will not be interrupted, place a sign outside the door. Provide large enough chairs for the parents to sit on, and arrange the chairs so that you are not sitting behind your desk. It is important that you provide an informal atmosphere so that the parents will feel more comfortable during the conference.

### Conducting the Conference

You want to accomplish three primary objectives during the conference: establish and maintain rapport with the parents, share information, and plan a course of action with them. Specific guidelines for these objectives follow (Gronlund, 1974a, pp. 40–43), with comments.

### ESTABLISHING AND MAINTAINING RAPPORT

1. *"Create a friendly informal atmosphere."* This approach gives parents time to overcome their initial anxiety and allows them to see you in a less formal role.

2. *"Maintain a positive attitude."* It is important that you communicate directly and indirectly that your primary goal is to help their child, not simply to criticize or point out weaknesses. Use language such as "there are some areas that need improvement" when identifying weaknesses. Try not to make the parents defensive by avoiding statements like "According to the test results, he is doing about what I would expect." Parents will respond positively or negatively to the type and tone of communication you use.

3. *"Use language that is understandable to parents."* Stay away from "educationese." Do not assume that parents understand technical words. Be careful in presenting test information, and help parents to understand what the tests measure, what the test scores mean, and how test information is used. Finally, point out that test scores are not exact measures of behavior or ability.

4. *"Be willing to listen to parents."* Sometimes teachers are so concerned about completing their agenda that they forget about the

concerns of the parents. The more you listen, the more credibility you may develop as an individual who is sincerely interested in helping. Use Gordon's reflective listening techniques discussed in Chapter 11. Some parents may become emotional and wander into areas of concern other than the purpose of the conference. However, as their emotion subsides, you can get them redirected to the main issue of the conference.

5. *"Be honest and sincere with parents and do not betray confidences."* Be tactful but tell parents what you think, and do not promise anything that you cannot deliver. Most important, if parents communicate some confidential information about their personal or family life, you have a responsibility to honor their confidence by not talking about the child or family in the teachers' lounge or with other parents. Also, it is usually best to avoid comparisons with other children when communicating with parents.

## SHARING INFORMATION

1. *"Begin by describing the student's strong points."* This approach serves two purposes. It helps in developing rapport with the parents and provides information for the parents when their child asks, "What did the teacher say about me?"

2. *"Describe the areas needing improvement in a positive and tactful manner."* At this time you should present information you have prepared from the student's cumulative folder and/or classroom work. Avoid generalizations that cannot be supported by the information available.

3. *"Encourage parents to participate in the conference."* You will not need to worry about the involvement of some parents because they will ask questions, give advice, and offer recommendations without any encouragement by you. There will also, however, be parents who will answer most questions with "yes" or "no" answers. In this situation, you need to ask more open-ended questions such as, "How does Susan feel about social studies?" "How does Henry prepare for tests?"

4. *"Be cautious about giving advice."* A teacher can easily project a know-it-all image and give simple solutions to difficult problems. Questions pertaining to correct ways to handle discipline problems at home are commonly raised by parents. In responding, present information in terms of alternative approaches, pointing out that typically there is no one best way to rear children. Suggest different approaches that other parents have used to deal with the situation or problem. If parents want information dealing with educational matters, you can be more specific in offering advice on tutoring and remedial strategies.

**PLANNING A COURSE OF ACTION**

The final phase of the conference is summarizing what has been discussed and planning a course of action. Parents should never leave a conference without any idea as to what should be done to help their child.

1. *"Begin the conclusion phase of the conference with a brief overall summary."* By beginning the summary, you communicate to the parents that the conference is coming to an end and you set the stage for planning a course of action.

2. *"Have parents participate in planning a course of action."* Discuss what can be done at home in addition to what you plan to do at school. You might also discuss plans for another conference at some later time to evaluate the progress that will have been made since the first conference.

3. *"Review your conference notes with parents."* Some school districts require teachers to fill out a form after a conference with parents. If so, review the content covered during the conference. Even if no formal report is required by the school, a summary will help you and the parents to organize notes before the end of the conference.

4. *"End the conference on a positive note."* At the end of the conference, you should thank the parents for coming and showing interest in their child. Invite them to visit the class when possible, or call you if they have further questions.

## GRADES: HELP OR HINDRANCE?

In Chapter 10, Hill and Wigfield's (1984) recommendations for reducing anxiety in school were discussed. One of their suggestions entailed abolishing letter grades at the elementary school level, substituting instead information on the child's achievement, effort, social development, and specific strengths and weaknesses in each subject area. Concerned over the pressure of grades and the premature labeling of young children as failures, the Board of Education for the Los Angeles Unified School District recently voted to abolish letter grades in the early elementary grades and replace them with a system that reported whether students performed satisfactorily or needed to improve.

Soon after this change, the following article by Robert Butterworth and Daniella Alloro, co-directors of Contemporary Psychology Associates in Los Angeles, appeared in the opinion section of the *Herald Examiner*, a newspaper in Los Angeles. As you read the article, identify some of the issues regarding grading that need to be discussed.

## Changing "F" to "N" Only Disguises the Fact That a Student Is Failing

BY ROBERT BUTTERWORTH AND DANIELLA ALLORO

The Los Angeles School Board's decision to change the grading structure in the early elementary grades is a smokescreen to disguise reality and carries with it the danger of erupting into a nationwide trend.

The board's decision to eliminate "F," the failing grade, and substitute "N," for needs improvement was made to protect the young child from a loss of self-esteem associated with a failing grade. Yet it is difficult to understand how self-esteem can be enhanced when we disguise the fact that a child is failing in school.

In some respects, the F grade may be the best friend the parents of a failing child have. The early years of school are crucial in educational development. At this time, future academic- and work-performance patterns are established. It is also the best period to correct problems that may exist in the child.

As psychologists who work with children, we understand that a failing grade is only a symptom of other problems. It is essential that parents have a real understanding of the child's academic status so that if difficulties do exist, they can be treated. There are many reasons why children fail at school.

Learning disorders, family difficulties, emotional problems—all can contribute. Yet by just focusing on the self-esteem issue of failing grades, we pretend to cure the symptoms but overlook the disease.

It isn't the failing grade that makes a child feel like a failure; this is accomplished by parents before children start school. Low self-esteem and a feeling of being a failure comes from random, non-directed punishment and criticism. A failing grade in school is the logical consequence of specific behavior.

Has this newly adopted grading system worked before? Remember the '60s, when many universities decided to throw out the letter grades and adopt "pass-fail" grading? Did it work? Ask students who were competing with other students to get into medical school. Many of them were eliminated because they couldn't be academically ranked. Graduate schools need an accurate gauge to pick the best people they can, and this is as much a fact of life in medical schools as it is in any other educational setting.

The school board says that the child suffers at the hands of his or her peers and teachers if he or she gets an F. Yet classmates and teachers know, based on classroom behavior, who the bright and slow pupils are.

By changing F to N, we are using a smokescreen from which children and parents will get the impression that the failure is minimized and not all that important. Not only do the consequences of having failed become a subject not treated, but the underlying deeper problems are avoided as well.

We have a duty and obligation as parents and educators to prepare our children for the contemporary world. Competition and high achievement may not be liked or favored by some, but they exist and will continue to exist. Jobs are getting scarcer. The competition in all areas of life is keener than ever before. Children should be prepared for it. Is it fair to protect our children from the reality of failure in the early years, only to have this reality resurface with a vengeance when they enter the real world?

There is no need to disguise grades. Schools have to develop better methods to screen and evaluate youngsters in the early grades. And schools and parents have to establish rewards for positive academic achievement. But for those students with academic problems, the focus should be on the underlying problems, not the external cosmetics, of the F grade.

This opinion article presented the classic arguments for the use of letter grades in school: the need to report academic progress to parents, to correct problems early in children's educational careers, to prepare children for competition in the real world, and to provide information to schools and institutions of higher learning.

There are other positions that you should be aware of. First, there are some educators and psychologists (primarily of a humanistic orientation) who are opposed to all external grading standards. They argue that the best evaluation is self-evaluation, because no one knows more about how much the individual learned than that individual. Second, there are individuals who are opposed to letter grades but who are not opposed to any form of external evaluation. These individuals would favor, in addition to self-evaluation, such procedures as written evaluation, pass-fail, credit-no credit, and various mastery approaches. The book *Wad-ja-Get: The Grading Game in American Education*, by Kirschenbaum, Simon, and Napier (1971), provides an excellent discussion of alternative grading systems.

Opponents of the letter-grade system raise a number of issues. First, the letters do not mean the same in all classes. A grade of A in one class may be worth a C in another. Thus educators overemphasize the amount of information communicated to the student and parents. Many of these educators would also argue that letter grades are not objective and that they do not ensure competency.

Second, there is evidence that self-esteem is affected by evaluation in school. To argue that low self-esteem comes from experiences in the home prior to school is to reject a great deal of social science research.

Third, students can be better prepared for the competition in the real world without experiencing failure and rejection early in school, which, in turn, leads to *less* learning rather than more learning. Also, there is no evidence that continual failure leads to greater motivation and more success in competition.

Fourth, the fact that letter grades are not used does not mean that the student and the parents cannot receive detailed information about educational achievement (see "Behavior Mastery Reports"). In fact, when you go to a doctor for a physical, you don't receive a grade on your health condition, but you learn a great deal by discussing your condition with the physician. The same can be said about alternative grading systems, which can provide more specific information about strengths and weaknesses without using a letter grade.

Finally, the argument used primarily at higher levels of education is: How will colleges or universities evaluate applicants without letter grades? A number of responses are given to this concern. One is that high school grades do not always predict success in college or in the marketplace. Another argument is that students from outstanding alternative schools with no-grades transcripts have had an acceptance rate equal to or better than that of graduates from traditional schools in the same school districts (Bellanca, 1977). Third, institutions of higher learning would also benefit from more detailed information concerning students in terms of written evaluations regarding academic strengths and weaknesses, as well as on effort, interests, attitudes, and behaviors. Fourth, there could be a compromise, whereby grades would begin at the junior high or high school level.

What are your beliefs about grading? Do letter grades provide an important standard of communication with parents and students? Do you think students would achieve more if grades were abolished? Would they be more motivated to learn? Do you think different procedures need to be established at different educational levels—elementary, junior high, and high school? How do these issues relate to your own learning and evaluation experiences?

## PROMOTION AND RETENTION OF STUDENTS

**What are the factors that should be considered in promotion and retention decisions?**

With the emphasis on minimum competency testing, mastery learning, and a general focus on improving students' levels of achievement, one of the oldest issues in education is again receiving considerable attention in the literature. The primary question is stated as follows: Should students who do not meet the basic content objectives repeat the grade level? This is one of the most important decisions that you may be involved in during the school year.

Throughout the history of public education in the United States, various points of view have dominated educational practice. For example, in the early 1900s the average retention rate for all grades was 16%, but by the 1930s it had dropped to 4 to 5%. In the 1960s the notion of "social promotion" became prevalent. Instead of repeating a grade, the student would be promoted to the next grade and given remedial instruction to acquire the knowledge and skills that were not attained in the previous grade level (Medway, 1985).

In general, researchers reviewing the investigations on the effects of retention (especially in kindergarten) have concluded that it *does not* lead to improved achievement and better personal adjustment (see Holmes & Matthews, 1984; Shepard & Smith, 1988). When students with similar problems and backgrounds are compared, the students who are retained don't achieve any better than low-achieving students who are promoted. The research does indicate that the benefits of retention are greatest for the first and second grades when the children and their parents are supportive of retention.

By now you may be thinking: "Well, if the research doesn't support retention, why is it used?" First, school districts are under considerable political pressure to demonstrate to the public that they are dealing with the problem of low achievement, and retention is one way to make this point. Second, each student's situation must be analyzed separately. In some situations the evidence indicates more strongly that the student would benefit from retention. Remember that when research investigations are undertaken, the purpose is to make generalizations based on a large sample of individuals. Thus the general finding that retention is not effective should not lead one to conclude that no student will benefit from retention, only that most students will not benefit.

Most school districts have a committee to make recommendations about retention. This committee may include the school principal, teacher, parent, school psychologist, and counselor. The committee's responsibility is to collect relevant information before a recommendation is made. For example, it is important that the school psychologist evaluate the teacher's instructional effectiveness and to determine whether remedial methods were attempted to improve the student's achievement. If the student has not received the proper instruction, retention would be unfair and unwise (Medway, 1985).

**THINKING ABOUT THE TEACHING-LEARNING MODEL**

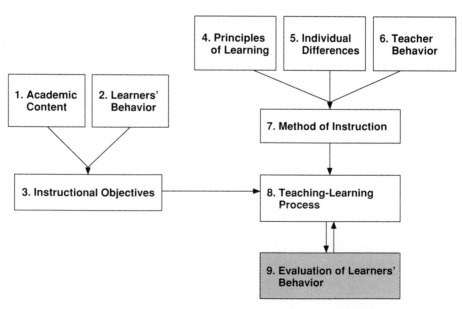

*Source: Adapted from Hunter, 1971, in Allen and Seifman.*

In Chapter 1, I reported that teachers state that one of their major problems is relating to parents. Chapter 10 discussed one of the factors influencing teachers' sense of efficacy: their relations with parents. It is clear that teachers need to develop skills to interact effectively with parents. Conducting productive parent-teacher conferences can be an important step toward developing a greater sense of efficacy.

One of the first contacts teachers have with parents generally involves reporting and evaluating student progress. The classroom application on preparing and conducting parent conferences should be helpful in establishing a positive climate for dialogue with parents. Also remember some of the comments made about parents of exceptional children in Chapter 5. These parents can be under a great deal of pressure in dealing with education and child-rearing problems. If you use the ideas from humanistic psychology (i.e., focus on a person's perceptions), you may better understand the concerns of parents. Finally, the humanistic teacher's reliance on genuineness, trust, and empathic understanding, and the active listening skills identified by Gordon, are useful teacher behaviors for interacting with adults as well as children. If you practice these skills during conferences with parents, you may find that you are able to communicate more effectively with them.

A recent study by Smith and Shepard (1988) shows how teacher beliefs influence their decisions regarding student retention. These researchers found that teachers in schools with different retention rates tended to hold different beliefs regarding child development and school policies. The beliefs ranged from assumptions described as "nativist" (the idea that development and learning are strongly influenced by internal processes that cannot be accelerated by teacher involvement) to "remediationist" (the belief that learning and development can be influenced by educational intervention). Schools in which teachers hold nativist beliefs retained a higher proportion of students than schools in which teachers hold remediationist beliefs.

In Chapter 10, I first mentioned the link between student motivation and evaluation. Students' self-perceptions of ability, their sense of efficacy, and level of test anxiety are influenced by their evaluation experiences. For example, Natriello and Dornbusch (1985) found that student effort can be encouraged and increased by an effective evaluation system. They point out that the lack of frequent and challenging teacher evaluation of students' academic work can lead to low student effort and achievement.

There are other individual differences to consider in developing evaluation systems. For example, Bolocofsky and Mescher (1984) investigated the effects of different standards—individually referenced, criterion-referenced, and norm-referenced—for students who differed in their self-esteem and locus of control. They found that these students performed differently under different kinds of standards. Individually referenced standards were more effective with students of low self-esteem and internal locus of control. Criterion-referenced standards were more effective with students of low self-esteem and external locus of control. Norm-referenced standards were more effective with students of high self-esteem, regardless of locus of control.

Students who receive unsatisfactory evaluations often misunderstand the criteria by which they are to be evaluated (Natriello, 1982). Therefore, it is important for the teacher to review carefully the criteria used to judge performance and discuss the questions students may have about their work.

Grading is one aspect of an evaluation system that can affect student behavior because grading communicates information to students about their academic and personal competencies. For example, absolute standards can be fine. However, if the standards are perceived as unattainable by some students, they may give up and expend only minimal effort in their academic work (remember information in Chapter 10 about the impact of student attributions). Norm-referenced letter grades can provide students with information as to how well they achieved in relation to their peers, but students who do poorly on early tests often reduce their time and effort in the course when they realize they cannot achieve a high grade.

Suppose your college instructor gives you two exams, each worth 50% of your final grade, and you receive a C on the first test early in the semester. Would this grade play any role in your work habits in this course for the rest of the semester? Think about other examples of how grading policies and procedures influence student motivation, attention, and work habits. Remember that grades generally do not motivate low achievers to excel in the classroom. Therefore, consider the issues on grading and evaluation discussed in this book before you develop your own system.

## KEY POINTS

1. A frequency distribution for a test is a table summarizing how often each score occurs.
2. The mean is the arithmetic average of a set of scores.
3. The median is the middle score in a distribution.
4. The mode is the score with the highest frequency of occurrence.
5. The standard deviation is a measure of the dispersion, or variability, of the scores from the mean.
6. A raw score is the number of items answered correctly on a test.
7. A percentile rank indicates a person's rank in a group in terms of the percentage of individuals at or below that person's score.
8. Grade-equivalent scores indicate the average performance of students at different grade levels.
9. Percentile ranks and grade-equivalent scores cannot be added or averaged because they do not form equal intervals at all points along the scale.
10. Standard scores represent test scores that have fixed means and standard deviations.
11. The basic standard score is the z score, which is calculated by dividing

the standard deviation into the difference between a given raw score and the mean of all the scores.

12. A T score is obtained by multiplying a z score by 10 and adding 50.

13. A normal, or bell-shaped, curve is a mathematical model that symbolically represents the way in which many human characteristics are distributed.

14. Stanines are scores that represent the normal curve divided into nine parts. Each part, or percentage, of the distribution is a stanine.

15. The standard error of measurement estimates the amount of error in a test score.

16. Grades can be based on comparative or absolute standards.

17. The variability of scores on each test can influence the weighting of the test when determining each student's final grade.

18. Preparing and conducting parent conferences are important teaching skills.

19. Educators differ in their beliefs regarding the benefits of student grades.

20. Careful consideration should be given before a student is retained at a particular grade level. Research findings indicate that, in most situations, retention does not lead to improved achievement or better personal adjustment.

## KEY TERMS

frequency distribution, p. 548
measures of central tendency, p. 548
mean, p. 548
medium, p. 548
mode, p. 548
variability, p. 550
range of scores, p. 550
standard deviation, p. 550
raw score, p. 551
derived score, p. 551
percentile rank, p. 551
grade-equivalent score, p. 551
standard score, p. 551
z score, p. 553
T score, p. 553
deviation IQ, p. 554
normal distribution (curve), p. 554
stanines, p. 555
standard error of measurement, p. 555
cumulative record, p. 559
norm-referenced evaluation, p. 563
behavioral mastery reports, p. 566

## SUGGESTIONS FOR FURTHER READING

Kroth, R. L., & Simpson, R. L. (1977). *Parent conferences as a teaching strategy*. Denver: Love. Good suggestions for effective parent-teacher conferences.

Lyman, H. B. (1986). *Test scores and what they mean* (4th ed.). Englewood Cliffs, NJ: Prentice-Hall. A detailed discussion of the interpretation of test scores.

The following references discuss alternative procedures for grading:

Gronlund, N. E. (1974). *Improving marking and reporting in classroom instruction*. New York: Macmillan.

Kirschenbaum, H., Simon, S., & Napier, R. (1971). *Wad-ja-get? The grading game in American education*. New York: Hart.

Terwilliger, J. S. (1971). *Assigning grades to students*. Glenview, IL: Scott, Foresman.

## FOLLOW-UP ACTIVITIES

### 1. Interpret Achievement Test Scores

Your school system has administered the Elementary Reading Test for grades 3 and 4 from the Elementary Battery of the Metropolitan Achievement Tests to all third-grade students in October, and you now have the scores for each student. A portion of the score sheet is provided below. What does it mean?

Which student does each of the following statements describe?

a. Scored close to the average third grader in the October testing.
b. Was more than a year above third-grade level in Word Knowledge.
c. Scored very well in Reading; only 15% of the standardization group did better.
d. About 40 percent of the students in the country scored higher in Word Knowledge.
e. With the total score scale divided into nine segments, the student scored the second from the top in Word Knowledge.

|  |  | Word Knowledge | Reading |
|---|---|---|---|
| **Sims, Fred** | Grade equivalent | 4.8 | 4.4 |
|  | Percentile rank | 95 | 85 |
|  | Standard score | 55 | 53 |
|  | Stanine | 8 | 7 |
| **Simmons, Mary** | Grade equivalent | 3.2 | 3.1 |
|  | Percentile rank | 60 | 45 |
|  | Standard score | 44 | 41 |
|  | Stanine | 6 | 5 |

_____ 2. Interpret Information from a Cumulative Record

In June, Fred North's parents make an appointment with you, his English teacher, to discuss his academic progress. They want him to become a doctor but are afraid that he will not get into college if his academic work continues to decline. Given the information from a part of his cumulative record that follows, how would you start this meeting? What would you tell his parents about his potential and his academic progress? What recommendations would you make? You may want to consult reference materials for information about the standardized tests used by the school.

_____ 3. Interpret a Grade Summary Sheet

Given the grade summary sheet that follows for a sample of eighth-grade social studies students, determine the teacher's primary basis for assigning

---

## CUMULATIVE RECORD
## CENTRAL JUNIOR HIGH SCHOOL

Name: Fred North
Age: 13
Grade: 7

### Test Record

| **Intelligence tests** | | IQ | Grade Level |
|---|---|---|---|
| *Group* | | | |
| California Test of Mental | Language | 77 | 6th |
| Maturity | Performance | 96 | |
| *Individual* | | | |
| Wechsler Intelligence | Verbal | 81 | 6th |
| Scale for Children | Performance | 99 | |
| | Full Scale | 88 | |

| | | Grade equivalent scores | |
|---|---|---|---|
| **Achievement tests** | | | |
| California Achievement Tests | Total reading | 5.6 | 7th |
| taken in October) | Total arithmetic | 7.3 | |
| | Total language | 6.1 | |

### Academic Record

| **Subject** | Final Grades | Grade Level |
|---|---|---|
| English | C− | 7th |
| Mathematics | C+ | 7th |
| Social Studies | D | 7th |
| Science | B | 7th |

Work habits: below average.

grades. Are there inconsistencies in grading priorities? If so, how would the teacher defend them? What are possible sources of teacher bias? Could the grading system be made more equitable? If so, how?

---

**GRADE SUMMARY SHEET**

**Grade/Subject:** Eighth Grade/Social Studies
**Grading Period:** First Six Weeks

| Name | Pre-test | Post-test | Grades on Group Reports | Individual Project Reports | Students Self-evaluation | Final Grade |
|------|------|------|------|------|------|------|
| Ames, Sally | 90% | 89% | A− | A | A | A |
| Brooks, Sid | 42 | 67 | B+ | C+ | A | B |
| Colton, Billy | 72 | 82 | A− | A+ | B | A |
| Courtes, Sally | 86 | 86 | B+ | B | A | B |
| Debs, Sam | 54 | 57 | B | C | B | C |
| | | | | | | |
| | | | | | | |
| | | | | | | |
| | | | | | | |
| | | | | | | |
| Williams, Tom | 70 | 80 | B | B+ | A | B |
| Young, John | 70 | 80 | B | B+ | A | B |
| Zimmer, Alice | 62 | 72 | A− | B+ | B | A |

---

———————— 4. **Evaluate Grading Methods and Procedures**

   a. What effect do grades have on you? Think about the courses you had in high school or those that you are now taking. Would you have behaved differently had you not been graded in any of them? In which courses would you not have altered your performance, regardless of whether you had been graded?

   b. What experiences have you had with pass-fail and absolute standards (A = 90–100%, B = 80–90%, and so on)? What do you consider the advantages and disadvantages of each? How did these grading priorities dispose you toward learning?

   c. Discuss what you believe was an unfair grading system used by a teacher. Defend your position, and point out how the system could be improved.

   d. Should a grade represent student achievement only, or should it also include the student's effort and work habits? Explain.

# Glossary

Words set in *italics* are defined elsewhere in the Glossary.

**academic learning time (ALT).** A subset of *time-on-task* (engaged time). ALT is the amount of time a student spends on academic tasks while performing at a high rate of success.

**accommodation.** Piaget's term for the modification or reorganization of existing cognitive structures (*schemata*) to deal with environmental demands.

**achievement test.** A test that measures how much a student has learned in a subject area.

**acronyms.** *Mnemonics* that use the first letter in each word of a list to form a word.

**action sequence.** A sequence of behaviors or cognitive actions to be taken to reach a goal. Regrouping and borrowing in subtraction are examples of action-sequence knowledge.

**active listening.** A type of communication in which teachers summarize and paraphrase what students have said so that the students feel that they have been understood.

**adaptation.** Changes in an organism in response to environmental demands. Adaptation comprises *assimilation* and *accommodation*.

**adjunct questions.** Questions asked just before or after the presentation of text or lecture material regarding important points of the material. These questions may be asked by the teacher, asked by the students themselves, or embedded within the text.

**advance organizers.** Introductory information intended to facilitate a student's learning by providing a framework and organization for the material to be learned.

**affective domain.** One of the categories of educational objectives for student attitudes, values, and emotional growth. The affective domain includes five basic categories: receiving, responding, valuing, organization, and characterization by a value.

**affective strategies.** Learning strategies that involve getting ready to learn and eliminating undesirable affect. They include focusing attention, maintaining motivation, and managing time.

583

allocated time. The time that a teacher designates for a particular learning task.

androgyny. A condition that comprises both male and female traits.

anorexia nervosa. An eating disorder in which individuals (primarily female) starve themselves to maintain a slim figure. The illness causes a distortion in one's perceptions of body image.

anxiety. The emotional state associated with apprehension or fear.

applied behavior analysis. A scientific method of behavioral change using principles of *operant conditioning* and directed toward clinically or socially significant behavior in a setting such as a hospital or school.

aptitude by treatment interaction (ATI). Research that focuses on how different aptitudes matched with different instructional methods affect learning. The result of this interaction indicates that a particular teaching method may not be equally effective with all students.

aptitude test. A test used to predict how well a student will learn unfamiliar material. A scholastic aptitude test, which measures learning potential, is an example.

assertive discipline. A method of *classroom management* developed by Canter that emphasizes the rights of teachers to teach and the rights of students to learn.

assimilation. Piaget's term for the process of making sense of experiences and perceptions by fitting them into previously established cognitive structures (*schemata*).

associativity. An operation wherein several classes can be combined in any order to produce the same results.

attribution. An individual's perception of the causes of his or her own success or failure.

authoritarian parenting style. A method of child rearing in which parents attempt to control their children's behavior and attitudes to conform to strict rules of conduct. They use punitive measures when their children fail to conform and don't discuss standards with them.

authoritative parenting style. A method of child rearing in which parents direct their children's activities by establishing firm rules and standards but are willing to discuss the reasons behind their regulations. These parents don't threaten their children, and are loving, consistent, and respectful of their children's independent decisions.

automaticity. The result of overlearning behaviors to the point that they can be carried out without conscious thought.

baseline. The natural occurrence of a behavior before intervention.

behavioral mastery reports. Reports that measure competency by assessing specific behavior.

behavioral objectives. Statements regarding the specific changes educators intend to produce in student behavior.

behavior-disordered. A category in special education for students exhibiting one or more of the following behaviors over a substantial period: inability to learn that cannot be explained by intellectual, sensory, or health factors; difficulty in establishing positive interpersonal relationships; frequent inappropriate behavior; a general mood of unhappiness or depression; frequent physical complaints.

behavior modification. Interventions designed to change behavior in a precisely measurable manner.

**bilingual education.** Classroom instruction in two languages (e.g., English and a student's native language).

**branching program.** Programmed material that, in contrast to a *linear program*, presents a variety of alternative routes through the material.

**chunking.** Grouping of data so that a greater amount of information may be retained in *short-term memory*.

**classical conditioning.** A procedure in which the *conditioned stimulus*, after being paired with the *unconditioned stimulus* often enough, can then be substituted for it. It is often called "stimulus substitution."

**classroom management.** Teacher behaviors and activities that encourage learning in the classroom.

**coaching.** A program of test preparation to increase scores on specific tests.

**cognition.** The process or faculties by which knowledge is acquired and manipulated (e.g., thinking or remembering).

**cognitive behavior modification.** A technique based on behavioral and cognitive theory that changes behavior by modifying an individual's inner, self-directive speech.

**cognitive domain.** A part of Bloom's *Taxonomy of Educational Objectives*. Bloom divides the objectives in the cognitive domain into six categories: knowledge, comprehension, application, analysis, synthesis, and evaluation.

**cognitive style.** The consistent way in which an individual responds to a wide range of perceptual tasks.

**combinativity.** An operation in which two or more classes are combined into a larger group. It is sometimes called "classification."

**combinatorial reasoning.** An ability developed at the formal operations stage that enables an individual to isolate individual factors and possible combinations of factors that may determine the solution to a problem.

**comprehension-monitoring strategies.** The metacognitive process whereby the reader ensures that material read has been understood adequately to satisfy the goals of the reading assignment.

**computer-assisted instruction (CAI).** The use of a computer as tutor to present information, give students opportunities to practice what they learn, evaluate student achievement, and provide additional instruction.

**computer-managed instruction (CMI).** The use of a computer for managerial purposes in instruction, such as determining error rates, student progress, and class averages and making assignments based on the diagnosis of student weaknesses. In many instruction programs *computer-assisted instruction* (CAI) and CMI are used in an integrated manner.

**concept learning.** The acquisition of *pattern-recognition knowledge* involving the learning of a rule or rules for classifying a number of objects into mutually exclusive categories based on one or more salient characteristics of the objects.

**conceptual tempo.** A *cognitive style* referring to the speed with which subjects make a response to tasks and the number of errors they make in the response. See *impulsive*; *reflective*.

**concrete operations stage.** The third of Piaget's four major stages, characterized by children's ability to think logically, but only about concrete problems and objects.

**conditioned response.** A response elicited by a *conditioned stimulus*. The response is similar but not identical to its associated *unconditioned response*.

**conditioned stimulus.** A stimulus that does not initially elicit a response but through its pairing with an *unconditioned stimulus* acquires the capability of eliciting the same response as the latter.

**connectionism.** A term used by Thorndike to explain a type of learning that is concerned with the formation of bonds (connections) between stimuli and responses.

**conservation.** A Piagetian term for the realization that certain properties of an object (e.g., weight and length) remain the same regardless of changes in its other properties (e.g., shape and position).

**construct validity.** The degree to which a test measures specific psychological traits or constructs (e.g., intelligence, attitude, anxiety).

**contents.** A term used by Guilford to describe the content of a person's intellect— auditory, visual, symbolic, semantic, or behavioral.

**content validity.** The ability of a test to adequately sample a specific universe of content.

**contingency contracting.** A written document in which a teacher and student agree that when a student satisfactorily behaves in some specified way or completes some specified work, he or she will be able to engage in a stated amount of some privilege, preferred activity, or other reinforcer. It is sometimes called "behavioral contracting."

**continuing motivation.** The tendency to return to and continue working on tasks away from the classroom without the supervision or control of the teacher.

**control group.** A group in an experimental study that receives no special treatment.

**convergent thinking.** A term used by Guilford to describe the type of thinking in which an individual produces a single response to a specific question or problem.

**correlation.** A measure of the degree of relationship between two variables.

**creativity.** The capacity of individuals to produce novel or original answers or products.

**criterion-referenced measurement; criterion-referenced testing.** A testing procedure in which an individual's performance is based on whether specific objectives have been achieved.

**criterion-related validity.** The extent to which scores on a test are in agreement with (concurrent validity) or predict (predictive validity) some given criterion measure. An example is the Scholastic Aptitude Test (SAT), which predicts grade-point average.

**culture.** The ways in which a group of people think, feel, and react in order to solve problems of living in their environment.

**cumulative record.** A file on a student that includes such information as family data, health, academic grades, standardized test scores, attendance, and teacher comments.

**curve.** See *normal distribution*.

**decenter.** The ability to take into consideration two or more details or dimensions (e.g., length and width) at the same time.

**declarative knowledge.** Knowledge about things. Declarative knowledge is composed of *rote learning* and *meaningful learning*.

**decoding.** The process of translating a symbol back into its original form, such as translating a letter into its sound or a word into its meaning.

**dependent variable.** A variable in an experimental study that may change as a result of the manipulation of the *independent variable*.

**derived score.** A *raw score* that has been converted to another scale.

**deviation IQ.** An intelligence test score based upon the difference, or deviation, between an individual's score and the average score for persons of the same chronological age.

**diagnostic test; diagnostic evaluation.** A test designed to assess those skills and abilities that are important in learning a particular subject. Diagnostic tests are widely used in reading and mathematics.

**direct instruction.** An instructional method that emphasizes the mastery of basic skills by placing a clear focus on academic goals, wide coverage of content, selection of instructional goals, monitoring of student progress, structuring of learning activities, immediate feedback, and creation of an environment that is task-oriented but relaxed.

**disabled.** A term describing children with a physical problem or problems that limit their ability to perform certain tasks.

**discipline.** The degree to which students behave appropriately, are involved in classroom activities, and are task-oriented.

**discovery learning.** The learning of new information largely as a result of the learner's own efforts.

**discrimination learning.** The restriction of responding to certain stimulus situations and not others.

**discriminative stimulus.** A stimulus ($S^D$) in the presence of which a given response is likely to be reinforced.

**disequilibrium.** Piaget's term for the state, or condition, occurring when, in the process of *assimilation*, the individual cannot adapt to the environment. Disequilibrium forces the individual into *accommodation*.

**distributed practice.** *Rote-learning* trials divided among short and frequent periods.

**divergent thinking.** A term used by Guilford to describe the type of thinking wherein an individual produces multiple responses or solutions (often non-traditional) to a single question or problem. Divergent thinking is associated with *creativity*.

**educable mentally retarded (EMR).** A label for mildly retarded children, who are often educated in regular classrooms.

**Education for All Handicapped Children Act (P.L. 94-142).** A federal law that mandates specific educational procedures and rights for handicapped children.

**egocentrism.** Piaget's term for describing children in the *preoperational stage*, who have difficulty in assuming the point of view of others.

**elaboration strategies.** Integration of meaningful *declarative knowledge* into *long-term memory* through adding detail, creating examples, making associations with other ideas, and drawing inferences.

**eliciting effect.** A type of imitative behavior in which the observer does not copy the model's responses but simply behaves in a related manner.

**empathic understanding.** Sensitivity to and awareness of the feelings, motives, attitudes, and values of others.

**enactive.** Bruner's first stage of cognitive development, in which children understand the environment through physical action on that environment.

**encoding.** The *short-term memory* process of transforming incoming information into episodic or semantic form and associating it with old knowledge for storage in *long-term memory*.

**entry behavior.** The knowledge, skills, or attitudes that a learner brings into a new learning situation.

**episodic memory.** Information in *long-term memory* that is stored in the form of images.

**equilibration.** A motivation principle in Piaget's theory that identifies humans as active and exploratory in attempting to impose order and meaningfulness on experiences. This order or balance occurs through the processes of *assimilation* and *accommodation*.

**equivalent forms.** Forms having nearly the same level of difficulty. Two tests are equivalent forms if, for example, the items are different on each test, or form, but all items are representative of the same universe of test items. They are a measure of *reliability*.

**evaluation.** The process of obtaining information to form judgments so that educational decisions can be made.

**exceptional.** A term describing children whose performance deviates from the norm—above or below—to the extent that special education is needed.

**executive processes.** The part of the information processing system, based on *metacognition*, that controls the flow of information and implements *cognitive strategies* to reach a learning goal.

**experimental group.** A group receiving special treatment in an experimental study.

**experimental research.** An investigation that explores cause-and-effect relationships.

**expressive objectives.** Eisner's approach in which teachers define learning activities for students but do not specify exactly what the students might learn from these activities. Eisner believes that it is not always possible to predict the outcome of activities.

**external locus of control.** A feeling that one has little control over one's fate, and the failure to perceive a cause-and-effect relationship between actions and consequences.

**extinction.** In *operant conditioning*, the gradual disappearance of reinforcing events that maintain a behavior. In *classical conditioning*, extinction results when a *conditioned stimulus* is no longer paired with an *unconditioned stimulus*.

**extrinsic motivation.** Motivation influenced by external events such as grades, points, or money.

**factor analysis.** A statistical technique that groups responses on a test instrument into several categories, or factors. Guilford used factor analysis in developing the *Structure of Intellect* model.

**fading.** The gradual removal of *prompts* so that the learner can respond to a *discriminative stimulus* ($S^D$) without additional assistance.

**field-dependent.** A *cognitive style* in which the individual operates in a global manner and is distracted by, or sensitive to, background elements.

**field-independent.** A *cognitive style* in which the individual is capable of overcoming the effects of distracting elements (the field) when attempting to differentiate relevant aspects of a particular situation.

**fixed-interval schedule.** A *reinforcement* schedule in which a predetermined, fixed-time interval must occur between each reinforced response regardless of the number of responses the subject makes.

**fixed-ratio schedule.** A schedule of *reinforcement* in which a predetermined, fixed number of responses must occur between each reinforced response.

**formal operations stage.** Piaget's final stage of cognitive development, characterized by children's increasing ability to employ logical thought processes.

**formative test; formative evaluation.** The measurement of student achievement before or during instruction for the purpose of planning instruction or assessing student progress.

free recall. A type of *rote learning* in which information is recalled without any specific order or association with other stimuli.

frequency distribution. A table that summarizes how often each score on a test occurs.

gifted and talented. A category in special education that defines individuals who give evidence of high-performance capability in certain areas. These areas include intellectual ability, creative ability, specific academic competence, leadership ability, or special talent in the performing and visual arts. These students may require educational services or activities not ordinarily provided by the school.

goal structure. The way in which students relate to one another and to the teacher while working toward the attainment of instructional goals. Three widely used goal structures are cooperative, competitive, and individualistic.

grade-equivalent score. A score expressed in terms of the school-grade placement of students whose *raw scores* are typical of students at that particular grade level. For example, a grade-equivalent score of 4.5 means that the student's raw score is average for students in the fifth month of the fourth grade.

group contingency. A rule that specifies exactly how a consequence, positive or negative, is applied to a group.

handicapped. A term describing children who have a physical disability or behavioral characteristic so severe that they are hindered in school situations and require special help to profit from instruction.

hearing-impaired. Having a hearing loss significant enough to require special education or training. The term includes both deaf and hard-of-hearing persons.

hemisphericity. The identification of the two halves of the human brain. The two halves appear to control different functions, although they are connected and work together. For most people the right hemisphere, or half, of the brain appears to be involved with spatial relations, imagery, and nonverbal problem solving. The left side is involved with verbal abilities and sequential processing.

heritability. The extent to which differences in a trait (e.g., intelligence) are attributed to inheritance.

hierarchy of needs. Maslow's classification of human needs.

hypothesis. A statement about the relationship among variables.

hypothetico-deductive reasoning. The ability to formulate many alternative hypotheses in dealing with a problem and to check data against each of the hypotheses to make an appropriate decision.

i +1. Krashen's term for the distance between actual language development (represented by i) and potential language development (represented by i +1).

iconic. The form of children's representation of knowledge in Bruner's second level of cognitive development, in which children begin to form concrete mental images of their environment.

identity. An operation involving recognition that physical substances retain their volume or quantity, even when moved or reorganized, as long as nothing is added or taken away.

identity achievement. Described by Marcia as one of the four alternative states during Erikson's identity versus role confusion stage. The adolescent has a strong sense of commitment to life choices after careful consideration of options.

**identity diffusion.** Described by Marcia as one of the four alternative states during Erikson's identity versus role confusion stage. The adolescent has not made any firm commitments to any ideology, occupation, or interpersonal relationship and is not currently thinking about such commitments.

**identity foreclosure.** Described by Marcia as one of the four alternative states during Erikson's identity versus role confusion stage. The adolescent selects a convenient set of beliefs and goals without carefully considering the alternatives. An example would be accepting one's parents' choice of life-style and career without considering other options.

**identity moratorium.** Described by Marcia as one of the four alternative states during Erickson's identity versus role confusion stage. The adolescent considers alternative choices, experiences different roles, but has made no final decision regarding his or her identity.

**I-messages.** Gordon's strategy for changing student behavior, in which a teacher describes the problem behavior, the concrete effect the behavior is having on the teacher, and the way the behavior makes the teacher feel.

**imitation.** See *observational learning*.

**impulsive.** A dimension of *conceptual tempo*, describing rapid responders who make a moderate number of errors.

**independent variable.** A variable that is manipulated or modified in an experimental study.

**index of difficulty.** The ratio of the number of students who answered an item correctly divided by the total number of students tested. It is used in *item analysis*.

**index of item discrimination.** A measure used in *item analysis*, determined by subtracting the proportion of high scorers who answered an item correctly from the proportion of low scorers who answered correctly. High and low scorers are usually determined by the top and bottom thirds of the distribution.

**individual intelligence test.** An intelligence test administered to one individual at a time by a trained specialist.

**individualized education program (IEP).** A written document that details a yearly instructional plan for a handicapped child. It is required by federal law.

**information processing.** The study of specific thinking processes that underlie intelligent behavior or *cognition*.

**information processing system.** The cognitive structure through which information flows, is controlled, and is transformed during the process of learning.

**inhibitory-disinhibitory effect.** A type of imitative behavior resulting either in the suppression (inhibition) or appearance (disinhibition) of previously acquired behavior.

**inquiry learning.** A process that is similar to *discovery learning*. Students learn strategies to manipulate and process information, test hypotheses, and apply their conclusions to new content or situations.

**instructional objectives.** See *behavioral objectives*.

**intelligence.** The capacity or set of capacities that allows an individual to learn, to solve problems, and/or to interact successfully with his or her environment.

**intelligence quotient (IQ).** A term originally defined as an individual's mental age divided by his or her chronological age. It is rarely used in this sense today. The term "IQ" is still used to mean an intelligence test score.

**internal locus of control.** A feeling of control over one's fate, and the belief that effort and reward are correlated.

**intrinsic motivation.** Motivation influenced by personal factors such as satisfaction or enjoyment.

**item analysis.** The process of evaluating single test items in respect to certain characteristics. See *index of difficulty; index of item discrimination*.

**jigsaw method.** A procedure that emphasizes and reinforces cooperation among students.

**key-word method.** A *mnemonic* formed by associating the two parts of a *paired associate* through the use of visual imagery.

**Kohlberg's stages of moral reasoning.** A theory of moral development based on three levels of moral reasoning, each of which has substages.

**language disorder.** Difficulties with the linguistic code or rules and conventions for linking symbols and symbol sequences.

**latchkey children.** Children or adolescents who are without supervision for long periods of time before or after school.

**law of effect.** Thorndike's finding that the connections between stimuli and responses are strengthened by satisfying outcomes.

**law of exercise.** Thorndike's finding that the repetition of a learned response strengthens the bond between the stimulus situation and the response.

**learned helplessness.** A situation in which individuals learn over time, through constant failure, that they cannot control the outcome of events affecting their lives.

**learning.** A process by which behavior is either modified or changed through experience or training.

**learning disabilities.** A wide variety of disorders in which a student has learning problems that cannot be attributed to emotional difficulties, retardation, or sensory impairment.

**learning, or cognitive, strategies.** Techniques or methods students use to help them learn, including *affective, comprehension-monitoring, elaboration, organizational,* and *rehearsal strategies*.

**learning style.** Individual differences that influence learning in classroom situations. It is similar to *cognitive style*.

**least restrictive educational environment.** The educational setting most like the regular classroom in which an individual can succeed.

**lesson plan.** A detailed outline of the objectives, content, procedures, and evaluation of a single instructional period.

**linear program.** Programmed material presented in a manner so that all learners progress through the material in the same order.

**loci method.** A *mnemonic* involving the association of each item of a *serial recall* task with a particular location in a mental image created by the learner.

**locus of control.** Individuals' perception of who or what is responsible for the outcome of events and behavior in their lives.

**long-term memory (LTM).** The part of the *information processing system* that retains encoded information for long periods.

**mainstreaming.** The return to the regular classroom, for all or part of the school day, of exceptional children previously educated in self-contained, special classrooms.

**massed practice.** *Rote-learning* trials that are grouped into long, massive practice periods.

**mastery learning.** An instructional strategy that allows students to study material until they master it. It uses alternative instructional materials and diagnostic tests.

**matrix notes.** A system of note taking in which the student fills in information in the cells created by vertical and horizontal headings.

**mean.** The arithmetic average of a group of scores. The mean can be distorted by extreme scores. It is a *measure of central tendency*.

**meaningful learning.** The learning of concepts, procedures, or ideas from sources such as textbooks and lectures.

**measurement.** The process of assigning numbers to behavior according to certain rules or specifications to determine individual differences in the behavioral characteristic being measured.

**measures of central tendency.** Statistical measures that are intended to describe the typical score of a distribution. The three measures of central tendency are the *mean, median,* and *mode.*

**median.** A *measure of central tendency* defined as the middle score in the distribution. Half of the scores lie above the median and half lie below the median.

**mental age.** A concept used in intelligence testing as a basis for determining the level of an individual's mental functioning. Mental age is based on the number of questions answered correctly by one individual compared with other individuals of the same age.

**mental retardation.** A significantly subaverage general intellectual function existing concurrently with deficits in adaptive behavior and manifested during the developmental period.

**metacognition.** Knowledge of one's own cognitive processes and ability to regulate these processes.

**minimal brain damage.** A term used by some specialists, who subscribe to the controversial belief that learning disabled children suffer from some form of brain injury.

**minimum competency testing; minimum competency standards.** A testing program designed to evaluate the mastery of specified academic knowledge before granting promotion to the next grade level or graduation from high school.

**mnemonics.** Techniques that impose a useful link between new data and visual images or semantic knowledge. Mnemonics are useful for improving *serial recall* or *paired-associate learning.*

**mode.** A *measure of central tendency* that is defined as the most frequently occurring score.

**modeling.** A type of learning in which individuals observe and then imitate the behavior of others.

**moral dilemmas.** Problem situations that require individuals to make decisions that are used to assess their level of moral development.

**motherese.** A language used by caretakers who wish to communicate with their children. It involves the simplification of speech by using short, slow, and repetitive phrases.

**multicultural education.** An educational reform and process whose major goal is to change educational institutions so that male and female students; *exceptional* students; and students from all ethnic, cultural, and racial groups have an equal chance to achieve academically in school.

**negative reinforcement.** The termination of an unpleasant condition following a desired response. The termination serves to reinforce the desired response.

**negative transfer.** Increased difficulty in learning caused by a task's having stimuli similar to, but responses different from, a previously learned task.

**Nonstandard English.** An English dialect that deviates from the standard pronunciation, vocabulary, and grammar.

**normal distribution (curve).** A symmetric distribution of test scores in which most scores lie in the center, and scores decline in frequency as they move away from the center.

**norm-referenced evaluation.** A rating based on an individual's performance when compared to the performance of others on the same test.

**norm-referenced measurement; norm-referenced testing.** See *norm-referenced evaluation*.

**norms.** Test results from a sample of students similar to those who will take the test. For teachers to compare their students with the norming sample, the students must be similar in background to the normative group.

**object permanence.** Piaget's term for children's understanding that objects continue to exist apart from the children's perception of them.

**observational learning.** A process in which responses are learned by observing the behavior of others. It is sometimes called *modeling* or *imitation*.

**open education.** A type of teaching in which students have a great deal of choice about what work to do and about when and how they do the work. It is also called "open classroom."

**operant.** A term used by Skinner to describe responses not elicited by any known stimulus. Such behaviors as walking or writing a letter are operants because no known specific stimulus elicits them. It contrasts with *respondent*.

**operant conditioning.** A type of learning that involves an increase in the probability that a response will occur as a function of *reinforcement*.

**operations.** Actions implemented as the result of logical mental thought processes rather than through physical manipulations.

**organization.** Piaget's term for the ability of organisms to systematize, or organize, their physical and psychological processes into coherent systems.

**organizational strategies.** *Learning strategies* that impose structure on material via hierarchical and other relationships among the material's parts.

**overlapping.** The ability of a teacher to do two or more things at once.

**overlearning.** Continuing practice or drill after a student reaches the desired level of performance.

**paired-associate learning.** A type of *rote learning* referring to recall of information associated with a stimulus, such as remembering the capital city for each state in the United States.

**part learning.** The process of breaking up a large learning task into smaller segments for easier learning.

**pattern-recognition knowledge.** *Procedural knowledge* having to do with the recognition of patterns of stimuli. Two important types of pattern-recognition skills are identifying examples of a concept and recognizing the conditions calling for the execution of an *action sequence*.

**peg-word method.** The formation of a *mnemonic* by the association of a series of visual images with *serial recall* information.

**percentile rank.** The percentage of scores equal to or lower than a given score in a distribution.

**permissive parenting style.** A method of child rearing in which parents make few demands on their children, allowing them to regulate their own behavior.

**Personalized System of Instruction.** An individually based, student-paced form of *mastery learning* developed by Keller. It involves five features: self-pacing, unit mastery, a minimum of lecturers, an emphasis on written assignments, and the use of proctors.

**person-centered education.** An approach to instruction, favored by Rogers, that focuses on individual feelings, attitudes, and values. Students are given a great deal of choice in deciding what and how they want to learn.

**placement evaluation.** A process of determining performance at the beginning of instruction to decide where a student should begin in the instructional sequence.

**positive reinforcement.** A procedure that maintains or increases the rate of a response by presenting a stimulus (a positive reinforcer) following the response.

**positive transfer.** Facilitation of learning that occurs when a new learning task involves the same stimuli and responses as a previously learned task.

**Premack's principle.** A principle that states that contingent access to preferred activities serves as a reinforcer for the performance of low-frequency behaviors. "If you eat your vegetables (low-frequency behavior), you can go out and play (preferred activity)."

**preoperational stage.** The second stage in Piaget's theory of cognitive development, in which the lack of logical operations forces children to make decisions based on their perceptions.

**primary reinforcement.** The process of using a stimulus that is reinforcing in the absence of any learning. Such stimuli as food and water are primary reinforcers.

**proactive inhibition.** An explanation for the forgetting that takes place when previous learning interferes with the retention of new information.

**procedural knowledge.** Knowledge about how to do things, composed of *pattern-recognition* and *action-sequence* knowledge.

**products.** A term used by Guilford to describe the result of applying different operations to different contents.

**programmed instruction.** An instructional procedure in which material is arranged in a particular sequence and in small steps, or frames. Programs require the learners to respond, and provide them with immediate knowledge of results.

**prompting.** The presentation of an additional stimulus (e.g., a cue) to increase the probability that an appropriate response will be made in the presence of a *discriminative stimulus* ($S^D$).

**propositional reasoning.** The ability to deal with statements or propositions that describe concrete data. This type of thinking occurs during the *formal operations stage*.

**prosocial behavior.** The demonstration of positive social behavior such as helping, sharing, and cooperating.

**psychometric.** An approach to the study of intelligence that uses statistical procedures to identify the factors or mental structures (e.g., reasoning and spatial ability) that are responsible for individual differences on tests.

**psychomotor domain.** Objectives involving physical ability.

**psychosocial crises.** Erikson's psychological tasks, or dilemmas, which have their roots in the demands of society and which individuals experience over the course of their lives.

**psychosocial moratorium.** A period of delay granted by society to someone not ready to meet obligations. The fact that adolescents are not held responsible for all their behavior is an example of a psychosocial moratorium.

**puberty.** The biological changes that lead to reproductive maturity. Its onset is identified by such factors as the growth of body hair, voice changes in males, and menstruation and breast development in females.

**punishment.** A procedure in which an aversive stimulus is presented immediately following a response, resulting in a reduction in the rate of response.

**range of scores.** A measure of dispersion calculated by subtracting the highest and lowest scores in a distribution.

**raw score.** A test score that identifies the number of correct responses.

**Reality Therapy (RT).** A counseling approach by Glasser based on the principle that human problems arise when the primary needs of love and worth go unfulfilled.

**reciprocal determinism.** The mutual influence of the individual and the environment on each other.

**reflective.** A dimension of *conceptual tempo*. Slow responders who tend to make few errors are considered to be reflective.

**regular education initiative.** An attempt to restructure special education so that the regular classroom would serve as the primary setting for special education services. A regular education initiative also attempts to include all special needs students (e.g., economically disadvantaged and non-English-speaking) in one basic program rather than establishing separate programs for each type of need.

**rehearsal strategies.** The process of repeating information over and over in *short-term memory* in order to retain it.

**reinforcement.** See *negative reinforcement; positive reinforcement*.

**reinforcing stimulus.** A stimulus used as a reinforcer. A reinforcer is defined solely by the fact that it increases or maintains the behavior upon which it is contingent.

**reliability.** The extent to which a test is consistent in measuring what it is supposed to measure.

**resource room.** A special education classroom to which students come from regular classes to receive academic help to remediate their particular learning problems.

**respondent.** A term used by Skinner in contrast to the term *operant*. A respondent is a response that is elicited by a known stimulus and requires no previous learning.

**response cost.** The removal of previously earned tokens or points in a *token economy* intervention program.

**response generalization.** A condition whereby a behavior becomes more probable in the presence of a stimulus or situation as a result of a similar behavior having been strengthened in the presence of that stimulus or situation.

**retroactive inhibition.** The interference of new material with the retention of previously learned material.

**reversibility.** In Piaget's theory, the process of performing an action and then restoring the original condition.

**reward.** An object, stimulus, or outcome that is perceived as being pleasant and may be reinforcing.

**rote learning.** The learning of disconnected or arbitrary verbal material (e.g., a list of states and their capitals or the U.S. presidents in chronological order). It includes *free recall, paired-associate learning*, and *serial recall*.

**schemata.** Cognitive structures created through the abstraction of previous experience. Schemata function in the comprehension and recall of data and can aid learning or be responsible for many types of distortion in recall.

**secondary reinforcement.** A process that uses a stimulus that is not originally reinforcing but that acquires reinforcing properties when paired with a primary reinforcer. Money is a secondary reinforcer.

**self-actualization.** Maslow's term for the psychological need to develop one's capabilities and potential in order to enhance personal growth.

**self-concept.** The total organization of the perceptions individuals have of themselves. See *self-esteem.*

**self-efficacy.** The belief that one can successfully execute the behavior required to produce a particular outcome.

**self-esteem.** The value, or judgment, individuals place on their behavior. Self-esteem and *self-concept* are often used interchangeably in educational literature.

**self-fulfilling prophecy.** A phenomenon in which a teacher's expectations lead to differential behavior by the teacher toward certain students; the teacher's attitude may help produce the "expected" behavior in the students.

**self-reinforcement.** A procedure in which individuals reinforce their own behavior.

**semantic memory.** Verbal information stored in *long-term memory.* Semantic memory is composed of *declarative knowledge* and *procedural knowledge.*

**sensorimotor stage.** Piaget's first stage of intellectual development, in which the child moves from the reflexive activities of reaching, grasping, and sucking to more highly organized forms of activity.

**serializing.** The process of ordering objects in terms of one or more properties (e.g., placing objects in a series from small to large).

**serial position effect.** The process by which the position of material in a list affects the ease with which the material can be recalled. A person is more likely to remember information placed at the beginning (primacy effect) or at the end (recency effect) of a list than information placed in the middle.

**serial recall.** A type of *rote learning*—specifically, recall of ordered information, such as the names, in chronological order, of the U.S. presidents.

**set effect.** The failure to process important information as a result of the automatic execution of an *action sequence.*

**shaping.** A technique whereby individuals are taught to perform complex behaviors that were not previously in their repertoire. The method involves analyzing the desired behavior and dividing it into small, easily identifiable behaviors that can be readily reinforced. It is also termed "successive approximations."

**short-term memory (STM).** The part of the *information processing system* in which conscious mental activity is carried out. Information is held in short-term memory for only a few seconds.

**short-term sensory store (STSS).** The part of the *information processing system* that briefly stores information from the senses.

**signal continuity.** The ability of a teacher to move lessons along at a brisk pace and to alert students to what they should attend to.

**significant difference.** A difference based on a level of probability (e.g., $p < .01$) established before an investigation begins.

**social learning theory.** Bandura's theory to explain learning in naturalistic settings. The theory explains how individuals acquire complex skills and abilities through observing the behavior of others.

**socioeconomic status (SES).** A ranking to determine social position in a society. In the United States, SES is determined by objective indices such as father's and/or mother's occupation, father's and/or mother's educational background, and the family's material resources (e.g., what the family owns). Sometimes the more subjective term—"social class"—is used to describe high or low status to individuals.

**sociolinguistics.** The study of language in its social context.

speech disorder. Problems associated with production of the oral symbols of language.

split-half reliability. A method of *reliability* obtained by correlating the odd and even items on a test and then applying the Spearman-Brown correction formula. Reliability of the total test = 2 × reliability for odd items divided by 1 + reliability for even items.

spontaneous recovery. The re-emergence of behavior after a period of *extinction*.

SQ3R system. A system for improving comprehension and retention of text material. Students are encouraged to Survey the material, develop Questions about it, Read and then Review the text, and, finally, practice Recalling the important points of the text.

standard deviation. A measure of the spread of scores around the *mean* of the distribution.

standard error of measurement. An estimate of the amount of error in a test score.

standardized test. A test commercially prepared by measurement experts who have carefully studied all test items used in a large number of schools.

standard score. A score described in terms of *standard deviation* units from the *mean* of the distribution.

stanines. Intervals on a nine-point scale of *standard scores*.

stimulus generalization. A process whereby once a particular *conditioned stimulus* is associated with a response, other, similar stimuli are able to elicit the response.

stress. An unpleasant personal condition produced by a stimulus situation.

Structure of Intellect. Guilford's organization of *intelligence* into three major factors—*operations, contents, and products*.

successive approximations. See *shaping*.

summative test; summative evaluation. The measurement of student achievement at the end of an instructional unit.

symbolic. Bruner's highest level of knowledge representation and thinking, in which the individual can deal with abstract concepts.

table of specifications. A two-way chart that relates desired learning outcomes to course content; helps ensure *content validity* in planning test questions.

task analysis. The identification of the subordinate skills and knowledge that learners must acquire in order to achieve an educational objective.

Taxonomy of Educational Objectives. A classification system developed by Bloom that divides objectives into two domains: *cognitive* and *affective*. A third domain—*psychomotor*—has been developed by other individuals.

teacher efficacy. The belief, held by many teachers, that they have the ability to educate all types of students.

teacher expectations. Inferences made by teachers about their students' present and future academic achievement and classroom behavior.

teacher-made test. An *achievement test* constructed by classroom teachers to measure the specific goals or objectives of particular courses.

teaching. A system of actions intended to induce learning.

teaching machine. A mechanical device incorporating a programmed learning format.

test. A measurement containing a series of questions, each of which has a correct answer.

test-retest reliability. A type of *reliability* measure obtained by administering the same test a second time, after a short interval, and correlating the two sets of scores.

**test-wiseness training.** A program to teach students general test-taking skills for use on any test.

**time-on-task.** The time a student spends actually engaged in an academic task.

**time-out.** A behavioral control method that involves removal of a disruptive student from the classroom or to an isolated part of the classroom.

**token economy.** Reinforcing students through the use of *behavior modification* procedures—specifically, by supplying tokens that can later be exchanged for some reinforcement.

**transductive reasoning.** Piaget's term to describe thought in the *preoperational stage* when the child moves from the particular to the particular without touching on the general (i.e., the child sees a relationship between particular instances when in fact there is none).

**T score.** A *standard score* in a distribution with a *mean* of 50 and a *standard deviation* of 10.

**unconditioned response.** The unlearned, biological reaction evoked by an *unconditioned stimulus*.

**unconditioned stimulus.** A stimulus that naturally elicits a particular response.

**unit plan.** A detailed outline for a series of interrelated *lesson plans* on a particular topic of study that lasts from two to four weeks.

**validity.** The appropriateness of the interpretation of a test score with regard to a particular use.

**values clarification.** A humanistic approach to moral education designed to help individuals to understand the relationship between their beliefs and their behavior and to become more aware of their values.

**variability.** The spread, or dispersion, of scores in a distribution.

**variable-interval schedule.** A schedule providing *reinforcement* following the first correct response after different lapses of time.

**variable-ratio schedule.** A schedule of *reinforcement* in which a predetermined number of responses, varied from one time to another, must occur between each reinforced response.

**vicarious reinforcement.** Observation of positive consequences received by another person or model that leads to matching behavior by the learner. A teacher uses vicarious reinforcement to modify behavior when he or she states to the class: "Look how well row No. 1 has cleaned up their desks" and the rest of the rows begin cleaning their desks.

**visual impairment.** A difficulty in clearly distinguishing forms or discriminating details by sight at a specified distance, resulting in the need for special methods and materials.

**wait-time.** The period of time that a teacher waits for a student to respond to a question.

**with-it-ness.** A teacher's ability to communicate to students that he or she knows what is happening in the classroom.

**working memory.** A term for *short-term memory* that emphasizes the function of STM in conscious mental work, such as solving math problems.

**zone of proximal development.** Vygotsky's description for the difference between an individual's current level of development and his or her potential level of development.

**z score.** A *standard score* in a distribution with a mean of 0 and a *standard deviation* of 1.

# References

Abramson, L., Seligman, M., & Teasdale, J. (1978). Learned helplessness in humans: Critique and reformulation. *Journal of Abnormal Psychology, 87*, 49–74.

Abramson, M., Willson, V., Yoshida, R. K., & Hagerty, G. (1983). Parents' perceptions of their learning disabled child's educational performance. *Learning Disability Quarterly, 6*, 184–194.

Adams, M. J. (1989). Thinking skills curricula: Their promise and progress. *Educational Psychologist, 24*, 25–77.

Adler, S. (1979). *Poverty children and their language.* New York: Grune & Stratton.

Ahrons, C. R., & Rodgers, R. H. (1987). *Divorced families: A multidisciplinary view.* New York: Norton.

Aiken, E. G., Thomas, G. S., & Shennum, W. A. (1975). Memory for a lecture: Effects of notes, lecture rate and information density. *Journal of Educational Psychology, 67*, 439–444.

Ainsworth, N. (1984). The cultural shaping of oral discourse. *Theory into Practice, 23*, 132–137.

Airasian, P. W., & Madaus, G. J. (1972). Functional types of student evaluation. *Measurement and Evaluation in Guidance, 4*, 221–233.

Alatis, J. E., & Staczek, J. J. (Eds.). (1985). *Perspectives on bilingualism and bilingual education.* Washington, DC: Georgetown University Press.

Alberto, P., & Troutman, A. C. (1990). *Applied behavior analysis for teachers: Influencing student performance* (3rd ed.). Columbus, OH: Merrill.

Allen, D., & Seifman, E. (Eds.). (1971). *The teacher's handbook.* Glenview, IL: Scott, Foresman.

Almy, M. (1969). *Ways of studying children.* New York: Teachers College Press.

Ambert, A. N., & Melendez, S. E. (1985). *Bilingual education: A sourcebook.* New York: Garland.

Ames, C. (1981). Competitive versus cooperative reward structures: The influence of individual and group performance factors on achievement attributions and affect. *American Educational Research Journal, 73*, 411–418.

Ames, C. (1987). The enhancement of student motivation. In M. L. Maehr & D. A. Kleiber (Eds.), *Advances in motivation and achievement: Enhancing motivation* (Vol. 5). Greenwich, CT: JAI Press.

Ames, C. (1990). Motivation: What teachers need to know. *Teachers College Record, 91,* 409–421.

Ames, C., & Ames, R. (1981). Competitive versus individualistic goal structures: The salience of past performance information for causal attributions and affect. *Journal of Educational Psychology, 73,* 411–418.

Ames, C., & Ames, R. (1985). Goal structures and motivation. *Elementary School Journal, 85,* 40–51.

Ames, C., & Archer, J. (1988). Achievement goals in the classroom: Students' learning strategies and motivation processes. *Journal of Educational Psychology, 80,* 260–267.

Ames, C., & Felker, D. W. (1979). Effects of self-concept on children's causal attributions and self-reinforcement. *Journal of Educational Psychology, 71,* 613–619.

Ames, R., & Ames, C. (Eds.). (1984). *Research on motivation in education: Vol. 1. Student motivation.* Orlando, FL: Academic Press.

Ames, R., & Ames, C. (1990). Student motivation in the classroom. In B. F. Jones & L. Idol (Eds.), *Dimensions of thinking and cognitive instruction: Implications for educational reform* (Vol. 2). Hillsdale, NJ: Erlbaum.

Anderson, J. R. (1982). Acquisition of cognitive skill. *Psychological Review, 89,* 369–406.

Anderson, J. R. (1983). Cognitive styles and multicultural populations. *Journal of Teacher Education, 29,* 2–9.

Anderson, J. R. (1985). *Cognitive psychology and its implications.* New York: Freeman.

Anderson, L. M., Brubaker, N. L., Alleman-Brooks, J., & Duffy, G. G. (1984). *Making seatwork work* (Research Series No. 142). Institute for Research on Teaching. East Lansing: Michigan State University.

Anderson, L. M., Evertson, C., & Brophy, J. (1979). An experimental study of effective teaching first-grade reading groups. *Elementary School Journal, 71,* 193–223.

Anderson, R. C., & Biddle, W. B. (1975). On asking people questions about what they are reading. In G. H. Bower (Ed.), *Psychology of learning and motivation* (Vol. 9). New York: Academic Press.

Anderson, T. H., & Armbruster, B. B. (1984). Studying. In P. D. Pearson (Ed.), *Handbook of reading research.* White Plains, NY: Longman.

Andre, T., & Phye, G. D. (1986). Cognition, learning, and education. In G. D. Phye & T. Andre (Eds.), *Cognitive classroom learning: Understanding, thinking, and problem solving.* New York: Academic Press.

Andre, T., & Thieman, A. (1988). Level of adjunct question, type of feedback, and learning concepts by reading. *Contemporary Educational Psychology, 13,* 296–307.

Andrews, G. R., & Debus, R. L. (1978). Persistence and the causal perception of failure: Modifying cognitive attributions. *Journal of Educational Psychology, 70,* 154–166.

Arlin, M. (1984). Time, equality, and mastery learning. *Review of Educational Research, 54,* 65–86.

Armbruster, B. B. (1986). Schema theory and the design of content-area textbooks. *Educational Psychologist, 2,* 253–267.

Arnold, R. (1968). The achievements of boys and girls taught by men and women teachers. *Elementary School Journal, 68,* 367–371.

Aronson, E., & Carlsmith, J. (1962). Performance expectancy as a determinant of actual performance. *Journal of Abnormal and Social Psychology, 65,* 178–182.

Ashton, P. T., & Webb, R. B. (1986). *Making a difference: Teachers' sense of efficacy and student achievement.* White Plains, NY: Longman.

Aspy, D. N. (1972). An investigation into the relationship between teachers' actual knowledge of learning theory and their classroom performance. *Journal of Teacher Education*, 23, 21–24.

Atkinson, J. W. (1964). *An introduction to motivation*. Princeton, NJ: Van Nostrand.

Atkinson, J. W., & Feather, N. T. (1966). *A theory of achievement motivation*. New York: Wiley.

Atkinson, R. C. (1975). Mnemotechnics in second-language learning. *American Psychologist*, 30, 821–828.

Au, K. H., & Mason, J. M. (1981). Social organizational factors in learning to read: The balance of rights hypothesis. *Reading Research Quarterly*, 17, 115–152.

Ausubel, D. P. (1968). *Educational psychology: A cognitive view*. New York: Holt, Rinehart and Winston.

Baer, D. M., Peterson, R. F., & Sherman, J. A. (1967). The development of imitation by reinforcing behavioral similarity to a model. *Journal of the Experimental Analysis of Behavior*, 10, 405–416.

Baer, D. M., Wolf, M. M., & Risley, T. R. (1968). Some current dimensions of applied behavior analysis. *Journal of Applied Behavior Analysis*, 1, 91–97.

Bailey, D. B., & Worley, M. (1984). *Teaching infants and preschoolers with handicaps*. Columbus, OH: Merrill.

Bandura, A. (1967, March). Behavioral psychotherapy. *Scientific American*, pp. 78–86.

Bandura, A. (1969). *Principles of behavior modification*. New York: Holt, Rinehart and Winston.

Bandura, A. (1977). *Social learning theory*. Englewood Cliffs, NJ: Prentice-Hall.

Bandura, A. (1982). Self-efficacy mechanism in human agency. *American Psychologist*, 37, 122–147.

Bandura, A. (1986). *Social foundations of thought and action: A social cognitive theory*. Englewood Cliffs, NJ: Prentice-Hall.

Bandura, A., Grusec, J., & Menlove, F. (1967). Vicarious extinction of avoidance behavior. *Journal of Personality and Social Psychology*, 5, 16–23.

Bandura, A., & Kupers, C. J. (1964). The transmission of patterns of self-reinforcement through modeling. *Journal of Abnormal and Social Psychology*, 69, 1–9.

Bandura, A., & Perloff, B. (1967). Relative efficacy of self-monitored and externally imposed reinforcement systems. *Journal of Personality and Social Psychology*, 7, 111–116

Bandura, A., & Walters, R. H. (1963). *Social learning and personality development*. New York: Holt, Rinehart and Winston.

Bangert-Drowns, R. L., Kulik, J. A., & Kulik, C. C. (1983). Effects of coaching programs on achievement test performance. *Review of Educational Research*, 55, 571–585.

Bangert-Drowns, R. L., Kulik, J. A., & Kulik, C. C. (1985, April). *Effectiveness of computer-based education in secondary schools*. Paper presented at the annual meeting of the American Educational Research Association, Chicago.

Bank, B., Biddle, B., & Good, T. L. (1980). Sex roles, classroom instruction, and reading achievement. *Journal of Educational Psychology*, 72, 119–132.

Banks, J. A. (1989). Multicultural education: Characteristics and goals. In J. A. Banks & C. M. McGee Banks (Eds.), *Multicultural education: Issues and perspectives*. Boston: Allyn & Bacon.

Barnes, B., & Clawson, E. (1975). Do advance organizers facilitate learning? Recommendations for further research based on the analysis of thirty-two studies. *Review of Educational Research*, 45, 637–659.

Barnett, W. S. (1985). Benefit-cost analysis of the Perry Preschool Program and its policy implications. *Educational Evaluation and Policy Analysis, 7,* 333–342.

Baron, R. M., Tom, D., & Cooper, H. M. (1985). Social class, race and teacher expectations. In J. Dusek (Ed.), *Teacher expectancies.* Hillsdale, NJ: Erlbaum.

Barrish, H. H., Saunders, M., & Wolf, M. M. (1969). Good behavior game: Effects of individual contingencies for group contingencies on disruptive behavior in a classroom. *Journal of Applied Behavior Analysis, 2,* 119–124.

Bar-Tal, D. (1978). Attributional analysis of achievement-related behavior. *Review of Educational Research, 48,* 259–271.

Barth, R. S. (1971). So you want to change to an open classroom? *Phi Delta Kappan, 53,* 97–99.

Bartlett, E. J. (1972). Selecting preschool language programs. In C. B. Cazden (Ed.), *Language in early childhood education.* Washington, DC: National Association for the Education of Young Children.

Bash, M. S., & Camp, B. W. (1980). Teacher training in the think aloud classroom program. In G. Cartledge & J. F. Milburn (Eds.), *Teaching social skills to children.* New York: Pergamon.

Baskin, E. J., & Hess, R. D. (1980). Does affective education work? A review of seven programs. *Journal of School Psychology, 18,* 40–50.

Battle, E., & Rotter, J. (1963). Children's feeling of personal control as related to social class and ethnic group. *Journal of Personality, 31,* 482–490.

Baumrind, D. (1966). Effects of authoritative parental control on child behavior. *Child Development, 37,* 887–907.

Baumrind, D. (1967). Child care practices anteceding three patterns of preschool behavior. *Genetic Psychology Monographs, 75,* 43–88.

Baumrind, D. (1971). Harmonious parents and their preschool children. *Developmental Psychology, 4,* 99–102.

Beal, C. R. (1989). Children's communication skills: Implications for the development of writing strategies. In C. B. McCormick, G. Miller, & M. Pressley (Eds.), *Cognitive strategy research: From basic research to educational applications.* New York: Springer-Verlag.

Beane, J. R. (1985/1986). The continuing controversy over affective education. *Educational Leadership, 43,* 26–31.

Becker, W. C., & Gersten, R. (1982). A follow-up of Follow Through: The later effects of the direct instruction model on children in fifth and sixth grades. *American Educational Research Journal, 19,* 75–92.

Becker, W. C., Madsen, C. H., Arnold, C. R., & Thomas, D. R. (1967). The contingent use of teacher attention and praise in reducing classroom behavior problems. *Journal of Special Education, 1,* 287–330.

Bee, H. (1989). *The developing child* (5th ed.). New York: Harper & Row.

Bellanca, J. A. (1977). *Grading.* NEA Professional Studies. Washington, DC: National Education Association. ERIC Report No. ED 143 673.

Belleza, F. S. (1981). Mnemonic devices: Classification, characteristics and criteria. *Review of Educational Research, 51,* 247–275.

Bell-Gredler, M. E. (1986). *Learning and instruction: Theory into practice.* New York: Macmillan

Bem, S. (1974). The measurement of psychological androgyny. *Journal of Consulting and Clinical Psychology, 42,* 155–162.

Bem, S. (1975). Sex-role adaptability: One consequence of psychological androgyny. *Journal of Personality and Social Psychology, 31,* 634–643.

Bem, S. (1981). Gender schema theory: A cognitive account of sex typing. *Psychological Review, 88*, 354–364.

Bem, S. (1984). Androgyny and gender schema theory: A conceptual and empirical integration. In T. B. Sonderegger (Ed.), *Nebraska symposium on motivation: Psychology and gender.* Lincoln: University of Nebraska Press.

Benbow, C. P., & Stanley, J. C. (1980). Sex differences in mathematical ability: Fact or artifact? *Science, 210*, 1262–1264.

Bennett, W. J. (1986). *First lessons: A report on elementary education in America.* Washington, DC: U. S. Government Printing Office.

Benninga, J. S. (1988). An emerging synthesis in moral education. *Phi Delta Kappan, 69*, 415–418.

Berdine, W. H., & Blackhurst, A. E. (Eds.). (1985). *An introduction to special education.* Boston: Little, Brown.

Berns, R. M. (1989). *Child, family, community.* New York: Holt, Rinehart and Winston.

Biehler, R. F. (1974). *Study guide: Psychology applied to teaching* (2nd ed.). Boston: Houghton Mifflin.

Bjorklund, D. F. (1989). *Children's thinking: Developmental function and individual differences.* Pacific Grove, CA: Brooks/Cole.

Black, K. N. (1979, January). What about the child from a one-parent home? *Teacher,* pp. 24–28.

Blakeslee, T. R. (1980). *The right brain: A new understanding of the unconscious mind and its creative powers.* Garden City, NY: Anchor.

Block, J. H., & Anderson, L. W. (1975). *Mastery learning in classroom instruction.* New York: Macmillan.

Block, J. H., & Burns, R. B. (1976). Mastery learning. In L. Shulman (Ed.), *Review of research in education* (Vol. 4). Itasca, IL: Peacock.

Block, J. H., Efthim, H. E., & Burns, R. B. (1989). *Building effective mastery learning schools.* White Plains, NY: Longman.

Bloom, B. S. (1968). Learning for mastery. *[UCLA-CSEIP] Evaluation Comment, 1,* 1–12.

Bloom, B. S. (1971). Affective consequences of school achievement. In J. H. Block (Ed.), *Mastery learning: Theory and practice.* New York: Holt, Rinehart and Winston.

Bloom, B. S. (1974). An introduction to mastery learning theory. In J. H. Block (Ed.), *School, society and mastery learning.* New York: Holt, Rinehart and Winston.

Bloom, B. S., Englehart, N. D., Furst, E. J., Hill, W. H., & Krathwohl, D. R. (1956). *Taxonomy of educational objectives: Handbook I. Cognitive domain.* New York: McKay.

Bluming, M., & Dembo, M. (1973). *Solving teaching problems: A guide for the elementary school teacher.* Santa Monica, CA: Goodyear.

Blyth, D. A., Simmons, R. G., & Bush, D. (1978). The transition into early adolescence: A longitudinal comparison of youth in two educational contexts. *Sociology of Education, 51*, 149–162.

Bolocofsky, D. N., & Mescher, S. (1984). Student characteristics: Using student characteristics to develop effective grading practices. *The Directive Teacher, 6*, 11–23.

Bond, L. (1989). The effects of special preparation on measures of scholastic ability. In R. L. Linn (Ed.), *Educational measurement* (3rd ed.). New York: Macmillan.

Bondy, E. (1984). Thinking about thinking: Encouraging children's use of meta-cognitive processes. *Childhood Education, 60,* 234–238.

Borg, W. R., & Gall, M. D. (1989). *Educational research: An introduction* (5th ed.). White Plains, NY: Longman.

Borko, H., & Shavelson, R. J. (1990). Teacher decision making. In B. F. Jones & L. Idol (Eds.), *Dimensions of thinking and cognitive instruction: Implications for educational reform* (Vol. 1). Hillsdale, NJ: Erlbaum.

Borkowski, J. G., Carr, M., Rellinger, E., & Pressley, M. (1990). Self-regulated cognition: Interdependence of metacognition, attributions, and self-esteem. In B. F. Jones & L. Idol (Eds.), *Dimensions of thinking and cognitive instruction: Implications for educational reform* (Vol. 1). Hillsdale, NJ: Erlbaum.

Boshes, B., & Myklebust, H. R. (1964). A neurological and behavioral study of children with learning disorders. *Neurology, 14,* 7–12.

Bouchard, T. J., Jr., & McCue, M. (1981). Familial studies of intelligence: A review. *Science, 212,* 1055–1059.

Bouvier, L. F., & Agresta, A. J. (1987). The future Asian population of the United States. In J. T. Fawcett & B. V. Carino (Eds.), *Pacific bridges: The new immigration from Asia and the Pacific Islands.* New York: Center for Migration Studies.

Boyer, E. L. (1983). *High school: A report on secondary education in America.* New York: Harper & Row.

Brainerd, C. J. (1978). The stage question in cognitive-develomental theory. *The Behavioral and Brain Sciences, 2,* 173–213.

Bransford, J. D. (1979). *Human cognition: Learning, understanding and remembering.* Belmont, CA: Wadsworth.

Brodsky, C. M. (1954). *A study of norms for body form: Behavior relationships.* Washington, DC: Catholic University of America Press.

Bronfenbrenner, U. (1974). *Longitudinal evaluations: A report on longitudinal evaluations of pre-school programs: Is early intervention effective?* (Vol. 2, Publication No. OHD 74–25). Washington, DC: Dept. of Health, Education and Welfare.

Brookover, W., Beamer, L., Efthim, H., Hathaway, D., Lezotte, L., Miller, S., Passalacqua, J., & Tornatsky, L. (1982). *Creating effective schools: An in-service program for enhancing school learning climate and achievement.* Holmes Beach, FL: Learning Publications.

Brookover, W., Patterson, A., & Thomas, S. (1965). *Improving academic achievement through students' self-concept enhancement, self-concept of ability and school achievement* (Project No. 1636). Washington, DC: U.S. Department of Health, Education and Welfare, Office of Education.

Brookover, W., Schweitzer, K., Schneider, J., Beady, C., Flood, P., Wisenbaker, J. (1978). Elementary school social climate and school achievement. *American Educational Research Journal, 15,* 301–318.

Brooks-Gunn, J., & Matthews, W. S. (1979). *He & she: How children develop their sex-role identity.* Englewood Cliffs, NJ: Prentice-Hall.

Brophy, J. E. (1979). Teacher behavior and its effects. *Journal of Educational Psychology, 71,* 733–750.

Brophy, J. E. (1981). Teacher praise: A functional analysis. *Review of Educational Research, 51,* 5–32.

Brophy, J. E. (1985a). Teacher-student interaction. In J. Dusek (Ed.), *Teacher expectancies.* Hillsdale, NJ: Erlbaum.

Brophy, J. E. (1985b). Interactions of male and female students with male and female teachers. In L. C. Wilkinson & C. B. Marrett (Eds.), *Gender influences in classroom interaction*. Orlando, FL: Academic Press.

Brophy, J. E., & Evertson, C. M. (1976). *Learning from teaching: A development perspective*. Boston: Allyn & Bacon.

Brophy, J. E., & Good, T. L. (1974). *Teacher-student relationships: Causes and consequences*. New York: Holt, Rinehart and Winston.

Brophy, J. E., & Rohrkemper, M. (1981). The influence of problem ownership on teachers' perceptions of and strategies for coping with problem students. *Journal of Educational Psychology, 73*, 295–311.

Brophy, J. E., Rohrkemper, M., Rashid, H., & Goldberger, M. (1983). Relationships between teachers' presentations of classroom tasks and students' engagement in those tasks. *Journal of Educational Psychology, 75*, 544–552.

Brown, A. L. (1980). Metacognitive development and reading. In R. J. Spiro, B. C. Bruce, & W. F. Brewer (Eds.), *Theoretical issues in reading comprehension: Perspectives from cognitive psychology, linguistics, artificial intelligence, and education*. Hillsdale, NJ: Erlbaum.

Brown, A. L., & Smiley, S. S. (1977). Rating the importance of structural units of prose passages: A problem of metacognitive development. *Child Development, 48*, 1–8.

Brown, F. G. (1983). *Principles of educational and psychological testing* (3rd ed.). New York: Holt, Rinehart and Winston.

Brown, H. D. (1987). *Principles of language learning and teaching* (2nd ed.). Englewood Cliffs, NJ: Prentice-Hall.

Bruner, J. (1960). *The process of education*. Cambridge, MA: Harvard University Press.

Bruner, J. (1961). The act of discovery. *Harvard Educational Review, 31*, 21–32.

Buenning, M., & Tollefson, N. (1987). The cultural gap hypothesis as an explanation for the achievement patterns of Mexican-American students. *Psychology in the Schools, 14*, 264–271.

Buike, S. (1980). *Teacher decision making in reading*. (Research Series No. 79). East Lansing: Michigan State University, Institute for Research on Teaching.

Buros, O. K., et al. (Eds.). (1938–1978). *Mental measurements yearbook* (Vols. 1–8). Lincoln: University of Nebraska Press.

Butterworth, R., & Alloro, D. (1986, March 21). Changing "F" to "N" only disguises the fact that a student is failing. *Los Angeles Herald Examiner*.

Caldwell, J. H., Huitt, W. G., & Graeber, A. O. (1982). Time spent in learning: Implications from research. *Elementary School Journal, 82*, 471–480.

Canter, L. (1976). *Assertive discipline: A take-charge approach for today's educator*. Seal Beach, CA: Canter and Associates.

Canter, L. (1989). Assertive discipline: A response. *Teachers College Record, 90*, 631–638.

Cardenas, J. A. (1986). The role of native-language instruction in bilingual education. *Phi Delta Kappan, 67*, 359–363.

Carin, A. A., & Sund, R. B. (1985). *Teaching science through discovery* (5th ed.). Columbus, OH: Merrill.

Carpenter, R. L., & Apter, S. (1988). Research integration of cognitive-emotional interventions for behaviorally disordered children and youth. In M. C. Wang, M. C. Reynolds, & H. J. Walberg (Eds.), *Handbook of special education: Vol 2. Mildly handicapped conditions*. New York: Pergamon.

Carroll, J. B. (1963). A model of school learning. *Teachers College Record, 64,* 723–733.

Carter, R. (1952). How valid are marks assigned by teachers? *Journal of Educational Psychology, 43,* 218–228.

Carter, T. P., & Chatfield, M. L. (1986). Effective bilingual schools: Implications for policy and practice. *American Journal of Education, 95,* 200–234.

Cartwright, G. P., Cartwright, C. A., & Ward, M. E. (1984). *Educating special learners* (2nd ed.). Belmont, CA: Wadsworth.

Casanova, U. (1987). Ethnic and cultural differences. In V. Richardson-Koehler (Ed.), *Educators' handbook: A research perspective.* White Plains, NY: Longman.

Case, R. (1985). *Intellectual development: Birth to adulthood.* New York: Academic Press.

Case, R., & Griffin, S. (1989). Child cognitive development: The role of central conceptual structures in the development of scientific and social thought. In C. A. Hauert (Ed.), *Developmental psychology: Cognitive, perceptual, motor and neurological perspectives.* Amsterdam: North Holland.

Case, R. S. (1978). Intellectual development from birth to adulthood: A neo-Piagetian interpretation. In R. W. Siegler (Ed.), *Children's thinking: What develops?* Hillsdale, NJ: Erlbaum.

Cazden, C. B., Carrasco, R., Maldonado-Guzman, A. A., & Erickson, F. (1980). The contribution of ethnographic research to bicultural-bilingual education. In J. E. Alatis (Ed.), *Current issues in bilingual education.* Washington, DC: Georgetown University Press.

Center for Social Organization of Schools (1984, November). *School uses of microcomputers: Reports from a national survey* (Issue No. 6). Baltimore: Johns Hopkins University.

Chalfant, J. (1989). Learning disabilities: Policy issues and promising approaches. *American Psychologist, 44,* 392–398.

Chapman, J. W. (1989). Learning disabled children's self-concepts. *Review of Educational Research, 58,* 347–371.

Charles, C. M. (1989). *Building classroom discipline: From models to practice* (3rd ed.). White Plains, NY: Longman.

Chase, C. I. (1974). *Measurement for educational evaluation.* Reading, MA: Addison-Wesley.

Chomsky, N. (1965). *Aspects of a theory of syntax.* Cambridge, MA: MIT Press.

Claiborn, W. (1969). Expectancy effects in the classroom: A failure to replicate. *Journal of Educational Psychology, 60,* 377–383.

Clarizio, H. F. (1980). *Toward positive classroom discipline.* New York: Wiley.

Clark, C. M., & Elmore, J. L. (1981). *Transforming curriculum in mathematics, science, and writing: A case study of teacher yearly planning* (Research Series No. 99). East Lansing: Michigan State University, Institute for Research on Teaching.

Clark, C. M., & Peterson, P. L. (1985). Teacher thought processes. In M. C. Wittrock (Ed.), *Handbook of research on teaching* (3rd ed.). New York: Macmillan.

Clark, C. M., & Yinger, R. J. (1979). *Three studies of teacher planning* (Research Series No. 55). East Lansing: Michigan State University, Institute for Research on Teaching.

Clark, R. E. (1982). Antagonism between achievement and enjoyment in ATI studies. *Educational Psychologist, 17,* 92–101.

Clark, R. E. (1983). Reconsidering research on learning from media. *Review of Educational Research, 53,* 445–459.

Clifford, M. M. (1986a). The comparative effects of strategy and effort attributions. *British Journal of Educational Psychology, 56,* 75–83.

Clifford, M. M. (1986b). The effects of ability, strategy, and effort attributions for educational, business, and athletic failures. *British Journal of Educational Psychology, 56,* 169–179.

Cohen, E. G. (1982). Expectation states and interracial interaction in school settings. *Annual Review of Sociology, 8,* 209–235.

Cohen, E. G. (1986, April). *Treating status problems in the cooperative classroom.* Paper presented at the annual meeting of the American Educational Research Association, San Francisco.

Cohen, S. (1973). Educational psychology: Practice what we preach! *Educational Psychologist, 10,* 80–86.

Cohen, S. A., Hyman, J. S., Ascroft, L., & Loveless, D. (1989, March). *Comparing effects of metacognition, learning styles, & human attributes with alignment.* Paper presented at the annual meeting of the American Educational Research Association, San Francisco.

Cole, R. (1979). Minimum competency testing for teachers: Confusion compounded. *Phi Delta Kappan, 61,* 29.

Coleman, J., Campbell, E., Hobson, C., McPartland, J., Mood, A., Weinfield, F., & York, R. (1966). *Equality of educational opportunity.* Washington, DC: U.S. Government Printing Office.

Coleman, J. S. (1961). *The adolescent society.* New York: Free Press.

Coles, G. S. (1978). The learning-disabilities test battery: Empirical and social issues. *Harvard Educational Review, 48,* 313–340.

Collins, A. M., & Quillian, M. R. (1969). Retrieval time from semantic memory. *Journal of Verbal Learning and Verbal Behavior, 8,* 240–247.

Collins, J. (1982, March). *Self-efficacy and ability in achievement behavior.* Paper presented at the annual meeting of the American Educational Research Association, New York.

Combs, A. W. (1979). *Myths in education.* Boston: Allyn & Bacon.

Combs, A. W. (1981). Humanistic education: Too tender for a tough world? *Phi Delta Kappan, 62,* 446–449.

Combs, A. W. (1982). *A personal approach to teaching: Beliefs that make a difference.* Boston: Allyn & Bacon.

Combs, A. W., & Avila, D. L. (1985). *Helping relationships: Basic concepts for the helping professions* (3rd ed.). Boston: Allyn & Bacon.

Combs, A. W., Avila, D. L., & Purkey, W. W. (1971). *Helping relationships: Basic concepts for the helping professions.* Boston: Allyn & Bacon.

Combs, A. W., Blume, R. A., Newman, A. J., & Wass, H. L. (1974). *The professional education of teachers* (2nd ed.). Boston: Allyn & Bacon.

*Congressional Record,* October 10, 1978, H-12179.

Cook, L. K., & Mayer, R. E. (1983). Reading strategies training for meaningful learning from prose. In M. Pressley and J. R. Levin (Eds.), *Cognitive strategy research: Educational applications.* New York: Springer-Verlag.

Cooper, H. (1989). *Homework.* White Plains, NY: Longman.

Cooper, J. O., Heron, T. E., & Heward, W. L. (1987). *Applied behavior analysis.* Columbus, OH: Merrill.

Coopersmith, S. (1967). *The antecedents of self-esteem.* San Francisco: Freeman.

Corno, L. (1986, April). *Self-regulated learning and classroom teaching.* Paper presented at the annual meeting of the American Educational Research Association, San Francisco.

Corno, L. (1987). Teaching and self-regulated learning. In D. C. Berliner & B. V. Rosenshine (Eds.). *Talks to teachers.* New York: Random House.

Corno, L. (1989). Self-regulated learning: A volitional analysis. In B. J. Zimmerman & D. H. Schunk (Eds.), *Self-regulated learning and academic achievement: Theory, research, and practice.* New York: Springer-Verlag.

Corrao, J., & Melton, G. B. (1988). Legal issues in school-based behavior therapy. In J. C. Witt, S. N. Elliott, & F. M. Gresham (Eds.), *Handbook of behavior therapy in education.* New York: Plenum.

Costa, A. L. (1984). A reaction to Hunter's knowing, teaching, and supervising. In P. L. Hosford (Ed.), *Using what we know about teaching.* Alexandria, VA: Association of Supervision and Curriculum Development.

Costa, A. L. (Ed.). (1985). *Developing minds: A resource book for teaching thinking.* Alexandria, VA: Association for Supervision and Curriculum Development.

Cote, R. W. (1973). Behavior modification: Some questions. *Elementary School Journal, 24,* 45–47.

Cott, A. (1972). Megavitamins: The orthomolecular approach to behavioral disorders and learning disabilities. *Academic Therapy, 7,* 245–258.

Council of State Directors of Programs for the Gifted (1987). *The 1987 state of the states Gifted and Talented Education Report.* Washington, DC.

Covington, M. V. (1983). Motivated cognitions. In S. G. Paris, G. M. Olson, & H. W. Stevenson (Eds.), *Learning and motivation in the classroom.* Hillsdale, NJ: Erlbaum.

Covington, M. V. (1984). The self-worth theory of achievement motivation: Findings and implications. *Elementary School Journal, 85,* 5–20.

Covington, M. V., & Beery, R. (1976). *Self-worth and school learning.* New York: Holt, Rinehart and Winston.

Covington, M. V., & Omelich, C. (1979). Effort: The double-edged sword in school achievement. *Journal of Educational Psychology, 71,* 169, 182.

Cox, W. F., Jr., & Dunn, T. G. (1979). Mastery learning: A psychological trap? *Educational Psychologist, 14,* 24–29.

Crandall, V. C., Katkovsky, W., & Crandall, J. J. (1965). Children's beliefs in their own control of reinforcement in intellectual-academic situations. *Child Development, 36,* 91–109.

Cronbach, L. J., & Snow, R. E. (1977). *Aptitudes and instructional methods: A handbook for research on interactions.* New York: Irvington.

Crooks, T. J. (1988). The impact of classroom evaluation practices on students. *Review of Educational Research, 58,* 438–481.

Cruickshank, D. R., & Callahan, R. C. (1983). The other side of the desk: Stages and problems of teacher development. *Elementary School Journal, 83,* 251–258.

Cummins, J. (1981). The role of primary language development in promoting educational success for language minority students. In *Schooling and language minority students: A theoretical framework.* Los Angeles: State of California, Office of Bilingual Bicultural Education.

Curwin, R., & Mendler, A. N. (1988). Packaged discipline programs: Let the buyer beware. *Educational Leadership, 46,* 68–71

Curwin, R., & Mendler, A. N. (1989). We repeat, let the buyer beware: A response to Canter. *Educational Leadership, 46,* 83.

D'Amato, J. (1986). "We cool, tha's why": *A study of personhood and place in a class of Hawaiian second graders*. Unpublished doctoral dissertation, University of Hawaii, Honolulu.

Dansereau, D. F., Collins, K. W., McDonald, B. A., Holley, C. D., Garland, J., Dickhoff, G., & Evans, S. H. (1979). Development and evaluation of a learning strategy training program. *Journal of Educational Psychology, 71,* 64–73.

Das, J. P., Kirby, J., & Jarman, R. F. (1975). Simultaneous and successive syntheses: An alternative model for cognitive abilities. *Psychological Bulletin, 82,* 87–103.

Datta, L., Schaefer, E., & Davis, M. (1968). Sex and scholastic aptitude as variables in teachers' ratings of the adjustment and classroom behavior of Negro and other seventh-grade students. *Journal of Educational Psychology, 59,* 94–101.

Davis, E. D. (1984). Should the public schools teach values? *Phi Delta Kappan, 66,* 358–362.

Davis, J. M., Wilson, M., & Sandoval, J. (1988). Strategies for the primary prevention of adolescent suicide. *School Psychology Review, 17,* 559–569.

Davis, W., & Phares, E. (1969). Parental antecedents of internal-external control of reinforcement. *Psychological Reports, 24,* 427–436.

Day, J. D., Cordon, L. A., & Kerwin, M. L. (1989). Informal instruction and development of cognitive skills: A review and critique of research. In C. B. McCormick, G. E. Miller, & M. Pressley (Eds.), *Cognitive strategy research: From basic research to educational applications.* New York: Springer-Verlag.

deBono, E. (1985). The CoRT thinking program. In J. Segal, S. Chipman, & R. Glaser (Eds.), *Thinking and learning skills: Vol. 1. Relating instruction to research.* Hillsdale, NJ: Erlbaum.

DeCecco, J. P. (1968) *The psychology of learning and instruction.* Englewood Cliffs, NJ: Prentice-Hall.

DeCharms, R. (1981). Personal causation and locus of control: Two different traditions and two uncorrelated measures. In H. M. Lefcourt (Ed.), *Research with the locus of control construct: Vol. 1. Assessment methods.* New York: Academic Press.

Deci, E. L., Nezlek, J., & Sheinman, L. (1981). Characteristics of the rewarder and intrinsic motivation of the rewardee. *Journal of Personality and Social Psychology, 40,* 1–10.

Dembo, M. H., & Gibson, S. (1985). Teachers' sense of efficacy: An important factor in school improvement. *Elementary School Journal, 86,* 173–184.

Dembo, M. H., Sweitzer, M., & Lauritzen, P. (1985). An evaluation of group parent education: Behavioral, PET, and Adlerian programs. *Review of Educational Research, 55,* 155–200.

Deno, E. (1973). *Instructional alternatives for exceptional children.* Reston, VA: Council for Exceptional Children.

Derry, S. J., & Murphy, D. A. (1986). Designing systems that train learning ability: From theory to practice. *Review of Educational Research, 56,* 1–39.

Devine, T. G. (1987). *Teaching study skills: A guide for teachers.* Boston: Allyn & Bacon.

Devin-Sheehan, L., Feldman, R. S., & Allen, V. L. (1976). Research on children tutoring children: A critical review. *Review of Educational Research, 46,* 355–358.

Deyhle, D. (1987). Learning failure: Tests as gatekeepers and the culturally different child. In H. T. Trueba (Ed.), *Success or failure? Learning and the language minority child.* Cambridge, MA: Newbury House.

Dinkmeyer, D., & McKay, G. (1976). *Systematic training for effective parenting.* Circle Pines, MN: American Guidance Service.

Divoky, D. (1988). The model minority goes to school. *Phi Delta Kappan, 70,* 219–222.

Dowling, C. (1981). *The Cinderella complex.* New York: Summit.

Doyle, W., Hancock, G., & Kifer, E. (1972). Teachers' perceptions: Do they make a difference? *Journal of the Association for the Study of Perception, 7,* 21–30.

Doyle, W., & Rutherford, B. (1984). Classroom research on matching learning and teaching styles. *Theory into Practice, 23,* 20–25.

Dreikurs, R., & Soltz, V. (1964). *Children: The challenge.* New York: Hawthorn.

Duckworth, E. (1964). Piaget rediscovered. In R. E. Ripple & V. N. Rockcastle (Eds.), *Piaget rediscovered: A report of the conference on cognitive skills and curriculum development.* Ithaca, NY: Cornell University, School of Education.

Duckworth, K. E. (1976, April). *Instructional differentiation and the institutionalization of student activity in the classroom.* Paper presented at the annual meeting of the American Educational Research Association, San Francisco.

Duffy, G. G., & Roehler, L. R. (1987). Improving reading instruction through the use of responsive elaboration. *The Reading Teacher, 40,* 514–520.

Duffy, G. G., & Roehler, L. R. (1989). Why strategy instruction is so difficult and what we need to do about it. In C. B. McCormick, G. E. Miller, & M. Pressley (Eds.), *Cognitive strategy research: From basic research to educational applications.* New York: Springer-Verlag.

Duffy, G. G., & Roehler, L. R. (1990). *Improving classroom reading instruction: A decision-making approach* (2nd ed.). New York: Random House.

Dulay, H., Burt, M., & Krashen, S. (1982). *Language two.* New York: Oxford.

Dunn, L. M. (1973). Children with mild general learning disabilities. In L. M. Dunn (Ed.), *Exceptional children in the schools* (2nd ed.). New York: Holt, Rinehart and Winston.

Dunn, R., & Dunn, K. (1972). *Practical approaches to individualizing instruction.* West Nyack, NY: Parker.

Dusek, J. B., & Joseph, G. (1985). The bases of teacher expectancies. In J. Dusek (Ed.), *Teacher expectancies.* Hillsdale, NJ: Erlbaum.

Dutton, W. H. (1962). Attitude change of elementary school student teachers and anxiety. *Journal of Educational Research, 55,* 380–382.

Dweck, C. S. (1985). Intrinsic motivation, perceived control, and self-evaluation maintenance: An achievement goal analysis. In C. Ames & R. Ames (Eds.), *Research on motivation in education: Vol. 2. The classroom milieu.* Orlando, FL: Academic Press.

Ebel, R. L., & Frisbie, D. A. (1986). *Essentials of educational measurement* (4th ed.). Englewood Cliffs, NJ: Prentice-Hall.

Eccles, J. S., & Blumenfeld, P. (1985). Classroom experiences and student gender: Are there differences and do they matter? In L. C. Wilkinson & C. B. Marrett (Eds.), *Gender influences in classroom interaction.* Orlando, FL: Academic Press.

Eccles, J. S., & Jacobs, J. E. (1986). Social forces shape math attitudes and performances. *Signs, 11,* 367–389.

Eccles, J. S., & Midgley, C. (1989). Stage-environment fit: Developmentally appropriate classrooms for young adolescents. In C. Ames & R. Ames (Eds.), *Research on motivation in education: Vol. 3. Goals and cognitions.* San Diego: Academic Press.

Educational Testing Service. (1973). *Making the classroom test: A guide for teachers.* Princeton, NJ: Author.

Educational Testing Service. (1975). *Hidden figures test—CF-1* (Rev.). Princeton, NJ: Author.

*Education of the Handicapped* (Vol. 12). (1986, January 8). Arlington, VA: Capitol Publications.

Edwards, B. (1979). *Drawing on the right side of the brain: A course in enhancing creativity and artistic confidence.* Los Angeles: Tarcher.

Eisner, E. W. (1969). Instructional and expressive educational objectives: Their formulation and use in curriculum. In W. J. Popham, E. W. Eisner, H. J. Sullivan, & L. L. Tyler (Eds.), *Instructional objectives.* (AERA Monograph Series on Curriculum Evaluation), Chicago: Rand McNally.

Eisner, E. W. (1983). The art and craft of teaching. *Educational Leadership, 4,* 4–13.

Elawar, M. C., & Corno, L. (1985). A factorial experiment in teachers' written feedback on student homework: Changing teacher behavior a little rather than a lot. *Journal of Educational Psychology, 77,* 162–173.

Electronic Learning's Inservice Workshop (1983). *Part III: Evaluating software.* Electronic Learning, 3, 1c-8c.

Elkind, D. (1968). Adolescent cognitive development. In J. F. Adams (Ed.), *Understanding adolescence: Current developments in adolescent psychology.* Boston: Allyn & Bacon.

Elkind, D. (1974). *Children and adolescents: Interpretive essays on Jean Piaget* (2nd ed.). New York: Oxford.

Elkind, D. (1980). Investigating intelligence in early adolescence. In M. Johnson & K. Rehage (Eds.), *Toward adolescence: The middle school years. Seventy-ninth Yearbook of the National Society for the Study of Education* (Part I). Chicago: University of Chicago Press.

Elkind, D. (1981). *The hurried child: Growing up too fast too soon.* Reading, MA: Addison-Wesley.

Elkind, D. (1986). Formal education and early childhood education: An essential difference. *Phi Delta Kappan, 67,* 631–636.

Elliott, E. S., & Dweck, C. S. (1981). *Children's achievement goals as determinants of learned helplessness and mastery-oriented achievement patterns: An experimental analysis.* Unpublished manuscript, Harvard University, Cambridge, MA.

Ellis, E. S. (1986). The role of motivation and pedagogy on the generalization of cognitive strategy training. *Journal of Learning Disabilities, 19,* 66–70.

Ellis, R. (1985). Teacher-pupil interaction in second language development. In S. Glass & C. Madden (Eds.), *Input in second language acquisition.* Rowley, MA: Newbury House.

Ellis, R. (1986). *Understanding second language acquisition.* Oxford: Oxford University.

Emery, R. E. (1988). *Marriage, divorce, and children's adjustment* (Vol 14). Newbury Park, CA: Sage.

Emmer, E. T. (1987). Classroom management and discipline. In V. Richardson-Koehler (Ed.), *Educators' handbook: A research perspective.* White Plains, NY: Longman.

Emmer, E. T., Evertson, C. M., & Anderson, L. M. (1980). Effective classroom management at the beginning of the school year. *Elementary School Journal, 80,* 219–231.

Englemann, S. E. (1977). Sequencing cognitive and academic tasks. In R. D. Kneedler and S. G. Tarver (Eds.), *Changing perspectives in special education.* Columbus, OH: Merrill.

Englert, C. S. (1984). Measuring teacher effectiveness from the teacher's point of view. *Focus on Exceptional Children, 17,* 1–15.

Enright, R., Lapsley, M., & Levy M. (1983). Moral education strategies. In M. Pressley & J. R. Levin (Eds.), *Cognitive strategy research: Educational applications*. New York: Springer-Verlag.

Erikson, E. H. (1963). *Childhood and society* (2nd ed.). New York: Norton.

Erikson, E. H. (1968). *Identity: Youth and crisis*. New York: Norton.

Evertson, C. M. (1982). Differences in instructional activities in higher- and lower-achieving junior high English and math classes. *Elementary School Journal, 82*, 329–350.

Evertson, C. M., & Emmer, E. (1982a). Effective management at the beginning of the school year in junior high classes. *Journal of Educational Psychology, 74*, 485–498.

Evertson, C. M., & Emmer, E. (1982b). Preventive classroom management. In D. L. Duke (Ed.), *Helping teachers manage classrooms*. Alexandria, VA: Association for Supervision and Curriculum Development.

Evertson, C. M., Emmer, E. T., Clements, B. S., Sanford, J. P., & Worshem, M. E. (1989). *Classroom management for elementary teachers* (2nd ed.). Englewood Cliffs, NJ: Prentice-Hall.

Fearn, L., & McCabe, R. E. (1975). *Human development programs: Supplementary idea guide*. La Mesa, CA: Human Development Training Institute.

*Federal Register. See* U.S. Office of Education.

Feingold, B. F. (1975a). Hyperkinesis and learning disabilities linked to artificial food flavors and colors. *American Journal of Nursing, 75*, 797–803(a).

Feingold, B. F. (1975b). *Why your child is hyperactive*. New York: Random House.

Felker, D. B., & Dapra, R. A. (1975). Effects of question type and question placement on problem solving ability from prose material. *Journal of Educational Psychology, 67*, 380–384.

Fennema, E. (1983). Success in mathematics. In M. Marland (Ed.), *Sex differentiation and schooling*. London: Heinemann.

Feshbach, N. (1969). Student teacher preferences for elementary school pupils varying in personality characteristics. *Journal of Educational Psychology, 60*, 126–132.

Feuerstein, R. (1980). *Instrumental Enrichment: An intervention program for cognitive modifiability*. Baltimore: University Park Press.

Field, D. (1987). A review of preschool conservation training: An analysis of analyses. *Developmental Review, 7*, 210–251.

Fischer, K. W. (1980). A theory of cognitive development: The control and construction of hierarchies of skills. *Psychological Review, 87*, 477–531.

Fischer, K. W., & Pipp, S. L. (1984). Process of cognitive development: Optimal level and skill acquisition. In R. J. Sternberg (Ed.), *Mechanisms for cognitive development*. New York: Freeman.

Fisher, C. W., & Berliner, D. C. (Eds.). (1985). *Perspectives on instructional time*. White Plains, NY: Longman.

Fisher, C. W., Filby, N., Marliave, R. S., Cahen, L. S., Dishaw, M. M., Moore, J. E., & Berliner, D. C. (1978). *Teaching behaviors, academic learning time and student achievement: Final report of Phase III-B, Beginning Teacher Evaluation Study*. San Francisco: Far West Laboratory for Educational Research and Development.

Flavell, J. H. (1963). *The developmental psychology of Jean Piaget*. Princeton, NJ: Van Nostrand.

Flavell, J. H. (1976). Metacognitive aspects of problem solving. In L. Resnick (Ed.), *The nature of intelligence*. Hillsdale, NJ: Erlbaum.

Flavell, J. H. (1979). Metacognition and metacognitive monitoring: A new area of cognitive developmental inquiry. *American Psychologist, 34*, 906–911.

Flavell, J. H. (1985). *Cognitive development* (2nd ed.) Englewood Cliffs, NJ: Prentice-Hall.

Fleming, E., & Anttonen, R. (1971). Teacher expectancy or My Fair Lady. *American Educational Research Journal, 8,* 241–252.

Fogel, A., & Melson, G. (1988). *Child development: Individual, family, and society.* St. Paul: West.

Fowler, R. L., & Barker, A. S. (1974). Effectiveness of highlighting for retention of text material. *Journal of Applied Psychology, 59,* 358–364.

Fraenkel, J. R. (1976). The Kohlberg bandwagon: Some reservations. In D. Purpel and K. Ryan (Eds.), *Moral education . . . It comes with the territory.* Berkeley, CA: McCutchan.

Frase, L. T. (1973). Integration of written text. *Journal of Educational Psychology, 65,* 252–261.

Frazier, B. H. (1969). *Design of a microeconomy system for correcting delinquent behavior patterns in institutionalized children.* Paper presented at the Conference of Behavioral Engineering in Therapeutic Environments, Washington, DC, Walter Reed Army Medical Center.

Friedlander, B. (1975). Some remarks upon "open education." *American Educational Research Journal, 12,* 465–468.

Friedman, M., & Rosenman, A. H. (1974). *Type A behavior and your heart.* New York: Knopf.

Fry, P., & Lupart, J. (1987). *Cognitive processes in children's learning.* Springfield, IL: Thomas.

Frymier, J. (1988). Understanding and preventing teen suicide: An interview with Barry Garfinkel. *Phi Delta Kappan, 70,* 290–293.

Fuhrmann, B. S. (1986). *Adolescence, adolescents.* Boston: Little, Brown.

Fuller, F. F., & Brown, O. H. (1975). Becoming a teacher. In K. Ryan (Ed.), *Teacher Education: The Seventy-fourth Yearbook of the National Society for the Study of Education* (Part II). Chicago: University of Chicago Press.

Furth, H. G. (1973). *Deafness and learning: A psychosocial approach.* Belmont, CA: Wadsworth.

Gage, N. L., & Berliner, D. C. (1988). *Educational Psychology* (4th ed.) Boston: Houghton Mifflin.

Gagné, E. D. (1985). *The cognitive psychology of school learning.* Boston: Little, Brown.

Gagné, R. M. (1977). *The conditions of learning* (3rd ed.). New York: Holt, Rinehart and Winston.

Gagné, R. M. (1980). Learnable aspects of human thinking. In A. E. Lawton (Ed.), *The psychology of teaching for thinking and creativity.* Columbus, OH: 1980 Yearbook of the Association for the Education of Teachers in Science Education.

Gagné, R. M. (1985). *The conditions of learning* (4th ed.). New York: Holt, Rinehart and Winston.

Gall, M. D., & Ward, B. A. (Eds.). (1974). *Critical issues in educational psychology.* Boston: Little, Brown.

Gallagher, J. J. (1975). *Teaching and gifted child* (2nd ed.). Boston: Allyn & Bacon.

Gallagher, J. J. (1989). A new policy initiative: Infants and toddlers with handicapping conditions. *American Psychologist, 44,* 387–391.

Gallimore, R., Boggs, J. W., & Jordan, C. (1974). *Culture, behavior and education: A study of Hawaiian-American.* Beverly Hills, CA: Sage.

Gamoran, A., & Berends, M. (1987). The effects of stratification in secondary schools: Synthesis of survey and ethnographic research. *Review of Educational Research, 57,* 415–435.

Gardner, W. I. (1974). *Children with learning and behavior problems: A behavior management approach*. Boston: Allyn & Bacon.

Garger, S., & Guild, P. (1984). Learning styles: The crucial differences. *Curriculum Review, 23*, 9–12.

Gasper, K. L. (1980). The student perspective. *Teaching Political Science, 7*, 470–471.

Gaudry, E., & Spielberger, C. D. (1971). *Anxiety and educational achievement*. New York: Wiley.

Gelardo, M. S., & Sanford, E. E. (1987). Child abuse and neglect: A review of the literature. *School Psychology Review, 16*, 137–155.

Gelman, R., & Gallistel, C. R. (1978). *The child's understanding of number*. Cambridge, MA: Harvard University Press.

Getzels, J. W., & Jackson, P. W. (1962). *Creativity and intelligence*. New York: Wiley.

Giaconia, R. M., & Hedges, L. V. (1982). Identifying features of effective open education. *Review of Educational Research, 52*, 579–602.

Gibbs, J. C., Arnold, K. D., Burkhart, J. E. (1984). Sex differences in the expression of moral judgment. *Child Development, 55*, 1040–1043.

Gibson, M. A. (1987). The school performance of immigrant minorities: A comparative view. *Anthropology & Education Quarterly, 18*, 262–275.

Gibson, S., & Dembo, M. (1984). Teacher efficacy: A construct validation. *Journal of Educational Psychology, 76*, 569–582.

Gick, M. L., & Holyoak, K. J. (1987). The cognitive basis of knowledge transfer. In S. M. Cormier & J. D. Hagman (Eds.), *Transfer of learning: Contemporary research and applications*. New York: Academic Press.

Gilliam, J. E., & Coleman, M. C. (1981). Who influences IEP committee decisions? *Exceptional Children, 47*, 642–644.

Gilligan, C. (1982). *In a different voice: Psychological theory and women's development*. Cambridge, MA: Harvard University Press.

Gilligan, C., & Attanucci, J. (1988). Two moral orientations: Gender differences and similarities. *Merrill-Palmer Quarterly, 34*, 223–237.

Ginsburg, H. P., & Opper, S. (1988). *Piaget's theory of intellectual development* (3rd ed.). Englewood Cliffs, NJ: Prentice-Hall.

Givner, A., & Graubard, D. S. (1974). *A handbook of behavior modification for the classroom*. New York: Holt, Rinehart and Winston.

Glass, R. M., Christiansen, J., & Christiansen, J. L. (1982). *Teaching exceptional students in the regular classroom*. Boston: Little, Brown.

Glasser, W. G. (1965). *Reality Therapy: A new approach to psychiatry*. New York: Harper & Row.

Glasser, W. G. (1969). *Schools without failure*. New York: Harper & Row.

Glasser, W. G. (1972). *The identity society*. New York: Harper & Row.

Glasser, W. G. (1985). *Control theory*. New York: Harper & Row.

Glasser, W. G. (1990). The quality school. *Phi Delta Kappan, 71*, 424–435.

Gleason, J. B. (1985). Studying language development. In J. B. Gleason (Ed.), *The development of language*. Columbus, OH: Merrill.

Glick, P. C., & Lin, S. (1986). Recent changes in divorce and remarriage. *Journal of Marriage and the Family, 48*, 737–747.

Glickman, C., & Wolfgang, C. (1979). Dealing with student misbehavior: An eclectic review. *Journal of Teacher Education, 30*, 7–13.

Glynn, S. M., & Divesta, F. J. (1977). Outline and hierarchical organization as aids for study and retrieval. *Journal of Educational Psychology, 69*, 89–95.

Goldstein, A. P., Sprafkin, R. P., Gershaw, N. J., & Klein, P. (1980). *Skill-streaming the adolescent*. Champaign, IL: Research Press.

Gollnick, D., Sadker, M., & Sadker, D. (1982). Beyond the Dick and Jane syndrome: Confronting sex bias in instructional materials. In M. P. Sadker & D. M. Sadker (Eds.), *Sex equity handbook for schools*. White Plains, NY: Longman.

Good, T. L. (1979). Teacher effectiveness in the elementary school: What we know about it now. *Journal of Teacher Education, 30,* 52–64.

Good, T. L., & Brophy, J. E. (1978). *Looking in classrooms* (2nd ed.). New York: Harper & Row.

Good, T. L., & Brophy, J. E. (1987). *Looking in classrooms* (4th ed.). New York: Harper & Row

Good, T. L., & Brophy, J. E. (1990). *Educational psychology: A realistic approach* (4th ed.). White Plains, NY: Longman.

Good, T. L., & Grouws, D. (1975). *Process-product relationships in fourth-grade mathematics classroom: Final Report of National Institute of Education Grant.* (NEG-00–3-0125). Columbia: University of Missouri.

Good, T. L., Grouws, D., & Ebmeier, H. (1983). *Active mathematics teaching.* White Plains, NY: Longman.

Good, T. L., & Marshall, S. (1984). Do students learn more in heterogeneous or homogeneous groups? In P. Peterson, L. C. Wilkinson, & M. Hallinan (Eds.), *The social context of instruction: Group organization and group processes.* New York: Academic Press.

Goodlad, J., & Klein, M. F. (1970). *Behind the classroom door.* Worthington, OH: Jones.

Gordon, C. J., & Braun, C. (1985). Metacognitive processes: Reading and writing narrative discourse. In D. L. Forrest-Pressley, G. E. Mackinnon, & T. G. Waller (Eds.), *Metacognition, cognition, and human performance: Vol. 2. Instructional practices.* Orlando, FL: Academic Press.

Gordon, I. J. (1966). *Studying the child in school.* New York: Wiley.

Gordon, T. (1974). *T.E.T.: Teacher effectiveness training.* White Plains, NY: Longman.

Gordon, T. (1975). *P.E.T.: Parent effectiveness training.* New York: Hawthorn.

Gorman, R. M. (1974). *The psychology of classroom learning.* Columbus, OH: Merrill.

Graham, S., & Long, A. (1986). Race, class and the attributional process. *Journal of Educational Psychology, 78,* 4–13.

Greenwood, G. E., & Parkay, F. W. (1989). *Case studies for teacher decision making.* New York: Random House.

Gresham, F. M. (1981). Social skills training with handicapped children. *Review of Educational Research, 51,* 139–176.

Gresham, F. M. (1984). Social skills and self-efficacy for exceptional children. *Exceptional Children, 51,* 253–261.

Gresham, F. M. (1988a). Social competence and motivational characteristics of learning disabled students. In M. C. Wang, M. C., Reynolds, & H. J. Walberg (Eds.), *Handbook of special education: Vol 2. Mildly handicapped conditions.* New York: Pergamon.

Gresham, F. M. (1988b). Social skills: Conceptual and applied aspects of assessment, training, and social validation. In J. C. Witt, S. N. Elliott, & F. M. Gresham (Eds.), *Handbook of behavior therapy in education.* New York: Plenum.

Gronlund, N. E. (1974a). *Improving marking and reporting in classroom instruction.* New York: Macmillan.

Gronlund, N. E. (1974b). *Individualizing classroom instruction.* New York: Macmillan.

Gronlund, N. E. (1985a). *Measurement and evaluation in teaching* (5th ed.). New York: Macmillan.

Gronlund, N. E. (1985b). *Stating objectives for classroom instruction* (3rd ed.). New York: Macmillan.

Gross, T. (1985). *Cognitive development*. Monterey, CA: Brooks/Cole.

Grossman, H. J. (Ed.). (1983). *Classification in mental retardation*. Washington, DC: American Association of Mental Deficiency.

Guilford, J. P. (1959). Three faces of intellect. *American Psychologist, 14,* 469–479.

Guilford, J. P. (1988). Some changes in the Structure-of-Intellect model. *Educational and Psychological Measurement, 48,* 1–4.

Guskey, T. R. (1985). *Implementing mastery learning*. Belmont, CA: Wadsworth.

Guskey, T. R., & Gates, S. L. (1986). Synthesis of research on the effects of mastery learning in elementary and secondary classrooms. *Educational Leadership, 43,* 73–80.

Hackett, G. (1985). Role of mathematics self-efficacy in the choice of math-related majors of college women and men: A path analysis. *Journal of Counseling Psychology, 32,* 47–439.

Hakuta, K. (1986). *Mirror of language: The debate on bilingualism*. New York: Basic Books.

Hakuta, K., & Garcia, E. E. (1989). Bilingualism and education. *American Psychologist, 44,* 374–379.

Hall, E. T. (1959). *The silent language*. Garden City, NY: Doubleday.

Hall, E. T. (1966). *The hidden dimension*. Garden City, NY: Doubleday.

Hall, E. T. (1969). Listening behavior: Some cultural differences. *Phi Delta Kappan, 50,* 379–380.

Hallahan, D. P., & Kauffman, J. M. (1988). *Exceptional children: Introduction to special education* (4th ed.). Englewood Cliffs, NJ: Prentice-Hall.

Hamachek, D. E. (1978). *Encounters with the self* (2nd ed.). New York: Holt, Rinehart and Winston.

Hamachek, D. E. (1985). *Psychology in teaching, learning, and growth* (3rd ed.). Boston: Allyn & Bacon.

Hamaker, C. (1986). The effects of adjunct questions on prose learning. *Review of Educational Research, 56,* 212–242.

Hamilton, R. J. (1985). A framework for the evaluation of the effectiveness of adjunct questions and objectives. *Review of Educational Research, 55,* 47–85.

Hammond, J. M. (1981, February). Children, divorce, and you. *Learning,* pp. 83–91.

Hamner, T. J., & Turner, P. H. (1985). *Parenting in contemporary society*. Englewood Cliffs, NJ: Prentice-Hall.

Haney, W., & Madaus, G. (1978). Making sense of the competency testing movement. *Harvard Educational Review, 48,* 462–484.

Hanson, S. L., & Ginsburg, A. L. (1988). Gaining ground: Values and high school success. *American Educational Research Journal, 25,* 334–365.

Harley, R. K. (1973). Children with visual disabilities. In L. M. Dunn (Ed.), *Exceptional children in the schools* (2nd ed.). New York: Holt, Rinehart and Winston.

Harnisch, D. L., Hill, K. T., & Fyans, L. J. (1980, April). *Development of a shorter, more reliable, and more valid measure of test motivation*. Paper presented at the annual meeting of the National Council on Measurement in Education, Boston.

Harris, L. J. (1985). Teaching the right brain: Historical perspectives on a contemporary educational fad. In L. J. Harris (Ed.), *Hemispheric function and collaboration in the child*. New York: Academic Press.

Harrow, A. J. (1972). *A taxonomy of the psychomotor domain: A guide for developing behavioral objectives*. New York: McKay.

Harter, S. (1981). A new self-report scale of intrinsic versus extrinsic orientation in the classroom: Motivational and informational components. *Developmental Psychology, 17,* 300–312.

Harvey, G. (1986). Finding reality among the myths: Why what you thought about sex equity in education isn't so. *Phi Delta Kappan, 67,* 509–512.

Haskins, R. (1989). Beyond metaphor: The efficacy of early childhood education. *American Psychologist, 44,* 274–282.

Hathaway, W. E. (1980). Testing teachers. *Educational Leadership, 38,* 210–215.

Havighurst, R. J (1970). Minority subcultures and the law of effect. *American Psychologist, 25,* 313–322.

Hawkins, J., Pea, R. D., Glick, J., & Scribner, S. (1984). "Merds that laugh don't like mushrooms": Evidence for deductive reasoning by preschoolers. *Developmental Psychology, 20,* 584–594.

Hearold, S. (1986). A synthesis of 1043 effects of television on social behavior. In G. Comstock (Ed.), *Public communications and behavior* (Vol. I). New York: Academic Press.

Hembree, R. (1988). Correlates, causes, effects, and treatment of test anxiety. *Review of Educational Research, 58,* 47–77.

Henry, J. (1963). *Culture against man.* New York: Random House.

Hersh, R. H., Miller, J. P., & Fielding, G. D. (1980). *Models of moral education: An appraisal.* White Plains, NY: Longman.

Hersh, R. H., Paolitto, D., & Reimer, J. (1979). *Promoting moral growth.* White Plains, NY: Longman.

Hess, R., Shipman, V., Brophy, J., & Bear, R. (in collaboration with A. Adelberger). (1969). *The cognitive environments of urban preschool children: Follow-up phase* Chicago. (Mimeo, final report).

Hetherington, E. M., & Anderson, E. R. (1988). The effects of divorce and remarriage on early adolescents and their families. In M. D. Levine & E. R. McAnarney (Eds.), *Early adolescent transitions.* Lexington, MA: Heath.

Hetherington, E. M., Cox, M., & Cox, A. (1982). Effects of divorce on parents and children. In M. Lamb (Ed.), *Nontraditional families.* Hillsdale, NJ: Erlbaum.

Heward, W. L., & Orlansky, M. D. (1988). *Exceptional children: An introductory survey of special education* (3rd ed.). Columbus, OH: Merrill.

Higgs, T., & Clifford, R. (1982). The push toward communication. In T. Higgs (Ed.), *Curriculum, competence, and the foreign language teacher. ACTFL Foreign Language Education Series* (Vol. 13). Lincolnwood, IL: National Textbook.

Hill, K. T., & Wigfield, A. (1984). Test anxiety: A major educational problem and what can be done about it. *Elementary School Journal, 85,* 105–126.

Hilliard, A. G. (1989, January). Teachers and cultural styles in a pluralistic society. [Special issue]. *Education Today,* 65–69.

Hirsch, E. D. (1987). *Cultural literacy: What every American needs to know.* Boston: Houghton Mifflin.

Hirsch, E. D. (1989). *A first dictionary of cultural literacy: What our children need to know.* Boston: Houghton Mifflin.

Hocevar, D., & Bachelor, P. (1989). A taxonomy and critique of measurements used in the study of creativity. In J. A. Glover, R. Ronning, & C. Reynolds (Eds.), *Handbook of Creativity Research.* New York: Plenum.

Hocevar, S. P., & Arnold, D. (1979). In S. P. Hocevar and C. L. Fox (Eds.), *Trainer's manual for: Module one: Understanding handicapping conditions: Strategies for improving awareness and acceptance of handicapped students in the regular classroom.*

Los Angeles: University of Southern California, California Regional Resource Center, School of Education.

Hoffman, L. W. (1989). Effects of maternal employment in the two-parent family. *American Psychologist, 44,* 283–292.

Hoge, R. D. (1988). Issues in the definition and measurement of the giftedness construct. *Educational Researcher, 17,* 12–16, 22.

Holmen, M. G., & Docter, R. F. (1974, January/February). Criticisms of standardized testing. *Today's Education, 63,* 50–58, 60.

Holmes, C. T., & Matthews, K. M. (1984). The effects of nonpromotion on elementary and junior high school pupils: A meta-analysis. *Review of Educational Research, 54,* 225–236.

Holt, J. (1982). *How children fail* (rev. ed.). New York: Delta.

Homme, L., Csanyi, A. P., Gonzales, M. A., & Rechs, J. R. (1979). *How to use contingency contracting in the classsroom.* Champaign, IL: Research Press.

Hops, H., & Cobb, J. A. (1973). Survival behaviors in the educational setting: Their implications for research and intervention. In L. A. Hammerlynk, L. C. Handy, & E. J. Mash (Eds.), *Behavior change.* Champaign, IL: Research Press.

Howe, L., & Howe, M. M. (1975). *Personalizing education: Values clarification and beyond.* New York: A & W Visual Library.

Hoy, W. K. (1967). Organizational socialization and student teacher and pupil control ideology. *Journal of Educational Research, 61,* 153–155.

Hudgins, B. B., Phyl, G. D., Schau, C. G., Theisen, G. L., Ames, C., & Ames, R. (1983). *Educational psychology.* Itasca, IL: Peacock.

Hughes, J. N. (1988). *Cognitive behavior therapy with children in schools.* New York: Pergamon.

Humes, A. (1983). Research on the composing process. *Review of Educational Research, 53,* 201–216.

Humphrey, J. H., & Humphrey, J. N. (1985). *Controlling stress in children.* Springfield, IL: Thomas.

Hunt, J. McV. (1961). *Intelligence and experience.* New York: Ronald Press.

Hunt, J. McV. (1964). The psychological basis for using preschool enrichment as an antidote for cultural deprivation. *Merrill-Palmer Quarterly, 10,* 209–248.

Hunter, M. C. (1971). *The teaching process.* In D. Allen & E. Seifman (Eds.), *The teacher's handbook.* Glenview, IL: Scott, Foresman.

Hunter, M. C. (1973). Appraising teaching performance: One approach. *National Elementary Principal, 52,* 60–62.

Hunter, M. C. (1982). *Mastery teaching.* El Segundo, CA: TIP Publications.

Hunter, M. C. (1986). Comments on the Napa County, California, Follow Through Project. *Elementary School Journal, 87,* 173–179.

Hunter, M. C. (1988/1989). "Well acquainted" is not enough: A response to Mandeville and Rivers. *Educational Leadership, 46,* 67–68.

Huston, A. C., Watkins, B. A., & Kunkel, D. (1989). Public policy and children's television. *American Psychologist, 44,* 424–433.

Hutton, L. A., & Levitt, E. E. (1987). An academic approach to the remediation of mathematics anxiety. In R. Schwarzer, H. M. van der Ploeg, & C. D. Spielberger (Eds.), *Advances in test anxiety research* (Vol. 5). Lisse: Swets and Zeitlinger.

Hyde, A. A., & Bizar, M. (1989). *Thinking in context: Teaching cognitive processes across the elementary school curriculum.* White Plains, NY: Longman.

Inhelder, B., & Piaget, J. (1958). *The growth of logical thinking from childhood to adolescence*. New York: Basic Books.

Jackson, N. E., Robinson, H. B., & Dale, P. S. (1977). *Cognitive development in young children*. Monterey, CA: Brooks/Cole.

Jackson, P. (1968). *Life in classrooms*. New York: Holt, Rinehart and Winston.

Jackson, P., & Lahaderne, H. (1967). Inequalities of teacher-pupil contacts. *Psychology in the Schools, 4,* 204–211.

Jackson, P., Silberman, M., & Wolfson, B. (1969). Signs of personal involvement in teachers' descriptions of their students. *Journal of Educational Psychology, 60,* 22–27.

Jacob, E., & Jordan, C. (1987). Moving to dialogue. *Anthropology & Education Quarterly, 18,* 259–261.

Jacobsen, D., Eggen, P., & Kauchak, D. (1989). *Methods for teaching: A skills approach* (3rd ed.). Columbus, OH: Merrill.

Jaeger, R. M. (1989). Certification of student competence. In R. L. Linn (Ed.), *Educational measurement* (3rd ed.). New York: Macmillan.

Jaynes, J. (1975). Hello, teacher . . . A review of Fred S. Keller, "The history of psychology: A personalized system of instruction" and Fred S. Keller, "Selected readings in the history of psychology: A PSI companion." *Contemporary Psychology, 20,* 629–631.

Jensen, A. R. (1969). How much can we boost IQ and scholastic achievement? *Harvard Educational Review, 39,* 1–123.

Jensen, A. R. (1980). *Bias in mental testing*. New York: Free Press.

Jensen, A. R. (1985). Compensatory education and the theory of intelligence. *Phi Delta Kappan, 66,* 554–558.

Jenson, W. R., Sloane, H. N., & Young, K. R. (1988). *Applied analysis in education: A structured teaching approach*. Englewood Cliffs, NJ: Prentice-Hall.

Johnson, D. (1972). *An investigation of sex differences in reading in four English-speaking nations* (Tech. Report No. 109). Madison: University of Wisconsin, Research and Development Center for Cognitive Learning.

Johnson, D. I., & Spielberger, C. D. (1968). The effects of relaxation training and passage of time on measures of state- and trait-anxiety. *Journal of Clinical Psychology, 24,* 20–23.

Johnson, D. W. (1979). *Educational psychology*. Englewood Cliffs, NJ: Prentice-Hall.

Johnson, D. W., & Johnson, R. T. (1987). *Learning together and alone: Cooperation, competition, and individualization* (2nd ed.). Englewood Cliffs, NJ: Prentice-Hall.

Johnson, D. W., & Johnson, R. T. (1989). Cooperative learning. In L. W. Anderson (Ed.), *The effective teacher*. New York: Random House.

Johnson, D. W., Johnson, R. T., Holubec, E. J., & Roy, P. (1984). *Circles of learning: Cooperation in the classroom*. Arlington, VA: Association for Supervision and Curriculum Development.

Johnson, K. R., & Ruskin, R. S. (1977). *Behavioral instruction: An evaluative review*. Washington, DC: American Psychological Association.

Johnson, R. T., Johnson, D. W., & Holubec, E. (Eds.). (1987). *Structuring cooperative learning: Lesson plans for teachers*. Edina, MN: Interaction.

Jones, B. F. (1986). Quality and equality through cognitive instruction. *Educational Leadership, 43,* 5–11.

Jones, B. F., Palincsar, A. S., Ogle, D. S., & Carr, E. G. (Eds.). (1987). *Strategic teaching and learning: Cognitive instruction in the content areas*. Elmhurst, IL: North Central Regional Educational Laboratory.

Jones, M. C., & Bayley, N. (1950). Physical maturing among boys as related to behavior. *Journal of Educational Psychology, 41,* 129–148.

Jones, M. C., & Mussen, P. H. (1958). Self-conceptions, motivations, and interpersonal attitudes of early- and late-maturing girls. *Child Development, 29,* 491–501.

Jourard, S. M., & Secord, P. F. (1955). Body-cathexis and the ideal female figure. *Journal of Abnormal and Social Psychology, 50,* 243–246.

Joyce, B., & Weil, M. (1972). *Models of teaching.* Englewood Cliffs, NJ: Prentice-Hall.

Kagan, J. (1966). Understanding the psychology of mental growth. *Grade Teacher Magazine, 79,* 123–130.

Kagan, J., Rosman, B. L., Day, D., Albert, J., & Phillips, W. (1964). Information processing in the child: Significances of analytic and reflective attitudes. *Psychological Monographs, 78* (1, Whole No. 578).

Kagan, S. (1984). Interpreting Chicano cooperativeness: Methodological and theoretical considerations. In J. L. Martinez, Jr., & R. H. Mendoza (Eds.), *Chicano psychology* (2nd ed.). New York: Academic Press.

Kahn, S. B., & Weiss, J. (1973). The teaching of affective responses. In R. Travers (Ed.), *Second handbook of research on teaching.* Chicago: Rand McNally.

Kakuta, K. (1986). *Mirror of language: The debate on bilingualism.* New York: Basic Books.

Kamp, S. H., & Chinn, P. C. (1982). *A multiethnic curriculum for special education students.* Reston, VA: Council for Exceptional Children.

Kampwirth, T. J., & Bates, M. (1980). Modality preference and teaching methods: A review of the research. *Academic Therapy, 15,* 597–605.

Katkovsky, W., Crandall, V. C., & Good, S. (1967). Parental antecedents of children's beliefs in internal-external control of reinforcements in intellectual achievement situations. *Child Development, 38,* 765–776.

Kauffman, J. M., Pullen, P. L., & Akers, E. (1986). Classroom management: Teacher-child-peer relationships. *Focus on Exceptional Children, 19,* 1–10.

Kaufman, A. S., & Kaufman, N. L. (1983). *Kaufman Assessment Battery for Children (K-ABC).* Circle Pines, MN: American Guidance Service.

Kavale, K., & Forness, S. R. (1983). Hyperactivity and diet treatment: A meta-analysis of the Feingold hypothesis. *Journal of Learning Disabilities, 16,* 165–173.

Kaye, E. (1979). *The ACT guide to children's television.* Boston: Beacon Press.

Kazdin, A. E. (1978). Methodology of applied behavior analysis. In A. C. Catania & T. A. Brigham (Eds.), *Handbook of applied behavior analysis: Social and instructional processes.* New York: Irvington.

Kazdin, A. E. (1987). Treatment of antisocial behavior in children: Current status and future directions. *Psychological Bulletin, 102,* 187–203.

Keat, D. B. (1972). Broad spectrum behavior therapy with children: A case presentation. *Behavior Therapy, 3,* 454–459.

Kedar-Voivodas, G. (1983). The impact of elementary children's school roles and sex roles on teacher attitudes: An interactional analysis. *Review of Educational Research, 53,* 415–437.

Keefe, J. W. (1982). *Assessing student learning styles: An overview.* In *Student learning styles and brain behavior.* Reston, VA: National Association of Secondary School Principals.

Keller, F. S. (1968). Goodbye teacher . . .! *Journal of Applied Behavior Analysis, 1,* 79–89.

Kelley, M. L., & Carper, L. B. (1988). Home-based reinforcement procedures. In

J. C. Witt, S. N. Elliott, & F. M. Gresham (Eds.), *Handbook of behavior therapy in education*. New York: Plenum.

Kellogg, J. B. (1988). Forces of change. *Phi Delta Kappan, 70,* 199–204.

Kelly, T. J., Bullock, L. M., & Dykes, M. R. (1977). Behavioral disorders: Teachers' perceptions. *Exceptional Children, 43,* 316–318.

Kendall, P., & Braswell, L. (1985). *Cognitive-behavioral therapy for impulsive children.* New York: Guilford.

Kersh, M. E. (1972). *A study of mastery learning in elementary mathematics.* Paper presented at the annual convention of the National Council of Teachers of Mathematics, Chicago.

Kershner, J., Hawks, W., & Grekin, R. (1977). *Megavitamins and learning disorders: A controlled double-blind experiment.* Unpublished manuscript, Ontario Institute of Studies in Education.

Kiewra, K. A. (1985). Investigating notetaking and review: A depth of processing alternative. *Educational Psychologist, 20,* 23–32.

Kiewra, K. A. (1989a). Matrix notes. *Educational Technology, 29,* 55–56.

Kiewra, K. A. (1989b). A review of note-taking: The encoding-storage paradigm and beyond. *Educational Psychology Review, 1,* 147–172.

Kirschenbaum, H., Simon, S., & Napier, R. (1971). *Wad-ja-get? The grading game in American education.* New York: Hart.

Klausmeier, H. J. (1976). Instructional design and the teaching of concepts. In J. R. Levin & V. L. Allen (Eds.), *Cognitive learning in children.* New York: Academic Press.

Klein, S. (Ed.). (1985). *Handbook for achieving sex equity through education.* Baltimore: Johns Hopkins University Press.

Kline, D. F. (1977). *Child abuse and neglect: A primer for school personnel.* Reston, VA: Council for Exceptional Children.

Knight, G. P., & Kagan, S. (1977). Acculturation of prosocial and competitive behaviors among second- and third-generation Mexican-American children. *Journal of Cross-Cultural Psychology, 8,* 273–284.

Kohlberg, L. (1964). Development of moral character and moral ideology. In M. L. Hoffman & L. W. Hoffman (Eds.), *Review of child development research.* New York: Russell Sage Foundation.

Kohlberg, L. (1976). Moral stages and moralization. In T. Lickona (Ed.), *Moral development and behavior: Theory, research, and social issues.* New York: Holt, Rinehart and Winston.

Kolesnik, W. B. (1975). *Humanism and/or behaviorism in education.* Boston: Allyn & Bacon.

Komarovsky, M. (1953). *Women in the modern world: Their education and their dilemmas.* Boston: Little, Brown.

Kopp, C. B., & McCall, R. B. (1982). Predicting later mental performance for normal, at-risk, and handicapped infants. In P. B. Baltes & O. G. Brim, Jr. (Eds.), *Life-span development and behavior* (Vol. 4). New York: Academic Press.

Kounin, J. (1970). *Discipline and group management in classrooms.* New York: Holt, Rinehart and Winston.

Kozol, J. (1972). *Free schools.* Boston: Houghton Mifflin.

Krashen, S. (1982). *Principles and practice of second language acquisition.* Oxford, Eng.: Pergamon.

Krashen, S., & Biber, D. (1988). *On course: Bilingual education success in California.* Sacramento: California Association for Bilingual Education.

Krashen, S., & Terrell, T. (1983). *The natural approach: Language acquisition in the classroom*. Oxford, Eng.: Pergamon.

Krathwohl, D. R., Bloom, B. S., & Masia, B. (1964). *Taxonomy of educational objectives: Handbook II. Affective domain*. New York: McKay.

Kubany, E. S., Gallimore, R., & Buell, J. (1970). The effects of extrinsic factors on achievement-oriented behaviors: A non-Western case. *Journal of Cross-Cultural Psychology, 1,* 77–84.

Kuhn, D., Langer, J., Kohlberg, L., & Haan, N. S. (1977). The development of formal operations in logical and moral judgment. *Genetic Psychology Monographs, 95,* 97–188.

Kulhavy, R. W., & Swenson, I. (1975). Imagery instructions and the comprehension of text. *British Journal of Educational Psychology, 45,* 47–51.

Kulik, J. A., Kulik, C. C., & Bangert-Drowns, R. L. (1985, April). *Effectiveness of computer-based education in elementary schools*. Paper presented at the annual meeting of the American Educational Research Association, Chicago.

Kulik, J. A., Kulik, C. C., & Cohen, P. A. (1979). A meta-analysis of outcome studies of Keller's personalized system of instruction. *American Psychologist, 34,* 307–318.

Labov, W. (1969). Some sources of reading problems for Negro speakers of Nonstandard English. In J. C. Baratz & R. W. Shuy (Eds.), *Teaching black children to read*. Washington, DC: Center for Applied Linguistics.

Labov, W. (1970). *The study of Nonstandard English*. Champaign, IL: National Council of Teachers of English.

Labov, W. (1974). Academic ignorance and black intelligence. In M. D. Gall & B. A. Ward (Eds.), *Critical issues in educational psychology*. Boston: Little, Brown.

Landesman, S., & Ramey, C. (1989). Developmental psychology and mental retardation: Integrating scientific principles with treatment practices. *American Psychologist, 44,* 409–415.

Larkins, A. G. (1981). Minimum competency tests: A negative view. In H. D. Mehlinger & O. L. Davis (Eds.), *The social studies: Eightieth Yearbook of the National Society for the Study of Education* (Part II). Chicago: University of Chicago Press.

Larrivee, B. (1985). *Effective teaching behaviors for successful mainstreaming*. White Plains, NY: Longman.

Lawton, J. P., & Wanska, S. K. (1977). Advance organizers as a teaching strategy: A reply to Baines and Clawson. *Review of Educational Research, 47,* 233–244.

Lazar, I., Darlington, R., Murray, H., Royce, J., & Snipper, A. (1982). Lasting effects of early education: A report from the Consortium for Longitudinal Studies. *Monographs of the Society for Research in Child Development, 47* (Serial No. 195).

Leacock, E. B. (1969). *Teaching and learning in city schools: A comparative study*. New York: Basic Books.

Lee, P. C. (1973). Male and female teachers in elementary schools. *Teachers College Record, 75,* 75–98.

Lefcourt, H. M. (1966). Internal versus external control of reinforcement: A review. *Psychological Review, 65,* 206–220.

Lefcourt, H. M. (1982). *Locus of control: Current trends in theory and research* (2nd ed.). Hillsdale, NJ: Erlbaum.

Leinhardt, G., Seewald, A., & Engel, M. (1979). Learning what's taught: Sex differences in instruction. *Journal of Educational Psychology, 71,* 432–439.

Lembo, J. M. (1969). *The psychology of effective classroom instruction*. Columbus, OH: Merrill.

Leming, J. S. (1981). Curriculum effectiveness in moral/values education: A review of research. *Journal of Moral Education, 10*, 147–164.

Lemlech, J. K. (1988). *Classroom management* (2nd ed.). New York: Harper & Row.

Leonard, G. B. (1968). *Education and ecstasy*. New York: Dell.

Lepper, M. R., & Gurtner, J. (1989). Children and computers: Approaching the twenty-first century. *American Psychologist, 44*, 170–179.

Lepper, M. R., & Hodell, M. (1989). Intrinsic motivation in the classroom. In C. Ames & R. Ames (Eds.), *Research on motivation in education: Vol. 3. Goals and cognitions*. San Diego: Academic Press.

Lerner, J. W. (1984). *Learning disabilities: Theories, diagnosis, & teaching strategies* (4th ed.). Boston: Houghton Mifflin.

Lerner, R. M., & Gillert, E. (1969). Body build identification, preference, and aversion in children. *Developmental Psychology, 1*, 456–463.

Lesser, G. S., Fifer, G., & Clark, D. H. (1965). Mental abilities of children from different social-class and cultural groups. *Monographs of the Society for Research in Child Development, 30* (4, Serial No. 102).

Lester, F. K., & Garofalo, J. (1986, April). *An emerging study of sixth-graders' metacognition and mathematical performance*. Paper presented at the annual meeting of the American Educational Research Association, San Francisco.

Levin, J. R. (1986). Four cognitive principles of learning-strategy instruction. *Educational Psychologist, 21*, 3–17.

Levy, J. (1982). *Children thinking with whole brains: Myth and reality*. In *Student learning styles and brain behavior*. Reston, VA: National Association of Secondary School Principals.

Levy, J. (1983). Research synthesis on right and left hemispheres: We think with both sides of the brain. *Educational Leadership, 40*, 66–71.

Lewellen, A. (1980). *The use of quiet rooms and other time-out procedures in the public school: A position paper*. Matton, IL: Eastern Illinois Area of Special Education.

Liben, L. S., & Signorella, M. L. (Eds.). (1987). *Children's gender schemata*. San Francisco: Jossey-Bass.

Licht, B. G., & Dweck, C. S. (1983). Sex differences in achievement orientations: Consequences for academic choices and attainments. In M. Marland (Ed.), *Sex differentiation and schooling*. London: Heinemann.

Lickona, T. (1988). Educating the moral child. *Principal, 68*, 6–10.

Liebert, R. M., & Sprafkin, J. (1988). *The early window: Effects of television on children and youth*. New York: Pergamon.

Lillie, D. L., Hannum, W. H., & Stuck, G. B. (1989). *Computers and effective instruction*. White Plains, NY: Longman.

Linn, M. C., & Petersen, A. C. (1985). Facts and assumptions about the nature of sex differences. In S. Klein (Ed.), *Handbook for achieving sex equity through education*. Baltimore: Johns Hopkins University Press.

Lipman, M. (1985). Thinking skills fostered by Philosophy for Children. In J. W. Segal, S. F. Chipman, & R. Glaser (Eds.), *Thinking and learning skills: Vol. 1. Relating instruction to research*. Hillsdale, NJ: Erlbaum.

Lips, H. M. (1988). *Sex and gender: An introduction*. Mountain View, CA: Mayfield.

Lloyd, J. W. (1988). Direct instruction. In M. C. Wang, M. C. Reynolds, & H. J. Walberg (Eds.), *Handbook of special education: Vol 2. Mildly handicapped conditions*. New York: Pergamon.

Lockheed, M. E., & Hall, K. P. (1976). Conceptualizing sex as a status characteristic: Application to leadership training strategies. *Journal of Social Issues, 32*, 111–124.

Lockheed, M. E., & Klein, S. S. (1985). Sex equity in classroom organization and climate. In S. Klein (Ed.), *Handbook for achieving sex equity through education*. Baltimore: Johns Hopkins University Press.

Lockwood, A. (1978). The effects of values clarification and moral development curriculum on school age subjects: A critical review of recent research. *Review of Educational Research, 48*, 325–364.

Loeber, R., & Dishion, T. J. (1983). Early predictors of male delinquency: A review. *Psychological Bulletin, 102*, 187–203.

London, P. (1987). Character education and clinical intervention: A paradigm shift for U.S. schools. *Phi Delta Kappan, 68*, 667–673.

Long, L., & Long, T. (1983). *The handbook for latchkey children and their working parents*. New York: Arbor House.

Long, L., & Long, T. (1989). Latchkey adolescents: How administrators can respond to their needs. *NASSP Bulletin, 73*, 102–108.

Loper, A. B., & Murphy, D. M. (1985). Cognitive self-regulatory training for underachieving children. In D. L. Forrest-Pressley, G. E. Mackinnon, & T. G. Waller (Eds.), *Metacognition, cognition, and human performance: Vol. 2. Instructional practices*. Orlando, FL: Academic Press.

Los Angeles Unified School District. (1981). *Individualized education program* (Form 27.808–2). Los Angeles: Author.

Lovitt, T. C. (1978). The learning disabled. In N. G. Haring (Ed.), *Behavior of exceptional children* (2nd ed.). Columbus, OH: Merrill.

Ludwig, D. J., & Maehr, M. L. (1967). Changes in self-concept and stated behavioral preferences. *Child Development, 38*, 453–467.

Luria, A. (1961). *The role of speech in the regulation of normal and abnormal behaviors*. New York: Liveright.

Lynch, D. O., & Smith, B. C. (1972, April). *To change or not to change item responses when taking tests: Empirical evidence for test takers*. Paper presented at the annual meeting of the American Educational Research Association, Chicago.

Lynn, R. (1982). IQ in Japan and the U.S. shows a growing disparity. *Nature, 297*, 222–223.

Maccoby, E. E., & Jacklin, C. N. (1974). *Sex differences revisited: Myth and reality*. Paper presented at the annual meeting of the American Educational Research Association, Chicago.

Mace, F. C., & Kratochwill, T. R. (1988). Self-monitoring. In J. C. Witt, S. N. Elliott, & F. M. Gresham (Eds.), *Handbook of behavior therapy in education*. New York: Plenum.

Madaus, G. F. (1981). NIE clarification hearing: The negative team's case. *Phi Delta Kappan, 63*, 92–94.

Madden, N. A., & Slavin, R. E. (1983). Mainstreaming students with mild handicaps: Academic and social outcomes. *Review of Educational Research, 55*, 519–659.

Madsen, C. H., Becker, W. C., Thomas, O. R., Koser, L., & Plager, E. (1968). An analysis of the reinforcing function of "sit down" commands. In R. K. Parker (Ed.), *Readings in educational psychology*. Boston: Allyn & Bacon.

Maehr, M. (1976). Continuing motivation: An analysis of a seldom considered educational outcome. *Review of Educational Research, 46*, 443–462.

Maehr, M. (1978). Sociocultural origins of achievement motivation. In D. Bar-Tal & L. Saxe (Eds.), *Social psychology of education: Theory and practice*. Washington, DC: Hemisphere.

Maehr, M. (1984). Meaning and motivation: Toward a theory of personal investment. In R. E. Ames & C. R. Ames (Eds.), *Research on motivation in education: Vol. 1. Student motivation*. Orlando, FL: Academic Press.

Mager, R. F. (1978). *Preparing instructional objectives*. Belmont, CA: Fearon.

Mager, R. F. (1984). *Preparing instructional objectives*. Belmont, CA: Lake.

Mandeville, G. K., & Rivers, J. L. (1988/1989). Effects of South Carolina's Hunter-based PET program. *Educational Leadership, 46,* 63–66.

Marcia, J. E. (1967). Ego identity status: Relationship to change in self-esteem, "general maladjustment," and authoritarianism. *Journal of Personality, 35,* 118–133.

Marcia, J. E. (1980). Identity in adolescence. In J. Adelson (Ed.), *Handbook of adolescent psychology*. New York: Wiley.

Marland, M. (1983). School as sexist amplifier. In M. Marland (Ed.), *Sex differentiation and schooling*. London: Heinemann.

Marland, S. P. (1972). *Education of the gifted and talented*. Washington, DC: U.S. Office of Education.

Marsh, H. W. (1987). The big-fish-little-pond effect on academic self-concept. *Journal of Educational Psychology, 79,* 280–295.

Marsh, H. W. (1989). Age and sex effects in multiple dimensions of self-concept: Preadolescence to early adulthood. *Journal of Educational Psychology, 81,* 417–430.

Marsh, H. W. (1990). A multidimensional, hierarchical model of self-concept: Theoretical and empirical justification. *Educational Psychology Review, 2.*

Marsh, H. W., Byrne, B. M., & Shavelson, R. J. (1988). A multifaceted academic self-concept: Its hierarchical structure and its relation to academic achievement. *Journal of Educational Psychology, 80,* 366–380.

Marsh, H. W., & Parker, J. (1984). Determinants of student self-concept: Is it better to be a relatively big fish in a small pond even if you don't learn to swim as well? *Journal of Personality and Social Psychology, 47,* 213–237.

Marsh, H. W., & Peart, N. (1988). Competitive and cooperative physical fitness training programs for girls: Effects on physical fitness and on multidimensional self-concepts. *Journal of Sport and Exercise Psychology, 10,* 390–407.

Marsh, H. W., & Shavelson, R. J. (1985). Self-concept: Its multifaceted, hierarchical structure. *Educational Psychologist, 20,* 107–125.

Martin, G., & Pear, J. (1988). *Behavior modification: What it is and how to do it* (3rd ed.). Englewood Cliffs, NJ: Prentice-Hall.

Martinez, M. E., & Mead, N. A. (1988). *Computer competence: The first national assessment*. Princeton, NJ: Educational Testing Service.

Maslow, A. H. (1968). *Toward a psychology of being* (2nd ed.). New York: Van Nostrand.

Mattox, B. A. (1975). *Getting it together: Dilemmas for the classroom*. San Diego: Pennant Press.

Mayer, G. R., Butterworth, T. W., Spaulding, H. L., Hollingsworth, P., Amorim, M., Caldwell-McElroy, C., Nafpaktitis, M., & Perez-Osorio, X. (1983). *Constructive discipline: Building a climate for learning*. Downey, CA: Office of the Los Angeles County Superintendent of Schools.

Mayer, R. E. (1979a). Can advance organizers influence meaningful learning? *Review of Educational Research, 49,* 371–383.

Mayer, R. E. (1979b). Twenty years of research on advance organizers: Assimilation theory is still the best predictor of results. *Instructional Science, 8,* 133–167.

Mayer, R. E. (1981). *The promise of cognitive psychology*. San Francisco: Freeman.

Mayer, R. E. (1985a, April). *Recent research on teacher beliefs and its use in the improvement of instruction*. Paper presented at the annual meeting of the American Educational Research Association, Chicago.

Mayer, R. E. (1985b). Mathematical ability. In R. J. Sternberg (Ed.), *Human abilities: An information-processing approach*. New York: Freeman.

Mayer, R. E. (1987). Instructional variables that influence cognitive processes during reading. In B. K. Britton & S. M. Glynn (Eds.), *Executive control processes in reading*. Hillsdale, NJ: Erlbaum.

Mayer, R. E. (1988). Learning strategies: An overview. In C. E. Weinstein, E. T. Goetz, & P. A. Alexander (Eds.), *Learning and study strategies: Issues in assessment, instruction, and evaluation*. San Diego: Academic Press.

McClelland, D. C. (1965). Toward a theory of motive acquisition. *American Psychologist, 20,* 321–333.

McCord, W., McCord, J., & Howard, A. (1963). Familial correlates of aggression in nondelinquent male children. *Journal of Abnormal and Social Psychology, 62,* 79–93.

McCormack, S. (1989). Response to Render, Padilla, and Frank: But practitioners say it works! *Educational Leadership, 46,* 77–79.

McDonald, F. (1965). *Educational psychology* (2nd ed.). Belmont, CA: Wadsworth.

McDonald, F., & Elias, P. (1976). *The effects of teacher performance on pupil learning, beginning teacher evaluation study: Phase II* (Final report: Vol. I). Princeton, NJ: Educational Testing Service.

McGinnis, E., Goldstein, A. P., Sprafkin, R. P., & Gershaw, N. J. (1984). *Skill-streaming the elementary school child*. Champaign, IL: Research Press.

McGinnis, E., Sauerbry, L., & Nichols, P. (1985). Skill-streaming: Teaching social skills to children with behavioral disorders. *Teaching Exceptional Children, 17,* 160–167.

McKey, R. H., Condelli, L., Ganson, H., Barrett, B., McConkey, C., & Plantz, M. (1985). *The impact of Head Start on children, families and communities: A final report of the Head Start Evaluation, Synthesis and Utilization Project*. Washington, DC: CSR.

McLaughlin, B. (1978). The monitor model: Some methodological considerations. *Language Learning, 28,* 309–332.

McLaughlin, T. F., & Malaby, J. E. (1972). Intrinsic reinforcers in a classroom token economy. *Journal of Applied Behavior Analysis, 5,* 263–270.

McNeese, M. C., & Hebeler, J. R. (1977). The abused child: A clinical approach to identification and management. *Clinical Symposia, 29,* 1–36.

Medway, F. J. (1985). To promote or not to promote? *Principal, 64,* 22–25.

Meeker, M. N. (1969). *The structure of intellect: Its interpretations and uses*. Columbus, OH: Merrill.

Mehrens, W. A., & Lehmann, I. J. (1984). *Measurement and evaluation in education and psychology* (3rd ed.). New York: CBS College Publishing.

Meichenbaum, D., & Asarnow, J. (1979). Cognitive-behavioral modification and metacognitive development: Implications for the classroom. In P. C. Kendall & S. D. Hollon (Eds.), *Cognitive-behavioral interventions: Theory, research, and procedures*. New York: Academic Press.

Meichenbaum, D., & Goodman, J. (1971). Training impulsive children to talk to themselves: A means of developing self-control. *Journal of Abnormal Psychology, 77,* 115–126.

Mercer, J. R. (1971). Sociocultural factors in labeling mental retardates. *Peabody Journal of Education, 48*, 188–203.

Mercer, J. R. (1973). *Labelling the mentally retarded*. Berkeley: University of California Press.

Mercer, J. R., & Lewis, J. F. (1978). *System of multi-cultural pluralistic assessment: Conceptual and technical manual*. Riverside, CA: Institute for Pluralistic Assessment Research and Training.

Merrill, M. D. (1983). Component display theory. In C. M. Reigeluth (Ed.), *Instructional-design theories and models: An overview of their current status*. Hillsdale, NJ: Erlbaum.

Messick, S. (1976). *Individuality in learning: Implications of cognitive styles and creativity for human development*. San Francisco: Jossey-Bass.

Messick, S. (1981). Evidence and ethics in the evaluation of tests. *Educational Researcher, 10*, 9–20.

Messick, S. (1982). Issues of effectiveness and equity in the coaching controversy: Implications for educational and testing practice. *Educational Psychologist, 17*, 67–91.

Messick, S., & Jungeblut, A. (1981). Time and method in coaching for the SAT. *Psychological Bulletin, 89*, 191–216.

Meyen, E. L. (1988). A commentary on special education. In E. L. Meyen & T. M. Skrtic (Eds.), *Exceptional children and youth* (3rd ed.). Denver: Love.

Milakofsky, L., & Patterson, H. D. (1979). Chemical education and Piaget. *Journal of Chemical Education, 56*, 87–90.

Miller, G. A. (1956). The magical number seven, plus or minus two: Some limits on our capacity to process information. *Psychological Review, 63*, 81–97.

Miller, H. L., & Woock, R. R. (1970). *Social foundations of urban education*. Hinsdale, IL: Dryden Press.

Miller, N. E., & Dollard, J. (1941). *Social learning and imitation*. New Haven, CT: Yale University Press.

Millman, J. (1970). Reporting student progress: A case for a criterion-referenced working system. *Phi Delta Kappan, 52*, 226–231.

Millman, J., Bishop, C., & Ebel, R. (1965). An analysis of test-wiseness. *Educational and Psychological Measurement, 25*, 707–726.

Mitchell, J. V., Jr. (Ed.). (1983). *Tests in print III*. Lincoln: University of Nebraska Press.

Mitchell, J. V., Jr. (Ed.). (1985). *The ninth mental measurements yearbook*. Lincoln: University of Nebraska Press, Buros Institute of Mental Measurements.

Moores, D. F. (1987). *Educating the deaf: Psychology, principles and practices* (3rd ed.). Boston: Houghton Mifflin.

Moran, M. R. (1978). *Assessment of the exceptional learner in the regular classroom*. Denver: Love.

Morgan, S. R. (1987). *Abuse and neglect of handicapped children*. Boston: Little, Brown.

Moroney, R. M. (1981). Public school policy: Impact on families with handicapped children. In J. L. Paul (Ed.), *Understanding and working with parents of children with special needs*. New York: Holt, Rinehart and Winston.

Morris, J. (1968). Diary of a beginning teacher. *National Association of Secondary School Principals, 52*, 6–15.

Morris, R. J., & Kratochwill, T. R. (1983). *Treating children's fears and phobias: A behavioral approach*. New York: Pergamon.

Mowrer, O. H. (1960). *Learning theory and the symbolic processes*. New York: Wiley.

Moynihan, D. P. (1986). *Family and nation.* New York: Harcourt Brace Jovanovich.

Muller, T., & Espenshade, T. (1985). *The fourth wave.* Washington, DC: Urban Institute Press.

Mussen, P. H., & Jones, M. C. (1957). Self-conceptions, motivations, and interpersonal attitudes of late and early maturing boys. *Child Development, 28,* 243–256.

National Assessment of Educational Progress (1986). *The writing report card: Writing achievement in American schools.* Princeton, NJ: Educational Testing Service.

National Center for Health Statistics (1985, September). *Monthly Vital Statistics Report.* Washington, DC.

National Commission on Excellence in Education (1983). *A nation at risk.* Washington, DC: U.S. Department of Education.

National Education Association. (1961). *Central purposes of American education.* Educational Policies Commission of the National Education Association. Washington, DC: Author.

National Education Association. (1983). *Academic preparation for college.* Educational Policies Commission of the National Education Association. Washington, DC: Author.

National Society to Prevent Blindness (1977). *Signs of possible eye trouble in children* (Publication No. G-112). New York: Author.

Natriello, G. (1982). *Organizational evaluation systems and student disengagement in secondary schools: Final Report to the National Institute of Education.* St. Louis, MO: Washington University.

Natriello, G., & Dornbusch, S. (1985). *Teacher evaluative standards and student effort.* White Plains, NY: Longman.

Nelson, C. M., & Rutherford, R. B. (1988). Behavioral interventions with behaviorally disordered students. In M. C. Wang, M. C. Reynolds, & H. J. Walberg (Eds.), *Handbook of special education: Vol 2. Mildly handicapped conditions.* New York: Pergamon.

Nicholls, J. G. (1984). Conceptions of ability and achievement motivation. In R. E. Ames & C. R. Ames (Eds.), *Research on motivation in education: Vol. 1. Student motivation.* Orlando, FL: Academic Press.

Nichols, P. L., & Chen, T. C. (1981). *Minimal brain dysfunction: A prospective study.* Hillsdale, NJ: Erlbaum.

Nolan, C. Y. (1961). Legibility of ink and paper color combinations for readers of large type. *International Journal for the Education of the Blind, 10,* 82–84.

Nolan, J. D. (1974). The true humanist: The behavior modifier. *Teachers College Record, 76,* 335–343.

Noland, T. K. (1985). *The effects of ability grouping: A meta-analysis of research findings.* Unpublished doctoral dissertation, University of Colorado, Boulder.

Oakes, J. (1985). *Keeping track: How schools structure inequality.* New Haven, CT: Yale University Press.

Oakes, J. (1987). Tracking in secondary schools: A contextual perspective. *Educational Psychologist, 22,* 129–153.

Ogbu, J. (1987). Variability in minority school peformance: A problem in search of an explanation. *Anthropology & Education Quarterly, 18,* 312–334.

Olsen, L. (1988). Crossing the school house border: Immigrant children in California. *Phi Delta Kappan, 70,* 211–218.

Orlich, D. C., Harder, R. J., Callahan, R. C., Kravas, C. H., Kauchak, D. P., Pendergrass, R. A., & Keogh, A. J. (1985). *Teaching strategies: A guide to better instruction* (2nd ed.). Lexington, MA: Heath.

Packard, R. G. (1975). *Psychology of learning and instruction.* Columbus, OH: Merrill.

Palincsar, A. S. (1986). Metacognitive strategy instruction. *Exceptional Children, 53,* 118–124.

Palincsar, A. S., & Brown, A. L. (1984). Reciprocal teaching of comprehension and comprehension monitoring activities. *Cognition and Instruction, 1,* 117–175.

Palincsar, A. S., & Brown, A. L. (1989). Classroom dialogues to promote self-regulated comprehension. In J. Brophy (Ed.), *Teaching for understanding and self-regulated learning* (Vol. 1). Greenwich, CT: JAI Press.

Palincsar, A. S., Brown, A. L., & David, Y. M. (in press). *Facilitative guide to reciprocal teaching.* Ann Arbor: University of Michigan Press.

Palincsar, A. S., Brown, A. L., & Martin, S. M. (1987). Peer interaction in reading comprehension instruction. *Educational Psychologist, 22,* 231–254.

Pallas, A. M., Natriello, G., & McDill, E. L. (1989). The changing nature of the disadvantaged population: Current dimensions and future trends. *Educational Researcher, 18,* 16–22.

Palomares, V. H., & Ball, G. (1974). *Human development program.* La Mesa, CA: Human Development Training Institute.

Paris, S. G., & Byrnes, J. P. (1989). The constructivist approach to self-regulation and learning in the classroom. In B. J. Zimmerman & D. H. Schunk (Eds.), *Self-regulated learning and academic achievement: Theory, research and practice.* New York: Springer-Verlag.

Pascarella, E. T., Walberg, H. J., Junker, L. K., & Haertel, G. D. (1981). Continuing motivation in science for early and late adolescents *American Educational Research Journal, 18,* 439–452.

Pascual-Leone, J. (1970). A mathematical model for the transition rule in Piaget's developmental stages. *Acta Psychologica, 32,* 301–345.

Pascual-Leone, J. (1989). Organismic processes for neo-Piagetian theories: A dialectical causal account of cognitive development. In A. Demetriou (Ed.), *The Neo-Piagetian theories of cognitive development: Toward an integration.* Amsterdam: North Holland.

Patten, J. V., Chao, C. I., & Reigeluth, C. M. (1986). A review of strategies for sequencing and synthesizing instruction. *Review of Educational Research, 56,* 437–471.

Patterson, G. R., DeBaryshe, B. D., & Ramsey, E. (1989). A developmental perspective on antisocial behavior. *American Psychologist, 44,* 329–335.

Patterson, G. R., & Guillion, M. E. (1971). *Living with children.* Champaign, IL: Research Press.

Patterson, J. H., & Smith, M. (1986). The role of computers in higher-order thinking. In J. A. Culbertson & L. L. Cunningham (Eds.), *Microcomputers and education: Eighty-fifth Yearbook of the National Society for the Study of Education* (Part I). Chicago: University of Chicago Press.

Peters, R. S. (1975). Why doesn't Lawrence Kohlberg do his homework? *Phi Delta Kappan, 56,* 678.

Peterson, N. L., & Cooper, C. S. (1989). Parent education and involvement in early intervention programs for handicapped children. In M. J. Fine (Ed.), *The second handbook on parent education: Contemporary perspectives.* San Diego: Academic Press.

Peterson, P. (1979). Direct instruction reconsidered. In P. Peterson & H. J. Walberg (Eds.), *Research in teaching*. Berkeley, CA: McCutchan.

Peterson, P., Marx, R., & Clark, C. (1978). Teaching planning, teacher behavior, and student achievement. *American Educational Research Journal, 15,* 417–432.

Philips, S. U. (1983). *The invisible culture: Communication in classroom and community on the Warm Springs Indian Reservation*. White Plains, NY: Longman.

Phillips, B. N. (1978). *School stress and anxiety: Theory, research, and intervention*. New York: Human Sciences Press.

Phillips, B. N., Hindsman, E., & McGuire, C. (1960). Factors associated with anxiety and their relation to the school achievement of adolescents. *Psychological Reports, 7,* 365–372.

Phillips, B. N., Martin, R. P., & Meyers, J. (1972). Interventions in relation to anxiety in school. In C. D. Speilberger (Ed.), *Anxiety: Current trends in theory and research*. New York: Academic Press.

Phillips, J. L. (1969). *The origins of intellect: Piaget's theory*. San Francisco: Freeman.

Piaget, J. (1952). *The child's conception of number*. London: Humanities Press.

Piaget, J. (1964). Development and learning. In R. E. Ripple & V. N. Rockcastle (Eds.), *Piaget rediscovered: A report of the conference on cognitive skills and curriculum development*. Ithaca, NY: Cornell University, School of Education.

Piaget, J., & Szeminska, A. (1952). *The child's conception of number* (C. Gattegno & F. M. Hodgson, Trans.). New York: Humanities Press.

Plowden Report. (1967). *Children and their primary schools: A report of the Central Advisory Council for Education*. London: H.M. Stationery Office.

Plowman, P. D. (1971). *Behavioral objectives*. Chicago: Science Research Associates.

Popham, W. J., & Baker, E. L. (1970). *Systematic instruction*. Englewood Cliffs, NJ: Prentice-Hall.

Poteet, J. A. (1973). *Behavior modification: A practical guide for teachers*. Minneapolis: Burgess.

Prawat, R., & Nickerson, J. (1985). Relationship between teacher thought and action and student affective outcomes. *Elementary School Journal, 85,* 529–540.

Premack, D. (1959). Toward empirical behavior laws: I. Positive reinforcement. *Psychological Review, 66,* 219–233.

Pressley, M., Goodchild, F., Fleet, J., Zajchowski, R., & Evans, E. D. (1989). The challenges of classroom strategy instruction. *Elementary School Journal, 89,* 301–342.

Pressley, M., Snyder, B. L., & Cariglia-Bull, T. (1987). How can good strategy use be taught to children? Evaluation of six alternative approaches. In S. M. Cormier & J. D. Hagman (Eds.), *Transfer of learning: Contemporary research and application*. New York: Academic Press.

Preston, R. (1962). Reading achievement of German and American children. *School and Society, 90,* 350–354.

Ramirez, M., & Castaneda, A. (1974). *Cultural democracy, bicognitive development, and education*. New York: Academic Press.

Reigeluth, C. M., & Stein, F. S. (1983). The elaboration theory of instruction. In C. M. Reigeluth (Ed.), *Instructional-design theories and models: An overview of their current status*. Hillsdale, NJ: Erlbaum.

Reiling, E., & Taylor, R. (1972). A new approach to the problem of changing initial responses to multiple-choice questions. *Journal of Educational Measurement, 9,* 67–70.

Render, G., Padilla, N. M., & Frank, H. M. (1989a). Assertive discipline: A critical review and analysis. *Teachers College Record, 90,* 607–630.

Render, G., Padilla, N. M., & Frank, H. M. (1989b). What research really shows about assertive discipline. *Educational Leadership, 46,* 72–75.

Renzulli, J. S. (1982). What makes giftedness? *Phi Delta Kappan, 60,* 180–184, 261.

Report of the Ad Hoc Committee to Define Deafness and Hard-of-Hearing. (1975). *American Annals of the Deaf, 120,* 509–512.

Reppucci, N. D., & Haugaard, J. J. (1989). Prevention of child sexual abuse: Myth or reality. *American Psychologist, 44,* 1266–1275.

Resnick, L. B., & Klopfer, L. E. (Eds.) (1989). *Toward the thinking curriculum: Current cognitive research: 1989 Yearbook of the Association for Supervision and Curriculum Development.* Alexandria, VA: ASCD.

Rest, J. R. (1983). Morality. In J. Flavell and E. Markman (Eds.), *Cognitive development* (Vol. 4), (P. H. Mussen, General Ed.), *Manual of child psychology.* New York: Wiley.

Reynolds, C. R., & Jensen, A. R. (1983). WISC-R subscale patterns of abilities of blacks and whites matched on full scale IQ. *Journal of Educational Psychology, 75,* 207–214.

Reynolds, M. C. (1962). A framework for considering some issues in special education. *Exceptional Children, 28,* 367–370.

Richard-Amato, P. A. (1988). *Making it happen: Interaction in the second language classroom. From theory to practice.* White Plains, NY: Longman.

Richardson, J. L., et al. (1989). Substance use among eighth-grade students who take care of themselves after school. *Pediatrics, 84,* 556–566.

Rickards, J. P. (1979). Adjunct postquestions in text: A critical review of methods processes. *Review of Educational Research, 49,* 181–197.

Rickards, J. P., & August, G. J. (1975). Generative underlining strategies in prose recall. *Journal of Educational Psychology, 67,* 860–865.

Robinson, F. (1970). *Study guide for Ausubel/Robinson: School learning.* New York: Holt, Rinehart and Winston.

Robinson, F. P. (1970). *Effective study.* New York: Harper & Row.

Roehler, L. R., & Duffy, G. G. (1984). Direct explanation of comprehension processes. In G. G. Duffy, L. R. Roehler, & J. Mason (Eds.), *Comprehension instruction: Perspectives and suggestions.* White Plains, NY: Longman.

Roffman, A. J. (1983). *The classroom teacher's guide to mainstreaming.* Springfield, IL: Thomas.

Rogers, C. R. (1969). *Freedom to learn.* Columbus, OH: Merrill.

Rogers, C. R. (1983). *Freedom to learn for the 80's.* Columbus, OH: Merrill.

Romberg, T. A., & Carpenter, T. P. (1986). Research on teaching and learning mathematics. In M. C. Wittrock (Ed.), *Handbook of research on teaching* (3rd ed.). New York: Macmillan.

Rose, B. C. (1980). Child abuse and the educator. *Focus on Exceptional Children, 12,* 1–16.

Rosen, B., & D'Andrade, R. (1959). The psychosocial origins of achievement motivation. *Sociometry, 22,* 185–218.

Rosenbaum, J. (1980). Social implications of educational grouping. *Review of Educational Research, 8,* 361–401.

Rosenholtz, S. J., & Simpson, C. (1984). The formation of ability conceptions: Developmental trend or social construction? *Review of Educational Research, 54,* 31–63.

Rosenshine, B. V. (1980). How time is spent in elementary classrooms. In C. Denham & A. Lieberman (Eds.), *Time to learn*. Washington, DC: U.S. Department of Education.

Rosenshine, B. V. (1983). Teaching functions in instructional programs. *Elementary School Journal, 83*, 335–351.

Rosenshine, B. V. (1986). Synthesis of research on explicit teaching. *Educational Leadership, 43*, 60–69.

Rosenshine, B. V., & Berliner, D. (1978). Academic engaged time. *British Journal of Teacher Education, 4*, 3–16.

Rosenthal, R. (1985). From unconscious experimenter bias to teacher expectancy effects. In J. Dusek (Ed.), *Teacher expectancies*. Hillsdale, NJ: Erlbaum.

Rosenthal, R., & Jacobson, L. (1968). *Pygmalion in the classroom*. New York: Holt, Rinehart and Winston.

Rossel, C., & Ross, J. M. (1986). *The social science evidence on bilingual education*. Boston: Boston University Press.

Rothenberg, J. (1989). The open classroom reconsidered. *Elementary School Journal, 90*, 69–86.

Rothkopf, E. Z., & Billington, M. J. (1979). Goal-guided learning from text: Inferring a descriptive processing model from inspection times and eye movements. *Journal of Educational Psychology, 71*, 310–327.

Rothrock, D. (1982). The rise and decline of individualized instruction. *Educational Leadership, 39*, 528–531.

Rotter, J. (1966). Generalized expectancies for internal versus external control of reinforcement. *Psychological Monographs, 80* (1, Whole No. 609).

Rowe, M. (1969). Science, silence, and sanctions. *Science and Children, 6*, 11–13.

Rowe, M. B. (1974). Wait-time and rewards as instructional variables: Their influence on language, logic, and fate control: Part 1. Wait-time. *Journal of Research in Science Teaching, 11*, 81–97.

Rudner, L. (1988). Teacher testing—An update. *Educational Measurement: Issues and Practices, 7*, 16–19.

Rumbaut, R. G., & Weeks, J. R. (1986). Fertility and adaptation: Indochinese refugees in the United States. *International Migration Review, 20*, 439–446.

Ryan, K. (1970). The first year of teaching. In K. Ryan (Ed.), *Don't smile until Christmas*. Chicago: University of Chicago Press.

Ryan, K. (1986). The new moral education. *Phi Delta Kappan, 68*, 228–233.

Ryan, R. M., Connell, J. P., & Deci, E. (1985). A motivational analysis of self-determination and self-regulation in education. In C. Ames & R. Ames (Eds.), *Research on motivation in education: Vol. 2. The classroom milieu*. Orlando, FL: Academic Press.

Ryan, R. M., & Grolnick, W. (1984). *Origins and pawns in the classroom: A self-report and projective assessment of childrens' perceptions*. Unpublished manuscript, University of Rochester, Rochester, NY.

Sadker, M. (1974). Elements of sex bias in schools. In M. Gail & B. Ward (Eds.), *Critical issues in educational psychology*. Boston: Little, Brown.

Sadker, M., & Sadker, D. (1986). Sexism in the classroom: From grade school to graduate school. *Phi Delta Kappan, 67*, 512–515.

Samson, G. E. (1985). Effects of training in test-taking skills on achievement test performance: A quantitative synthesis. *Journal of Educational Research, 78*, 261–266.

Sando, J. (1973). Educating the native American: Conflict in values. In L. Branford,

L. Baca, & K. Lane (Eds.), *Cultural diversity and the exceptional child*. Reston, VA: Council for Exceptional Children.

Sarason, S. B., Davidson, K. S., Lighthall, F. F., Waite, R. R., & Ruebrush, B. K. (1960). *Anxiety in elementary school children*. New York: Wiley.

Sarnacki, R. E. (1979). An examination of test-wiseness in the cognitive test domain. *Review of Educational Research, 49,* 252–279.

Sattler, J. M. (1988). *Assessment of children* (3rd ed.). San Diego: Sattler.

Sattler, J. M., & Gwynne, J. (1982). White examiners generally do not impede the intelligence performance of black children: To debunk a myth. *Journal of Consulting and Clinical Psychology, 50,* 196–208.

Savell, J. M., Twohig, P. T., & Rachford, D. L. (1986). Empirical status of Feuerstein's "Instrumental Enrichment" (FIE) technique as a method of teaching thinking skills. *Review of Educational Research, 56,* 381–409.

Scarr, S., & Kidd, K. K. (1983). Developmental behavior genetics. In M. M. Haith & J. J. Campos (Eds.), *Handbook of child psychology: Infancy and developmental psychobiology* (Vol. 2). (P. H. Mussen, General Ed.). New York: Wiley.

Scarr, S., & Weinberg, R. A. (1976). IQ test performance of black children adopted by white families. *American Psychologist, 31,* 726–739.

Scarr, S., & Weinberg, R. A. (1983). The Minnesota Adoption Studies: Genetic differences and malleability. *Child Development, 54,* 260–267.

Schlaefli, A., Rest, J. R., & Thoma, S. J. (1985). Does moral education improve moral judgment? A meta-analysis of intervention studies using the Defining Issues Test. *Review of Educational Research, 55,* 319–352.

Schneider, W., & Pressley, M. (1989). *Memory development between 2 and 20*. New York: Springer-Verlag.

Schoenfeld, A. H. (1983). The wild, wild, wild, wild, wild world of problem solving. *For the Learning of Mathematics, 3,* 40–47.

Schoenfeld, A. H. (1985). Metacognitive and epistemological issues in mathematical understanding. In E. A. Silver (Ed.), *Teaching and learning mathematical problem solving: Multiple research perspectives*. Hillsdale, NJ: Erlbaum.

Schoenfeld, A. H. (1989). Teaching mathematical thinking and problem solving. In L. B. Resnick & L. E. Klopfer (Eds.), *Toward the thinking curriculum: Current cognitive research*. Washington, DC: Association for Supervision and Curriculum Development.

Schumacker, J. B., Deshler, D. D., Alley, G. R., & Warner, M. M. (1983). Toward the development of an intervention model for learning disabled adolescents: The University of Kansas Institute. *Exceptional Education Quarterly, 4,* 45–74.

Schumacker, J. B., Deshler, D. D., & Ellis, E. S. (1986). Intervention issues related to the education of LD adolescents. In J. K. Torgeson & B. Y. L. Wong (Eds.), *Learning disabilities: Some new perspectives*. New York: Academic Press.

Schunk, D. H. (1986, April). *Self-regulation through overt verbalization during cognitive skill learning*. Paper presented at the annual meeting of the American Educational Research Association, San Francisco.

Schunk, D. H. (1989). Self-efficacy and cognitive skill learning. In C. Ames & R. Ames (Eds.), *Research on motivation in education: Vol. 3. Goals and cognitions*. San Diego: Academic Press.

Schwebel, M. (1975). Formal operations in the first year college student. *Journal of Psychology, 91,* 133–141.

Seaberg, D. I. (1974). *The four faces of teaching: The role of the teacher in humanizing education*. Santa Monica, CA: Goodyear.

Semmel, M. I., Gottlieb, J., & Robinson, N. M. (1979). Mainstreaming: Perspectives on educating handicapped children in the public school. In D. C. Berliner (Ed.), *Review of research in education* (Vol. 7). Washington, DC: American Educational Research Association.

Serbin, L. A. (1983). The hidden curriculum: Academic consequences of teacher expectations. In M. Marland (Ed.), *Sex differentiation and schooling*. London: Heinemann.

Shade, B. J. (1982). Afro-American cognitive style: A variable in school success. *Review of Educational Research, 52*, 219–244.

Shapiro, J., Kramer, S., & Hunerberg, C. (1981). *Equal their chances: Children's activities for non-sexist learning*. Englewood Cliffs, NJ: Prentice-Hall.

Sharon, S., et al. (1984). *Cooperative learning in the classroom: Research in desegregated schools*. Hillsdale, NJ: Erlbaum.

Shavelson, R. J. (1973). What is the basic teaching skill? *Journal of Teacher Education, 14*, 144–151.

Shavelson, R. J., Hubner, J., & Stanton, G. (1976). Self-concept: Validation of construct interpretations. *Review of Educational Research, 46*, 407–441.

Shepard, L. A., & Smith, M. L. (1988). Escalating academic demand in kindergarten: Counterproductive policies. *Elementary School Journal, 89*, 135–145.

Short, E. J., & Weissberg-Benchell, J. A. (1989). The triple alliance for learning: Cognition, metacognition, and motivation. In C. B. McCormick, G. E. Miller, & M. Pressley (Eds.), *Cognitive strategy research: From basic research to educational applications*. New York: Springer-Verlag.

Shumsky, A. (1968). Individual differences in learning styles. In A. Shumsky (Ed.), *In search of teaching style*. Norwalk, CT: Appleton-Century-Crofts.

Sieber, J., O'Neil, H., & Tobias, S. (1977). *Anxiety, learning and instruction*. Hillsdale, NJ: Erlbaum.

Siegel, I. E. (1969). The Piagetian system and the world of education. In D. Elkind & J. H. Flavell (Eds.), *Studies in cognitive development: Essays in honor of Jean Piaget*. New York: Oxford.

Silverman, S., & Kimmel, D. (1972). The effects of immediate feedback on the behavior of teachers in training. *School Application of Learning Theory, 4*, 16–23.

Simmons, R. G., Blyth, D. A., Van Cleave, E. F., & Bush, D. M. (1979). Entry into early adolescence: The impact of school structure, puberty and early dating on self-esteem. *American Sociological Review, 44*, 948–967.

Simmons, R. G., Rosenberg, F., & Rosenberg, M. (1973). Disturbance in the self-image at adolescence. *American Sociological Review, 38*, 553–568.

Simon, S. B., Howe, L. W., & Kirschenbaum, H. (1972). *Values clarification: A handbook of practical strategies for teachers and students*. New York: Hart.

Skinner, B. F. (1948). *Walden two*. New York: Macmillan.

Skinner, B. F. (1953). *Science and human behavior*. New York: Macmillan.

Skinner, B. F. (1954). The science of learning and the art of teaching. *Harvard Educational Review, 24*, 86–97.

Skinner, B. F. (1957). *Verbal behavior*. Englewood Cliffs, NJ: Prentice-Hall.

Skinner, B. F. (1958, October). Teaching machines. *Science, 128*, 969–977.

Skinner, B. F. (1973). The free and happy student. *Phi Delta Kappan, 55*, 13–16.

Skinner, B. F. (1986). Programmed instruction revisited. *Phi Delta Kappan, 68*, 103–110.

Skodak, M., & Skeels, H. M. (1945). A follow-up study of children in adoptive homes. *Journal of Genetic Psychology, 66*, 21–58.

Slater, A. M., & Kingston, D. J. (1981). Competence and performance variables in the assessment of formal operational skills. *British Journal of Educational Psychology, 51,* 163–169.

Slavin, R. E. (1983). *Cooperative learning.* White Plains, NY: Longman.

Slavin, R. E. (1985). Team-assisted instruction: A cooperative learning solution for adaptive instruction in mathematics. In M. C. Wang & H. J. Walberg (Eds.), *Adapting instruction to individual differences.* Berkeley, CA: McCutchan.

Slavin, R. E. (1987). Mastery learning reconsidered. *Review of Educational Research, 57,* 175–213.

Slavin, R. E. (1988). *Educational psychology: Theory into practice* (2nd ed.). Englewood Cliffs, NJ: Prentice-Hall.

Slavin, R. E. (1990). *Cooperative learning: Theory, research, and practice.* Englewood Cliffs, NJ: Prentice-Hall.

Slavin, R. E., & Karweit, N. (1984). Mastery learning and student teams: A factorial experiment in urban general mathematics classes. *American Educational Research Journal, 21,* 725–736.

Slavin, R. E., Karweit, N. L., & Madden, N. A. (1989). *Effective programs for students at risk.* Boston: Allyn & Bacon.

Sloane, H. N., Gordon, H. M., Gunn, C., & Mickelsen, V. G. (1989). *Evaluating educational software: A guide for teachers.* Englewood Cliffs, NJ: Prentice-Hall.

Smart, K. L., & Bruning, J. L. (1973, August). *An examination of the practical import of the Von Restorff effect.* Paper presented at the annual meeting of the American Psychological Association, Montreal. (ERIC Document ED 102 502)

Smith, B. O. (1960). A concept of teaching. *Teachers College Record, 61,* 229–241.

Smith, C. R., Wood, F. H., & Grimes, J. (1988). Issues in the identification and placement of behaviorally disordered students. In M. C. Wang, M. C. Reynolds, & H. J. Walberg (Eds.), *Handbook of special education: Vol 2. Mildly handicapped conditions.* New York: Pergamon.

Smith, E. L., & Sendelbach, N. B. (1979, April). *Teacher intentions for science instruction and their antecedents in program materials.* Paper presented at the annual meeting of the American Educational Research Association, San Francisco.

Smith, F. M., & Adams, S. (1972). *Educational measurement for the classroom teacher* (2nd ed.). New York: Harper & Row.

Smith, M. L., & Shepard, L. A. (1988). Kindergarten readiness and retention: A qualitative study of teachers' beliefs and practices. *American Educational Research Journal, 25,* 307–333.

Smith, R. M. (1982). *Learning how to learn: Applied theory for adults.* New York: Cambridge University Press.

Snowman, J. (1984). Learning tactics and strategies. In G. D. Phye & T. Andre (Eds.), *Cognitive instructional psychology.* Orlando, FL: Academic Press.

Sosniak, L. A. (1987). Gifted education boondoggles: A few bad apples or a rotten bushel? *Phi Delta Kappan, 68,* 535–538.

Sowell, E. J., & Casey, R. J. (1982). *Research methods in education.* Belmont, CA: Wadsworth.

Spearman, C. (1927). *The abilities of man: Their nature and measurement.* New York: Macmillan.

Spears, H. (1973). Kappans ponder the goals of education. *Phi Delta Kappan, 55,* 29–32.

Spence, J., & Helmreich, R. (1978). *Masculinity and femininity.* Austin: University of Texas.

Staffieri, J. R. (1967). A study of social stereotype of body image in children. *Journal of Personality and Social Psychology, 7*, 101–103.

Stallings, J., & Krasavage, E. M. (1986). *Peaks, valleys and plateaus in program implementation: A longitudinal study of a Madeline Hunter Follow-Through Project.* Nashville, TN: Vanderbilt University, Peabody Center for Effective Teaching.

Stallings, J., Robbins, M., Presbrey, L., & Scott, J. (1986). Effects of instruction based on the Madeline Hunter model on students' achievement: Findings from a Follow-Through Project. *Elementary School Journal, 86*, 571–587.

*Standards for educational and psychological testing.* (1985). Washington, DC: American Psychological Association.

*Stanford Achievement Tests* (7th ed.). (1982). San Diego: Harcourt Brace Jovanovich.

Steinberg, C. (1985). *TV facts.* New York: Facts on File.

Stern, P., & Shavelson, R. (1981). *The relationship between teachers' grouping decisions and instructional behaviors: An ethnographic study of reading instruction.* Resources in Education (ERIC Document Reproduction Service No. ED 210 971)

Sternberg, R. J. (Ed.). (1985). *Human abilities: An information-processing approach.* New York: Freeman.

Sternberg, R. J. (1986). *Intelligence applied: Understanding and increasing your intellectual skills.* New York: Harcourt Brace Jovanovich.

Sternberg, R. J. (1987a). A day at developmental downs: Sportscast for race #2—Neo-Piagetian theories of cognitive development. *International Journal of Psychology, 22*, 507–529.

Sternberg, R. J. (1987b). Teaching intelligence: The application of cognitive psychology to the improvement of intellectual skills. In J. B. Baron & R. J. Sternberg (Eds.), *Teaching thinking skills: Theory and practice.* New York: Freeman.

Sternberg, R. J. (1988). *The triarchic mind: A new theory of human intelligence.* New York: Viking.

Sternberg, R. J., & Bhana, K. (1986). Synthesis of research on the effectiveness of intellectual skills programs: Snake-oil remedies or miracle cures? *Eductional Leadership, 44*, 60–67.

Sternberg, R. J., & Davidson, J. E. (Eds.). (1986). *Conceptions of giftedness.* New York: Cambridge University Press.

Stipek, D. J. (1988). *Motivation to learn: From theory to practice.* Englewood Cliffs, NJ: Prentice-Hall.

St. John, N. (1971). Thirty-six teachers: Their characteristics and outcomes for black and white pupils. *American Educational Research Journal, 8*, 635–648.

Stober, S. F. (1985, April). *A metacognitive perspective of conceptual tempo.* Paper presented at the meeting of the Society for Research in Child Development, Toronto.

Stodolsky, S. S., & Lesser, G. S. (1967). Learning patterns in the disadvantaged. *Harvard Educational Review, 37*, 548–593.

Strain, P. S., & Kerr, M. M. (1981). *Mainstreaming of children in schools: Research and programmatic issues.* New York: Academic Press.

Strauss, S. (1972). Inducing cognitive development and learning: A review of short-term training experiments—the organismic-developmental approach. *Cognition, 1*, 329–357.

Strein, W. (1988). Classroom-based elementary school affective education programs: A critical review. *Psychology in the Schools, 25*, 288–296.

Strenio, A. L., Jr. (1981). *The testing trap.* New York: Rawson, Wade.

Strickland, B. R. (1989). Internal-external control expectancies: From contingency to creativity. *American Psychologist, 44*, 1–12.

Sue, S., & Padilla, A. (1986). Ethnic minority issues in the United States: Challenges for the educational system. In *Beyond language: Social and cultural factors in schooling language minority students*. Los Angeles: California State University, Evaluation, Dissemination and Assessment Center.

Sullivan, E. V. (1967). *Piaget and the school curriculum: A critical appraisal* (Bulletin No. 2). Toronto: Ontario Institute for Studies in Education.

Summers, M. (1977). Learning disabilities . . . A puzzlement. *Today's Education, 66*, 42.

Suran, B. G., & Rizzo, J. (1979). *Special children: An integrative approach*. Glenview, IL: Scott, Foresman.

Sutherland, K. (1979). Accuracy vs. fluency in the second language classroom. California Association of Teachers of English to Speakers of Other Languages. *CATESOL Occasional Papers, 5*, 25–29.

Tarver, S. G., & Hallahan, D. P. (1976). Children with learning disabilities: An overview. In J. M. Kauffman & D. P. Hallahan (Eds.), *Teaching children with learning disabilities: Personal perspectives*. Columbus, OH: Merrill.

Tenbrink, T. D. (1974). *Evaluation: A practical guide for teachers*. New York: McGraw-Hill.

Tennyson, R. D., & Park, O. (1980). The teaching of concepts: A review of instructional design literature. *Review of Educational Research, 50*, 55–70.

Terman, L. M., & Oden, M. (1925). *Genetic studies of genius: Mental and physical traits of a thousand gifted children*. Stanford, CA: Stanford University Press.

Terman, L. M., & Oden, M. (1954). *Genetic studies of genius: The gifted group at midlife. Thirty-five years' follow-up of the superior child*. Stanford, CA: Stanford University Press.

Terwilliger, J. S. (1971). *Assigning grades to students*. Glenview, IL: Scott, Foresman.

Test, D. W., Heward, W. L., & Orlansky, M. D. (1980). *A teacher's guide to Howard and Orlansky's exceptional children*. Columbus, OH: Merrill.

Tharp, R. (1989). Psychocultural variables and constants: Effects on teaching and learning in schools. *American Psychologist, 44*, 349–359.

Thatcher, D. A. (1972). Ask not what you can do for the machine. *Phi Delta Kappan, 53*, 509–511.

Thorndike, E. L. (1913). *Educational psychology*. New York: Columbia University, Teachers College Press.

Thorndike, E. L. (1927). *The measurement of intelligence*. New York: Columbia University, Teachers College Press.

Thorndyke, P. W., & Stasz, C. (1980). Individual differences in procedures for knowledge acquisition from maps. *Cognitive Psychology, 12*, 137–175.

Thurstone, L. L. (1938). *Primary mental abilities*. Chicago: University of Chicago Press.

Tobias, S. (1979). Anxiety research in educational psychology. *Journal of Educational Psychology, 71*, 573–582.

Tobias, S. (1980). *Paths to programs for intervention: Math anxiety, math avoidance, and reentry mathematics*. Washington, DC: Institute for the Study of Anxiety in Learning.

Tobias, S. (1985). Computer-assisted instruction. In M. C. Wang & H. J. Walberg (Eds.), *Adapting instruction to individual differences*. Berkeley, CA: McCutchan.

Tobin-Richards, M. H., Boxer, A. H., & Petersen, A. C. (1983). The psychological significance of pubertal change: Sex differences in perception of self during early adolescence. In J. Brooks-Gunn & A. C. Petersen (Eds.), *Girls at puberty: Biological and psychological perspectives*. New York: Plenum.

Torrance, E. P. (1962). *Guiding creative behavior*. Englewood Cliffs, NJ: Prentice-Hall.

Torrance, E. P. (1965). *Rewarding creative behavior*. Englewood Cliffs, NJ: Prentice-Hall.

Torrance, E. P. (1970). *Encouraging creativity in the classroom*. Dubuque, IA: Brown.

Torrance, E. P. (1972). Creative kids. *Today's Education, 61*, 22–29.

Troike, R. C. (1978). Research evidence for the effectiveness of bilingual education. *National Association for Bilingual Education Journal, 3*, 13–24.

Trojcak, D. A. (1977). Implementing the competency of sequencing instruction. In J. Weigand (Ed.), *Implementing teacher competencies*. Englewood Cliffs, NJ: Prentice-Hall.

Underwood, B. J. (1961). Ten years of massed practice on distributed practice. *Psychological Review, 68*, 229–247.

Underwood, B. J., & Ekstrand, B. R. (1966). An analysis of some shortcomings in the interference theory of forgetting. *Psychological Review, 73*, 540–549.

United States Department of Education (1989). *Eleventh annual report to Congress on the implementation of the Education of the Handicapped Act*. Washington, DC.

United States Department of Health, Education and Welfare. (1970). *Statistics for 1966 on blindness in the model reporting area*. Washington, DC: U.S. Government Printing Office.

United States Office of Education (1977). *Implementation of Part B of the Education of the Handicapped Act*. Federal Register, 42, 42474–42518. Washington, DC: U.S. Government Printing Office.

Urman, H. N. (1982). *Ethnic differences and the effects of test-wiseness training on verbal and math achievement*. Unpublished doctoral dissertation, University of Southern California, Los Angeles.

Van Riper, C. (1978). *Speech correction: Principles and methods* (6th ed.). Englewood Cliffs, NJ: Prentice-Hall.

Vargas, J. S. (1986). Instructional design flaws in computer-assisted instruction. *Phi Delta Kappan, 67*, 738–744.

Veenman, S. (1984). Perceived problems of beginning teachers. *Review of Educational Research, 4*, 143–178.

Vogt, L. A., Jordan, C., & Tharp, R. G. (1987). Explaining school failure, producing school success: Two cases. *Anthropology & Education Quarterly, 18*, 276–286.

Vygotsky, L. S. (1962). *Thought and language*. Cambridge, MA: MIT Press.

Vygotsky, L. S. (1978). Interaction between learning and development. In M. Cole, S. Scribner, V. John-Steiner, & E. Sonberman (Eds.), *Mind in society: Development of higher psychological processes*. Cambridge, MA: Harvard University Press.

Wadsworth, B. (1978). *Piaget for the classroom teacher*. White Plains, NY: Longman.

Wadsworth, B. (1989). *Piaget's theory of cognitive and affective development* (4th ed.). White Plains, NY: Longman.

Wagner, R., & Sternberg, R. S. (1984). Alternative conceptions of intelligence and their implications for education. *Review of Educational Research, 54*, 179–223.

Walberg, H., & Thomas, S. (1972). Open education: An operational definition and validation in Great Britain and the U.S. *American Educational Research Journal, 9*, 197–208.

Walker, J. E., & Shea, T. (1988). *Behavior management: A practical approach for educators* (4th ed.). Columbus, OH: Merrill.

Walker, L. J. (1984). Sex differences in the development of moral reasoning: A critical review. *Child Development, 55,* 677–691.

Wallach, M. A., & Kogan, N. (1965). *Modes of thinking in young children: A study of the creativity-intelligence distinction.* New York: Holt, Rinehart and Winston.

Wallerstein, J. S., Corbin, S. B., & Lewis, J. M. (1988). Children of divorce: A ten-year study. In E. M. Hetherington & J. Arasteh (Eds.), *Impact of divorce, single-parenting and stepparenting on children.* Hillsdale, NJ: Erlbaum.

Wallerstein, J. S., & Kelly, J. B. (1980). *Surviving the breakup.* New York: Basic Books.

Walters, R. H., Parke, R. D., & Cane, V. A. (1965). Timing of punishment and the observation of consequences to others as determinants of response inhibition. *Journal of Experimental Child Psychology, 2,* 10–30.

Wang, M. (1980). Adaptive instruction: Building on diversity. *Theory into Practice, 19,* 122–128.

Wang, M. C., Reynolds, M. C., & Walberg, H. J. (1988). Integrating the children of the second system. *Phi Delta Kappan, 70,* 248–251.

Waterman, A. S. (1982). Identity development from adolescence to adulthood: An extension of theory and a review of research. *Developmental Psychology, 18,* 341–358.

Wax, M. L. (1969). *Indian education in Eastern Oklahoma* (Research contract report No. O.C. 6–10–260 and B/A No. 5–05650–2-12–1). Washington, DC: U.S. Department of Education.

Webb, N. (1982). Peer interaction and learning in cooperative small groups. *Journal of Educational Psychology, 74,* 642–655.

Webb, N. (1985). Verbal interaction and learning in peer-directed groups. *Theory into Practice, 24,* 32–38.

Webb, N. (1987, April). *Helping behavior to maximize learning.* Paper presented at the annual meeting of the American Educational Research Association, Washington, DC.

Webb, N. M., & Kenderski, C. M. (1985). Gender differences in small-group interaction and achievement in high- and low-achieving classes. In L. C. Wilkinson & C. B. Marrett (Eds.), *Gender influences in classroom interaction.* Orlando, FL: Academic Press.

Weiner, B. (1972). *Theories of motivation.* Chicago: Rand McNally.

Weiner, B., Frieze, I., Kukla, A., Reed, L., Rest, S., & Rosenbaum, R. (1971). Perceiving the causes of success and failure. In E. E. Jones (Ed.), *Attribution: Perceiving the causes of behavior.* Morristown, NJ: General Learning Press.

Weiner, B., & Kukla, A. (1970). An attributional analysis of achievement motivation. *Journal of Personality and Social Psychology, 15,* 1–20.

Weinstein, C. E., & Mayer, R. E. (1985). The teaching of learning strategies. In M. Wittrock (Ed.), *Handbook of research on teaching* (3rd ed.). New York: Macmillan.

Weinstein, R. (1989). Perceptions of classroom processes and student motivation: Children's views of self-fulfilling prophecies. In C. Ames & R. Ames (Eds.), *Research on motivation in education: Vol. 3. Goals and cognitions.* San Diego: Academic Press.

Whelan, R. J., & Gallagher, P. A. (1972). Effective teaching in children with behavior disorders. In N. G. Haring & A. H. Hayden (Eds.), *The improvement of instruction.* Seattle: Special Child Publications.

Wherry, J. N. (1983). Some legal considerations and implications for the use of behavior modification in the schools. *Psychology in the Schools, 20,* 46–51.

White, S., & Tharp, R. G. (1988, April). *Questioning and wait-time: A cross-cultural analysis.* Paper presented at the annual meeting of the American Educational Research Association, New Orleans.

Wigfield, A., & Eccles, J. S. (1989). Test anxiety in elementary and secondary students. *Educational Psychologist, 24,* 159–183.

Willig, A. C. (1985). A meta-analysis of selected studies on the effectiveness of bilingual education. *Review of Educational Research, 55,* 269–317.

Willig, A. C., Harnisch, D. L., Hill, K., & Maehr, M. (1983). Sociocultural and educational correlates of success-failure attributions and evaluation anxiety in the school setting for black, Hispanic, and Anglo children. *American Educational Research Journal, 20,* 385–410.

Willis, S. (1972). *Formation of teachers' expectations of students' academic performance.* Unpublished doctoral dissertation, University of Texas, Austin.

Winograd, P., & Hare, V. C. (1988). Direct instruction of reading comprehension strategies: The nature of teacher explanation. In C. E. Weinstein, E. T. Goetz, & P. A. Alexander (Eds.), *Learning and study strategies: Issues in assessment, instruction, and evaluation.* San Diego: Academic Press.

Winterbottom, M. R. (1953). *The relation of childhood training in independence to achievement motivation.* Unpublished doctoral dissertation, University of Michigan, Ann Arbor.

Witkin, H. A., Moore, C., Goodenough, D., & Cox, P. (1977). Field-dependent and field-independent cognitive styles and their educational implications. *Review of Educational Research, 47,* 1–64.

Wittrock, M. C. (1966). The learning by discovery hypothesis. In L. S. Shulman and E. R. Keislar (Eds.), *Learning by discovery: A critical appraisal.* Chicago: Rand McNally.

Wolfe, P. (1984). *Instructional skills trainers' manual.* Napa, CA: Napa County Office of Education.

Wood, P., Bruner, J., & Ross, G. (1976). The role of tutoring in problem solving. *Journal of Child Psychology and Psychiatry, 17,* 89–100.

Workman, E. A. (1982). *Teaching behavioral self-control to students.* Austin, TX: PRO-ED.

Workman, E. A., & Hector, M. (1978). Behavior self-control in classroom settings: A review of the literature. *Journal of School Psychology, 16,* 227–236.

Wrightsman, L. S. (1962). The effects of anxiety, achievement, motivation, and task importance upon performance on an intelligence test. *Journal of Educational Psychology, 53,* 150–156.

Wynne, E. A. (1988). Balancing character development and academics in the elementary school. *Phi Delta Kappan, 69,* 424–426.

Youngs, B. B. (1985). *Stress in children: How to recognize, avoid and overcome it.* New York: Arbor House.

Zahorik, J. A. (1975). Teachers' planning models. *Educational Leadership, 33,* 134–139.

Zander, A., & Forward, J. (1968). Position in group, achievement motivation, and group aspirations. *Journal of Personality and Social Psychology, 8,* 282–288.

Zeuli, J. S., & Floden, R. E. (1987). Cultural incongruities and inequities of schooling: Implications for practice from ethnographic research. *Journal of Teacher Education, 38,* 9–15.

Zigler, E., & Valentine, J. (Eds.). (1979). *Project Head Start: A legacy of the war on poverty.* New York: Free Press.

# Author Index

# Subject Index